INSIDERS' ►GUIDE

PHOENIX

by

Lori Rohlk Pfeiffer

&

Paul Morris

The Insiders' Guide®
An imprint of The Globe Pequot Press
P.O. Box 480
Guilford, CT 06437-0480
(800) 582-2665
www.insiders.com

•

Sales and Marketing: The Globe Pequot Press
P.O. Box 480
Guilford, CT 06437-0480
(800) 582-2665
www.falcon.com

•

SECOND EDITION
1st printing

•

•

Printed in the United States of America

•

Front photo: sunset with cactus-courtesy of Jensen Associates, Inc.
Back photo: Camelback Inn Resort-Debbie Ross
Photo band (left to right): mountains with flowers-Al Richmond, courtesy of Flagstaff
Convention & Visitors Bureau; riders-courtesy of Jensen Associates, Inc.;
saquaro blossom-David Moore, courtesy of Scottsdale CVB; dancer-courtesy of Heard Museum;
sombrero man with boy-courtesy of Festival of the West;
Spine photo: calf roper-courtesy of Scottsdale CVB

•

Publications from *The Insiders' Guide*® series are available at special discounts for
bulk purchases for sales promotions, premiums, or fundraisings. Special editions,
including personalized covers, can be created in large quantities for special needs.
For more information, please contact The Globe Pequot Press.

ISBN 1-57380-183-6

About the Authors

Lori Rohlk Pfeiffer

When she first visited a friend in the Phoenix area in 1995, writer Lori Rohlk Pfeiffer felt jealous because she hadn't thought of moving to Arizona first. She soon remedied the oversight and married her friend; they just finished building their dream house in Mesa. An avid art aficionado and an enthusiastic, if not hardy, hiker and rock climber, Lori enjoys exploring the area's byways and flyways with her husband, Dr. Matthias Pfeiffer.

Lori grew up in Iowa but doesn't miss the snow. She received her bachelor's degree in mass communication from Buena Vista College in Storm Lake, Iowa, in 1988. She worked at newspapers and edited her alumni magazine before earning a master's degree in United States history from the University of Nebraska-Lincoln in 1998.

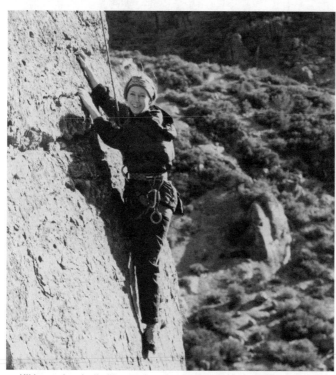

Hiking and rock climbing are favorite activities for Lori and her husband.

Photo: Lori Rohlk Pfeiffer

As a freelance writer, Lori specializes in trends, travel, and business. Her articles have been published in regional and national magazines like *Arizona Highways*, *PHOENIX Magazine*, *Valley Guide Quarterly*, *Working Woman*, *Black Enterprise*, and *America West Airlines Magazine*. Lately, the desert muse has tugged her toward exploring creative nonfiction essays.

Paul Morris

Paul Morris arrived in the Sonoran desert of Phoenix in 1961. Growing up among the saguaros, he has learned to love the monsoon rains, owns no umbrella, and likes to swim late at night, looking up at the stars over Tempe. When he is not typing, he is an avid birder, always studying the hummingbirds on his patio and looking forward to the arrival of the white-winged doves each spring.

Paul writes about food and lifestyle and his work can be found in *Valley Guide Quarterly*, *Scottsdale Magazine*, *East Valley Magazine*, *Where Magazine*, *Guest Informant*, *Phoenix New Times*, and other regional publications.

He also teaches creative writing at Arizona State University. His poems, creative nonfiction, and translations appear in many journals including *Fever Dreams: An Anthology of Contemporary Arizona Poetry*. In 1991 he was awarded a Creative Writing Fellowship in poetry, and in 1997 he received an Artist Project Grant from the Arizona Commission on the Arts. He lives in Tempe with his wife Rebecca Ross and a cat named Trouble (who also watches birds).

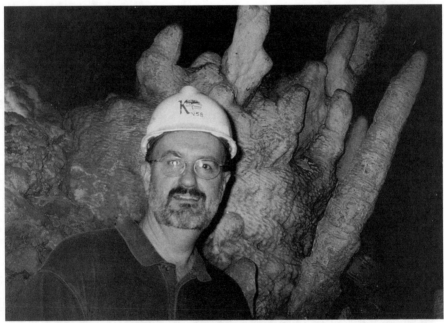

Paul Morris enjoys unique adventures, like touring Kartchner Caverns . . . before it was opened to the public.

Photo: Ron Bimrose

Acknowledgements

For their input, expertise, and assistance in many forms, we thank all who helped with the production of this book. These include Howard Boice, Debi Bridges, Jean-Pierre Brietta, Matt Burdick, Tracey Cates, Marguarite Clark, Sally Cooper, Brooke Cromwell, Jennifer Franklin, Angie Harvey, Susan Gear, Rand Hubbell, Margo Kesler, Valerie Lee, Wendie Marlais, Juliet Martin, James McKnight, Jean McKnight, Beckie Mayberry, Mike Nevarez, Maryfrances Piattoni, Peter Pfeiffer, Lora Robinson, Bonnie Ruscetti, Suzanne Sperl, Jaye Stimson, Marcheta Strunk, Michelle Walyuchow, and Ruth Young. We also acknowledge the research and writing of Salvatore Caputo and Deborah Ross who created the first edition of this work.

Paul would like to thank William "Skip" Boyer for his friendship, Lori Pfeiffer for being a terrific collaborator, and his cat Trouble for trying to help him type.

Lori would like to thank Bob Early and Bruce Ellingson for their encouragement; co-author Paul Morris for making the project so much fun; colleagues Bev Harvey; Sonya Goodwin Hemmings, Stephanie Lyncheski, Bonnie Smith, Barbara Riggs, and Pam Waterman for their friendship; and her parents, Eldon and Norma Rohlk, for always having books in the house.

A bouquet of thanks goes to Erika Serviss of Falcon Publishing for her keen editorial eye and patience.

We also gratefully acknowledge the assistance of our spouses, Rebecca Ross and Matthias Pfeiffer, for their culinary and proofreading skills as well as their patience, encouragement, and love.

—Lori Rohlk Pfeiffer and Paul Morris

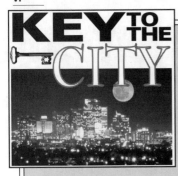
KEY ^{TO} **THE CITY**

Vital Statistics

Governor:
Jane Hull

Phoenix City Mayor:
Skip Rimza

State Capital:
Phoenix

Area Cities:
Phoenix, Scottsdale, Paradise Valley, Tempe, Mesa, Gilbert, Chandler, Glendale, Cave Creek, and Sun City

Population:
2.8 million in the greater Phoenix area

Area:
2,000 square miles

Nickname:
Valley of the Sun

Average Temperatures:
January: 65 F. 39 F
July: 105 F 79.5 F

Average Rainfall:
7.66 inches

Days of Sunshine:
300 days

City Founded:
October 26, 1870

State Founded:
Arizona entered the Union on February 14, 1912, as the 48th state. The state flower is the saguaro cactus blossom, the state tree is the palo verde, and the state bird is the cactus wren.

Major Universities:
Arizona State University, University of Phoenix, Ottawa University, and 10 colleges within the Maricopa Community College District: Phoenix College; Mesa Community College; Gateway Community College; Scottsdale Community College; Glendale Community College; Rio Salado Community College; South Mountain Community College; Chandler-Gilbert Community College; Estrella Mountain Community College; and Paradise Valley Community College

Important Dates in History:
1885—Arizona State University, the oldest institution of higher learning in Arizona, founded.

1889—Phoenix named as Arizona's capital
1911—Roosevelt Dam, a reservoir that helps supply the Valley's water, completed
1959—Phoenix experiences a boom in new construction and enters a period of steady growth

Community Honors:
1993—Best Run City in the World award from the Carl Bertelsmann Foundation
2000—Best Managed City, *Governing Magazine*

Time Zone:
Arizona is on Mountain Standard Time and does not change its clocks for daylight saving time. So Arizona is on Mountain time half the year and on Pacific time during daylight savings time.

Dress Codes:
The focus is on comfortable and casual and comfortable. Only a few restaurants require a tie and jacket for gentlemen. A sweater or lightweight jacket is advisable for cool evenings from December through March.

Major Area Industries:
High-tech manufacturing, tourism, and construction

Famous Sons, Daughters, and Residents:
Frank Luke, W.W. I Ace Pilot
Ira Hayes, U.S. Marine who raised the flag on Iwo Jima
Barry Goldwater, politician
Frank Lloyd Wright, architect
Steve Allen, entertainer
Marty Robbins, country singer
Paul Harvey, radio personality
Glen Campbell, entertainer
Erma Bombeck, humorist
Bil Keene, cartoonist
Alice Cooper, rock musician
Francine Reed, blues singer
Steven Spielberg, film maker
David Spade, comedian

State/City Holidays:
Labor Day, Thanksgiving, Christmas, New Year's Day, Martin Luther King, Jr. Day, Memorial Day, Independence Day, Veterans Day

Chamber of Commerce:
Phoenix Chamber Of Commerce
201 N Central Ave., #2700
Phoenix, AZ 85073-8001
(602) 254-5521

Major Airports:
Phoenix Sky Harbor International Airport, served by 23 airlines

Public Transportation:
Phoenix offers bus service throughout the majority of the metro area.
Valley Metro: (602) 253-5000

(Continued on next page)

Military Bases:
Luke Air Force Base

Driving Laws:
Seat belts must be worn. Children must be in car seats until they weigh 40 lbs or more. High occupancy lanes are for cars with two or more people.

Alcohol Law:
You must be 21 years old to purchase alcoholic beverages. Bars are open until 1 AM. You can purchase alcohol on Sunday after 10 AM.

Daily Newspapers:
The Arizona Republic is the largest daily newspaper with a circulation of nearly 500,000. Call (602) 444-8000 or visit www.azcentral.com.

Sales Tax:
7.05%

Room Tax:
11.07%

Visitor Centers:
Downtown Phoenix
Visitor Information Center
50 N. Second St.
(Second & Adams Streets)
Hours: Monday through Friday, 8 AM to 5 PM

Biltmore Visitor Information Center Located at the Biltmore Fashion Park
2404 E. Camelback Rd.
(24th St. & Camelback Rd.)
Phoenix, AZ 85016
Hours: Monday through Friday, 10 AM to 6 PM; Weekends, 12 to 5 PM
Visitor Hotline:(602) 252-5588

Time and Temperature:
National Weather Service forecast office offers information about weather around the state: (602) 379-4000 for updated information.

Phoenix weather information is also available at www.weather.com

Table of Contents

Directory of Maps

CENTRAL ARIZONA

GREATER PHOENIX

DOWNTOWN PHOENIX

Arizona Veterans
Memorial Coliseum

Heard Museum

Phoenix Art Museum

51

West McDowell Road

East McDowell Road

10

East Roosevelt Street

North 1st Avenue

North 3rd Street

North 7th Street

West Van Buren Street

East Van Buren Street

17

American West
Arena

East Washington Street

West Buckeye Road

East Buckeye Road

17 60

South 7th Avenue

South Central Avenue

South 7th Street

West Grand Avenue

CHANDLER

North Alma School Road

North McQueen Road

West Galveston Street

East Galveston Street

87

West Chandler Boulevard

East Chandler Boulevard

South McQueen Road

West Frye Road

East Frye Road

GLENDALE

West Bell Road

East Bell Road

● Sun City

60

North 59th Avenue

17

West Olive Avenue

West Dunlap Avenue

PHOENIX ★

West Glendale Avenue

Grand Avenue

10

West Buckeye Road

MESA

East McKellips Road

SALT RIVER

202

101

North Alma School Road

North Country Club Drive

Center Street

North Mesa Drive

East Brown Road

West University Drive

East University Drive

West Main Street

South Dobson Road

East Main Street

87

West Broadway Road

East Broadway Road

West Southern Avenue

South Country Club Drive

East Southern Avenue

South Mesa Drive

60

SCOTTSDALE

TEMPE

Botanical Garden

Van Buren Street

143

Washington Street

202

The Phoenix Zoo

Scottsdale Road

Hayden Road

McKellips Road

North Mill Avenue

Curry Rd.

McClintock Drive

Salt River

North Priest Drive

Tempe Town Lake

Rio Salado Pkwy.

Sun Devil
Stadium

West University Drive

East University Drive

ASU

Tempe
St. Luke's
Hospital

East Apache Blvd.

10

East Broadway Road

South Priest Drive

South Hardy Drive

South Mill Avenue

South Rural Road

East Southern Avenue

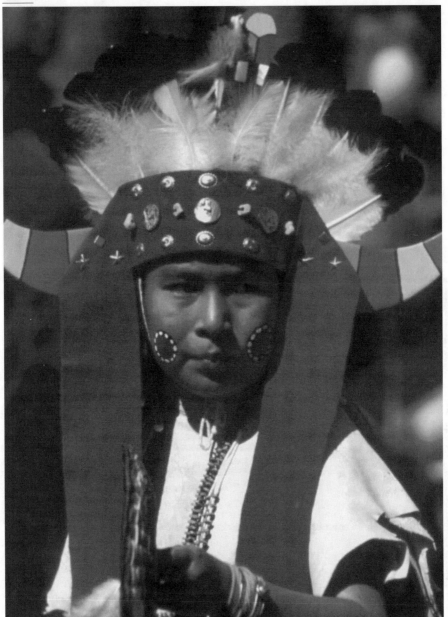

Visitors can enjoy colorful music and dance performances during the Heard's many events and Saturday programming. Pictured is a member of the Hopi Tewa Senom Dance Group.

Photo: Courtesy of the Heard Museum

Area Overview

Welcome to the desert and the Valley of the Sun. You're going to have a good time here and we hope this book will help you find your way around and introduce you to the best the area has to offer. The Valley is big and covers a lot of territory and we thought we'd begin by telling you a bit about the history of the area and then touch on the various cities and geographic regions. You'll be surprised by the diversity of people, cultures, and experiences that you'll discover.

People have visited the Phoenix area for thousands of years and decided to stay but living here has always been dependent upon access to water. Through the past millennia, civilization in the Valley of the Sun has risen and fallen with irrigation. Centuries before Christ, the Hohokam people began to develop an agrarian culture in the arid Valley, whose desert soil hardens within a few inches of the surface. A scant 6 inches of rain falls in the Sonoran Desert each year, just enough to wet the top, percolate through, and still leave a shovel-busting crust. The Hohokam dug through the hardpan to build the 250 miles of canals that now form the basis of the Valley's modern canal system. In fact, most of the Valley's irrigation systems follow the paths of these original canals. The Hohokam eventually left the area, leaving behind their waterways to fill with dirt until the next group of people arrived.

The continued growth of the Valley of the Sun still depends on vast waterworks that would make Rome's aqueduct builders envious. And in the last decade, the Central Arizona Project canal diverted water from the 200-miles-distant Colorado River over the Valley's desert acres. In addition, vast reserves of runoff from rain and snow in Arizona's northern mountains are stored behind Roosevelt Dam northeast of the Valley.

Made livable with water and air conditioning, the Valley draws people like a magnet year after year. Some come for the 300 or so days of sunshine the Valley enjoys each year. Others seek the economic opportunity that this booming desert capital offers. Some come to reinvent themselves in the same way that the pioneers threw off their old lives to find something new in the West. They come to get away from bad weather, bad memories, and bad jobs. Even though about a third of Maricopa County residents leave each year, the influx of newcomers is so great that the Valley keeps growing.

The migration out of the county happens for many of the same reasons that people are coming in. Since so many people move here for work, they have no roots in the Valley and, therefore, when a better job comes up elsewhere, they move there. Job transfers in interstate corporations also play a part. Many of Arizona's major employment fields— such as tourism and the high-tech industry—traditionally attract very mobile employees.

Maricopa County enjoyed the largest population growth of the state's 15 counties from 1993 to 1999, gaining more than 500,000 residents. The county's annual growth rate from 1997 to 2000 was approximately 3.4

LOOK FOR:
- **Phoenix**
- **Southeast Valley**
- **Northeast Valley**
- **Northwest Valley**
- **Southwest Valley**

percent. The U.S. Census Bureau estimated the county's 2000 population at approximately 3 million. Where do you put all these people? Unlike the already high-density population centers of the East and West coasts, most cities in the Valley of the Sun are relatively young with no natural growth boundaries. With few exceptions, the cities have nearly free reign to expand and gulp up unincorporated land as they wish in order to accommodate and promote growth. However, growth cannot be allowed to continue unchecked and boosterism and conserving open spaces are not mutually exclusive concepts. Within recent years, the debate over growth boundaries has been fierce, with groups like the Sierra Club attempting to initiate growth management boundaries and policies that actually have some judicial teeth.

As recently as 1950, the city of Phoenix encompassed just 17 square miles and had a population of about 100,000. Since then, the city has pursued an aggressive policy of annexation, which has expanded its area by nearly 400 square miles. As of July 1, 1999, the Census Bureau estimated the population of Phoenix at 1,220,710, making it the sixth-largest city in the United States.

The Valley's other cities have been just as aggressive in their growth and land annexation. Mesa, the second largest city in the Valley, had a population of 16,670 in 1950. From the early city center around Main and Center Streets, it has expanded to the edge of Maricopa County on the east. Traveling from Mesa's west end to its east end takes nearly a half-hour of driving at the posted 55 mph speed limit on the Superstition Freeway (Interstate 60). Mesa, with a 1999 population estimated at 361,895, is the third-largest city in Arizona, behind Phoenix and Tucson. Similarly, Tempe grew to 159,220 in 1999 from 7,684 in 1950; Scottsdale to 195,495 from 2,032; Glendale to 196,820 from 8,179; and Chandler to 160,165 from 3,799.

The strong economy has fueled this growth. The United States Department of Commerce Bureau of Economic Analysis (BEA) ranks Arizona as first in the nation in its real gross state product (GSP). From 1992 through 1998, Arizona's GSP grew 7.5% compared to 3.9% nationally. According to the BEA, strength in high-tech manufacturing and in business services—two industries identified with the New Economy—contributed to the rapid growth. The Valley's economic focus has shifted away from agriculture—though Maricopa County remains one of the largest cotton-producing counties in the nation—to the service industry, tourism, and high-tech manufacturing. Agriculture began to give way to a defense economy during World War II. After the war the defense industries, such as aerospace, shifted to peacetime production. Electronics companies came to the Valley in profusion in the 1950s, and the high-tech and computer industries followed in the 1980s and 1990s.

As of August 2000, Maricopa County's unemployment rate continued to be good, dropping as low as 2.6% during the summer. About 1,565,300 people are employed in nonfarm industries the Phoenix metropolitan area, according to The Arizona Department of Economic Security. Service industries—such as banking, real-estate, and government—represented the largest employment category, with 514,100 workers. Manufacturing jobs at such major employers as Boeing, Honeywell, Motorola, and Intel employed 164,300, and the booming construction industry employed 114,200.

The Valley has also become a sports Mecca. This is one of a handful of metropolitan areas to have franchises for all four major-league sports—baseball, football, basketball and hockey—a claim that even the monstrous Los Angeles metroplex has been unable to make since both the Rams and Raiders deserted la-la land. (See our Spectator Sports chapter.)

As much as the mayors and loyal residents of other Valley cities may bristle, Phoenix has always been the Valley of the Sun's 900-pound gorilla, the hub around which its commerce revolves—so much so that many people refer to the entire Valley of the Sun as Phoenix. Even people who live as far afield as Apache Junction and Avondale have been heard to tell outsiders, "I live in Phoenix."

So just what is the Valley of the Sun? To most, the Valley represents the urbanized portions of Maricopa County. The Valley covers 2,000 square miles, and Phoenix represents about 470 of

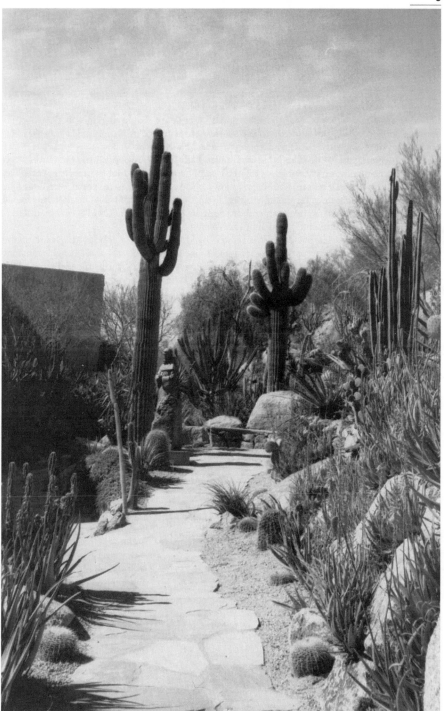

Phoenix wears its desert surroundings as a complement to the Southwestern-style buildings.

Photo: Penny Kleingartner

those. Maricopa County includes 24 incorporated cities and towns, not to mention 32 unincorporated communities. Cities and towns within the county are Avondale, Buckeye, Carefree, Cave Creek, Chandler, El Mirage, Fountain Hills, Gila Bend, Gilbert, Glendale, Goodyear, Guadalupe, Litchfield Park, Mesa, Paradise Valley, Peoria, Phoenix, Queen Creek, Scottsdale, Surprise, Tempe, Tolleson, Wickenburg, and Youngtown. Unincorporated cities include Chandler Heights, Sun City, Sun City West, and Sunflower. From east to west, it stretches 45 miles from Apache Junction to Goodyear. From north to south, it stretches about 40 miles from the northern boundary of Phoenix to Chandler. The outer orbit of the Valley's growth has touched Carefree and Cave Creek in the foothills north of Phoenix, Fountain Hills in the foothills northeast of Scottsdale, and Buckeye to the southwest. Although Wickenburg is about 40 miles northwest of the Sun Cities, it is sometimes considered part of the Valley.

The continuing growth of the urbanized Valley has almost surrounded the Salt River Pima Maricopa Indian Community, which is located east of Scottsdale and south of north Scottsdale. The reservation's southeastern boundary follows the Salt River's path north of Mesa. The reservation also touches on Tempe at Hayden Road, south of Scottsdale. The Fort McDowell Indian Community touches the north end of Fountain Hills, while the Gila River Indian Reservation marks the southern end of much of the Valley.

In many ways Sky Harbor Airport, operated by the City of Phoenix, is the heart of the Valley. Its eastbound flight paths have sparked noise complaints and a seemingly constant battle with the city of Tempe. Yet the sight of the virtually constant air traffic seems symbolic of the Valley's economic vitality. The Valley is a place where, more often than not, shiny new buildings win out over preserving the past. It's a place where people and governments are not afraid to use the latest technology.

Still, it's important to remember that the Valley of the Sun is not just Phoenix, and that although the housing developments that are consuming the desert landscape at the rate of an acre an hour sometimes seem stultifyingly similar, each city does have its own character, history, and attractions.

Phoenix

As of 1985, Phoenix adopted an "urban village plan" as part of the city's general plan. The idea was that the city had nine distinct areas in which city services and business cores were situated or needed to be situated. The city in its annexations had gobbled up many distinctive neighborhoods such as Maryvale, which began as an affordable bedroom community for young married couples and families when it was developed by John F. Long in the late 1950s and early 1960s, and South Phoenix, where the Valley's African-American and Hispanic populations concentrated.

As was the case with many cities, the central business district of Phoenix became less important as suburbs like Maryvale and Deer Valley arose. Unlike the case in older and more densely packed metropolitan areas like New York City, Phoenix swallowed its suburbs and neglected its epicenter. The malls in its far-flung neighborhoods helped keep people from heading downtown to do business. Aside from the office workers who went there, Phoenix's downtown was a ghost town after dark through most of the 1980s.

The urban village concept seemed like hokum to some critics, and it's certainly too soon to tell what effect it will

have on eight of the nine villages. However, the plan's adoption coincided with major efforts to revitalize downtown, which was one of the nine villages included in the concept. Ever since Phoenix Suns owner Jerry Colangelo decided to build America West Arena in downtown Phoenix, the center of the city has become more vibrant and lively. Although it's still not loaded with nightlife, downtown has been enlivened by the presence of the Phoenix Symphony, the Herberger Theater Center, the Orpheum Theater, Web Theater, and the Arizona Center (an open-air, two story outdoor mall with a number of restaurants and clubs), all of which have given people some genuine reasons to head (or stay) there after dark.

A few other clubs and restaurants also have benefited from the rise in foot traffic, which is but a trickle compared with that in other major cities, yet far greater than it was in the 1980s. Bank One Ballpark, the home of the Arizona Diamondbacks, opened in March 1998 and has further boosted downtown's fortunes.

As a city, though, Phoenix remains a huge suburb with interesting pockets of old-time housing such as Encanto Village. There are some very good parks, such as Papago Park, and some strangely desolate ones. For example, Margaret T. Hance Park, a mile-long, treeless expanse built to cover Interstate 10's incursion through downtown (the freeway moves through a tunnel beneath the park) seems unused much of the time. Patriot's Square in downtown Phoenix sits atop an underground parking garage. Since it only covers a city block, it seems packed, especially at lunchtime. There's more brick than grass in it, but it remains a downtown oasis.

The freeway system has improved mobility around the Valley, but people tend to play and shop close to home, and a number of malls serve that purpose—Desert Sky and Maryvale malls on the west side; Metrocenter in the north-central section; Chris-Town Mall in the central section; the Colonnade and Town & Country shopping center and the Biltmore Fashion Park, all off Camelback Road and the Squaw Peak Parkway (State Route 51); Paradise Valley Mall in the northeastern section; and Arcadia Crossing in the eastern section—and much more shopping has grown up around them. (We provide an overview of shopping hot spots in our Shopping chapter.)

Although Phoenix's neighborhoods are built primarily on a grid and many housing developments are built cookie-cutter style, geographic and economic diversity provide character. In the northeastern part of the city, middle-class to upper-middle-class neighborhoods are punctuated by mountains—Camelback, Squaw Peak, North Mountain, and others. South Phoenix also features some prime housing in the foothills of South Mountain, but as you head north toward the Salt River, the increasing tension of crime-ridden neighborhoods can be felt in the flatlands. Nevertheless, along stretches of Baseline Road in South Phoenix, you'll experience an almost pastoral feeling with small remaining farms and orchards. There's a cozy claustrophobia to Phoenix's Paradise Valley neighborhood, which cannot be confused with the upscale town of the same name that sits to the neighborhood's southeast.

The high-rises of the Central Avenue corridor stand in stark contrast to the many old single-story houses just blocks away. A little farther north on Central Avenue, some housing sits on big lots near large apartment complexes—rarely more than two stories tall—and the number of trees increases radically. These are relatively old, established neighborhoods. Far to the west, where housing is relatively new, one can feel an unsettled quietude. The neighborhoods sit flat in the slope toward the Agua Fria River, and the houses are far enough apart that they still seem unsheltered, like pioneer dwellings on the desert floor.

In other words, this gorilla city doesn't have a single face. Whatever the fate of the urban-village concept, the planners who created it were certainly right about the diversity of the styles and needs of the city's neighborhoods.

Southeast Valley

Mesa

The Southeast Valley consists of sprawling Mesa, landlocked Tempe, and newly rising Chandler, Gilbert, and Guadalupe. Some even consider far-flung Apache Junction, a city in Pinal County, to be part of the Valley.

The Southeast Valley is one of the key centers of housing growth, with goods and services following on the heels of new housing builds. Since so much of this area was agricultural mere decades ago, there are few old commerce centers to serve as anchors. Instead, strip malls sprout along the major thoroughfares, spaced on a grid of one-mile squares. Mesa, Tempe, and Chandler all have core downtown areas that are pedestrian-friendly, but in some neighborhoods in the Southeast Valley it's a daunting task to walk almost anywhere, and local mom-and-pop stores or newsstands are nowhere to be seen.

Mesa is the giant of the southeast Valley. The city was founded by Mormons from Utah and Idaho. They settled on this broad plateau, or mesa, in May of 1878 and sought to name the settlement in its honor. However, the post office wouldn't recognize the name "Mesa" because a town named Mesaville existed in Pinal County. The settlers decided to name their community Hayden, after Charles Trumbull Hayden, who at the time ran a ferryboat across the Salt River. This caused confusion in the mails because of an old post office called Hayden's Ferry, so the settlers renamed their town Zenos, after a prophet in the Book of Mormon, in 1886. When Mesaville went out of existence in 1888, the settlers promptly changed the name of the community back to Mesa.

Mormon culture remains dominant in Mesa, giving it a different ambiance from Phoenix and the rest of the Valley. It's not uncommon to see Mormon missionaries, dressed neatly in white shirts and dark ties, riding bicycles and spreading the word.

Given the city's size, the downtown is small and quiet at night. This is not to say that the city is a Mormon city; it's far from it. The influx of population in recent years makes it nearly as heterogeneous as other parts of the Valley. However, the Mormon influence has given rise to the perception that it's a good place for young families to settle. The city also has a larger share of winter visitors and older residents living in trailer parks.

Tempe

Tempe began when Charles Trumbull Hayden built a flour mill and established a ferry service across the Salt River in 1871. Soon, a small community grew up around these enterprises, and the post office recognized it as Hayden's Ferry and Hayden's Mill. The growing settlement took the name Tempe after the suggestion of "Lord" Darrell Duppa. Duppa had a penchant for Greek names, having named Phoenix, and he suggested that Hayden's Ferry be renamed Tempe because to him it resembled the Vale of Tempe in Greece. Hayden became one of the trustees of the Territorial Normal School, which became Tempe's major asset. The Normal School evolved over the next six decades to become Arizona State University (see our Education chapter). Today, the university is central to Tempe's active downtown scene along Mill Avenue, which has been revived in the past decade and is full of cafes, restaurants, and shopping spots. The presence of students makes Tempe one of the best towns in Arizona for aspiring musicians.

The university's Sun Devil Stadium is the site of ASU Sun Devil football and the NFL's Arizona Cardinals games. It annually hosts the Fiesta Bowl and was the site of Super Bowl XXX. The stadium also is one of the few venues to have hosted both a papal Mass and Rolling Stones concerts. Large concert scenes from Barbara Streisand's *A Star Is Born* were filmed there, as were scenes in U2's movie *Rattle and Hum*. Other university facilities, such as Gammage Auditorium, also provide easily accessible cultural activities, ranging from touring Broadway plays to classical and pop concerts. The university is also the home of KAET (Channel 8), the Valley's PBS station.

Tempe is unique among the Valley's major cities in that it cannot annex any neighboring land. It is landlocked by Phoenix on the west, Scottsdale on the north, Mesa on the east, and Chandler on the south. However, the city has been making the most of undeveloped land within its limits. The Arizona Mills Mall opened in late 1997 at the junction of the Superstition Freeway (Interstate 60) and Interstate 10. It is the largest mall in Arizona and boasts a range of outlet stores, high-tech play areas, and restaurants.

The newest Tempe attraction is the Tempe Town Lake, where the once-dry Salt River was dammed to create a two-mile long recreation area perfect for biking, jogging, skating, canoeing, sailing, and paddle-boating.

Aside from Phoenix, Tempe is the only Valley city to be host to two major-league sports teams. The NFL's Arizona Cardinals play at ASU's Sun Devil Stadium (as do the school's Sun

INSIDERS' TIP

Cars and trucks in Maricopa County are tested every two years for polluting exhaust emissions and to make sure that emission-control devices are working. New residents need only a registration or title when testing the vehicle. Emission testing stations are open on weekdays, 8 AM to 7 PM, and on Saturday, from 8 AM to 5 PM. For information about locations near you, call (602) 470-4646.

Devils), and Major League Baseball's Anaheim Angels play spring-training games at Tempe Diablo Stadium.

Chandler

Chandler is named after Alexander John Chandler, a Canadian who settled in Arizona in 1887. He was the territory's first veterinary surgeon, a post he held until 1892. In the interim, he became one of the Valley's largest landholders. His Chandler Ranch covered about 18,000 acres, and in 1911 he sold his land in plots of 10 to 160 acres. The city of Chandler was established a year later.

The community retained its agricultural character until about 1980, when a building boom propelled it into its status one of the fastest-growing communities in the state. Chandler has become home to several high-tech manufacturers, including Intel. The city continues to revitalize its downtown on Arizona Avenue with such projects as the Chandler Center for the Arts, which was completed in the early 1990s. The San Marcos Hotel, with some updating, was re-established as the major draw of Chandler's downtown. The hotel, isolated as it was from the rest of the Valley in Chandler's early days, was one of the first to promote itself as a resort for winter visitors. Dr. Chandler lived out his final days at the San Marcos.

INSIDERS' TIP

If you're a celebrity watcher, Scottsdale is one place where you're likely to run into some. Whether you're out shopping, browsing in art galleries, or taking in the nightlife, keep your eyes wide and you just might spot a star.

Gilbert

Gilbert was established in 1912 on land donated by Robert Gilbert. It, too, was an agricultural community. In fact, it was known as the Hay Capital of the World until 1920. In 1980,

Camelback Mountain over the orange trees looks inviting from this Arcadia neighborhood.

Photo: Debbie Ross

Gilbert had 5,717 residents. In 1999, the U.S. Census Bureau reported its population to be 160,165. The fastest-growing community in Arizona, Gilbert has suffered some growing pains. The city is taking in new students faster than it can fund new classrooms, and hopes to attract more businesses to balance the residential growth.

Guadalupe

Also part of the Southeast Valley is Guadalupe. A tiny "landlocked" community, Guadalupe's 1999 population was 5,390, one of the smallest in the Valley. It boasts one of the more colorful municipal histories. Guadalupe was established by members of the Yaqui tribe who fled Mexico in the late 1800s to escape dictator Porfirio Diaz's attempts to relocate them to the Yucatan, which was far from their ancestral home in northwestern Mexico. The name comes from the Virgin of Guadalupe, the patron saint of Mexico. The town's chief landmarks are the mission-style Our Lady of Guadalupe Church and the Yaqui Temple. Today, Yaqui descendants and Mexican-Americans comprise the majority of the town's residents. Public school students go to school in Tempe, which nearly encircles Guadalupe. With an unemployment rate at around 15 percent, Guadalupe officials are seeking more businesses to employ their residents.

Queen Creek

Beyond what is commonly considered the Valley, the farming community of Queen Creek maintains a bucolic lifestyle southeast of Gilbert. The biggest event of the year in the community is Country Thunder, a three-day festival of country music that's heavily attended by RV campers (see our Annual Events chapter). With Gilbert rapidly growing and Williams Gateway Airport growing to its north, Queen Creek may soon be enveloped to become part of the Valley's mainstream instead of remaining on the fringe.

Apache Junction

East of Mesa, all the way in Pinal County, Apache Junction sits at the foot of the Superstition Mountains like an appendix to the Valley. Formerly a fairly relaxed community, Apache Junction has the Valley's growth gene as well. With growth came new zoning restrictions that rankled some longtime residents. Primarily known for the many senior citizens who winter here in trailer and RV parks, Apache Junction may be changing its character as more families settle in the town. Although it is 45 minutes from downtown Phoenix, Apache Junction is likely to be considered part of the Valley's mainstream in the coming years.

Sun Lakes

The unincorporated retirement community of Sun Lakes is wedged between the southern end of Chandler and the northeastern boundary of the Gila River Indian Reservation. When the community was established in 1972 by developer Robson Communities, it was well-separated from Chandler development and not thought of as part of the Valley. Today, the population of roughly 14,000 enjoys golf courses, swimming pools, tennis courts, health clubs, fishing lakes, craft studios, social clubs, and dining facilities. Although separated from downtown Phoenix by a 35-minute drive up Interstate 10, local seniors have little or no need to leave the area to sustain their lifestyle.

Gila River Native American Reservation

The Gila River Native American Reservation marks the Valley's southern end. The reservation covers 650 square miles—more than half the size of the Valley—but it houses only about 12,000 mostly agrarian residents. Although technically outside the Valley, the northern end of the reservation houses attractions that bring in hundreds of thousands of visitors annually. Firebird International Raceway and two casinos have allowed the tribe to improve many community services and add a hospital and fire department.

Northeast Valley

The Northeast Valley is considered the Valley's most upscale region. It includes large estates in Paradise Valley and newly developed high-end communities located in land recently annexed by the city of Scottsdale. This area is miles from the Salt River bottom, and, in its gradual slope upwards to the Mogollon Rim, foothills become an important geographical feature.

Scottsdale

Scottsdale is top dog in the Northeast Valley. On its eastern side, the city mostly borders the Salt River Pima-Maricopa Native American Community, and to the south it is hemmed in by Tempe. Early in its development it squabbled with Phoenix over annexation rights to various tracts on its west side. In the past decade, Scottsdale annexed a huge amount of land to the north, which brought communities of ranchers and desert dwellers into its chic fold.

In 1881, Major Winfield Scott homesteaded on the site of the city that would one day carry his name. When Scott retired from the military, he promoted his ranch and the surrounding area as a rest cure and agricultural center. Scottsdale became the official name in 1896, when local settlers sought to establish a school district.

Scottsdale was relatively slow to develop but has boomed in the years since World War II. It was one of the first cities to revitalize its downtown, billing itself as "the West's most Western town." Art galleries abound in downtown Scottsdale, catering to both cowboy-art and modern-art lovers. The downtown is eminently friendly to foot traffic, and Scottsdale Fashion Square Mall offers another area for upscale shopping not too far from the town center. Although the Galleria, an ambitious higher-end shopping mall, stands empty as the city's biggest white elephant, other forward-looking ideas promoted by the city have been successful in defining Scottsdale.

The greenbelt that runs for a dozen miles down the Indian Bend Wash made a virtue out of a flooding problem. Since the wash floods during any significant rain, filling it in for development would have been unwise. Instead, the city devised an alternative plan that turned it into a strip of parkland with jogging and bicycle paths and other recreational facilities that would not be unduly affected by the occasional flooding. Floodwaters would irrigate the grass and would be contained by the wide channel.

Central to the city's image as a cultural leader is the Scottsdale Center for the Arts, which features two art galleries and an 800-seat auditorium (see our Arts chapter). The arts facility is part of the Scottsdale Civic Center complex, also known as the Scottsdale Mall, which includes City Hall, the Scottsdale Library, and other municipal facilities. It is adjacent to Scottsdale Stadium, which hosts the San Francisco Giants during spring training and two teams in the Arizona Fall Baseball League. Another Scottsdale landmark is Taliesin West, a winter residence built by Frank Lloyd Wright in 1937, making Wright's presence a powerful force in the city's cultural fabric. He's claimed almost as a native son. Scottsdale is also home to the Scottsdale Air Park, a busy industrial park that surrounds Scottsdale Municipal Airport around Frank Lloyd Wright Boulevard.

The town of Paradise Valley, nestled among the hills between north Phoenix and north Scottsdale, may be the Valley's most exclusive community. Residents can see the back of

INSIDERS' TIP

If you listen to the metro traffic alerts on the local radio stations (and you will once you begin driving during the rush hours), you'll find them confusing at first. The voice will reel off a list of numbers and names: the 101, the 202, the short stack, the deck-park tunnel, the Superstition.... These names will sound a bit like a secret code until you've spent 10 minutes with a map of the Valley. Pay close attention to the freeways. Each has a number you'll soon learn as you motor around. You can speed up the process by referring to our Getting Here, Getting Around chapter.

Camelback Mountain and look up at a formation called the Praying Monk. The large estates of the community, incorporated in 1961, house many of the Valley's celebrities—Alice Cooper, Geordie Hormel (the heir to the Spam fortune), former major leaguer Joe Garagiola, and *Family Circus* cartoonist Bil Keane, just to name a few.

As Billie Holiday sang, "Them that's got shall get!" The 13,315 well-heeled residents of Paradise Valley, where most recent figures show that the median home value was $650,000 and the median household income was $137,284, pay no property tax. The town earned some infamy among local drivers when it became the first municipality in the Valley to install photo-radar to help its small police force crack down on speeders along Lincoln Boulevard. The mountainside street offers wonderful views of the Valley's lights at night, and it is the main thoroughfare through Paradise Valley from Phoenix to Scottsdale.

Carefree

As Scottsdale and Phoenix aggressively annex toward the north, the Valley almost includes the foothill towns Carefree and Cave Creek, which are almost always mentioned in the same breath. Gordon Lightfoot's song "Carefree Highway" refers to the highway that connects Carefree to Interstate 17, miles to the west. Carefree, established in 1959, is a planned community of luxury homes that rests in the northwestern shoulder of Scottsdale, just northeast of the very northeastern tip of Phoenix. The home of the Boulders Resort (see our Resorts chapter), the town has huge boulders as topographical features. In 1999, the Census Bureau listed Carefree's population 2,615.

INSIDERS' TIP

Be sure to take along plenty of water on all excursions during the summer in Arizona—even if you're just planning to drive or walk a short distance. It's amazing how fast you can dehydrate in the desert heat. If you're waiting for a tow truck in the case of a breakdown, water can feel heaven sent.

Cave Creek

Cave Creek, on the other hand, was founded in 1874, when prospectors found gold to the northeast. Unlike other communities that became ghost towns after a gold rush, Cave Creek was a good area for ranching. The Cave Creek Wash, which flows year round, and lush springs nearby helped provide water and grazing areas for cattle. The town, just west of Carefree and just north of Phoenix, offers Valley residents a quick, admission-free getaway to the Old West in its Frontier Town, a group of Western-style shops, and its old-timey saloons. Cave Creek's 1999 population was listed as 3,605.

Fountain Hills

Similarly, Scottsdale's growth has nearly brought Fountain Hills into the Valley. From northeast Scottsdale, Shea Boulevard travels through a pass in the McDowell Mountains to enter Fountain Hills. The McDowells form a natural boundary between the mountain community and the Valley. Fountain Hills prides itself on being far from the hubbub and crime of the urban center. It was one of "Ten Great Places to Raise a Family," in the May 1997 issue of *Parenting* magazine. When building began in 1970, unincorporated Fountain Hills was seen as being attractive to retirees. The plan called for the then-unincorporated community to expand to 70,000 residents by the time it was built out. Times changed, though, and the market for that type of community evaporated. Now, the town, which was incorporated in 1989, offers upscale, low-density neighborhoods. Its population is a mix of retirees, winter visitors, and families. In 1999, the Census Bureau estimated Fountain Hills' population at 17,280 . Fountain Hills cannot annex any land because it is surrounded by the McDowell Mountains, McDowell Mountain Park, the Fort McDowell Indian Community, and the Salt River Pima-Maricopa Indian Community. The town takes its name from its fountain, which can spew a plume of water more than 560 feet into the air. Boosters claim that it is the world's tallest fountain and it was designed both as a landmark and a means to disperse the town's effluent.

Taliesin West: Architect Frank Lloyd Wright's Personal Favorite

Eleven of Frank Lloyd Wright's buildings are listed by *The Architectural Record* as among the top 100 significant in the world, but the architect's personal favorite was his architectural school in Scottsdale, Arizona—Taliesin West.

From 1927, when he first visited the Phoenix area to consult on the Arizona Biltmore Resort, to his death in 1959 at the age of 91, the charm of the Sonoran desert lured Wright to Arizona every winter. He built Taliesin West in the late 1930s and it was during his tenure there, he completely one-third of his designs and his controversial architect achieved the recognition he had long pursued.

Taliesin West, now a National Historic Landmark, nestles on 600 acres of desert land. A stroll around the grounds, led by informed tour guides—some of them former Wright apprentices—offers insight into Wright's genius. The school trains about 35 students each year, still has an on-site architectural firm, and the on-site archives of Wright's drawing and writings draw researchers from around the world. Filmmaker Ken Burns spent two years there researching Wright for a PBS documentary that aired in 1999.

The handful of buildings that comprise Taliesin West recline below the mountains, their profile harmonizing with the desert's rocks and plants. Wright's philosophy of organic design found its spiritual home in Arizona, and he believed the cactus epitomized good design. In a 1940 article for *Arizona Highways*, he wrote: "The Arizona desert is no place for the hard box-walls of the houses of the Middle West and East. Here all is sculptured by wind and water, patterned in color and texture."

The desert also supplied building materials. Wright worked side-by-side with his apprentices in the backbreaking work of gathering rocks and sand to create his unique "desert masonry." Hard, flat-sided rocks found in the area, called Taliesin quartzite, were unsuitable for cutting, but he used them to create a textured surface on the thick, concrete walls throughout the campus.

Hands-on work was an integral part of Wright's education philosophy, and his students still learn by doing. Many continue the tradition of constructing their own desert digs in which they live while studying at the school. In Wright's time, students worked hard but they also played hard, because the teacher felt that learning how to socialize formally provided good training for the architecture business.

One center of social activity was the living room, dubbed "The Garden Room," whose 56-foot-long space is made even more dramatic by its sloping, translucent roof and spine of windows. Other points of interest on the Taliesin West grounds include the Cabaret Cinema, the Music Pavilion, the Seminar Theater, and Wright's private office. One of Wright's works, the historic Sun Cottage, consists of three large circular rooms framed by glass walls and clustered around a breezeway.

Throughout Taliesin West, redwood timbers crown the buildings and canvas roofs allow sunlight to diffuse through the rooms. His rooms are filled with furniture that he designed. The entrances to his buildings are hidden and mysterious; entryways to rooms are low, opening suddenly into spaciousness and light.

Taliesin West was a work in progress while Wright lived, because the master was forever improving on his designs. Today, his desert camp provides a glimpse into the creative life of a man whose vision is still ahead of its time.

Taliesin West is located at 1261 Frank Lloyd Wright Boulevard in Scottsdale. For more information about tours, call (480) 860-2700 ext. 495, or visit www.franklloydwright.org.

Because of Fountain Hills' growth, the Fort McDowell Indian Community to the northeast of town is slowly being brought into the Valley's sphere as well. The small community has about 800 registered members. Revenues from tribal enterprises such as the Fort McDowell Casino, a tribal farm, a gas station on the busy Beeline Highway (State Route 87), Fort McDowell Adventures (a tourist destination that offers horseback riding and other activities in the desert), and Fort McDowell Sand and Gravel have helped the community improve its infrastructure and the income of its members.

Salt River Pima-Maricopa Indian Community

Where does the mostly agricultural Salt River Pima-Maricopa Indian Community fit in? It's either the very southern part of the Northeast Valley or the very northern part of the Southeast Valley. Although it has fingers that shoot down south of Tempe's northern boundary, the reservation for the most part is east of Scottsdale, which also bounds the reservation on the north. For the most part, the Salt River marks its southern boundary just north of Mesa and Tempe. Although it is considered the most urbanized of Arizona's reservations, when you pass through the sparsely populated agricultural landscape you feel as though you have left the Valley.

The community's chief crops are cotton, melons, potatoes, onions, and carrots. Along its boundaries with Mesa, Tempe, and Scottsdale, little shops do heavy business selling cigarettes free of state sales tax. The reservation also benefits from a 140-acre shopping center known as the Pavilions, the largest on Native American land in the nation. The shopping center sits right across from north Scottsdale at Indian Bend and Pima Roads, so it draws a good business from the city.

To some extent, Northeast Phoenix is also seen as part of the Northeast Valley. With deluxe areas such as the Arizona Biltmore within it, Northeast Phoenix shares the Northeast Valley's reputation for glitzy affluence.

Northwest Valley

After the Southeast Valley, the Northwest Valley is enjoying the area's greatest growth spurt. Houses are being built farther and farther out. For our purposes, the Northwest Valley

Modern structures surround the historic State Capitol.

Photo: Penny Kleingartner

includes Glendale, Peoria, Sun City, Sun City West, Youngtown, El Mirage, and Surprise. The housing boom, mostly appealing to young families and retirees, has spawned a major upsurge in amenities in the area in the past decade.

The key to the Northwest Valley's development has always been roads. For most of its existence, Grand Avenue, which also doubles as several highways including Interstate 60, was the main drag that opened commercial development. Acres of industrial buildings line the highway as it progresses northwestward as the only major road in the Valley that proceeds on an angle to the squared-off grid system. Grand Avenue touches on downtown Glendale and downtown Peoria, then offers easy access to Sun City, Sun City West, Surprise, and Youngtown before heading for Wickenburg and Nevada.

The Loop 101 freeway, which begins at Camelback Road and 99th Avenue, heads north to approximately Bell Road and 83rd Avenue before jogging east to connect with Interstate 17. The corridor served by this relatively new freeway has been the center for the Northwest Valley's growth. The Arrowhead Towne Center in Glendale is convenient to residents of Peoria and the Sun Cities, as well as Glendale, and has been the focal point of commercial growth in the area.

Glendale

With an estimated population of 196,820 in 1999, Glendale is the third largest city in the Valley, fourth largest in the state, and obviously the big dog in the Northwest Valley. It was established in 1892 by members of the Church of the Brethren, but the reason church members had for naming the area Glendale has been lost. For the longest time, the city had a reputation as a blue-collar community. and the housing was on a par with that offered in Maryvale. The image of downtown was of a railroad crossing tying up traffic at the triple intersection of Grand, Glendale, and 59th Avenues. The city hired a full-time marketing director in 1987, and its downtown has undergone revitalization, building a reputation as a premiere antiquing destination. The city's library offers notable public arts programming. The city is the home of the American Graduate School of International Management, and since the 1980s has also housed Arizona State University's West Valley campus, a gem that also offers easily accessible cultural activities to the community.

To accommodate its rapid growth, Glendale annexed many square miles of unincorporated land to the southwest, including Luke Air Force Base. When Luke Air Force Base was built in 1941, it was expected to be a major economic plum. Unexpectedly, World War II boosted its value. Unlike Williams Air Force Base, which was downsized out of the Southeast Valley due to post-Cold War defense cutbacks, Luke continues to pump money into the economy of the Northwest Valley. However, with Glendale's commercial and residential growth, it has become a target of noise complaints and safety concerns because of flight training missions based there.

Peoria

Peoria was first settled by Chauncey Clark, who settled there from Peoria, Illinois, in the late 1800s. A primarily agricultural settlement, the city began to boom in the 1980s, attracting about 400 newcomers a month as housing developments marched over acres previously planted in cotton and other crops. Owing to its young-family orientation, the Peoria schools number among the best in the Valley. The city also opened the Peoria Sports Complex, a spring-training facility along the popular retro-style ballpark lines of Camden Yards, whose proximity to Arrowhead Towne Center has further fueled economic growth along Loop 101. As Peoria's population has grown, Grand Avenue has also developed as a popular business corridor. The city has reached northward in its growth and swallowed up Lake Pleasant and Lake Pleasant Regional Park, one of the most popular weekend destinations among boating and fishing enthusiasts (see our Recreation chapter).

Sun City and Sun City West

Sun City and Sun City West are developed as far as they can be. They are unincorporated

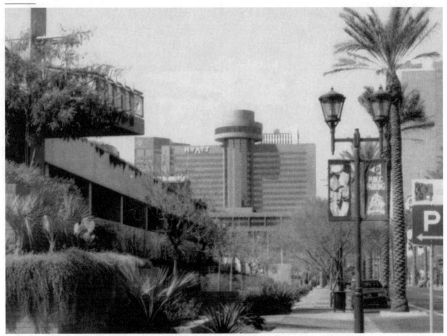

The changing skyline reflects a revitalized downtown Phoenix.

Photo: Penny Kleingartner

retirement communities established in the past four decades by builder Del Webb. The primary way to reach these communities is via Bell Road, which runs east to west across the Valley, connecting Sun City West to north Scottsdale far away to the east. The streets are designed in twisting, sometimes circular mazes that are nearly surrounded by golf courses. The speed limits are low, and golf carts have the right of way. Besides the golf courses, recreation centers form the center of social activity in the Sun Cities, and the community's recreation center boards act as a sort of low-level governmental body (see our Retirement chapter).

Shopping and restaurants are available, but the primary attraction of these retirement communities is the low-key lifestyle they offer, which is augmented by easy access to the attractions of Phoenix. Owned and operated by ASU, the 7,000-seat Sundome Center for the Arts offers frequent cultural and entertainment programs, mostly to residents of the Sun Cities since they are so isolated (although popular acts such as the Judds have drawn people from across the Valley). The Sundial Auditorium offers classical music performances.

Youngtown

With an ironic name, Youngtown was the Valley's first master-planned retirement community, begun on 320 acres in 1954. Youngtown was incorporated six years later, when Sun City opened. The community, which is virtually fully developed, encompasses a wedge-shaped area, surrounded by Sun City to the east, El Mirage to the north and west, and Peoria to the south. Since 1995, its annual population growth rate has been 0.8 percent, among the lowest in the Valley. Fortunately, most residents treasure Youngtown's small-town ambiance, so being landlocked is a blessing here.

EL Mirage

El Mirage, on the west bank of the Agua Fria River, was settled by migrant farm workers in the early 1930s. A working-class community, many residents have roots that reach back to the city's founding. It's estimated that 75 percent of the town's 5,770 residents are Hispanic, and El Mirage retains a Mexican-American flavor. The city's population growth rate has been even lower than Youngtown's, averaging 0.3 percent annually since 1995. However, city fathers are looking to attract more businesses, particularly distributors and manufacturers. The Santa Fe Railroad and Grand Avenue (Interstate 60) run parallel to one another through the center of El Mirage.

Surprise

Surprise, on the other hand, has become one of the fastest growing cities in Maricopa County, with an average annual population increase of 18.5 percent since 1995. In 1999, the U.S. Census Bureau estimated Surprise's population at 18,830. It had been 10,737 in 1995. The story goes that one of the city's first settlers back in 1929 said that it would be a surprise if the settlement became a city. Development has been spurred by both family-style and retirement communities. However, Sun City Grand, the latest development by Sun City founder Del Webb Corp., could tilt the community's demographic profile toward the older end of the spectrum. The 3,700-acre Sun City Grand sits on a triangle bounded by Bell Road to the south, Grand Avenue to the northeast and the proposed Estrella Freeway (Loop 303) to the west. Plans call for Sun City Grand to house 17,600 residents in 9,800 homes when it is fully developed. Thanks to annexations in the past 15 years, Surprise cradles Sun City West to its northeast and touches Sun City to its east. El Mirage sits to the southeast. Surprise has plenty of room to grow because unincorporated county land stretches from its northwest and southwest boundaries.

INSIDERS' TIP

How can you get a feeling for life in the different Valley communities? Spend time on foot, walking through the various downtown areas. Have a cup of coffee on the outdoor patio of a coffeehouse or restaurant and just people watch for a while. Try this on the weekend and a weekday. Visit during different times of the day. See who passes by you. Is the pace of life slow or fast? Is it quiet or noisy? What are the ages of the people you see? Then sit back and imagine your life among these people.

Southwest Valley

Phoenix's headlong growth has pushed its fingers into the Southwest Valley, touching such previously outlying cities as Litchfield Park, Goodyear, Avondale, and Tolleson. The pace of development in these communities has almost made Buckeye, which is about 35 miles west of downtown Phoenix, part of the Valley's mainstream.

Litchfield Park

Litchfield Park's main claim to fame is the Goodyear Tire and Rubber Company and its aircraft subsidiary. The company purchased the land that became Litchfield Park and Goodyear during World War I to grow cotton for use in its wartime products. In 1941, as Luke Air Force Base was being established to the north, the government set up a defense plant run by Goodyear Aircraft Corporation in Litchfield Park.

In the late 1960s, the city developed a master plan that changed its character from agricultural and defense-oriented to a suburban residential. It has since become home to many retired military personnel. The Wigwam Resort, which features three championship golf courses, is Litchfield Park's major employer (with 700 employees) and offers a five-star getaway for locals and visitors alike. Life is easygoing out here, even though Interstate 10 puts downtown Phoenix just 25 minutes away.

Goodyear

The completion of Interstate 10 in the early 1990s sparked a building boom in the town of Goodyear. Although the Goodyear company stopped growing cotton there at the end of World War II, the town remains primarily an agricultural community south of Litchfield Park. But that

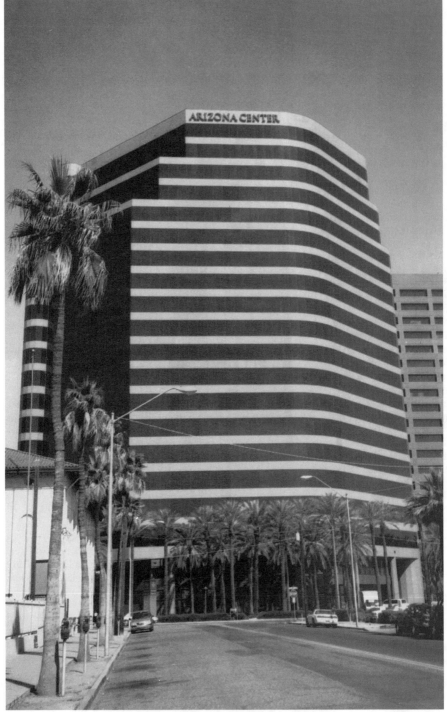

The Arizona Center is a downtown Phoenix landmark.

Photo: Penny Kleingartner

already is rapidly changing. *The Arizona Republic* says that Goodyear is expected to be the fastest growing community in the Valley over the next 40 years. Indeed, its average annual population growth rate of 17.9 percent since 1995 is surpassed only by Surprise (18.5 percent) in the Northwest Valley and Gilbert (18.8 percent) in the Southeast Valley. Family-oriented residential growth is expected to further deplete the area's farmland, and service industries geared to those residents are already booming. In 1999, Goodyear's population reached 14,305.

INSIDERS' TIP

Mall culture may be at its most developed in the Valley of the Sun. Some people save on their summer utility bills by going to an air-conditioned mall and spending the day there. There are even clubs of mall-walkers, who don their tennies and walk around the promenades for the exercise value more than the shopping values.

Avondale

Avondale was first settled by an outlaw named Billy Moore back during Frontier settlement, but it wasn't incorporated as a city until 1946. It remains mainly an agricultural community, but like Goodyear to its west, it is undergoing a transformation. City planners want light industry and commercial enterprises to balance residential growth. The plan appears to be working. Its annual average growth rate of 8.3 percent since 1995 is relatively modest compared with Goodyear's. However, in 1999 Avondale had an estimated 28,650 residents and thus was already nearly twice as large as Goodyear was in 1999, which had 14,305. Avondale's growth has encompassed Phoenix International Raceway, which used to sit on unincorporated county land. The raceway, a major draw on the NASCAR circuit, generates a good deal of revenue and traffic for all of the Southwest Valley.

Tolleson

At a scant six square miles, Tolleson sits just a few miles south and west of Desert Sky Mall in the Maryvale section of Phoenix. It, too, has a history as a farming community that has been changed by Interstate 10. Today, a Federal Express service center to serve all of Arizona and a major grocery-store distribution center are among the large employers taking advantage of the access the freeway provides. The community of 4,675 residents is mostly Hispanic.

INSIDERS' TIP

It's legal to make a right turn on a red-light in the Valley if you make sure to come to a complete stop first. Check the on-coming traffic and then proceed to turn if safe. Many of the Valley communities have left-turn signals, but the ones in Scottsdale are slightly different. The left-turn arrow are timed to follow (rather than proceed) the green light for the traffic traveling through the intersection.

Buckeye

At the far west limit of the Valley's expanse, almost to the Palo Verde Nuclear Generating Station, Buckeye is a giant, 100-square-mile agricultural community with a 1999 population of 5,035. Annexation plans call for the town to expand to 500 square miles by 2005. Plans also call for a mix of residential and commercial building to augment the town's agricultural base. However, that's all in the future for now. The average annual population growth rate has been 1.3 percent since 1995.

Getting Here, Getting Around

LOOK FOR:
- Traveling By Car
- Public Transportation
- Air Travel
- Private Transportation
- Taxis and Limousines

As a frontier settlement, Phoenix served more as a milepost than a destination point for settlers heading to California. Traveling on the region's first roads was a dusty, bumpy affair and those going by wagon between Phoenix and Tempe had to allow at least a half day to make the trip.

With the area's current cachet as a tourist hot spot and high-tech center, those cowtown days are gone. However, during peak rush hours—from 6 to 9 AM in the morning and 3 to 6 PM in the afternoon—unsuspecting travelers can still be snarled in wagon-pace traffic on one of the Valley's beleaguered interstates. A world-class airport, rationally laid out streets, and clear vistas make the Valley of the Sun welcoming for travelers, but newcomers will quickly realize that the freeway system is racing to keep up with the population explosion. In the 1970s, when an interstate system that would connect Phoenix with Los Angeles was proposed, opponents successfully campaigned against it. Our Valley was left in the dust in terms of freeway construction.

The Arizona Department of Transportation has worked in conjunction with other public and private entities to speed up highway construction and introduce alternative methods of transportation. Interstates 202 and 101 are about ten years ahead of schedule and they will eventually loop around the entire metropolitan area. New HOV (High Occupancy Vehicle) lanes are being introduced to encourage carpooling and many companies allow their employees to telecommute.

The Valley leads the pack in building Intelligent Transportation Systems or "smart highways," which—in the not-so-distant-future—will triple the amount of traffic that can travel on a road. In the meantime, visitors may not realize they are driving on smart corridors that tie together disparate traffic signals and computer systems, but they already benefit from faster commutes, fewer accidents, reduced fuel consumption, and lower levels of pollution.

If caught in a traffic jam, drivers are advised to keep their cool and avoid tailgating or other confrontational (and accident-causing) behavior. Although road rage is not the norm in Arizona, the mantle of the wild and wooly West has not disappeared altogether; many desert denizens do pack guns. To keep from becoming an accident statistic, the Arizona Department of Public Safety posts safety tips on its website.

Travelers should note that the Valley's streets are laid out on a grid system, which makes navigation simpler. Major streets are spaced about a mile apart both on an east-west and a north-south axis, creating a grid of square-mile blocks across most of the Valley. (The major exception to the rule is Grand Avenue, which cuts diagonally across the west Valley.) When you know the Valley well, a simple mention of the nearest major cross streets will make it easy for you to plot your route in your head. You'll also know the travel time almost immediately.

Some travelers get away from it all by flying above the crowd. In addition to Phoenix Sky Harbor International Airport, if you can pilot your own plane or are being flown in on a company jet, you can land at one of eight airports around the Valley, which often feature their own on-site amenities, like restaurants.

A trip by air reveals how much of the Valley sprawls: development already covers 3,000 square miles and new buildings gobble up additional desert acreage daily. Although downtown Phoenix remains a major center, the Valley, by and large, is decentralized. This legacy of the automobile presents a challenge for those who eschew a vehicle, though mass transit services are constantly improving. For example, Phoenix voters recently approved a mass transit system. Until light rail comes to town, consider taking a bus, carpooling, biking, or even walking. Using alternative modes of transportation will help us all in improving Phoenix's air quality and maintaining the quality of life that draws visitors here.

Traveling By Car

Interstates and Highways

Visitors will find that there are many interesting sites within the Valley that pique their interest or, they may want to venture out on day trips to explore the rest of Arizona. Whatever the case, the Valley's collection of Interstates and highways provide the quickest way to go. Here's some information that will help you familiarize yourself with major roads.

Interstate 10
- Also called: Papago Freeway, west of the I-17 interchange in Phoenix; Maricopa Freeway, east the I-17 interchange.
- Serves: The cities of Phoenix, Tempe, and Chandler.
- Connects: Los Angeles, to the west of Phoenix; Tucson, to the southeast.
- Orientation: Mostly east-west, except in Chandler, where it travels north-south before angling southeastward to Tucson. Note that even if you are traveling south for a few miles, the sign still reads "east."
- Special notes: I-10 twice crosses paths with I-17 to form a loop around downtown Phoenix, once at the southern end of I-17 near Phoenix Sky Harbor International Airport, and again at a major interchange know as "the stack," about a half-mile south of McDowell Road, near 23rd Avenue.

Interstate 17
- Also called: Black Canyon Freeway, north of the junction with I-10; Maricopa Freeway, where it converges with I-10.
- Serves: Phoenix, Glendale, and Peoria.
- Orientation: North-south, except where it becomes an east-west corridor through South Phoenix after rounding the Durango Curve, in the vicinity of 23rd Avenue and Durango Street.

- Special notes: Inside the Valley, use this route to get to Arizona State University West. Outside the Valley, it offers the most direct route to Sedona, Flagstaff, and other northern points.

U.S. Highway 60
- Also called: Superstition Freeway.
- Serves: Tempe, Mesa, Gilbert, and Apache Junction.
- Connects: The East Valley with Miami, Globe, and Native American Reservations on the east side of the state. Continues to New Mexico.
- Orientation: East-west.
- Special notes: Good way to reach Fiesta Mall and the Superstition Springs Mall, both in Mesa. The western portion of the Superstition converges with Grand Avenue.

State Route 87
- Also called: Beeline Highway.
- Serves: Chandler, Gilbert, Mesa, Fountain Hills, and Sun Lakes.
- Connects: The East Valley with Payson to the north and it picks up I-10 southeast of the Valley near Picacho.
- Orientation: Mostly north-south.
- Special notes: This route is a good way to reach Fountain Hills and some of Arizona's cooler northern escapes. North of town, the Beeline Highway becomes a four-lane, sometimes-divided highway, beginning at the intersection of McDowell Road and Country Club on the Salt River Pima-Maricopa Native American Community. In town, the Beeline Highway is a regular city street—Country Club in Mesa and Arizona Avenue in Chandler.

State Route 51
- Also called: Squaw Peak Freeway.
- Intersects: Phoenix and Paradise Valley.
- Connects: I-10 and Loop 202 near downtown Phoenix with north Phoenix.
- Orientation: North-south.

• Special notes: This newly constructed, three- and four-lane route is a good alternative when I-17 is jammed. Elevated portions of this highway offer nice views of the Phoenix skyline and Squaw Peak. Some of the side walls feature public art, such as decorative pots.

Loop 202

• Also called: Red Mountain Freeway.
• Intersects: Phoenix, Tempe, and Mesa.
• Connects: Downtown Phoenix with north ern Mesa.
• Orientation: East-west.
• Special Notes: Offers good access to Phoe- nix Sky Harbor International Airport, down- town Tempe, and Arizona State University. It connects with Loop 101, which in turn links with U.S. 60. Offers a nice view of the new Tempe Town Lake and ASU's Sun Devil Stadium.

State Route 143

• Also called: Hohokam Expressway.
• Intersects: Phoenix and Tempe.
• Connects: Loop 202 with I-10.
• Orientation: North- south.
• Special notes: This short stretch of road offers ac- cess to the eastern en- trance of the Phoenix Sky Harbor International Air- port.

State Route 153

• Also called: Sky Harbor Expressway.
• Intersects: Phoenix and Tempe.
• Connects: Washington and University Streets on the east end of the airport.
• Orientation: North-south.
• Special Notes: This fairly new, short stretch of road offers access to the Phoenix Sky Har- bor International Airport.

Loop 101

• Also called: Agua Fria Freeway, between I- 10 and I-17 on its western end in Glendale; the Pima Freeway, between I-17 and Loop 202 on the northern end in Scottsdale; the Price Freeway, south of Loop 202 on the eastern part of the loop in Mesa. Known generally as the Outer Loop.
• Intersects: Glendale and Peoria, on its west-

ern end; Phoenix and Scottsdale on its north- ern end; Mesa, Tempe, and Chandler on its eastern end.
• Connects: On its western end, I-10 with I- 17; on its northern end, I-17 with 56th Street; on its eastern end, U.S. 60 in Mesa with Shea Road in Scottsdale.
• Orientation: North-south and east-west.
• Special notes: Within the decade, Loop 101 will form a horseshoe around the north end of the Valley and connect with Loop 202, making it a breeze to travel between such far-flung Valley outposts as Apache Junc- tion and Sun City. Since it is under con- struction, Loop 101 may be built farther out than indicated at this printing. On the Pima section, Loop 101 provides a handy way to reach destinations in Scottsdale if you want to avoid the traffic on Scottsdale Road— just take any exit and drive west a couple miles.

HOV Lanes

Take note of the lanes marked by diamonds on I-10, I-17, and Loop 202— they function as High Oc- cupancy Vehicle lanes during rush-hour traffic, Monday through Friday, 6 to 9 AM and 3 to 7 PM. Unless you have a passen- ger, are traveling by mo- torcycle, or have an auto- mobile that uses alterna- tive fuel, you will be tick- eted for driving in HOV lanes during those speci- fied hours. These lanes are mighty convenient during rush-hour times. For example, you can zip by creeping traffic on I- 10 from Chandler Boulevard on the south through 91st Avenue on the west. One cau- tion: keep an eye out for cars in the regular lane that are tempted to zip into the HOV lane. If a collision occurs, the difference in the speed of the two vehicles can be deadly.

> **INSIDERS' TIP**
> Use logic when finding Valley addresses. By and large, an even number indicates that an address is on the west or north side of a respective street. An odd number indicates that an address is on the east or south side of a street. Of course, there are exceptions to the rule, but mostly the excep- tions are on cul-de-sacs.

Driving Tips

Even though you will see speeders all around you, remember that posted limits on freeways are 55 miles per hour within the entire metro- politan area. We all like to get there as quickly as we can, but speeding does not save consider-

If you are venturing into rugged terrain, signing up for a guided tour in a four-wheel drive vehicle saves wear and tear on your own car.

Photo: Courtesy of the Phoenix Convention and Visitors Bureau

able time. In addition, the Valley's jam-packed freeways can fluster newcomers, especially since seasoned residents don't yield the right of way as often as they do in the Midwest. Be aware of your exits and the possibility that you may have to cut across several lanes of traffic to reach them. If you don't get over early enough and find yourself cut off, stay on the freeway until the next exit, then double back. Keep a wary eye out for others who might indulge in high-speed lane changes.

Surface Streets

Grand Avenue—Most of the Valley is on a grid system, with major thoroughfares marking each square mile. The major exception is Grand Avenue, which is also called U.S. Highway 60, linking Phoenix to Wickenburg and points north. Grand Avenue's southern end is at Seventh Avenue and Van Buren Street, and it proceeds at a diagonal northwestwardly across the West Valley, traveling from downtown Phoenix to downtown Glendale and Peoria and just southwest of the Sun Cities as it heads out of the Valley.

Central Avenue—Although it is not the geographical center of Phoenix, Central Avenue is central to the street-numbering system. The numbered avenues (First Avenue, Second Avenue, etc.) are north-south thoroughfares west of Central. The numbered streets (First Street, Second Street, and so on) are north-south thoroughfares on the east side of Central. Central Avenue is also the major corridor linking downtown Phoenix with uptown Phoenix, two major areas of high-rise business development.

Van Buren Street—An east-west thoroughfare that runs through downtown Phoenix, Van Buren Street is like Central Avenue in that it's the center point for the north-south streets. For example, north of Van Buren, Central Avenue becomes North Central Avenue. South of Van Buren, it becomes South Central Avenue.

Public Transportation

Valley Metro
Regional Public Transportation Authority, 302 N. First Ave., Phoenix
• **(602) 253-5000**
• **www.valleymetro.maricopa.gov**

Valley Metro is the regional identity of the public transit system. This umbrella name was adopted by each city's Regional Public Transportation Authority (RPTA), so the public could experience and interact with a seamless, coherent system.

Buses are equipped with bike racks. Smoking is not allowed. All buses are wheelchair accessible, although not all buses can accommodate all types of wheelchairs. For detailed information on wheelchair accessibility, call the Community Forum at (602) 223-4100.

Routes

Valley Metro buses link 12 Valley communities. Bus frequency varies from every five minutes to every hour, depending on the route and the time of day. As of August 2000, 63 local routes run from early morning until early evening. Actual hours of operation differ according to the routes. Connections are usually easy because most routes are generally north-south or east-west and intersect with one another.

As of August 2000, 21 express routes connect outlying areas with downtown Phoenix. Designed for business commuters, they head inbound to downtown during the morning rush hour, and outbound during the afternoon rush. All of them stop at free park-and-ride lots.

All routes run Monday through Friday, and 57 local routes run on Saturday. Tempe and Phoenix buses run on Sundays and on holidays, thanks to funding initiatives passed by voters. The Bus Book, which contains route and fare information and route maps, can be picked up on any Valley Metro bus, at Central Station at Central Avenue and Van Buren Street in downtown Phoenix, or at the libraries and municipal buildings of the participating cities. It is updated twice a year. The Online Bus Book is available at www.bus.maricopa.gov.

Fares and Transfers

Fares are $1.25 for a local route and $1.75 for an express route. Bring exact change. Transfers are free and are good for an hour after the route reaches the end of the line, a nice deal when trying to cross the Valley by bus. Reduced fares of 60 cents per ride are available for youths ages 6 to 18, seniors 65 and older, and persons with disabilities. Children younger than

6 ride free. For information on reduced fares, bus routes, ticket books, and passes, call (602) 253-5000 from 4 AM to 10 PM on weekdays and Saturdays, and from 6 AM to 8 PM on Sundays and holidays.

Shuttles

DASH, the Downtown Area SHuttle

This shuttle service runs every 6 to 12 minutes in downtown Phoenix, from 6:30 AM to 5:30 PM, weekdays. From 11 AM to 2 PM, it connects the State Capitol with downtown as well. The shuttle is free. Call Valley Metro for more information, (602) 253-5000.

FLASH
the Free Local Area Shuttle

FLASH runs through downtown Tempe and around the Arizona State University campus. As the name says, the fare is free. Buses run every 10 minutes or so from 7 AM to 8 PM Monday through Thursday, and from 7 AM to 6 PM on Friday. During the summer, from mid-May through late August, hours are 7 AM to 6 PM Monday through Friday. FLASH routes running in a clockwise direction are called FLASH Forward, while those running in a counterclockwise direction are called FLASH Back. For more information call Valley Metro, (602) 253-5000.

FLASH Lite on MILL

FLASH is an additional service on Mill Avenue, serving Tempe Town Lake, downtown Tempe, ASU/Gammage Auditorium, and the Papago area. For just Mill Avenue service, it runs approximately every 10 to 15 minutes, seven days a week, from 7 AM to Midnight. It serves the Phoenix Zoo and the Desert Botanical Garden on Saturday and Sunday, from 8 AM to 8 PM. It serves the Papago Center business park Monday through Friday, from 7 AM to 6 PM. For more information call Valley Metro, (602) 253-5000.

FAST
the Free Airpark Shuttle Transfer

FAST serves the Scottsdale Airpark and the fare is free. FAST operates in two directions.

INSIDERS' TIP

If you get caught in a dust storm, pull off the road, turn off your lights, and take your foot off the brake. When visibility is low, you don't want other motorists to mistakenly plow into you because they see your lights think you are still driving. During Arizona's monsoon season, flooding can render roads impassable and deadly. Never enter a flooded wash. For more driving safety tips, visit www.dps.state.az.

FAST Forward runs in a clockwise direction, while FAST Back runs in a counter-clockwise direction. FAST runs approximately every 10 minutes, Monday through Friday, 6 AM to 7 PM. For more information call Valley Metro, (602) 253-5000.

GUS, the Glendale Urban Shuttle

GUS serves Glendale's central corridor. GUS costs a quarter to ride, and runs Monday through Saturday, 9 AM to 6 PM. For more information, call (602) 647-8569. (Please note that, because this GUS operates from a cellular phone, the area code differs from Glendale's area code.) For more information call Valley Metro, (602) 253-5000.

Rideshare

The Valley Metro Rideshare program was developed to fight vehicle-emitted air pollution. It can help Valley residents set up carpools, vanpools, telecommuting, and compressed work schedules. Call (602) 262-7433 for information.

Dial-a-Ride

The dial-a-ride service is available in many communities in the Phoenix metropolitan area. Although it is geared to meet the needs of seniors 65 and older and persons with disabilities, some dial-a-ride systems are available for use by the general public. The Dial-a-Ride Guide is available upon request at (602) 253-5000. Alternative formats are available and callers with text telephone machines can call (602) 261-8208.

People who have a disability that prevents them from using or accessing the regular bus service may qualify for special service under the Americans with Disabilities Act (ADA). They must apply in advance to Valley Metro for certification and must call the respective dial-a-ride at least one day in advance to schedule their service. The certification process may take up to 21 days to complete and may require verification of disabilities from a doctor or other medical professional. Information about ADA eligibility may be obtained by calling (602) 495-5777.

Valley Metro buses offers a convenient way of getting around and using them helps reduce air pollution.

Photo: Penny Kleingartner

Here are the Dial-a-Ride numbers for the communities they serve:

El Mirage Dial-a-Ride, (623) 937-0500, serves the general public from 8 AM to 5 PM Monday through Friday with no holiday service.

Glendale Dial-a-Ride, (623) 930-3500, serves the general public from 7:30 AM to 5 PM Monday through Friday with no holiday service. Extended service hours for those qualifying under the Americans with Disabilities Act (ADA) run from 6 AM to 10 PM Monday through Friday and from 6 AM to 9 PM on Saturday. Those seeking ADA service should call Glendale Dial-a-Ride at (623) 930-3515.

Guadalupe Special Services, (480) 730-3092, serves senior citizens and persons with disabilities from 8 AM to 4:30 PM, Monday through Friday, with no holiday service.

East Valley Dial-a-Ride, (480) 633-0101, serves senior citizens and persons with disabilities. Days and hours of operation vary from city to city. In the cities of Chandler, Gilbert, and Mesa, service is from 4 AM to 7 PM on weekdays, and from 6 AM to 7 PM on Saturdays, with no service on Sundays or holidays. In the cities of Scottsdale and Tempe, service is from 4 AM to midnight, seven days a week, except holidays.

Maricopa County Special Services, (602) 336-6699, provides services as needed to senior citizens, low-income residents, TANF recipients, and persons with disabilities. No holiday service is provided.

Paradise Valley ADA Service, (602) 257-0338, serves only persons with disabilities and runs from 5 AM to 8 PM, Monday through Saturday, with no holiday service, unless a fixed route service is provided.

Peoria Dial-a-Ride, (602) 412-7435, serves the general public from 6 AM to 6 PM Monday through Friday with no holiday service. Extended ADA service hours are from 5 AM to 8 PM Monday through Friday.

Phoenix Dial-a-Ride, (623) 773-7435, serves seniors and persons with disabilities seven days a week. Weekday service is provided from 5 AM to midnight, with service requests taken as late as 10 PM. Weekend service is provided until 10 PM, with service requests taken until 9 PM. Reservations for ADA service must be made at least one day in advance and can be made between 8 AM and 6 PM.

Sun Cities Area Transit System (SCAT), (623) 977-8363, serves the general public from 7:15 AM to 6:45 PM, Monday through Friday, and from 7:15 AM to 4:45 PM, Saturday, Sunday, and holidays. Extended ADA service hours are from 5 AM to 8 PM Monday through Friday.

Surprise Dial-a-Ride, (623) 583-1688, serves the general public from 8 AM to noon and from 1 to 5 PM, Monday through Friday, with no holiday service.

A variety of passenger transportation is available for travelers heading to and from airports.

Photo: Penny Kleingartner

Air Travel

Phoenix Sky Harbor International Airport
3400 Sky Harbor Blvd., Phoenix
- **(602) 273-3300**
- **www.phx.skyharbor.com**

As anyone who looks up at the Valley skies can tell you, Sky Harbor is busy. It's the fifth busiest airport in the United States and the 11th busiest in the world. It accommodates 1,400 commercial flights a day, serving an average of 36 million people annually. Sky Harbor also serves general aviation, corporate, cargo, and military planes.

The airport began operating in 1929, and in 1935 the City of Phoenix purchased the airport, which then stood on 285 acres. Terminal 1 opened October 13, 1952, and began Sky Harbor's ascent to its current status. The airport handled 296,066 passengers in the first year Terminal 1 was open. In 1961, it served 920,096 passengers. Terminal 2 was built in 1962 for $2.7 million, just as Sky Harbor broke the one-million-passenger-per-year mark. The city strove to make the terminal a lovely gateway to Phoenix and commissioned the late Paul Coze to create a three-panel mosaic mural, known as The Phoenix. It still greets passengers in Terminal 2 today. The passenger rate grew to three million in 1971, so planning began for the construction of Terminal 3, which opened in 1979. Growth continued, and the Phoenix City Council authorized construction of Terminal 4 in 1986. The $248 million terminal and four-level parking garage opened in 1990, and Terminal 1 was closed. In 1991, Terminal 4 alone handled 15.4 million passengers, 70 percent of the airport's traffic.

There are 99 gates and 17,000 parking spaces at the airport. Currently, Sky Harbor has three runways, its newest one, which opened in 2000, carries a price tag of $128 million. With passenger traffic at about 31.5 million annually, it's a good idea to arrive at the airport about 90 minutes before your flight is scheduled to leave. A free shuttle travels from economy parking to the terminals every six minutes.

The airport is only five minutes from downtown Phoenix. It's almost centrally located in the Valley and has good access to freeways. Sky Harbor is open 24 hours a day, and car rentals, food service, and catering are available.

Here are the airlines that serve Phoenix Sky Harbor International Airport and their terminals:

Aeromexico/Aerolitoral—Terminal 4
Air Canada—Terminal 2
Air Jamaica—Terminal 4
Alaska—Terminal 2
American—Terminal 3
America West and America West Express—Terminal 4
American Trans Air—Terminal 3
British Airways—Terminal 4
Continental—Terminal 4
Delta—Terminal 3
Frontier—Terminal 3
Mesa—Terminal 4
Midwest Express—Terminal 3
Northwest/KLM—Terminal 3
Shuttle by United—Terminal 2
Southwest—Terminal 4
Sun Country—Terminal 3
Sunrise—Terminal 2
TWA—Terminal 2
United—Terminal 2
US Airways—Terminal 2

Ground Transportation

All rates listed below are the maximum allowed under contract with Sky Harbor. Passengers are encouraged to negotiate for better rates.

Taxis
AAA Cab, Courier Cab, and Yellow Cab have contracts to provide service to Sky Harbor passengers at the following rates: First mile $3; each additional mile $1.50; with an airport surcharge of $1. There should be no extra charges for more than one passenger in a party or for baggage. You may choose any taxi you wish from the waiting line.

SuperShuttle
SuperShuttle operates 24 hours a day and offers airport-to-door service. Vans depart every 15 minutes to all areas of the Valley from 9 AM to 9 PM and with less frequency from 9 PM to 9 AM. Flat rates are charged to each geographical area being served and range from $10 to $35 for a single passenger, with a $6 charge for additional passengers within a group. Call (602) 244-9000 or (800) 258-3826 (outside Arizona) for information. To get to the airport via SuperShuttle, call at the same time you make your airline reservations.

Limousines
AAA, AM, Affordable, Aries, Arizona Chauffer, Carmel, Empire, Esquire, Love, Luxe,

Manhattan, Monarch, Prince, and TLC offer limousine service from Sky Harbor. Their rates are set by mileage and range from $15 to $50. These rates include transport of one or two in a party to the same address. Each additional passenger is $7 a head. Feel free to negotiate with the drivers for a lower rate, especially if you wait for other passengers to load and share the fare. Limousines are also available for $30 an hour, with a minimum charge of two hours.

VIP or Private Services

A number of companies operate as private carriers from Sky Harbor. Before you make arrangements with a particular company, check to see if they are permitted to operate from the airport, and verify all facets of your arrangement with them.

Valley Metro

The Red Line and bus route No. 13 both stop at the airport and provide connections to the entire Valley. Call (602) 253-5000 for information.

Phoenix Dial-a-Ride

Dial-a-Ride provides service seven days a week to seniors 65 and older and persons with disabilities. Weekday service is provided from 5 AM to midnight, with service requests taken as late as 10 PM. Weekend service is provided until 10 PM, with service requests taken until 9 PM. Reservations for ADA service must be made at least one day in advance, between the hours of 8 AM and 6 PM. For more information, call (602) 253-4000.

Courtesy Rides

Many hotels and resorts provide free pickup and drop-off service for their patrons. To check with your place of accommodation, a courtesy phone center for many hotels and resorts is adjacent to the baggage claim areas in the passenger terminals.

Wheelchair Accessibility

Taxis and limousines will transport passengers using wheelchairs as long as the wheelchairs or other appliances can be folded to fit in the trunk with the luggage. Lift-equipped service for passengers in wheelchairs is available from the SuperShuttle, and passengers should call (602) 244-9000 or, from outside Arizona, (800) 331-3565 for this service. The Valley Metro bus routes that stop at Sky Harbor are also lift-equipped, as are interterminal buses at the airport. Rental cars with hand controls are available from Avis and Hertz. Avis recom-

mends advance notice, and Hertz needs 48 hours' notice. For private carriers, contact the particular companies to find out their wheelchair accessibility.

Parking

Each terminal has its own parking area and all are wheelchair accessible.

Terminal 2—The short-term parking area sits north of the terminal and features 360 spaces for hourly parking and 2,053 spaces for daily parking. Hourly rates are $1 per half hour, with a $15 maximum, and a $15 lost-ticket fee. Daily rates are $7 per day.

Terminal 3—The parking garage adjoins the terminal to the east. It features 2,274 spaces on six levels. Rates are $1 per half hour, $15 for a daily maximum, and $15 for a lost-ticket fee. The garage cannot accommodate vehicles more than seven feet in height.

Terminal 4—The parking garage sits above the terminal. It has 3,090 regular spaces on four levels and features a 228-space lot for high-profile vehicles that are seven feet or taller. Rates are $1 per half hour, with a $15 daily maximum, and a $15 lost-ticket fee.

In addition, the airport offers two economy lots for long-term parking. The lot west of Terminal 2 can hold 1,567 vehicles and can accommodate vehicles more than 7 feet high. The lot east of Terminal 4 has 5,700 spaces and can accommodate high-profile vehicles as well as vehicles up to 32 feet in length. Both lots have shuttle service to the terminals. Rates are $1 per half hour, with a daily maximum of $4, and a minimum lost-ticket fee of $4.

Rental Cars

A number of rental-car companies have counters in the terminals at Sky Harbor, while a number of other companies rent cars at the airport but do not have counters inside the terminals. Whether they have counters on site or not, all of them will shuttle you from the airport to their lots outside Sky Harbor when you arrive (and vice versa when you depart). The following are some of the companies that serve the airport. Use the courtesy phones at the airport to call the companies that don't have on-site counters.

Advantage Rent-A-Car:
    Terminal 2, (602) 267-8982
    Terminal 3, (602) 267-8997
    Terminal 4, (602) 220-0332
Alamo Rent-A-Car, (602) 244-0897
Avis Rent-A-Car, (602) 273-3222
Budget Rent-A-Car, (602) 267-4000
Discount Car and Truck Rentals, Radisson

Hotel, I-10 and University Drive, Phoenix, (602) 437-3477

Enterprise Rent-A-Car, 2738 E. Washington Street, Phoenix, (602) 225-0588

Hertz Rent-A-Car, (602) 267-8822

National Car Rental, (602) 275-4771

Thrifty Car Rental, 4114 E. Washington St., Phoenix, (602) 244-0311

U-Save Auto Rental, (602) 267-9505

Other Valley Airports

In addition to Phoenix Sky Harbor International Airport, numerous smaller airports in the Valley serve general aviation traffic, such as corporate and private planes. These airports, known as "relievers," draw a good measure of the general-aviation traffic that would otherwise be served by Sky Harbor.

Chandler Municipal Airport
2380 Stinson Way, Chandler
• (480) 782-3540

A general-aviation airport, Chandler handles about 221,000 takeoffs and landings a year. Its control tower is open from 6 AM to 9 PM. There are hangars, shaded tiedowns, and open tiedowns. About 360 planes are based there, as well as one medical helicopter. Airport-based businesses include an avionics shop, full-service fuel pumps, a repair shop, and three flight schools. Sightseeing tours are available.

Glendale Municipal Airport
6801 N. Glen Harbor Blvd., Glendale
• (623) 930-2188

The Glendale airport is home base for about 260 planes, both corporate and private, and handles about 134,000 takeoffs and landings per year. Though primarily a general-aviation airport, it is home to about 20 businesses, ranging from airplane hangar sales to an aviation insurance adjuster, and serves two medical evacuation helicopters. A restaurant and gift shop is on site. The airport also features two flight schools, a terminal, maintenance services, and a Hertz rental car service. The control tower

operates daily from 7 AM to 8 PM. For charter flights, call Global Aviation at (623) 877-4762.

Mesa Falcon Field
4800 E. Falcon Dr., Mesa
• (480) 644-2444

Falcon Field handles approximately 190,000 general-aviation takeoffs and landings a year. Falcon Field, which opened in 1941, was used originally by the U.S. War Department to train combat pilots for the British Royal Air Force. When World War II ended, the City of Mesa took over the airport. Today, 900 planes are based there, along with 30 aviation-related businesses, and 50 general commercial enterprises. The control tower operates from 6 AM to 9 PM, and the airport features a gift shop, a pilot shop, maintenance, fuel, and rental-car services. It's also home to the Champlin Fighter Aircraft Museum and the Confederate Air Force Museum. In addition, Falcon Field operates a helipad, used mostly by business people heading to meetings in downtown Mesa, which is a few miles away.

Phoenix Deer Valley Airport
702 W. Deer Valley Rd., Phoenix
• (602) 869-0975

The City of Phoenix Aviation Department, which runs Sky Harbor, has also run this general-aviation airport in the north central part of the Valley since 1971. It averages about 220,000 takeoffs and landings per year. The control tower operates from 6 AM to 9 PM. The airport offers fuel sales, overnight parking, an aircraft maintenance bay, and a conference room.

Phoenix Goodyear Airport
1658 S. Litchfield Rd., Goodyear
• (623) 932-1200

The City of Phoenix Aviation Department, which oversees Sky Harbor, has managed this airport since 1968. The airport was built in 1943 and originally operated by the U.S. Navy. It served as a support facility for the nearby aircraft division of the Goodyear Tire and Rubber Company. In 1951, the Navy expanded the airport as a base for military aircraft storage, which

INSIDERS' TIP

If you yearn for the thrill of speed but want to avoid getting a ticket, stop by the Bob Bondurant School of High Performance Driving. Launched by the former racing champion, the Valley school has trained more than 60,000 students, from teenagers to professional racing drivers. Celebrities like Tom Cruise, Paul Newman, Clint Eastwood, and Candice Bergen have all learned how to handle high-performance cars for movies. We lesser-known mortals can benefit from a few safety tips. For more information, call (480) 961-0143.

was its mission until 1965, when the U.S. General Services Administration took over with plans to phase it out. The major tenant is Lufthansa Airlines' Airline Training Center. The airport serves the general-aviation needs of western Maricopa County, and air traffic peaked at 202,356 takeoffs and landings in 1991. The control tower operates from 6 AM to 9 PM. The airport offers fuel sales, overnight parking, a flight planning and lounge area, an aircraft wash rack, and a conference room.

Scottsdale Municipal Airport
15000 N. Airport Dr., Scottsdale
- **(480) 312-2321**

Scottsdale Municipal Airport handles approximately 180,000 takeoffs and landings a year. It is surrounded by the Scottsdale Airpark, an industrial park that is home to 25 national/regional corporations and nearly 1,200 small- and medium-size businesses. Commercial charters take off on sightseeing tours from the airport, handling about 8,000 passengers annually. The control tower operates from 6 AM to 10 PM. The airport features an array of specialty shops, maintenance support and repairs, a rental car company, limousine services, conference rooms, a pilot lounge, and aircraft cleaning and storage. A number of flight schools are based there as well.

Williams Gateway Airport
5835 S. Sossaman Rd., Mesa
- **(480) 988-1013**
- **www.flywga.org**

Williams Gateway Airport is on the site of former Williams Air Force Base, which was closed down in post-Cold War Department of Defense budget cuts. It handles approximately 240,000 takeoffs and landings per year—including corporate, cargo, general-aviation, and military aircraft. A major economic hub for the area, the airport has about 25 business tenants, including aircraft maintenance, modification, and testing services. It also offers pilot training. The terminal is being remodeled and passenger services are planned for the near future.

The control tower is operated daily from 6 AM to 9 PM. Facilities include fuel sales, a pilot lounge, VIP lounge, pilot shop, and a cafe. Arizona State University's east campus is also here.

Private Transportation

Arizona Shuttle Service
5350 E. Speedway Blvd., Tucson
- **(520) 795-6771, (800) 888-2749**
- **www.arizonashuttle.com**

Arizona Shuttle Service runs 13 luxury vans—complete with television and VCRs—between Phoenix Sky Harbor International Airport and Tucson. At the airport, it has offices in Terminals 2, 3, and 4. The company offers 36 runs a day, virtually around the clock on the half hour from Phoenix. Fares are $22 one way and $40 round trip, with senior and student rates available. Children under 12 accompanied by parents are charged $15 one way (no round-trip discount). Unaccompanied children pay the full adult fare.

El Paso-Los Angeles Limousine Express
Roosevelt and Seventh Sts., Phoenix
- **(602) 254-4101**

El Paso-Los Angeles Limousine Express has four buses leaving nightly for El Paso, Los Angeles, and Las Vegas. Las Vegas tickets cost $20 one way. Tickets for El Paso and Los Angeles are $35 one way and $65 round trip, with special children's rates available. You're advised to purchase tickets in advance, especially for weekend departures, as the buses fill rapidly.

Greyhound Bus Lines
2115 E. Buckeye Rd., Phoenix
- **(602) 389-4200**
- **www.greyhound.com**

Greyhound can get you here from anywhere in the United States. You'll arrive at its main terminal in Phoenix or around the Valley in

---

INSIDERS' TIP

Concerned about the environment? Because 95 percent of the Valley's air pollution comes from automobiles, ask your car rental agency about renting something that uses alternative fuels. These vehicles are perfect for short trips around the Valley, though they are not recommended for taking on long trips outside the metropolitan area. The Valley tallies 35 electric fueling stations, eight natural gas fueling stations, and 40 propane fueling stations. For a full list, call the Arizona Department of Commerce at (602) 280-1402, or visit www.azcommerce.com.

Glendale, Chandler, or Mesa. For route and fare information, call (800) 231-2222. For information in Spanish, call (800) 531-5332.

Payson Express
(602) 256-6464

Payson Express is a reservation-only, door-to-door service that shuttles passengers between the Valley and Payson. It leaves Payson at 8 AM and departs from the Valley for Payson at 1:30 PM. Service runs daily, except on Sundays, and 24-hour notice is required. Prices vary. As an example, a one-way trip from Sky Harbor can range from $25 to $30 for a single passenger and from $45 to $50 for a round trip. Each additional person helps reduce the per-person price.

Sedona Phoenix Shuttle Service, Inc.
P.O. Box 3342, Sedona 86340
• (520) 282-2066

Providing service between Phoenix and the Verde Valley area, this company has representatives at each terminal in Phoenix Sky Harbor International Airport. It offers seven trips daily from the airport, costing $55 one way and $60 for a round trip. Children under 12 ride for half price. The Service prefers that you make reservations at least one week in advance.

Taxis and Limousines

Because of the distances involved in getting around the Valley, taxis, whose fares are based on miles traveled, are not the most popular option. Most Valley dwellers use them as a last resort—usually when cars have given up the ghost in the middle of the night, and batteries have so little juice left that even a tow-truck driver can't get them jump-started.

Few cabs cruise for fares here since there are so few locations where enough people congregate to make the endeavor worthwhile. Besides that, hailing a cab is pretty much a lost art among Valley dwellers. If you want a cab, you'll find them lined up at the airport or in front of your downtown hotel. Otherwise,

you'll have to give the cab company a call. Rates vary from company to company, although fares hover around $3 for the first mile and $1.50 for each additional mile. (A number of taxi companies offer a variety of services, including limousine rentals, package deliveries, and courier services.)

The following taxi companies serve the entire Valley 24 hours a day:

AAA Cab, (602) 437-4000
Ace Taxi, (602) 254-1999
Alpha Cab, (602) 232-2000
Checker Cab, (602) 257-1818
Discount Cab, (602) 266-1110
Tender Loving Care Taxi, (602) 222-2228
Yellow Cab, (602) 252-5252

On the other end of the spectrum, limousines are as popular here as anywhere because they make a nice splurge for a special occasion—at least, for most of us. Limos are generally rented by the hour, with at least a two-hour minimum rental. Some companies require a higher minimum at busy times, such as weekends and the holiday season. Fares also vary by the type of limo being rented. A 10-passenger limo is going to cost more than a six-passenger one. You can get a decent limo in Arizona for from $45 to $65 an hour, with the two-hour minimum, not including gratuity and tax. Of course, you can always splurge even more than that—ask for a TV or a bar or food service or all of the above. In addition, most limousine companies also offer van and sedan rentals on similar terms.

Here are some of the limousine companies that serve the Valley:

Arizona Limousines, (602) 267-7097
Carey Phoenix Limousine (602) 996-1955
Desert Rose Limousine Service, (623) 780-0159
Driver Provider, (480) 998-7517
Hollywood Limousines, (602) 585-6528
Premiere Limousines, (480) 957-4533
Scottsdale Limousine, (480) 946-8446
Sky Mountain Limousines, (480) 830-3944
Starlight Limousines, (480) 905-1234
Valley Limousine, (602) 254-1955

History

Although the Valley's runaway growth within the last few decades makes it seem like a young city, the Phoenix metropolitan area is heir to a rich and varied cultural history. Certainly, very few historical buildings have survived our hell-bent-for-leather development, but the observant visitor or newcomer will be able to look beyond the façade and catch a glimpse of the past.

Historical clues about Arizona's history include the ruins of early human settlements; petroglyphs scrawled on rocks; Spanish missions and presidios; defunct copper mines; ranches that now run more tourists than cattle; and ancient canal beds. Beyond material objects, a living history can be seen in the thriving folkways of our people, including multilingual speakers who still honor their ancestral languages; artisans who preserve time-worn skills like weaving, lapidary work, and pottery making; and festivals that celebrate traditions ranging from ostrich farming to Easter.

One of the reoccurring themes you'll find in our desert is, naturally, water. Irrigation has always played a pivotal role in human settlement in the Valley, not only for the waves of European descendants who eventually settled here, but for the earliest humans who passed this way, somewhere between 20,000 and 40,0000 years ago. Those Paleo-Indians disappeared about 12,000 years ago, possibly because they depleted the region's game, but other settlers took their place.

The Hohokam (hoe-hoe-CALM) were the first to settle the Salt River Valley for a long period. No one knows what the Hohokam called themselves; the name we use is a Pima word for "those who came before." The Hohokam farmed the Valley and dug a series of irrigation canals, about 250 miles' worth, to grow food. These canals formed the basis of the modern canal system that helped Phoenix rise from the desert. Their crops included many staples, such as maize, cotton, beans, and tobacco. It's estimated that 50,000 Hohokam lived in the Valley in the peak period around A.D. 1000. We can tell from the remains of their settlements that Hohokam life was relatively prosperous, thanks to their constructive use of the Salt River's waters. The ruins of courts they built for ball games reveal that they enjoyed leisurely pursuits, not unlike those we indulge in today.

After about 1,700 years of tilling the Valley, the Hohokam disappeared, roughly 90 years before Columbus sailed to America. No one knows why they left, but speculations place blame on drought, flooding, or war. Where they went is also unknown, although the Hohokam are thought to be the ancestors of the Pima and Tohono O'odham Indians of central and southern Arizona. The Valley had no permanent residents from the time the Hohokam left until Anglo settlers came.

The Founding of Phoenix

The Spanish arrived in what is now Arizona in 1539. Conquistadors and Catholic priests explored the area and warred with—and enslaved—the native peoples. The territory that is today Arizona was claimed for New Spain, although the crown's hold on the land was tenuous. The

Valley itself lay virtually forgotten during the rule of the Spanish crown. In 1821, Mexico won its independence from Spain, and Arizona became part of the new country of Mexico. Neither Spain nor Mexico settled the Valley. Tucson, about 120 miles south of present-day Phoenix, was the seat of Hispanic culture in Arizona. The Spanish presence in Tucson began when Father Eusebio Kino, a Jesuit priest, arrived in the late 1600s. Since there already existed a relatively stable Indian settlement called Stjukshon, Kino saw it as an appropriate place to establish the mission of San Xavier del Bac and begin converting Indian souls to Christendom. By the end of the 1700s, the Spanish had established an army outpost there. In contrast, the Spanish virtually ignored the Salt River Valley area, leaving it to occasional Pima and Maricopa Indian settlements, who sometimes traveled from their traditional lands around the Gila River to farm near the Salt.

After gaining its independence from Spain, Mexico and the United States clashed as the latter sought to expand Westward. American settlers living in the present-day region of Texas, which was a Mexican state, instigated and fought a successful rebellion in 1836. In 1845, the independent Republic of Texas joined the Union. During this period, the United States, high on Manifest Destiny, fought directly with Mexico as well. After bitter warfare, the Treaty of Guadalupe Hidalgo was signed on February 2, 1848.

In this treaty, Mexico officially recognized the United State's claim on Texas, and ceded much of what is today the Southwestern United States to its northern neighbor. These lands included the present-day states of Arizona, California, and New Mexico. The United States government established the New Mexico Territory as an administrative unit whose vast territory included most of present-day Arizona. Part of Arizona, south of the Gila River, was acquired in the Gadsden Purchase of 1854 and duly added to the New Mexico Territory.

The Arizona region was a long way from the Territorial capital at Santa Fe, which meant that much of what passed for law and order—a Federal administrative and military presence—lacked teeth. A number of settlers wanted the Arizona region to become a separate United States territory, so that their local concerns could be aired adequately in Washington.

In 1861, an ad-hoc congress of Territory boosters met in Tucson—then the largest settlement in Arizona—and voted to form a territory of the Confederacy. The Confederate States agreed and established a garrison in Tucson. In June of 1862, James H. Carleton, commander of the Union's California Column, reached Tucson after engaging in only one skirmish at Picacho Pass and reclaimed the area for the Union. This move did not abate local sentiment that Arizona split from the New Mexico Territory. Organized legal efforts eventually prevailed, and the United States established the Arizona Territory on February 24, 1863.

During the New Mexico Territorial years, the Valley was seen as little more than a stopping point between Prescott, which later became the first and third Territorial capital of Arizona, and Tucson, which became the second Arizona capital. No one suspected that the Valley, home to virtually no permanent residents since A.D. 1400, would become the site of the fourth and final Territorial capital.

In 1865, the United States Army established Fort McDowell on the Verde River, 18 miles north of the Salt River, to ward off Apache attacks on Anglo settlers in the area, who were mostly miners. John Y.T. Smith came to the area as the post's sutler (or supplier) and secured a contract to supply the fort with hay he found growing wild in the Valley. He was the first white settler to build a house in the Valley, which was near the river where the eastern end of Sky Harbor Airport stands today.

Although much of Smith's hay was growing in the remnants of the Hohokam canals, he overlooked the potential the canals represented. In 1867, a former Confederate soldier named Jack Swilling visited Smith and realized that the remnants of the Hohokam canals could be cleaned and used as the foundation for a much larger agricultural settlement.

INSIDERS' TIP

Remnants of the ancient Hohokam culture survive at The Pueblo Grande Museum and Cultural Park, 4619 E. Washington Street, Phoenix, (602) 495-0900. Visitors can tour the ruins and ponder why the Hohokam suddenly disappeared around A.D. 1400.

In 1867, with funding from backers in Wickenburg, Swilling established the Swilling Irrigating and Canal Company. The next year, Frenchy Sawyer became the Valley's first farmer since the Hohokam. Swilling began operations near present-day Tempe, but soon moved near Smith's Station.

HISTORY

As the settlement grew, a naming committee was formed and its members proposed a number of alternatives. Swilling was partial to Stonewall, after the Civil War hero, Stonewall Jackson. Based on the idea that they would be drawing water from the Salt River, someone suggested Salina. The eloquent "Lord" Darrell Duppa, an eccentric British stockholder in Swilling's company, made the suggestion that stuck. He said the site should be named Phoenix, because they envisioned the city rising out of the remnants of the Hohokam settlement, in much the way the bird of myth rose from its ashes. On June 15, 1869, the Phoenix Post Office was established, giving the name its first official use.

As expected, Swilling's enterprise attracted settlers who met to establish an official town site on October 15, 1870. In December, the first town lot (at the corner of First Street and Washington) fetched $104. After more than four centuries, the secret of the Hohokam—that the Valley was a great place to live if you irrigated it—was out.

The Young City

Entrepreneurs boosted Phoenix at every opportunity, and the settlers who followed them were likewise industrious. The boosters succeeded in making Phoenix the seat of newly formed Maricopa County in 1871. The city itself incorporated in 1878.

The canal system continued to be expanded and improved. The Arizona Canal, completed by the Arizona Canal Company in 1885, was the largest yet, and the first to depart from the Hohokam routes. New canals fueled new settlement and vice versa, in a continual upward cycle. From the 50 or so residents at Smith's Station when Swilling's company was formed, Phoenix's population climbed into the thousands.

When the Southern Pacific Railroad's transcontinental main line was built through Arizona in the late 1870s, it passed 30 miles south of Phoenix through a depot settlement called Maricopa. Phoenix's boosters, realizing the value the rail connection would have to the city's growth, built a road to Maricopa for stagecoaches and freight wagons in 1879. By 1886, they needed more than a road, and a group of promoters found financing in Chicago and San Francisco for the Maricopa and Phoenix Railroad, a rail line that would eventually connect Phoenix to the Southern Pacific line. The new line reached Phoenix on July 4, 1887.

The railroad spur, the city's convenient location in the center of the territory, and its mild winter weather all played a part in its ascension to being named Arizona's capital. The capital had moved three times since 1863, when it was established at Fort Whipple outside the site that would become Prescott. Tucson became the capital in 1867, but Prescott grabbed the designation in 1877. In the end, Phoenix won because Prescott, at an elevation of 5,347 feet, was much colder, and the Legislature members preferred warmer weather for their January sessions. In 1889, Phoenix, which had not existed when the Arizona Territory was first established, became the final Territorial capital. At that time, it had 3,000 residents.

The presence of Federal, territorial, and county governments in Phoenix was good for business. First of all, the governmental bodies employed more people, whose trade in goods and services poured money into the local economy. In addition, having all the levels of government nearby made it easier for businesses to track down deeds, to get necessary permits, or to file lawsuits—which made the city even more attractive to developers. In fact, in the year after Phoenix became the capital, the city had $448,000 worth of building projects.

The city that drew on the Hohokam's ideas was, ironically, intolerant of nonwhite ethnic groups, especially Native Americans. In 1881, a city ordinance made it illegal for Native Americans to be in town after dark if not in the employ of a white resident. In an effort to indoctrinate tribal members, the federal government opened the Phoenix Indian School in 1891, which had 41 students the first year. Likewise, Hispanics who settled in the city found themselves barred from the Anglo community and power structure, so their lives revolved around their own social and Catholic religious activities. The Chinese, trying to escape prejudice

INSIDERS' TIP

The Arizona Historical Society's headquarters at 1300 N. College Avenue, Tempe, (480) 929-0292, doubles as a museum that focuses on the history of the Valley of the Sun and the central Arizona region. The society also maintains museums in Tucson and Flagstaff.

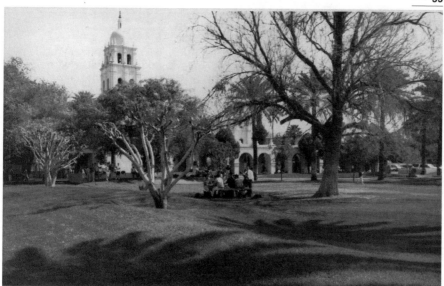

Spanish missions like the San Xavier del Bac, which dates from the late 1600s, played a pivotal role in early European settlement of the area. This mission is now the St. Frances Xavier.

Photo: Penny Kleingartner

in California, moved to Phoenix in some numbers in the 1880s. The prejudice wasn't as great in Arizona as it was in California, but the Chinese still kept to themselves in a small Chinatown. Today the region celebrates its Asian heritage with special events at various spots throughout the metropolitan center. See our Annual Events chapter for more information.

The Twentieth Century Dawns

As the new century approached, Phoenix boosters weren't satisfied with having just one railroad line coming into town. In 1895, after four years of work, the Santa Fe, Prescott, and Phoenix Railroad connected Phoenix to Prescott and, farther north, to Ash Fork, which was on the Santa Fe Railroad's transcontinental line. This move established Phoenix as a railroad hub within the Valley and throughout Arizona.

However, as much as boosters touted Phoenix's considerable attractive qualities, they could do nothing about the unpredictability of the weather. In the summer, the heat was barely tolerable. In the early 1890s, floods raged through the southern half of the city. In the latter part of the decade, drought ruined farmers.

Much of the West suffered from that drought and, soon afterward, cries for federal assistance led to the institution of the huge Federal dam projects that stabilized many Western cities' water situations. The Federal Salt River Project sponsored the Roosevelt Dam, built south of the confluence of the Salt River and Tonto Creek about 65 miles northeast of Phoenix. The process of building the dam, from acquiring rights of way to completion, took seven years. The dam was completed in February 1911, and the artificial lake it created gave Phoenix a reservoir that covered more than 16,000 acres. Roosevelt Dam also offered the city its first reliable flood control system and hydroelectric power source.

With the advent of electrification, Phoenix became as modern as a city could be and growth scurried along new trolley lines. By 1910, the city's population topped 11,000 people. It was the commercial center of a Valley that included the smaller towns of Tempe, Mesa, Scottsdale, Glendale, and Peoria, and would soon include Gilbert and Chandler. On February 14, 1912, Phoenix became a state capital with Arizona's admission as the 48th state of the Union.

At the turn of the twentieth century, lung patients seeking a rest cure flocked to Phoenix because of its low humidity, mild winter weather, and clean air. Through the 1920s, institutions

Sandra Day O'Connor

One of Arizona's proudest moments came in July 1981, when former President Ronald Reagan nominated Sandra Day O'Connor, a judge on the state's Court of Appeals, to the U.S. Supreme Court. Arizonans were overjoyed that one of their own—a rancher's daughter who had risen to become a lawyer, state legislator, and jurist—was the woman who had been tapped to break the Supreme Court's 191-year, men-only tradition.

In making the nomination, Reagan fulfilled a campaign promise to appoint a woman to the court. It was not a token appointment, he said at the time, but the selection of someone who met the high standards he demanded of all court appointees. A televised press conference featured Reagan describing O'Connor as a "person for all seasons" who possessed the "temperament, fairness, intellectual capacity, and devotion to the public good, which have characterized the 101 brethren who have preceded her."

After intense confirmation hearings during which opponents tried to paint her as being too liberal for the court, she won a 99-0 vote in the Senate and was sworn in September 1981. The American public seemed to approve: In her first year as a justice, she received 60,000 letters, more than any one member in the court's history.

O'Connor has said in interviews that the outpouring of support, especially from women, deeply touched her and that she hoped her appointment signaled to women their unlimited opportunities.

O'Connor has also said that, earlier in her life, she never expected to be where she is today. She

Sandra Day O'Connor grew up on an Arizona ranch and rose to become the first female Supreme Court Justice.

Photo: Courtesy of the Arizona Historical Society

had thought the state appellate judgeship would be the pinnacle of her career and that "I would live the balance of my life in our adobe house on the desert."

The life of this history maker began simply enough. Born Sandra Day in El Paso, Texas, in 1930, she was the first child of a second-generation cattle rancher. She grew up on the 150,000-acre Lazy-B Ranch near Duncan, Arizona, which is on the Arizona-New Mexico border. Thanks to tutoring from her mother, Sandra began to read at age 4 and continued to be an avid reader. In addition, it is said that by the time she was 8, she could brand cattle, ride a horse, drive a tractor, and fire a rifle. Her parents sent her to live with her grandmother and go to school in El Paso, because they felt the schools in their area were inadequate. She excelled as a student, graduating from high school at 16, then enrolling at Stanford University.

After receiving an undergraduate degree in economics, she enrolled in Stanford's law school, an unusual step for a young woman of the 1950s. She graduated third in her law school class, which, by coincidence, included William H. Rehnquist, who one day would become her colleague on the Supreme Court.

In 1952 she married John Jay O'Connor III, a fellow law student. She began interviewing with law firms in San Francisco and Los Angeles, none of which seemed willing to hire a female lawyer. She received one job offer—to work as a legal secretary. She kept looking and found a law clerk's job in the office of the San Mateo, California, county attorney. She was soon promoted to deputy county attorney.

After her husband's Army stint in Germany, O'Connor settled in Phoenix in 1957. The next decade was a mixture of part-time work in her private law practice, young motherhood (she gave birth to three sons), and increasing participation in Maricopa County's Republican Party activities. In 1965, she became an assistant attorney general for the state, and, in 1969, she was appointed to fill a vacant seat in the Arizona Senate. She subsequently won election to two full terms in the Senate, rising to majority leader. She was the first woman in the state to hold that post. She made her mark as a politician, winning admiration for her professionalism. It's interesting to note that O'Connor urged the passage of the Equal Rights Amendment when it came before the state Legislature for ratification in 1972.

By 1975, O'Connor returned to law and became a Maricopa County Superior Court judge. That work won her much recognition and led to her being named to the Arizona Court of Appeals in 1979, which proved to be the springboard for her ascension to the Supreme Court.

As a justice on the highest court of the land, O'Connor has been hard to peg as categorically conservative. There have been times when she has been the swing vote on an important issue, or when the opinions she has written have shown a moderate philosophy. Among the issues before the court that have thrown her into the spotlight are states' rights, abortion, affirmative action, sex discrimination, civil rights, and freedom of information. *The New York Times* once described O'Connor as a "sometime conservative with a moderate, even progressive streak" and "a determined woman but not a dogmatic one." It has also been said that O'Connor asks hard questions of attorneys and expects thoughtful, well-informed answers.

The year 2000 marks the 19th anniversary of O'Connor's appointment to the bench. Her commitment to public service has taken her far away from her beloved desert home. But her roots in Arizona are still strong, thanks to her many family ties here, along with friendships in political and legal circles. She remains a favorite daughter of the Grand Canyon State and she has been honored by having Arizona's new Federal Building and United States Courthouse named after her.

HISTORY

like the Phoenix Sanitarium promoted themselves nationally. Many of these institutions, such as Good Samaritan and St. Joseph's Hospitals, eventually offered the Valley more general hospital services.

World War I prompted a change in Valley agriculture. Cotton, used in the manufacture of tires and airplane fabric, was vital to the war effort. The Goodyear Tire and Rubber Corporation of Akron, Ohio bought two huge parcels of land near Phoenix. One was 27 miles southeast of Phoenix and was known as Goodyear (not to be confused with the present-day town of Goodyear located west of Phoenix). The other, west of the Agua Fria River, was known as Litchfield.

The historic Heritage House in downtown Phoenix offers visitors a rare example of Victorian architecture.

Photo: Penny Kleingartner

Cotton soon surpassed alfalfa as the primary cash crop of the Valley. By 1920, even though the cotton market went bust, Phoenix, with 29,000 people, had gained and retained its position as the largest city in the state. Its old rival, Tucson, had slipped in 1920 to being the second largest city at 20,000. The cotton bust prompted banks to offer loans to encourage crop diversification, and Valley farmers went headlong into citrus and dairy farming and planted the first alfalfa and grain crops.

In the 1920s, transportation in Phoenix improved. The Southern Pacific Railroad completed a new mainline through Phoenix in 1926. The first airline flights from Phoenix started in 1927, with two destinations—Tucson and Los Angeles—and, in September 1929, Phoenix Sky Harbor Airport was dedicated. Paved roads became more important as automobile ownership grew, and a paved highway to Los Angeles was completed in 1928. Phoenix had 86 miles of paved roads by 1929. The magazine *Arizona Highways* launched in 1925 to promote the state's scenic byways.

A group of promoters known as the Phoenix-Arizona Club began in 1919 to tout Phoenix as "the city where winter never comes." Tourism revenues climbed. The San Carlos and the Westward Ho hotels opened in 1928 to handle the increasing numbers of visitors. When the Arizona Biltmore resort opened in 1929, it was six miles outside of the Phoenix city limits.

INSIDERS' TIP

The westernmost battle of the Civil War—and the only one to take place in Arizona—was the Battle of Picacho Pass, fought near the peculiar split peak of Picacho. Picacho Peak looms over Interstate 10, approximately halfway between Phoenix and Tucson, and is the site of a state park. Today, no battles are waged; the wildflowers are plentiful, and it's a great place to hike.

Air Conditioning Changes Everything

The Great Depression affected Phoenix and the Valley more mildly than it did other urban areas, but nonetheless, unemployment rose in the early early 1930s. The New Deal policies of Franklin D. Roosevelt, elected in 1932, made the Federal government the Valley's biggest employer by 1935. The New Deal public works' projects involved improvements to the Valley's water-supply system, including dam renovations, and the building of the Bartlett Dam on the Verde River. That put the Valley's business growth on the upswing again. Even with the disruption of the Depression, Phoenix continued to grow.

In 1934, a Valley ad agency coined the phrase "Valley of the Sun." As boosters hoped, the moniker eventually replaced the "Salt River Valley" nickname, because the new phrase appealed to tourists and newcomers seeking relief from rain and snow.

Air conditioning changed Valley lifestyles radically, beginning in the 1930s. Necessity being the mother of invention, the heat in Phoenix prompted local companies to develop coolers.

Seven restored ranch buildings grace the grounds of Historic Sahuaro Ranch, which gives insight into day-to-day living of early Anglo and Hispanic settlers.

Photo: Courtesy of Glendale Tourism Division

HISTORY

Although Willis Carrier began manufacturing refrigerant-based mechanical air conditioners in 1915, the operating costs kept them from gaining much of a foothold in Valley homes. The evaporative cooler of the 1930s, an efficient device in Phoenix's low humidity, was considerably less expensive to run and offered an affordable alternative. Though simple, the system was an improvement on old-fashioned air-conditioning methods, by which Arizonans would sleep in wet sheets or hang wet blankets across an outdoor sleeping porch and hope for a breeze.

In the early 1940s, the Department of War opened two air bases in the Valley. Luke Field, in the far West Valley, was north of Litchfield Park and eight miles west of Glendale. Higley Field, renamed Williams Field in 1942, opened at a site south of Mesa and east of Chandler. During the war, desert-combat training camps opened west of Phoenix as well. The thousands who trained at these installations also were introduced to the Valley of the Sun and many returned for good after the war.

As it had been during World War I, Goodyear was an important employer in World War II. Goodyear operated a government-owned airplane-parts plant south of Litchfield Park in 1941. Other defense contractors followed.

When the war ended, Phoenix continued to attract defense contractors. The Valley's high-tech era began when a Motorola research and development facility opened in 1948, which established the pattern of the Valley's so-called "clean" industrialization. Motorola used mechanical refrigeration, as opposed to evaporative cooling, in its plants, and a Motorola executive wrote in a local business review in 1954 that the company believed refrigeration was "the complete solution" to Phoenix's staggering heat. By that time, the mass production of air conditioners had lowered the per-unit cost to levels affordable to the average working-class family. This development, perhaps more than any other—except the availability of water—cemented Phoenix's growth.

In the late 1950s, Phoenix boomed on every front and the Valley developed at an awe-inspiring rate. New communities sprouted, such as Maryvale for young families and the Sun Cities for retirees, as did shopping centers and office buildings. Towering high-rises soon lined Central Avenue, the city's main corridor of commerce.

The city aggressively annexed land and, by 1960, had expanded to 187 square miles. This urban sprawl sent downtown Phoenix into decline, as retail centers migrated with the population growth. Other problems included increased air pollution, whose haze was thick enough to obscure the view of the mountains in the distance. Despite the rampant growth, Phoenix civic leaders dragged their feet in building freeways in the Valley. In 1960, a plan that called for building 140 miles of freeway over 20 years was rejected as being too expensive.

Though they did not have the foresight to build freeways, Phoenix boosters did support the Central Arizona Project, a Federal project to transport water to the Valley from the Colorado River on the western boundary of Arizona. First proposed in 1947, the canal was finally completed in the 1980s.

INSIDERS' TIP

A number of museums in the area focus on Arizona's diverse heritage. Some lesser-known gems include the Carver/Phoenix Union Colored High School Museum and Cultural Center, Phoenix, which gives voice to the Valley's African-American experience, (602) 254-7516; the Museo Chicano/Chicano Museum, Phoenix, with changing exhibits on Latino culture, (602) 257-5539; and the Hoo-Hoogam Ki Museum, on the Salt River Pima-Maricopa Native American Community near Scottsdale, which celebrates the culture of the Pima and Maricopa tribes, (480) 850-8190.

Metropolis in the Desert

From the 1960s through the 1980s, Valley leaders took the peculiar stance of being pro-growth without giving regard to developing either a mass-transit system or a freeway system. Driving anywhere in the Valley became an ordeal in the stop-and-start traffic. Since the 1980s, the Valley has tried to make up for lost time in freeway construction, with projects being sped up about ten year's ahead of schedule. The final link of Interstate 10, connecting Florida to California, was completed here in 1990.

It would be easy to say that the poor transportation situation hampered Phoenix's downtown development, especially since, during the 1960s and 1970s, the area followed national patterns of people abandoning urban cores for life in the suburbs. Despite the skyscrapers, which by the early 1970s included the 40-story Valley Bank Center, the city's shopping malls became social centers for most residents. Park Central, Chris-Town, Thomas Mall, and MetroCenter, all were more important to the fabric of the city than the downtown.

The city's downtown deterioration seems to have halted, and new loft living spaces are beginning to lure dwellers to the urban core. This revitalization was encouraged by many construction projects, including the new Phoenix Civic Plaza, which included Phoenix Symphony Hall. In 1992, the Phoenix Suns basketball franchise tired of its digs in the Veterans Memorial Coliseum, three miles north of downtown, and opened the America West Arena in downtown Phoenix. That, and the opening of the Arizona Center and the Herberger Theater Center, brought enough entertainment venues to downtown that other merchants followed suit. By 1996, the arena was home to the NHL's Phoenix Coyotes. In 1997, the Orpheum Theater, one of the hallmarks of Phoenix's past, reopened. The downtown area's third major-league franchise, the Arizona Diamondbacks, began playing baseball in April 1998 in the Bank One Ballpark, a few blocks from the America West Arena. A new library opened, the Phoenix Art Museum expanded, and the Arizona Science Center moved and expanded—all within a reasonable drive or bus ride from downtown. Revitalization efforts continue with the construction of the new Sandra Day O' Connor Federal Building and United States Courthouse in 2000.

Phoenix may be the center of the Valley of the Sun, but its growth fueled the development other cities—Mesa, Tempe, Scottsdale, Glendale, Peoria, Gilbert, and Chandler. They are all among the largest cities in mostly rural Arizona, with only Tucson, Yuma, and Flagstaff in the same population ballpark. By 1990, Phoenix had grown to 983,403 people, and Mesa, at 288,104, was the third-largest city in the state. The population of Maricopa County was 2,346,610, most of that concentrated in the Valley of the Sun. (For more information on the cities in the Valley, see our Area Overview chapter.)

As the century turned, the Valley's growth showed no sign of abating. That means the most basic challenges—ensuring dependable water, energy, and transportation in the Valley—remain unchanged since the city's early days. However, a new generation of boosters is evaluating Arizona's quality of life, and more thoughtful strategies to preserve natural desert spaces, decrease air pollution, introduce efficient means of transportation, preserve pride in ethnic traditions, and build communities, have gained broader acceptance. These are all hopeful signs that more Valley residents think Arizona's historical legacy is worth preserving for future generations.

HISTORY

Hotels and Motels

LOOK FOR:
- Phoenix
- Southeast Valley
- Northeast Valley
- Northwest Valley

Price code

With each location listed in this chapter you will find a pricing guide ranging from one to four dollar signs. The code is based on the price for a one-night, double-occupancy stay in high season, which is January through April. Rates do not include tax. Room tax ranges from 10.3 percent in Phoenix to 10.45 percent in Scottsdale.

$	Less than $100
$$	$100 to $150
$$$	$151 to $250
$$$$	251 and higher

As a mecca for sunworshippers and tourists, Phoenix and the Valley have been working hard at creating places for all those guests to stay. Seems like there is a new hotel going up every few miles and occupancy rates still remain high. The Phoenix area has been enjoying a boom in hotel construction since the mid-1990s, and several of the places listed in this chapter have opened in the last few years. This tremendous growth in hotels is generally good news for the tired traveler. Lots of hotels and motels means ferocious competition in rates so there are plenty of good values to be found.

This chapter includes older hotels that have retained their special character while keeping their amenities and services up-to-date. You'll also find many familiar national and regional hotel and motel chains that appeal to budget-conscious vacationers as well as business travelers. However, these listings cannot cover the Valley's many motels and hotels. If you see a favorite chain listed here but aren't sure whether it's the location you want, be sure to inquire with toll-free operators about the chain's other properties in the Phoenix area.

The best places to stay tend to be areas around the Valley where there are clusters of newer hotels and motels. Examples include: the area off Arizona Highway 143 near Phoenix Sky Harbor International Airport; the Interstate 17 corridor near Metrocenter in Phoenix; the Superstition Freeway corridor through Mesa; Apache Boulevard in Tempe; the Interstate 10 corridor about 5 miles west of downtown Phoenix; the Camelback Road corridor in east-central Phoenix; the I-10 corridor near Arizona Mills shopping center in Tempe; the area near Arrowhead Towne Center and the Peoria Sports Complex in Glendale and neighboring Peoria; downtown Scottsdale; and north Scottsdale from Shea to Frank Lloyd Wright Boulevards.

Notice that we didn't mention downtown Phoenix. There are a handful of great hotels near Central Avenue, and we list them here. But boosters of downtown have long wished for more rooms, not only to meet the needs of Phoenix's healthy convention industry, but also to keep up with downtown's increasing popularity with leisure travelers.

So think about what part of the vast Valley you would like to make your home base during your vacation stay. Then study the listings under the various geographic areas. Each of the four corners of the Valley has certain commendable features.

All the hotels and motels in this chapter offer smoking and non-

INSIDERS' TIP

Here's a bit of movie trivia concerning old Phoenix hotels: The tall hotel with the antennas that you see in the opening scenes of Alfred Hitchcock's *Psycho* is the Westward Ho at 618 N. Central Avenue, which dates from 1928. It is no longer a hotel, but a senior citizens' home.

smoking rooms. Most have set aside wheelchair-accessible rooms as well. Expect to find cable or satellite TV, with many accommodations offering in-room movies for a small fee. In many cases children stay free as long as they're in the same room as their parents. Small pets are allowed at some hotels and motels; we'll tell you which locations accept them, and you can assume the others do not. If there are certain amenities that are particularly important to you, be sure to ask for details when you call for reservations.

All the accommodations in this chapter accept major credit cards. Many offer senior, group, or corporate discounts. Be sure to ask about these when you call. Because golf is such a popular activity in the Valley of the Sun, we have mentioned a few properties that offer golf packages with your stay.

Prices are based on high-season, double-occupancy rates. Take note, though, that prices go down considerably as summer approaches and stay low at least through Labor Day. So if you're considering a trip to Phoenix in the summer, you'll be pleased with the price of a room. Yes, it's hot then, but almost every accommodation in town has a swimming pool—or pools—and there's always the comfort of air conditioning. If you will be here in our balmier, non-triple-digit weather, remember to make reservations for lodging as soon as possible. Rooms fill up especially fast in February and March.

Of course, the Valley has options other than hotels and motels. Several upscale hotels are listed here, but if you desire a resort vacation, check the luxurious offerings in our Resorts chapter. Fans of the bed-and-breakfast experience should see our Bed and Breakfast Inns chapter. Those traveling in recreational vehicles or vacationers who don't mind roughing it should turn to our RV Parks and Campgrounds chapter.

Phoenix

Courtyard by Marriott
$$–$$$ • 2101 E. Camelback Rd., Phoenix
• (602) 955-5200, (800) 321-2211
• www.marriott.com

The area near 24th Street and Camelback Road is a great place for accommodations because of all the nearby shopping and fine dining. Courtyard by Marriott is one of the more economical options in that area and within walking distance of Biltmore Fashion Park and the Esplanade retail/restaurant areas. It adjoins the Town & Country Shopping Center. The four-story hotel, built in 1990, has 144 rooms and 11 suites. Amenities include a swimming pool in the courtyard, a hot tub, and an exercise room. In your guest room you'll find a coffee maker, desk, and complimentary newspaper on weekdays. The hotel serves a reasonably priced breakfast buffet.

Crowne Plaza
$$–$$$ • 100 N. First St., Phoenix
• (602) 257-1525, (800) 2CROWNE
• www.basshotels.com/crowneplaza

There were years when downtown Phoenix was a less desirable area and its few high-rise hotels had a hard time competing with newer accommodations in suburbia. But in this decade, downtown has become the hot place to be. Existing hotels have been beautifully renovated, and new ones are on the way. The

19-story Crowne Plaza is a good option for those who like the ambiance and convenience of staying downtown. Within walking distance are the convention and entertainment facilities of Phoenix Civic Plaza, the Herberger Theater Center, America West Arena and the shops and restaurants of Arizona Center. The 532 rooms are quite spacious and offer you a choice of one king or two queen beds, all redone with contemporary furnishings. Some suites and rooms with balconies are available. The Crowne Plaza Club executive level offers extra concierge service, evening cocktails, and complimentary breakfasts. Within the hotel are a gift shop, beauty salon, breakfast café, and restaurant. Other amenities include a massage studio and half-acre recreation deck with a jogging track, an outdoor pool, and a sauna.

DoubleTree Guest Suites
$$–$$$$ • 320 N. 44th St., Phoenix
• (602) 225-0500, (800) 800-3098
• www.hilton.com/doubletree/

Proximity to Phoenix Sky Harbor International Airport makes this a good bet for those traveling by air. The hotel also is near several office towers known as the Gateway Center, the Pueblo Grande Museum, and the new Chinese Cultural Center. Plus, 44th Street provides easy access to the freeways into downtown Phoenix and to Scottsdale. The six-story DoubleTree has 242 two-room suites furnished with microwaves, wet bars, refrigerators, and voice messaging. A complimentary breakfast buffet adds to the amenities, as do the fitness center, the on-site restaurant, and a large swimming pool surrounded by palm trees.

Embassy Suites Phoenix—Biltmore
$$–$$$$ • 2630 E. Camelback Rd., Phoenix
• (602) 955-3992, (800) EMBASSY
• www.embassysuites.com

The pinkish exterior of this hotel draws your attention if you're near the Biltmore Fashion Park shopping center. But you'll be even more dazzled by the interior: A giant atrium called the Sonoran Oasis features waterfalls, pools of koi fish, and four-story desert-theme murals. Palms and many other trees are in abundance, plus the atrium offers pleasant, brightly colored sitting areas. Rooms of this five-story hotel look out on the atrium, and the hotel's complimentary breakfasts are served there as well. The Omaha Steakhouse on the premises has been a popular addition to the Biltmore area's many dining options. Lodging consists of 232 two-room suites, each outfitted with a wet bar, microwave, refrigerator, well-lit work/dining area, and sleeper sofa in the living room. Each room also has two telephones with dataports and voice mail, two TVs, a coffee maker, a hair dryer, an iron, and ironing board. A fitness room and outdoor swimming pool also are at your disposal. Ask about special rates at the nearby Biltmore Country Club golf course.

Hilton Phoenix Airport
$$–$$$ • 2435 South 47th St.
• (602) 894-0326, (800) 445-8667
• www.hilton.com

Located just 1.5 miles from Sky Harbor International Airport, the Hilton Phoenix Airport offers rooms or suites featuring a Southwestern-style decor. For the business traveler, this full-service hotel offers dual phone lines and modem hook-ups in the rooms, as well as meet-

The Fountain Court at the Hyatt Regency looks across the lake to a golf course surrounded by palms and water.

HOTELS AND MOTELS

ing or banquet space for up to 500 people. Other amenities include private balconies, premier cable, heated outdoor pool and spa, on-site rental car desk, fitness center, a full-service restaurant, and a sports bar and grill for more casual dining. If you can stay awhile, the luxurious Concierge Level features king-size beds, whirlpool baths in some rooms, and an exclusive lounge serving complimentary cocktails, hors d'oeuvres, and breakfast. The Hilton is located ten minutes or less from a wide variety of sports, shopping, and dining opportunities.

Holiday Inn—Phoenix West
$$ • 1500 N. 51st Ave., Phoenix
• (602) 484-9009, (800) HOLIDAY
• www.holidayinn.com

This attractive Holiday Inn is done in Pueblo-style architecture with long balconies on the three upper floors and archways on the ground floor. Inside, it offers more Southwestern touches with native plants, ceramic tiles, pastel colors, and various artworks. The 144 rooms are decorated in Southwestern shades of turquoise and rose. In-room amenities include a coffee maker, a hair dryer, a makeup mirror, an iron, and ironing board. There are several suites with their own Jacuzzis or private balconies. Also, you can ask for a room with a desk/work area and dataport. A heated pool, whirlpool, sauna, and exercise room are on the premises. The Coyote Grill atrium restaurant serves Mexican food and other fare. The hotel's location gives you easy access to I-10, and you are only about 5 miles west of downtown.

Homewood Suites
$$$ • 2001 E. Highland Ave., Phoenix
• (602) 508-0937, (800) 225-5466
• www.homewoodsuites.com

This hotel specializes in extended stays, but you can book a room for just one night. Rates decrease for those staying longer than six days, and there is also a special 30-day rate. All 124 rooms are suites in this four-story hotel, which opened in 1997. It's in a prime location near the Camelback Corridor of businesses, retail stores, and restaurants. Three shopping malls—Town & Country, Camelback Colonnade, and Biltmore Fashion Park—are within walking distance. It's eight miles to downtown Phoenix via the Squaw Peak Parkway. Lodging is a choice between a Homewood Suite, with one king-size or two double beds in the bedroom and fold-out sofa in the living room plus a fully equipped kitchen and dining area, or the Master Suite, where the main difference is the larger living room with fireplace. You can also get a Master Suite with two bedrooms. The hotel rate includes complimentary breakfast, evening social hour, and use of an exercise room, gas grills, and a laundry room. A swimming pool, basketball court, and business center with computers are available for guests to use. Pets are allowed.

Hotel San Carlos
$$–$$$ • 202 N. Central Ave., Phoenix
• (602) 253-4121, (800) 528-5446

Clark Gable, Marilyn Monroe, Mae West, Spencer Tracy, and Carole Lombard slept here. The San Carlos is full of interesting stories, especially from its heyday in the 1930s and '40s. It was built in 1928 in an Italian Renaissance Revival design, and it was the city's first high-rise, fully air-conditioned hotel with an elevator. Its commitment to preservation has put the hotel on the registry of Historic Hotels of America. It's close to the sporting events, museums, and restaurants of downtown. Hotel service is European-style, with the aim of offering more personalized attention and hospitality. On the premises are a small bistro, an Irish pub, and a coffeehouse. A small swimming pool and sundeck are on the roof of the seven-story hotel. First-floor sitting areas have 1930s-era charm with dark woods and crystal chandeliers. There are 121 rooms and 11 suites, all with coffee makers and dataport telephones, but they're not as spacious as modern hotel rooms. Refrigerators and microwaves are available upon request. Continental breakfast is complimentary.

Hyatt Regency Phoenix
$$$ • 122 N. Second St., Phoenix
• (602) 252-1234
• www.hyatt.com

Long a top player in the downtown Phoenix hotel scene, the Hyatt Regency is a dominant structure in the downtown skyline—a 24-floor building of dark sandstone and glass topped by a popular rotating restaurant called the Compass Room (see our Restaurants chapter). The hotel itself has 712 rooms, including 45 VIP and business suites. A ride on the glass elevators that slice through the middle of the building affords spectacular views of downtown Phoenix and the Valley beyond. The lobby's huge seven-story atrium is a stunning showcase for hanging abstract sculptures and other artworks. The rooms are tastefully appointed and include in-room coffee makers. In addition to the Compass Room, the Hyatt has a more casual restaurant and a lounge. You'll also find an outdoor swimming pool, a whirlpool, exercise rooms, a concierge desk, and a car-rental desk. Early reservations are important, as the Hyatt is right across from Phoenix Civic Plaza and fills quickly when major conventions are in town.

InnSuites Hotel—Phoenix
$$–$$$ • 1615 E. Northern Ave., Phoenix
• 997-6285, (800) 752-2204
• www.innsuites.com

The InnSuites chain of hotels in Arizona and California touts its good service and full slate of amenities. This location is near Squaw Peak and the mountain preserve of north-central Phoenix. As such, it's quite scenic while being close to the Camelback Corridor of shops, restaurants, and offices. Amenities at this 122-suite hotel include complimentary continental breakfast and refreshments, nearby walking and jogging trails, a swimming pool, spa, and exercise room. There are several types of rooms of various sizes, with options on having a king- or queen-size bed and a sleeper sofa and/or a love seat. The Jacuzzi Suite includes a whirlpool tub. You'll find in-room coffee and tea, juice in your refrigerator, and popcorn for your microwave. Pets are allowed. Other InnSuites

locations are at 1651 W. Baseline Road in Tempe, near I-10, (800) 841-4242; and at 7707 E. McDowell Road in Scottsdale, near Eldorado Park, (800) 238-8851.

Lexington Hotel
$$ • 100 W. Clarendon Ave., Phoenix
• (602) 279-9811, (800) 537-8483

This is the day and age when a hotel's exercise and fitness facilities might be the amenities that draw you to it. The Lexington's City Square Sports Club, at 45,000 square feet, encompasses all kinds of fitness machines, an indoor basketball court, 11 racquetball courts, an aerobics studio, a whirlpool, a sauna, a steam room, and an outdoor pool. The Courtside Cafe serves a breakfast buffet daily. Another attractive aspect of the Lexington is its location, in Phoenix's uptown financial district. You're midway between downtown and busy Camelback Road. As for the rooms, there are 180 of them divided between a seven-story building and an adjacent three-story building. It's possible to ask for a room with a poolside patio in the cabana wing. Other amenities include beauty salon and an underground garage. Microwaves, refrigerators, and coffee makers are available for rent upon request.

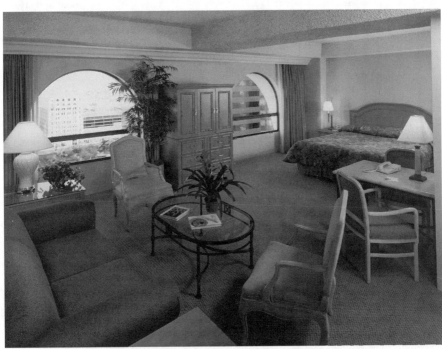

A view of the Valley accompanies the amenities at the Crowne Plaza.

Photo: Courtesy of the Crowne Plaza

Phoenix Inn
$$–$$$ • **2310 E. Highland Ave., Phoenix**
• **(602) 956-5221, (800) 956-5221**

With a great location just two blocks from 24th Street and Camelback Road, the Phoenix Inn specializes in mini-suites—spacious rooms with a king-size bed and sitting area. There are 82 such rooms in the four-story, sand-colored hotel. In addition, there are 24 rooms with two queen beds and a sitting area; eight king suites with a corner Jacuzzi; three family suites with two queen beds, a sitting area, and a separate king bedroom; and three presidential suites, which are full two-room suites. All rooms include microwave, refrigerator, coffee maker, hair dryer, iron/ironing board, dataport, and voice mail. A swimming pool, Jacuzzi, and workout room are available for use by all guests. The hotel's sunny breakfast room is the place for a complimentary buffet of pastries, cereal, and fruit every morning. A complimentary airport shuttle is available upon request.

Radisson Hotel—Phoenix Airport
$$ • **3333 E. University Dr., Phoenix**
• **(602) 437-8400, (800) 333-3333**
• **www.radisson.com**

The Radisson is one of a cluster of hotels that has opened near I-10 south of Phoenix Sky Harbor International Airport in the last decade or so. With its mirrored glass and concrete incorporated into a modern Southwestern design, the six-floor hotel makes an impressive-looking destination. Inside, the rooms surround an expansive lobby, made inviting by an atrium effect, many plants, and comfortable furniture. The 163 rooms include 13 suites; all have in-room coffee makers, hair dryers, dataports, and pleasing Southwestern artworks. There's a large pool, whirlpool, sauna, and fitness center. Conveniences also include a free airport shuttle and a car-rental desk on the property. The Radisson's restaurant and lounge are called Cafe de Tryst and W.E. Tryst.

Residence Inn by Marriott
$$–$$$ • **8242 N. Black Canyon Hwy., Phoenix**
• **(602) 864-1900**
• **www.marriott.com**

Many vacationers planning extended stays in Phoenix like the homelike atmosphere of rooms in the Residence Inn chain. This location gives you easy access to I-17 through northwest Phoenix. Metrocenter and its village of stores, restaurants, and entertainment are about a mile away via the freeway. Marriott says that Residence Inn's suite floor plans are 50 percent larger than the typical hotel room. Each of the 168 suites has a fully equipped kitchen with full-size appliances, separate living area, full bath, and sleeper sofa. Floor plan options include studio style, a one-bedroom suite, a two-bedroom suite with a fireplace, and a penthouse with a loft-style upper floor. Continental breakfast is complimentary. Plus, there is a weekly social hour. Other amenities include a swimming pool and the Sport Court for tennis, volleyball, and basketball.

Ritz-Carlton
$$$–$$$$ • **2401 E. Camelback Rd., Phoenix**
• **(602) 468-0700. (800) 241-3333**
• **www.ritzcarlton.com**

The 11-story, rose-colored Ritz-Carlton is one of the main buildings to anchor 24th Street and Camelback Road, probably the ritziest intersection in the city. Hotel brochures point out that a rental car is unnecessary for guests because of all the first-class shopping, entertainment, and dining that is within walking distance. Examples include Biltmore Fashion Park, the gourmet restaurant Christopher's, Roy's, Morton's, Hard Rock Cafe, and the AMC Esplanade movie theaters. Golf is also quite accessible, as concierges can arrange for tee times at the Biltmore Country Club a few blocks away. The hotel has 281 beautifully appointed guest rooms, including 14 suites and a private Club Level with extra services. Dark woods and colors of rose and mauve predominate in the hotel's decor, which is quite ornate, down to the wall moldings, gilded frames on artwork, and the many immense chandeliers. The lobby is a wonderful place for intimate conversations, with the space divided into drawing rooms with overstuffed chairs and museum-quality Old World paintings. Each guest room features a marble bath, a refreshment bar, three telephones, an in-room safe, plush terry bathrobes, and full maid service twice a day. The hotel has two restaurants, one of which is quite formal and the other of which has a bistro feel. The swimming pool area has a grill-style cafe for al fresco dining, and the Lobby Lounge serves afternoon tea and cocktails. Other amenities include a fitness center, lighted tennis court, and pro shop.

Royal Palms
$$$–$$$$ • **5200 E. Camelback Rd., Phoenix**
• **(602) 840-3610, (800) 672-6011**
• **www.royalpalmshotel.com**

In the late 1920s, when New York financier

and world traveler Delos Cooke and his wife, Florence, decided to make Phoenix home, they commissioned the building of a mansion in grand Spanish Colonial style. Years later, the mansion and its additional casitas were transformed into a hotel that attracted the rich and famous seeking Phoenix sun and solace at the base of Camelback Mountain. But the years took their toll, and the Royal Palms Inn, as it was known until recently, lost clientele to the Valley's newer resorts and hotels. Now it is back in the spotlight, grander than ever thanks to a multimillion-dollar restoration project completed in 1997. Buildings on the nine-acre property were given an exterior face-lift— Italian-stained terra-cotta walls and tiled roofs to recapture the feeling of a Mediterranean-style estate. In addition, some of the best landscape designers in town went to work on the property's orange and palm tree groves, flower gardens, outdoor fireplaces, and fountains. Interior designers carefully revamped the furnishings of the main building and casitas. Touches such as textured walls, tapestry fabrics, deep jewel colors, and handcrafted artifacts help recall the Royal Palms' heyday in the 1940s and '50s. The nine-hole golf course gave way to residential development, but guests can enjoy the swimming pool, tennis court, and fitness center. The Mediterranean restaurant T. Cook's is arguably one of the best dining rooms in town (see our Restaurants chapter).

Lodging consists of 34 standard rooms on the plaza, 34 plaza suites, 28 standard casitas, 15 deluxe casitas, and four villas, all built around the original Cooke mansion. The deluxe casitas in the West Courtyard are the most sumptuous, with a master bedroom suite, luxurious bath, and patio. Other rooms feature king-size beds, mini refrigerators, and bathrooms with a tub and pedestal sink.

Sheraton Crescent Hotel
$$$–$$$$ • 2620 W. Dunlap Ave., Phoenix
• (602) 943-8200, (800) 423-4126
• www.sheraton.com

The Sheraton Crescent has the rich ambiance of a grand downtown hotel, even though it is not downtown. Instead it's in the I-17 technology/commerce corridor of northwest Phoenix. The interstate makes it fairly convenient to central Phoenix attractions (15 to 20 minutes in non-rush hours), and you'll find the large Metrocenter shopping mall just a few blocks from the hotel. The seven-story building sits on nicely landscaped 13 acres, but the interior is downright opulent with its use of marble, stone, glass, and inviting furniture under twinkling chandeliers. There are 342 guest rooms, 12 of which are suites and two of which are top-floor penthouse suites. All have been recently renovated. The two top floors have controlled elevator access, and guests on those floors have exclusive concierge service, complimentary continental breakfast, and evening cocktails. In the other rooms, you'll find high-quality furnishings; a balcony or terrace; a bathroom with Italian marble; two telephones with computer-link and voice-mail capability; an in-room coffee maker; an in-room safe; a hair dryer; and an iron and ironing board. The bistro Indigo serves breakfast, lunch, and dinner.

On-site recreation includes two lighted tennis courts, sand volleyball, basketball and racquetball/squash courts, and a health and fitness center with steam rooms and a sauna. Golfers enjoy preferred tee times at nearby courses. At the swimming pool, the family will enjoy Monsoon Mountain, said to be one of the longest hotel water slides in the Phoenix area.

INSIDERS' TIP

Arizona is one of the few regions of the country that does not change its clocks for Daylight Savings Time. So if you are here on the first Sunday in April or the last Sunday in October, realize that national reminders about the time change do not apply to you—while you're here at least.

Wyndham Metrocenter Hotel
$$–$$$ • 10220 N. Metro Parkway East, Phoenix
• (602) 997-5900, (800) WYNDHAM
• www.wyndham.com

Like the Sheraton Crescent, the Wyndham Metrocenter Hotel serves the accommodation needs of business travelers in the I-17 high-tech corridor. But leisure travelers will love the fact that it's right next door to Metrocenter, with its shops, restaurants, and movie theaters, and down the street from Castles 'N Coasters amusement park. The hotel itself is quite luxurious, with a large, lush central courtyard leading out to an Olympic-size swimming pool. The 284 rooms are spread over five floors and include 18 suites. You can ask for a poolside Cabana Suite if you want to live it up. All rooms have coffee makers, hair dryers, radios and TVs, irons and ironing boards, and telephones with dataport and voice mail. Guest services include a car-rental desk, a gift shop, and an on-call massage therapist. The Coppercreek Bar and Grill is open for breakfast, lunch, and dinner, and an area called the Library offers cocktails and hors d'oeuvres. Another nice touch: the health club is open 24 hours.

Southeast Valley

Best Western Dobson Ranch Inn
$$$ • 1666 S. Dobson Rd., Mesa
• (480) 831-7000, (800) 528-1234
• www.bestwestern.com

A pleasant destination in Mesa for almost 20 years, the Spanish-style Dobson Ranch Inn boasts lovely courtyards with fountains and

Close to shopping at Fiesta Mall, Mesa Pavilion Hilton has an eight-story atrium.

Photo: Courtesy Mesa Convention and Visitors Bureau

flower gardens, and its 10 acres are crisscrossed with jogging and walking paths. Fronting the inn is the popular restaurant Monti's at the Ranch, serving steaks and continental cuisine. The inn is convenient to the Superstition Freeway and Fiesta Mall. Right down the road is the Dobson Ranch Golf Course. The inn has 213 rooms, with a standard room offering a sitting area and large dressing area. Executive king rooms include a king-size bed, refrigerator, and coffee maker. The two-room suites include a refrigerator, coffee maker, microwave, and an additional TV and phone. Other amenities at the inn include a swimming pool, two

spas, an exercise room, complimentary buffet breakfast, complimentary welcome cocktail, and free daily newspaper delivered to your door.

Best Western Inn of Tempe
$$ • 670 N. Scottsdale Rd., Tempe
• (480) 784-2233, (800) 528-1234
• www.bestwestern.com

Opened in 1997, this four-floor hotel is popular with business and leisure travelers who want easy access to the Valley's freeways. It's busy whenever major events at Arizona State University bring people to town. The 103 rooms are accessed from interior corridors, and guests have the option of queen- or king-size beds. There are in-room coffee makers, dataports, and voice mail systems. The indoor lap pool has resistance waves for those who like a workout, and the hotel also features an exercise room with five spas. A Denny's restaurant shares the property. Small pets are allowed.

Best Western Grace Inn
$$ • 10831 S. 51st St., Phoenix
• (602) 893-3000, (800) 843-6010
• www.bestwestern.com

The six-story Grace Inn is in the ever-growing Ahwatukee area of southern Phoenix. It is close to I-10 and nearby neighborhood shops, restaurants, and malls. Swimming and tennis are on the property; golf courses are quite accessible via the freeway. The hotel's spacious rooms have a Southwestern flavor, and guests can choose a king-size bed or two double beds. Larger one-bedroom suites offer separate sleeping quarters and living areas, and the kitchens have a microwave. For more money, there's a Plaza Level of suites with complete concierge amenities. All rooms have coffee makers and refrigerators. A restaurant on the property offers Southwestern specialties for breakfast, lunch, and dinner. You'll also find a lounge for happy hour and beverage service at the pool.

Country Suites By Carlson, Tempe
$$ • 1660 W. Elliot Rd., Tempe
• (480) 345-8585, (800) 456-4000

This location is a good bet if you like suite-style accommodations and want to be close to

I-10. The 250 rooms range from studio rooms to one- or two-bedroom suites, all with kitchen facilities. The decor is modern country, with lots of floral fabrics, silk plants, and light woods. The continental breakfast is free. You'll also find a generously sized swimming pool and spa. Pets are allowed, although the hotel asks for a deposit when you check in.

Days Inn—East Mesa
$–$$ • 5531 E. Main St., Mesa
• (480) 981-8111, (800) 325-2525
• www.daysinn.com

Families will like the casualness and comfort of this attractive Days Inn, located in a growing area of the East Valley. It has 61 guest rooms and suites, with your choice of one or two extra-long queen beds. A family suite includes a sleeper sofa and breakfast nook with microwave, refrigerator, and wet bar. The outdoor pool is heated and has a nearby Jacuzzi. The continental breakfast is complimentary.

Econo Lodge
$–$$ • 2101 E. Apache Blvd., Tempe
• (480) 966-5832, (800) 207-1317
• www.econolodge.com

This 12-year-old motel is reasonably priced and has 40 clean, no-frills rooms with a choice of one or two double beds. The motel has an outdoor pool and offers a complimentary continental breakfast. The location is good if you seek proximity to Arizona State University and downtown Tempe with its many shops, restaurants, and nightlife.

Fiesta Inn
$$–$$$ • 2100 S. Priest Dr., Tempe
• (480) 967-1441, (800) 528-6481

This 33-acre resort-style hotel is a bit off the beaten path yet full of amenities and close to the freeways and Arizona State University. Golfers like the inn's practice facility with a lighted driving range, a practice bunker, and chipping and putting greens. Lessons are available. For other recreation, there are three lighted tennis courts, a swimming pool, and Jacuzzi, an exercise room, and a full-service health club within walking distance of the inn. On the premises find a longtime Valley restaurant called Dale Anderson's The Other Place, serving breakfast, lunch, and dinner. Happy hour in the Kachina Lounge includes complimentary hors d'oeuvres. The 270 Southwestern-style guest rooms are divided into 156 standard rooms, 110 mini-suites, and four full suites. All rooms have hair dryers, small refrigerators, in-room coffee, irons, and ironing boards. Com-

plimentary limousine service to Phoenix Sky Harbor International Airport is available. Golf packages are available, too.

Hawthorn Suites
$$ • 5858 W. Chandler Blvd., Chandler
• (480) 705-8881, (800) 527-1133

Travelers planning an extended stay in the Valley probably will like the rates of Hawthorn Suites, a chain new to the area. Rates are discounted for stays of five nights or longer. The Chandler location opened in summer 1998, and the suites feature king-size beds in your choice of one- or two-bedrooms. Other pluses in each room: a living room, a fully equipped kitchen with full-size appliances, dual phone lines, full-size ironing board and iron, coffee maker, and toaster. All rooms are reached by an interior corridor. The hot/cold breakfast buffet is complimentary, plus there's an evening social hour every Wednesday. Recreation amenities include an outdoor heated pool, fitness center, and barbecue area. The well-landscaped grounds also have a small convenience store and laundry room. A hotel shuttle will take you to some of the sights within a 5-mile radius, including the Gila River Casino and Arizona Mills shopping mall.

Holiday Inn Express—Tempe
$$ • 5300 S. Priest Dr., Tempe
• (480) 820-7500, (800) HOLIDAY

There's a nicer-than-average lobby at this Holiday Inn Express, with its terra-cotta tile floors, atrium, plants, and pottery giving a feel of casual Southwestern style. The four-story motel has 160 rooms, recently redecorated, with king or queen beds. Guests enjoy free breakfast, and the outdoor pool area includes a spa. Those traveling in RVs or trucks will find ample parking. Another plus is the proximity of Arizona Mills, the Valley's newest shopping mall, at Priest Drive and the Superstition Freeway. Pets are allowed.

La Quinta Inn
$–$$ • 911 S. 48th St., Tempe
• (480) 967-4465
• www.laquinta.com

A convenient location two miles south of Phoenix Sky Harbor International Airport makes this La Quinta a popular choice for business and leisure travelers. The 129 rooms have a bright look with an earth-tone decor. Rooms come with either two full-size or one king-size bed and, in some cases, also with a recliner and workstation. You can upgrade to a suite, which has a small microwave and a refrigerator. All rooms have a coffee maker, and Nintendo is available if you ask. In addition to the requisite swimming pool, there's a small putting green in the courtyard. The inn's continental breakfast is free, or you can head to the Denny's restaurant next door. Transportation to and from the airport is complimentary as well.

Mesa Pavilion Hilton
$$$ • 1011 W. Holmes Ave., Mesa
• (480) 833-5555, (800) HILTONS
• www.hilton.com

It calls itself a business hotel with resort flair, but Mesa's Hilton is an attractive place with appeal for leisure travelers, too. Rooms look out on an eight-story atrium with a curved glass ceiling and lots of palm trees and upscale furnishings. The Hilton is close to Fiesta Mall, a major retail crossroads in the East Valley. For recreation, enjoy the outdoor pool and whirlpool, a nine-hole executive golf course, and a fitness center. There are 263 rooms, 63 of which are suites. All are decorated in soft pastels and have a refrigerator, hair dryer, coffee maker, iron and ironing board, oversize desk, voice mail, and two phones with modem capability. Those staying in the more expensive suites enjoy a concierge lounge, complimentary continental breakfast, and evening cocktails. The Zuni Grill Restaurant serves breakfast, lunch, dinner, and Sunday brunch, and the Atrium Lounge is a piano bar with live jazz music. In the lobby find a gift shop and airline reservations desk.

Mezona Inn
$$ • 250 W. Main St., Mesa
• (480) 834-9233

For a medium-priced motel, Mezona Inn has an above-average swimming pool area, where vacationers can sun themselves in a well-landscaped courtyard. Many of the inn's 136 rooms look out on the courtyard. Rooms come with one king or two queen beds plus a refrigerator, coffee maker, hair dryer, and makeup mirror. Some rooms have irons and ironing boards. The Mezona is in downtown Mesa—easy to reach from the freeway if you are traveling by car. Fiesta Mall is about a 10-minute drive away.

Microtel Inn
$ • 255 N. Kyrene Rd., Chandler
• (480) 705-8882, (888) 771-7171
• www.microtelinn.com

Microtel Inns specialize in no-frills, budget accommodations with interior access to guest rooms. The Chandler location—convenient to I-10—opened in 1998, offering 72 rooms and

giving guests a choice of one or two queen beds. The gray-and-white three-story motel has a New England cottage look. The grounds include a heated pool, Jacuzzi, and an extensive vending machine area. The rooms are small but have desks and modem hookups. Coffee is available in the lobby 24 hours.

Sheraton Mesa
$$–$$$ • 200 N. Centennial Way, Mesa
• (480) 898-8300, (800) 325-3535
• www.sheraton.com

This 12-story hotel is a classy addition to downtown Mesa, which has sometimes been criticized for being lackluster. Visitors and locals patronize its restaurants: Quail Run, serving breakfast, lunch and dinner in casual Southwestern ambiance, and Dos Lobos Cantina, serving Mexican food. The Sheraton has 273 guest rooms and suites, all with in-room coffee, minibars, and a simple but cheery floral decor. The two executive floors offer upgraded amenities, continental breakfast, and evening cocktails. You will probably want a car to venture out to the East Valley shopping malls, tourist attractions, and entertainment. A few small museums and Town Center boutiques are within walking distance.

Super 8 Motel
$ • 3 E. Main St., Mesa
• (480) 834-6060
• www.super8.com

This unobtrusive little property, situated where Center and Main Streets intersect in the middle of downtown Mesa, is a good deal for the budget-conscious. The motel has 78 rooms, all with queen-size beds except for the five king-size rooms. Besides the outdoor pool, extras include the coffee and tea available in the office around the clock and the free continental breakfast.

Tempe Mission Palms
$$–$$$ • 60 E. Fifth St., Tempe
• (480) 894-1400, (800) 547-8705

Here's a little bit of California in the heart of Old Town Tempe. The Mission Palms hotel is done in Mission-style architecture with a lovely courtyard where dozens of palm trees tower above you. Interior appointments are very Southwestern, with the lobby's Native American-inspired pictographs and earth-tone colors. The four-story hotel has 303 guest rooms decorated in shades of teal and plum. Several restaurants, coffeehouses, nightclubs, and boutiques are within walking distance on the popular and trendy Mill Avenue. Or take advantage of the on-site restaurant, called Arches Café, and the Monster Bar lounge. Other amenities include a swimming pool, a fitness center, and two lighted tennis courts. Tee times and transportation to the nearby Arizona State University Karsten Golf Course can be arranged. Guests also receive complimentary transportation to and from Phoenix Sky Harbor International Airport.

Travelodge Suites
$–$$ • 4244 E. Main St., Mesa
• **(480) 832-5961**
• **www.travelodge.com**

This motel underwent extensive renovations after being taken over by the Travelodge chain in 1997. Coffee makers and refrigerators are standard in the 79 rooms, where you have a choice of one or two queen-size beds. The one-bed version has a full kitchen, and the rooms with two beds have space for a microwave. Or you can ask for a full-fledged suite with separate living and sleeping areas. Recreational amenities include an outdoor pool, a Jacuzzi, and shuffleboard. A laundry area is available for guests to use. Pets are allowed for an additional fee if they weigh less than 50 pounds.

Twin Palms
$$$–$$$$ • 225 E. Apache Blvd., Tempe
• **(480) 967-9431, (800) 367-0835**

You can find several chain motels and hotels on the stretch of Apache Boulevard between Arizona State University and the Mesa city limits, but the Twin Palms stands out as something refreshingly different. It's a pinkish, seven-story tower, independently owned, sitting directly across from the ASU campus. The hotel says it offers "European hospitality," meaning that it aims to cater to guests' needs with a more personalized approach. Rooms offer higher-quality furniture with contemporary styling. There are 139 rooms and one king suite. Rooms have in-room coffee makers and dataport phones. Other amenities include complimentary use of ASU's massive Recreation Complex, a complimentary newspaper, an outdoor pool, and free 24-hour van transportation to Phoenix Sky Harbor International Airport. Fronting the hotel is a 24-hour International House of Pancakes. Inside the hotel is a bar and lounge.

Northeast Valley

Comfort Inn
$$ • 7350 E. Gold Dust Ave., Scottsdale
• **(480) 596-6559**
• **www.comfortinn.com**

Near the bustling north Scottsdale intersection of Shea Boulevard and Scottsdale Road, this three-story Comfort Inn puts you fairly close to two major shopping malls and many good restaurants, as well as several premier golf courses. In fact, golf packages are available. Just a few years old, the location has 124 rooms, with the options of a king-size bed, two queen-size beds, a king bed combined with a study area, or a suite with its own whirlpool. All rooms have refrigerators, and you can ask for Nintendo. The large outdoor pool has an adjacent whirlpool. The motel serves a complimentary continental breakfast.

Comfort Suites
$–$$ • 3275 Civic Center Blvd., Scottsdale
• **(480) 946-1111**
• **www.comfortinn.com**

Thanks to a robust tourism industry in Scottsdale, many reasonably priced accommodations have recently been built, including this one just south of downtown. The three-story, all-suite inn has a pleasing pueblo-style exterior, and the lobby is a small but lovely homage to Southwestern decor, with a beehive fireplace, Santa Fe-style light-wood furniture, and Native American objets d'art. The 60 rooms are junior suites, meaning that a half-wall separates the living and sleeping areas. Rooms include a refrigerator and microwave. A continental breakfast is complimentary. For leisure hours, there's an indoor pool and spa, plus an outdoor spa and sundeck. Restaurant options abound along nearby Scottsdale Road.

Hampton Inn—Old Town Scottsdale
$$ • 4415 N. Civic Center Plaza, Scottsdale
• **(480) 941-9400, (800) 426-7866**
• **www.hamptoninn.com**

This five-story Hampton Inn is in a quiet corner of downtown Scottsdale near professional and business offices. Yet it's within walking distance of Old Town Scottsdale, which

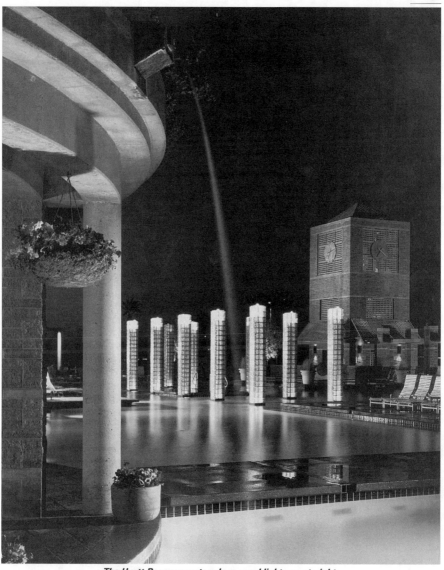

The Hyatt Regency water playground lights up at night.

Photo: Courtesy of Hyatt Regency Scottsdale

has boutiques and art galleries, and Scottsdale Fashion Square, filled with department stores, smaller shops, and restaurants. The lobby is on the second floor, allowing for parking spaces underneath it. Don't underestimate the pleasure of shaded parking if you're here in the summer. The outdoor pool is small but pleasant enough. Guests receive a complimentary continental breakfast. The 126 rooms, which include nine king deluxe suites, are decorated in deep reds and blues.

Inn at the Citadel
$$$–$$$$ • 8700 E. Pinnacle Peak Rd., Scottsdale
• (480) 585-6133, (800) 927-8367

If you're not set on staying close to major tourist attractions, you might want to consider this intimate inn, 30 miles from downtown Phoenix in what's known as the Pinnacle Peak area of north Scottsdale. There is quite a bit of new neighborhood development around the Pueblo-style inn, but it doesn't spoil the spectacular view of the McDowell Mountains. The 11 suites are appointed with antique-style furnishings and original artwork. Some suites have fireplaces, others have balconies, and some have both. One suite offers a private hot tub on a terrace with a good view. Guests are served complimentary continental breakfasts. In the same complex are an upscale restaurant and a market cafe. Nearby are boutiques and art galleries.

Motel 6 Scottsdale
$ • 6848 E. Camelback Rd., Scottsdale
• (480) 946-2280
• www.motel6.com

This is not your usual Motel 6 beckoning you from the freeway. This 122-room location is nestled along Camelback Road as the thoroughfare heads into the heart of Scottsdale. Just steps away is the posh Scottsdale Fashion Square, with its mix of major department stores, boutiques, and trendy restaurants (see our Shopping chapter). And fronting the motel is a remarkably good (and popular) pancake house. The rooms are decorated in light woods and Southwestern colors. You have the option of two full beds or a queen-size bed. The swimming pool offers a pleasant respite under the palms. Pets are allowed.

Quality Suites
$$$ • 3131 N. Scottsdale Rd., Scottsdale
• (480) 675-7665, (800) 228-5151
• www.qualitysuites.com

An all-suite, three-floor hotel, Quality is one of the newcomers to the downtown Scottsdale accommodations scene. It opened in early 1998 with 171 two-room suites, where you have your choice of a king-size or two queen-size beds. Suites come in several floor plans and include kitchenettes. You can upgrade to a Tycoon Business Suite featuring executive desks, well-lit work areas, and computer connections. Each suite comes with a wet bar, an iron and ironing board, two TVs, a microwave, a coffee maker, and two telephones. The complimentary breakfast buffet offers toast, waffles, cereal, pastries, yogurt, and fruit. For recreation enjoy an exercise room and swimming pool. Or you can stroll into Old Town Scottsdale, about a one-mile walk.

Rodeway Inn
$-$$ • 7110 E. Indian School Rd., Scottsdale
• (480) 946-3456
• www.rodeway.com

This location places you near a major cross-roads of downtown Scottsdale—Indian School and Scottsdale Roads—close to shopping, restaurants, and art galleries. That makes it quite a good deal. The motel has undergone both exterior and interior renovations in the last few years. The L-shaped building has two floors, with rooms looking out on a swimming pool. Management is friendly and offers amenities such as free continental breakfast, free coffee 24 hours a day, and a refrigerator and microwave in all rooms. The 65 rooms come with your choice of double beds, king beds, or queen beds; a few rooms have been set aside as suites. Ask about golf packages.

Scottsdale Hilton Resort and Villas
$$$-$$$$ • 6333 N. Scottsdale Rd., Scottsdale
• (480) 948-7750, (800) 528-3119
• www.hilton.com

Although it is a compact 20 acres and 187 rooms, the Scottsdale Hilton is a resort-like hotel with beautiful grounds, a relaxing pool area, and impeccably decorated rooms. Adjacent to the hotel is a complex of boutiques and restaurants called Hilton Village, and the exclusive Borgata shopping area is across the street (see our Shopping chapter). The hotel itself has Griff's restaurant, serving up American fare. It's named after hotel owner Merv Griffin of television fame. On the grounds is the Fleming's Steakhouse, a wonderful restaurant for beef and wine lovers. Other amenities include four lighted tennis courts, a fitness center, a gift shop, a beauty salon, and a car-rental desk. Concierges can arrange tee times at one of Scottsdale's many golf courses. The guest rooms range upward from the standard room to rooms with a pool view, poolside rooms with a patio, and luxury suites. Also on the grounds are 45 two-bedroom, two-bath villas that feature full-size living rooms, dining rooms, and kitchens. For an additional cost, you can ask for a private spa.

Scottsdale's 5th Avenue Inn
$$ • 6935 Fifth Ave., Scottsdale
• (480) 994-9461, (800) 528-7396

At 20 years old, the Spanish Colonial-style 5th Avenue Inn is showing its age a bit on the outside, but the room interiors have been refurbished recently, and you can't beat the location if you plan to spend time browsing the many boutiques along Fifth Avenue. The inn is just behind a Village Inn pancake house. Amenities include the quiet, sunny pool area, complimentary continental breakfast, and free coffee around the clock. The inn is three stories and has 92 rooms, furnished with either king or queen beds.

Sunburst Resort
$$$–$$$$ • 4925 N. Scottsdale Rd., Scottsdale
• (480) 945-7666, (800) 528-7867

The Sunburst, a resort-like hotel, offers some of the same ambiance of major Scottsdale resorts on a smaller scale. It consists of five, two-story structures in a nicely landscaped setting along busy Scottsdale Road, just a few blocks north of Camelback Road. The location puts you in walking distance of plenty of shopping, restaurants, and nightlife. The lobby has a striking, sunlit appearance with lots of wood furniture and bright colors. The 210 rooms have a contemporary Southwestern decor. Rooms include refrigerators and private balconies. There's a lot of activity around the Sunburst's new sand-beach pool. A restaurant and bar on the premises also keep things lively.

Northwest Valley

Best Western Inn of Sun City
$$ • 11201 Grand Ave., Sun City
• (623) 933-8211, (800) 253-2168
• www.bestwestern.com

There are plenty of shopping, dining, and recreational opportunities in the Sun City area for tourists of all ages. Plus, the recent expansion of the Valley freeway system makes it easier to get from Sun City to other points. Downtown Phoenix, for instance, is between a half-hour and 45 minutes away. This Best Western has 75 rooms furnished with either a king bed or two double beds. The majority of rooms include a microwave, refrigerator, and coffee maker. The inn also has a one-room kitchenette with one queen-size bed as well as a larger three-room apartment with twin beds

in the bedroom, and a queen sofa bed in the living room plus a full kitchen. All rooms are eligible for discounted rates for those staying seven consecutive nights or longer. The two-story motel has a swimming pool.

Hampton Inn
$$ • 8408 W. Paradise Ln., Peoria
• (623) 486-9918
• www.hamptoninn.com

Arrowhead Towne Center, one of the Valley's newer shopping malls, has fostered a boom in retail, office, and residential development in the surrounding area. One new building is this five-story Hampton Inn, which opened in early 1998. The mall is close by and so is Peoria Sports Complex, site of spring-training baseball games, and other events (see our Spectator Sports chapter). The 112 rooms here come with either two queen beds or one king bed. Standard features include coffee maker, microwave, and refrigerator. The inn has an outdoor pool and whirlpool plus a laundry room for guests' use. Continental breakfast is complimentary. Pets are allowed.

Windmill Inn at Sun City West
$–$$ • 12545 W. Bell Rd., Surprise
• (623) 583-0133, (800) 547-4747

This all-suite hotel has a few intriguing amenities you don't always find, including the free use of bicycles, free use of a lending library of best-selling books, and, free coffee and muffin plus a newspaper delivered to your door every morning. The 127 two-room suites are 500 square feet and come with either a king-size bed or two double beds, along with double sinks in the bathroom, a wet bar, a microwave, a refrigerator, two TVs, three telephones, a desk area, and a sleeper sofa. Guests also have the use of laundry facilities. Adding to the amenities are the swimming pool and whirlpool. Pets are accepted.

Resorts

LOOK FOR:
- The Famous Five
- Even More Resorts

Price Code

Resorts were asked for their double-occupancy, daily rates in high-season (generally considered to be January to April, but in some cases including fall months and May). Because resorts tend to offer a variety of accommodations, we have given you dollar codes that represent the range from a standard room to suites, casitas, and luxury villas. Prices indicated here do not include tax, room service, incidental fees or fees for golf, spas, and other amenities. Remember that off-season rates can be dramatically lower than what you see here.

$ $151 to $200
$$ $201 to $300
$$$ $300 to $500
$$$$ $500 and higher

VISIT US TODAY!
www.insiders.com

A hundred years ago, when winter vacationers first spread out their lawn chairs at Phoenix hotels to soak up the desert sun, they probably had no inkling of what lay ahead for the Phoenix hotel industry. From those simpler times have evolved sumptuous, top-rated resorts in Phoenix, Scottsdale, and other areas of the Valley that attract millions of people and pump billions of dollars into the local economy. In Scottsdale in particular, the long row of resorts and high-end hotels along Scottsdale Road help make tourism the largest economic activity in that city.

Modern resorts don't just have a pool—they have several pools, many of which resemble small lakes. They pay great attention to details in furnishings and architecture, always striving to raise the lodging experience. They always offer golf, if not by building one or two championship courses on their own properties, then by arranging access and trips to nearby courses. You'll always find tennis, notable restaurants, and a full array of guest services, including around-the-clock room service. It's no wonder that Valley resorts have been showered with awards and accolades in surveys, travel guides, and national magazines.

Happily for those of us who appreciate the desert and Arizona's heritage, the fancy resorts respect Southwestern style. We're not Hawaii, after all. Attention is given to desert landscaping, for the most part. Tribute is paid to the state's Native American and Spanish roots through architecture, all kinds of art, and often through the food served in restaurants.

INSIDERS' TIP

Live music at the resorts attracts Valley residents and visitors alike. Musicians bring jazz, blues, and light rock to clubs such as Remington's at the Scottsdale Plaza Resort, Different Pointe of View at the Pointe Hilton at Tapatio Cliffs, and the Lobby Bar of the Hyatt Regency at Gainey Ranch.

Staying at a Valley resort can be a once-in-a-lifetime experience. The resorts offer great choices for a honeymoon or romantic getaway, going so far as to offer special, all-inclusive packages. Some visitors are lucky enough to come to a resort as part of a business meeting or convention. Even if a resort is not in your vacation budget, you might think about splurging on a fine dinner or Sunday brunch in one of the restaurants, or just relax by sipping cocktails at sunset in one of the lounges. If you're just in for a brief visit, be sure to take some time to walk the main grounds to enjoy the flower gardens and water features

All of the top-rated resorts recognize the importance of offering the spa experience. Steam rooms, massages, facials, whirlpools, lap swimming pools, fitness machines, and free weights are the kinds of ultimate indulgences that well-heeled vacationers seek. The Boulders, for instance, offers a special massage with hot rocks. At the Biltmore, you can get a purification treatment based on Native American healing rituals and amenities such as juice bars, aerobics classes, shiatsu, reflexology, aromatherapy, wraps, manicures, and pedicures. You can pick your pleasure in hour-long sessions or day-long packages. Also realize that more and more, a resort's dining options contribute to how highly it's rated.

This chapter touches on several award-winning restaurants, but look to our Restaurants chapter for more detailed information.

In recent years, hotels and resorts have made great strides in setting aside smoke-free rooms and providing wheelchair-accessible accommodations. Be sure to ask about these features when making reservations. All resorts listed here accept major credit cards. There are no restrictions on bringing children to the resorts, although, as you'll see from our descriptions, some are more kid-friendly than others.

This chapter describes a variety of resorts, starting with what we consider to be the most exclusive, "The Famous Five."

The Famous Five

Think of it: A place to luxuriate in the sun, have all kinds of amenities at one's fingertips, and let money be no object. This ideal resort vacation is within the means of some lucky travelers, who often make it their sole purpose in coming to Phoenix. Chances are they will pick one of these five resorts, all with interesting histories, lovely settings, and national, if not international, fame. These are what the industry calls total-destination resorts: Once you arrive, there's enough right around you to fully entertain you so you may never venture away from the resort grounds.

Prices for these resorts vary greatly. Assume that the simplest room during high season will cost at least $300 a night, and that prices per night for double occupancy are more typically around $500. For a two-bedroom villa, say, at the Arizona Biltmore, you could pay $1,700. But remember that these are high-season prices, usually lasting from January to April. If vacation plans (and tolerance of the weather) permit you to travel here in the hotter months, the price tag can be much lower. For instance, at the Phoenician, a premium room that goes for more than $500 from January to June can go for $350 in the dead of summer. The Scottsdale Princess has lower rates from April to June and from September to January and even lower rates from mid-June to the end of August. In the slowest part of the year, you could nab a standard room for about $150, less than half the high-season rate, and grab The Presidential Suite, on the other hand, for $1,350 ($2,750 in high season). It's also possible to catch some deals around the winter holidays. Many of the resorts offer special bargains on

One of the best things to do during a resort vacation is to relax and do absolutely nothing at all.

Photo: Courtesy of Arizona Biltmore

RESORTS

stays between Thanksgiving and New Year's eve. When choosing a resort, inquire whether the rate varies with how good the view is from your room. The best views command the highest rates. Just remember, you might spend more time by the pool than in your room so you might be happier without the expensive view. If you're a serious tennis or golf player, or serious about indulging in a resort's spa, ask about programs that include the cost of those activities with your room rate. All resorts offer creative packages that will combine sports or spa pleasures with the cost of your room.

Arizona Biltmore
$$$–$$$$ • 24th St. and Missouri Ave., Phoenix
- **(602) 955-6600, (800) 950-0086**
- **www.arizonbiltmore.com**

Open since 1929, the Arizona Biltmore—crowned "The Jewel of the Desert" at its grand-opening gala—is a cherished part of Phoenix history. Even visitors to town who are not guests of the hotel should see it to appreciate the way it helped lay the foundation for the Valley of the Sun's resort industry and to ap-

preciate it as an architectural gem. Vestiges of Frank Lloyd Wright can be seen all through the interior and exterior since the Biltmore was designed by one of Wright's apprentices, Albert Chase McArthur. (The extent of Wright's own involvement as "consulting architect" is not known, but that just adds to the hotel's mystique.) The ambiance is one of functional elegance. The geometrically stylized image of a palm tree trunk that's sculpted into many of the exterior concrete blocks sets a theme that's used repeatedly in the decor and landscaping. The lobby has remarkable stained-glass windows, balconies, and Wright-inspired furniture and lighting.

Other interesting facts about the Biltmore: Every U.S. president since 1930 has stayed at the Biltmore; chewing-gum magnate William Wrigley and his heirs owned the resort for four decades; and in 1996, the resort completed a five-year, $50 million renovation and expansion project. The Biltmore continues to be an award-winning resort because its amenities and services keep up with modern times, but face-lifts over the years have not marred its architectural integrity. Although at its debut the

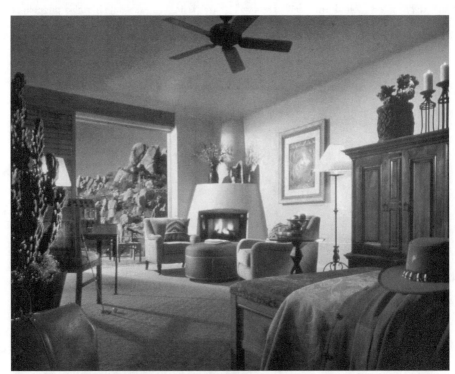

The Casita Guestroom, like this one at the Four Seasons Resort, offers additional space and comforts during your stay.

Biltmore was virtually on the outskirts of town, Phoenix's phenomenal growth has now placed it at the center of the action. It's only 15 minutes by freeway from downtown and is just a skip away from the Camelback Corridor, a prime retail, restaurant, and office district.

The Biltmore's 620 rooms are furnished in a style reminiscent of Wright's. New to the resort are one- and two-bedroom villas with full kitchens, indoor and outdoor dining areas, and fireplaces. The Biltmore's 39 acres make it a relatively compact resort. Still, there's space for the Biltmore Athletic Club, along with two championship golf courses at the adjacent Arizona Biltmore Country Club. There's also an 18-hole putting course; three restaurants, including Wright's, featuring impeccable New American cuisine; two bars; eight tennis courts; and an elegant spa offering therapeutic treatments, fitness equipment, steam rooms, and a full-service beauty salon. The resort has become more kid-friendly over the years. The Paradise Pool features a 92-foot water slide enclosed in twin towers. The Kids Kabana offers a range of supervised activities. Lawn games include croquet, volleyball, chess, and shuffleboard, and there are pleasant trails for jogging, strolling, and biking. You will also find poolside private cabanas and swim-up beverage service as well as a salad and sandwich bar.

The Boulders

$$$$ • 34631 N. Tom Darlington Dr., Carefree
- **(480) 488-9009, (800) 553-1717**
- **www.grandbay.com/properties/boulders**

When celebrities want to be seen, they stay at the Arizona Biltmore. When they want privacy, they sneak away to The Boulders. Or so goes the scuttlebutt in Phoenix resort circles. The Boulders, set in the foothills of the far northeast Valley, is logistically the best place to get away from it all without leaving civilization. It's the kind of place Microsoft founder Bill Gates chose for a retreat. And "Andrew Harper's Hideaway Report," a travel newsletter that goes out to business executives, has ranked The Boulders the best American resort, in addition to the many other honors it has received over the years.

Carefree, as its name suggests, is a small, laid-back town with beautiful hillside homes about 30 miles north of central Phoenix. The Boulders is on the main route into town and has a 24-hour security gate. Its name pays tribute to the geological curiosity at its center: a 90-foot-high mound of boulders. Elsewhere on the grounds are other rock outcroppings. When

the resort was designed and built in the early 1980s, painstaking care was taken to make it as unobtrusive as possible within its desert surroundings. The adobe-style buildings are low-slung and painted to closely match the color of the boulders. Almost all the landscaping is indigenous to the area.

A network of trails on resort grounds lets guests enjoy the mountain scenery, including the reported 350 species of birds and other wildlife in the area. The list of amenities is pages long, topped by The Boulders' two 18-hole championship golf courses. Designed by Jay Morrish, they've won kudos from *Golf* magazine and *Golf Digest*. In harmony with the surroundings, the fairways are covered in local grasses. Staff at the Boulders says service is just as important as amenities. With an eye toward anticipating their guests' every need, the staff keeps detailed preference histories—for instance, who likes feather pillows and who likes synthetic. Concierges welcome questions and relish opportunities to help guests arrange off-resort excursions, such as daytrips to the Grand Canyon or hot-air ballooning.

The 160 guest casitas are nestled into the terrain, and each has a fireplace and private patio. Families and golf groups can take advantage of the 35 one-, two-, or three-bedroom villas, complete with laundry facilities and kitchens. All units are furnished in earth tones, and all have wet bars, large dressing and bathroom areas, and wood-beam ceilings.

Dining is exceptional, with five restaurants to choose from, including the casually elegant Palo Verde and The Latilla, offering a more formal menu and views of a waterfall. There are eight tennis courts, with tennis pros offering private lessons and weekly clinics. You'll also find three swimming pools and rock-climbing sessions that guide you up the boulders formation, which is estimated to be 12 million years old. The Sonoran Spa offers enticing facials, massages, and fitness machines. The resort opened the luxurious Golden Door Spa in 1999. It's a short stroll away from the boutiques and galleries of El Pedregal Festival Marketplace or a short drive to the touristy town of Carefree. Complimentary shuttles get you around the 1,300-acre resort. Native American art is showcased in the main lodge and dining areas, and the staff even conducts art tours. The world-famous Heard Museum has a satellite museum featuring their renowned collection of Native American art. Transportation to Sky Harbor and Scottsdale airports is available, or you can fly your private plane right into Carefree Airport.

The Phoenician

$$$–$$$$ • 6000 E. Camelback Rd., Scottsdale
- **(480) 941-8200, (800) 888-8234**
- **www.thephoenician.com**

"Opulence" is the word to best describe the Phoenician. Looking around, you get the sense that no expense was spared in its design and furnishing, from the $7.7 million collection of paintings, tapestries, antiques, and bronze sculptures inside and on the grounds to the oval pool tiled in mother-of-pearl and surrounded by lush landscaping with waterfalls, lagoons, and fountains. And then there are touches such as crystal chandeliers, marble floors and walls, and Italian linens. It's unexpectedly palatial for a metropolitan area with such humble beginnings as Phoenix. Yet guests can easily find serenity and relaxation, along with topnotch services, beautiful nighttime views, great golf, and one of the best restaurants in town, all with majestic Camelback Mountain as backdrop.

The Phoenician is better understood through a quick look at its beginnings. It opened in 1988, the "house" that Charles Keating built, as he envisioned building a resort like no other. But when Keating's savings and loan empire crumbled and landed him in federal prison, the resort became the property of the Resolution Trust Corp. Recently it's come under the wing of ITT Sheraton Corp. as part of its "Luxury Collection."

The Phoenician is huge, laid out on 250 acres with 654 rooms and suites. Most of the accommodation is in the main building, supplemented by more secluded areas with casitas, suites, and villas. Rooms are furnished with expensive rattan furniture, Berber carpets, oversized bathrooms with Italian marble, in-room safes, telephones with voice mail and modem capabilities, and limited-edition prints. The resort boasts nine pools and a 165-foot water slide. Guests can stroll through a two-acre cactus garden. A 27-hole golf course, putting green, and clubhouse are also on site, as is the Tennis Garden with 12 courts, an automated practice court, and a Wimbledon-like grass court. Staff can arrange for hikes up Camelback Mountain, croquet, lawn bowling, lawn chess, and billiards provide other amusements.

As for restaurants, the modern French cuisine at Mary Elaine's (named for Keating's wife) is perhaps one of the most expensive and outstanding restaurants in town . The Terrace Dining Room's Italian fare and Windows on the Green's Southwestern food are popular options. Many Phoenix residents know about the charming afternoon teas in the Tea Court. In addition, you can enjoy a poolside cafe, ice cream parlor, the 19th Hole Snack Bar, and the Thirsty Camel Lounge. The Centre for Well-Being is a large spa, offering 13 kinds of massages, scrubs and mud packs, facial care, and exercise equipment. For children ages 5 to 12, the resort runs the Funicians Kids Club, where daily themes get them swimming, hiking, making crafts, and playing games under staff supervision. No stone's left unturned: You'll also find a beauty salon, a few boutiques, 24-hour room service, concierge service, and airport transportation.

Fairmont Scottsdale Princess

$$$–$$$$ • 7575 E. Princess Dr., Scottsdale
- **(602) 585-4848, (800) 344-4758**
- **www.fairmont.com**

The Scottsdale Princess is probably best known for its association with the Phoenix Open, a key tournament on the PGA tour that annually draws tens of thousands of spectators. It's played on the adjacent TPC Stadium Course. The resort is part of the exclusive chain of Princess Hotels, also located in Bermuda, the Bahamas, and Acapulco. The Arizona location blends opulence with Southwestern sensibilities. It's built to resemble a Mexican Colonial estate, with lots of arched openings, balconies, railings, and red-tiled roofs. Its terra cotta color complements the beautiful view of the McDowell Mountains. The Princess is on 450 acres in ever-expanding north Scottsdale and has about 650 guest rooms, suites, casitas, and villas. It has the largest hotel ballroom in Arizona, making it a popular place for business conferences. Another prime feature is the Marquesa, the resort's much-heralded restaurant serving Catalan cuisine.

Golf is the big draw here. In addition to the course used for the PGA tour, there's another 18-hole championship course; the Tournament Players Club of Scottsdale operates both. Tennis gets attention here, too, with seven courts, including a stadium court that annually hosts a couple of important tournaments. Other opportunities for recreation include three swimming pools, indoor basketball, sand/water volleyball, a fitness trail, and fishing. Besides the Marquesa, the resort has six other restaurants, including La Hacienda, popular for its Mexican food and strolling mariachis; a grill at the golf clubhouse; a poolside cafe; and a country-western nightclub. Shopping is well-covered, too, with boutiques carrying sports clothing and other fashions, Southwestern gifts, and Indian jewelry. You can indulge yourself in the Spa &

Fitness Center with a Turkish steam bath, herbal wraps, or a loofah buff. And how about a Massage in Symphony, where two massage therapists work on one guest, using long, flowing strokes in unison? On the grounds of the Princess are several distinct gardens. Enjoy two cactus gardens, a plaza with 300 decorated pots and a fragrance garden with jasmine, orchid trees, and citrus trees. All rooms have terraces, wet bars, refrigerators, and oversized bathrooms. The 125 casitas are grouped near the tennis courts, while the 75 villas are on the opposite end. Families can take advantage of the Kids Club, which offers supervised activities for kids ages 5 to 12 on weekends.

> **INSIDERS' TIP**
>
> What is a resort casita? Think of it as a mini-house and a home away from home. Often the casitas are individual, stand-alone structures or large guest rooms joined in small groupings with other casitas, townhome-style, to create a greater sense of privacy. Often they have their own patios, fireplaces, living rooms, and kitchens.

The Wigwam
**$$$ • 300 Indian School Rd.,
Litchfield Park**
• (602) 935-3811, (800) 327-0396
• www.wigwamresort.com

Of the top-five resorts, some say the Wigwam comes closest to capturing the essence of Arizona and the lure of the West. It couldn't exist anyplace but here. This once-private club was built in 1918 to lodge visiting executives of the Goodyear Tire and Rubber Co. and was way out in the country back then. By 1929, it opened to the public, with room for 24 guests. Now expanded to 75 acres, it still carries reminders of a more rugged, cowboy era. Much of the original building from 1918 has been incorporated into the Main Lodge, including a sitting room with a large stone fireplace that is both cozy and rustic.

This is the only one of the resorts described in this chapter that is in the West Valley. Litchfield Park is a growing area, and thanks to freeways, the Wigwam is now only 20 minutes from downtown Phoenix. Also distinguishing it from other resorts is the fact that it's the only one in Arizona with three golf courses on its property. The Gold and Blue courses were designed by Robert Trent Jones, and Arizona's "Red" Lawrence designed the Red course. All of the courses, especially the Gold one, have been praised by those in the know. Also, the Wigwam is home to the nationally known Jacobs' Golf Schools, which run four- and five-day golf sessions. (See our Golf chapter.)

Accommodations are arranged in clusters of casitas—331 in all, plus about 70 suites. To say "Southwest," the interiors are decorated with distressed-wood furnishings, stone fireplaces, leather chairs, Mexican ceramic tiles, and Indian-style pottery and baskets. The casitas themselves are made of adobe. Get a taste of Arizona in the Wigwam's best restaurant, the award-winning Arizona Kitchen, where the chef uses ingredients common to the desert and to Native American cooking. Also on the premises are the Terrace Dining Room, plus a casual restaurant with a view of the golf course, and a poolside cafe. The resort has two pools, the main one more suited for group activities and for having fun on the water slide. The second pool is quieter, nestled among palm trees and flower gardens. Other recreational amenities include nine tennis courts, horseback riding, volleyball, croquet, and trap and skeet shooting. For families on vacation, there's Camp Pow Wow, a supervised recreation program for children ages 5 and older. It's available major holidays, during spring break, and Memorial Day through Labor Day.

Four Seasons Resort at Troon North
**$$$–$$$$ • 10600 E. Crescent Moon Dr.,
Scottsdale**
• (480) 515-5700
• www.fourseasons.com

Despite the fame of the above resorts, the new Four Seasons can give any resort in the Valley a run for its money. The location is spectacular—surrounded by acres and acres of pristine desert scenery. With 210 guest rooms and suites, arranged in Southwestern casitas, the luxurious accommodations offer views of desert, mountain, and cityscapes. The good news for golf fanatics is the resort offers preferred tee times on the two renowned golf courses at Troon North. Three restaurants and a lounge provide a wide range of culinary options. The 9,500-square-foot health club and spa offers sauna, steam, and massage therapy.

Even More Resorts

Well, maybe you haven't won that lottery yet. Don't despair—there are plenty of other

RESORTS

great resorts in the Valley that are a notch down in pricing yet provide many of the same amenities and services. And some travelers might rate a few of these resorts even higher than the aforementioned Famous Five. Golfers should note that resorts without courses on site can help you get preferred tee times at nearby public and private courses.

The choices of Valley resorts are abundant, and this is only a sampling of resorts listed by geographic area, with price ranges included. Again, they are concentrated in Scottsdale, with some in north Phoenix and the East Valley. You may also want to refer to our Accommodations chapter for a look at hotels and inns with a resort ambiance.

Phoenix

Hermosa Inn
$$$–$$$$ • 5532 N. Palo Cristi Rd., Paradise Valley
• (602) 955-8614 (800) 241-1210
• www.hermosainn.com

Quietly hidden among the cactus-studded, multimillion-dollar estates of Paradise Valley is the small Hermosa Inn, with 35 casitas and Lon's, an award-winning restaurant, brimming with hacienda charm. The dream project of cowboy artist Lon Megargee, the place was hand-built with adobe bricks in the 1930s. Megargee turned it into his home, studio, and guest ranch, and called it Casa Hermosa, or handsome house. Megargee's paintings hang throughout the lobby and restuarant. The inn was extensively renovated in the mid-1990s, and today it's popular not only as an inn, but also as the home of Lon's, a secluded restaurant serving rustic American cuisine (see our Restaurants chapter). Guests of the inn enjoy a pool, outdoor spas, and tennis; golf at nearby courses can be arranged. The four types of casitas, from least expensive to most expensive, are: Rancho, offering one bedroom, a sitting area, and patio; Casita, a king bedroom with a fireplace and patio or a junior queen suite; Hacienda, a one-bedroom suite with a fireplace, wet bar, mini-kitchen, and patio; and Villa, a two-bedroom, two-bathroom suite with a fireplace, wet bar, kitchen, and private patios. All lodging includes continental breakfast at Lon's. The Hermosa Inn is convenient to both central Phoenix and Scottsdale.

Pointe Hilton Squaw Peak Resort
$–$$$ • 7677 N. 16th St., Phoenix
• (602) 997-2626, (800) 572-7222
• www.pointehilton.com

The resort's proximity to the Phoenix

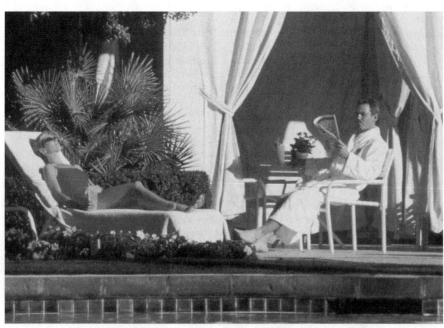

Let your cares drift away as you unwind by an Arizona oasis, resort-style.

Photo: Courtesy of Arizona Biltmore

Mountain Preserve and the second-highest point in the city, Squaw Peak, gives a scenic setting to this relatively centralized location. Opened in 1976, this is the oldest of the two Pointe Hilton resorts in the Valley. It reportedly was the first all-suite resort in the country. Architects gave it a Spanish-Mediterranean look, and the many courtyards and gardens are great for a stroll. The 564 units include mostly two-room suites and some casitas. New to the resort is the Hole-in-the-Wall River Ranch, where families can enjoy tubing amid rocks, fountains, and waterfalls. You'll also find a 136-foot slide, a children's camp, a retail area whimsically called Rodeo Drive, and a putting course. Golf is available a few miles away, and four tennis courts are on the premises. The spa and fitness center are good places to unwind from all this fun. Restaurants include Lantana Grille, offering American favorites; the Hole-in-the-Wall, serving Western grub from a 1940s-era ranch house; and Aunt Chilada's, serving authentic Mexican food.

The Pointe Hilton Tapatio Cliffs Resort
$$–$$$ • 11111 N. Seventh St., Phoenix
• (602) 866-7500, (800) 572-7222
• www.pointehilton.com

"Tapatio" means "a place of peace and contentment." This resort is nestled into North Mountain Park, offering tranquil views of desert mountains, desert flora, and cliffs. The 584 suites of the Spanish-Mediterranean-style resort take advantage of the views. So does its best restaurant, Different Pointe of View, where tables are on terraced rows, all facing a floor-to-ceiling window for a beautiful panorama of the Valley. The restaurant is known for its wine cellar as well as its fine American/continental food. The Falls is a three-acre water feature of waterfalls, free-form swimming pools, an enclosed waterslide, and an open-air restaurant pavilion. The centerpiece is a 40-foot waterfall that cascades into 12 meandering pools, a design inspired by Havasupai Falls in the Grand Canyon. There are eight recreational pools in all, plus 11 tennis courts, a fitness room, a full-service spa and salon, an 18-hole golf course, and horseback riding. This Pointe also has a Western-theme restaurant called the Waterin'

INSIDERS' TIP
Several of the Scottsdale resorts listed in this chapter are served by Ollie the Trolley. The shuttle runs up and down Scottsdale Road and Lincoln Drive and can take you to the shops and art galleries of downtown Scottsdale. An all-day pass is $5 per person, and the trolley runs Monday through Saturday during tourist season.

Hole. As for the two-room suites, each features a private balcony. A special Concierge Level with upgraded services and amenities is available upon request.

Southeast Valley

Arizona Golf Resort and Conference Center
$$–$$$ • 425 S. Power Rd., Mesa
• (480) 832-3202, (800) 528-8282
• www.azgolfresort.com

As the name implies, this 186-room resort is for golf lovers. Resort staff can direct you to several nearby courses, but you'll probably be just as happy with the championship course on the property. It's nicely landscaped with three lakes and mature trees and is a par 71 course. The best accommodation deals are packages that include two to six rounds of golf. Guest rooms include one- or two-bedroom suites, many with private patios or balconies that overlook the fairways. Nongolfers receive reduced rates. Amenities include a fitness center, tennis, a pool, and volleyball. The resort's two restaurants are Annabelle's, featuring prime rib and seafood, and Anna's Grill, with lighter, Southwestern fare. The East Valley location is distant from Phoenix and Scottsdale, but it's only a mile from the large Superstition Springs Shopping Center.

The Buttes
$$ • 2000 Westcourt Way, Tempe
• (480) 225-9000, (800) 843-1986
• www.wyndham.com

Advertised as a "mountaintop resort," The Buttes is actually nestled in the saddle of the Tempe Buttes. That means the resort is nicely elevated above the city and the nearby crossroads of two major freeways. We're talking hills, not mountains. Even so, the four-story resort has a well-designed, curvilinear look, and the sunset views from its premier restaurant, Top of the Rock, are almost unparalleled. The huge pool area uses the rocks as a design element, and for kids, there's an aquatic playground and 115-foot water slide. This is a popular resort because it's close to Sky Harbor Airport. On a

How We Live: The Southwestern Lifestyle

Some winter day you'll be relaxing in a Mexican-tiled room bursting with sunlight, enjoying a glass of sun tea, watching the hummingbirds visit a feeder, and you'll say to yourself, "I could never do this in Cleveland!" The truth is, you've hit upon some of the many pleasures of living in a Sunbelt city like Phoenix. Such days are possible—in fact, likely—in the middle of winter. The sun defines our way of life. Longtime residents know it, and newcomers quickly learn it. The things we do in harmony with the climate all contribute to the definition of a Southwestern lifestyle.

The good life here begins by knowing that many outdoor activities and household projects are better left for the cooler months. June through September are for traveling to the nearby mountains, or staying home and splashing in the pool, and relaxing inside air-conditioned comfort, much like hunkering down for the winter in the Snowbelt. Southwestern lifestyle means taking advantage of our glorious non-summer months by getting outside and enjoying the gorgeous outdoors, whether it's a round of golf or an in-line skating date, hiking or rock climbing, or taking the time to plant your vegetable garden. Locals keep tabs on winter rainfall so that they'll know how colorfully the desert will bloom in the spring. (With all the wildflowers, desert trees, and cactuses, it's usually a spectacular display.) You'll begin to acquaint yourself with the native flora and appreciate how shrubs, trees, and grasses are planted with water conservation in mind. It's about seeing the beauty of desert landscaping for homes, roadways, and buildings. Learning the names of indigenous animals is also important. Yes, we have coyotes, roadrunners, quail, jackrabbits, cactus wrens,

The Valley's luxury resorts reflect our Southwestern style.

Photo: Debbie Ross

lizards, snakes, scorpions, and javelinas. The animals around here can be both wondrous and mysterious.

To enjoy all that nature has to offer here, there are several essentials. One is good outdoor furniture—chairs, chaise lounges, umbrellas, and tables that you know will get good use. A good outdoor grill is a must-have too. Many homeowners have grills built into brick or stone walls complementing their backyard design or make do with simpler portable charcoal or propane grills. During the summer months, many people refuse to turn on their ovens for fear of heating up the already warm house. What's a cook to do? Just fire up the grill and cook under the blue skies.

Backyards bring us to swimming pools. Despite their proliferation in residential areas—from an airplane they look like thousands of turquoise dots—pools are not essential, but certainly a great pleasure, and actually quite common. There are two schools of thought. Some Phoenicians couldn't live without them, and find their time in the water rejuvenating and refreshing. Others find their upkeep daunting and worry about pool safety, especially with small children at home. Some homeowners compromise by buying townhomes with common pool areas or by building small water features on their properties, such as fountains, ponds, or hot tubs. People without private pools cool off in the summer at public pools, water parks, country clubs, or become very good friends with the neighbors who have pools.

During the Valley's many pleasant evenings, the Southwestern lifestyle is brought out onto patios with ceramic luminarias, or candleholders, and Guadalajara firepots (large cone-shaped ceramic pots for burning wood). Lots of brightly colored Mexican pots and terra-cotta containers filled with cactuses and flowers add to the scene. It's not unusual to see twinkly strings of white lights adorning backyards year round. Another Southwestern twist is to decorate indoors and out with strings of mini-lights that look like red chile peppers.

While you're enjoying the outdoors, don't forget the sunscreen. You can find it at stores year round, in a variety of strengths and aromas. The midday sun can be intense, even in temperatures of 60 or 70 degrees. Of course, in summer, people don't even step outside without sunscreen, a hat, sunglasses, or a combination of those.

In addition, locals display their Southwestern lifestyle inside their homes. Homes and hotels gravitate toward the casual elegance of Southwestern design. Also known as Santa Fe style, it incorporates the color palette of the desert, such as terra cotta and turquoise, and lots of ceramic tile flooring and wood furniture. Interior designers say contemporary, Mission, country, and Spanish Colonial styles all fit well in Southwestern homes. Peruse some of the unique furniture and accessories shops in the Valley of the Sun, and you'll see how the style encompasses wrought-iron tables and lamps; large urns filled with cactuses or brightly colored paper flowers; chairs and tables with cowhide stretched over them; polished pewter vases, photo frames, and dinnerware; placemats and tablecloths in bright Mexican-inspired stripes; colorful hand-blown Mexican glasswear; rugs that pay homage to Indian weaving on the floor and on walls; knickknack shelves holding Mexican folk art; large rustic wooden antiques; and hand-forged copper pots.

Once you've found a place dressed in Southwestern style, it's time to dress like the natives yourself. Casual is the word, but not too casual. Worn-in but not worn-out jeans are good, as are khaki pants, shorts, and polo shirts. Contrary to popular belief, all Arizonans do not wear cowboy hats. But if they're for you, you'll be pleased by the selection at area retail outlets. Arizona is also a good place to buy cowboy boots—the kind that John Wayne would be proud to wear. Scan advertisements for stores specializing in Western wear and don't miss the shops specializing in custom-made boots and belts. Also consider how stylish you would look in Arizona's official neckwear, the bola tie. The classic bola tie is a black leather string

RESORTS

(Continued on next page)

that holds a clasp of turquoise set in silver. But stores here sell many wonderful variations that range from small and tasteful to immense and gaudy. You might even find one with a scorpion preserved in a globe of clear plastic.

Speaking of turquoise, you probably won't be in Arizona too long before you break down and buy an authentic piece of turquoise jewelry. It could be a showy squash blossom necklace, a belt buckle, a silver-and-turquoise watchband, or a simple silver ring inlaid with turquoise and other stones native to the Southwest. The pieces can be pricey, but are worth having, both for their beauty and Native American craftsmanship.

The Southwestern lifestyle means learning to talk the talk. Since Arizona's Native American and Hispanic populations have influenced everything from architecture to apparel to food, you'll discover a whole new vocabulary being used. While you're absorbing all these new words with non-English origins—for instance, saguaro (sah-WAH-ro) and gila (HEE-la)—take a few moments to learn how to pronounce them. This is especially true at the many fine Valley restaurants, where you'll be confronted with words like pollo (POY-oh) and mole (MOH-lay). Many of the menus will have a glossary that will explain the language and certainly, your server will be happy to translate. The words are easy to pick up once you start.

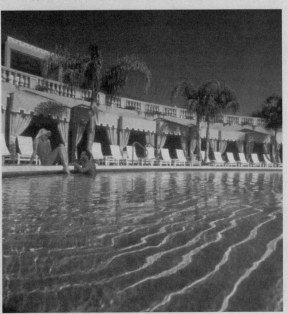

Many of the area's resorts—such as the Phoenican in Scottsdale—offer an elaborate labyrinth of play pools, spas, and fountains that rival ancient Roman spas.

Photo: Courtesy of the Scottsdale Convention and Visitors Bureau

Southwestern food is a natural offspring of the Southwestern lifestyle. We're talking Mexican food, Native American fare, (don't miss out sampling Navajo frybread—puffed, fried dough served with honey or beans) and nouvelle Southwestern cuisine that takes advantage of the many products harvested here. A perfect example of Southwestern cuisine is this item from the menu at Arizona Kitchen, the Wigwam Resort's four-star restaurant: filet mignon of beef dusted with guajillo chile powder in a prickly pear Merlot sauce. Of course, it doesn't get that fancy in Southwestern homes, but every good kitchen probably has a Mexican cookbook, a constant supply of tortillas (handmade or store-bought), and several varieties of salsa. And party hosts always bring out a circular platter of chips and salsa. Many people take pride in making their own recipes for salsa, heating them up with chiles or cooling them down with tomatoes.

By the way, if you like to drink beer at parties or restaurants, it's appropriate to ask for a Mexican beer. Many restaurants stock imported brands like Negro Modelo, Bohemia, and Pacifica, in addition to the more commonly known Corona. Or you may choose to drink margaritas, a frozen lime drink made with tequila and triple sec, then served in a salt-rimmed glass. For nonalcoholic drinks, try sun tea, which is brewed by simply placing it in the sun for a few hours and letting the summer heat do the preparation. People here drink it in all kinds of fruit flavors.

Relaxation and socialization in the Southwest is, by and large, not suits and ties, or cocktail dresses and overstuffed chairs in fancy parlors. You can find that at certain resorts, restaurants, or private clubs, but more typically, it's friends gathered in a backyard, casually dressed in jeans, shorts, T-shirts, sandals, and sundresses. Enjoy the laid-back atmosphere. Just don't forget the sunscreen. Come live the Southwestern life.

mere 25 acres it manages to fit 353 rooms, four tennis courts, a fitness center, a volleyball court, and a gift shop. The decor in the rooms is Southwestern style. You'll pay a bit more for a good view. Note to baseball fans: The resort is adjacent to the Tempe Diablo Stadium, the spring-training home of the Anaheim Angels.

Sheraton San Marcos Resort
$–$$$ • 1 San Marcos Pl., Chandler
• (480) 963-6655, (800) 325-3535
• www.sheraton.com

Known as Arizona's original golf resort, the stately San Marcos has been around 80 years, long enough to land the hotel on the National Register of Historic Places. It was designed in the Mission Revival style of architecture popular after the turn of the century. The architect was Arthur Benton of California, an associate of Frank Lloyd Wright's. In fact, it's said Wright spent considerable time at the San Marcos construction site. Today the San Marcos commands an attractive corner of downtown Chandler, which once was a farming community but is now one of the Valley's fastest-growing suburbs.

The almost 300 rooms and suites have been recently renovated. On the resort's 123 acres is an 18-hole championship golf course, where mature landscaping makes for a pleasant oasis in the desert. Also on the grounds are a putting green, a driving range, lighted tennis courts, golf and tennis pro shops, gift shops, an exercise room, and two pools. Dining options range from an upscale restaurant to a cafe to a clubhouse grill. If you have a chance to wander around the conference facilities of the resort,

INSIDERS' TIP

When the temperatures climb in the Valley, the prices begin to fall at the various resorts. Summer is when the locals take their vacations at the resorts, enjoying the terrific warm-season values out by the pools. You can wear your sunglasses and pretend that you're a celebrity for a weekend because you'll get the same first-class service that the resort offers in the more expensive seasons.

you'll notice that meeting rooms are named after illustrious former guests of the San Marcos, including Clark Gable, Errol Flynn, and Gloria Swanson.

Northeast Valley

Carefree Inn
$–$$$$ • 37220 N. Mule Trail Rd., Carefree
• (480) 488-5300, (800) 637-7200

If you like the idea of being close to the mountains near the town of Carefree, this small, nicely hidden-away resort is a good choice. You'll enjoy learning the names and whereabouts of such landmarks as Black Mountain, Elephant Butte, and Skull Mesa. The 177 rooms include standard ones with good views, casitas, and luxury villas. Close at hand are several championship golf courses. The inn also caters to bicyclists with tours of the Carefree/Cave Creek area. Spa services, two pools, five tennis courts, a retail shop, a small desert botanical garden, and a fitness center are on site. The restaurant, Minerva's, is elegantly decorated, distinctively Western, and has been recognized by travel guides. Through concierge services, you can strike out on desert jeep tours, hot-air balloon rides, or horseback riding trips.

Doubletree La Posada Resort
$$–$$$$ • 4949 E. Lincoln Dr., Scottsdale
• (602) 952-0420, (800) 222-8733
• www.hilton.com/doubletree

As resort swimming pools go, this place has one of the largest around. The half-acre Lagoon Pool features four waterfalls cascading over big red boulders. Under one waterfall is the weight room and sauna; nearby is the Grotto Bar, if you're seeking a picturesque place for a repast. At a million gallons and the size of a football field, the Lagoon Pool is the largest swimming pool in Arizona and one of the largest in North America, hotel officials say. The resort has many other recreational amenities: a smaller pool, six tennis courts, racquetball, volleyball, and two putting greens. In addition, the resort helps guests get their fill of golf by arranging preferred tee times at off-property championship courses.

At 32 acres, La Posada is relatively small, but it has enough room for 252 casita-like rooms and 10 suites, all with semiprivate patios. The architecture aims for a Southwestern feel by incorporating Spanish and Native American design elements. You'll find lots of archways, columns, red-tiled roofs, and terra cotta color. Buildings are almost entirely single-story, with casitas grouped in quadrants to give the place a residential feel. Restaurant options include the poolside Cafe Laguna, which serves breakfast, lunch, and light dinner, and the Garden Terrace, serving Mediterranean continental cuisine. La Posada's location at the northern base of Camelback Mountain near Tatum Boulevard makes it convenient not only to Scottsdale, but also to Phoenix and Paradise Valley.

Doubletree Paradise Valley Resort
$–$$ • 5401 N. Scottsdale Rd., Scottsdale
• (480) 947-5400, (800) 222-TREE
• www.hilton.com/doubletree

This is one of the most architecturally attractive resorts on Scottsdale Road. The design incorporates sculpted concrete blocks in a purplish gray for a look that is reminiscent of a Frank Lloyd Wright structure. The central courtyards and pool area of the 22-acre resort are artfully done, with lots of palm trees, fountains, gardens, and waterfalls. The colorful and airy restaurant, EnFuego, offers fusion cuisine with Caribbean and Pacific-Rim influences. The 387 rooms have been redecorated recently, and all have either patios or balconies. Other amenities include two other restaurants, a lounge

with live entertainment, a health club, saunas, a massage service, two indoor racquetball courts, two tennis courts, and a gift shop. The city's main mall, Scottsdale Fashion Square, is within walking distance. Golfing at the McCormick Ranch course is a few minutes' drive away.

Hyatt Regency Scottsdale at Gainey Ranch
$$$–$$$$ • 7500 E. Doubletree Ranch Rd., Scottsdale
• (602) 991-3388, (800) 233-1234
• www.hyatt.com

Strikingly beautiful inside and out, this Hyatt resort will take you slightly away from the hubbub on Scottsdale Road and into the upscale, lushly landscaped Gainey Ranch—a cluster of office parks, residential development, and retail centers. The main building of the 27-acre resort is a four-story double H shape, and it houses most of the 493 rooms and suites. The construction is elegantly modern concrete block and glass with copper and wood accents. A huge, moveable wall of glass off the lobby takes advantage of the view—gardens and fountains in the foreground and the McDowell Mountains in the background. The Hyatt's collection of art includes Native American works, bronzes, paintings, pre-Columbian artifacts, and a giant sand painting on the roof of the ballroom. As for restaurants, the Golden Swan overlooks a lagoon, and the Ristorante Sandolo features singing waiters and complimentary rides on a sandolo boat. Golf is available at the three nine-hole courses of the adjacent Gainey Ranch Golf Club. But guests are likely to get sidetracked by the Hyatt's water playground with its white sand beach, three-story slide, 10 swimming pools, aqueduct, spa, cold-plunge pools, waterfalls, and other features. The intent is to give guests the feeling of luxuriating in an ancient Roman bath. Also on the grounds are eight tennis courts and the Regency Spa, offering aerobics, exercise equipment, saunas, massages, and facials. Jogging and cycling trails are also available. Children can enjoy Camp Hyatt Kachina, where the emphasis is on learning about the culture and geography of Arizona. Deluxe accommodations include casitas

INSIDERS' TIP
During any resort stay, take a moment to stop by and meet the concierge. Usually located off the main lobby, the concierge's job is to help you enjoy your stay. The concierge knows how to get tickets for sporting events and concerts, where the best tacos can be found, and where to locate just about anything you seek. They also know everything about the resort and can make reservations for you at the spa for a massage session or get you saddled up for a sunrise trailride from the stables.

RESORTS

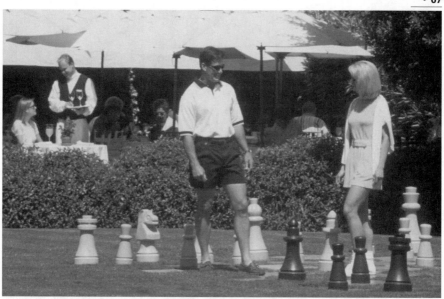

Only in Arizona can you get a tan while playing an intellectual game of chess.

Photo: Courtesy of Arizona Biltmore

and the Regency Club, an area of the third floor where guests receive VIP service.

Marriott's Camelback Inn
$$$–$$$$ • 5402 E. Lincoln Dr., Scottsdale
• (480) 948-1700, (800) 24-CAMEL
• www.marriott.com

This resort has a lovely, laid-back feel to it, even though it's packed with sophistication and topnotch amenities. A tower above the lobby bears the words "Where Time Stands Still." Guests can relax amid 125 acres in the scenic crook between Camelback Mountain and the Mummy Mountain of Paradise Valley. The hacienda-like resort has earned many awards since opening in 1936. It has needed upkeep over the years, though, with the most recent renovation project totaling $35 million and taking four years. Room interiors were redecorated, and a large pool with fun water features was added, among other things. The property has about 400 adobe-style casitas with private patios or balconies, plus two dozen suites with sundecks and two dozen suites with private pools. Amenities include six tennis courts, a golf pro shop, a nine-hole pitch-and-putt course, and five restaurants. The two golf courses are a short distance by car. Also worth noting is the full-service spa, with all kinds of body-pampering therapies. Open since 1989, it was the first spa of its kind in the Valley and is still one of the nicest.

Marriott's Mountain Shadows Resort & Golf Club
$$ • 5641 E. Lincoln Dr., Scottsdale
• (480) 948-7111, (800) 782-2123
• www.marriott.com

Although not an ostentatious resort, Mountain Shadows is a fine choice for golfers. The on-site, 18-hole executive course has nice views of Camelback Mountain and Paradise Valley. Or you can go off-property a short distance to try out two championship courses where Mountain Shadows guests are welcome. Other recreational amenities include

INSIDERS' TIP

When the relatives visit from out of town, take them out one afternoon to high tea at The Phoenician Resort. Served off the lobby, with a spectacular view of the Valley, the tea features exquisite finger-sized sandwiches, your own personal pot of tea, wonderful pastries with Devonshire cream, and decadent sweets—all served on fine china. You can munch and chat while listening to soothing piano music. It's guaranteed to impress those out-of-town visitors. Call (480) 941-8200 for reservations and information.

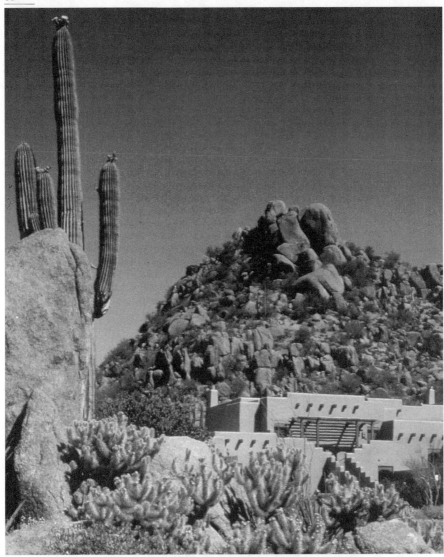

Designed to blend flawlessly into the surrounding desertscape, the accommodations at the Four Seasons embrace the surrounding environment.

Photo: Courtesy of Four Seasons Resort Scottsdale at Troon North

RESORTS

three pools, a putting green, sand volleyball, and a fitness center. The resort appeals to tennis players, too, with eight championship Plexiplave tennis courts, which are lighted and open for evening play. The tennis pro can arrange round-robin tennis or match you with a partner. The pro also gives free clinics to resort guests or private instruction for a fee. A sports shop on the premises is stocked with tennis sportswear and souvenirs. Accommodations at this 40-year-old resort stretch out over several acres to encompass 337 guest rooms and suites,

all with recently updated decor. Restaurants on the premises offer a choice of casual meals or fine dining.

Radisson Resort Scottsdale
$$–$$$$ • 7171 N. Scottsdale Rd., Scottsdale
• (480) 991-3800, (800) 333-3333
• www.radisson.com

Proximity to downtown Scottsdale makes this 76-acre resort an attractive option. On the premises are 318 guest rooms, villas, and bilevel suites. There are three swimming pools, the fanciest of which is a double-size Olympic pool shaped in an almost perfect circle. The pool is surrounded by deck chairs and palm trees, evoking an idyllic setting. Adding to the generous mix of recreational amenities are 21 tennis courts and two 18-hole golf courses. Restaurants at the resort are noteworthy: a semiformal dining room called Andre's, serving breakfast, lunch, dinner, and Sunday brunch either inside or on the patio; a French-style patisserie with coffee and pastries in the lobby; and Taps, a pub featuring a dozen microbrews on tap.

An area of the resort called the Arroyo is a small replica of an Old West town, with storefronts and hitching posts made to look like a scene from a John Wayne movie. The Arroyo is used for group functions of up to 900 people, and it's there that the resort caters Western-theme dinners of mesquite-grilled steaks. A full-service spa rivals those at larger resorts, and includes Swedish massages, aromatherapy, and body wraps.

Regal McCormick Ranch Resort & Villas
$$–$$$$ • 7401 N. Scottsdale Rd., Scottsdale
• (480) 948-5050, (800) 243-1332

A large lake gives this resort a beautiful and almost surreal setting in the desert. Called Camelback Lake, it's open to resort guests who want to rent canoes, paddle boats, or sailboats, or even try fishing. Across the lake is the McCormick Ranch Golf Club, which offers guests two championship courses and one of the Southwest's largest driving ranges. In addition to golf, enjoy a pool and whirlpool, four tennis courts, sand volleyball, and a fitness center. Another option is one of the 51 lakeside villas. All rooms have private patios or balconies and feature a Southwestern decor. There are two main restaurants, one of which, the Piñon Grill serves American/continental cuisine with a Southwestern flair and has won raves from local restaurant critics.

Renaissance Cottonwoods Resort
$$–$$$ • 6160 N. Scottsdale Rd., Scottsdale
• (480) 991-1414
• www.renaissancehotels.com

This 25-acre resort is tucked into a nice little niche next to The Borgata, an enclave of exclusive shops designed to look like a centuries-old Italian village. That means fun window-shopping and two great restaurants—Mancuso's and Café Terra Cotta—are a quick walk away. The Cottonwoods has a low-slung, adobe look and offers 171 casitas as well as suites. Each of the more expensive suites has a private spa on its patio. All have Southwestern decor with wood-beamed ceilings. For recreation, there are two pools, four tennis courts, and a jogging trail. For those seeking golf, the resort can arrange tee times at one of the well-known championship courses in the area. Choices include the Camelback Golf Club, the Arizona Biltmore Country Club, Stonecreek Golf Club, and Eagle Mountain, all with varying greens fees. The Cottonwoods staff prides itself on the services to guests, such as delivering a newspaper and complimentary continental breakfast with your morning wake-up call.

Scottsdale Plaza Resort
$$–$$$$ • 7200 N. Scottsdale Rd., Scottsdale
• (480) 948-5000, (800) 832-2025
• www.scottsdaleplaza.com

This resort, in the style of a Mediterranean villa, prides itself on the way its 400 rooms and suites are arranged to give a residential feel. Lots of arched walkways, stone fountains, and courtyards add to the ambiance. Its main restaurant, Remington's, is a popular nightspot, while J.D.'s Lounge is an English-style sports pub. For recreation, the resort has five swimming pools, lighted tennis courts, a putting green, and indoor racquetball. It has an outdoor whirlpool that is said to be the largest hotel spa in Arizona. The health club has a sauna, exercise equipment, and massage services. For golf lovers, the resort can arrange for preferred tee times at about two dozen courses in the Valley, including Eagle Mountain, Arizona State University's Karsten course, and Scottsdale Country Club.

As for accommodation choices, the range starts with 224 guest rooms, then moves up to 27 patio suites, which offer a private patio overlooking a courtyard. Similar in pricing are the 85 villa suites, which also have private patios. The 58 bi-level suites offer two bathrooms, skylights, and balconies along with the private patio. At the high end of the spectrum are the exclusive Executive Lodge suites, 10 suites offered in four different floor plans. Each is designed as a private residence with extra attention to details, such as four to five telephones, a whirlpool bath, original artwork on the walls, and other fancier furnishings.

Bed and Breakfast Inns

With all the first-class resorts, luxury hotels, and budget motels vying for your tourist dollar in the Valley of the Sun, you might not be aware of the genteel alternative of staying at a bed and breakfast. Many seasoned travelers, accustomed to bed and breakfast experiences in Europe, New England, and other places, prefer only bed and breakfasts. They'll not be disappointed in Arizona. Scenic spots such as the Grand Canyon, Sedona, Prescott, and the mountains near Tucson are filled with bed and breakfasts offering ranch-house settings, hacienda digs, and even the quaintness of Victorian mansions.

The Valley of the Sun, however, is another story. You won't find too many bed and breakfasts in this metropolis of office parks, shopping centers, and sprawling neighborhoods. Those that do exist operate almost in anonymity, often not known even to their neighbors. Ruth Young, who has operated the Mi Casa Su Casa Reservation Service for two decades, says there are a few bed and breakfast inns in the rest of Arizona that emulate the expansive country inns of New England, with 15 to 20 guest rooms and a full slate of amenities. And there are many inns with 10 or so rooms in the rest of the state, but not here. The three commercial bed and breakfast inns in Phoenix have five or six rooms, and although they may seem modest by European standards, they offer well-appointed rooms, lovely settings, privacy, and personal attention.

Another accommodation category in the Phoenix area is referred to

Price Code

Our pricing indicates the average cost of accommodations during the high season (Labor Day through Memorial Day) minus tax and fees for added services.

$	Less than $125
$$	$125 to $150
$$$	$150 to $200
$$$$	$200 and higher

Lodging often can be found off the beaten track in the surrounding suburbs like this bed and breakfast in a quiet northeast Phoenix neighborhood.

Photo: Courtesy of Mi Casa Su Casa Bed and Breakfast Reservation Service

Many Phoenix area bed and breakfast inns utilize period furniture and furnishing to enhance your visit.

Photo: Courtesy of Maricopa Manor

as host homes or guesthouses, and these are usually operated by couples who have enjoyed traveling to bed and breakfasts themselves and now want to reciprocate, so to speak. In a small way, they want to show Arizona hospitality to U.S. and international visitors, much like people elsewhere once opened their doors to them. Guests and hosts alike enjoy the opportunity to get to know each other. The hosts put up guests either in rooms within the main house, or in small guesthouses on their property. Private entrances and kitchenettes are frequently available. Guests can take care of breakfasts themselves if they want, and can come and go as they please. If they do want their hosts to fix breakfasts, they're often treated to feasts of waffles topped with fresh fruit, made-to-order omelets, and luscious pastries.

You'll find that many of the bed and breakfast inns are great deals, in addition to being a fun way to see how Arizonans live. Some of the properties are on large acreage and offer scenic views of the Valley; some have convenient, in-town locations; and some let you see the varied Phoenix residential architecture.

To find out about host homes, contact one of the bed and breakfast reservation services listed in this chapter. These homes tend not to advertise and prefer that all their bookings come through a reservation service. That way, the service can ask and answer questions as needed to ensure the guests receive the bed and breakfast amenities they're looking for.

In giving the price ranges, we assume your trip will be in high season, from September to May. But if you'll be here in summer, you can come across good discounts. Arizona Trails says the low-season rates for the properties it represents can range from $60 to $195 a night. The bed and breakfast inns listed here accept credit cards. When choosing a guesthouse, ask the reservation service whether credit cards are accepted.

INSIDERS' TIP

If you're traveling outside the Phoenix area and would like to stay at bed and breakfast inns around the state, you'll want to request a directory from the Arizona Association of Bed and Breakfast Inns. Call (800) 284-2589 or visit www.arizona-bedbreakfast.com. More than 60 locations are listed.

Reservation Services

The reservation services

At the Maricopa Manor, towering palm trees and white stucco walls create a romantic Southwestern ambiance.

Photo: Courtesy of Maricopa Manor

listed here are free to callers. All promise that they have inspected and approved the bed and breakfast properties they represent and know them inside and out. In cases where the bed and breakfast withholds its address and/or phone number to maintain privacy, we have listed the appropriate reservation service. Roxanne Boryczki, owner of Arizona Trails Bed & Breakfast Reservation Service, says that anyone needing the home's phone number in an emergency can contact the service, which will quickly relay a message. Guests receive the site's phone number and directions upon confirming their reservations.

Arizona Trails Bed & Breakfast Reservation Service
Fountain Hills
- (480) 837-4284, (888) 799-4284
- www.arizonatrails.com

Arizona Trails, established in 1996, handles more than 150 properties around the state. In the Valley that list includes 10 bed and breakfast inns and a number of guesthouses in Phoenix, Scottsdale, Tempe, Fountain Hills, and Cave Creek. Owner Roxanne Boryczki says she offers callers a good mix of properties in regard to amenities, location, and price. Many of the bed and breakfasts are in scenic locations, even though they might be a long drive from the

center of Phoenix. The service keeps track of such things as the age of the house, its decor, availability of kitchen appliances, recreational amenities, convenience to shopping, and tourist attractions, and whether the guesthouse has a private entrance. In addition, hosts are rated on their friendliness, the cleanliness of their accommodations, the safety of the surrounding area, and their breakfasts. The price range of these bed and breakfasts is $75 to $200 a night, double occupancy, and the reservation service is free. Arizona Trails is a member of the Arizona Association of Bed and Breakfast Inns and the Professional Association of Innkeepers International.

Mi Casa Su Casa/Old Pueblo Bed & Breakfast Reservation Service
Tempe
- (480) 990-0682, (800) 456-0682
- www.azres.com

Ruth Young has owned Mi Casa Su Casa since 1981, so she knows the industry. Mi Casa Su Casa lists more than 300 bed and breakfasts in four states but specializes in Arizona. The list includes 65 properties in the Phoenix metropolitan area and 65 in the Tucson area. They range from modest homes in quiet neighborhoods to million-dollar homes on large properties. The geographic range includes Phoenix as well as Tempe, Scottsdale, Mesa, Fountain Hills, and Carefree/Cave Creek. Host homes have only one or two guest rooms or a separate guest cottage. Some have magnificent views of the city from the mountain preserves, and some are near mostly undeveloped desert lands. Callers may inquire about heated swimming pools, spas, fireplaces, king- or queen-size beds, and the type of breakfasts served. One guest room affiliated with this service has won an Arizona Society of Interior Designers award. Double occupancy rates range from $60 to $300 a night, except for a luxury property in Fountain Hills that goes for $350 a night. The reservation service is free.

Inns and Guesthouses

Phoenix

Camelback Mountain Bed & Breakfast Guesthouse
$$$ • Contact: Arizona Trails
• (480) 837-4284

This luxury home perched on the south side of Camelback Mountain was built in the style of famed architect Frank Lloyd Wright. Windows afford great views of the city at night, and interior decoration is contemporary and elegant. The one guest room has a queen-size bed; a cozy sitting area with TV, VCR, and stereo; a kitchenette; a private bath; and a spa on the patio. Also available for use are a swimming pool and game room. The owners serve a continental breakfast and keep complimentary juices and water bottles on hand. Tee times can be arranged for golfers. No pets are allowed. Smoking is allowed outside the house. Inquire about bringing children.

Harmony House Bed & Breakfast Inn
$–$$ • 7202 N. Seventh Ave., Phoenix
• (602) 331-9554, (877) 331-9554

The Tudor-style Harmony House was built in 1934 as a doctor's residence among acres of citrus trees. Back then it was on the outskirts of Phoenix. Today it offers easy access to central Phoenix. Guests have their choice of five rooms. The Rose Room features Victorian-style decor in forest green and deep rose, a rose-carved king-size bed, a crystal chandelier, and a private bath with a shower and pedestal sink. The Madison Library offers a similar Victorian feel. The Country Garden is upstairs and has charming dormer windows, a king-size brass bed, and a private bath with a pedestal sink, bath, and shower. The Lindsay Room is more secluded, with lots of sunlight, a hunter green decor, a queen-size bed, and an extensive private bath. The Banta Suite has a private bathroom and a

Some bed and breakfast inns embrace the surrounding desert in their landscaping.

Photo: Courtesy of Mi Casa Su Casa Bed and Breakfast Reservation Service

Once you get past the austere desert landscaping in front of many inns, you'll often be surprised by lush green yards and private sitting areas.

Photo: Courtesy of Mi Casa Su Casa Bed and Breakfast Reservation Service

knotty-pine bedroom with an adjoining living room to sleep an additional two people. Full breakfasts are served in a family-style dining room or kitchen nook. The Harmony House is a nonsmoking inn. Pets are not allowed. Children older than 12 are welcome.

Maricopa Manor
$–$$$ • 15 W. Pasadena Ave., Phoenix
• (602) 274-6302, (800) 292-6403
• www.maricopamanor.com

This is an unexpected oasis near the busy intersection of Central Avenue and Camelback Road, yet it has been a highly popular bed and breakfast inn for several years. The Spanish-style manor house was built in 1928, and the grounds are filled with palm trees and flower gardens. Guests can relax outdoors on the deck, at the pool, or in one of the gathering rooms. The Library Suite has a canopied king-size bed, shelves of leather-bound books, a private deck entrance, and a desk. The Victorian Suite is done in satins, lace, and antiques and has a quaint sitting room with a breakfast table. The Palo Verde Suite

has a large bedroom with a king-size canopied bed plus a guest room with a spool bed. Reflections Past is a large suite with a fireplace in the living room and a bedroom done in tapestry fabrics. Reflections Future, with a queen-size bed, offers a large living room, sunroom, kitchen, breakfast area, and private entrance. The Manor Suite is a luxury suite with a three-sided fireplace between the bedroom and living room plus a dining table, chairs, and a desk. The bathroom has a shower and double whirlpool tub. Other suites are offered. All suites have a private bath, cable TV, and telephone. The continental breakfasts feature homemade breads and fresh fruit. Children are welcome. Smoking is allowed outside in designated areas. Pets are not allowed.

Southeast Valley

The Hydeout Bed & Breakfast
$ • Contact:
Arizona Trails,
(480) 837-4284

This modest Tempe property, about 10 minutes from Arizona State

INSIDERS' TIP

Did you enjoy your romantic bed and breakfast stay? Hang on to those business cards! Weekends at these plush homes-away-from-home are a popular and different gift for newlyweds and others who are celebrating. Of course, the price might make such a gift more feasible as a group offering from the office or a gang of friends.

University, offers a two-room suite with a queen-size brass bed and country/antique decor. The sitting room is done in Southwestern style, and the private bath has both a tub and shower. The suite also comes with a mini refrigerator, microwave, coffee maker, and TV/VCR. Guests are welcome to swim in the pool. And here's something you don't find too often with Phoenix accommodations—the hosts speak German. No pets are allowed, and smoking is permitted outside only. Children are welcome, as long as they know how to swim, as the pool is not gated. The menu for breakfast varies each day.

Northeast Valley

Hideout at RedBuck Ranch
$$$$ • 30212 N. 154th St., Scottsdale
• Contact: Arizona Trails, (480) 837-4284

Opened in 1997, the Hideout is hidden in the northernmost reaches of Scottsdale, near the Tonto National Forest, and touts itself as a luxurious Western guest ranch. The view stretches uninterrupted for miles and can be enjoyed from the private veranda of the ranch's one guesthouse. Inside that four-room guesthouse you'll find a bedroom with a custom-made, king-size "mountain man" bed of hand-hewn logs; a full bathroom with a red, claw-foot slipper tub and a shower surrounded by a rock wall; a living room with a pullout sofa bed, TV/VCR and gas fireplace; and a kitchen with a wagon-wheel breakfast bar and flagstone countertop. Oh, and don't forget the washer and dryer. The ranch's swimming pool

has two waterfalls and a spa. The hosts serve continental breakfasts on weekdays and full breakfasts on weekends, the latter known as a Ranch Hand's breakfast, complete with eggs, biscuits and gravy, sausage, and coffee. Horse lovers will be glad to know that the ranch will stable your horse overnight. For golfers, the hosts can arrange tee times at one of Scottsdale's championship courses. It's OK to bring kids if they're 16 or older. Smoking is allowed outdoors only.

Sleepy Hollow Bed & Breakfast
$ • 5522 E. Tapekim Rd., Cave Creek
• (480) 488-9402

This reasonably priced bed and breakfast is fairly new and is in a neighborhood of large properties with desert landscaping. The Sleepy Hollow is at the end of a gravel road, but access to Interstate 17 is only 10 minutes away. It features three guest rooms—two upstairs and one downstairs—in a home filled with antiques and Southwestern wares. The owners also display their antique-doll collection. A porch at the back of the house is a comfortable place for stargazing. Also on the premises is an indoor hot tub. The common living room has a TV/VCR, fireplace, and bar stocked with bottled water and juice. The rooms, called the Owl's Nest, the American, and the Dream Catcher, all have queen-size beds and private baths. The Dream Catcher has a sliding door leading to a patio. Breakfast consists of a continental buffet on weekdays and helpings of eggs, pancakes, or waffles on weekends. Smoking is allowed only outside. Pets are not allowed. Children are welcome.

RV Parks and Campgrounds

For those who like to explore the country from a home on wheels, the Phoenix area provides a great place for a break from the highway, especially during the winter months when the desert sun's power has diminished. There are recreational vehicle parks aplenty in the Valley—the Yellow Pages list more than 100. Many nestle in locations with mountain views, and come equipped with perks like grocery stores, recreational activities, and spacious shower facilities. Some RV parks are downright luxurious, protected by security gates and enhanced with championship golf courses and resort-like landscaping. The largest of these parks boast between 1,500 and 2,000 spaces. The range of quality and rates offers something for everyone's taste and pocketbook.

Most of the RV parks are in the outlying communities of the northwest and southeast Valley, like east Mesa and the Sun Cities. That's also where most snowbirds, or winter-only residents, like to flock. In fact, Apache Junction, a few miles east of Mesa, is composed primarily of retirees who call their RVs and mobile homes home at least part of the year. Consequently, the Valley's RV parks tend to fill with older or retired folks who stay for two to three months, sometimes longer. They hail from snowy climes such as North Dakota, Minnesota, Iowa, and Canada. Repeat visitors often live in park models, which are sized like large RVs and have similar interior appointments, but are not designated for open-road use. Often, these models can be distinguished from RVs by their peaked roofs.

If you're planning to winter in Phoenix at one of these parks, you'll want to make your reservations early—even as much as a year ahead of time. The months of April and October are less crowded than winter. Because space is more available during the hot summer months, you can often find good summer rates if you ask around. If you enjoy your visit to the Valley enough to consider making the transition from resort to RV park, find an RV community you like and reserve a space for the following year.

Some RV parks—especially the large ones with golf courses and other classy amenities—cater to the 55-plus crowd. In accordance with the Fair Housing Act, these parks stipulate that at least one resident of the recreational vehicle must be 55 or older. Although your living quarters won't be multigenerational, these parks compensate by providing a full slate of activities—ranging from softball leagues to computer clubs—to keep their community members busy. In this respect, the scene resembles the lifestyles of the mobile-home communities listed in our Retirement chapter. Folks make a park their home-away-from-home and return to it year after year, developing a sense of community within the neighborhood. Of course, RV parks are pleased to have year-round residents as well. Mobile-home communities that dedicate a certain percentage of their spaces to RVs are another option for visitors, whatever their age. Consult the listings in our Retirement chapter.

The following list of RV parks provides a sampling of amenities and prices, and is intended to give a short overview by region. When scouting out accommodations, be sure to ask whether the park accepts only certain types of RVs and if it accepts overnighters as well as long-term guests. Also, many parks offer discounts, such as to members of the Good Samaritan Club, that are worth asking about. For a directory of about RV parks, not only the Valley, but also other popular Arizona destinations, write for a copy of the publication, Welcome RV'ers Discover Arizona! 2000, at 3030 N. Third St., Suite 200, Phoenix, AZ 85012, or call the association at (602) 241-8525.

At the end of this chapter, we list options for those campers who prefer car camping or rough camping.

RV Parks

Southeast Valley

Apache Palms RV Park
1836 E. Apache Blvd.,
Tempe
• (480) 966-7399

This small, modest park with 72 spaces is modern, friendly, and will put you close to the action in downtown Tempe. Amenities include a swimming pool, spa, showers, and a laundry room. Rates are $29 nightly and $130 weekly for an elite site with full hookups; rates go down in the summer. Pets are welcome.

Gold Canyon RV Ranch & Golf
7151 E. U.S. Hwy. 60, Apache Junction
• (480) 982-5800

A desert setting of 73 acres at the base of the Superstition Mountains makes this an alluring location. And did we mention the nine-hole golf course? The 756 spaces are open to those 45 and older, although most spaces are taken by winter and year-round residents. In addition to a 40,000-square-foot activity center with swimming and crafts areas, you'll find a golf pro shop, steam room, sauna, and tennis courts. Pets are allowed but limited to one area of the park. Rates are $600 monthly, $1,200 for two months, $1,500 for three months, $1,800 for four months, $2,100 for five months, and

$2,800 annually. Only the monthly rate includes electricity. Nightly and weekly rates are $32 and $217 respectively.

Mesa Regal RV Resort
4700 E. Main St., Mesa
• (480) 830-2821, (800) 845-4752

A huge, 55-plus RV resort, Mesa Regal offers loads of activities, clubs, and recreational amenities for seniors. Perks include four swimming pools, a library, a computer room, and saunas. The Mesa Regal occasionally has room for short-term visitors among its 2,005 spaces. Rates are $33 per night, $189 weekly, and $498 monthly (electricity extra). A pet section is available.

Orangewood Shadows RV Resort
3165 E. University Dr., Mesa
• (480) 832-9080, (800) 826-0909
• www.orangewoodshadows.com

This 55-plus resort prides itself on its recreational amenities and activities for seniors, including group excursions, shuffleboard, heated pools, spas, and a recently added exercise room. The majority of its residents are winter visitors who return from year to year. Thus, you should call early to reserve one of its 474 spaces. Daily and weekly rates, including electricity, are $31 and $170, respectively. The monthly rate is $460, and the annual rate is $2,517, with electricity extra. No pets are allowed.

Schnepf Farms RV Park
24810 S. Rittenhouse Rd., Queen Creek
• (602) 987-3333
• www.schnepffarms.com

Here's an unusual find off the beaten path— RV spaces set amid a peach orchard. The Schnepf family leases out spaces for 25 full RV hookups, 10 to 12 partial hookups, and a large area for dry camping on their 250-acre farm. Guests can partake of the many attractions that bring out locals and others, including pick-your-own produce, a country store, petting zoo, and picnic area. The farm holds several festivals throughout the year and leases its land for the annual Country Thunder country music extravaganza in April, which means some dates

INSIDERS' TIP
You don't need to own your own RV to enjoy the state's wonderful RV parks. Two Valley companies that offer RV rentals include: Cruise America, Inc., 11 W. Hampton Ave., Mesa 85210, (480) 464-7300; or Leisure Time Coaches, 2219 W. Deer Valley Rd., Phoenix 85027, (623) 582-5869. You can also find parts and supplies for your RV in any number of stores on Mesa's Main Street.

are unavailable for campers. Rates are $15 nightly for a full hookup, $12 nightly for a partial hookup, and $10 nightly for dry camping. Weekly and monthly rates are available; maximum length of stay, though, is 45 days. Children and pets are welcome. Schnepf Farms is open October through March, and is closed in the summer.

Tempe Travel Trailer Villa
1831 E. Apache Blvd., Tempe
• **(480) 968-1411**

This 160-unit park caters mostly to permanent residents, who must be 18 or older, except for short-term visits. It's reasonably priced, clean, and in a convenient location near Arizona State University and downtown Tempe. You'll find a laundry area, swimming pool, and showers. Full hookup rates are $20 daily, $122 weekly, $360 monthly, and $2,112 yearly; electricity is extra. Special summer rates are available. Small pets are allowed.

Valle del Oro RV Resort
1452 S. Ellsworth Rd., Mesa
• **(480) 984-1146**
• **www.azresorts.com**

This 55-plus park boasts 200 activities each week during high season, making it a popular choice for older winter visitors. A golf coordi-nator leads trips to nearby courses. Also available are pools, a spa, tennis, a library, and theater, and an arts and crafts building. The 1,802 spaces have full hookups, and the rates are $35 daily, $185 weekly, $505 monthly, and $3,150 annually; electricity is not included in the monthly or annual rates. Guests are allowed one pet, not to exceed 40 pounds.

Northeast Valley

WestWorld of Scottsdale
16601 N. Pima Rd., Scottsdale
• **(480) 312-6810**

Horse lovers, take note. This city-owned park near The Princess resort is the site of some of the nation's largest horse shows. About 400 RV sites are open to the public on a space-available basis. Those traveling with horses can take advantage of overnight stabling too. Those who didn't bring a horse can rent one for a trail ride at Trail Horse Adventures, (800) 723-3538. If golf is your thing, ask about the 18-hole course, at Sanctuary Golf Course, (480)502-8200, www.sanctuarygolfaz.com. Pets and children are welcome at WestWorld. Shower facilities are available. Full-hookup nightly rates are $15 for RVs 39 feet or less; otherwise rates are $20. There are no weekly or monthly rates

Arizona's RV parks offer many amenities to visitors and residents.

Photo: Penny Kleingartner

since this park is intended for short stays, with a 21-day maximum.

Northwest Valley

North Phoenix RV Park
2550 W. Louise Dr., Phoenix
• (623) 581-3969

This park, in the northwestern stretches of the city limits, is convenient to Interstate 17 and the Deer Valley Road exit. Under new management, the park boasts 200 spaces to accommodate RVs, with a few cabins available for rent as well. Amenities include showers, a laundry room, a lounge, a swimming pool, and a store selling propane and other supplies. Pets and children are welcome, and those who desire more seclusion can ask for the no-kids section. Rates are $25 daily, $115 weekly, and $295 monthly, with electricity extra in all cases. Ask about special summer rates.

Pleasant Harbor RV Resort
8708 W. Harbor Blvd., Peoria
• (602) 269-0077, (520) 501-1035
• www.pleasantharbor.com

Yes, there are lakes in the Phoenix area. This resort is at Lake Pleasant, an intriguing desert setting popular with local boating and fishing enthusiasts. On cool fall and spring weekends, sailors with the Arizona Yacht Club turn out in full regatta and their colorful sails, unfurled against a backdrop of the Bradshaw Mountains, add drama to the setting. The relatively new RV park puts you 300 yards from the lake on the east side behind the marina, which is available for those pulling boats. In addition, the 200-space park boasts a clubhouse, an activities slate in high season, pools, spas, lawn bowling, shuffleboard, laundry facilities, a general store, and organized tours. It's adult-oriented, but there are no age restrictions. Many people stay three months or longer. All spaces have full hookups, with rates of $25 nightly, $150 weekly, $420 monthly, $1,000 for three months, and $2,500 annually. Discounts are available to those staying longer than three months. Newer sites for larger RVs cost more. One or two pets are allowed per site.

> **INSIDERS' TIP**
> A recent survey out of Arizona State University found that 50 percent of the state's winter visitors, or snowbirds, live in mobile home, RV, or travel-trailer parks while here. In 1996, about 75 percent of the state's snowbirds roosted in the East Valley. Apache Junction alone has approximately 100 mobile-home and RV parks.

Pueblo El Mirage RV Resort & Country Club
11201 N. El Mirage Rd., El Mirage
• (623) 583-0464, (800) 445-4115

An 18-hole golf course designed by Fuzzy Zoeller is the centerpiece of this 1,200-space resort, which is geared to winter visitors and year-round residents age 55 and older. In addition to golf, guests can take advantage of the on-site restaurant, pools and Jacuzzis, exercise rooms, billiards, lawn bowling, arts and crafts, dances, and a computer club. With a full-time activity director on board, there's no time for boredom. Full-hookup rates are $27 daily, $190 weekly, $475 monthly, and $2,300 yearly. Special spots on the golf course are available at higher rates. Small pets are allowed.

Sunflower RV Resort
16501 N. El Mirage Rd., Surprise
• (623) 583-0100

This gated resort near the Sun Cities is mostly for 55-plus seniors living in park models, who tend to return every winter. About 250 of the park's 1,156 spaces are available for short-term leases to those seniors with any kind of RV. Amenities are ample: an Olympic-size lap pool, spas, a Jacuzzi, a eucalyptus steam bath, organized activities, shuffleboard, tennis, horseshoes, exercise rooms, a wood shop, a ballroom, a library, and modem connections. Pets are welcome. Call for rates.

Southwest Valley

Destiny Phoenix RV Park
416 N. Citrus Rd., Buckeye
• (623) 853-0537, (888) 667-2454

This campground has easy access to Interstate 10, about 5 miles west of Goodyear. This family campground welcomes all ages. Its 284 spaces are open all year and amenities include a pool and spa, shuffleboard, and classes and social get-togethers in high season. The rate for one night with a full hookup starts at $33; weekly rates change according to the size of the RV and the season. Two pets are allowed as long as they're medium-sized or smaller.

RV PARKS AND CAMPGROUNDS

Campgrounds

The best place for tent camping or rough camping from a truck or RV is in the mountain parks managed by Maricopa County. Not only are they scenic, but they also put you at a distance—though not a great one—from the city's hustle and bustle. The mountains that surround Phoenix aren't terribly tall or verdant with trees, yet they showcase the beautiful Sonoran desert, with its multitude of cactus species, hardy trees, and wildlife like hawks and coyotes. The parks attract out-of-state visitors and locals for their campsites, hiking trails, horseback riding trails, and picnic sites. All county park campgrounds limit stays to 14 days and generally charge a $2 vehicle entry fee. Usually, they ask that RVs be no longer than 35 feet. Note that the heat often forces county campgrounds to close in June, July, and August. For information beyond what is listed here, write to Maricopa County Parks and Recreation, 3475 W. Durango Street, Phoenix, 85009, or call (602) 506-2930.

INSIDERS' TIP

The happy RV camper will avoid rush-hour traffic, which peaks from 6 to 9 AM and again between 3 PM to 6 PM. If you must drive at these times, first check out traffic conditions and road closures across the state by calling (888) 411-ROAD or on the Web at www.azfms.com.

Cave Creek Recreation Area
32nd St., 1.5 miles north of Carefree Hwy.
• **(623) 465-0431**

A small but scenic recreation area, the Cave Creek park has picnic areas, a horse staging area, and more than 11 miles of trails. Several old mine shafts lie within the park, but they are off limits. The park has 38 camping sites, all with water and electrical hookups. The comfort stations have showers, and a park host is on the premises. Cost is $15 nightly, plus $5 to use the dump station.

Estrella Mountain Regional Park
Estrella Pkwy., 5 miles south of I-10
• **(623) 932-3811**

RV'ers take note—this 19,000-acre park, about 18 miles southwest of Phoenix, now not only offers a few areas for rough camping from a tent but has added a new group campsite with spots for 700 RVs. The camp is located near the new track for competitive mountain biking, running, and equestrian use. There is a $3 vehicle entry fee. Amenities in the park include 56 acres of lawns with picnic tables, a golf course,

Palm trees grace the lots of this RV community in the desert.

Photo: Penny Kleingartner

restrooms, playground equipment, two lighted ball fields, and a rodeo arena. Also find an amphitheater overlooking the picnic area at this park, which is heavily used for group functions. The many trails are for hikers, bicyclists, and horseback riders. The picnic areas, but not the campgrounds, have comfort stations.

Lake Pleasant Regional Park
99th Ave., 15 miles north of Sun City
• (520) 501-1702

A variety of camping options are available in this 23,000-acre park northwest of the Valley. Popular with boaters, this Park contains 76 sites for RVs, and each site has a picnic table, grill, and ramada (an open shelter). The rate of $15 nightly includes water and electricity. There are no dump stations in this county park, but nearby Pleasant Harbor will accommodate that need for a $5 fee. For primitive camping, there's space along the lake's shoreline for $5 a night. Also, there are about three dozen other sites for tent and RV camping, some with limited access to water and electricity and some with full hookups. Nightly rates range from $8 to $15 at these sites.

INSIDERS' TIP
A few desert survival tips from the Maricopa County Parks system: Carry at least one gallon of water per person per day. Plastic gallon jugs are handy and portable. If you have water, drink it. Do not ration it. If water is limited, avoid talking, eating, and smoking and do not take salt.

McDowell Mountain Regional Park
McDowell Mountain Rd.,
4 miles north of Fountain Hills
• (480) 471-0173

This county park, 15 miles northeast of Scottsdale, rates as one of the most scenic, with an abundance of vegetation and majestic mountain views. Elevation within the park ranges from 1,600 to 3,000 feet. Camping areas are divided into a family campground, group campground, and youth group area, with 80 sites altogether. The nightly rate is $15, including water and electricity. Showers are available, and the dump station charges a $5 fee.

Usery Mountain Recreation Area
Usery Pass Rd., 12 miles northeast of Mesa
• (480) 984-0032

In addition to an extensive hiking and horse-back-riding trail system, this recreation area also has an excellent archery range and 50 picnic sites. The area's Buckhorn Family Campground offers 73 sites, several comfort stations, and two campground hosts. A few of the spaces are wheelchair accessible. Individual campsites have electric and water hookups, a grill, and picnic table. Cost is $15 nightly, including hookup. The dump station costs $5 to use.

White Tank Mountain Regional Park
Olive Ave., 15 miles west of Peoria
• (623) 935-2505

Comprising more than 26,000 acres of Sonoran desert mountains, this is the largest park in the Maricopa County park system. Elevations range from 1,400 feet at the park entrance to 4,000 feet at the highest peak. You'll find plenty of picnic areas, ramadas for use by large groups, a mountain bike trail system, a horse staging area, and two wheelchair-accessible trails. The family campground has 40 sites, each with a picnic table and grill. There are no electrical hookups and no dump stations. Comfort stations have showers. Cost is $15 nightly.

Another Option

Lost Dutchman State Park
Near Goldfield Ghost Town,
5 miles north of Apache Junction
• (602) 982-4485

You will be in the midst of legends and lore about down-on-their-luck gold miners at this 35-site park for tents and RVs, at the base of the Superstition Mountains. Campers will find shower facilities but no hookups. The cost is $10 per night.

Restaurants

Price Code

The price code symbol in each restaurant listing gives you a broad idea about the cost of dinner entrees for two, not including beverages, appetizers, desserts, tax and tip. Obviously, your own bill at a given restaurant may be higher or lower, depending on what you order and on fluctuating prices. These symbols provide a general guide.

$	Less than $12
$$	$12 to $25
$$$	$26 to $50
$$$	$51 and more

Trying to pick a good restaurant out of the Yellow Pages could be quite a daunting task if you're unfamiliar with the Phoenix area. After all, there are thousands of restaurants listed. But we're here to help. Within this limited space we have listed dozens of restaurants that cover a broad spectrum of choices from upscale, continental dining to neighborhood take-out eateries. Naturally, we had to keep the list to our personal favorites and to places heartily recommended by friends. As a visitor or new resident in the Valley, don't be shy about asking folks for their restaurant recommendations. They are bound to know of wonderful places off the beaten track, and they very well might steer you away from restaurants that are hyped as being great but actually aren't. Why bother with a so-so restaurant when there are so many great places to eat out there?

Restaurateurs are constantly opening places in the Valley, capitalizing on new trends in dining. Breweries serving food have taken off here, as have Pacific Rim restaurants (serving a medley of Asian and American foods with a seafood emphasis). Ever-growing Phoenix is an attractive place to set up business, but it also sees its share of restaurant failures. It's a volatile dining scene, which we thought could best be described to you by limiting our list to restaurants that have been open at least a year at the time of this writing. Just keep your eyes open as you drive around the Valley, or read reviews in local newspapers and magazines to stay current on what's hot and what's not on the dining scene.

Be aware that many restaurants cut back on their hours from June to August, when tourist traffic dies down. Realize, too, that restaurants sometimes close suddenly for reasons beyond the quality of their food. Or they change hours. Or change menus. Or change names. It doesn't hurt to call a restaurant before heading to it.

Do call for reservations on weekends in high season, from January to April. Even weeknight reservations might be in order, especially for places with well-known chefs or for those in high-traffic areas such as 24th Street and Camelback Road in Phoenix or downtown Scottsdale.

We've arranged this chapter by geographical regions and types of cuisine. In the mood for a certain kind of food? First find the appropriate geographic area—Phoenix proper, Southeast Valley, Northeast Valley, or Northwest Valley, then look for the various cuisine categories under those areas. Try to browse the whole chapter, though, because a restaurant that intrigues you might be listed in one geographic area yet have a second location better suited to your needs.

We created a category called American Fusion to incorporate the many restaurants that succeed on culturally diverse menus—the places that offer pizza next to tamales and sirloin steak next to grilled eggplant. The menus reflect the melting pot that is American food. Mexican food is a regional specialty, so we have included many options in that category. Many restaurants say their cuisine is Southwestern. The term can be a bit vague, but generally it means food that blends Mexican, Spanish, Anglo, and Native American ingredients and cooking styles, usually presented with special touches like brightly colored pepper slices or fruit salsas. To simplify matters, we have grouped Southwestern-style eateries under American Fusion. Folks from other parts of the country and world who want a taste of the Old West—in terms of both atmosphere and culinary offerings—can find those restaurants under the Western category. Casual steakhouses are in this category too. We've also squeezed in a couple of Cajun and Spanish restaurants. Other categories include Continental and Fine Dining (which includes several luxury hotel and resort restaurants), Seafood, Italian and Pizza, Breakfast, Bakeries, Sandwich Shops, and, last but not least, Asian—in which you'll be surprisingly pleased at the number of Japanese, Chinese, and Thai restaurants. If we have left out a category you're interested in, by all means, check the current Yellow Pages. The Valley is growing increasingly sophisticated in ethnic offerings, and new restaurants open practically every week.

Valley residents often complain that we have too many chain restaurants. Actually, we found in compiling this list that there are plenty of good non-chain restaurants if you take the time to search them out. This chapter does include a few regional chains, names that might not be familiar to you if you hail from the Midwest or Eastern United States. They are in the list because their quality of food warrants their inclusion. We do not, however, list national chains because you already know what to expect from those places.

Unless we note otherwise, assume that the establishments in this chapter accept major credit cards. Most restaurants have smoking and nonsmoking sections. Wheelchair accessibility is usually not a problem.

Phoenix

American Fusion

Coopers'Town
$$ • 101 E. Jackson St., Phoenix • (602) 253-7337

Alice Cooper, Phoenix's hometown hero of rock 'n' roll fame, opened a casual American eatery near Bank One Ballpark and America West Arena. Billed as "eat-ertainment," the restaurant/bar features not only rock memorabilia, but also sports memorabilia. Cooper is one of many savvy businesspeople capitalizing on the increased downtown foot traffic associated with the Arizona Diamondbacks and other sports teams. He and his partners have renovated an old warehouse for this restaurant venture. Joining ribs, chicken, and burgers on the menu are two-foot-long hot dogs, steak grilled on a shingle and—even wackier—a barbecue feast served in a trash can lid. Look for items served in hubcaps too. (Clean ones, of course.) You can also hear live music here and sometimes famous musicians will sit in with the band. Lunch and dinner are served daily.

Eddie Matney's Epicurean Trio
$$$ • 2398 E. Camelback Rd. Phoenix • (602) 957-3215

Chef Eddie Matney specializes in bold makeovers of American classics with Mediterranean influences. Examples include a veal chop with sun-dried cherry chipotle au jus; seared tenderloin encased in country mashed potatoes; baked meat loaf; Southwestern-style chicken; and seafood cioppino pot pie. He calls his creations "New American." Lunch and dinner are served daily.

Hard Rock Cafe
$$ • 2621 E. Camelback Rd., Phoenix • (602) 956-3669

Ogle the memorabilia from the many pop, rock, country, and heavy-metal artists. See the glass-encased costumes from Madonna and Stevie Nicks. Study the signed guitars from Johnny Cash, Waylon Jennings, Tom Petty, Kurt Cobain, and others. Stare at the Cadillac perched above the restaurant's centerpiece bar. Be amazed by all the signed gold records. Listen to the nostalgic mix of rock music. See for yourself why Hard Rock Cafe is an international phenomenon. And enjoy a decent meal of American and Southwestern fare served by friendly waitstaff. Best bets include the chicken sandwiches and meal-sized salads, along with barbecue chicken and fresh fish of the day. Oh yes, the wait for a table is long when it's tourist season. Pass the time by posing for a snapshot in front of the Hard Rock's metal phoenix rising from the fire—a can't-miss-it sight along Camelback Road. Lunch and dinner are served seven days a week

Omaha SteakHouse
$$$–$$$$ • 2630 E. Camelback Rd., Phoenix • (602) 553-8970

Familiar with Omaha Steaks International, which sells certified prime Midwestern corn-fed beef through mail order? This is the company's first restaurant venture, and it's a fine way to have someone else cook the T-bone or the rib eye. The restaurant has lovely surroundings in the atrium of the Embassy

Suites Biltmore. The menu goes beyond steaks to include shrimp-and-ahi-tuna brochette, rotisserie chicken, rack of lamb, and other items. Side dishes are refreshingly diverse: Lyonnaise potatoes, asparagus with Hollandaise, snow peas with red pepper, and more. The steakhouse is open daily for lunch and dinner.

The Original Hamburger Works
$ • 2801 N. 15th Ave., Phoenix
• (602) 263-8693

True to name, this casual central Phoenix restaurant dishes out tasty and juicy meat patties, tended to over mesquite charcoal and cooked to your specification. Select what kind of bun and cheese you want, then dress 'em up at the condiment table. Also on the menu are chicken breast and broiled fish sandwiches, and there's a full-service bar. The grill's going daily for lunch and dinner.

Sam's Cafe
$$$ • 455 N. Third St., Phoenix
• (602) 252-3545

Reliably good food makes this a bustling eatery in downtown's Arizona Center. The restaurant has a Southwestern theme, but the entrees delve into quite a few different cuisine categories. Always on the table are addictive breadsticks served with a spiced cream cheese spread. Favorite items include chicken-fried tuna, grilled salmon, poblano-chile chicken chowder, chicken Caesar salad, and noodles in a spicy peanut sauce. The cafe's signature is a chocolate tamale, your sweet, complimentary ending to the meal—white chocolate and chopped pecans wrapped in small cornhusks. Lunch and dinner are served daily. Other locations are at Biltmore Fashion Park, 2566 E. Camelback Road, Phoenix, (602) 954-7100; and 10010 N. Scottsdale Road in Scottsdale, (480) 368-2800.

Tom's Tavern
$-$$ • 2 N. Central Ave., Phoenix
• (602) 257-1688

Tom's is big on burgers and fries and blue-plate specials, all of which you can down while rubbing shoulders with the mayor of Phoenix and other politicos known to hang out there. Dark wood, booths, and a long bar add to the tavern feel. The restaurant, in an office tower, is open Monday through Friday for breakfast, lunch, and dinner.

Asian

The Bamboo Club
$$-$$$ • 2596 E. Camelback Rd., Phoenix
• (602) 955-1288

This restaurant in Biltmore Fashion Park offers trendy Pacific Rim cuisine in a club-like atmosphere. The furnishings have a bamboo theme, and you can opt for friendly surroundings at the long bar downstairs or more intimate dining upstairs in the mezzanine. Dishes are served Asian style—platters come to the table and are meant to be passed around and shared. Various kinds of seafood and meats are steamed, grilled, or cooked in a sizzling wok. A popular appetizer is the Spicy Crackling Calamari Salad, which is calamari cooked in a wok with garlic sauce, peppers, and mushrooms then served on a bed of Napa cabbage. Popular entrees include the orange scallops, shrimp on crispy spinach, or Hong Kong steak flambéed with brandy. Another Bamboo Club—this one with a cigar room—is at 8624 E. Shea Boulevard in Scottsdale, (480) 998-1287. Both are open Monday through Saturday for lunch and dinner and Sunday for dinner only.

Bamboo Express
$, no credit cards • 4231 E. Thomas Rd., Phoenix
• (602) 955-1088

"Express" it definitely is, with a kitchen that whips out Chinese favorites faster than you can say, "An order of General Tsao's Chicken, please." Dinner specials include the crispy and tangy General Tsao's, chicken with broccoli, and sweet and sour pork, all served with an egg roll, a crab angel (crab and cream cheese in a deep-fried won ton) and fried rice. There are two dozen items to choose from, all reasonably priced. Lunch specials for $3.50 include teriyaki chicken and chow mein. Bamboo Express is suitable for take-out or for dining in. The location is a former bank branch, turned into a pleasant little pastel-toned dining area with green plants and a goldfish tank. Lunch and dinner are served daily.

INSIDERS' TIP
Scattered around the Valley are small, freestanding taco shops that serve reasonably priced, reliably tasty Mexican food. An added convenience is quick service and, often, drive-through windows. Filiberto's has several locations, but also look for names such as Rolberto's, Aliberto's, and Los Betos.

Big Wong
$$ • 616 W. Indian School Rd., Phoenix
• (602) 277-2870

A fun name, authentic foods that draw a large Chinese-American clientele, and a casual atmosphere are just a few things that make Big Wong a hit. The simple exterior gives way to a pleasant interior that borders on elegant with nicely set tables and lots of Asian adornments on the walls. Many of the familiar dishes are on the menu, or you can go more exotic with entrees made in a clay pot, such as shrimp with vermicelli. Also recommended are the noodle dishes and steamed chicken in ginger sauce. The restaurant is open for lunch and dinner daily.

Gourmet House of Hong Kong
$$ • 1438 E. McDowell Rd., Phoenix
• (602) 253-4859

This is the place for authentic Hong Kong and Cantonese dishes. Be ready for rudimentary decor with Formica tables and tiled floor, but know you're in for the real thing when it comes to the food. Hand-lettered signs on the walls offer lots of specials (all written in Chinese, though). The lunch "Big Plate" is a bargain, with entree plus soup, crab angels, egg roll, and rice for about $5. There are lots of noodle dishes for both lunch and dinner. If take-out is your choice, you'll find the service is quite fast. Lunch and dinner are served daily.

Little Shanghai
$–$$ • 4017 E. Indian School Rd., Phoenix
• (602) 957-7666

With all the hoopla that accompanies the opening of trendy Chinese, Japanese, and Pacific Rim restaurants in the Valley, it's easy to overlook the small, neighborhood restaurants that keep on serving regular customers, in the same unpretentious style as they have for years. Little Shanghai is such a restaurant—nicely appointed with green plants, primly set tables, and dim lighting, but nothing spectacular. The Szechwan, Shanghai, and Mandarin cuisine is generously portioned and dependably good. Specialties include tangerine beef; Yui-Shan spicy chicken in a cucumber-and-mushroom sauce; shrimp with cream sauce; and moo-shu pork. You can ask for a pot of green tea to be served with your meal. Lunch is served Monday through Friday and dinner every day.

Pho Bang
$ • 1702 W. Camelback Rd., Phoenix
• (602) 433-9440

Vietnamese food is the specialty here, so be

RESTAURANTS

The striking décor of the Latilla at The Boulders recalls its surounding Sonoran setting.

Photo: Courtesy of The Boulders Resort

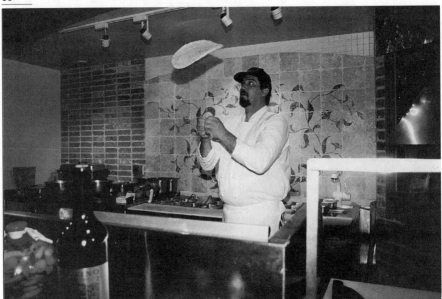

DeFrancesco's Ristorante offers authentic Italian cuisine and pizza.

Photo: Courtesy of DeFrancesco's Ristorante, Margo Media

prepared to sample spring rolls, hearty noodle soups with beef, vermicelli salads, summer rolls, Vietnamese-style grilled shrimp, and other delicacies. Rice bowls are a good lunch option. The ambiance is rather plain, on the order of Formica and vinyl, but tidy enough. Pho Bang, which you can find in a small shopping center with other Vietnamese-oriented businesses, serves lunch and dinner daily.

Thai Lahna
$–$$ • 3738 E. Indian School Rd., Phoenix • (602) 955-4658

One of the older Thai restaurants in town, Thai Lahna still packs them in at this small, simply decorated location in an east Phoenix strip shopping center. On the spiciness spectrum, the cooks can prepare your order to the fire-breathing extreme, make it on the mild side, or give you something in between. Recommended dishes include any of the curries, the Pad Thai (thin noodles stir-fried with chicken, shrimp, egg and bean sprouts), the soups, and the house special of barbecue chicken in a Thai-style chile sauce. Check out the lunch specials Monday through Friday. Dinner is served every day but Sunday.

Tokyo Express
$ • 914 E. Camelback Rd., Phoenix • (602) 277-4666

Tokyo Express opened about 1980 at a tiny location in east Phoenix and proved to be on the cutting edge of Americans' desire for healthy Japanese-style meals of meat and vegetables over rice. Over the years, the first location has expanded, and seven other locations have opened. It has, arguably, the best teriyaki chicken in town—still ringing in at less than $3. In addition, many Phoenicians had their first experience with sushi thanks to Tokyo Express. We list the Camelback Road location because it's in central Phoenix and because it's next door to an affiliate, the Cherry Blossom Bakery, (602) 248-9090, which always offers interesting tarts, fruit cakes, and carrot cake. Other locations of Tokyo Express are at 3517 E. Thomas Road, Phoenix, (602) 955-1051; 5130 N. 19th Avenue, Phoenix, (602) 433-1311; 4105 N. 51st Avenue, Phoenix, (602) 245-1166; 1120 S. Dobson Road, Mesa, (480) 898-3090; 13637 N. Tatum Boulevard, Phoenix, (602) 996-0101; 267 E. Bell Road, Phoenix, (602) 564-9585; and 9100 E. Indian Bend Road, Scottsdale, (480) 948-7500. All locations are open daily for lunch and dinner.

Bakeries

Barb's Bakery
$ • 2929 N. 24th St., Phoenix • (602) 957-4422

While the trendy coffeehouses with big bakery counters spring up in the suburbs, Barb's Bakery tools along just fine at its decades-old location near Thomas Road and 24th Street. It has a small sit-down area for coffee and pastries or spinach-and-cheese croissants, but mostly this is a take-out place for all kinds of muffins, breads, pies, and sweet rolls. The bakery does a brisk business in cakes for special occasions too. It's open Monday through Saturday through the breakfast and lunch hours.

Karsh's Bakery
$ • 5539 N. Seventh St., Phoenix
• (602) 264-4874

A busy bakery with an immense wholesale business along with counter service, Karsh's specializes in Jewish breads—ryes, challahs and bagels—along with European-style pastries and cookies. Chocoholics will delight in the brownies, tortes, and chocolate coffee rings. Sorry, you'll have to get your cappuccino elsewhere. The bakery is open until 6 PM every day but Sunday, when it closes at 4 PM.

Old Heidelberg Bakery and Euro Market
$ • 2210 E. Indian School Rd., Phoenix
• (602) 224-9877

This 30-year-old German bakery recently relocated to new digs closer to downtown and added "Euro Market" to its name to reflect the line of European canned goods, jams, chocolates, and other items that it now carries. The baked goods are as scrumptious and reasonably priced. You'll find Danishes, strudels, cookies, and a great selection of hard rolls and breads baked the European way. A sidelight: The store sells German-language newspapers and magazines. The market is open 9:30 AM to 6 PM Tuesday through Friday and 9:30 AM to 5 PM Saturday.

Barbecue

Honey Bear's
$$ • 5012 E. Van Buren St., Phoenix
• (602) 273-9148

"You don't need no teeth to eat our meat" goes the motto of Honey Bear's, which enjoys a brisk catering business along with busy counter service. Customers order at the counter for food to take out or eat in. Honey Bear's dining room is nothing fancy but is usually filled with a nice diversity of families and singles. Specialties include pork ribs, chicken, and hot links—all cooked to a just-right tenderness. And that tangy Tennessee-style bar-

becue sauce! Spicy barbecue beans, described as "Cow-Bro Beans" are a recommended side dish. Recently opened is a second location in a former International House of Pancakes at 2824 N. Central Avenue in uptown Phoenix, (602) 279-7911. Both are open daily for lunch and dinner.

Cajun

Baby Kay's Cajun Kitchen
$$ • 2119 E. Camelback Rd., Phoenix
• (602) 955-0011

Surprised to see a Cajun restaurant in the desert? You'll be surprised, too, at the number of desert dwellers who flock to Baby Kay's for jambalaya, catfish, gumbo, etouffee, and other specialties from the red-hot heart of New Orleans. You say it's food with more heat than a 110-degree day? We can take it! Baby Kay's is easy to find in Town & Country Shopping Center. On weekends, just listen for the guitarist playing blues.. Outdoor seating on the mall's red-brick plaza is available. Baby Kay's is open for lunch and dinner Monday through Saturday.

Continental and Fine Dining

Christopher's Fermier Brasserie & Paola's Wine Bar
$$$–$$$$ • 2596 E. Camelback Rd., Phoenix
• (602) 522-234

Christopher's has a sterling reputation for culinary excellence at this prime location at the Biltmore Fashion Square. The cuisine is French based and c'est magnifique! Here are a few menu items, better appreciated by giving their entire titles: roasted, herbed veal loin with artichokes, sweetbreads and Portobello mushroom; Wapiti elk chop with celery root risotto, horseradish flan and black currant brown butter sauce; magret of duck with foie gras, Asian cabbage and a light sherry vinegar sauce; and sautéed lobster with baby bok choy in a ginger-infused black bean sauce. Of the desserts, we've only tried the chocolate mousse tower, but it was unforgettable in terms of presentation and to-die-for taste. The restaurant serves dinner nightly.

The Compass
$$$ • 122 N. Second St., Phoenix
• (602) 440-3166

This revolving restaurant atop the 24-story

Hyatt Regency in downtown Phoenix is an excellent choice for those wanting to complement a special night at the symphony, theater, or ballet with a special meal. The Herberger and Orpheum Theaters and Symphony Hall are within walking distance. And the view from The Compass—which makes one clockwise rotation every hour—is incredible. Brass plaques on the windows point out some of the city landmarks you can see from this vantage point. Entrees include roast prime rib of beef, pan-seared salmon, sliced duckling, and pork saltimbocca. Lunch is served Monday through Saturday, when the emphasis is on sandwiches and salads; Sunday brings a fancy brunch. Dinner is served nightly.

Different Pointe of View
$$$$ • 11111 N. Seventh St., Phoenix
• (602) 863-0912

The astounding view from the hills of north Phoenix or the regional American cuisine? Which is it that makes Different Pointe of View a great place for a romantic evening out? It's a toss-up, really. This restaurant at the Pointe Hilton Tapatio Cliffs Resort has a terraced design allowing every table to enjoy a good view. (Sunset dining is recommended.) Plus, the menu is certain to please, with entrees such as herb-crusted rack of lamb, tenderloin of Angus beef, roasted Muscovy duck breast, and pecan-smoked venison. The thrill of the evening might be dessert if you choose Bananas Foster prepared in a flaming frying pan. Dinner is served nightly.

Harris'
$$$$ • 3101 E. Camelback Rd., Phoenix
• (602) 508-8888

The eye-catching stucco, red tile, and brick exterior of this large restaurant looks as if it could be someone's lovely Southwestern estate. Inside are high wood-beam ceilings, chandeliers, draperies, and comfortable chairs. Large slabs of meat being hung for dry-aging are displayed behind glass at the front of the restaurant, a reminder that this is a great place for steak and prime rib. The menu also includes lobster, salmon, and chicken. Harris' serves lunch Monday through, and dinner Monday through Saturday.

Lon's at the Hermosa
$$$ • 5532 N. Palo Cristi Rd., Phoenix
• (602) 955-7878

You can get away from it all at this intimate Southwestern-style dining room at the Hermosa Inn, which is tucked into a Paradise Valley residential area. The restaurant is named for Lon Megargee, a cowboy artist who developed this property as a hacienda and studio, then turned it into lodging. The contemporary cuisine features pan-seared scallops on broccoli risotto; breast of duck with foie gras sauce; and wood-grilled salmon with polenta. Lunch and dinner are served Sunday through Friday; it's dinner only on Saturday.

Morton's of Chicago
$$$$ • 2501 E. Camelback Rd., Phoenix
• (602) 955-9577

Fairly new to the Phoenix area, Morton's is an elegant steakhouse with the style and attitude of Chicago transplanted to the desert. You can't go wrong with Morton's prime-grade beef and rib-eye steak. Finish with souffle for two, available in such flavors as Grand Marnier and raspberry. Dinner is served nightly.

RoxSand
$$$ • 2594 E. Camelback Rd., Phoenix
• (602) 381-0444

One of the big draws in the restaurant-rich Biltmore Fashion Square is RoxSand, a two-level establishment with stylishly modern decor and lots of contemporary art. The name behind the restaurant is RoxSand Scocos, whose culinary creations have put her on the A list of Phoenix-area chefs for several years (see our Close-up in this chapter). The house specialty is air-dried duck with buckwheat crepes, pistachio onion marmalade, and three sauces. Also recommended are the braised veal with polenta and the gourmet pizzas. The vegetarian options are quite extensive too. Desserts such as chocolate tortes and fruit tarts will be hard to pass up. Lunch and dinner are served daily.

T. Cook's
$$$–$$$$ • 5200 E. Camelback Rd., Phoenix
• (602) 808-0766

With the recent renovation of Royal Palms, an old-time east Phoenix inn, came a makeover for its restaurant—in regard to both decor and food. The result is a stunner—a beautifully appointed, romantic dining room with topnotch food. The brick walls are painted a soft tangerine color, accented by original tile murals. The focal point of the restaurant is a massive stone fireplace with a rotisserie spit producing many of the signature items on the menu. The theme is "rustic Mediterranean cuisine," which encompasses items such as rosemary-tied pork loin with baked apples and Tuscan green beans; Cornish game hen coq au vin; and a Mediterra-

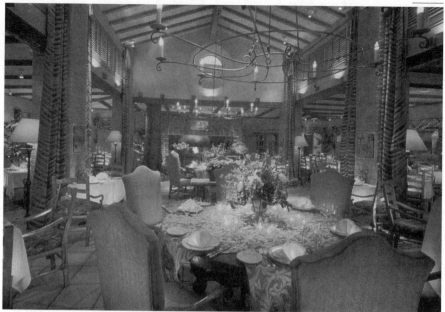

Brunch is more than a meal at T. Cooks at the Royal Palms.

Photo: Courtesy of Royal Palms, Cooper Lee Marketing

nean antipasto platter for two. In addition to lunch and dinner daily, T. Cook's serves breakfasts and Sunday brunch.

Vincent on Camelback
$$$$ • 3930 E. Camelback Rd., Phoenix • (602) 224-0225

Vincent is so well-known and respected that it doesn't have to go to great lengths to promote itself. The chef is Vincent Guerithault, a longtime Phoenix resident who, some might say, put Phoenix on the culinary map. Among his many awards is the James Beard Foundation's "Best Chef Southwest" award (see our Close-up in this chapter). Vincent has worked in different locations over the years but is now settled into a small, modest-looking restaurant next to a convenience store in east Phoenix. The interior, though, is decorated like a lovely country French cottage. The food is known for Southwestern ingredients prepared in a classical French manner. Vincent's signature dishes include duck tamale, grilled lobster with habanera pasta, smoked salmon quesadilla, and roasted corn soup. The menu also features artfully prepared lamb and chicken dishes. Don't miss dessert, with wonderful French pastries and a crème brûlée served in a taco-like shell. Lunch is served Monday through Friday, and dinner is served Monday through Saturday.

Cuban

Havana Cafe
$$–$$$ • 4225 E. Camelback Rd., Phoenix • (602) 952-1991

In the 1980s, Chef B.J. Hernandez introduced Valley residents to flavorful Cuban cuisine. Her intimate restaurant has been drawing crowds ever since, and praise goes to such dishes as Ropa Vieja (shredded beef braised with vegetables and red wine), the moros (Cuban black beans and rice), the paella, Arroz con Pollo (chicken with saffron rice and chorizo sausage), and black bean soup. In the 1990s she opened an offshoot called Havana Patio Cafe at 6245 E. Bell Road in Scottsdale, (480) 991-1496. Lunch is served Monday through Saturday and dinner is served nightly.

Italian and Pizza

DeFrancesco's Ristorante
$ • 4117 N. 16th St., Phoenix • (602) 279-7409

Look for the red awning to lead you into a warm and cozy home-style dining room. Personal family photographs adorn the walls and the exhibition kitchen is centerstage with a wood-burning pizza oven. The family recipes include chicken marsala, tomato basil angel hair, and, of course, pizzas. Open for lunch Tuesday through Friday, and dinner Tuesday through Saturday.

Focaccia Fiorentina
$ • 123 N. Central Ave., Phoenix
• (602) 252-0007

Step up to the counter and survey the varieties of plump pasta and simmering sauces behind the glass. Then make your choice. Indecisive types can order a plate with half of one sauce and half of another. Sandwiches on focaccia bread—using ingredients such as imported air-dried beef, Genoa salami, and fontina cheese—are also topnotch, with a taste rarely duplicated at your local sub shop. Located in cozy, brightly decorated quarters, the eatery fills up at lunchtime with office workers so be willing to share a table. Open for lunch Monday through Friday.

Lombardi's
$$$ • 455 N. Third St., Phoenix
• (602) 257-8323

If you work downtown and the boss wants to take you out to lunch, immediately suggest Lombardi's, an upscale Italian eatery facing the gardens at Arizona Center. Of course, it's also a fine choice for a nice dinner downtown before or after a cultural or sports event. On the menu are grilled chicken breast, breaded veal scaloppini, scampi with pasta, Italian-style beef tenderloin, and other entrees. Or choose from the assortment of pastas—risotto, fettuccine, cappellini, or rigatoni—prepared with meat or seafood in various sauces. Tiramisu makes a great dessert. Lunch and dinner are offered daily.

Pizzeria Bianco
$$$ • 623 E. Adams St., Phoenix
• (602) 258-8300

Chef and owner Chris Bianco has won much acclaim for his Neapolitan-style pizza made in wood-fired ovens with toppings such as wood-roasted mushrooms and homemade fennel sausage. Individually sized pizzas, inventive salads, and sandwiches make this a great lunch spot, although you'll have to wait in line with the downtown workers who flock here. The

pizzeria is in a historic building that's part of Heritage Square, next to the Arizona Science Center. It serves lunch Tuesday through Friday, and dinner Tuesday through Sunday.

Raffaele's
$$-$$$ • 2999 N. 44th St., Phoenix
• (602) 952-0063

Raffaele's is tucked into the elegant-looking Concord Place office complex at Thomas Road and 44th Street, which offers a pleasant parklike setting. The chef and owner is an Italian named Raffaele Contacessi, who comes up with creative variations on Italian standbys. Menu favorites include a chicken and rigatoni dish in a light cream sauce, seafood in tomato-basil sauce on angel hair pasta, and a dish combining broiled Italian sausage and sautéed chicken in a balsamic vinegar sauce. In addition, Raffaele comes up with evening specials. The restaurant is open for lunch and dinner Monday through Friday, and for dinner only on Saturday.

Streets of New York
$-$$ • 4757 E. Greenway Rd., Phoenix
• (602) 788-0787

Streets of New York is a 20-year-old Arizona restaurant chain with 17 Valley locations. When you're in the mood for pizza with a bit of panache, this is a good choice. In addition to New York-style pizzas with traditional toppings, Streets of New York offers "Uptown Gourmet" pizzas in varieties such as chicken cacciatore, four-cheese, and garlic shrimp. Calzones, chicken wings, and pasta dinners are tasty too. Most locations have patio seating as well as informal dining rooms where the TV is often tuned into a sports channel. Take-out and delivery services are available. The above location is near an Albertsons store at Tatum Boulevard and Greenway Road. Consult the Yellow Pages for other locations.

Mexican

Aunt Chilada's
$$ • 7777 South Pointe Pkwy., Phoenix
• (602) 431-6470

You can tell from the name that this is a

INSIDERS' TIP

The dress code at most Valley restaurants ranges from very casual (nice shorts, jeans, and sandals are fine) to semi-casual (the kinds of things you would wear on a "casual Friday" at the office). Things get especially relaxed in the summer. Do get dressed up, though, for the restaurants in this chapter marked with four dollar signs. Call the restaurant if you're unsure about jackets, ties, and dresses.

RESTAURANTS

fun restaurant. It's gaily decorated and long known for good Sonoran-style Mexican food. Chef Jesse Gonzales puts his heart into the food and uses his family's recipes for solid results. Enchiladas come in cheese, red meat, chicken, and seafood versions. Of course, standbys like tacos, burros, and fajitas are also on the menu. Whet your appetite with the warm tortilla chips and award-winning salsa. The Margaritas—served in a giant cone-shaped, salt-rimmed glass—are awfully wicked too. You can find Aunt Chilada's off Baseline, just west of I-10. Lunch and dinner are served daily.

Blue Burrito Grille
$ • 3118 E. Camelback Rd., Phoenix
• (602) 955-9596

"Mexican food redefined" is Blue Burrito's motto because it's successfully shown that burritos and enchiladas don't have to be laden with cheese and sour cream to be delicious. The emphasis here is on charbroiled meats, black beans without lard, and vegetarian variations on standard Mexican fare. Many "Heart Smart" meals are available, meaning they're a good option for those watching saturated fats and cholesterol. A family favorite is the Big Blue Burrito, filled with steak or chicken, beans, rice, guacamole, and more, and big enough to serve two. The establishment serves lunch and dinner daily. The Camelback location is the original, but you can find a newer location at 7318 E. Shea Boulevard, Scottsdale, (602) 951-3151.

La Salsa
$ • 10855 N. Tatum Blvd., Phoenix
• (602) 948-2600

Healthful Mexican food is the goal of the California-based La Salsa chain, which uses charbroiled skinless chicken, extra-lean steak, lard-free black beans, and freshly made tortillas. Favorites include the Original Gourmet Burrito, blending chicken, cheese, and guacamole, and the soft tacos in corn tortillas—choose from chicken, steak, or mahi mahi versions. Don't start eating without investigating the salsa bar, where you'll find five salsas, rated in their spiciness from one to five chile peppers. A second location is inside Scottsdale Fashion Square at 7014 E. Camelback Road, (480) 994-4112. Both are open daily for lunch and dinner.

Los Dos Molinos
$$ • 8646 S. Central Ave., Phoenix
• (602) 243-9113

This is a good choice for experiencing fiery

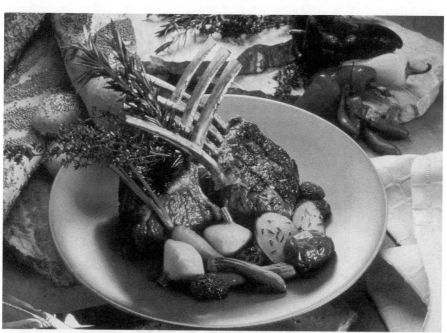

Menu specialties, like this one at Different Point of View, will tempt you to sample the Southwestern touch again and again.

Photo: Courtesy of Point Hilton Tapatio Cliffs Resort

RESTAURANTS

hot Mexican food (when in Arizona, do as Arizonans do) and for getting a look at an old hacienda once occupied by old-time cowboy movie star Tom Mix. Enjoy the scenic drive near South Mountain Park while you're at it. As for the tasty menu selections in this family-run restaurant, house specialties include New Mexican-style ribs and green chile enchiladas. Lunch and dinner are served Tuesday through Saturday.

Manuel's
$ • 2820 E. Indian School Rd., Phoenix
• (602) 957-7540

To those of us who view comfort food as a combination plate of tacos, enchiladas, rice, and beans (with guacamole on the side), the Manuel's chain hits the spot. The restaurant has been in the Valley for almost 35 years and at last count had eight locations. Count on a festive and colorful decor and friendly, efficient service. If you are watching calories and cholesterol, Manuel's has options such as fajitas and Mexican-style salads. Lunch and dinner are served daily. Additional locations: In Phoenix, 3162 E. Indian School Road, (602) 956-1120; 1111 W. Bell Road, (602) 993-8778; 5509 N. Seventh Street, (602) 274-6426; and 12801 N. Cave Creek Road, (480) 971-3680. In Tempe, 1123 W. Broadway Road, (480) 968-4437, and 2350 E. Southern Avenue, (480) 897-0025. In

Glendale, 5670 W. Peoria Avenue, (623) 979-3500.

Pan y Mas
$ • 3111 E. Greenway Rd., Phoenix
• (602) 992-8899

A small, family-run operation, Pan y Mas specializes in Yucatan-style dishes. The simple surroundings are enlivened by a wall-length mural and touches of red, white, and green, the colors of the Mexican flag. Through a small window to the kitchen, you can watch tortillas being shaped and grilled and, wow, are they good. Recommended are the quesadillas with cheese, chicken, or carnitas (shredded pork); the chicken enchilada in a mole (or spiced chocolate sauce); and the Yucatan-style chicken tacos. The bakery counter does a brisk business, offering Mexican-style cookies and doughnuts, and fruit-filled empanadas, or turnovers. Lunch and dinner are served Monday through Saturday.

Pico Pica Tacos
$, no credit cards • 3945 E. Camelback Rd., Phoenix
• (602) 912-0048

Pico Pica is as fun as its name sounds. Although it's a small place tucked into an Arcadia neighborhood shopping center, it's always enlivened by the sound of Mexican pop music

Part of the Southwestern resort experience is the chance to dine with romantic views of the city lights.

Photo: Courtesy of The Phoenician

The Valley's Celebrity Chefs

Rarely does a week go by in the columns of the Phoenix area news media that a local chef is not mentioned. Will RoxSand win that national culinary award? Will Eddie redo the interior of his restaurant? Will Christopher change his fall menu?

Gossip columnists and restaurant reviewers write about chefs with such regularity and familiarity because so many have been elevated to the status of celebrity chefs. Several have achieved national fame, winning prestigious culinary awards, writing cookbooks, and even appearing on cable TV food shows.

Thanks to the growing sophistication of the Phoenix area's restaurant scene over the last decade, many of the country's best and brightest chefs have settled here to work or have added locations of their restaurant chains here. And the Valley benefits from their presence.

You're probably curious about which "name" chefs are associated with the Valley. Here's a quick rundown on who's who and who's where, although you should be aware that restaurants are often in a state of flux, and two of the chefs mentioned here were without restaurants at the time of this writing.

One of the Phoenix area's best-loved chefs, Eddie Matney, known for his delicious twists on standard American food, is a popular character in his own right. Visit his restaurant and you're almost sure to see him walking around the room, greeting regulars, and making new friends. He's energetic and passionate about his work. Matney's ebullience about food and frequent public appearances helped stir up business for his restaurant. It probably didn't hurt that in 1995 Matney was a *Cosmopolitan* bachelor of the month, either. (He recently married, by the way.)

Christopher Gross has worked in the Valley since the 1970s and has apprenticed with chefs in California, England, and France. His knowledge of classic and international cooking methods helped make Christopher's an enormous success. Gross was the 1995 winner of the best chef in the Southwest award from the James Beard Foundation, and has been featured in national food magazines.

Things are cooking as well, at Vincent on Camelback, opened in 1986 by nationally known chef Vincent Guerithault at 40th Street and Camelback Road. This is a favorite destination for Valley residents seeking a special night out enjoying Southwest and French cuisine in intimate surroundings. In a 30-year career, Guerithault has received several awards, including the nod from the James Beard Foundation. Longtime Valley residents know of Vincent's work at other restaurants from the early 1980s. Many consider him the grand master of the Valley's community of chefs. It's interesting to note that as a teenager in France, Guerithault once worked alongside Wolfgang Puck.

One globally known chef opening a restaurant here in 1998 was Roy Yamaguchi. Roy's Restaurant, part of an international chain serving Pacific Rim food with a Hawaiian influence, opened in Scottsdale and immediately drew crowds. His restaurant and concept has proved so popular, he soon opened another location at the Camelback Esplande.

But as for the Valley's own celebrity chefs, the list must include RoxSand Scocos, whose restaurant, RoxSand, at Biltmore Fashion Park, is always packed and always a culinary adventure. Scocos, a James Beard Award nominee, is known for fusion cuisine that explores Southwestern, Asian, and French cooking. She is frequently involved in community events featuring chefs.

Erasmo "Razz" Kamnitzer began working in the Phoenix area in the 1980s and in 1995 opened Razz's Restaurant and Bar, featuring contemporary international cuisine based on French and classical cooking techniques. The Venezuelan-born

(Continued on next page)

RESTAURANTS

Kamnitzer is a seventh-generation chef, and Razz's north Scottsdale customers like the effusive personality he injects into his work. He loves talking food with dinner guests. He has appeared on cable TV's Food Network and has been written up in national food magazines. Kamnitzer and his wife, Bobbi Jo Haynes, founded a charity event—a combination gourmet dinner and art auction—that annually raises money to fight sexual abuse.

If you're around the Valley long enough, you will frequently hear chefs' names mentioned in conjunction with charity events. Chefs have gathered together to help raise money for the American Heart Association, as well as for an Arizona charity supporting emotionally troubled teens.

A PBS television series called *Savor the Southwest* brought further limelight to some of the chefs mentioned here. The 13-part series featured Southwestern chefs including: Guerithault; Scocos; Wiley; Donna Nordin of Cafe, Terra Cotta in Scottsdale; Lenny Rubin of the Medizona restaurant in the Scottsdale Princess resort; and Robert McGrath, of the Roaring Fork.

As a visitor or newcomer to the Valley, keep your eyes and ears open for news about these chefs and others. It's a good way to get to know the best restaurants in town. You also can learn about these chefs' culinary creations in more detail by picking up *The Arizona Chefs' Dine In—Dine Out Cookbook*, featuring 140 recipes from 35 chefs from around the state. The cookbook is available from AJ's Fine Foods, a Valley chain of upscale grocery stores.

and the bright interior colors. It's decorated to the max with folk art, Day of the Dead trinkets, Mexican rugs, and paper cutouts, posters, and primitive-looking masks. A Frida Kahlo fan? So are the owners of this establishment, as you can see from the many works of this revered Hispanic artist on the walls. As for food, you'll feel exotic trying the California-style tacos—not just meat varieties, but also potato and fish tacos—or zesty specialties of the house such as mole (meat in a spicy, chocolate-based sauce), carnitas (pork spiked with chiles), and calabacitas (stuffed zucchini). Even the more well-known enchiladas and flautas have a special flair, and the restaurant advertises its use of healthful ingredients. On the beverage end, there are Margaritas made from scratch, Mexican beers, and aguas frescas, or homemade fruit drinks. The restaurant is open daily for lunch and dinner; take-out service is available.

Richardson's
$$ • 1582 E. Bethany Home Rd., Phoenix
• (602) 265-5886

Mexican food of the Southwest has an offshoot called New Mexican cooking, which takes advantage of the range of flavors and heat in various kinds of chiles. Richardson's—through its imaginative enchiladas, quesadillas, and burritos—shows why it has some of the best New Mexican cooking in town. Beyond that, though, it also offers distinctive specialties of the house such as pan-fried top sirloin in a whis-

key-lime sauce, swordfish in jalapeño hollandaise, and cilantro paella. The restaurant's seating surrounds a bar, which makes for a lively ambiance. Lunch and dinner are served daily.

Tee Pee Mexican Food
$ • 4144 E. Indian School Rd., Phoenix
• (602) 956-0178

This bustling eatery and bar isn't too exciting on ambiance, but it has been a successful east Phoenix neighborhood hangout since the 1960s. The burritos, tacos, tamales, and chimichangas are reliably good, and this might be the place to try your first Mexican beer. The Indian School location, 602 E. Lincoln St. Phoenix, (602) 340-8787, is open daily for lunch and dinner.

Sandwich Shops

The Farm at South Mountain
$$ • 6106 S. 32nd St., Phoenix
• (602) 276-6360

A stop at this small outdoor cafe, set amid a pecan grove and gardens, can get you away from the hustle and bustle of the city. Enjoy views of South Mountain as you sit on picnic benches. Try the pecan turkey Waldorf salad, the organic turkey sandwich, or the mesquite-grilled eggplant. Also recommended are the muffins, pecan pie, and lemonade. Breakfast and lunch are served Tuesday through Sunday. There is an herb shop on the premises, and farm-fresh produce is sold Saturday.

Kohnie's
$ • 4233 E. Camelback Rd., Phoenix
• (602) 952-9948

This family-run Arcadia neighborhood lunch spot is tiny, with a few tables inside and a few next to the parking lot along busy Camelback Road. But personnel are friendly to regulars and first-timers alike. It's a good place to grab a flavored coffee and pastry on the way to work. The lunch menu offers imaginatively prepared soups, salads, and sandwiches plus fresh pasta occasionally. To accompany your coffee, tea, or soda, try one of Kohnie's scones. At last count, the cafe was churning out 23 varieties, from lemon to raisin to jalapeño-cheese (although not all 23 kinds are available every day). The cafe is open for quick breakfasts Monday through Saturday, and for brunch on Sunday. Lunch is until 2 PM Monday through Friday.

MacAlpine's Soda Fountain and Espresso Bar
$ • 2303 N. Seventh St., Phoenix
• (602) 252-7282

In existence since 1928, MacAlpine's boasts an old-time drugstore soda fountain and antique jukebox for good measure. Enjoy the ambiance in this small eatery while trying the hamburgers, tuna sandwiches, cherry phosphates, vanilla cola, and homemade pie. You can catch breakfast, lunch, or an early dinner Monday through Thursday; breakfast, lunch, or dinner Friday and Saturday; and breakfast Sunday.

The Teeter House
$$ • 622 E. Adams St., Phoenix
• (602) 252-4682

Unique among Phoenix's many lunch spots, the Teeter House offers sandwiches, salads, and afternoon tea in one of the Victorian houses of Heritage Square, a downtown block of historic homes. The interior is carefully appointed to be a throwback to Victorian times. Long black dresses and top hats are not required, however. Downtown office workers frequently stop by for things like the roast beef-and-cheese salad or a turkey and Havarti on a croissant. Reservations are advised for afternoon tea, in which servers bring on the scones, pastries, fruit, and finger sandwiches to accompany your favorite brew. The Teeter House is open for lunch and tea Tuesday through Sunday.

That's a Wrap!
$ • 2022 N. Seventh St., Phoenix
• (602) 252-5051

When the trend of wrapped sandwiches hit American menus in the early 1990s, this little spot near downtown showed how to create wraps with pizzazz. The selection has grown to 22 kinds of wraps, combining meats, seafood, sauces, and vegetables in several kinds of thin wraps and incorporating flavors from around the globe. The Scottsdale Wrap, for instance, is composed of mahi mahi, shrimp, mushrooms, snow peas, onions, and jasmine rice, topped with garlic sauce and Brie. Accompaniments to the wraps include coffee drinks and smoothies. The restaurant has another location at 2765 N. Scottsdale Road in Scottsdale, (480) 941-0484. Lunch and dinner are offered.

Seafood

Oyster Grill
$$–$$$ • 455 N. Third St., Phoenix
• (602) 252-6767

Bright colors and stylized ocean images all around make for a fun decor at Oyster Grill in the Arizona Center. You can sit at the oyster bar for a light meal, or choose a table for a full meal. Dinner items include shrimp-feta pizza, fresh salmon, and seafood kebabs. Chicken and pasta dishes round out the menu. Lunch and dinner are served daily.

Steamers
$$$ • 2576 E. Camelback Rd., Phoenix
• (602) 956-3631

The Biltmore Fashion Park location makes Steamers an upscale seafood restaurant, but it's a wise choice if you're hankering for quality fresh seafood, whether it's dinner for two or a family gathering. Recommended dishes include the tuna crusted with mustard seed; prawns stuffed with feta, artichokes, and pine nuts; and the day's fresh catch, grilled to your

INSIDERS' TIP
If you're in one of our many Japanese take-out restaurants, you might notice signs saying that sushi delicacies are not available for carryout in the summer months. This is for your protection, as raw fish can easily spoil in the triple-digit heat.

RESTAURANTS

liking. Meals are accompanied by wonderful cheese scones. Lunch and dinner are served daily.

Spanish

Altos
$$$ • 5029 N. 44th St., Phoenix
• (602) 808-0890

"Cuisine of the New Spain" is the way Altos describes its food, a way of saying that it combines the best of Old World Spain—with its emphasis on seafood and pork—and the best of Mexican cooking traditions, with their spicy flair. The menu is an exotic adventure in itself, with terms you won't fathom unless you ask—and the servers are happy to translate. The restaurant is known for its authentic paellas mixing various seafood, sausage, vegetables, and saffron rice. There are also lamb and filet mignon dishes and tapas, which are small, appetizer-size delicacies. And the atmosphere is a swirl of vibrant colors—deep gold, orange, and green, in a classy combination with wood-beam ceilings and white tablecloths, along with bull-fighting-themed prints and sculptures. Yet it's a small place with a handful of tables inside and on the patio. Altos is popular for lunch Monday through Friday and for dinner nightly.

Western

Bill Johnson's Big Apple
$$ • 16810 N. 19th Ave., Phoenix
• (602) 863-7921

Bill Johnson's is a fixture on the Valley's restaurant scene, with lots of red-bandana and cowboy-hat ambiance. The servers wear holsters and toy pistols, so tip big. The steak and chicken are expertly cooked and highly popular due to Johnson's way with barbecue sauce. It's so good it's bottled and sold in stores. For dessert, apple pie á la mode is a fitting ending. Other locations are at 3757 E. Van Buren Street, Phoenix, (602) 275-2107; 3101 W. Indian School Road, Phoenix, (602) 277-6291; 950 E. Main Street, Mesa, (480) 969-6504; and 3110 N. Arizona Avenue, Chandler, (480) 892-2542. Breakfast, lunch, and dinner are served daily.

Rustler's Rooste
$$–$$$ • 7777 S. Pointe Pkwy., Phoenix
• (602) 431-6474

The "rooste" in this case is a butte at the Pointe Hilton Resort on South Mountain. It's a scenic setting for a fun, casual Western-style steakhouse, where there's often live country music playing. The restaurant features down-home steaks, barbecue ribs, and seafood served in hearty portions. Lunch and dinner are served daily.

Southeast Valley

American Fusion

American Grill
$$–$$$ • 1233 S. Alma School Rd., Mesa
• (480) 844-1918

Open since 1987, American Grill, across from Fiesta Mall, has a steady clientele of East Valley residents seeking classic American food in a classy atmosphere. The grill is all dark woods and brass, with high-backed booths and chandeliers. Baby back ribs, meat loaf, and medallions of beef are good examples of its fare. But don't overlook the starters—we like the clam chowder in a hollowed-out round of Italian bread, the barbecue shrimp, and cheddar fritters. The menu frequently rotates in a few entrees reflecting regional American cooking, such as Creole dishes or California cuisine. American Grill is open for lunch and dinner Monday through Saturday, and for dinner Sunday.

Crocodile Cafe
$$ • 525 S. Mill Ave., Tempe
• (480) 966-5883

The Crocodile Cafe's location puts you in the middle of the action along Mill Avenue, so expect crowds on weekend evenings. The restaurant prides itself on "California Cooking," a style combining fresh ingredients with creative marinades, vinaigrettes, and salsas. Many dishes are prepared over an oak-wood grill. The diversity says "California" too—everything from pizza and calzones to massive salads and Mama's Meatloaf Sandwich. Quesadillas made with chicken or duck are good, as are the burgers and pasta dishes. The restaurant is open daily for lunch and dinner.

The Weather Vane
$–$$ • 7303 E. Main St., Mesa
• (480) 830-2721

Food from the heartland is the theme at the Weather Vane, operating since 1990 in east Mesa. The chicken-fried steak is recommended, or for something a bit fancier at a reasonable price, try the prime rib, or fish of the day. Customers come in especially for the restaurant's

RESTAURANTS

signature dessert, blackberry cobbler. Lunch and dinner are served daily.

Asian

Happy Bowl Samurai
$, no credit cards • 5136 S. Rural Rd., Tempe
• (480) 838-2211

The Japanese-language newspapers near the counter and the autographed photos of Japanese baseball stars are a good sign that this is the real thing from the Far East. We recommend the shrimp and vegetable tempura, the chicken teriyaki, and the curry-flavored udon, which are thick noodles, served in a ceramic soup bowl. You can purchase items la carte or obento, which means you get side dishes of egg roll, rice, fruit, and noodles. The cooler is full of imported carbonated beverages and juices that are fun to investigate. The restaurant is fairly small but more gaily decorated than your typical Japanese fast-food establishment. Lunch and dinner are available Monday through Saturday.

Mint Thai Cafe
$$ • 1111 N. Gilbert Rd., Gilbert
• (480) 497-5366

This tidy little authentic Thai restaurant in a small shopping center is a prime example of the growing sophistication of dining options in the Gilbert area. House specialties include Thai-style pork chops, Sizzling Beef, and a number of spicy seafood entrees. The Mussaman curry, a Thai beef stew, is tasty, as are the chicken satay appetizers, and curry noodles. Dessert is cool-down time with a dish of homemade coconut ice cream or Thai custard. The restaurant is open for lunch Monday through Saturday, and for dinner nightly.

P.F. Chang's China Bistro
$$–$$$ • 740 S. Mill Ave., Tempe
• (480) 731-4600

Immensely popular for its food and ambiance, P.F. Chang's packs 'em in on weekends at its two locations. The Tempe location in a renovated red-brick building from the city's early days is notable for its two giant statues of horses and a Chinese mural. The food is a pleasing array of Cantonese, Szechwan, and Hunan cooking, from moo-shu pork to honey shrimp to kung pao chicken. The other location is in Scottsdale Fashion Square at 7014 E. Camelback Road, (602) 949-2610. Lunch and dinner are served daily.

Saki's Pacific Rim Cafe on Mill
$$$ • 740 S. Mill Ave., Tempe
• (480) 968-7300

You can't miss this restaurant on Mill Avenue—just look for the pillar spouting flames. It's on the same block of Old Town Tempe as P.F. Chang's. Saki's has a large sushi bar downstairs that faces an oblong aquarium. The sushi and sashimi varieties number in the dozens—which means you will not only have to ponder whether you want salmon, tuna, eel, scallop, shrimp, or sea urchin, but also what you would like it rolled with and whether you want it cooked, raw, presented in a salad, or tempura-style. You could be there a while. Items beside sushi run the gamut from chicken to filet mignon to noodle dishes. Lunch decisions are a little less complicated, with choices such as chicken curry, seafood tempura, and salmon teriyaki. Similar dishes are available at dinner. The patio upstairs has a misting system to cool down summer diners and heaters to keep winter customers toasty. Saki's is popular at happy hour, where trendies try sake bombers—Japanese beer with shots of hot Japanese wine. Dinner is served Monday through Saturday and lunch, Monday through Friday. Another location, Sushi on Shea, is at 7000 E. Shea Boulevard in Scottsdale, (480) 483-7799. A Scottsdale Fashion Square location, Kona Grill, (480) 429-1100, serves up great food, too.

Breakfast

Farm House
$, no credit cards • 397 S. Gilbert Rd., Gilbert
• (480) 926-0676

A small white farmhouse serving a hearty breakfast from old family recipes sounds too good to be true. But this rustic place still exists even as the once-sleepy town of Gilbert explodes in population. The menu includes eggs, sausage, bacon, pancakes, French toast, Belgian waffles, omelets, home-fried potatoes, and homemade granola. The lunch menu includes sandwiches, burgers, salads, and homemade soups. Or you might catch a lunch special such as meat loaf or chicken and biscuits. The Farm House is open for breakfast and lunch Monday through Saturday.

Mitchell's Ripe Tomato Cafe
$ • 745 W. Baseline Rd., Mesa
• (480) 892-4340

The decor of this homey diner celebrates the bold colors of ripe tomatoes, with red booths against green paneling, red-and-green barstools, and green mini-blinds. If that doesn't perk you up for the day, the huge omelets—some served in their own skillet—surely will. Mitchell's is a longtime Chicago establishment that found its way to Mesa in the 1980s. Noted restaurant critic Mimi Sheraton once praised Mitchell's breakfasts, as a news clipping near the entrance will attest. Omelet flavors include shredded beef, seasoned chicken, and green chili and cheese. Fortunately, they are served through the lunch hour, as are various American-diner style sandwiches, burgers, and salads. Breakfast and lunch are served daily.

Continental and Fine Dining

Top of the Rock
$$$–$$$$ • 2000 Westcourt Way, Tempe • (480) 431-2370

Many view Top of the Rock as tops in elegant dining in the Southeast Valley. It's perched up high as part of The Buttes resort, from which you can correctly conclude that the view of the Valley is wonderful and particularly romantic at sunset. Menu items include mesquite-grilled tenderloin and prawns; pesto-crusted swordfish; and veal chop with saffron orzo. Dinner is served nightly. Sunday brunch is a popular option.

Mexican

Guedo's Taco Shop
$ • 71 E. Chandler Blvd., Chandler • (480) 899-7841

Some say Guedo's (pronounced WE-do) has the best soft-shell tacos around. The freshly made corn and flour tortillas are delicious, and the meat is tender and saucy. Cheese crisps are also a good choice and can be filled with beans, chiles, sour cream, avocado, or a combination. For beverages, check out the good selection of Mexican soda pop and beers, or try horchata, a milky, cinnamon-flavored drink. The salsa bar—with three kinds of salsa, lime slices, onions, shredded cabbage, and cilantro for dressing up your tacos—is attractively draped with a serape, and the colors of the Mexican flag are put to good use in the decor. The Chandler location, in an adobe-style building, is a bit cramped, but you have your choice of indoor or patio seating. Lunch and dinner are served Tuesday through Saturday. Guedo's other location is at 108 W. Broadway Road in Mesa,

(480) 461-3660. It has more limited hours—from 11 AM to 6 PM Tuesday through Saturday.

Macayo Depot Cantina
$$ • 300 S. Ash Ave., Tempe • (480) 966-6677

Macayo's Mexican Restaurants is a family-owned chain that has been operating in Arizona for more than 50 years. It has seven locations in the Valley—all with a colorful, South-of-the-border feel—but we like this one because it has the added attraction of having been transformed from the old Tempe railroad station. The tracks are still just a few steps away. Many of the architectural details of the Territorial-style depot have been preserved. Also, the outdoor seating creates a great cantina atmosphere on most balmy evenings. The food is hearty, and we recommend the chimichangas and fajitas. Macayo's also sells special Margarita mugs. Additional locations: 11107 N. Scottsdale Road, Scottsdale, (480) 596-1181; 4001 N. Central Avenue, Phoenix, (602) 264-6141; 1909 W. Thunderbird Road, Phoenix, (602) 866-7034; 7829 W. Thomas Road, Phoenix, (602) 873-0313; 1920 S. Dobson Road, Mesa, (480) 820-0237; and 12637 S. 48th Street, Phoenix, (602) 598-5101. All are open daily for lunch and dinner.

Rosa's Mexican Grill
$, no credit cards • 328 E. University Dr., Mesa • (480) 964-5451

If you believe Mexican food utilizes only beef, pork, and chicken, then this might be just the place to learn otherwise. Specialties of the house include seafood tacos (using grilled fish or shrimp) and Shrimp Mazatlan (incorporating pineapple salsa). Traditional tacos, burros, enchiladas, and tostadas are also available. The restaurant's name was chosen as a way for owners Dennis and Liz Sirrine to pay homage to their grandmothers, both of whom were named Rosa. The Sirrines learned about Mexican food preparation from them and studied at the Culinary Institute of America in San Francisco as well. Rosa's is open for lunch and dinner Tuesday through Saturday.

Serrano's
$–$$ • 1955 W. Guadalupe Rd., Mesa • (480) 756-2992

If you're feeling a bit out of the loop as to exactly what Sonoran-style Mexican food is, here's a good place to learn all about it and please your palate in the process. Serrano's is an established local chain with concentration in the Southeast Valley. The extensive menu has many dishes featuring shredded and cubed meats served the Sonoran way with lots of cheese and chiles. They come wrapped in corn or flour tortillas, with spicy rice and refried beans on the side. In addition to the requisite enchiladas, tacos, quesadillas, and burros, find Especiales de la Casa such as carnitas, thin slices of charbroiled pork loin, and Pollo Rojo, charbroiled chicken breast covered with a spicy sauce. All meals are preceded by tasty tortilla chips served with a nice chunky salsa and a bean-and-cheese dip. Don't go overboard on those, though, because Serrano's portions are huge. The restaurant is open daily for lunch and dinner. Additional locations: 141 S. Arizona Avenue, Chandler, (480) 899-3318; 6440 S. Rural Road, Tempe, (480) 345-0044; 1964 E. McKellips Road, Mesa, (480) 649-3503; 1021 S. Power Road, Mesa, (480) 854-7455; 959 N. Val Vista Drive, Gilbert, (480) 507- 5027; and 3941 E. Chandler Boulevard, Phoenix, (602) 706-8442.

Sandwich Shops

The News Cafe
$ • 4810 E. Ray Rd., Phoenix
• (602) 592-0400

You don't have to be a newspaper junkie to hang out at this establishment, but you'll certainly be tempted to relax and open up one of the many newspapers lying around as you sip your coffee or tea. And you will probably get a kick out of the sandwich names: Tuna Melt Tattler, BLT Bulletin, Vegetarian Voice...you get the idea. Magazine racks bear many titles for sale, from Architectural Digest to Utne Reader. This location is open daily for breakfast and lunch. The smaller, but original News Cafe is at 5053 N. 44th Street in Phoenix, (602) 852-0982. It's open daily for breakfast and lunch, as well as Tuesday through Friday evenings for sandwich/soup/salad specials.

Pita Jungle
$–$$ • 1250 E. Apache Blvd., Tempe
• (480) 804-0234

If you would just as soon have your sandwich on pita bread, this place is for you. It's popular with vegetarians, but chicken, turkey, and tuna are on the menu as well, in sandwich concoctions that show a Greek and Italian influence. Specialties include falafel, baba ghanoush (broiled eggplant), and stuffed grape leaves. The restaurant is fairly small and made intimate by lots of paintings and photographs by local artists on the walls. Pita Jungle is in a funky little shopping center near Arizona State University that also houses a tattoo parlor. The restaurant is open daily for breakfast, lunch, and dinner. Recently opened is a second location at 1949 W. Ray Road in Chandler, (480) 855-3232.

Western

Monti's La Casa Vieja
$$$ • 3 W. First St., Tempe
• (480) 967-7594

In calling this a Western restaurant, we're talking old-time Arizona charm, not boot-stompin' and sawdust-on-the-floor. Monti's is where Tempe edges toward the Town Lake, in the historic Hayden family home, the oldest surviving building in the Salt River Valley. Charles Hayden, founder of Tempe, built the home in the 1870s, about the time he erected the flour mill across the street. His son, Carl Hayden, was a beloved U.S. senator and statesman. The building became a restaurant by 1924. It's been Monti's for decades and has a faithful clientele. You are sure to enjoy the steaks— Monti's trademark—and you will be steeped in history as you survey the photographs of old Tempe on the walls. A related restaurant is Monti's at the Ranch, at the Dobson Ranch Inn, 1644 S. Dobson Road in Mesa, (480) 831-8877. Both are open daily for lunch and dinner.

Northeast Valley

American Fusion

Arcadia Farms
$$ • 7014 E. First Ave. and
7007 E. First Ave., Scottsdale
• (480) 941-5665

Arcadia Farms occupies two restored homes across the street from each other in downtown Scottsdale and serves up American, bistro -style dishes. There is both indoor and outdoor seating, but when the weather is nice it's hard to resist the patio dining amid the lovely trees on the grounds. The menu ranges from grilled shrimp skewers to salmon medallions on soba noodles to grilled beef tenderloin. Homemade breads and desserts are quite enjoyable. Lunch and dinner are served Monday through Saturday.

Bandera
$$ • 3821 N. Scottsdale Rd., Scottsdale • (480) 994-3524

Generous portions and reasonable prices—not to mention the best rotisserie chicken we've tasted—make this a popular spot in Old Town Scottsdale. Be sure to try the country-style mashed potatoes with chives, the chile corn bread, and the cole slaw with peanut dressing. The wild mushroom meat loaf is another popular entree. The restaurant is open daily for dinner only. If you're in the mood for a take-out dinner, Bandera has a very efficient drive-through service; call ahead to order, and they'll have it ready for you when you drive up.

Cafe Terra Cotta
$$$ • 6166 N. Scottsdale Rd., Scottsdale • (480) 948-8100

Chef Donna Nordin is one of Arizona's pioneers in capitalizing on the rich variety of local food-preparation traditions and regional ingredients to create distinctive Southwestern dishes. By Southwestern, we mean food blending American, Hispanic, Anglo, and Native American styles. The resulting menu at Cafe, Terra Cotta (there's another one in Tucson, where Nordin is based) offers such treats as tortilla soup; soft-shell crabs in blue cornmeal; calamari with papaya-tequila dressing; and wood-fired rock shrimp pizza. The restaurant's

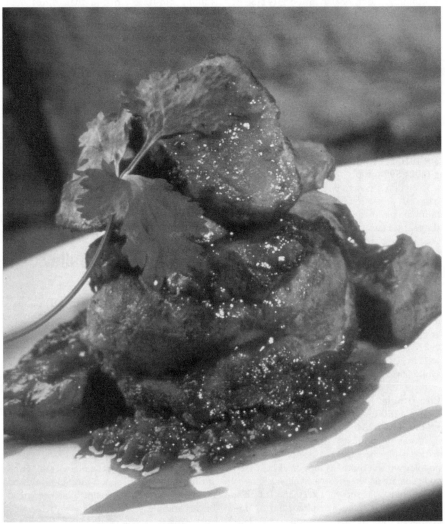

Grilled beef tenderloin is a house specialty at the Roaring Fork.

Photo: Courtesy of Roaring Fork, Margo Media

RESTAURANTS

interior plays with bold colors of the Southwest such as turquoise and coral, and is classy without being stuffy. Since the restaurant is in the Borgata shopping center, those choosing patio seating will have views of the goings-on at the boutiques. The Borgata, by the way, is a re-creation of an Italian village. Lunch and dinner are served daily.

Hops! Bistro & Brewery
$$$ • 8668 E. Shea Boulevard, Scottsdale
• (480) 998-7777

There's an exclamation point after Hops! for a reason—the microbrewery beer is a must-have with your meal. The varieties run the gamut from light, fruit-flavored beers (raspberry ale, for instance), to dark ales and stouts. The food is a pleasing blend of pastas and pizzas, and steak, seafood, and chicken specialties, many of them prepared with the house beers. Lunch and dinner are served daily.

The Palo Verde
$$$$ • 34631 N. Tom Darlington Dr., Carefree
• (480) 488-9009

Bright interior colors and lovely views of the Valley from the hills of the Boulders resort make the Palo Verde a good choice, especially if you're intrigued by Southwestern cooking at its toniest. Specialties include smoked lamb shank with pumpkin puree; marinated Arizona ostrich with salsa; pan-roasted snapper with cactus tartar sauce; and red-chile marinated quail. Lunch dishes are a little more mainstream, tending toward salads, sandwiches, and pastas served on thick ceramic plates. Lunch and dinner are served daily.

Pinon Grill
$$$ • 7401 N. Scottsdale Rd., Scottsdale
• (480) 948-5050

Setting and food make for a memorable experience at Pinon Grill, which is in the Regal McCormick Ranch resort. We suggest seating on the patio, with its romantic views of a large artificial lake. The interior of the restaurant is nice, too, with a Southwestern-casual feel. Entree favorites include the Baked Mexican Shrimp, butterfly shrimp stuffed with spinach and goat cheese; ahi tuna steak with cantaloupe salsa; and veal chop marinated in lime and chiles. Side dishes and corn bread are tastefully presented. Rounding out the fare are innovative appetizers—scallops on blue tortilla shells, for example—chile corn bread, prickly pear Margaritas, and yummy dessert crepes. Dinner is served nightly.

Roaring Fork
$$$$ • 7243 E. Camelback Rd., Scottsdale,
• (480) 947-0795

Named after a river in Colorado, this restaurant is under the steady hand of Chef Robert McGrath. The food concept is described as American Western cuisine so you can enjoy a cast-iron skillet of cornbread with each meal, smoked trout on buttermilk corn cakes, and rib eye steak slathered in blueberry barbecue sauce. Try the Big-Ass hamburger. Lunch and dinner are served daily.

Windows on the Green
$$$$ • 6000 E. Camelback Rd., Scottsdale
• (480) 941-8200

The award-winning chefs at The Phoenician demonstrate their expertise with Southwestern fare at this semi-casual restaurant overlooking the resort's golf course. The menu emphasizes indigenous ingredients, such as cilantro, jicama, and Nopales cactus combined with traditional meats and wild game. Lunch and dinner are served daily.

Asian

Malee's on Main
$$ • 7131 E. Main St., Scottsdale
• (480) 947-6042

Some find this restaurant a bit on the snooty side, being as it is in the heart of Scottsdale's gallery district. We don't recommend it for families with young children, but we can say it has dependably good and artfully served Thai dishes, ranging from meats in lemongrass and mint to satays to curries. Thai iced tea with or without cream makes a most soothing accompaniment if you like your dishes spicy. Malee's (pronounced MAH-ly) is open daily for lunch and dinner.

Roy's Restaurant
$$$ • 7001 N. Scottsdale Rd., Scottsdale
• (480) 905-1155

Born and raised in Japan and now based in Hawaii, chef and author Roy Yamaguchi has achieved international fame for his cuisine combining elements of European cooking, Pacific seafood, and Asian ingredients and seasonings (see our close-up in this chapter). A few menu examples: lemongrass tempura chicken with Thai sticky rice; blackened ahi tuna; oak-fired filet mignon; and duck pizza. If you're tantalized enough to try it, we suggest making reservations well in advance. Dinner is served nightly and lunch, Monday through Friday.

Roy's just opened a second location at the Camelback Esplanade, 2501 E. Camelback Rd., in Phoenix, (602) 381-1155.

Barbecue

Don & Charlie's
$$ • 7501 E. Camelback Rd., Scottsdale
• (480) 990-0900

Just remember this four-letter word when considering Don & Charlie's—ribs. Many locals say this longtime establishment in downtown Scottsdale serves the best-tasting ribs around. The prime rib, New York sirloin, and lamb chops are also recommended. Sports memorabilia sets the pace for the decor. Don & Charlie's is open for dinner only, but they're open seven days a week.

El Paso Bar-B-Que Company
$$–$$$ • 8220 N. Hayden Rd., Scottsdale
• (480) 998-2626

For "bar-b-que with an attitude" this restaurant has become quite popular among Valley residents. Special seasonings and the low heat of a pecan-wood pit are the secrets to El Paso's success, the menu explains. We've enjoyed the baby back ribs, beef ribs, and smoked chicken, but be forewarned that the portions are humongous. For something a little different, try the barbecue salmon or lamb barbacoa, which is smoked overnight, Mexican-style. There are sandwich, salad, and burger selections, along with a kid's menu and plenty of alcoholic and nonalcoholic beverages. The decor in the huge Scottsdale location is fairly sophisticated for a barbecue house—with Southwestern fabrics, log columns, ironwork accents, and cowboy paintings. Lunch and dinner are served daily. Other locations: 4921 E. Ray Road, Phoenix, (602) 705-5050, and 4303 W. Peoria Avenue, Glendale, (623) 931-2438.

Tom's BBQ Chicago Style
$ • 7919 E. Thomas Rd., Scottsdale
• (480) 947-6440

Chicago rib tips are the specialty at Tom's BBQ, which has several individually owned locations around the Valley. Meats are slowly

cooked over mesquite wood for lots of flavor and are served with cole slaw, potato salad, barbecue-baked beans, and rolls. For those who don't eat red meat, the chicken dinner is a good option. Whatever your choice, you can feed a family of four for less than $25, which makes this an attractive place on weeknights for working couples with starving kids. The Scottsdale location is conveniently situated in a strip shopping center on the southwest corner of Thomas and Hayden Roads. Find other locations

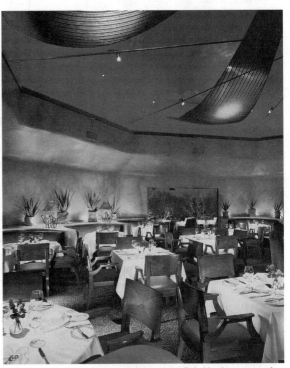

Southwestern fare is the specialty of the Palo Verde room at the Boulders Resort.

Photo: Courtesy of The Boulders Resort

in Chandler, Glendale, Mesa, Tempe, and west Phoenix. Hours may vary by location, but the Scottsdale restaurant is open for lunch and dinner daily.

Breakfast

First Watch
$ • 4422 N. 75th St., Scottsdale
• (480) 941-8464

First Watch gets your day going with an extensive selection of egg dishes and pancakes. There are also several heart-healthy options.

Oak furniture and contemporary country decor give it a homey feel. And the constantly poured coffee and tea help you kick it into gear too. It's open seven days a week for breakfast and lunch. Other locations: 9645 N. Black Canyon Highway, Phoenix, (602) 943-3232; 1 N. First St., downtown Phoenix, (602) 340-9089; and 61 W. Thomas Road, Phoenix, (602) 265-2092.

The Good Egg
$ • 6149 N. Scottsdale Rd., Scottsdale
• (480) 991-5416

Breakfast dishes are imaginatively prepared at this regional chain whose restaurants go by either The Good Egg or The Eggery. You can find omelets, pancakes, and waffles, along with frittatas, a lighter version of omelets called "crepeggs," and Mexican specialties such as huevos rancheros. Many menu items meet nutritionists' guidelines for low-cholesterol meals. Breakfast and lunch (primarily sandwiches and salads) are served daily. This Good Egg is conveniently located in the Hilton Village shopping area. Other locations: 2957 W. Bell Road, Phoenix, (602) 993-2797; Park Central Mall, Thomas Road and Central Avenue, Phoenix, (602) 248-3897; 906 E. Camelback Road, Phoenix, (602) 274-5393; 13802 N. Scottsdale Road, Scottsdale, (480) 483-1090; and 34422 N. Scottsdale Road, Scottsdale, (480) 595-1044. Find The Eggery at: 5109 N. 44th Street, Phoenix, (602) 840-5734; 4326 E. Cactus Road, Phoenix, (602) 953-2342; and 50 E. Camelback Road, Phoenix, (602) 263-8554.

The Original Pancake House
$ • 6840 E. Camelback Rd., Scottsdale
• (480) 946-4902

Oven-baked apple pancakes and Dutch Babies are a specialty at this cheery breakfast place next to a Motel 6. The crepes are also a good bet as are, naturally, the good ol' buttermilk pancakes. Hours are 7 AM to 2 PM daily.

British

The Olde English Inn
$$–$$$ • 7111 E. Thomas Rd., Scottsdale
• (480) 941-4915

In 1996, Marilyn and Dick Neal from Essex, England, took on the daunting task of retooling a Chinese restaurant near Scottsdale Road into an English pub like the one they ran in Essex for many years. The plastered walls, long beams, and stonework recall the half-timbered houses of the English countryside, and the Neals shipped over lots of pub memorabilia such as tankards and copper implements. More important, the food is authentic, with all the Anglophile favorites—steak and kidney pie, cottage pie, bangers and mash, and fish and chips. For those not quite into pub food, there are chicken and pasta dishes, and various sandwiches and salads. The bar area boasts more than a dozen British and imported draft beers, which, as the British know, are best enjoyed with a round of billiards or darts, also provided at this establishment. Lunch and dinner are served Tuesday through Sunday with dinner only on Monday.

Continental and Fine Dining

Golden Swan
$$$$ • 7500 E. Doubletree Ranch Rd., Scottsdale
• (480) 991-3388

Travel magazines have bestowed accolades upon the Golden Swan, the centerpiece restaurant of the Hyatt Regency Scottsdale. Chefs specialize in regional American cuisine while allowing distinctively local ingredients and cooking traditions to shine through. Examples include beef fajitas with Southwestern herb butter; grilled lamb chop glazed with jalapeño honey mustard and rolled in pistachios; and herb-marinated range chicken baked in an Arizona red-clay pot. The restaurant has a Euro-contemporary feel, with marble and stone floors, ceiling-high glass walls, and black and jewel tones as color accents. Outdoor dining is in a charming pavilion alongside a lagoon inhabited by black swans. Dinner is offered nightly.

The Marquesa
$$$$ • 7575 E. Princess Dr., Scottsdale
• (480) 585-4848

Imagine yourself in the Catalonia region of Spain, dining on the finest of regional food, immaculately presented. That's what you'll experience at The Marquesa, one of the Valley's best restaurants. The surroundings are Old World-elegant, almost museum-like with the many paintings on the walls. Fare includes sweet red peppers stuffed with crabmeat and cheese; monkfish in a tomato tapenade and white bean sauce; and Paella Valenciana, which is lobster, chicken, pork, shellfish, and Spanish sausage in saffron rice. Dinner is served nightly. The Marquesa is also recognized for its wonderful outdoor Sunday brunch, which exudes a Spanish-marketplace air. The restaurant is closed mid-June through mid-September.

Mary Elaine's
$$$$ • 6000 E. Camelback Rd., Scottsdale
• (480) 941-8200, (480) 423-2530

This is one of the Valley's most celebrated restaurants, thanks to the extraordinary food and special ambiance at The Phoenician resort. You'll be bowled over by the modern French cuisine of Mary Elaine's. The menu changes seasonally, but can include dishes such as Dover sole, squab, rack of lamb, and veal tenderloin. The elegant rooms that form Mary Elaine's have splendid views of the city lights, and all around are gold-framed paintings and sparkling chandeliers. This may be the priciest restaurant in the Valley, but everyone agrees it's worth it! Dinner is served Monday through Saturday.

Razz's Restaurant & Bar
$$$ • 10321 N. Scottsdale Rd., Scottsdale
• (623) 905-1308

Razz's is named for its chef, Erasmo "Razz" Kamnitzer, a Venezuelan and seventh-generation restaurateur who believes in healthy cooking with pizzazz (see our Close-up in this chapter). He uses all kinds of meats, seafood, produce, pasta, herbs, and spices to produce meals low in cholesterol and fat yet intense in flavor. Examples include duck cakes; escargot Bourguignone; nut-encrusted roasted pork tenderloin; halibut Veracruz; and ahi tuna with seasoned soba noodles. Kamnitzer is an exuberant man who likes to schmooze with his customers, which makes Razz's a fun place for a great meal. Dinner is served Tuesday through Saturday.

Italian and Pizza

California Pizza Kitchen
$$ • 10100 N. Scottsdale Rd., Scottsdale
• (480) 596-8300

Pizza with zing is how we think of CPK's selection of more than two dozen wood-fired pizzas, in flavors such as Thai chicken, shrimp scampi, grilled eggplant, and even the less adventurous pepperoni. The menu for this Western U.S. chain of restaurants also includes pasta dishes—would you believe kung pao spaghetti?—and nicely presented salads. A second Valley location is at 2400 E. Camelback Road, Phoenix, (602) 553-8382. Lunch and dinner are available daily.

Oregano's Pizza Bistro
$$ • 3622 N. Scottsdale Rd., Scottsdale
• (480) 970-1860

Oregano's is a hot spot on weekend evenings for its casual Italian bistro feel and inventive pizzas. Thin-crust or Chicago stuffed pizzas come with traditional toppings or in varieties such as Cajun chicken pesto or Mexican pizza with chicken and green chiles. Hoagies and pasta dishes are also on the menu. Recently opened is a Tempe location at 523 E. University Drive, (480) 858-0501. Oregano's is open daily for lunch and dinner.

NYPD Pizza
$$ • 8880 E. Via
• (480) 451-6973

Don't puzzle too long over why a restaurant goes by "NYPD" in the middle of Scottsdale. It stands for New York Pizza Dept., and the pies are made from Old World recipes—Old World as in Brooklyn, not Italy, the menu explains. Order the Greenwich Village (spinach, Roma tomatoes, and garlic), the Pizza Blanca (a white pizza featuring ricotta), or Da Works with, you know, the works. Or fahgeddaboutit and order another variety— even a calzone, some pasta, or an Italian sandwich. The dining room—done up in black-and-white checkerboard—and the take-out counter are open daily for lunch and dinner.

Ristorante Sandolo
$$$ • 7500 E. Doubletree Ranch Rd., Scottsdale
• (480) 991-3388

It's hard to resist the Venetian charm of this Italian bistro inside the Hyatt Regency Scottsdale. An informal indoor/outdoor cafe, it serves fettuccine Alfredo, mostaccioli Bolognese, and other pasta dishes, with a chopped Italian salad on the side. What's more, the waiters sing, and they'll arrange for you to ride in a gondola-style boat on the Hyatt's lake. The boatman, sings, too. Dinner is served nightly.

Mexican

Arizona Burrito Co.
$ • 6941 N. Hayden Rd., Scottsdale
• (480) 922-9466

You can pretty much design your own burrito at this small take-out or eat-in establishment, and chances are it will be heart-healthy. Almost half the menu items meet guidelines set by Heart Smart International.

Sautéed shrimp, vegetable medleys, barbecue chicken, and charbroiled steak are among the fillings for the burritos, along with rice, beans, and salsa. The ingredients are rolled into your choice of a white, wheat, spinach, or tomato basil tortilla. Then the burritos are foil wrapped to keep them warm and less messy to eat. A second location is at 4221 E. Chandler Boulevard, Phoenix, (480) 704-9127. Lunch and dinner are served daily.

Carlsbad Tavern
$$$ • 3313 N. Hayden Rd., Scottsdale • (480) 970-8164

Scottsdale certainly has its share of pretentious, pricey restaurants—which makes Carlsbad Tavern a refreshing change. The food—New Mexico-style Mexican with steak and pasta thrown in—is tasty and reasonably priced. The servers are friendly, in a neighborhood tavern kind of way. The newsprint menu pokes fun at "owner" Miguel Guacamole. The restaurant recently moved to new, larger digs in a clay-colored building, which you can't miss along Hayden Road. We recommend the blue-plate special of roasted chicken, the blue corn enchiladas, and the braised lamb grilled over wood in the New Mexican way. Entrees come with green-chile mashed potatoes and corn bread topped with prickly pear butter. Lunch and dinner are served Monday through Saturday, with dinner only on Sunday.

La Hacienda
$$$$ • 7575 E. Princess Dr., Scottsdale • (480) 585-4848

We place La Hacienda in the Mexican category with the advisory that it is a cut above most Mexican restaurants in fine-dining ambiance. But you would expect that at a restaurant on the grounds of the ritzy Scottsdale Princess resort. Just a short walk from the hotel lobby, the restaurant occupies a turn-of-the-century, freestanding Mexican ranch house. Expect first-class table settings, comfortable chairs, a beehive fireplace, extraordinary food, and strolling mariachis to set the tone. Consider spit-roasted suckling pig, grilled seafood, chicken, and beef, all prepared in traditional Mexican style. The place is also known for its coffee drinks that are ordered to cap off a meal. La Hacienda serves dinner nightly.

Old Town Tortilla Factory
$$–$$$ • 6910 E. Main St., Scottsdale • (480) 945-4567

In a renovated adobe cottage dating from 1933, Old Town Tortilla Factory is mega-popular with Valley residents because it's a funky place with nice twists on Mexican and American fare. With entree items like Shawnee Sea Bass and Stuffed Beef Filet, you can see it's not strictly the cheese crisp-enchilada-taco type of Mexican food. Even those items, though, are presented with flair. And the Tortilla Factory makes two dozen varieties of flour tortillas, using ingredients like sun-dried tomatoes and serrano chiles. The bar gets a lot of business, too, and it's quite popular with tequila aficionados, since the place serves almost 100 varieties of the Mexican liquor. Some of the high-end tequilas go for $500 a bottle. The restaurant is open Monday through Saturday for lunch and dinner and Sunday for dinner only.

Sandwich Shops

Chompie's
$$ • 9301 E. Shea Blvd., Scottsdale • (480) 860-0475

Chompie's is much more than a sandwich shop, but we include it in this category because its sandwiches are so good. The mile-high sandwiches in this kosher-style restaurant are stacked with your choice of tender corned beef, pastrami, turkey, cheeses, or combinations thereof—congratulations go to the diner who can finish a Chompie's sandwich in one sitting. The restaurant serves breakfast, lunch, and dinner Tuesday through Sunday (breakfast and lunch on Monday), which makes it tempting to stick around all day, working your way through lox on bagels, eggs, and blintzes for breakfast, then a potato knish and salad for lunch, and then for dinner, a beef brisket special or sweet and sour cabbage rolls. For dessert, you can saunter (or waddle) over to the bakery counter, with its myriad cakes and cookies. Chompie's is a popular neighborhood stop for bagels, which come in about 30 varieties. An additional location is at 3202 E. Greenway Road in Phoenix, (602) 971-8010.

Wildflower Bread Company
$ • 15640 N. Pima Rd., Scottsdale • (480) 991-5180

The owners of this fairly new bakery and sandwich shop in north Scottsdale say it's "where the aroma of fresh-baked bread alone solves all of the world's problems for awhile." We'll buy that, especially when it's bread in such varieties as good ol' multigrain or the more exotic ciabatta, foccacia, or wild mushroom. Or when the bread embraces sandwiches like chicken pesto and feta, or roast beef and bleu

RESTAURANTS

cheese. Also on the menu are salads, from Caribbean Cobb to Oriental chicken. There are cookies and biscotti to go with the good selection of coffees and teas. Counter service is available for breakfast, lunch, and dinner daily.

Seafood

Restaurant Oceana
$$$$ • 8900 E. Pinnacle Peak Rd., Scottsdale
• (480) 515-BASS

A wonderful seafood restaurant in the Pinnacle Peak area. Oceana features grilled ahi tuna with foie gras, Atlantic salmon, wood-fire roasted Maine scallops, and pan-seared cod in a bacon and leek broth. For diners who want to sample Chef Ercolino Crugnale's signature dishes, there are four- and five-course Tasting Menus with smaller portions of his seafood creations. Dinner is served daily.

Western

Crazy Ed's Satisfied Frog
$$$ • 6245 E. Cave Creek Rd., Cave Creek
• (480) 253-FROG

Things are always hoppin' at the Frog during tourist season. The restaurant shoots for a rollicking Western atmosphere, with sawdust on the floor, a saloon area, honky-tonk music, picnic tables covered with checkered tablecloths, a paper menu filled with cartoons and jokes, and shops on the premises selling Western souvenirs. The food ain't bad, either. We recommend the barbecue ribs or spit-roasted chicken. A children's menu is available. You can sample beers from Crazy Ed Chilleen's (he's a real person) microbrewery. And this is the home of Cave Creek Chili Beer, which features an Arizona-grown chili pepper hand-inserted into every bottle. Lunch and dinner are served daily.

Rawhide Steakhouse
$$ • 23023 N. Scottsdale Rd., Scottsdale
• (480) 502-5600

See how the West was fun at the Rawhide theme park, popular with tourists from all over the world. Then reward yourself with a steak from the restaurant in this re-created 1880s Western town. The baby back ribs and barbecue chicken are also good. We hear tell that the appetizers include deep-fried rattlesnake and

buffalo kebabs. We might need a beer from the saloon before we give that a try. Lunch is served Friday through Sunday (October through May), and dinner is served nightly year round.

Northwest Valley

American Fusion

Earl's Eating and Drinking Establishment
$ • 9852 W. Peoria Ave., Peoria
• (623) 977-7391

There's nothing terribly fancy about this longtime establishment, just wholesome American and Mexican food at reasonable prices. The mesquite-smoked meats with barbecue sauce are a favorite, as are the Mexican combination plates and the hearty breakfasts of eggs and chorizo (Mexican sausage). The full bar sells a lot of Margaritas and beer. The restaurant is open seven days a week for breakfast, lunch, and dinner.

Lenny Monti's Restaurant
$$ • 12025 N. 19th Ave., Phoenix
• (623) 997-5844

This family-style restaurant has been drawing crowds for 25 years, partly because Monti is a trusted name in steaks in the Valley. Lenny Monti belongs to the family that runs the well-known Monti's La Casa Vieja in downtown Tempe, but the two restaurants are not connected. This one is a great place for large family gatherings, kids included. Adults can choose steak, seafood, prime rib, mesquite-smoked chicken, or fried chicken, while children can feel grown up by ordering a small steak, shrimp, or chicken from the kids' menu. The restaurant serves lunch and dinner daily.

Lo Perchio's
$$ • 12425 W. Bell Rd., Surprise
• (623) 583-0600

This is one of the most popular restaurants in the Sun Cities area, owing to its moderate prices and traditional menu of steaks, prime rib, pasta, and fried seafood. To make the evening a bit more adventurous, try the fresh seafood of the day. The desserts are worth saving room for, especially if you're in the mood for lemon cake or carrot cake. Lo Perchio's is open daily for lunch and dinner as well as for a Sunday champagne brunch.

The elegant restaurants at The Phoenician offer remarkable dining.

Photo: Courtesy of The Phoenician

Mimi's Cafe
$$ • 7450 W. Bell Rd., Glendale
• (623) 979-4500

This restaurant chain out of California is rich in New Orleans French Quarter ambiance. It's a charming change of pace among the eateries fronting the large West Valley mall, Arrowhead Towne Center. For dinner you will have to decide between something light from their great selection of sandwiches and salads, or something more robust, such as chicken pot pie, beer-batter halibut, or roast pork loin and red cabbage. Especially recommended are the soups du jour, such as clam "chowda" and Caribbean black bean. Breakfast, lunch, and dinner are served daily. Other Valley locations are at 4901 E. Ray Road, Phoenix, (480) 705-4811; 1250 S. Alma School Road, Mesa, (480) 833-4646; and 8980 E. Shea Boulevard, Scottsdale, (480) 451-6763.

Breakfast

Kiss the Cook Restaurant & Antiques
$ • 4915 W. Glendale Ave., Glendale
• (623) 939-4663

Just a mile from downtown Glendale's antique district, Kiss the Cook has been dishing out homemade breakfast and lunch goodies since 1980. The family-operated restaurant has a country-cluttered feel, with all the antiques, dolls, birdhouses, and assorted knickknacks on display and for sale. Breakfast gets down to business with buttermilk pancakes from an old family recipe and omelets that you fill with your choice of three ingredients. Also on the table are homemade muffins and apple butter. For lunch, salads are a good choice; select from Cobb, salmon Caesar, Monterey chicken, and Cajun chicken salads, all made from scratch. The restaurant is open every day, for breakfast and lunch only.

German

Haus Murphy's
$$ • 5819 W. Glendale Ave., Glendale
• (623) 939-2480

Tucked into downtown Glendale's oldest commercial building (c. 1900) is a little bit of Germany, a colorful place serving schnitzel, sauerbraten, bratwurst, strudel, and other home-style favorites from Rhineland and Bavaria. Polka tunes and yodeling provide the

The menu at the Arizona Kitchen combines Native American traditions with local Arizona ingredients.

Photo: Courtesy of The Wigwam Resort

RESTAURANTS

background music, and weekends bring a strolling accordionist. Sure to catch your eye is the restaurant's vintage soda fountain. It was moved here from Florence, Arizona, where it was featured in the *Murphy's Romance*, starring James Garner and Sally Field. The menu also includes American fare such as chicken sandwiches, pasta, and burgers. *Ja wohl*, there's a good selection of German wines and beers. From the soda fountain, you can order things like cherry-flavored colas. Haus Murphy's is open for lunch daily, for dinner Monday through Saturday, and for lunch and early dinner (until 5 PM) on Sunday.

INSIDERS' TIP

The best advice we can give to visitors and newcomers who like to cruise around town for a restaurant until something strikes their fancy is to head for areas near the shopping malls, such as Metrocenter, Fiesta Mall, and Paradise Valley Mall. Other good bets: Cruise East Camelback Road in Phoenix or Scottsdale Road from Downtown to Shea Boulevard. All have good concentrations of restaurants—chains and local favorites.

Italian and Pizza

Cucina Tagliani
$$ • 17045 N. 59th Ave., Glendale
• (623) 547-2782

This Southern Italian-style restaurant is popular with West Valley families because of its great Pick-A-Pasta deal for $8.99. Diners choose from seven types of pasta and seven types of sauce, then customize their plates further with 20 different add-on items, from sausage, meatballs, and meat sauce to eggplant to bacon to scallops. Meals come with a house salad or soup, and focaccia bread. Other items such as sausage sandwiches, antipasto platters, and seafood linguine are also available. Lunch and dinner are served every day.

Mexican

Mayan's
$$ • 4323 W. Cactus Rd., Glendale
• (623) 978-5167

Formerly known as Minga's, this 12-year-old eatery serves Mexican favorites prepared without lard, additives, or fillers. In addition to combination plates and chimichangas, Mayan's has house specialties running the gamut from fajitas to halibut steak over Spanish rice to the Mighty Carne Asada (spiced beef) Burro. The restaurant's "Mesoamerican Ultra-Lite" specialties focus on vegetarian ingredients and fish prepared with an Aztec and Mayan theme. The vegetarian chimichanga, for instance, uses spiced and sautéed zucchini, bell pepper, onion, celery, carrots, and green chiles on an oven-roasted flour tortilla. Lunch and dinner are served Tuesday through Sunday.

Southwest Valley

The Arizona Kitchen
$$$–$$$$ • 300 E. Wigwam Blvd.,
Litchfield Park
• (623) 935-3811

Although this restaurant is off in distant Litchfield Park, it is well worth the drive. This centerpiece restaurant of the Wigwam resort features distinctive entrees such as sautéed medallions of turkey with jalapeño-jack cheese glaze and sun-dried cranberry ancho chile sauce; roasted pheasant glazed with coconut, jalapeños, and mint; and filet mignon dusted with chile powder in a prickly pear Merlot sauce. Plus, the restaurant often uses produce grown just a few miles away in the West Valley's agricultural fields. A dessert treat is a chocolate kahlua taco—the taco shell is a dark chocolate and the filling is fruit and Kahlua mousse. Dinner is served Tuesday through Sunday.

Nightlife

"Work hard and play hard!"

That's the motto of the people who frequent the Valley's nightclubs. Mostly, it's a young crowd out there—people with the energy to trip the light fantastic and dance until the cows come home. These are the folks that work a busy day, run home and change their clothes, and head out to meet up with friends to explore the good times available around the Valley.

Music lovers are fortunate to live here. On any given night, popular music concerts and other types of performances take place at America West Arena, Arizona Veterans Memorial Coliseum, the Celebrity Theatre, Chandler Center for the Arts, Gammage Auditorium, the Red River Music Hall, Scottsdale Center for the Arts, and the Sundome Center for the Performing Arts, among others. In the summer, you can add such outdoor venues as Desert Sky Pavilion and Mesa Amphitheater to the mix. That's not to mention the very occasional use of the 70,000-seat Sun Devil Stadium for occasional mega-concerts by the likes of the Rolling Stones or U2. See our Arts or Spectator Sports chapters for information on getting tickets.

Sometimes nightlife turns up in odd venues. In Glendale, the Public Library has a weekly folk-music coffeehouse. Every now and then, a pop concert like Tony Bennett or k.d. lang will show up at Phoenix Symphony Hall. The America West Arena will feature everything from the circus to Faith Hill and Tina Turner.

In addition, the Valley has just about every type of nightclub imaginable—country, rock, blues, comedy, sports. It also seems that every resort has a lounge with performers who are a far cry from Bill Murray's lounge lizard parody.

Unless you plan to visit downtown Tempe, don't expect to hit a lot of spots on a single club crawl. Things are just too spread out for that. Downtown Tempe, however, is just off the Arizona State University campus and as a result has numerous bars, nightclubs, and coffeehouses within easy walking distance of each other. Sometimes it seems the whole city is pounding out music.

Drinking and driving is never a good idea and in the Valley of the Sun, it's particularly bad. Valley police frequently set up roadblocks to check for DUI infractions, and they snag quite a few. There have been a number of high-profile drunk driving deaths that have stirred community resentment against drunk drivers. Call a cab or use the designated driver plan if you're out drinking.

For the most part, cover charges for the places listed in this chapter will be in the $3 to $10 range. Those prices go up when clubs are offering name acts.

The following list is purely subjective, a sample of what we consider the best places Phoenix and the Valley of the Sun have to offer, although there are many fine establishments not listed here. These are the places to start. Of course, we have the tourist havens like the Hard Rock Cafe on Camelback Road, just east of 24th Street in Phoenix. But since you know what to expect from the typical tourist destinations, in this chapter we'll stick to nonchain nightlife. When you're looking for current nighttime things to do, the best places to look are the calendars in Phoenix New Times, Get Out, and The Rep. All of them are published weekly on Thursday and are available for free at convenience stores and in their own freestanding boxes.

Blues Nightclubs

Phoenix

Char's Has the Blues
4631 N. Seventh Ave., Phoenix
• **(602) 230-0205**
Char's Has the Blues has a friendly, crowded, smoky atmosphere where the blues make you sweat and the brews cool you off. Char's has been voted "Best Blues R&B bar" for years in the weekly papers. You're not here to see concerts, but to dance on the postage-stamp-size dance floor when one of the local

bands gets really hot. When the bands are off stage, the atmosphere is conducive to genuine conversation like a regular corner bar. No cover on Mondays and Wednesdays.

Southeast Valley

The Melody Lounge
1126 N. Scottsdale Rd., Tempe
• **(480) 829-8129**
The Melody Lounge features blues and roots-rock bands two to three nights a week and disc jockeys through the weekend. The club's ambiance for blues is swell—you can play pool, enjoy a drink, and listen.

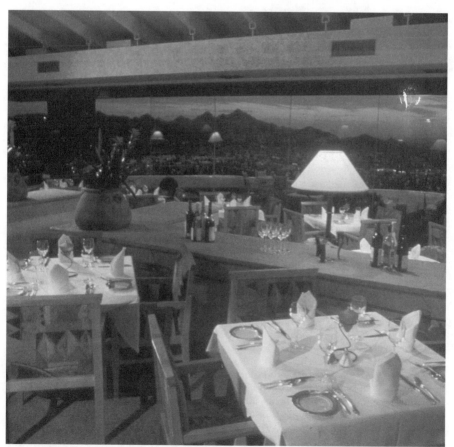

Set high on North Mountain, Different Pointe of View offers a popular lounge where the Khani Cole Band performs.

Photo: Courtesy of Different Pointe of View

Northeast Valley

The Blue Note Cool Cafe
8040 E. McDowell Rd., Scottsdale
• (480) 946-6227

Local blues bands play nightly at this club, which is funky by Scottsdale's immaculately hip standards. The Blue Note also hosts an open-mike night for up-and-coming blues talent. If you like the blues, you can't go wrong. Look for a $5 cover charge on the weekends.

Brew Pubs

Phoenix

Southeast Valley

Copper Canyon Brewing & Ale House
5940 W. Ray Rd., Chandler
• (480) 705-9700

Use Copper Canyon's six varieties of beer to wash down a menu that includes everything from stuffed salmon and veggie pasta to steaks, burgers, and pizzas. Our taste tends toward the Foothills Honey Blonde and the A-1 Amber Ale, which both have a pleasant tang to them. Although it's situated in a strip mall, Copper Canyon seems anything but storelike. The atmosphere is cool and dark, a refuge for enjoying the brews, and it attracts a mixture of young and middle-age professionals.

Four Peaks Brewing Co.
1340 E. Eighth St., Tempe
• (480) 303-9967

Four Peaks Brewing Co. is situated in what used to be the Borden's Creamery in Tempe, giving the place a hip, funky industrial warehouse atmosphere. Even the 72-foot-long bar seems lost in all that space. The brew pub caters to college and young urban professional crowds with 10 different varieties of beer. We recommend the Kiltlifter, a Scottish ale, for its rich body and the Four Peaks Pale, a pale ale, for its lighter taste. The brew pub serves food, including gourmet-style pizzas and sandwiches. Best of all, though, is the shrine to Elvis almost tucked away behind the right side of the bar (as you look in from the entrance). This kitschy

attraction takes on special significance after a pint or two.

Gordon Biersch Brewery & Restaurant
420 S. Mill Ave., Tempe
• (480) 736-0033

Part brew-pub, part restaurant, and part lounge, come here to hear live rock, blues, and reggae bands here a story above the Mill Avenue scene. The kitchen features American cuisine with Asian influences.

Mill Avenue Beer Company
605 S. Mill Ave., Tempe
• (480) 829-6775

With 100 beers available, the Mill Avenue Beer Company is really a brew-drinker's paradise. In addition, the menu is full of the munchies that go great with beer—from onion rings to bratwurst. Add in a friendly atmosphere, and Nirvana's just around the corner.

Coffeehouses

Phoenix

Fiddler's Dream
1702 E. Glendale Ave., Phoenix
• (602) 997-9795

This isn't your Seattle-type coffeehouse; it's a folk-music coffeehouse where the music is front and center. There's no sound system, and performers are asked to leave their amplifiers home too. The kitchen produces a few snacks to go with the java, and the atmosphere is friendly and relaxed. The low-tech presentation makes it the perfect place to listen, and then converse after a set.

Southeast Valley

Coffee Plantation
680 S. Mill Ave., Tempe
• (480) 829-7878

The Coffee Plantation chain took off after Seattle validated coffee for what's come to be known as Generation X. The one in Tempe remains an integral part of the Valley's music scene, offering an acoustic-music venue amid the electric clangor of Mill Avenue. The building has an open, airy feeling to it, while the

INSIDERS' TIP
Buy tickets to concert events in advance. You can usually save several dollars per ticket by not waiting until the day of the show.

NIGHTLIFE

Reservations Bet on Gaming

Valley folks used to satiate their desire for gambling by heading to Laughlin, Nevada, for a weekend getaway with the one-armed bandits, games of chance, and card games. Or they'd drive (or fly) a little deeper into Nevada and hit Las Vegas, the way much of the rest of America does. Otherwise, the alternatives were charity casino games played for prizes, not money, or betting on the races at Turf Paradise and Phoenix Greyhound Park (see our Spectator Sports chapter).

Now, though, casinos are much closer at hand. Four local Indian reservations have turned to casinos as a means of generating revenue and employment for their tribal members.

The path to the casinos was an interesting one that started with on-reservation bingo parlors back in the 1970s. The number of tribes with gaming activities grew steadily, until there was a court challenge. As tribes searched for new revenue sources in the wake of Reagan administration cutbacks, gaming became the hot solution. A federal court ruled in 1983 that states had no jurisdiction over regulatory affairs on Indian reservations. That's when Fort McDowell Indian Community, northeast of Fountain Hills, opened its Ba' Ja Bingo Hall. The first Indian bingo parlor serving the Valley was an instant success.

The growth of Indian gaming nationwide prompted Congress to pass the Federal Indian Gaming Regulatory Act of 1988. This created three classes of Indian gaming. Class 1 involved traditional or ceremonial Native American gaming, and it is completely under the jurisdiction of the tribes. Class 2 covers bingo and such numbers games as Lotto and non-bank card games (where the card players play against each other and not the house). This second class is under the jurisdiction of the National Indian Gaming Commission, which was also established by the 1988 law. Class 3 covers high-stakes gaming, including casinos, racing, blackjack and baccarat-style card games, slot machines, and jai alai. To run such games, a tribe must forge a compact with the state in which it is located.

The national law set conflicts in motion between Arizona and tribes that offered gaming. Asserting their sovereignty, tribes such as the Fort McDowell Indian Community began to offer video slots in addition to non-bank card games and bingo even though compacts had not been struck with the state. The state argued that Congress had no power to mandate negotiations between sovereign entities.

On May 12, 1992, federal officials raided reservations around the state and impounded video gaming machines. Fort McDowell was the site of the only major

Opened in 1994, Harrah's Ak-Chin brought a brand name to the local gaming scene.

(Continued on next page)

resistance. Tribal members used heavy equipment to blockade the trucks into which federal authorities had loaded the 349 machines seized from Fort McDowell's little casino. The tension was thick. A 10-day cooling off period was ordered. Tribes marched at the State Capitol.

The standoff is generally credited with forcing the state's hand in negotiating gaming compacts. Public sentiment appeared to strongly favor Indian gaming.

Eventually, tribal officials agreed to allow the machines to be shipped off the reservations until a gaming compact was reached. Poker and gaming continued at Fort McDowell even when the machines were impounded. The machines were returned to the tribe on August 27, 1992, in anticipation of a gaming compact. The compact was signed November 25, 1992. The tribe was allowed 475 video gaming machines. Fort McDowell was expected to earn $850 million over the course of the 10-year compact.

In the wake of the Fort McDowell compact, two other tribes near the Valley—the Gila River Indian Community and the Ak-Chin community—also signed compacts. Gila River's casino opened in a tent (or a sprung structure, as the industry calls them) and was so successful that it opened two permanent casinos in 1997.

The future of Indian gaming in Arizona is an open question. The Arizona Gaming Department held in August 1997 that poker games must be regulated by the state and not by the tribes, a position, that, if upheld, could invalidate existing gaming compacts and, in the most extreme possibility, end Indian gaming in the state.

Undaunted, the Salt River Pima-Maricopa Indian Community opened the doors to a casino for card games in 1998.

Here is a list of the Valley's nearby casinos:

Casino Arizona at Salt River
Salt River Pima-Maricopa Indian Reservation, 92nd St. and McKellips Rd.
• (480) 850-7777

The newest casino in the Valley is a large tent with 20,000 square feet of floor space and 240 tons of air-conditioning capacity. The casino opened in 1998 and features 42 card tables for all varieties of poker. There is also an instructional table, a piano bar lounge, and the Arizona Bistro Cafe for informal dining. To get there, take the Red Mountain Freeway to the Pima Freeway and head north one exit to McKellips Road. Head east to 92nd Street. The tent is impossible to miss as it stands in otherwise empty fields and is visible from the freeway. A permanent structure will open it doors in 2001.

Fort McDowell Casino
State Route. 87 and Fort McDowell Rd., Fort McDowell • (480) 843-3678

The granddaddy of local casinos is popularly known as "the Fort." It started out as the 17,000-square-foot Ba' Ja Bingo Hall in 1983. Today, Fort McDowell Casino features 150,000 square feet of floor space that handles an estimated 10,000 customers each day. The Fort features 475 video gaming machines, poker, keno, high-stakes bingo, and pari-mutuel wagering. It also has four food outlets—the Ba' Ja Food Court, the Deli, the Rotisserie, and the Red Rock Cafe, which features a seafood buffet every Tuesday and Friday night. To get there from downtown Phoenix, take the Red Mountain Freeway to the Pima Freeway and head north to McDowell Road. Take McDowell Road east to State Route 87 (the Beeline Highway), and turn left. Those coming from the northeast Valley can take Shea Boulevard out to the Beeline Highway and head north. The casino is on the southwest corner of the intersection of Fort McDowell Road and the Beeline Highway.

Gila River Casinos Arizona at Wild Horse Pass
I-10 and Maricopa Rd., Chandler • (520) 796-7777, (800) 946-4452

This permanent structure near the site of the original Gila River Casino tent boasts 167,000 square feet of floor space. It features a live poker room, high-stakes poker, a $50,000 live keno jackpot, a 1,500-seat bingo hall, and 500 video gaming machines. In addition, a restaurant, deli, and sports bar give patrons a chance to break from the gaming. To get there from central Phoenix, take Interstate 10 to the Maricopa Road exit and head west. Wild Horse Pass is on the north side of the road.

Gila River Casinos Arizona at Vee Quiva
51st Ave., Laveen • (520) 946-4452, (800) 946-4452

With the 66,000-square-foot Vee Quiva casino, the west Valley got into the gaming mode in December 1997. Vee Quiva features live poker, keno, a 500-seat bingo hall and 400 video gaming machines. There's also a restaurant, deli, and coffee shop. To get there from central Phoenix, take I-10 west to the 51st Avenue exit and head south. The casino, which has no physical address, is 4 miles south of Baseline Road on the east side.

Harrah's Phoenix Ak-Chin Casino
15406 Maricopa Rd., Maricopa • (520) 802-5000

Opened in 1994, Harrah's Ak-Chin brought a brand-name to the local Indian gaming scene. The casino offers 475 video gaming machines, keno, poker, and a 500-seat bingo hall. Food is available at the Range Steakhouse, the Dealers Choice Deli, the Harvest, and the Coyote Crossing Snack Bar. You'll also find a lounge, live entertainment, and a dance floor. To get there from central Phoenix, take I-10 to the Queen Creek Road exit (Exit 164). Turn right and follow Queen Creek Road to Maricopa Road and take a left. The casino is about 17 miles from the freeway exit.

---

lighting makes it feel like a shady refuge from Arizona's intense sun. There are tables outside as well.

Essenza Coffeehouse
1350 S. Longmore St., Mesa
• (480) 461-0445

One of the great attractions of Essenza Coffeehouse (besides the java, of course) are events like the poetry slam, which turns poetry reading into a wrestling-like competition. You have to see it to understand. Essenza also features acoustic music and an open-mike night.

Gold Bar
1707 E. Southern Ave., Tempe
• (480) 839-3082

Housed in a former bank, The Gold Bar offers opportunities to people watch, enjoy live music, or drink coffee in the vault. The atmosphere is relaxed and friendly.

Undici Undici Art Gallery & Coffee House
1111 S. Longmore St., Mesa
• (480) 962-4224

Undici Undici is another casual, yet upscale coffeehouse with the added twist of being an art gallery as well. You can find unusual gifts,

often by local artisans. A cold case full of mouthwatering desserts is available to accompany that perfect cup of coffee, and the live acoustic music.

Comedy Clubs

Southeast Valley

The Improv
930 E. University Dr., Tempe
• (480) 921-9877

In the Cornerstone Mall, within sight of Sun Devil Stadium, the Improv continues to attract crowds, while most of its mid- to late '80s rivals have disappeared from the Valley scene. Maybe the secret is location, or maybe it's an example of the Improv's brand-name appeal. Of course, the lineup of comics might have something to do with it. For example, in 1998 Rob Schneider of *Saturday Night Live* and *Men Behaving Badly* did his first nightclub show in six years at the Tempe club. The Improv, with a capacity of 400, books comedians from Thursday through Sunday. Dinner shows are at 8 PM each night, and Friday and Saturday feature a non-dinner show at 10 PM.

Country Nightclubs

Phoenix

Toolies Country
4231 W. Thomas Rd., Phoenix
• (602) 272-3100

When you step into the parking lot of Toolies Plaza, you'd never imagine that the strip mall holds one of the major country nightclubs of the Southwest. Step inside, though, and you know you're in for some serious honky-tonkin'. You can drink, eat, dance, and listen to top regional bands and the occasional national act. Owner Bill Bachand has an ear for young talent and got the likes of Garth Brooks, Patty Loveless, and a host of others to play here before they broke into the big-time. People still talk about the Brooks show at Toolies.

Mr. Lucky's
3660 N.W. Grand Ave., Phoenix
• (602) 246-0686

Mr. Lucky's owner, J. David Sloan, is a veteran country performer on the Valley scene. He's been around since Waylon Jennings was a local fixture, and one of his many bands backed up Lyle Lovett on his debut album.

The club has been a country mainstay even longer than Sloan. There's live music and dancing. If you're completely loco, Mr. Lucky's offers live bull riding out in the parking lot on the weekends.

Graham Central Station
33rd Ave. and Indian School Rd., Phoenix
• (602) 279-4226

If you're young, rowdy, and want to meet jean-wrapped, boot-wearing members of the opposite sex, the mammoth country palace known as Graham Central Station is your best bet. Blaring music played by a DJ sets the scene for the dancers and revelers.

Northeast Valley

Greasewood Flats
27000 N. Alma School Parkway, Scottsdale
• (480) 585-7227

This is as close as you can get to the Arizona cowboy experience. Way out by Pinnacle Peak, this joint is mostly open corrals with picnic tables, hay bales, and bonfires. You can dine on burgers, but people come here to dance to the live music under the stars. The turnoff is easy to miss and there's no telephone (the number above rings at another nearby bar). This is where the locals go and don't tell out-of-towners.

Buffalo Chip Saloon
6811 E. Cave Creek, Cave Creek
• (480) 488-9118

The cowboy boots nailed to the roof are a clue that you're in the right place. Dine on barbecue, dance to live music, and enjoy the cowboy culture.

Southeast Valley

Rockin' Rodeo
7850 S. Priest Rd., Tempe
• (480) 496-0799

Set up by the same people who created Graham Central Station in Phoenix, Rockin' Rodeo—built in the '90s—is even a more frenetic, bright lights, big city place. This is the place to meet people poured into stylish jeans. Neon art of wild horses and cowboys give the place a contemporary feel. The warehouse-size dance hall pulses to the Nashville beat, provided by DJs. Try the arm-wrestling machine or show up for a country-dance lesson. The club also goes in for events such as hard-body contests.

Country City
30 S. Robson St., Mesa
• (480) 644-1524

Country City is cut from the old cloth. It's as much a neighborhood bar as it is a nightclub, but there's live music, camaraderie, and dance lessons. True to the Mesa style, it's a humble sort of place with a down-home flavor that's missing in the big barns.

Northeast Valley

The Rockin' Horse
7316 E. Stetson Dr., Scottsdale
• (480) 949-0992

The Rockin' Horse is not strictly a country nightclub, although it has a country DJ most nights and a country band on weekends. This is a great place to hear American-roots music of any stripe. Steve Earle has played here, and so has Marshall Crenshaw. There's a postage-stamp-size dance floor that gets crowbar-tight when there's a big act, and the sight lines are bad when you're more than few dozen feet from the stage. Yet, the atmosphere and music make it worth the visit.

An evening of people watching can provide ample entertainment in Downtown Tempe. Grab a table at a sidewalk restaurant or hop from lounges to coffee shops in Tempe's easy-to-reach evening spots.

Photo: W. Scott Mitchell, courtesy of Tempe Convention and Visitors Bureau

NIGHTLIFE

Two clubs in one location, Radius and Axis are popular night spots.

Photo: Courtesy of Radius-Axis, Margo Media

Handlebar-J
7116 E. Becker Ln., Scottsdale
• (480) 948-0110

The Handlebar-J is another place with a long history. It's been in the Herndon family for two generations. It does a respectable restaurant trade, but its hallmark has been the Herndon family's music. Ray Herndon, who has played with J. David Sloan, Lyle Lovett, and McBride and the Ride, may be the best known of the Herndon Brothers Band members. Although the whole clan rarely gets together on stage, the Herndon Brothers Band remains among the Valley's country royalty. They play Wednesday through Sunday, while the other nights are filled with karaoke and dance lessons.

Dance Clubs

Southeast Valley

Axis/Radius
7340 E. Indian Plaza, Scottsdale
• (480) 966-2020

These two very fun, very cool clubs sit side by side and are connected by a glass catwalk.

Radius, featuring an ambiance which combines the Jetsons world with a retro '60s feeling, is the place for techno dance music, accompanied by a futuristic light show. Axis features live music, pool tables, dining, and an open-air patio.

Club Rio
430 N. Scottsdale Rd., Tempe
• (480) 894-0533

Club Rio sits on the edge of the Salt River, or Rio Salado, hence its name. The place is of airline-hangar proportions (35,000 square feet), so the dance floor is big. National acts from Todd Rundgren to Ice-T have played here, but most nights it's packed with dancers from ASU looking to groove in all the right places to top 40, techno, alternative, and modern rock. The outdoor terrace is an especially appealing place on cool evenings, even though it's right under the flight path to Sky Harbor Airport.

Northeast Valley

Anderson's Fifth Estate
6820 E. Fifth Ave., Scottsdale
• (480) 994-4168

Crowded little Anderson's always has a

good DJ mix whether it's on classic alternative night, swing night, or trash disco night. The dress on trash disco night is particularly outrageous, almost a game of "how high can you make a platform shoe before a person falls off?" In addition to the DJs, Anderson's features local bands on Thursdays and the occasional concert night.

Bobby McGee's
7000 E. Shea Blvd., Scottsdale
• (480) 998-5591

The dance floor's the thing at Bobby McGee's, although this is also a restaurant and bar. DJs get the crowds pumped up. McGee's also holds events such as martini nights and comedy nights, occasionally bringing in local acts.

Buzz Funbar
10345 N. Scottsdale Rd., Scottsdale
• (480) 991-3866

A relative newcomer to the scene, this upscale club has dancers moving to the groove of today's Top 40. The place also features a comfy upstairs room to hang out in.

Jazz Nightclubs

Phoenix

Different Pointe of View
11111 N. Seventh St., Phoenix
• (602) 863-0912

With any luck, Khani Cole and her band are still at Different Pointe of View when you read this. Her two albums on a small jazz label have drawn some favorable attention nationwide, and who knows when she'll itch to wander. She'll have to wander far, though, to find a better situation than the lounge at the Different Pointe of View restaurant. The room overlooks the Valley lights for a romantic atmosphere that would augment any singer's performance. It's part of the Pointe Hilton Tapatio Cliffs Resort, so you'll feel a little better (and more romantic) if you dress up a bit. In the Valley's casual style, anything from business casual attire to dress clothes fills that bill. As of this writing, Cole performs there Wednesday through Saturday.

INSIDERS' TIP

When attending big events at America West Arena and the Bank One Ballpark in Phoenix, get downtown early, park, and enjoy a restaurant meal. You'll get more for your dollar than you will at the pricey concession stands, and you'll avoid parking hassles. To avoid traffic on the way back, stop off for dessert or coffee.

Southeast Valley

Balboa Cafe
404 S. Mill Ave., Tempe
• (480) 966-1300

The Balboa Cafe isn't strictly a jazz club. However, jazz fans will want to note that the format features jazz in the early evening and alternative rock in the late hours. At least one night a week (it varies as to which night), a jazz band will be the featured act all night. Another of Mill Avenue's many hot spots, this one features both coffee and alcohol, a cyber-cafe area, and bar food.

Beeloe's Cafe & Underground Bar
501 S. Mill Ave., Tempe
• (480) 894-1230

This upscale spot is built below street level and a McDonald's, hence the name. Live bands provide a laid-back background of jazz and rhythm and blues as patrons dine and drink. The atmosphere is friendly, even cozy, with the sophistication that makes a jazz club, well, jazzy.

Latin Clubs

Northeast Valley

Tapas Papa Frita
6810 E. Fifth Ave., Scottsdale
• (480) 424-7777

Tapas Papa Frita is a restaurant that serves traditional Spanish food such as paella valenciana amid a contemporary Spanish decor. It's also the best place in the Valley to hear Latin music. We're taking a global view of Latin here, because Tapas not only features salsa and merengue, but also Brazilian flavors.

Southeast Valley

The Hola Cafe
2515 N. Scottsdale Rd., Scottsdale
• (480) 945-5900

This is one of the happening spots on the salsa dance scene. The club serves dinner, but

The Glories of Valley Pop

Phoenix isn't known as a regional music center the way that New Orleans, Detroit, San Francisco, Austin, or even (shudder) Tucson are. However, the Valley has produced members of both the Rock and Roll Hall of Fame and the Country Music Hall of Fame.

The hits that made Duane Eddy a rock 'n' roll guitar phenomenon were all recorded in an unobtrusive little studio called Ramsey Audio Recorders, which sat at the corner of Seventh Street and Weldon Avenue in Phoenix until 1964. Eddy racked up 13 Top 40 hits—including "Rebel Rouser," "Ramrod," and "Forty Miles of Bad Road"—while recording at Ramsey's from 1957 to 1962. The studio's unique reverb system played an important part in Eddy's bottom-heavy guitar sound. Producer Lee Hazlewood set up a speaker to feed the sound in the studio into an old water tank out in the building's parking lot. A microphone placed inside the tank recorded the original sound and its reverberations. Sometimes, Hazlewood would have to chase birds off the tank so that their chirping wouldn't bleed into the recordings.

Eddy was still in his teens when he met Hazlewood, an ambitious radio disc jockey in Coolidge, Arizona. Hazlewood liked Eddy's music and got him some bookings in Phoenix. Hazlewood became a DJ at Phoenix's Top 40 powerhouse KRUX and produced and co-wrote Sanford Clark's 1956 hit, "The Fool." Hazlewood struck out to Los Angeles to work for Dot Records for a year, and when he returned it was to work primarily as a record producer in Phoenix. By this point, Eddy was quite popular in Phoenix's booming country scene, and Hazlewood told him to write an instrumental. On their second shot, Eddy turned out "Rebel Rouser" and became Phoenix's first bona-fide rock 'n' roll guitar hero.

Marty Robbins, the country singer best known for the 1959 cowboy ballad "El Paso," was born Martin David Robinson in 1925 in Glendale, or more properly, in an area later annexed by Glendale. Robbins' early life was one of poverty, eased a bit by his grandfather's tales of the Old West. Robbins joined the Navy toward the end of World War II. Returning to civilian life in 1947, he took up the guitar and songwriting. He didn't abandon his day jobs, but did perform casual gigs around Phoenix, eventually landing a spot on KPHO radio, and eventually joining "Country Caravan," a show on KPHO-TV. Robbins' big break came in 1951 when Little Jimmy Dickens did a guest spot on "Country Caravan." Impressed by the Valley native, Dickens suggested that Columbia Records should sign Robbins. The major label took Dickens' advice, and soon Robbins left for his first recording session in Los Angeles. By 1953, he was a member of the Grand Ole Opry.

Phoenix has always had a thing for country, and both Eddy and Robbins could be on either side of the fence dividing country from rock 'n' roll. The city's cowboy past kept it firmly linked to country music, even though the Western aspect became an ever-decreasing part of country music (except for the hats so many male country singers wear). Waylon Jennings worked in the Valley for six years in the early '60s between working with Buddy Holly in the late '50s and signing with Chet Atkins at RCA in 1965. Tanya Tucker only played the Valley for a heartbeat but has been remembered as almost a native daughter ever since. Much later on, Lyle Lovett cut his first country album here, working with a group of musicians who knew Waylon back when.

However, there were always other kinds of music in town as well. Dyke and the Blazers may not be as well-known as the Hall of Famers, but they nearly immortalized a Phoenix street and nobody knows it! The Blazers were the O'Jays' backup band in the mid-'60s, but on one tour Arlester "Dyke" Christian and the Blazers were stranded in Phoenix when the O'Jays couldn't come up with the money to bring them back to Philadelphia. They made the most of a bad deal and began playing gigs in town. Phoenix became Dyke's home, and by 1967 he and the band had created the song "Funky Broadway" to celebrate the main drag through south Phoenix. It was a rhythm and blues hit for the Blazers, but Wilson Pickett's version of the song was even bigger, crossing over to the pop charts. Dyke and the Blazers had a few other hits, but Dyke was shot to death in Phoenix in 1971.

While Dyke was in the process of settling in Phoenix, another band, which would eventually become Alice Cooper, was doing everything it could to get thrown out. Neither the band nor its lead singer was then known as Alice Cooper, but even so, the lead singer says, they were definitely not in step with the Valley of the '60s. Burr-cut Republican Senator and presidential candidate Barry Goldwater was Arizona's political hero, and long-haired fellows who enjoyed the Yardbirds were just a bit too far out. Before they left town for fame and fortune, the band recorded some demos

(Continued on next page)

Alice Cooper is among the pop bands with origins in Phoenix.

Photo: Courtesy CBS Records, Inc.

NIGHTLIFE

at Ramsey's Audio Recorders at its then-new studio farther north on Seventh Street. (Alice Cooper wasn't the only rock group from Phoenix to trade in outrage. Members of two popular Phoenix bands who relocated to San Francisco birthed the Tubes.)

A big change happened in the '80s. Where it had always been wise for acts to leave the Valley if they wanted to attract a national following, the Valley suddenly became big enough to nurture its own bands. The Meat Puppets, a post-punk trio that Nirvana's Kurt Cobain would emulate, grew up here and left the Valley only to tour to a growing legion of underground rock fans. They were prophets without too much honor at home, but they were big enough to get London Records to sign them in 1990. A number of their albums earned glowing reviews in magazines like *Rolling Stone*. Cobain had them join in on some numbers on his band's MTV Unplugged album.

Another group that didn't have to leave the Valley to be signed by a national label was Flotsam and Jetsam, which hooked up with Elektra in 1988 and MCA in 1989. Although this metal quintet never quite broke beyond cult-hero status, its original bass player Jason Newsted joined metal superstars Metallica.

The most successful of the rock groups that didn't leave home were the tragicomic Gin Blossoms. A group that became synonymous with Tempe's "independent rock" scene, the quintet played a jangly brand of melodic rock that owed more than a passing nod to REM. Although they were the kingfish of this small pond, they always seemed to be on the verge of breaking up. Band members would stare daggers at one another on stage. Doug Hopkins, the band's most accomplished songwriter, was depressive and an alcoholic. After the group signed with A&M in 1990, his pugnacious attitude in the recording studio prompted the other members to kick him out of the band, even though he'd written most of the songs that were featured on the band's debut album. Hopkins formed another band and eventually left that one, too, apparently almost incapacitated by his own demons. He shot himself to death on the same December weekend in 1993 that Frank Zappa died. The rest of the Gin Blossoms issued a press release eulogizing Hopkins and continued to tour to keep the album selling. "New Miserable Experience," the Blossoms' debut, sold more than two million copies. The band's second album, "Congratulations, I'm Sorry," didn't do as well, and the road-worn band finally broke up in 1996.

CeCe Peniston, the rhythm and blues diva, also came out of Phoenix. A 1987 graduate of Trevor Browne High School on Phoenix's west side, she became Miss Black Arizona in 1989. When she sang background vocals on an album by Phoenix rapper Overweight Pooch, a talent scout at A&M was so impressed he asked Peniston to record. The result was "Finally," which became the title cut of her debut album in 1992.

This isn't the whole story of the Valley's music scene—which has shown a surprising love for jazz and blues—it's just the story of a few of the acts that made some waves on the pop charts. Not bad for a place that isn't known for its music.

NIGHTLIFE

the dancing starts at 10 PM. This is a great spot to watch people who really know how to dance.

The Bash on Ash
230 W. 5th St., Tempe
• (480) 966-8200

Ready to learn some new Latin or swing dance steps? Tuesday and Sunday nights feature salsa music with dance lessons from 8 to 9 PM. After 9 PM, you can take to the floor and move those hips.

Lounges

Phoenix

Chez Nous
675 W. Indian School Rd., Phoenix
• (602) 266-7372

Do you want to travel back to the early '60s? To the days of Kennedy's Camelot, when

Frank Sinatra and the Rat Pack were the models of the high life? Then clink a martini glass at Chez Nous. No, this isn't an incredible simulation '60s style; the club hasn't been touched by time since it opened up about three decades ago. You just know the banquettes and flocked wallpaper have been privy to thousands of illicit liaisons and one-for-the-road kiss-offs. Performers, usually duos or solos, play martini music every night.

The Merc Bar
2501 E. Camelback Rd., Phoenix
• (602) 508-9449
No advertising. No sign on the door. This lounge is hidden at the Camelback Esplanade beside the Houston's restaurant. Inside you'll find plush leather sofas, a dark soothing ambiance, and perfectly mixed cocktails. It's very chic.

Pop Concert Venues

Phoenix

America West Arena
201 E. Jefferson St.,
Phoenix
• (602) 379-7800
Built as the home of the popular Phoenix Suns basketball team, America West Arena can hold about 19,000 people in the basketball configuration, and a few thousand fewer for concerts, depending on the size of the performers' stage. For the best views and sound, you'll want to avoid the floor and the upper bowl. Head for seats about midway back in the lower bowl. Still, it's an arena, so sound quality generally is tolerable at best, but you're there for the spectacle, right?

Arizona Veterans Memorial Coliseum
1826 W. McDowell Rd., Phoenix
• (602) 258-6711
The old home of the Phoenix Suns also serves as an occasional concert venue and does nightly duty during the two weeks of the Arizona State Fair in October and November. The fair brings in all sorts of music and the prices are quite reasonable. This hall has seen better days, and the sound is very mushy the farther

you go from the stage. The best seats are in the lower rows about a quarter-way back from the stage.

Desert Sky Pavilion
2121 N. 83rd Ave., Phoenix
• (602) 254-7200
When it opened in November 1990, this amphitheater was touted as a year-round venue. After all, the Valley's weather would make outdoor wintertime concerts viable. Maybe so, but what touring act is geared up to do outdoor shows in the winter? Scratch that idea. Still, this is a classy venue, and considering its size (about 22,000 people at capacity), it's easy to get into and out of. The sound is pretty good, especially at dead center in the covered seats.

Celebrity Theatre
440 N. 32nd St., Phoenix
• (602) 267-9373
When it opened as the Star Theatre in the 1960s, this venue was the height of chic, a theater in the round setup with a stage that rotates on a turntable (although some acts opt not to have it turn). For many years, it was the premier small hall (about 2,500 seats) in Phoenix, especially for acts that could take advantage of its intimacy. The sound system strains when a heavy act plays there, but when the act is more mellow, the effect is absolute magic. Recently acquired by Toolies Country owner Bill Bachand, the theater has seen a bit of a return to its glory days. The Celebrity is a sentimental favorite of longtime Phoenix residents, although they are wary of the deteriorating neighborhood that surrounds it.

Orpheum Theatre
203 W. Adams St., Phoenix
• (602) 252-9678
The City of Phoenix bought the ancient (in Valley terms) movie theater in 1984 and reopened it in 1997 after extensive cleaning and refurbishing. Originally opened in 1929, the theater's furnishings and decor hearken back to the era when movie theaters were meant to be an experience. Check out the drifting clouds on the ceiling, generated by a projector. The 1,400-seat theater is now home to a variety of

INSIDERS' TIP
Dehydration is a real and serious concern in the desert heat. If you attend outdoor events in the summertime, bring water and avoid alcohol, which will dehydrate you quickly. Some concert venues are strict about what people can bring in and will inspect what you carry. Generally, they allow clear plastic water bottles with unbroken seals. When in doubt, call ahead.

NIGHTLIFE

performing arts events and is on the National Register of Historic Places.

Web Theater
600 E. Van Buren St., Phoenix
• (602) 253-7100

Web Theater is another venue with a history. Back in the 1930s through the '50s, Phoenix had no separate concert venues. The 2,000-seat auditorium at Phoenix Union High School became the city's substitute, bringing in the big names of the era. The property went unused for many years. With a new coat of paint, a lot of cleaning, and a modern sound system, Web Theater has become a good, downtown venue for touring contemporary jazz and roots-rock acts. The facility has also been updated for cybercasting concert events.

Southeast Valley

Chandler Center for the Arts
250 N. Arizona Ave., Chandler
• (480) 786-2680

A pleasant, community hall of about 1,500 seats, the Chandler Center hosts nostalgic pop events and the occasional contemporary touring act. Two seating sections are on turntables that can be turned around to make the hall smaller and more intimate. The acoustics are fairly good.

Gammage Auditorium
Mill Ave. and
Apache Blvd., Tempe
• (480) 965-3434

Frank Lloyd Wright designed this circular building. At roughly 3,000 seats, Gammage Auditorium feels intimate even in the balconies. It's not particularly welcoming to louder acts, but Bruce Springsteen's "acoustic" tour and Laurie Anderson's controlled technological avant-pop proved that this venue is just as good for live pop music as it is for the arts. You can catch touring road companies from Broadway like *The Lion King* and *Phantom of the Opera* as well as performances by opera divas and classical virtuosos.

Mesa Amphitheater
Center St. and University Dr., Mesa
• (480) 644-2560

There are no seats in this 4,000-capacity

amphitheater, just a pleasant grassy slope. So stretch out, watch the stars, and enjoy the music. This is the place to catch acts on their way up and acts on their way down. It's very casual, and people bring blankets.

Red River Music Hall
730 N. Mill Ave., Tempe
• (480) 829-6779

A 1,000-seat theater, the Music Hall was known as the Red River Opry when it opened, and its main stock-in-trade was a troupe that performed a nightly, Branson-type country-music revue. On summer nights, the Opry established a series of smooth-jazz concerts and country concerts by touring national acts as well as concert dates by pop performers. These series have continued, and the name changed to better reflect the diversity of entertainment offered. There really isn't a bad seat in the house, and the sound system is among the best.

Northeast Valley

Scottsdale Center for the Arts
7380 E. Second St., Scottsdale
• (480) 994-2787

At about 800 seats, the Scottsdale Center for the Arts offers an extremely intimate atmosphere for shows by jazz and folk-music performers, and a contemporary dance series brings in national companies. Touring swing bands also play here. In the summertime, performances in the outdoor amphitheater (within walking distance in the Scottsdale municipal complex) attract acts like the Chieftains and Queen Ida and her Zydeco Band. The sound in the auditorium is stellar, and all the seats provide excellent views of the stage; the sound in the amphitheater is good.

Northwest Valley

Sundome Center for the Performing Arts
19403 R.H. Johnson Blvd., Sun City West
• (623) 975-1900

Owing to its location in a retirement community, the 7,000-seat Sundome's bill of fare leans generally toward touring pop of another

INSIDERS' TIP

In Arizona, closing time is 1 AM. That doesn't mean you can't have a good long night out, but you've got to hurry up and get out there to do it.

NIGHTLIFE

era, from the McGuire Sisters to Victor Borge, but it has seen the likes of Garrison Keillor, The Judds, and Bill Cosby.

Rock Nightclubs

Phoenix

The Mason Jar
2303 E. Indian School Rd.
• (602) 956-6271

The Mason Jar's owner, Franco Gagliano, is a colorful guy. He's been known to pull the plug on acts that peeved him. Fortunately, Gagliano is canny enough to program heavy metal, big-hair rock, and even some alternative music in this venue that looks like an oversize basement rec room. The Mason Jar also has a reputation of being a place to catch national acts on the rise. Jane's Addiction played the Mason Jar on their first trip through Phoenix. You don't have to have any body-piercing or tattoos to go to the Jar, but you might see plenty while you're there. Bring your earplugs unless you're unconcerned about hearing loss.

Modified
407 E. Roosevelt, Phoenix
• (602) 252-7664

This is the local venue for the independent labels and alternative groups from the Valley. The walls feature contemporary paintings and the crowd often spills out onto the street. Even without a liquor license, the Modified experience is urban and cool.

Southeast Valley

Gibson's
410 S. Mill Ave., Tempe
• (602) 967-1234

Gibson's has been a fixture of the ever-changing Mill Avenue scene since the previous ownership opened it up as Chuy's in the late '80s. It's one of the few places still standing that the Gin Blossoms used to play before they became recording stars. The clientele is mostly college-age, and on most nights the place is packed by cover bands who play crowd favorites. A few national touring acts play Gibson's every month. Gibson's oddest feature is a second floor that acts like a balcony above the stage.

Nita's Hideaway
1816 E. Rio Salado Parkway, Tempe
• (480) 966-7715

Grungy? Yes. Fun? You bet! This is where up-and-coming bands stop just before making it to the big time. Keep an eye on the show listings because those are the names of the bands of tomorrow.

Hollywood Alley
2610 W. Baseline Rd., Mesa
• (480) 820-7117

The decor comes right out of '70s glam-band heaven, but the music is hard rock and edge of metal. Wear your earplugs. The place gets crowded when popular local bands are playing. In many ways Hollywood Alley reflects the Valley's blue-collar love of all heavy music. On top of that, the club serves good pizza to go with the beer and music.

Long Wong's Mill Avenue
701 S. Mill Ave., Tempe
• (480) 966-3147

Long Wong's is a Valley chain of buffalo-wings joints. The Mill Avenue branch also happens to be a humble, down-at-the-heels center of the local music scene. Playing Long Wong's won't guarantee you a recording contract, but the acts like the Gin Blossoms, who went from Tempe to national recording fame, have all played here at one time or another. It's a casual place that's packed with students when a popular band performs.

NIGHTLIFE

Shopping

The cultural diversity of the Valley of the Sun, coupled with its cachet as a travel destination, makes for a rich and varied shopping experience. Buying locally made arts and crafts—like Native American jewelry, Mexican pottery, kachinas, cowboy art, bola ties, and cowboy boots—yields one-of-a-kind finds and lasting mementos of your trip. If you are lucky enough to catch an artisan in action, your purchase will be even more meaningful and you'll have a good story to tell the folks at home.

In addition to Southwestern goods, the metropolitan area has nearly every item imaginable, from antique heirlooms to contemporary conversation pieces, teenage trends to evening designer wear, and kitchen classics to outdoor gadgets. Moreover, shopping areas are as plentiful here as jack rabbits in spring. Venues range from historic districts whose quaint shops offer unique and, often, high-end pieces, to mega malls that entice with competitive prices and large selections.

Each of the Valley's four corners sports at least one major mall—Phoenix itself has several—with a minimum of three large department stores anchoring a multitude of smaller shops. In addition, you can find even more shopping enclaves on the streets adjacent to the malls. Choose one mall and its outskirts to explore, and you can literally wander the area all day, shopping to your heart's content—or your budget's constraints. Malls are destination points for entertainment seekers, thanks to well-rounded offerings of restaurants, fast-food courts, cinemas, arcades, and, in a few cases, even playgrounds. Plus, malls provide a cool retreat from summer's heat when the sun prevents outdoor pursuits.

The area's open-air shopping districts provide a pleasant diversion for most of the year, whether you have some serious buying in mind or are just in the mood for a stroll and some window shopping. The Valley holds its own as an antique hunting destination, with centers in Glen-

The lush flower gardens at the Biltmore Fashion Park transform shopping into a tranquil excursion.

Photo: Ralph Rippe, courtesy of Biltmore Fashion Park

dale, Scottsdale, Mesa, and elsewhere. Outlet shopping opportunities have greatly increased in the Valley in the past decade. Even though the outlet malls listed here are on the fringes of the city, they are worth the drive if you're looking for bargains.

To maximize your shopping pleasure, we provide an overview—by geographic area—of the Valley's major shopping destinations. If you are on a mission to find a certain item not mentioned here, be sure to consult the Yellow Pages or ask another Insider. Since great little stores appear in unexpected places, don't be afraid to grab a map and go exploring. As the locals have known for years, you never know what treasures you'll discover.

Phoenix

Shopping Malls

Biltmore Fashion Park
24th St. and Camelback Rd., Phoenix
• **(602) 955-8400**
• **www.biltmorefashionpark.com**

Biltmore Fashion Park's luxurious setting mimics a ritzy Paris or London shopping district. The red-brick sidewalks, shaded walkways, fountains, outdoor cafes, and distinctive storefront architecture all exude elegance and Old World charm. The mall designation may be misleading—yes, it has major department stores mixed with specialty shops, but it also offers a pleasant place to dally and meet friends, even if shopping's not the main event. Don't forget to pick up a guide to the ground's five theme gardens.

Macy's, Saks Fifth Avenue, and The Galleries of Neiman Marcus comprise the major department stores, but a big draw for Phoenix residents and international visitors alike is the selection of intimate high-end stores, which include Gucci, Escada, Ann Taylor, Moda Georgio, Polo by Ralph Lauren, Cartier, and Cole-Haan. Even children's apparel goes trendy at places like OiLily and This Little Piggy Wears Cotton. Williams-Sonoma, Pottery Barn, and Restoration Hardware are fun stops for cooking and home-decorating enthusiasts. Other draws include the Banana Republic, which offers clothing and more, and The Sharper Image, with its fascinating array of high-tech gizmos. Borders Books & Music carries more than 200,000 book, music, and video titles, as well as 2,000 periodicals in 10 languages. It often offers live music. Borders' espresso bar and the children's activity area are great hangouts.

The Biltmore Fashion Park boasts more than 70 fine stores and eating establishments in all, with restaurants clustered on the east end of the mall (see our Restaurants chapter). Fare includes Japanese, Italian, Southwestern, and Transcontinental. Stores are open daily. The

Greater Phoenix Convention & Visitors Bureau runs an information booth near Saks Fifth Avenue. Valet service and free parking, much of it shaded, is available.

Camelback Colonnade
18th St. and Camelback Rd., Phoenix
• **(602) 274-7642**

The Colonnade, one of Phoenix's older shopping centers, has undergone a variety of makeovers through the years to compete with malls in suburban growth areas. Currently, it's a pleasant, not-too-sprawling mixture of large retail stores in an open-air setting, some reached through an indoor mall entrance and some having outdoor entrances. Two of its most popular stores are E & J's Designer Shoe Outlet, with designer shoes and handbags at prices rivaling wholesale, and Last Chance Bargain Shoes & Apparel, with low prices on racks and racks of items for women, men, and children. Returned, reconditioned, and refurbished items from Nordstrom department stores around the country are constantly trickling into Last Chance. Bargain hunters beware—some of the items have been previously worn or may have flaws.

Also find an Old Navy clothing store; Best Buy appliances, music, and computers; Stroud's Linens Outlet; Staples office supplies; Men's Wearhouse, which is a perfect place to pick up a tuxedo; Ulta 3 cosmetics store; and two department stores, Mervyn's and Marshall's. If you are hungry, join the locals at the popular Miracle Mile Deli for New York-style bagels and such. The Colonnade is open daily.

Chris-Town Mall
19th Ave. and Bethany Home Rd., Phoenix
• **(602) 242-9074**

Like the Colonnade, Chris-Town has shifted its stores and reshaped its philosophy over the years to stay competitive with newer, fancier malls. It just added CostCo Wholesale to its slate of anchors, which include Montgomery Ward and Wal-Mart. It also boasts a Dillard's Clearance Center, which carries unsold new merchandise shipped in from Dillard's department stores in the region. The mall has about 150 stores, a well-landscaped interior walkway with an abundance of mature trees, and a relatively new food court. The Chris-Town complex also has two movie theaters.

COFCO Chinese Cultural Center
668 N. 44th St., Phoenix
• (602) 244-8600

This intimate shopping, restaurant, and office complex offers a unique cultural experience where East Asia design meets Western sensibilities. The bold red exterior, green roof tiles, hand-carved pagodas, Feng shui statues, and an acre of traditional Chinese Gardens offer a tranquil refuge. The most interesting store is the Ranch 99 Market, which offers traditional Asian foods and hard-to-find items, from roast ducks to live clams. Oriental Factory Direct has clothing, books, jade, Feng shui products, silk clothes, and other gift items direct from Hong Kong. The Art Gallery carries Chinese art, such as rice paper paintings. Imperial Arts and Antiques features hand-painted porcelains and figurines. Yes! I Do, a photography and wedding shop, has a gorgeous selection of hand-made wedding gowns, in both Western and traditional Chinese styles.

Metrocenter
I-17 between Dunlap and Peoria Aves., Phoenix
• (602) 997-2641
• www.metrocentermall.com

When it opened in 1973, Metrocenter was not only one of Arizona's first major regional shopping malls, but was America's largest shopping mall. It's still no slouch. The two-level interior has been remodeled with marble inlay floors, palm trees throughout, and two dancing waterfalls that often stop shoppers in their tracks.

Among its 170 stores, you'll find the major department stores of Macy's, Dillard's, JCPenney, Sears, and Robinsons-May. Specialty stores include The Disney Store, B. Dalton Booksellers, Waldenbooks, and a NASCAR Thunder store specializing in racing paraphernalia. Clothing stores include Gap, Old Navy, Guess, Structure, Aeropostale, Arizona Outfitters, and Copper Rivet. The mall also offers

several Arizona gift stores, including Godber's Gifts.

The revamped food court, dubbed FoodWorks, features 10 eateries and a Ruby Tuesday restaurant. Harkins Theatres, near the food court, offers stadium seating, 12 screens, and the latest stereo sound system.

Inquire at the customer service center—on the lower level near Dillard's—for more information about merchants, bus schedules, and stroller rentals. The mall is open daily.

Metro Parkway, which circles Metrocenter, is lined with smaller shopping centers, restaurants, movie theaters, and the popular amusement park Castles 'N Coasters. Among the shops facing Metro Parkway is a large Barnes & Noble bookstore, at 10235 Metro Parkway East, (602) 678-0088. Other Valley Barnes & Noble locations are at 4847 E. Ray Road, Phoenix, 7685 W. Bell Road, Peoria, and 10500 N. 90th Street, Scottsdale.

INSIDERS' TIP

Shading your car while you shop becomes a high priority here at certain times of the year, so be savvy about seeking covered parking. Among the malls with the most covered parking or largest underground garages are Scottsdale Fashion Square, Biltmore Fashion Park, and Paradise Valley Mall.

Paradise Valley Mall
Tatum Blvd. and Cactus Rd., Phoenix
• (602) 953-2959
• www.westcor.com

In addition to being all on one level, Paradise Valley Mall has made its shopping experience more comfortable by adding plush seating areas throughout the mall to give shoppers frequent opportunities to sit and relax. A stream meanders through the recently remodeled food court and the "Recipe for a Healthy Me" children's playground. Its new outdoor patio also features lush landscaping. Anchored by Robinsons-May, Sears, JCPenney, Dillard's, and Macy's, the mall's 160 stores also include Banana Republic, Ann Taylor, Talbot's, Abercrombie and Fitch, Old Navy, Brookstone, Samuel's Jewelers, Big Fat Wow, and Brisa Hat Trader. Mall attractions also include a movie theater and a video game arcade.

Paradise Valley Mall is open daily, and should you need transportation assistance or have questions about the mall, you can find the Customer Service Center near the food court.

The corner of Tatum Boulevard and Cactus Road is also home to three smaller shopping centers, including the Village Fair North shopping center. There, you'll find a large Bookstar at 12863 North Tatum Boulevard, (602) 953-8066.

Shopping Districts

Arizona Center
Van Buren St. between Third and Fifth Sts., Phoenix
• **(602) 271-4000, (602) 949-4353**
• **www.arizonacenter.com**

By the 1970s, most department stores had vanished from downtown Phoenix. A handful of smaller specialty stores remained, but most Phoenicians shopped in neighborhoods closer to home. The downtown retail scene got a much-needed boost in the 1980s with the construction of the Arizona Center, a two-story, open-air collection of shops, restaurants, and nightclubs. Incorporated into the design are office towers and numerous gardens, sculptures, and fountains. The main garden, in a sunken area near Van Buren Street, offers a shady oasis for lunch breaks, people watching, or quiet contemplation. The restaurants and bars bustle, but the more sedate atmosphere in the shops provides a pleasant diversion if you're downtown.

The 50 shops include Lerner New York, Glory-B's, Jayne's Marketplace, The Leather Mill, Lil' People, and Arizona Beach Co. For Arizona books and gifts rustled up by a well-regarded state magazine publisher, check out the Arizona Highways Gift Shop. Other specialty shops include Flag World, with an extensive selection of the world's flags; The French Knot, which sells dolls, crystal, and hand-embroidered accessories; Oak Creek, with Southwestern home accessories; Sports Fan, featuring sports apparel; Angel Treasures, an angel-themed gift shop; the Phoenix International Raceway Gift Shop and Ticket office, which revs up with racing memorabilia; and Yippie-Ei-O, with its roundup of Western gifts and memorabilia.

Many retail carts are scattered about the Arizona Center selling everything from refrigerator magnets and T-shirts to wind chimes and posters.

The Gardenside Food Court packs them in during weekday lunch hours, and it is also open in the evening, making it a convenient place for a quick bite before catching a cultural or sporting event. A newer attraction is the AMC 24-screen theater, the only movie house in downtown Phoenix.

The mall is open daily, and provides a Guest Services Center in the food court. Find ample parking in the garage on Fillmore Street, which is open to Arizona Center customers, or try to find a spot along Third Street.

Town & Country Shopping Center
20th St. and Camelback Rd., Phoenix
• **(602) 955-6850**
• **www.townandcountryshops.com**

In the heart of the Camelback Corridor of retail and business complexes, Town & Country—with its charming blend of red-tiled roofs, courtyards, and fountains—makes a nice excursion. About two dozen shops, mostly on the small and eclectic side, are connected by walkways lined with red brick. Some interesting stops could include the Friends for UNICEF store, with clothing and gift items from around the world; The Herb Stop, which offers aromatherapy oils and a cornucopia of herbs; Lotions & Potions, with body-care items; Ye Olde Pipe & Tobacco Shoppe, for cigar and pipe aficionados; The Leather Center, which features furniture; Table Talk, a kitchen store; Jutenhoops, an eclectic gift shop with one of the best selections of greeting cards in town; and My Sister's Closet, which offers recycled designer apparel.

The larger stores in the vicinity include Linens 'N Things, Trader Joe's, and Bookstar. You'll find a coffeehouse, ice cream parlor, and a handful of restaurants in the area, along with a six-screen movie house. Most of the stores and restaurants are open daily.

Outlet Shopping

Prime Outlets at New River
I-17 at Anthem Way, Phoenix
• **(623) 465-9500**

When heading north on I-17 to the Prime Outlets at New River, you will feel like you're heading out on the open road to Flagstaff. The shops are 30 to 45 minutes from downtown and, surprisingly, still within in Phoenix city limits. Follow the signs and look for Exit 229.

You'll enjoy bargain hunting in the pleasant Southwestern-style setting, with its inviting landscaping and benches. The 90 stores have a wide enough variety to interest everyone in the family. If you are shopping for housewares, look for the Mikasa Factory Store, Black & Decker, Le Creuset, Springmaid-Wamsutta, and other stores. Women's apparel includes Ann Taylor Loft, Harolds, Jones New York, Polo Ralph Lauren, Donna Karan/DKNY, Casual Corner Woman, and Off 5th-Saks Fifth Avenue Outlet. For children, stop by the Oshkosh

B'Gosh Factory Store, Hartstrings, Carter's, and others. Men can stock up on clothes and accessories at Dockers Outlet, Geoffrey Beene, Gap, and Ashworths. Other stores are Publishers Warehouse, Sunglass Outlet, Gilbert Ortega Indian Arts, Bose Factory Store, and Reebok.

You also will find a food court and playground. Nearby, the Customer Service Center offers coupon books, stroller rentals, wheelchairs, and tourist information. The shops are open daily.

Antique Shopping

Antique Gatherings
3601 E. Indian School Rd., Phoenix
• **(602) 956-8203**

This large store gathers several antique dealers into one location. Each dealer has a designated space from which he or she displays and sells wares. You will be impressed by how tidy this store is, and it's a delight to browse here even if you're not in the market for antiques and collectibles. Walking from one dealer's area to another is like walking among various tastefully decorated sitting rooms from different eras. You get a quick sampling of the Victorian era, the American West, rural life, and more. Antique Gatherings dealers sell practically everything except the kitchen sink (and maybe that, too), including furniture, housewares, books, and dolls. Prepare to be smitten by fancy pillows, custom-made lamps, artwork, quilts, tea sets, and doll clothes.

A nice little bonus toward the back of the store is the Happy Cooker Cafe, which serves sandwiches and salads every day but Monday. Antique Gatherings is open daily.

The Brass Armadillo Antique Mall
12419 N. 28th Dr., Phoenix
• **(602) 942-0030**
• **www.brassarmadillo.com**

Here's a fun way to browse for antiques and collectibles all in one building. This mall—about a mile north of Metrocenter just off I-17 and Cactus Road—boasts more than 600 dealers and 39,000 square feet. Part of a chain of antique malls headquartered in the Midwest, the Brass Armadillo's easy-to-navigate design includes uncluttered booths and street signs named for states to guide your way.

Be prepared to lose track of time among the vast array of furniture, china, toys, glassware, dolls, vintage jewelry, collectible sports cards, and political memorabilia. If you want to learn more about your finds, you can browse the section of reference books on antiques and collectibles. The mall is open daily.

Downtown Glendale and Historic Catlin Court offer the perfect place to browse for antiques and enjoy time-honored traditions, such as breaking for afternoon tea.

Photo: Courtesy of the Glendale Tourism Division

Specialty Stores

Buffalo Exchange
730 E. Missouri St., Phoenix
- **(602) 523-0144**

Buffalo Exchange, a resale clothing store, has built a reputation among young adults as the place to find stylish clothing on the cheap. But the store has such a good turnover of merchandise and such a wide variety of duds for women and men that we recommend a visit for bargain shoppers of any age. If you're in the recycling mood, Buffalo Exchange will pay you cash for the used clothing that it accepts. The store has another location at 227 W. University Drive in Tempe, near Arizona State University. The stores are open daily.

Candle & Gift Factory Outlet
24th St. and Indian School Rd., Phoenix
- **(602) 508-8391**
- **www.cgfo.com**

It's not just the aroma of burning candles that makes a walk through this store a sensory experience. It's also the sounds of soft music and water trickling through indoor fountains, not to mention the eye-catching selection of candles, candleholders, luminarias, sconces, and candle chimneys. Scents include everything from florals to rich, chocolate "desserts." Many of the tapers, votives, pillars, and other candles have been made on site. The candleholders, baskets, and other gift items have been imported from all over the world. There is an especially good selection of folk art. Since this is a factory outlet, prices are reasonable. The store is open daily.

Do Wah Diddy
3642 E. Thomas Rd., Phoenix
- **(602) 957-3874**
- **www.dowahdiddy.com**

The '50s are where it's at in this fun store that celebrates its 20th year of collecting all things kitschy from the Eisenhower years. The small store is jam-packed with '50s furniture and accessories, '50s TV and movie memorabilia, kitchen doodads, and funky jewelry. Hip items from the '30s, '40s, '60s, and '70s don't get overlooked either. Do Wah Diddy also has a well-deserved reputation as the city's pink flamingo headquarters, in case you would like a flock for your yard. The store is only open the first full week of each month, Monday through Saturday, but you can also browse the store's wares in its booth at the Antiques Centre, Scottsdale, 2012 N. Scottsdale Road, (480) 675-9500.

Flax Company Inc.
1001 E. Jefferson St., Phoenix
- **(602) 254-0840**

This huge artists' supply store can prove invaluable in finding those perfect creative tools. It is patronized by both casual and serious artists. Flax flaunts one of the state's largest selections of fine writing instruments, picture frames, artists' paints, canvases, drafting supplies, art studio furniture, and equipment. You can honor your work by ordering a custom frame. It is open every day but Sunday.

Peppermint Bay
4905 E. Ray Rd., Ahwatukee
- **(480) 753-6412**

A sweetie of a sweets store, Peppermint Bay sells all kinds of candy either individually wrapped or in bulk. You can peruse the chocolates, candy bars, bubble gums, hard candies, jellybeans, and gummy bears while enjoying the bright decor. You'll wonder whether you've suddenly stepped into a Candyland game. The store has a good variety of sugar-free candies, too. Peppermint Bay is open every day and most evenings. If you shop at its other location, at the corner of Baseline and Stapley Roads in Mesa, you can take your candy into the AMC Theater.

The Astronomy Shoppe
3202 East Greenway Rd., Suite 1615, Phoenix
- **(602) 971-3170**
- **www.darkskyinc.com**

Arizona's clear nights have made it the perfect place for professional and amateur astronomers. The knowledgeable folks at The Astronomy Shoppe can recommend telescopes that are best-suited for your viewing needs. If you are lucky, one of its astronomy club mem-

INSIDERS' TIP

Traveling with children? Shopping malls are happy to loan out wheelchairs and baby strollers during your visit. Most malls also offer a courtesy escort service to help carry packages or accompany you to your car. Inquire at the mall's customer service center or look for rental kiosks and security stations near the food court.

bers (there are four active clubs in the area) might invite you on a star-gazing excursion. The store carries telescopes, books, eyepiece cases, and other accessories. An on-site technician can fix binoculars and telescopes.

Southeast Valley

Shopping Malls

Arizona Mills
Superstition Frwy. (U.S. Hwy. 60) and I-10, Tempe
- **(480) 491-9700**
- **www.arizonamills.com**

Arizona Mills opened to much media hoopla in late 1997, in part because it was Arizona's first shopping center from the Mills Corp., the developer of Ontario Mills near Los Angeles and elsewhere. The company brought "shoppertainment" to the Valley of the Sun, mixing outlet stores from dozens of nationally known retailers with a variety of entertainment venues and innovative restaurants. Arizona Mills strives to outshine the ordinary mall by conveying a lively, almost futuristic atmosphere. The walkway through its oval design wends through six theme neighborhoods that evoke an aspect of Arizona, from desert plants to ancient petroglyphs. Arizona artists designed many of the murals, mosaic tiles, metal sculptures, and pottery. Another fixture in the colorful and decor-intense mall is the profusion of video screens overhead, which blare commercials, mall promotions, and music videos. The shopping is fun, but be prepared for sensory overload.

The retailers, restaurants, and entertainment venues total 175, so there's plenty to see and do. Mall anchors include Nieman-Marcus Last Call, Burlington Coat Factory, Oshman's SuperSports USA, JCPenney Outlet Store, Marshall's, Linens 'N Things, and Off 5th-Saks Fifth Avenue Outlet. In women's apparel, other stores include Ann Taylor Loft, the Donna Karan Co. Store, and Kenneth Cole of New York. You'll also find a Guess? Factory Store, Big Dog Sportswear, and a Van Heusen Factory Outlet. There are a dozen housewares and furniture outlet stores, along with a half-dozen cosmetic stores. It may have more shoe stores than any other venue in the Valley, with options including Nine West Outlet, Skechers Outlet, Bostonian Clarks Shoe Outlet, and E&J's Designer Shoe Outlet.

Children can have a fun shopping experi-ence, too, exploring stores such as Funzy's, which carries cool toys, and Way to Glow!, which features glow-in-the-dark toys, puzzles, and T-shirts. Stop at Awesome Atom's, a branch of the store in downtown Phoenix's Arizona Science Center, or SanRio Surprise, which carries the latest must-haves.

Other interesting stops include Hi-Health World of Nutrition, which carries all manner of vitamins, supplements, packaged foods, and natural remedies as well as offering a juice bar. The Virgin Megastore is a good stop for compact discs and videos. The mall's newest offering, Hilo-Hattie, the Store of Hawaii, affords land-locked beach bums a selection of island clothing and foods.

There's a food court with an enormous seating area, plus a 24-screen cinema complex, an IMAX theater, and the extremely popular GameWorks, a giant arcade. Arizona Mills is open daily. It has two customer service centers, which also serve as Arizona Tourism Welcome Centers.

Fiesta Mall
Superstition Frwy. (U.S. Hwy. 60) and Alma School Rd., Mesa
- **(480) 833-4121**
- **www.shopfiesta.com**

Fiesta Mall has long been a handy location for Southeast Valley shoppers, with plenty of variety to meet shopping needs. In addition to the major department stores of Macy's, Dillard's, Robinsons-May and Sears, the mall houses specialty stores such as Abercrombie & Fitch, The Disney Store, Natural Wonders, Waldenbooks, Juxtapose, The Hat Club, Champs Sports, and Charlotte's Room, featuring gifts for girls. You can also find an Exclusively Arizona, which sells Arizona-made products. There are 150 stores in all, arranged in a two-level mall decorated with Southwestern colors. A food court and children's play area are also featured. The mall is open daily and covered parking is available.

For moviegoers, two cinema complexes are within two blocks of the mall. Just across the street from the mall, at 1361 S. Alma School Road, you'll find a large Borders Books & Music, (480) 833-2244, one of several in the Valley.

Superstition Springs Center
Superstition Frwy. (U.S. Hwy. 60) and Power Rd., Mesa
- **(480) 396-2570**
- **www.westcor.com**

The Valley's continued growth toward the

east has ensured the success of this regional mall, a pleasant destination with 130 stores. The major department stores are Dillard's, Robinsons-May, Mervyn's, JCPenney, and Sears. Several smaller shopping centers sit on the fringes of Superstition Springs Center, making the area a one-stop destination for most shopping needs.

As for the two-level mall, its stores include Lerner New York, The Limited, Petite Sophisticate, Bath & Body Works, Footlocker, Gapkids, Arizona Images, Waldenbooks, and B. Dalton Bookseller. The interior has a contemporary feel, and in good weather it's quite nice to take a breather from shopping by sitting in the outdoor plaza. Facing the plaza is a playground for children, which features large models of desert animals. There is also a mini botanical garden with a nature trail. Other family-friendly features include the full-size indoor carousel near the food court and a new play area with a slide shaped like a dog.

The customer service center is on the lower level near the JCPenney entrance, and the stores are open daily.

Shopping Districts

Mill Avenue
Downtown Tempe
• (480) 967-4877

Historic buildings, a mixture of shops, restaurants, offices, and a plethora of people watching opportunities, all combine to make Tempe a desirable place to wile away an afternoon. Several dozen shops line the Mill Avenue and the surrounding side streets, some tucked away in nooks and crannies. Tempe's central location in the heart of the Valley makes the Mill Avenue area a convenient meeting place; just grab a cup of something to sip at the Coffee Plantation or any of the other coffee shops, juice bars, and restaurants with outdoor seating areas. The student population from Arizona State University livens the place up, especially on weekend nights when it bustles like a sophisticated city several times its size.

Clothing, shoe shops, and other stores that cater to college students abound here. Specialty stores include Urban Outfitters, 545 S. Mill Avenue, filled with trendy home accessories, books, gifts, and clothing for the young set; Duck Soup, 740 S. Mill Avenue, a card and gift shop with a good selection of Arizona and ASU T-shirts, as well as posters, candles, Arizona food products, and jewelry; the Cap Co., 15 E. Sixth Street, offering shade for your head in

styles ranging from old-fashioned bowlers to sports team caps; Fiesta Chile Company, 640 S. Mill Avenue, whose food products will spice up your life; Mazar Bazaar, 514 S. Mill Avenue, which offers elegant imported designer clothes and accessories; Those Were the Days; 516 S. Mill Avenue, whose unique books and items look like finds from someone's attic; Campus Corner, at 603 S. Mill Ave., is a good place to get ASU apparel before the game. The nearby Gentle Strength Co-op, 234 W. University Dr., hits the spot with its selection of health food and cruelty-free products.

You'll also find several stores and restaurants connected to the Centerpoint office and retail development at Seventh Street and Mill Avenue, including a cinema complex. When you are done shopping and want to relax, the new Tempe Town Lake is a short stroll away.

Antique Shopping

Antique Plaza
114 W. Main St., Mesa
• (480) 833-4844

More than 100 dealers are packed into this two-story antiques mall with 20,000 square feet worth of exhibit space in downtown Mesa. Find all kinds of furniture from different eras, along with vintage jewelry, table linens, quilts, lamps, Depression glass, trains, toys, and similar small collectibles. Antique Plaza is open daily. There are eight other antique shops within walking distance. Free Public parking is available and a number of restaurants are located nearby.

Specialty Stores

Bookman's
1056 S. Country Club Dr., Mesa
• (480) 835-0505
• www.bookmans.com

This is Arizona's largest seller of used books and music. Bookman's has stores in Tucson, Flagstaff, and Sierra Vista, but this is its only store in the Valley. The selection is as complete as any of the book superstore chains—plus it has so many out-of-print titles that are often hard to find. There's a section devoted to new books, a large magazine section, and an area for used software. You can preview used CDs and cassettes at a listening station. A few chairs and couches are available if you become so engrossed in something that you need to sit down. The friendly personnel are willing to

A Taste of Arizona

In your hunt for souvenirs from your visit to this state, some of the best you'll come across will be edible. Arizona is bustling with small companies that turn out innovative food products, many of which have a definite Arizona identity.

One Arizona food success story is Goldwater's Taste of the Southwest, a Scottsdale company started several years ago by the family of former Senator Barry Goldwater. Salsas are its specialty, and they come in a wide range of flavors. Goldwater's was the first in the country to come out with fruit salsa, and now the line includes Paradise Pineapple and Mohave Mango. Goldwater's chunky, medium-spiced Sedona Red Salsa has been rated "excellent" by *The New York Times*. In addition, the company sells Bisbee Barbecue Sauce and The Senator's Chili, a dry mix for beans and beef created by the late senator himself. The products are available in stores around the country. They've even made a dent in the international market. Call (800) 488-4932 for retail locations or order from the Web at www.goldwater.net.

For something completely different, go home with a box of Fairytale Brownies. The Scottsdale company making these delights has established a lucrative national mail-order business, which you can reach by calling (800) 324-7982. The name comes from a story dreamed up about a fairy with a magic spoon who bakes "in the wee hours of night." The company's old family recipe has won raves from around the country. The 11 gourmet flavors—such as White Chocolate Chunk, Peanut Butter, and Espresso—are available in many Arizona food stores.

More sweet news comes from Glendale and the Cerreta Candy Co. A tour of the company's chocolate-making factory is a popular, mouth-watering diversion in downtown Glendale. The chocolates are available at Smitty's and Fry's supermarkets around the Valley.

A trip to Arizona isn't complete without tasting the salsa that's produced here.

Photo: Courtesy Goldwater's Foods of Arizona

Since Mexican food is a staple here, it's not surprising that many food companies specialize in salsas, tortillas, and tortilla chips. They can easily be found in Arizona groceries, and you'll have your choice of several variations—reduced-fat, reduced-salt, restaurant-style, black bean-style, lime-cilantro flavor, nacho flavor, and so forth. While in the snack aisle, you might try Poore Brothers Potato Chips. Again, it may be tough to decide which varieties to try—regular, jalapeño, salt and vinegar, or parmesan and garlic. The company is based in Goodyear.

Hot sauces of all sorts are popular too. Southwest Specialty Food Inc. in the West Valley makes a line of "Ass Kickin'" hot sauces and salsas, many of which contain habañero peppers, said to be 10 times as hot as jalapeños. With $10 million in annual sales, this company sells more than 90 different items in retail shops and by catalog in this country and abroad. Call (800) 536-3131 for a catalog.

Arizona Gunslinger Smokin' Hot Jalapeño Pepper Sauce has also made a name for itself. Its Phoenix-based makers have been distributing it nationally by mail order for almost a decade, and it's often found in airport shops. Gunslinger is made from red-ripened jalapeños, and its thicker consistency means it's suitable on all kinds of food, not just tacos and tostadas. Mail orders are taken at (800) 359-3912.

Other names to look out for: Mama Rosa's salsas and jellies, (800) 254-4774; Grand Canyon Cookies; Bill Johnson's Big Apple Barbecue Sauce, a 40-year-old recipe from the state's successful Big Apple restaurant chain; and Cave Creek Chili Beer, which boasts a serrano chili pepper hand inserted into every bottle. You can find this unusual beer in a Valley grocery store, or call Chili Beer at (800) 228-9742 for a list of retail shops.

What you take home doesn't necessarily have to be a manufactured food, though. Visit produce stands for homegrown citrus—different varieties of oranges as well as grapefruits, lemons, and tangerines—in the winter and spring. You'll also find dates, pecans, pistachios, piñon nuts, dried fruit, and honey. Arizona is the third-largest producer of citrus and vegetables in the United States.

And would you believe wine is produced in Arizona? The Sonoita-Elgin area of southern Arizona has been successfully making wines since the mid-1980s. Although the wines haven't yet captured more than the local market, they have won awards at various wine festivals. Check labels for these names: Sonoita Vineyards, Terra Rosa Vineyards, and Callaghan Vineyards.

About beverages, here's another thing you ought to know: The ubiquitous AriZona brand of flavored iced teas in the pretty pastel cans and decoratively wrapped bottles comes from eight plants all over the country, none of which are in Arizona.

You can easily find most of the products mentioned while browsing shops in areas popular with tourists, as well as specialty shops in malls. Suggested retailers are Shades of the West on Main Street in Old Town Scottsdale; the Pinnacle Peak General Store in north Scottsdale; Arizona Images, with several mall locations; Cost Plus locations; Exclusively Arizona at Fiesta Mall in Mesa; and the AJ's Fine Foods, with several locations in the Valley.

patiently sift through books and magazines you bring in for trade. Bookman's awards cash and/or store credit for materials it's willing to take off your hands. The store is open daily and most evenings.

Changing Hands Bookstore
• 6430 S. McClintock Dr., Tempe

This Valley institution used to be located in downtown Tempe but has now moved to a location a few miles south and taken its loyal following with it. The independent bookstore offers a noteworthy selection of new and used books for dedicated readers. A bin outside the store often offers freebies and frequent buyers can get discounts when their book card is filled with stamps. Changing Hands offers a number of educational activities for kids and features readings several times a month by local authors. Valley newcomers can keep up-to-date on activities and new releases through the store's newsletter, which features staff reviews.

The adjacent Wildflower Bread Company offers a good meeting point for book clubs, writing groups, and other literature lovers.

Cookies From Home
1605 W. University Dr., Suite 106, Tempe
- **(480) 894-1944**
- **www.cookiesfromhome.com**

This cookie bakery got its start in 1981 on Mill Avenue in downtown Tempe, then—thanks to a burgeoning mail-order business—moved to larger quarters in an industrial park. Most agree that these cookies are as good as home made. They come in eight different varieties and customer favorites include Hunka Chunka, Fudgies, and Snickerdoodles. The retail store in the new quarters is a great place to buy cookies by the pound or as gift packages. There are a variety of charming tins, baskets, decorated boxes, mugs, and cookie jars in which to present the treats. The store is open Monday through Saturday, but you can prolong the pleasure outside the state by ordering its treats online.

REI-Tempe
1405 W. Southern Ave., Tempe
- **(480) 967-5400**
- **www.rei.com**

Recreational Equipment, Inc.—just REI to those in the know—is the first stop for anyone wanting to explore Arizona's natural wonders. The store carries equipment and related clothing for camping, cycling, climbing, hiking, and more. Staff members often do the sports themselves, so they can help you make an intelligent selection. If you want to try out a sport, you can also rent equipment ranging from climbing shoes to kayaks. If you join the Seattle-based cooperative, you also get dividends at the end of the year. The store also has another location in Paradise Valley, at 12634 North Paradise Village Parkway West, (602) 996-5400.

Wide World of Maps
1444 W. Southern Ave., Mesa
- **(602) 844-1134**
- **www.maps4u.com**

This locally grown store carries just about any map your vagabond heart desires and is a vital stop for those who plan on hiking Arizona's rough terrain. If it doesn't carry what you need, Wide World of Maps can map it for you. Its inventory includes travel maps, guidebooks, cookbooks, books on local history, hiking books, topographical maps, atlases, globes, wall maps, CD Rom maps, and the latest Glo-

bal Position Systems and instruction on how to use them. The store also will laminate a map of your choice for maps that will be used alot. Wide World of Maps is open daily and has another location at 2626 W. Indian School Road in Phoenix, (602) 279-2323.

Zia Record Exchange
105 W. University Dr., Tempe
- **(480) 829-1967**
- **www.ziarocks.com**

Founded by Phoenix resident Brad Singer in the early 1980s, Zia has grown from a funky little place selling vinyl to an eight-store, statewide chain. Music lovers appreciate its no-frills approach to providing the widest possible selection of new and used CDs, cassettes, and LPs. Imports are well-represented here, and because the inventory is usually alphabetized without regard to genre, it's possible to spy a CD by a country singer snuggled next to one by a heavy metal artist. The local music scene mourned Singer's sudden passing in May 1998, but the stores continue on. Find other Zia's in the Valley at 807 W. Indian School Road in Phoenix, (602) 241-0313; 2510 W. Thunderbird Road in Phoenix, (602) 866-7867; and 10639 N. 32nd Street in Phoenix, (602) 482-3119.

Northeast Valley

Shopping Malls

Scottsdale Fashion Square
Camelback and Scottsdale Rds., Scottsdale
- **(480) 990-7800**
- **www.fashionsquare.com**

Once a tidy open-air shopping center serving Scottsdale residents, in the past decade Scottsdale Fashion Square has transformed into a ritzy indoor mall that, at 1.8 million square feet, is the largest mall in Arizona. The mall attracts people from all over the Valley, mainly because of its mix of high-powered department stores and classy boutiques.

But let's cut to the chase: Scottsdale Fashion Square has Arizona's only Nordstrom and Neiman Marcus. Its Robinson's-May store has been expanded and its Dillard's is the largest in the entire chain. A Sears has been recently added. There are 225 stores in all, of which 60 are exclusive stores. In the fall of 1998, Scottsdale Fashion Square not only opened Nordstrom but also finished construction of an enclosed bridge—filled with 50 stores—that connects Nordstrom on the south side of Camelback Road to the main mall on the north side of Camelback.

The ambiance inside the two-level mall makes for a decadent shopping experience. Palm trees tower nearly to the retractable glass ceiling. Fountains throughout the mall make Scottsdale seem more tropic than desert-like, including a two-story "rain curtain" in the center of the food court, which wraps around an open stairway. The food court itself is one of the best in the Valley because of its wide selection—from burgers to international fare that includes French, Mexican, Chinese, and Japanese fast food. The numerous sit-down restaurants and cafes in the mall draw evening diners.

Stores include Tiffany & Co., the famous New York jeweler; Crate & Barrel; Brookstone, gifts and gadgets; Banana Republic, clothing; Z Gallerie, featuring home-decorating accessories; The Museum Company, gifts inspired by famous works of art; Louis Vuitton; Bisou Bisuo; Coach Leatherware, Morgan; F.A.O. Schwarz toy store; the Field of Dreams sports memorabilia store; The Team Shop, Phoenix Suns memorabilia; Brentano's Bookstore; Emporio Optic; J. Crew clothing store; the Build-A-Bear Workshop; and the Everything But Water swimsuit store.

Also find the Scottsdale Kitchen Co., with all kinds of housewares; the Warner Bros. Studio Store; The Disney Store; Godiva Chocolatier; The Body Shop cosmetics store; and, for souvenir shoppers, Arizona Images and Arizona Territory. After a hard day of shopping, you can relax at the Day Spa at Nordstrom or Dillard's, or catch a flick at one of the mall's 12 cinemas. Special services provided by the mall include lockers, stroller rental, valet parking, and a roving concierge. The mall is open daily.

Shopping Districts

The Borgata
Lincoln Dr. and Scottsdale Rd., Scottsdale
- **(480) 998-1822**
- **www.westcor.com**

You'll do a double take when you spy this replica of a fourteenth century Italian village, complete with brick towers. The Borgata stands out in more than just the looks department; it guards an elegant array of high-fashion boutiques, jewelry stores, art galleries, and outdoor bistros. The 50 stores include Out of Hand, offering North American-made arts and crafts; Bradbury's Antique Bazaar; Stefan Mann

leather goods store; the Dance Centre, selling exercise togs; Impostors Jewelry, selling copies of famous jewelry; Clemons-Eicken, featuring collector figurines; The Beach House, selling swim wear to be seen in; and Koshari, featuring top-quality Native American arts and crafts. Each Friday, from October through April, The Borgata's cobblestone courtyard is transformed into a farmers market. The Christmas season brings an incredible display of twinkling white lights and other holiday decorations. The Borgata is open daily.

Carefree
Cave Creek and Tom Darlington Rds., Carefree
- **(602) 488-3381**

Located about 30 minutes north of downtown Scottsdale, the core of Carefree sports several small shops and boutiques that are similar to Scottsdale's Fifth Avenue, but on a smaller scale. They are clustered on Easy Street, Ho and Hum Roads, and Sundial Plaza—all within short walking distance of each other. Peruse stores such as like The Lemon Tree, 22 Easy Street, (480) 488-3894, which specializes in Hummels, Madame Alexander dolls, and other art collectibles; and Essentially Arizona, 42 Easy Street, (480) 488-5567, which offers Arizona gifts and novelties, including pottery and gift baskets. Stroll through the grounds of the Spanish Village, at the corner of Ho and Hum Roads, (480) 488-0350, and enjoy its specialty shops, clothing boutiques, galleries, and cafes. Most of the shops are open daily.

el Pedregal Festival Marketplace at the Boulders
Scottsdale Rd. and Carefree Hwy., Scottsdale
- **(480) 488-1072**
- **www.elpedregal.com**

With its Moroccon styling, el Pedregal Festival Marketplace harmonizes with its magnificent desert setting—rock-strewn terrain formed millions of years ago. Located where the new housing developments of north Scottsdale give way to the hills and boulders of Carefree, the shopping development is part of The Boulders resort, a short distance away by foot. One of the main attractions in el Pedregal is the Heard Museum North, which offers exhibitions on a smaller scale than the main Heard Museum in downtown Phoenix and whose gift shop features Native American arts and crafts. More than 36 artisan shops and galleries cluster in this two-level, distinctive building, which overlooks an amphitheater with grassy areas,

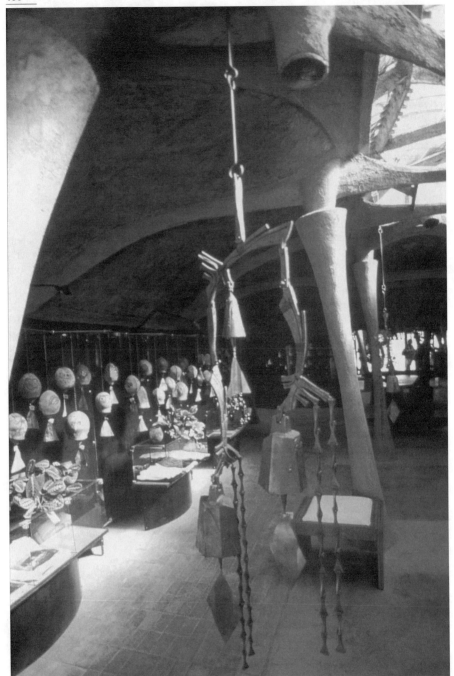

Soleri Bells—which are designed by esteemed Arizona architect Paolo Soleri and made by volunteers— make a unique souvenir. Proceeds go to support the experimental community, Arcosanti, he is building north of Phoenix. They can be purchased at Cosanti in Scottsdale.

Photo: Paul Markow, courtesy of Scottsdale Convention and Visitors Bureau

benches, and cafe tables. Galleries include Gallery 10, May Gallery, and Zuva Gallery, the latter featuring art and sculpture from South Africa. Other shops include the Mineral & Fossil Gallery, which appeals to the rock hound in your family; Canyon Lifestyles, which sells Southwestern accessories for the home; and Mother Nature's Trading Co.; with science kits for your burgeoning chemist or engineer. Three cafes and a restaurant round out the selection and special events, like the Spring Concert Series, make a visit even more memorable.

Fifth Avenue
Downtown Scottsdale
- **(480) 947-6423**
- **www.downtownscottsdale.com**

A number of thriving shopping districts thrive in downtown Scottsdale, each with its own special personality and charm. The merchants of Fifth Avenue cater to tourists and locals alike with a plethora of boutiques and galleries, many with merchandise unique to the Southwest. The Fifth Avenue shops run along three blocks of mostly shaded walkways—the fountain with four horses near the center of activity makes a prominent landmark. Shops line both sides of the street and it's worthwhile to explore the establishments on Third Avenue, Stetson Drive, Marshall Way, Craftsman Court, and Main Street. The shops are interspersed with many top-notch art galleries for which Scottsdale is famous. (See our chapter on The Arts for more information.)

Here are a few stops along the way to keep in mind as you browse: Irontiques at 7077 E. Main Street features early Americana such as old irons, trivets, banks, toys, and other collector's items. Kactus Jock, at 7121 E. Fifth Avenue, features sportswear made from natural fiber. Made in Arizona, at 7116 E. Fifth Avenue, deals in apparel, gifts, and souvenirs unique to our state. Debora Wayne Design, at 7140 E. Sixth Avenue, features the artist's fused glass jewelry in sterling silver settings. Hawaiian swimwear and luau items can be found at the Hawaiian Shop, 7124 E. Fifth Avenue. Scottsdale Stained Glass has glass art, collectibles, and figurines, along with art by well-known Arizona artist Ted DeGrazia. A store called Two Gray Hills Indian Pueblo, at 7142 E. Fifth Avenue, has a wide selection of Native American jewelry, rugs, and Kachinas. Sample Arizona-grown dates at Shalimar Date Gardens, 7021 E. Main Street. Cinch a good, custom-fitted swimsuit at Computerized Swimwear Systems, 4020 N. Scottsdale Road. Angel Wings and Other Things is an angel-themed gift shop at 7121 E. Fifth Avenue. Tierra del Lagarto, at 4248 N. Craftsman Court, sells imported art, furniture, and accessories. Essentially Books, 6957 E. Fifth Avenue, specializes in books on contemporary and Native American spirituality. Some stores are closed on Sunday or limit their hours during the summer.

Main Street
West Main St., downtown Scottsdale
- **(480) 947-6423**
- **www.downtownscottsdale.com**

The art gallery strip along West Main Street in Scottsdale boasts outstanding collections of arts and antiques. We'll explore the area's reputation more thoroughly in the chapter on The Arts, but note that masterpieces by many of the old Western masters are represented here, as well as work by folk artists, Native American artists, and contemporary artists. Some highlights include Husberg Fine Arts, at 713 E. Main, with its collection of Western artwork; and Guidon Books, at 7117 E. Main Street, which features a serious collection of antique Western and Civil War books, a well as collectible posters and maps.

Marshall Way Arts District
Marshall Way, downtown Scottsdale
- **(480) 947-6423**
- **www.downtownscottsdale.com**

The Marshall Way Arts District—between Craftsman Court and 3rd Avenue west of Scottsdale Road and north of Indian School Road—is an art lover's heaven. The galleries feature a diversity of media, from limited edition prints to art you can wear, all in a tree-shaded, upscale setting. Many internationally recognized artists displayed their work here, including those by master studio glass artist Dale Chihuly at the Vanier Galleries on Marshall, 4142 N. Marshall Way. If you are looking for distinctive jewelry, you might want to check out Jewelry by Gautheir, at 4211 N. Marshall Way. Dominique R. Paris, at 4151 N. Marshall Way, stocks

> **INSIDERS' TIP**
> For a directory of small bookstores in the Phoenix metropolitan area, including stores specializing in used and antiquarian books, call the Valley Independent Booksellers Association at (480) 976-4729. About 60 stores are listed.

SHOPPING

its women's boutique with the latest fashions shipped straight from Paris. If you get an urge to be creative yourself—or want to pen a perfectly elegant description of your travels to someone you left behind—stop by The Paper Place for fine stationary and writing instruments at 4130 N. Marshall Way.

Old Town
Four square blocks around Main St. and Brown Ave., downtown Scottsdale
• **(480) 947-6423**
• **www.downtownscottsdale.com**

Old Town Scottsdale encompasses many of the city's oldest buildings and their authentic, Western styling offers a unique flavor of the "West's most Western Town." The historic shopping district, with more than 150 stores, begins at the corner of Scottsdale Road and Main Street and feathers out a couple of blocks to the east and north. Across Scottsdale Road to the west are the Fifth Avenue shops, another fun shopping district mentioned earlier. Between the two, you are sure to find the perfect memento of your trip to this area or the perfect gift for a friend or relative.

A few Old Town Scottsdale shops to explore include Shades of the West at 7247 E. Main Street, which stocks boots, belts, hats, and Southwestern-made food products; Saba's Western Wear, at 3965 N. Brown Avenue, which has been outfitting cowboys and cowgirls since 1927; Cactus Cats, which offers gifts and apparel, at 7233 E. First Avenue; Lemonade Folk Art, showcasing many regional artists, at 7213 E. Main Street; the Cactus Hut, specializing in cactus gardens planted in Arizona pottery, located at 7249 E. First Avenue; and The Leather Mill, 7225 E. First Avenue, which specializes in jackets, belts, hats, boots, and office accessories. Within the Old West Outpost at the corner of First Avenue and Scottsdale Road, shoppers can find several stores that showcase Native American arts and crafts, as well as souvenirs, T-shirts, antiques, and memorabilia.

Scottsdale Pavilions
Pima and Indian Bend Rds., Scottsdale
• **(480) 991-6007**

Although its only major department stores are Mervyn's and Target, Scottsdale Pavilions has such a good selection of stores that it has fast become a popular destination since it opened a decade ago. It is on land owned by the Salt River Pima-Maricopa Native American Community and a portion of the revenues go to the tribe.

This open-air mall combines large, freestanding stores flanked by smaller stores, all

It's just like shopping in another century when you go to the Antique Emporium and Country Store in Glendale.

Photo: Courtesy of Glendale Convention and Visitors Bureau

on both sides of Indian Bend Road. Vendors include Pretty Papers, a stationery store; The Glass Table, which sells metal and glass furniture; Bunny's Shoes; Connelly Billiards, which sells billiard tables and home spas; Ulta 3 cosmetics store; Cost Plus, an imports store with home accessories and foods from around the world; Old Navy clothing store; Ross Dress for Less; Bookstar; Circuit City appliance store; Barbeques Galore; Van's Pro Shop for golfers; Cafe Au Clay pottery painting studio; a Sears Homelife furniture store; and Jennifer Convertibles, which sells fold-out sofas and futons.

Adjacent to the stores is Fiddlesticks Family Fun Park, an Arizona-grown amusement park with miniature golf, laser tag, and other rides and entertainment. Several chain and non-chain restaurants are interspersed throughout Scottsdale Pavilions. Shoppers can also catch a flick at the movie theater or dine at one of the patio-side restaurants in the food court. Most of the stores and entertainment venues are open daily.

Scottsdale Seville
7001 N. Scottsdale Rd., Scottsdale
• **(480) 905-8110**

This pastel-colored, Southwestern-style shopping center has several high-end boutiques, including Ap'ropo fashions and accessories; Destiny's Bride, a bridal shop; and Hot Rags fashions. One of the most popular stores is In Celebration of Golf, featuring golf equipment and clothing for all those taking advantage of the golf resorts and championship courses in Scottsdale. There's also a practice tee. For an eye-catching selection of kitchen accessories and whimsical gifts for the home, stop in at Two Plates Full. Most stores are open daily.

Antique Shopping

Antiques Super-Mall
1900 N. Scottsdale Rd., Scottsdale
• **(480) 874-2900**

Just two miles south of Old Town Scottsdale is a trio of antique stores boasting 600 dealers and 120,000 square feet. The largest of the three is the Antiques Super-Mall, housed in a former department store. Just a short walk away are Antique Trove, 2020 N.

INSIDERS' TIP
It is illegal and foolish to leave either a child or a pet waiting in the car for you while you run into a store. Summer temperatures can quickly cause oven-like conditions in the car's interior, and heat stroke is a quick killer.

Scottsdale Road, (480) 947-6074; and the Antique Centre, 2012 N. Scottsdale Road, (480) 675-9500. Independent antique dealers have their own booths within the stores, which encourages a mind-boggling variety of antiques and collectibles at prices ranging from inexpensive to thousands of dollars. On just one quick visit, you can eye hundreds of lamps, clocks, trunks, dressers, all kinds of china, folk art, and interesting collectible toys. The three stores are open daily.

Specialty Stores

Antigua Sportswear/Factory Outlet
9318 N. 95th Way, Scottsdale
• **(480) 860-8224**
• **www.antigua.com**

Antigua Sportswear is a well-known name in golf shirts made by the Scottsdale-based Antigua Group. This factory outlet store offers a large selection of shirts, jackets, sweatshirts, windshirts, and other golf sportswear for men and women. Befitting a factory store, the prices are very reasonable. Antigua is open Monday through Saturday.

Chief Dodge Indian Jewelry & Fine Arts
Papago Plaza, 1332 N. Scottsdale Rd., Scottsdale
• **(480) 970-1133**
• **www.chiefdodge.com**

For 30 years, this family-run establishment, which offers a wide selection of Native American arts and crafts, allows customers to buy directly from the artisans for a significant savings. Turquoise jewelry is in abundance here, as are crafts such as Kachinas, sand paintings, pottery, and baskets. The store also offers art restoration services and on-the-spot jewelry repair. It is open Monday through Saturday.

Pinnacle Peak General Store
8711 E. Pinnacle Peak Rd., Scottsdale
• **(480) 991-1822**
• **www.pinnaclepeakstore.com**

Step back in time at this old-fashioned general store, where you'll find a hodgepodge of groceries, gifts, and souvenirs, along with a soda fountain, gasoline station, restaurant, wine cellar, and even a weather station. The rustic store

A number of artists thrive and sell their wares in Scottsdale, which ranks as one of the top art destinations in the country. One of the best places to shop for unique gifts—especially studio glass art by masters such as Dale Chihuly—is the Museum Shop at the Scottsdale Center for the Arts.

Photo: Paul Markow, courtesy of Scottsdale Convention and Visitors Bureau

is set against the rugged backdrop of the McDowell Mountains in north Scottsdale. Among the items on sale are antiques (including Tiffany lamps), Arizona-made edibles for eating here or taking home, T-shirts, postcards, candles, cowboy hats, and even the requisite scorpions under glass. The store and restaurant are open daily.

SMoCA Museum Store
Scottsdale Museum of Contemporary Art, 7380 E. Second St., Scottsdale
• **(480) 874-4644**
• **www.scottsdalearts.org**

Voted "Best Museum Shop" by two Valley publications, shopping at the store's two locations within the Scottsdale Center for the Arts makes you feel good because proceeds support the center's programs. Its eclectic assortment of eye-popping home accessories, jewelry, art, T-shirts, books, and educational (but fun) toys should delight just about anybody on your shopping list. Many of the works are handmade by artists, such as studio art glass bowls or hand-painted ice cube tray clocks. Other items, such as neckties sporting Frank Lloyd Wright and Keith Haring designs, are inspired by famous creative types.

Sphinx Date Ranch
3039 N. Scottsdale Rd., Scottsdale
• **(480) 941-2261**
• **www.sphinxdateranch.com**

Date farming is quite successful in Arizona, as this little store can attest. Personnel offer samples of several plump date varieties to help you make your choice. Other products, such as cactus jellies and locally made candies, are also available. The store occupies the original home on the date ranch, although the dates now come in from elsewhere in the state. The store opens daily.

The Poisoned Pen
4014 N. Goldwater Blvd., Scottsdale
• **(480) 947-2974**
• **www.poisonedpen.com**

It's no mystery where book lovers go to buy their favorite whodunits. The Poisoned Pen is one of the largest mystery bookstores in the country. In business for more than a decade, the store not only tallies more than 12,000 titles, but it brings in top-rated mystery writers for book signings, hosts book clubs, has its own show on public access television, and even runs its own press. The Poisoned Pen is open daily.

Northwest Valley

Shopping Malls

Arrowhead Towne Center
Bell Rd. and 75th Ave., Glendale
• **(480) 979-7777**
• **www.westcor.com**
One of the Valley's newest regional malls, Arrowhead Towne Center serves the needs of residents in Glendale, the Sun Cities, and other new-growth areas stretching to the north and west. Nearby, you'll find the 4,500-acre master-planned community of Arrowhead Ranch, as well as the Peoria Sports Complex, Spring Training headquarters for the Seattle Mariners and the San Diego Padres.

Dillard's, Mervyn's, Robinsons-May, JCPenney, and Montgomery Ward anchor the mall, a high-tech looking, steel interior featuring a profusion of plants, skylights, and benches. Stores include Casual Corner, Lane Bryant, Victoria's Secret, B. Dalton Bookseller, Bag and Baggage, The Disney Store, The Gamekeeper, General Nutrition Center, Gymboree, Kay-Bee Toys, The Knife Shop, Legends in Turquoise, and Nava Hopi Gallery.

In addition to its 150 stores (open daily), shoppers can enjoy an outdoor amphitheater, carousel, two restaurants, a food court, and a movie theater.

Antique Shopping

Historic Downtown Glendale
Vicinity of 59th and Glendale Aves., Glendale
• **(623) 435-0556**
• **www.historic-glendale.net**
Named by *USA Today* as one of the top antique destinations in the country, Glendale's charming downtown, with its restored Craftsman bungalows and white picket fences, appears to have sprung from a Norman Rockwell painting. You can find about four dozen antique stores in the 16-square-block area of downtown. Shops that feature antiques, crafts, tearooms, and even a candy factory are often housed in carefully restored buildings from the early part of this century. To complete the picture, a trolley transports shoppers through the streets lined with old-fashioned storefronts, streetlights, and park benches in Old Towne and the Historic Catlin Court shopping districts. Old Towne surrounds historic Murphy Park. Catlin Court, which you'll find situated between Myrtle and Palmaire Avenues, and 57th Drive and 59th Avenue, is listed on the National Register of Historic Places.

Many of the stores are open seven days a week, but it's best to call ahead if you're interested in a particular store. Though the stores are too numerous to name, a few stops include The Apple Tree, 5811 W. Glendale Avenue, (623) 435-8486, with one of the larger selections of antiques and collectibles; Sandy's Dream Dolls, 7154 N. 58th Drive, (623) 931-1579, with new and old collectible dolls and bears; Angels, Angels, Angels, at 7149 N. 58th Drive, (623) 937-5717, with a collection of heavenly delights; and Bo's Funky Stuff, 5605 W. Glendale Avenue, (623) 842-0220, which specializes in 1950s memorabilia and art deco items.

> **INSIDERS' TIP**
> A number of imported imitations of Native American jewelry, arts, and crafts are finding their way into less-reputable stores. Educate yourself before you buy—look for an artist's signature and ask for a certificate of authenticity. When in doubt, buy from the artist directly.

Specialty Stores

Cowtown Boots
2710 W. Thunderbird Rd., Phoenix
• **(602) 548-3009**
• **www.cowtownboots.com**
After more than 30 years in the business, it's no surprise that almost everything you need to be outfitted in Western style is here at Cowtown, but its specialty is boots. More than 25,000 pairs are on hand, from standard cow leather to more exotic materials like snake, deer, bull, calf, mule, antelope, and ostrich. In addition to the Cowtown label of boots, find Dan

SHOPPING

Post, Texas, Chisholm, and ACME brands. Factory irregulars are usually on sale, for those looking for a great deal. The store is open daily. Cowtown's other Valley location is at 1001 N. Scottsdale Road, Tempe, (602) 968-4748.

Popular Outdoor Outfitters
2814 W. Bell Rd., Phoenix
• **(602) 863-2462**
• **www.popularoutdooroutfitters.com**
   This Arizona-based purveyor of outdoor gear sells practical items like, clothes, tents, and stoves, as well as just-for-fun goods like kayaks and fishing lures. Known for its good selection, Popular often has reasonable prices on hiking boots. Easily accessible from Interstate 17, the store is open daily. Check the Yellow Pages or its website for Popular's 14 other Valley locations.

Terri's Consign & Design Furnishings
5905 W. Bell Rd., Glendale
• **(602) 843-8030**
• **www.eterris.com**
   What started in 1979 as a place for people to sell their brand-name and designer furnishings has grown into the nation's largest consignment furniture superstore. The gently used and new items arrive daily from all over the world. Some pieces come from estates, model homes, and factory liquidations as well as from homeowners. So you'll find bargains on everything from dining room sets to framed fine art. Terri's has several other Valley locations, including 2049 W. Broadway Road, Mesa, (480) 969-5545; I-10 and Ray Road, Chandler, (480) 730-1200; 15000 N. Hayden Road, Scottsdale, (480) 998-2828; and 3333 W. Peoria Avenue, Phoenix, (602) 789-1212.

Southwest Valley

Shopping Malls

Desert Sky Mall
Thomas Rd. and 75th Ave., Phoenix
• **(623) 245-1400**
• **www.desertskymall.com**
   In the early 1990s, the old Westridge Mall

that serves west Phoenix was revamped into fancier digs—including two new courts and huge skylights—lending it a clean, airy ambiance that fits its mission as a community mall. The name "Desert Sky" links the mall to the nearby Desert Sky Pavilion, a popular outdoor concert venue. At 100 stores strong, the mall's department stores include Dillard's, Sears, Mervyn's, and Montgomery Ward. Other shopping venues include a Millers Outpost, Fuzziwigs Candy Factory, Tag Team, and Saba's Western Store. A new Six Shooters Sports Grill features an entertainment facility, and a movie theater is conveniently located on site. Open daily.

Outlet Shopping

Wigwam Outlet Stores
I-10 at Litchfield Rd., Goodyear
• **(623) 935-9730**
   Head west on I-10 bound for Los Angeles, and just 20 to 30 minutes from downtown Phoenix you will come to the Wigwam Outlet Stores, so named for their proximity to The Wigwam Resort in Litchfield Park. The stores can be reached from Exit 128 on Litchfield Road.
   There's a nice assortment of about 50 stores in this U-shaped shopping center. Familiar names include Big Dogs Sportswear, Adidas, Bugle Boy, Levi's Outlet by Most, Nine West Shoes, Rocky Mountain Chocolate Factory, Van Husen Direct, and Las Vegas Discount Golf & Tennis. A small food court in one corner of the shopping center features both indoor and patio seating. Stores are open daily.

Attractions

Are you a museum type? Phoenix has an impressive array of museums spotlighting art and artifacts, from kachina dolls to fighter planes. Are you an outdoorsy type? This area is brimming with attractions that let you enjoy the sunny weather Phoenix is so famous for, while learning something interesting about our city. Do you like to see the world by car? We can recommend a scenic drive up South Mountain or a jaunt into Paradise Valley. Have you come all the way to Arizona to get a taste of the Old West? This chapter rustles up your options in Wild West-theme attractions.

We have grouped this chapter's entries by geographic area so that you might consider spending a day in one part of the Valley in order to see one, two, three, or more of that area's attractions. For instance, if you're heading for the Desert Botanical Garden, consider piggybacking it with the Phoenix Zoo, both of which are in Papago Park. Or if you are touring downtown Scottsdale, that's a good jumping-off point for Frank Lloyd Wright's Taliesin West in north Scottsdale. How about a day seeing the sights of central and downtown Phoenix, such as the Heard Museum and the Arizona Science Center? Want to plan a day of antique hunting in downtown Glendale? Perhaps you could fit in a stop at the Deer Valley Rock Art Center.

So have a map handy as you read this chapter and think about marking your best route. We have given hours and admission prices for 2000, but you may want to call the attraction first to check for any changes.

See our Parks and Recreation chapter for more ideas on how to enjoy our beautiful desert scenery and balmy climate. Our Kidstuff chapter will give you a child's-eye view of our best museums and other attractions. Browse our Arts chapter if you'd like to take in some additional culture while you're here.

Whatever your plans for sightseeing, be sure to consider the weather. Some attractions are perfect for those occasional rainy winter days, and others, such as the Desert Botanical Garden, are just glorious on a fall or spring day.

LOOK FOR:
- **Phoenix**
- **Southeast Valley**
- **Northeast Valley**
- **Northwest Valley**

Phoenix

Arizona Science Center
600 E. Washington St., Phoenix
• (602) 716-2000

With about 350 interactive exhibits to explore, plus a giant-screen theater and planetarium, you could literally spend a day at the Arizona Science Center. It has proven wildly popular and exceeded attendance expectations since opening in 1997. City boosters rightfully consider it a major factor in the resurgence of downtown. The $47 million four-story structure is eye-catching both inside and out, with its futuristic concrete-and-glass design by noted architect Antoine Predock. Rising into the sky is a nine-story triangular peak, also called a fin, covered with aluminum.

The Science Center is about 10 times the size of the city's old science museum. The planetarium boasts one of the largest domes in the West and offers a 40-minute show called "Arizona Skies," along with changing shows exploring various intergalactic topics. The Irene P. Flinn Theater has a five-story screen using Iwerks technology, which offers a similar viewing experience to the Imax theaters.

The 350 or so exhibits are cleverly organized into galleries that explore human physiology, physical forces, transportation, geology, computers, and applied sciences. Almost all of the exhibits are hands-on, which is what makes the center so absorbing. Examples include: a physiology station in which you and a partner time yourselves in a wheelchair race; a geology exhibit where you create your own sand dunes; and a station where you simulate piloting an airplane. An area called the Fab Lab is a big draw with kids. They can pull themselves up a rope with a pulley, launch paper airplanes, and roll golf balls along a fast track.

Make time to check out the nifty games, puzzles, posters, books, and other items for sale in Awesome Atom's. The center has a food court with fast-food options, for those who are making a day of it. Also, the cafes of Heritage Square are just next door.

The Science Center exhibits are open 10 AM to 5 PM daily except Thanksgiving and Christmas. Admission is $6.50 for adults, $4.50 for seniors and children 4 to 12, and free for children 3 and younger. Higher-priced tickets combining the exhibits and admission to the Iwerks theater and/or planetarium are available.

Arizona State Capitol Museum and Wesley Bolin Memorial Plaza
1700 W. Washington St., Phoenix
• (602) 542-4581

As capitols go, Arizona's is a fairly modest granite building with a copper dome as its best feature. The white, winged figure atop the dome is called Victory Lady. The Capitol Museum is made up of all four floors of the original Capitol building, which dates to 1900. In fact, it was built 12 years before Arizona became a state. The Arizona Legislature, having outgrown the building in 1960, meets in newer quarters behind the Capitol. Stroll through the Capitol to see various murals executed over the decades to depict Arizona's history and scenery and its progress as a state. Also view the old Senate and House chambers, historical photos, and a statue of the state's first governor, George W.P. Hunt. More sights can be found on the Capitol grounds and the adjoining Wesley Bolin Plaza, a grassy, two-block area of sculptures and monuments. It is named after a former Arizona governor. On the eastern end of the plaza rests an anchor from the USS *Arizona*, sunk during the Japanese raid on Pearl Harbor in 1941. The anchor serves as a memorial to those who died aboard the battleship. You'll also find memorials to veterans of the Korean and Vietnam Wars. The plaza is accessible during daytime hours. Capitol Museum hours are 8 AM to 5 PM weekdays, and admission is free. Call to inquire about guided tours, which are given twice daily.

Burton Barr Central Library
1221 N. Central Ave., Phoenix
• (602) 262-4636

Several major metropolitan libraries with architectural significance have been built during the last decade, and Phoenix's central library is one of them. Opened in 1995, the five-story, multimillion-dollar structure was paid for through a city bond election for arts and cultural improvements. Residents looked at its simple exterior of corrugated copper and gray concrete and either loved it or hated it. Then, slowly but surely, the public trickled in, and by viewing it more closely, they began to understand the concept behind architect Will Bruder's organic design. It is a design inspired by the majesty of Arizona's many copper-colored mesas and rugged gray canyons, and it skillfully uses natural light in opposition to the notion that public libraries have to be dark and stuffy. The north side of the building has computer-controlled shades, or "sails," outside the windows that rotate and adjust to let in the right amount of light according to the time of day. Another remarkable feature is the main entry, where a glass elevator swooshes up and down the five floors while reflecting colored lights into the pool below it. The Great Reading Room on the top floor is considered the largest such room in North America. It's also where you'll notice how the roof is suspended by cables instead of resting on concrete pillars.

The Phoenix library system celebrated its 100th anniversary in 1998 and over the years has grown to 12 branches, in addition to new Burton Barr library, named after a longtime Arizona legislator. It replaces the old central library at McDowell Road and Central Avenue. The new library includes a good children's area, the Rare Book Room and the Arizona Room with resources on the history of the Southwest. Hours are 9 AM to 9 PM Monday through Wednesday, 9 AM to 6 PM Thursday through Saturday, and 1 to 5 PM Sunday.

Desert Botanical Garden
Papago Park, 1201 N. Galvin Pkwy., Phoenix
• (602) 941-1225

Sometimes Valley residents have a hard time

convincing outsiders that our Sonoran desert is a wonderland of trees, shrubs, and flowers. No, not in the magnolia and maple tree sense, but in the sense that we have an amazing variety of plants that can withstand this climate and still bloom brilliantly. The Desert Botanical Garden helps us make our case, immensely. It is one of the nation's few public gardens dedicated to desert plants. Its winding trails pleasantly take you through veritable forests and open your eyes to 4,000 species of cactus, succulents, trees, and flowers.

The garden opened in 1939 as both a showcase and conservation headquarters. Today its collection includes several rare, threatened, and endangered Southwestern species in addition to spotlighting common plants. After a leisurely morning or afternoon in the garden, you will be able to recognize and reel off names of flora such as the ocotillo, the jumping cholla, desert marigolds, the creosote bush, the palo verde tree, the yucca plant, and more. Each trail has signage not only bearing the names, but also explaining the plants' hardiness and desert life in general. Often you will find garden volunteers at information stations, displaying specimens you can touch.

The garden is organized around four trails. Plants & People of the Sonoran Desert Trail, which sheds light on desert dwellers' use of plants for food, fibers and construction, is one-third mile. The Sonoran Desert Nature Trail is a one-quarter-mile hillside trail focusing on the interactions among plants, birds, reptiles, insects, and mammals sharing the desert. The Desert Discovery Trail encompasses 20 acres and thousands of desert plants from around the world. On the trail are the Cactus House and Succulent House, which showcase plants inside greenhouses. The Center for Desert Living Trail demonstrates the beauty of desert landscaping and explains the water-efficiency of the Desert House, an actual residence within the garden.

At the garden you'll find a visitors center, a gift shop, a café, and a plant shop, which has a wonderful selection of plants to buy—instructions included. Also on the grounds is Webster Auditorium, one of the few remaining authentic examples of Pueblo Revival architecture in central Arizona.

Hours are 8 AM to 8 PM daily except during the summer, when you can beat the heat by arriving at 7 AM. Admission is $7.50 for adults, $6.50 for seniors, $1.50 for children ages 5 to 12, and free for those younger than 5. The garden frequently offers guided tours or schedules outdoor concerts; more information is available on the garden hotline, (480) 481-8184.

Hall of Flame Museum of Firefighting
6101 E. Van Buren St., Phoenix
- **(602) 275-3473**
- **www.hallofflame.org**

What a perfect name for the world's largest display of firefighting equipment. The Hall of

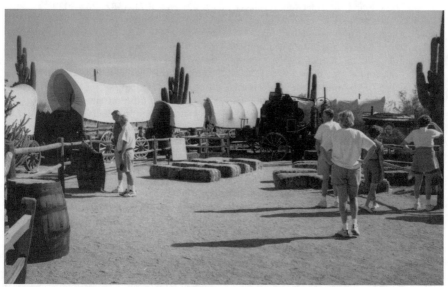

The prairie schooners are one of the many attractions at Rawhide.

Photo: Penny Kleingartner

Flame houses more than 100 restored pieces of hand-to-hand, horse-drawn and mechanized firefighting equipment dating from 1725 to 1961. The collection includes several well-preserved fire engines, including a fire truck that is safe for children to climb into and pretend to drive. Wannabe firefighters can dress up in coats, helmets, and other gear, or simply browse the four galleries to learn more about this honorable profession. The breadth of this museum is quite amazing. There's a gallery devoted to helmets, an area showing more than 2,000 fire department badges, fire safety exhibits, a game area, and an art gallery of firefighting-related scenes. The museum is open 9 AM to 5 PM Monday through Saturday and noon to 4 PM Sunday. Admission is $5 for adults, $4 for seniors, $3.50 for children 6 to 17, and free for children younger than 6.

Heard Museum
22 E. Monte Vista Rd., Phoenix
• **(602) 252-8848**
• **www.heard.org**

If you have time to see only one tourist attraction while you're in Phoenix, see the Heard Museum. No other museum in the world can provide insights into Native American culture the way the Heard can. It has an internationally renowned collection of Indian fine arts and crafts from throughout North America, with emphasis on the peoples of the Southwest. The more than 32,000 works of art and ethnographic objects span several centuries and are handsomely and informatively displayed. And all exhibits are presented with a quiet reverence for Native American ways of life.

The Heard Museum was founded in 1929 by Dwight B. and Maie Bartlett Heard, a prominent Phoenix couple who moved to the Valley from Chicago in the mid-1880s. The Heards were avid collectors of Native American artifacts and art, especially those of Southwestern cultures. Their decision to build a museum to share their exemplary collection was visionary. Today, the Heard Museum annually attracts 250,000 visitors from all over the world. It has outgrown its original building—of charming Spanish Colonial-style design—and has completed a multimillion-dollar expansion , adding three new galleries, a new auditorium for performances of Native American dance and music, and an Education Pavilion, among other things.

Visitors should spend time at "Native Peoples of the Southwest," the Heard's permanent exhibit chronicling the cultures of a number of tribes through art, artifacts, maps, information boards, and videos. Also see the Barry Goldwater collection of 437 historic Hopi kachina dolls, and the C.G. Wallace collection of more than 500 pieces of important Navajo and Zuni jewelry. A couple of galleries concentrate on contemporary paintings, prints, and sculptures by Native Americans, and these are also worth seeing. And here and there you will find art and artifacts from other parts of the world and other cultures, presented for their comparative value. Families ought to spend time in "Old Ways, New Ways," a hands-on exhibit area where youngsters step inside Indian structures, make crafts, and visit with artists.

The Heard Museum Shop & Bookstore is a showcase of Native American jewelry, textiles, pottery, and kachina dolls for sale. If you are a serious collector of Indian art, this is your place. The staff is knowledgeable about the things they sell and can often point you to the finer pieces.

See our Annual Events chapter for special events at the Heard, such as the World Championship Hoop Dance Contest, the Guild Indian Fair & Market and other events.

The Heard's hours are 9:30 AM to 5 PM Monday through Saturday and noon to 5 PM Sunday. Admission is $7 for adults, $6 for seniors, $3 for children 4 to 12, and free for children younger than 4.

Heritage Square
Sixth and Monroe Sts., Phoenix
• **(602) 262-5071, (602) 262-5029**

Heritage Square is a cherished niche in downtown Phoenix, a city block that contains the only remaining residential structures from the original townsite of Phoenix. As such, it is listed on the National Register of Historic Places. It's a grouping of eight restored Victorian houses in a pedestrian-only enclave, and you can find it in the shadow of the new Arizona Science Center and Bank One Ballpark.

The most eye-catching is the Rosson House, built in 1895, with its expansive veranda and an octagonal gray turret topped by an elaborate finial. The 10 rooms of the Rosson House feature pressed-tin ceilings and parquet floors. It's open for viewing from 10 AM to 3:30 PM Wednesday through Saturday and from noon to 3:30 PM Sunday. Tucked next to it is the Burgess Carriage House, which serves as the ticket office and gift shop. The charge for guided tours is $3 for adults, $2 for seniors, $1 for children 6 to 13, and free for children younger than 6.

In the Stevens House find the Arizona Doll

and Toy Museum, showcasing antique and modern dolls, dollhouses, and toys. An authentic-looking 1912 schoolroom features antique dolls propped in desks like students. There is a small admission charge of $2 for adults and 50 cents for children. Hours are 10 AM to 4 PM Tuesday through Saturday and noon to 4 PM Sunday. The museum is closed in August.

Heritage Square also features: the Teeter House Victorian Tea Room, offering lunch, tea and pastries and a high tea by reservation; Heritage House Café, a self-serve deli in what used to be a mule barn; the Silva House, which has exhibits about early life in Phoenix (admission is free); the Lath House Pavilion, erected in 1980 to facilitate the many outdoor festivals and farmers markets held at Heritage Square; the Duplex, a small house that serves as city offices; the Baird Machine Shop, dating from 1929 and now home of Pizzeria Bianco, a popular eatery; and Native Ring, which exhibits and sells fine Native American arts and crafts.

Mystery Castle
800 E. Mineral Rd., Phoenix
• **(602) 268-1581**

Built in 1930 in the foothills of South Mountain Park, Mystery Castle has been open for public tours ever since a 1948 *Life* magazine article put it on the map. The 8,000-square-foot castle, built from recycled bottles, old bricks, and granite, was built by an eccentric father as an act of love toward his young daughter. It has 18 rooms and 13 fireplaces. The daughter still lives there and conducts tours from 11 AM to 4 PM Thursday through Sunday. The castle is closed from July to September. Admission is $5 for adults, $2.50 for children ages 6 to 15, and free for children younger than 6.

Phoenix Art Museum
1625 N. Central Ave., Phoenix
• **(602) 257-1222, (602) 257-1880**
• **www.phxart.org**

Playing an increasingly larger role in the Valley's cultural life is the Phoenix Art Museum, with its permanent collection of 13,000 works spanning several centuries and representing many artistic styles and media as well as many world-renowned artists. The museum officially opened in 1959, although it had thrived as a small community arts center for two decades before that. By the 1980s, the museum began to outgrow its space. Thanks to a city bond election, the museum had funds to double its space and make several architectural improvements, which were completed in 1996.

There are several galleries worth seeing at the Phoenix Art Museum, including the Art of Our Time gallery, with works by Georgia O'Keeffe, Pablo Picasso, Frida Kahlo, Keith Haring, and others; the Western American Galleries, with many Realist paintings celebrating Western landscape and history; the European

Founded in 1929, the Heard Museum is renowned for its collection of Native American arts.

Photo: Courtesy of Heard Museum, Phoenix, Craig Smith

Galleries, with paintings and sculptures from the 14th century up to the Impressionists; the Art of Asia Galleries, with works spanning several hundred years; and the Thorne Miniature Rooms, miniature interior replications from America, England, France, and Italy.

Children will enjoy the hands-on Art Works Gallery, with games, puzzles, books, and videos that shed light on the museum's collection. You might want to stop by the Art Museum Cafe for light refreshments. The Museum Store is a shopper's delight with unusual gifts, art books, jewelry, and stationery.

The Phoenix Art Museum is open 10 AM to 5 PM Tuesday through Sunday, with hours extending until 9 PM on Thursday. Admission is $7 for adults, $5 for seniors and students, $2 for children ages 6 to 18, and free for children younger than 6. There is free admission on Thursdays.

Phoenix Museum of History
105 N. Fifth St., Phoenix
• **(602) 253-2734**

Drop into this museum's new home at Heritage and Science Park if you are visiting the Arizona Science Center or Heritage Square. It will give you a better appreciation of Phoenix's humble beginnings and rise to Sunbelt prominence. The emphases are on Territorial and early statehood days in Arizona, along with this area's proud multicultural heritage. Displays include Native American artifacts; the town's first jail; a 1920s living room; a look at Phoenix as turn-of-the-last-century haven for the chronically ill; and "aroma barrels" that recreate scents from the past. Sure to catch your eye is the stuffed ostrich, a reminder of the Valley's era as an ostrich-farming center. Cases hold dozens of smaller artifacts to admire, if you don't mind some leisurely browsing. The museum is open 10 AM to 5 PM Monday through Saturday and noon to 5 PM on Sunday. Admission is $5 for adults, $3.50 for seniors, $2.50 for children ages 7 to 12, and free for children 6 and younger.

Phoenix Zoo
Papago Park, 455 N. Galvin Pkwy., Phoenix
• **(602) 273-1341**

A little-known fact about the Phoenix Zoo: At 125 acres and 7,600 animals, it is the largest privately owned nonprofit zoo in the nation. Open since 1962, it is also internationally known for its efforts on behalf of saving endangered species. For instance, a zoo breeding and redistribution project begun in 1963 has increased the number of the Arabian oryx—a

type of antelope—from nine to its present world population of 1,400.

Set among the gently rolling hills, cactus, and craggy red rocks of Papago Park, the Phoenix Zoo draws about 1.2 million visitors a year. It's not unusual to find Valley families who visit the zoo several times a year. Exhibits are continually being updated and added. A recent addition is the Forest of Uco, featuring spectacled bears. With almost 400 species, the Phoenix Zoo specializes in animals that enjoy warm climates. Exhibit spaces closely resemble the animals' natural habitats. You can see how the spaces change as you move along the zoo's four distinct trails: the Tropics Trail, which is great for bird watching; the Africa Trail, with lions, tigers, and elephants; the Children's Trail and Harmony Farm, featuring farm animals and farm equipment, a small butterfly garden and playground; and the Arizona Trail, a must-see for out-of-state visitors. It's here you can view Mexican wolves, coyotes, desert birds, bats, and a spine-tingling array of snakes, scorpions, and other small creatures.

The Safari Train is a popular way to tour the zoo. It offers a 25-minute narrated tour by open-air bus. The zoo hosts special shows, guided walks, and classes year round. Ask about the day's events at the gate. If you're visiting in the summer, it's best to get there early in the morning before the animals take an afternoon siesta. There are several snack and beverage bars along the trails. Near the entrance is Trail's End Marketplace, with its fun collection of T-shirts, caps, toys, books, and other mementos.

Zoo hours are 9 AM to 5 PM daily, except from May 1 through Labor Day, when they change to 7 AM to 4 PM. Admission is $10 for adults, $9 for seniors, $5 for ages 3 to 12, and free for those 2 and younger. The Safari Train costs extra. Check our Annual Events chapter for details on two of the zoo's largest events, ZooLights at holiday time and Boo! At the Zoo at Halloween.

Pioneer Arizona Living History Museum
3901 W. Pioneer Rd., Phoenix
• **(623) 465-1052**

A mix of authentic buildings and historically accurate reproductions, Pioneer Arizona immerses you in life of the Arizona Territory at the turn of the twentieth century. Its 90 acres feature an 1880s schoolhouse, an 1890s exhibition hall and dress shop, and an 1870s opera house. A stroll down the dusty streets will also lead you to a blacksmith shop, sheriff's office and jail, church, ranch complex, and other buildings. And be sure to saunter through the swinging doors of the Whiskey Road to Ruin Saloon, dating from the mid-1800s. Some of the buildings were moved to the museum from other parts of Arizona, and some were constructed using building plans of the time. Adding to your visit will be the many costumed interpreters, including cowboys, lawmen, and Victorian ladies. The actors demonstrate crafts and stage melodramas. Pioneer Arizona is said to be the largest living history museum west of the Rockies. It is about 20 minutes north of central Phoenix, just off Interstate 17 at the Pioneer Road Exit. It's open 9 AM to 5 PM Wednesday through Sunday, but note that it is closed in July, August, and September. Admission is $5 for adults, $2.50 for children ages 6 to 12, and free for those younger than 6.

Pueblo Grande Museum and Cultural Park
4619 E. Washington St., Phoenix
• **(602) 495-0901**
• **www.pueblogrande.com**

Whenever we modern-day Phoenicians need a reminder that we were not the first to civilize this desert valley, we head over to Pueblo Grande. There we solemnly learn to understand and appreciate the world of the Hohokam Indians who flourished in this area for several centuries before mysteriously disappearing in the mid-fifteenth century. The museum, somewhat ironically, is just minutes from that icon of modern civilization, Phoenix Sky Harbor International Airport. Visitors can learn about the Hohokam's many crops, their extensive canal system for irrigation, their use of adobe construction, and their arts and crafts. Most important, once you've seen the indoor exhibits, you'll follow trails around the actual ruins of a Hohokam village that over the years has been unearthed by archaeologists. The Pueblo Grande also has an excellent gift shop with Native American arts and crafts. The museum is open 9 AM to 4:45 PM Monday through Saturday and 1 to 4:45 PM on Sunday. Admission is $2 for adults, $1 for children, and free for kids younger than 6.

South Mountain Park Scenic Drive
10919 S. Central Ave., Phoenix
• **(602) 495-0222**

South Mountain and the hills that surround it skirt the southern edge of the city of Phoenix. The city has preserved the area by turning it into a 16,500-acre park, a size that qualifies it as the largest municipal park in the world. It is home to more than 300 species of plant life and critters ranging from rabbits and coyotes to snakes and lizards.

You can drive to the summit of South Mountain, called Dobbins Lookout, by taking Central Avenue south from downtown. Once you pass the entrance gate to the park, simply follow the signs to the summit. The winding, two-lane road climbs for about five miles, taking you past picnic sites and trailheads. At the 2,330-foot summit, you will be rewarded by great views of the Valley, including the downtown skyline and the mountains to the east of the Valley. The views were even more spectacular before the Valley started having a smog problem. A springtime drive will introduce you to the desert's colorful wildflowers. The wet spring of 1998 produced one of the most beautiful wildflower displays ever, with lots of lupine, poppies, brittlebush, desert marigolds, and hedgehog cactuses in bloom along the road and on hillsides. The weather has been dryer since that time and the wildflowers have not been as prolific but that could change with the next season.

The visitors center at the base of the mountain is open daytime hours and can answer your questions about trails, picnic sites, and how to see the area's petroglyphs. Exhibits in the visitors center and the Interpretive Center look at area flora and fauna, mining heritage, and the contributions of the Civilian Conservation Corps.

Southeast Valley

Arizona Historical Society Museum
Papago Park, 1300 N. College Ave., Tempe
• **(480) 929-0292**

In Papago Park on the Tempe side is a large museum that is quite impressive from the outside, but is only partially completed inside. The Arizona Historical Society is struggling for private and government donations to build exhibits inside the 83,000-square-foot museum. It opened in 1996, with less than half of its space in use. In the meantime, though, visitors can spend about two hours touring what is there. That includes audiovisuals, maps, historic photographs, and a few hands-on exhibits looking at the agriculture, mining, and urban development of central Arizona in the nineteenth and twentieth centuries. One gallery focuses on World War II and its impact on the Valley, including personal letters and photographs from participants in the war effort. On the outdoor terrace is an interesting exhibit explaining the blood, sweat, and tears that went into building the Roosevelt Dam northeast of Phoenix—one of the first federal reclamation projects. Museum hours are 10 AM to 4 PM Monday through Saturday and noon to 4 PM on Sunday. Admission is free.

Champlin Fighter Museum
Falcon Field Airport, 4636 Fighter Aces Dr., Mesa
- **(480) 830-4540**
- **www.champlinfighter.com**

Aviation buffs aren't the only ones who will be awed by this comprehensive collection of historic and modern-day planes. Champlin, which houses its collection in three hangars at Falcon Field Airport, has been dubbed "the Smithsonian of fighter aircraft." The planes on view are from aircraft builders around the world. If you've never seen a British Sopwith Camel, here's your chance. Also on display are the German Messerschmitt 109E and Focke Wolf 190D, along with Soviet and Japanese aircraft. Jets on display include a Mig-21 and a McDonnell Douglas F4 Phantom. In all there are 33 flyable fighter aircraft from the World Wars and the Korean and Vietnam Wars. All have been beautifully preserved. You'll also find thousands of articles of aviation memorabilia, an art gallery, an automatic weapons collection, and a gift/book shop. The museum is open from 10 AM to 5 PM daily. Docent-led tours are optional, but are a good way to see the museum, because the docents add to the experience with their anecdotes about pilots and aircraft builders. Admission is $6.50 for adults, $3 for children 5 to 12, and free for those younger than 5.

Downtown Tempe
Tempe Convention and Visitors Bureau,
51 W. Third St., Tempe
- **(480) 894-8158,**
(800) 283-6734

College towns know how to be hip, and Tempe—home of Arizona State University—is the epitome of hip. The downtown and campus area blend coffeehouses, nightclubs, trendy restaurants, boutiques, bookstores, offbeat little stores, and office towers, primarily concentrated on Mill Avenue. All this activity makes for a thriving community of students, work-ers, and tourists who take to the streets all day and into the evening. In fact, downtown Tempe is bustling with nightlife, especially on weekends. But there's also a historic side to Tempe. Several brick buildings built earlier in the century in Victorian or Spanish Colonial Revival styles have been preserved, and new construction does a good job of harmonizing with them. A walking tour should include stops at: the Hayden Flour Mill, recognizable by its four silos; Monti's La Casa Vieja Steakhouse, the former home of Charles Hayden, founder of Tempe; Tempe City Hall, a modern, upside-down pyramid of glass and steel; the Andre Building (now housing Paradise Bar & Grill), one of the city's best examples of preservation; and the Laird and Dines Building, a recently renovated Tempe landmark that now incorporates restaurants, shops, and bars. On the way in or out of town, notice the Old Mill Avenue Bridge, dating from the 1930s.

Goldfield Ghost Town & Mine Tours
State Route 88 north of Apache Junction
- **(480) 983-0333**

Goldfield was a booming town back in the 1890s, thanks to a gold strike at the base of the Superstition Mountains. For five years, millions of dollars worth of high-grade ore was mined. In Goldfield's heyday, it boasted a hotel, boarding house, and three saloons. The boom went bust, of course, and the town looks quite battered by time now, but that's what ghost towns are all about. As a tourist attraction, Goldfield offers mine tours, gold panning, a nature trail, and exhibits of antique mining equipment. It is also the site of Arizona's only operating narrow gauge railroad, which takes you on a short scenic tour of the town. The town's Main Street has a steakhouse/saloon, an ice cream parlor, and several shops that are fun to browse. If you're there on a weekend, you might catch a gunfight (staged, of course). From Apache Junction in the far East Valley, Goldfield can be reached by driving north on Apache Trail (Arizona Highway 88). Goldfield is open 10 AM to 5 PM daily. Admission is free, with the various attractions priced individually.

INSIDERS' TIP
The white mansion on the hill near 24th Street and Lincoln Drive in Phoenix's ritzy Biltmore Estates neighborhood belonged to chewing gum magnate William Wrigley Jr. He built it in 1931 as a 50th wedding anniversary present for his wife. Currently the Wrigley Mansion is owned by Geordie Hormel, a Phoenix resident and heir to the Hormel meatpacking fortune.

Northeast Valley

Carefree/Cave Creek
Carefree/Cave Creek Chamber of
Commerce, 748 Easy St., Carefree
• (480) 488-3381

These two neighboring communities lie south of the Tonto National Forest and make fun excursions because of their scenic surroundings, boutiques, Western shops, and easygoing Southwestern ambiance. The half-hour drive from Scottsdale is scenic in itself. Head north on Scottsdale Road, and you'll see how acres of new development are interspersed with stretches of unspoiled desert. The McDowell Mountains draw your eye to the east, and the northern view spotlights the hills of the national forest. Several miles of Scottsdale Road north of Scottsdale have been designated the Desert Foothills Scenic Drive, and small signs tell you the names of the various desert plants that flourish in this area.

Using this route you'll reach Carefree first. The planned community was founded in 1956, and today it's dotted with expensive hillside homes. The world-class Boulders Resort is in Carefree, as is the upscale boutique/art gallery enclave called el Pedregal Marketplace. In the town center are several more boutiques and galleries, along with the K.T. Palmer Sundial, one of the largest sundials in the world. In tune with the town name, Carefree has fun with street names. Walk along Ho and Hum Roads, for instance, or Easy Street.

While Carefree is on the cosmopolitan side, Cave Creek is the country cousin. Find it by following the signs that point west to Cave Creek Road. You'll know you're there when you start to see storefronts and restaurants that hearken back to the Old West. Although there is modern residential development springing up all around it, the center of town is able to retain its quaint character. Cave Creek, too, is a fun place for souvenir shopping and antique hunting. A small museum shows Native American artifacts and mining and ranching displays. Take a break at one of the saloons on Cave Creek Road before heading back to the metropolis.

Downtown Scottsdale
Scottsdale Chamber of Commerce,
7343 E. Scottsdale Mall
• (480) 945-8481

Downtown Scottsdale is better seen by foot than by car. Scottsdale Road and the east-west roads that cross it are jam-packed with stores, restaurants, and galleries. Besides, traffic on Scottsdale Road slows to a crawl in high tourist season, so you might as well leave the car in one of the many public parking lots. Look at the lampposts and elsewhere, and you'll see signage that designates the different areas of downtown, including Old Town Scottsdale, West Main, Marshall Way, and Fifth Avenue. The latter three areas are the domain of shoppers and art connoisseurs and are well-worth your time if you are interested in souvenir hunting or in browsing the potpourri of galleries. See our Shopping and Arts chapters for more information.

A little background on Scottsdale: About 40 acres of virgin desert were turned into town lots in 1894, and a community was born, with a name honoring Army Chaplain Winfield Scott. For many decades, Scottsdale remained a farming and ranching community. Folks rode in by horse on dirt roads from Phoenix and hitched their steeds along what is now Scottsdale Road. This piece of history and others contribute to a slogan that the ultra-cosmopolitan Scottsdale still hangs onto today (perhaps in vain): "The West's Most Western Town."

Anyway, you do get a sense of the city's Old West heritage on a walking tour suggested by the Scottsdale Historical Society that includes these sites: the intersection of Brown Avenue and Main Street, site of the first general store and post office; the Little Red Schoolhouse on the Civic Center Mall, preserved from 1909 and home of the Historical Society; Cavalliere's Blacksmith Shop at 3805 N. Brown Avenue; and the building at 3933 N. Brown Avenue, built in 1923 as a pool hall.

INSIDERS' TIP
Spend the night at the Phoenix Zoo through a popular program called Night Camp. Chaperoned groups of youngsters 8 and older get to stay up late to walk the zoo trails and find nocturnal animals such as bats. They also participate in animal-related games and see wildlife up close with the help of zoo educators. After a full evening, kids camp out in the Education Building. Call the zoo at (602) 273-1341 for details.

Also be sure to walk around the Civic Center Mall, a modern complex of government buildings, a public library, a performing arts center that look out on gardens, fountains, sculptures, and the new Scottsdale Museum of Contemporary Art. It is a wonderfully conceived oasis and the site of many outdoor festivals and concerts.

Out of Africa Wildlife Park
Fort McDowell Rd., Fort McDowell
• **(480) 837-7779**
• **www.outofafricapark.com**

Think of Out of Africa not as a zoo but as a small version of Sea World that substitutes exotic tigers for the killer whales. The big cats can be seen in natural habitats developed for them at the park as well as in an unrehearsed show called Tiger Splash. Yes, they romp in the water with staff members and perform various tricks. Species include white tigers and Bengals. There are nine animal shows in all, which give the park a chance to show off its other inhabitants, including lions, coatis, foxes, bears, cougars, wolves, pythons, and exotic birds. But Tiger Splash, usually performed once daily, is the most popular. The grounds also include a cafe and gift shop. To get to Out of Africa, take the Beeline (Arizona Highway 87) north until you're 2 miles north of Shea Boulevard, then turn right on Fort McDowell Road. Winter hours (October 1 to Memorial Day) are 9:30 AM to 5 PM Tuesday through Sunday. Summer hours are 9:30 AM to 5 PM Wednesday through Sunday. In summer (from May to October) you might enjoy the park's dinner shows on the first Saturday of each month. Dinner (included in the admission price) is served from 6 to 7:15 PM, and the first show of the evening starts at 7:30 PM. Admission, which includes the shows, is $13.95 for adults, $12.95 for seniors, and $4.95 for ages 4 to 12. Children 3 and younger are admitted free.

Paradise Valley Scenic Drive
Town of Paradise Valley Offices,
6401 E. Lincoln Dr.
• **(480) 948-7411**

What's all this fuss about Paradise Valley? What makes it one of the most beautiful examples of mountainous Sonoran desert? See for yourself why the Town of Paradise Valley is the preferred address of the rich and famous. You can't get too close to the luxurious hillside homes because of security gates. But you can see them from a distance by starting at 24th Street and Camelback Road in Phoenix, then heading north toward Lincoln Drive. Take Lincoln east all the way to Scottsdale Road in Scottsdale, and you'll pass not only fine homes, but also a handful of first-class resorts, including Marriott's Camelback Inn and the DoubleTree La Posada. Turn south on Scottsdale Road, then go west on McDonald Drive for a few miles. The latter street turns into 44th Street, which will bring you back to Camelback Road. This drive affords fine views of Camelback Mountain, including the thumblike rock formation known as the Praying Monk; the Phoenix Mountain Preserve; and the Mummy Mountain range.

Rawhide
23023 N. Scottsdale Rd., Scottsdale
• **(480) 502-1880**
• **www.rawhide.com**

OK, pardner. Now's the time to dust off that cowboy hat and polish those Tony Lamas. Bring your camera, too, because Rawhide, an 1880s-style Western town, is a whole lot of fun if you're in the spirit of reliving the Wild West. With its zany shows by strolling costumed characters and authentic-looking storefronts on Main Street, Rawhide is considered one of Scottsdale's most popular attractions, annually drawing thousands of U.S. and foreign tourists. Featured on its 160 acres are stagecoach, train and burro rides, gold panning, a shooting gallery, several shops with Western wear and memorabilia, plus hourly stunt shows complete with explosions, fistfights, gunfights, and falls from buildings. In the Native American Village, watch members of the Apache, Navajo, Tohono O'dam, and Hopi tribes demonstrate traditional crafts and tell stories. Also view Native American structures built at the site using traditional materials. If you time your visit near dinner, you can grab some grub at the popular Rawhide Steakhouse. Hours change with the sea-

INSIDERS' TIP

You can't miss it if you're near the east side of Sky Harbor Airport at 50th and Van Buren Streets: Tovrea Castle is a maize-colored, tiered building on a cactus-studded hill. It was built in the 1920s by Italian immigrant Alessio Carraro and sold to cattle baron Edward Tovrea. Now owned by the City of Phoenix, the castle, often referred to as "the wedding cake," is under restoration and may open to the public for tours by 2001.

son, but in winter Rawhide is generally open 3 to 10 PM Monday through Thursday and 11 AM to 10 PM Friday through Sunday. Admission is $8 for adults, $7 for seniors, $5 for ages 5 to 11, and free for children younger than 3. Rawhide hosts many holiday-theme and special events throughout the year, often featuring live country music. Check our Annual Events chapter, or call the above number for more information.

Taliesin West
12621 Frank Lloyd Wright Blvd., Scottsdale
• **(480) 860-2700**
• **www.franklloydwright.org**

Frank Lloyd Wright's brilliance in creating organic architecture that harmonizes with its surroundings is perfectly exemplified at Taliesin West, Wright's personal winter home, studio, and architectural campus from 1937 until his death in 1959. The 600-acre site is nestled amid cactus and scrub, with wide-ranging views of Phoenix to the south and mountains to the east. The location was once considered quite remote for sightseers, but recent residential development in the far northeast Valley has

INSIDERS' TIP

Spend the night at the Phoenix Zoo through a popular program called Night Camp. Chaperoned groups of youngsters 8 and older get to stay up late to walk the zoo trails and find nocturnal animals such as bats. They also participate in animal-related games and see wildlife up close with the help of zoo educators. After a full evening, kids camp out in the Education Building. Call the zoo at (602) 273-1341 for details.

turned Frank Lloyd Wright Boulevard into a major thoroughfare.

At first glance, you may think Taliesin West looks quite strange. But the eccentricities of its design quickly grow on you as you learn how Wright and his apprentices gathered rocks from the desert floor and sand from the washes to use as building materials. You also will come to appreciate Wright's attention to detail and why he used light and space the way he did.

To see Taliesin West, you have your choice of four guided tours lasting from one to three hours. The one-hour Panorama Tour focuses on Wright's genius in integrating indoor and outdoor spaces. Visitors see the Cabaret Cinema, Music Pavilion, Seminar Theater, and Wright's private office, all linked by dramatic terraces, gardens, and walkways. You'll hear a general overview of Wright's theories of design and learn about the Taliesin Fellowship of architectural students. The tour is offered daily from 10 AM to 4 PM; no reservations are needed. Cost is $12.50 for adults, $11 for seniors and students, and $3 for children ages 4 to 12. Children younger than 4 are

Take a ride back in time at Rawhide, a re-created 1880's frontier town.

Photo: Penny Kleingartner

ATTRACTIONS

admitted free, but tours are not recommended for toddlers unless they are in strollers or in a parent's arms.

The 90-minute Insights Tour includes elements of the Panorama tour plus the dramatic Taliesin West Living Room, with its expansive windows linking it to the garden. Plus, you have an opportunity to sit in Wright-designed furniture. This tour is offered at 9 and 9:30 AM Monday through Saturday; no reservations are needed. Cost is $20 per person or $16 for seniors, students, and children.

Another option is the Nature of the Site Desert Walk, a 90-minute, in-depth explanation of how Wright's buildings are wedded to their surroundings. You will explore the desert trails that surround Taliesin West buildings and learn how desert vegetation and landforms were translated into design elements by Wright. Cost is $20, or combine it with one of the above-named tours for an additional cost. The walk is held at 11:15 AM and 1:15 PM Monday through Saturday, and reservations are suggested.

The three-hour Behind the Scenes Tour ($35 per person) allows you to chat with a Wright associate, have mid-morning refreshments in the Taliesin Fellowship dining room, and visit all the spots on the Insights tour. Reservations

are suggested for this tour, which is held at 9 AM Tuesday and Thursday.

The above tours are given October through May. Taliesin West is open in the summer, although the heat somewhat limits the number of tours. It's best for summer visitors to call ahead for times.

Be sure to stop in at the Taliesin West Bookstore, which stocks hard-to-find books and prints, along with a nice selection of Wright-inspired clothing and gifts.

Northwest Valley

Deer Valley Rock Art Center
3711 W. Deer Valley Rd., Phoenix
• (623) 582-8007

The Deer Valley Rock Art Center serves as a sanctuary for the 1,500 ancient petroglyphs to be found just on this 47-acre desert preserve. Operated by the Arizona State University Department of Anthropology, it provides public access to the Hedgpeth Hills petroglyph site via a quarter-mile nature trail. Signs along the way help interpret what you're seeing. You'll come away with a better understanding of the cultures that made the rock art—the Hohokam

The IMAX Theater in Tempe is a popular attraction.

Photo: Penny Kleingartner

Explore the past at the new Phoenix Museum of History near Heritage Square in downtown Phoenix.

Photo: Penny Kleingartner

and Patayan who inhabited the area from A.D. 300 to 1450. Morning viewing is recommended, and bring your binoculars. The visitors center has various exhibits, a video room, and gift shop. From October to April, the center is open from 9 AM to 5 PM Tuesday through Saturday and noon to 5 PM Sunday. Call about summer hours. Admission is $4 adults, $2 students and seniors, $1 for ages 6 to 12, and free for children younger than 6.

Downtown Glendale
**Glendale Chamber of Commerce,
7105 N. 59th Ave., Glendale
• (623) 937-4754**

The awnings, the shade of many trees, the brick sidewalks, and the well-preserved buildings all lend a pleasant ambiance to downtown Glendale, the area near 59th and Glendale Avenues. It is an antique-hunter's paradise, with about four dozen antiques shops within a few blocks of each other. It is said to be the largest concentration of antiques dealers in Arizona. The shops sell everything from Victorian-era furniture to automobile memorabilia to vintage telephones to elegant collectible figurines. Storefronts bear names like Arsenic & Old Lace, Bo's Funky Stuff, and Grandma's House. Also

scattered through downtown are plenty of specialty shops, such as one selling angel figurines or the shop specializing in hand-blown glass. Visitors always gravitate toward the four-block area known as Catlin Court, where century-old bungalows have been preserved and turned into shops and restaurants. Look for trolley stops if you would like a mobile tour of downtown the old-fashioned way. On Saturdays from October through May, Glendale stages a farmers market and crafts fair in Murphy Park.

For refreshments, your options include ice cream parlors, tearooms, and family-style restaurants. Or you could skip such formalities entirely and head straight to Cerreta Candy Co., 5345 W. Glendale Avenue, (623) 930-1000, where you can watch chocolates and other candies being made in this small, family-owned factory. Stop in anytime during retail hours of 8 AM to 6 PM Monday through Saturday. Boxed candies and chocolate by the pound are available for purchase.

Sahuaro Ranch
**9802 N. 59th Ave., Glendale
• (623) 939-5782**

Listed on the National Register of Historic Places, the 16-acre park known as Sahuaro

Ranch is designed to preserve one of the Valley's oldest and finest homesteads. The land was once part of a 640-acre fruit farm developed by a family from Peoria, Illinois, in the late 1800s. In the 1970s, the city of Glendale saved several acres from development and turned Sahuaro Ranch into a tourist attraction. You can admire seven original buildings, a lavish rose garden and the more than 100 peacocks that roam the grounds. Also on display is a small re-creation of the original fruit orchard as well as a miniature cotton gin, a restored vineyard, various artifacts in the Main House Museum, blacksmithing tools, and various artworks. The park itself is accessible all day every day, but guided tours of the exhibits are given by volunteers and are limited to Saturdays from 10 AM to 4 PM and Sundays from noon to 4 PM. The tours cost $3 for adults, $2 for teens, and are free to those 9 and younger.

INSIDERS' TIP

Arizona is rich in petroglyphs and pictographs, ancient Native American forms of communication. What's the difference between the two? Petroglyphs are etched into the rock, and pictographs are painted onto the rock. Explore the various symbols of prehistoric cultures at the Deer Valley Rock Art Center, South Mountain Park, Hayden Butte, and many sites outside the Phoenix area. And please heed this reminder from preservationists and archaeologists: Don't touch the rock art.

Wildlife World Zoo
165th and Northern Aves., Litchfield Park
• **(623) 935-9453**
• **www.wildlifeworld.com**

Billed as the place to see exotic animals, Wildlife World Zoo is worth seeing if you like an informal zoo that lets you encounter animals up close. The zoo actually began in 1974 as a breeding farm for rare and endangered species, then opened to the public 10 years later. The collection now runs the gamut from rare species of primates to gazelles, a rhino, a zebra, and a white tiger. Don't expect something on the scale of a municipal zoo, but a walk through the grounds allows you to see dozens of interesting animals in fenced enclosures—about 200 species in all. Many visitors come to see the impressive collection of birds, such as pheasants, toucans, macaws, cockatoos, stilts, and ostriches. Most of the birds are displayed in a large, walk-in aviary. The zoo houses reptiles, an aquarium, and a petting area for children. At the giraffe feeding station, you can mount a platform that puts you at eye-level with the giraffes, which then eat pellets out of your hand. You can also feed the lories, small parrots that like apple wedges. The zoo has guided tours, a snack bar, and a gift shop. It's open 9 AM to 5 PM daily, with admission prices of $10.95 for adults, and $5.95 for children ages 3 to 12. It's free to children younger than 3.

Kidstuff

Just as the lure of wealth fueled the imagination of the Old West's early settlers, the region's mystique still packs plenty of imaginative punch for kids. Our legends and lore, unforgettable landscapes, and unique cultural traditions make a rich and memorable experience for the young set. . . and plenty of photo opportunities for doting parents. Whether you hanker to ride a horse, inspect a rattlesnake, float down a river, pan for gold, eat hot foods, or bed down under the stars, there's plenty of family-friendly events and attractions.

Though the Phoenix metropolitan area is practically a living history textbook, Western-themed attractions are only part of the equation. The area offers a plethora of entertainment options, including playgrounds, arcades, fun parks, zoos, and toy shops. Phoenix has bragging rights to several world-class museums whose hands-on activities keep kids entertained. The Valley's vibrant arts community means that plenty of outlets exist for keeping those creative juices going—from hands-on art venues to special theater performances just for kids.

Keep in mind that the weather plays a big part in deciding how to have fun. From May through September, the temperature ranges too high to spend long periods of time outdoors—unless you plan to keep your cool in a pool, lake, or water theme park. Therefore, we suggest options for both indoor pursuits and outdoor adventures.

For more ideas, see our Spectator Sports chapter for places to watch professional sports year round. See our Parks and Recreation chapter to scope out ideal sites for desert hikes or for whiling away an afternoon.

LOOK FOR:
- **Indoor Pursuits**
  - –Museums
  - –Taste of the Old West
  - –Theater for Young Audiences
  - –Shopping
  - –Kid-Friendly Restaurants
  - –Other Indoor Retreats
- **Fun In The Sun**
  - –Appreciating Nature
  - –Amusement Pakrs
  - –Water Parks
  - –Other Parks

Indoor Pursuits

Museums

Phoenix

Arizona Science Center
600 E. Washington St., Phoenix
- **(602) 716-2000**
- **www.azscience.org**

The folks at the Arizona Science Center have fun down to a science. The nearly new, multi-million dollar structure houses four floor's worth of hands-on, engaging exhibits that make learning seem like second nature. Its futuristic concrete-and-glass design by noted architect Antoine Predock is worth a look in and of itself. It gets even better inside: look for a planetarium with one of the largest domes in the West; a theater with a five-story screen using Iwerks technology; and 350 exhibits cleverly organized into galleries that explore human physiology, physical forces, transportation, geology, computers, and applied sciences. Exhibits change frequently so families can stop by more than once. Experiments your budding Einsteins can try include making giant bubbles, testing paper airplanes, and measuring their skin in square inches. Near the food court, you'll find the center's store, Awesome Atom's, which is a required stop to stock up on gadgets for the thinking set. The Science Center exhibits are open 10 AM to 5 PM daily, except Thanksgiving and Christmas. Admission is $8 for adults, $6 for seniors and children ages 3 to 12, and free for children 3 and younger. Ask about special rates for large groups. Shows at the Iwerks theater and the planetarium cost extra. If you like what you see, the center runs a special summer camp for children 12 and younger, as well as continuing classroom programs for preschoolers during the winter months.

Hall of Flame Museum of Firefighting
6101 E. Van Buren St., Phoenix
• **(602) 275-3473**
• **www.hallofflame.org**

Fire trucks intrigue the child in all of us, but the array of firefighting gear at the Hall of Flame Museum will amaze even the most jaded museum-goer. Here's a chance to get a close-up view of more than 100 restored fire engines and firefighting apparatus dating from 1725 to 1961—said to be the world's largest such display. You can board a fire engine, slide down a firehouse pole, and dress up in firefighting gear. There's a gallery devoted to helmets, an exhibit of more than 2,000 fire department badges, fire safety exhibits, and a display of firefighting lithographs and prints by Currier and Ives and others. A kid's area teaches safety through activities geared for ages three and older. Perhaps the most intriguing display in the museum is an original Phoenix Call Center, whose working scanner still does duty. The museum is open

9 AM to 5 PM Monday through Saturday and noon to 4 PM Sunday. Admission is $5 for adults, $4 for seniors 62 and older, $3 for children 6 to 17, $1.50 for ages 3 to 5, and free for children younger than 3.

Heard Museum
2301 N. Central Ave., Phoenix
• **(602) 252-8848**
• **www.heard.org**

A recent expansion added even more pizzazz to this world-renowned museum, which provides one of the best ways to learn about the cultures and the arts of Native Americans of the Southwest. It has the largest selection of Katsinas (Kachina dolls) anywhere. The museum's 32,000 works of art and cultural artifacts will keep the whole family interested, though children will love the exhibits geared especially for them. Best of all, visitors learn not only about the past but find out about modern-day Native American life. Duck inside authentic houses—including a Navajo Hogan, an Apache Wickiup, and a Hopi-corn grinding room. Work on an oversize bead loom, design Zuni jewelry, visit a Kiowa dance arbor, and walk through a re-creation of a Zuni pueblo. Be on the lookout for demonstrations by Native American artists, as well as performances of Native American music and dance. In the Museum Shop and Bookstore, you'll find books for

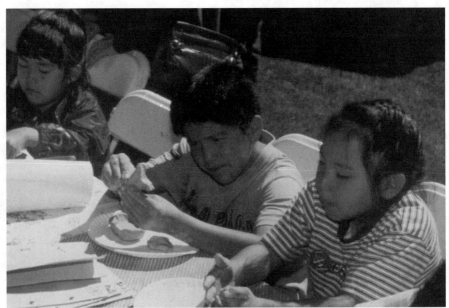

Hands-on crafts are a part of the fun at the Heard Museum's annual Guild Indian Fair & Market.

Photo: Courtesy of Heard Museum

young readers and toys that will continue to hold their interest at home. See our Annual Events chapter for special events at the Heard, such as the World Championship Hoop Dance Contest and the Guild Indian Fair & Market. The Heard opens daily from 9:30 AM to 5 PM, except for major holidays. Admission is $7 for adults, $6 for seniors, $3 for children 4 to 12, and free for those younger than 4. Guided tours are available and parking is free.

Pueblo Grande Museum and Archeological Park
4619 E. Washington St., Phoenix
• **(602) 495-0901**
• **www.pueblogrande.com**

Learn more about the Hohokam people whose villages once dotted the Valley more than six centuries ago. At the ruins of one of these villages, you can see the preservation work being done by archaeologists and wander among the interpretive exhibits both on the grounds and inside the museum. Kids can attend a workshop to become a junior archeologist or can be immersed in ancient studies at one of the park's archeology summer day camps held June through August. Petroglyph hikes outside the park, led by experts, also appeal to wannabe archeologists. Pueblo Grande is open 9 AM to 4:45 PM Monday through Saturday and 1 to 4:45 PM Sunday. Admission is $2 for adults, $1.50 for seniors, $1 for kids 6 to 12, and free for children 6 and younger. Sundays are free.

Southeast Valley

Arizona Museum for Youth
35 N. Robson St., Mesa
• **(480) 644-2467**

You can really kid around in this downtown Mesa museum, where youth enjoy an introduction to the world of fine arts. Named one of the country's best children's museums by *USA Today*, visitors can experiment with hands-on activities that stimulate creativity and artistic savvy. The museum plans to expand in 2001 and will be in new quarters for a period, so call ahead for its temporary location and hours.

Normally, fall, winter, and spring hours are from 1 to 5 PM, Tuesday through Friday; 10 AM to 5 PM, Saturday; and 1 to 5 PM, Sunday. Summer hours are 9 AM to 5 PM, Tuesday through Saturday; and 1 to 5 PM, Sunday. Admission is $2.50 per person and free for children younger than two.

Champlin Fighter Museum
4636 Fighter Aces Dr., Falcon Field, Mesa
• **(602) 830-4540**
• **www.champlinfighter.com**

See legendary fighter airplanes from all over the world up close in this three-hangar facility at Falcon Field Airport, which has been dubbed "the Smithsonian of fighter aircraft." The largest private collection of flyable vintage craft, 33 planes are represented from most of the United States' conflicts, beginning with the wood and canvas relics from World War I through the jets that flew during the Vietnam War. The stories of the pilots behind the planes come alive through articles of aviation memorabilia and an art gallery, though some parents with small children might find the automatic weapons collections a bit too glorified. A gift and book shop on the premises is a good stop to learn more about war in the sky. The museum is open from 8:30 AM to 3:30 PM daily. Docent-led tours are optional but offer valuable insight into the museum's collections. Admission is $6.50 for adults, $3 for children 5 to 12, and free for kids younger than 5.

Mesa Southwest Museum
53 N. Macdonald St., Mesa
• **(480) 644-2230**

At the newly expanded Mesa Southwest Museum, visitors can explore Arizona without ever leaving town. The 23-year-old natural history museum recently doubled its space and added several galleries. A 200 million-year-old Camarasaurus may be ancient history, but he's one of the stars of the museum's new Prehistoric Wing, which focuses on the age of dinosaurs. There, a three-story mountain presents a life-size peek at the Mesozoic Era—just watch out for the animated dinosaurs and the flash floods. Modern Arizona's beauty is revealed in the new *Arizona Highways* Magazine Gallery, a

INSIDERS' TIP

If your kids see rock climbers out and about and long to try it themselves, one safe way to learn the ropes is at an indoor climbing gym. The Phoenix Rock Gym, in Tempe's Aztech Court (1353 E. University), (480) 921-8322, will have them climbing the walls in no time. Check out their website at www.phoenixrockygym.com.

KIDSTUFF

permanent exhibit that features 45 top images from past issues of the magazine. Kids whose curiosity is piqued can get their kicks at the new Discovery Room, where computers, books, and classes offer answers to questions that might stump the adults in their entourage. The museum is open from 10 AM to 5 PM Tuesday through Saturday, and from 1 to 5 PM, Sundays. Admission is $4 for adults, $5 for seniors and students with an ID, $2 for children 3 to 12, and free for children younger than 3.

Taste of the Old West

Phoenix

Pioneer Arizona
Living History Museum
3901 W. Pioneer Rd., Phoenix
• (623) 465-1052

Did you know Arizona was the 48th state to join the Union? Here's a chance to experience what Arizona was like as a territory at the turn of the century, from a period of 1880 until it became a state in 1912. Pioneer Arizona is said to be the largest living-history museum west of the Rockies. Its 90 acres feature 29 historic buildings, including a schoolhouse, a sheriff's office and jail, a church, ranch complex, and a teacherage, which is a cabin where a teacher once lived. At the blacksmith shop, you'll see a real working blacksmith who has been plying his trade for nearly 25 years. You might even catch a melodrama playing in the Opera House. In the fall, costumed interpreters—cowboys, lawmen, and Victorian ladies—make the era come alive. The museum is about 20 minutes north of central Phoenix, just off Interstate 17 at exit 225. The museum is ramping up a full schedule of events, including Statehood Days, a Christmas lighting, and a Mountain Man Rendezvous. The grounds have a full-service restaurant, the Pioneer Café, and an antique shop. The museum plans to be open daily, from 9 AM to 5 PM. Admission is $5.75 for adults, $5.25 for seniors, $4 for children ages 6 to 12, and free for children younger than 6.

INSIDERS' TIP

A valuable resource for getting to know what Phoenix has to offer families is a monthly magazine called *Raising Arizona Kids*. It carries a comprehensive calendar of events and thoughtfully written articles about issues of concern to parents. The magazine is available at most Valley grocery stores and bookstores.

Southeast Valley

Goldfield Ghost Town & Mine Tours
State Route 88 (Apache Trail),
four miles north of Apache Junction
• (480) 983-0333

Flash back to the 1890s and get a feel for the excitement of the gold rush. Once a thriving town of 4,000 when gold fever was at its peak, Goldfield offers underground mine tours, gold panning, a nature trail, exhibits of antique mining equipment, and a narrow gauge train ride. If you're there on a weekend, you might catch a gunfight (staged, of course). From Apache Junction in the far East Valley, Goldfield can be reached by driving north on the Apache Trail, also known as State Route 88. Goldfield is open 10 AM to 5 PM daily. A steakhouse and saloon are open until midnight. Admission is free, with the various attractions priced individually.

Northeast Valley

Rawhide
23023 N. Scottsdale Rd., Scottsdale
• (480) 502-1880
• www.rawhide.com

One of Scottsdale's most popular attractions, Rawhide draws tourists from the United States and abroad, all of whom hanker for a glimpse of the Wild West. The 1880s-era town comes complete with passenger stagecoach, train rides, burro and horse rides, a rock climbing wall, a water corral, gold panning, a shooting gallery and arcade, and mechanical bull dubbed the Widowmaker. Gunfighters roam the streets (character actors, we presume) and might challenge your tyke to a shoot out. The antics at the Six-Gun Theater are as good as any Spaghetti Western, with plenty of cliff-hanging stunts like roof rolls and explosions. Learn more about Native American traditional dances and costumes at the Spirit of the West Theater. If time allows, browse through the Western-style shops, visit the petting ranch, watch a working blacksmith, and grab some grub at the steakhouse. Rawhide is open daily but hours change according to sea-

A petting ranch, ghost town, and little red schoolhouse await youngsters at Rawhide's Kids' Territory.

Photo: Penny Kleingartner

son, so call ahead to check its hours and annual events. Admission is $8 for adults, $7 for seniors, $5 for ages 5 to 11, and free for children younger than 3.

Theater for Young Audiences

If you are in the mood for an afternoon of imaginative entertainment, you and your family can catch a theatrical show. The Valley is home to a number of theater troupes whose offerings are geared for kids, many of whom feature child actors. Childsplay, a resident company of the Herberger Theater Center with an international reputation, is perhaps best known in the state. The Valley's children's theater offerings include pared-down adult fare, musicals, fairy tales, and—at the Great Arizona Puppet Theatre—there's even puppetry. Note that most companies go on hiatus for the summer, save for small productions by kids in summer camps or workshops. If you are a Valley newcomer, your kids might want to take a shot at the stage themselves.

Childsplay
• (602) 350-8101

Named by *American Theatre* magazine as one of the four leading theaters for young audiences in the nation, Childsplay has been entertaining

the young and young-at-heart since 1977. A recent sampling of shows included *Time Again in Oz*, which revisited Frank Baum's classic works; *The Velveteen Rabbit*, a fanciful story about a toy that comes to life; and *The Boxcar Children*, about a family trying to stay together in an abandoned boxcar. In addition to the classics, Childsplay's themes can provoke essential family conversations, especially with works like *And Then They Came for Me*, about hidden children of the Holocaust. Catch performances at the Herberger Theater Center, 222 E. Monroe Street, Phoenix, (602) 252-8497; at the Tempe Performing Arts Center, 132 E. 6th. Street, Tempe, (480) 350-8101; or at the Scottsdale Center for the Arts, 7380 E. 2nd Street, Scottsdale, (480) 994-2787. Ticket prices range from $11 to $18, and performance times vary.

Cookie Company
100 E. McDowell Rd., Phoenix
• (602) 254-2151

An affiliate of Phoenix Theatre, the Cookie Company built a stellar reputation for taking old stage favorites and putting a modern spin on them. Recent shows included *Charlotte's Web*, *The Sleeping Beauty*, and *Holidays on the Prairie*. The Cookie Company, made up primarily of adult actors, has also tackled fables, fairytales, and contemporary works. Its Saturday afternoon performances are often presented in both English and Spanish and tickets cost $7.50. And the theater is aptly named—audiences chomp on cookies and milk after each performance during a meet-the-actors reception.

Greasepaint Scottsdale Youtheatre
Stagebrush Theatre, 7020 E. Second St., Scottsdale
- **(602) 990-7405**
- **www.greasepaint.org**

Founded in 1984 by Wendy Leonard, a director with many years of experience in children's theater, Greasepaint is known for its reliably fun productions and its ability to nurture young talent. Recent performances included *Tom Sawyer, The King and I, The Little Princess, Camelot,* and *Oklahoma.* Performances usually take place on weekends on its home stage at the Stagebrush Theatre, with tickets ranging from $10 to $12. Aspiring thespians should check out the company's summer workshops.

Great Arizona Puppet Theater
302 Latham St., Phoenix
- **(602) 262-2050**

These puppeteers have been delighting audiences since 1983. They create and manipulate all kinds of artfully constructed puppets, including rod puppets, hand puppets, and marionettes. The theater's shows often celebrate Arizona culture. Recent productions have included *Hotel Saguaro, The Elves and the Shoemaker, Trouble at Haunted Mountain,* and *The Christmas Mouse.* The theater also occasionally hosts guest puppeteers from around the country, such as Chinese Puppet Master Yang Hui. Summer performances are 10 AM and 2 PM, Wednesday through Saturday; and 2 PM on Sundays. Fall performances are 10 AM, Tuesday through Friday; 10 AM and 2 PM, Saturday; and 2 PM, Sundays. Tickets cost $5, but go up when a guest artist performs.

Mesa Youtheatre
155 N. Center St., Mesa
- **(480) 644-2242**

Award-winning Mesa Youtheatre, under the direction of Jennifer Akridge, strives to present plays that speak to kids at their level, yet still challenge their minds. Costumes, set designs, and staging further demonstrate the theater's professionalism. Their repertoire—with classics like *Really Rosie, Alice in Wonderland,* and *Summer of the Swans*—encompasses both comedy and drama suitable for ages five and older. Performances usually take place Friday through

Kids enjoy the act at the Mesa Youtheatre, where productions like Really Rosie *bring down the house.*

Photo: Courtesy of Mesa Arts Center

Sunday, and tickets are $9 for adults and $7 for students. Acting and drama classes are also available for toddlers to adults.

Oxymoron'Z Star Theater
7117 E. McDowell Rd., Scottsdale
• **(480) 423-0120, (480) 874-1698**
• **www.startheaterprod.com**

Oxymoron'Z improvisational theater is funny enough for adults but clean enough for kids. Its shows steer clear of raw language and crude situations, and alcohol and smoking is prohibited on the premises. Fast paced and interactive, members of the audience yell out suggestions for scenes, games, and exercises. Catch the show playing every Friday and Saturday night at 8 PM. Tickets cost $8 for adults, $7 for seniors and children. Reservations required. If your kids get an itch for show business after the show, sign them up for classes and workshops.

Shopping

In this section we list a few of our favorite toy stores and specialty shops for kids. These stores may not be as well-known or as huge as places like Toys 'R' Us, the Disney Store, KAY-BEE, and Warner Bros, which are also in the Valley, but you're bound to find something that's both fun and educational. Two of the especially family-friendly malls are listed along with a few specialized bookstores. If you don't see your favorite store here, see our Shopping chapter for a more extensive listing of Valley malls.

Phoenix

Brainstorms
Paradise Valley Mall, 4550 E. Cactus Rd., Phoenix
• **(602) 996-8088**

This store has a both a serious and a fun side. You'll find books and kits on astronomy, anatomy, zoology, and other science areas that are educational and fun. It also includes kid-pleasing, absurd, wacky, and gross items, such as fake eyeballs, pillows made of shredded money, or rubber hands you toss around like

balls. Arts and crafts items, nursery toys, puppets, games, and puzzles also fill this compact store.

Gardner's Book Service
16461 N. 25th Ave., Phoenix
• **(602) 863-6000**
• **www.gbsbooks.com**

This store may be hard to find because it doesn't advertise and is literally a warehouse of educational resources, but once you peek inside the 12,000-square-foot treasure trove you'll agree it's worth the effort. The store is actually geared toward book distributors, teachers, and librarians—who receive discounts on purchases—but family shoppers are welcome. The selection includes juvenile fiction for all levels of readers, picture books, young adult novels, and nonfiction.

Hobby Bench
Paradise Valley Mall, 4550 E. Cactus Rd., Phoenix
• **(602) 996-7200**
• **www.hobbybench.com**

This is a toy store as much as a hobby store. It carries many brand-name toys, such as BRIO, LEGO, and Playmobil, but it also has an immense variety of arts and crafts items for all skill levels. Here's the best place to add to your model train set, and the best place to find model-building kits for your budding rocket scientist or aviator. Hobby Bench has two other Valley locations: 8058 N. 19th Avenue, Phoenix, (602) 995-1755; and 4240 W. Bell Road, Phoenix, (602) 547-1828.

Southeast Valley

Arizona Mills
Superstition Frwy.
(U.S. Hwy. 60) and I-10, Tempe
• **(480) 491-9700**
• **www.arizonamills.com**

The Valley's newest mall is full of manufacturers' outlets that appeal to adult shoppers, but it also has a kid-friendly side, notably because it contains GameWorks arcade, an IMAX theater, which shows interesting shows on faraway places, and a 24-screen movie house. The

Rainforest Cafe delights with the sights and sounds of an actual Amazon rainforest. Stores your kids will like include Funzy's, which carries cool toys; Way to Glow!, which lights up with glow-in-the-dark paraphernalia; and Awesome Atom's, a branch of the store at the Arizona Science Center. Arizona Mills can be reached from Interstate 10 near the junction with Interstate 60.

Atomic Comics
1310 W. Southern Ave., Suite 3, Mesa
- **(480) 649-0807**
- **www.atomiccomics.com**

The Valley has several good comic-book stores, but this is one of the best, offering a stock of more than one million comics. It also features comic-related video games, collectible cards, and action figures. It sponsors Pokemon seminars and tournaments on Saturdays. Atomic Comics has two other Valley locations: 3029 W. Peoria Avenue, Suite CC, Phoenix, (602) 395-1066; and 5965 W. Ray Road, Suite 19, Chandler, (480) 940-6061.

Imaginarium
Fiesta Mall, 1445 W. Southern Ave., Mesa
- **(480) 649-1711**
- **www.imaginarium.com**

In addition to brand-name toys and wooden train sets for fun and learning, Imaginarium's galaxy of toys includes books, CDs, and cassettes for kids. You'll also find educational games, unusual jigsaw puzzles, and nifty arts and crafts kits. The staff "toyologists" are happy to help you find something special, and they encourage you to play with the toys that are scattered on floors and tables. The store also hosts art-making programs once a month.

Superstition Springs Center
Power Rd. and Interstate 60, Mesa
- **(480) 396-2570**

This mall makes a nice destination for a family outing not only because it houses several major department stores and dozens of specialty stores, but also because it has a couple of nice features for those moments when you're shopped-out and need a respite. Young children can take a break by riding the carousel near the food court or by exploring the new indoor play area. Another play area outside, below the food court, features rocks to climb on and tunnels to skinny through, plus a slide that looks like a Gila monster. A pleasant sitting area, a botanical garden, and a short nature trail with marked sites that explain desert plants, completes the picture.

Northeast Valley

FAO Schwarz
Scottsdale Fashion Square,
7014 E. Camelback Rd., Scottsdale
- **(480) 423-9980**
- **www.faoschwarz.com**

The big name in toys back East has only one Arizona location, in one of the Valley's trendiest malls. You'll find a lot of brand-name toys, along with hard-to-find, limited-edition collectibles, such as dolls. Sometimes it's fun just to look in the window at all the big, furry, and fabulous stuffed animals this store carries.

Northwest Valley

Sunpath Children's Bookshop
7150 N. 57th Dr., Historic Catlin Court, Glendale
- **(623) 435-1500**

Sunpath's cozy, friendly store beckons young children to stay awhile, share a book aloud, and find a special book to take home. Rocking chairs and a circus tent with perchable pillows means everyone can get comfortable. To keep things fresh, Sunpath sponsors events like storytelling times and treasure hunts. It's geared for infants through 12-year-olds, though the store also has parenting and teacher resource sections. Sunpath is in the historic Catlin Court district of antique and specialty shops in downtown Glendale. It is open limited hours, from 10 AM to 2 PM, Tuesday through Saturday, and other times by appointment.

Kid-Friendly Restaurants

Phoenix

Chuck E. Cheese
8039 N. 35th Ave., Phoenix
- **(602) 973-1945**
856 S. Alma School Rd., Mesa
- **(480) 834-9322.**
8890 E. Indian Bend Rd., Scottsdale
- **(480) 951-1991**

This is a chain restaurant, but the kiddie rides, arcade games, and a ball pit make this a popular choice when the little ones get to choose the restaurant. Chuck E. Cheese and his mechanical puppet band pop out onto a stage every now and then to perform a few numbers and crack jokes. Pizza is the specialty, but sub sandwiches and a salad bar are also on the menu. The restaurants are open daily for lunch and dinner.

Ed Debevic's
2102 E. Highland Ave., Phoenix
• **(602) 956-2760**

You want atmosphere? You got atmosphere, plus plenty of fast-talking, insult-hurling, and bubble gum-chewing waiters and waitresses. The fabulous 1950s sets the theme at this chain restaurant, as you can guess from the retro attire, jukebox, linoleum, and signs on the walls. Expect burgers, fries, chicken, and spaghetti, diner-style, with enough variety for kids' fussy tastes. Be sure to order a genuine milk shake, served in a tall metal cup. The restaurant is open daily for lunch and dinner.

Rustler's Rooste
Pointe Hilton South Mountain Resort, 7777 S. Pointe Parkway
• **(602) 431-6474**

Your gang will enjoy hanging out at this taste of the Old West atop South Mountain, which offers great food and wide-open views of the city. If you can wrest your kids away from the popular slide, you can pick out Valley landmarks. Authentic touches include a barn-wood exterior, sawdust on the floor, and ranch and farm implements on the walls. Entertainment includes a live country band and colorful characters who wander from table to table, telling tall tales, and performing magic tricks.

Northeast Valley

Pinnacle Peak Patio Steakhouse
10426 E. Jomax Rd., Scottsdale
• **(480) 585-1599**
• **www.pppatio.com**

Your youngsters will experience a blast from the past when they are deputized by the Old Timer at this Western-themed restaurant. In addition to receiving their own badge, there's a coloring book, and a kids menu to amuse them—or you can challenge them to count the ties that have been cut from the necks of naïve tenderfoots and hung from the ceiling. Hint: there's close to a million. A Valley institution since 1957, the Pinnacle Peak Patio serves steak, chicken, and ribs.

Other Indoor Retreats

Phoenix

Burton Barr Central Library
1221 N. Central Ave., Phoenix
• **(602) 262-4636**

We recommend a stop at Phoenix's main library because of its fine selection of children's books and because of its fanciful design. The five-story library is copper and concrete on the outside, with lots of natural light flowing into the inside. If you're interested in architecture,

KIDSTUFF

These might be actors but your kids will get a taste for frontier justice at Rawhide.

we recommend checking out the Great Reading Room on the fifth floor, where you can inspect the cable-suspended roof more closely. And believe it or not, on the way to the library's restrooms, you can see a body heat-sensitive fiberoptic display along translucent walls. In addition, the glass elevators reflect colored lights as they swoosh up and down. The children's area has lots of cozy, creative sitting places, thanks to a city of Phoenix public art program that enlisted artists to design the furniture and book kiosks.

Ice Chalet
3853 E. Thomas Rd., Phoenix
• **(602) 267-0591**
• **www.icechalet.com**

Ice-skating might not be as popular in Phoenix as it is in colder climes, but it sure feels good on a hot day. The Ice Chalet is inside The Desert Palms Power Center and has public skating sessions during both days and evenings, with skating lessons on weekend afternoons. Day skating sessions are 1 to 4:30 PM, Monday through Friday; from noon to 3 PM, Saturdays; and from 1 to 4 PM on Sundays. Evening skating sessions are from 7 to 9 PM, Tuesdays and Thursdays; and 7 to 9 PM, Fridays and Saturdays. Admission is $5.50 for adults, $2.50 for children 6 and younger, and $2.50 for skate rental. Sunday afternoons, you can get a special family package for $24, which includes admission and skate rentals for a family of four.

Jungle Jim's Playland
4961 W. Bell Rd., Phoenix
• **(602) 439-9200**
2726 S. Alma School Rd., Mesa
• **(480) 820-8300**
•**www.jeepers.com**

Also known as Jeepers, Jungle Jim's Playland has the feel of a mini state fair with all its amusement park rides, video games, noise, and colored lights. Luckily for all those families looking for something to do on a hot day in the Valley, it's all indoors. The playlands are geared to children 12 and younger, offering small but fast roller coasters, carousels, and other kiddie rides. Preschoolers like the three-level soft playground with tunnels, chutes, and ladders. Both locations have a Pizza Hut. Hours are 11 AM to 8 PM, Sunday through Thursday; 11 AM to 10 PM, Fridays; and 10 AM to 10 PM, Saturdays. You can buy individual ride tickets or passes. Weekend passes are available for $6.99, and weekday passes cost $5.99, with toddlers under 36 inches getting a $2 discount. A $19.95 weekday special is good for parties, because it includes 20 ride tickets, 20 tokens, and a large, one-topping pizza.

Laser Quest
3335 W. Peoria Ave., Phoenix
• **(602) 548-0005**
2035 S. Alma School Rd., Mesa
• **(480) 752-0005**

Laser Quest is part of a national chain capitalizing on the new high-tech game of laser tag, in which participants chase each other around a maze in the dark, shooting laser guns at each other for almost a half-hour. Totally cool, say kids and adults who have tried it. Laser tag is hot, so expect to wait in line. Hours vary, depending on the season, but are typically 5 to 10 PM Monday through Thursday; 5 PM to midnight, Fridays; 10 AM to midnight, Saturdays; and noon to 10 PM, Sundays. It opens a few hours earlier in the summer. The cost is $6.50 per person, and you get to keep your personalized scorecard.

Mystery Castle
800 E. Mineral Rd., Phoenix
• **(602) 268-1581**

Once upon a time in the 1930s, a daddy decided to build a dream castle for his little princess. He built it in the desert, of native stone. It took 15 years to complete and has 18 rooms, 13 fireplaces, parapets, and many nooks and crannies. Inside and out, it looks like a castle and, at 8,000 square feet, is large enough to host royalty. Today, Mary Lou Gulley still lives in the castle her father built for her and conducts tours. Her fairytale abode is now on the Historical Registry and has been spotlighted by various media. Tour hours are 11 AM to 4 PM, Thursday through Sunday. Cost is $5 for adults, $4 for seniors and children ages 6 to 15, and free for children younger than 6. It is open October through June.

Southeast Valley

Kiwanis Park Wave Pool
6111 S. All-America Way, Tempe
• **(480) 350-5201**

This indoor pool at Kiwanis Community Park is not a full-fledged water park, but it has continuous waves and a giant water slide. It's popular on those days when it's just too hot to be outside, yet you can take away a bit of the chill from swimming with a few moments of sunning on the pool's outdoor deck. Hours vary by the season; sometimes the wave pool is only open on weekends. Admission is $6 for adults, and $3 for children ages 3 to 17. The pool is not recommended for toddlers. Tube rentals, snacks, and beverages are available.

Oceanside Ice Arena
1520 N. McClintock Dr., Tempe
• **(480) 947-2470**
• **iskateaz.com**

At a cool 50 degrees Farenheit, Oceanside provides a nice escape for East Valley residents.

Public skating sessions vary week to week, though. You can usually get in during the afternoons or evenings, but call ahead for hours. Admission is $4 for adults and $3 for children 12 and younger. Figure skate rentals are $3.50 and hockey skate rentals are $4.50. Inquire about lessons for beginning skaters or children's hockey.

Northeast Valley

Alltel Ice Den
9375 E. Bell Rd., Scottsdale
• **(480) 585-7465**

Attention, fans of NHL hockey. The Phoenix Coyotes' practice ice rink is open for public skating several times a week. The ice is almost exactly like the America West Arena rink in downtown Phoenix, where the Coyotes play their home games. The facility offers figure skating and hockey programs for children and adults, plus a pro shop, concessions area, and restaurant. Public sessions vary by the season, but usually last two hours every weekday, with the addition of two-hour evening sessions Thursday through Sunday. Admission is $7 for adults and $5 for those 6 to 15, with skate rental being an additional $4 for hockey skates or $3 for figure skates. Kids under 5 skate for $5, skate

KIDSTUFF

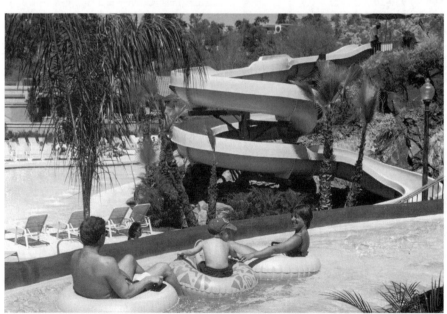

This family enjoys a leisurely tube down the Cactus rock river, a 1,000-foot long river canal that wraps around scenic mountain buttes, fountains, and waterfalls at The Pointe Hilton Squaw Peak Resort.

Photo: Courtesy of The Pointe Hilton Resorts

rental included. Friday and Saturday evening sessions cost $8. A family of four can skate on Wednesdays and Sundays for $28, skate rental included.

Scottsdale Civic Center Library
3839 Civic Center Blvd., Scottsdale
• (480) 994-2476, (480) 994-2449

This large library is a focal point of Scottsdale's Civic Center Mall, and its children's area is one of the most eye-appealing Valley libraries. It's designed to resemble a giant pop-up book, complete with cutout trees, clouds hanging from the ceiling, a castle facade, a reading tower with a drawbridge, carpeting in the color of a forest floor, and a "stream" running through shelving areas. Cozy seating can be found in the picture book area. In the young-adult fiction area, find an oversized chess set available for anyone's use, and just around the corner is a dollhouse on display. The library is open 9 AM to 9 PM, Monday through Thursday; 10 AM to 6 PM, Friday and Saturday; and 1 to 5 PM, Sunday.

Northwest Valley

Cerreta Candy Co.
5345 W. Glendale Ave., Glendale
• (623) 930-1000

This red-brick building is a landmark in downtown Glendale, but we're much more interested in what goes on inside—the making of delicious Cerreta chocolates and candies. You can stop in anytime during retail hours of 8 AM to 6 PM Monday through Saturday to watch candy being made at this family-owned factory. TV screens near the candy-making machines show a video that helps explain the process. Of course, boxed candies and chocolate by the pound are available for purchase on your way out.

Fun in the Sun

Appreciating Nature

Phoenix

Deer Valley Rock Art Center
3711 W. Deer Valley Rd., Phoenix
• (623) 582-8007

Better your understanding of the symbol-ism and beauty of rock art, or petroglyphs, and the earliest inhabitants of this region at the Deer Valley Rock Art Center, where you can view more than 1,500 petroglyphs along a quarter-mile path through a desert preserve. From October through April, the center is open from 9 AM to 5 PM, Monday through Saturday; and noon to 5 PM, Sunday. Guided tours are available at 10 AM on Saturdays. From May through September, the center is open from 8 AM to 2 PM, Tuesday through Friday; 9 AM to 5 PM, Saturday; and noon to 5 PM, Sunday. Admission is $4 for adults, $2 for students and seniors, $1 for ages 6 to 12, and free for those younger than 6. Kids can also explore the past more deeply at the Deer Valley Rock Art Center's summer day camp.

Desert Botanical Garden
Papago Park, 1201 N. Galvin Pkwy., Phoenix
• (602) 941-1225
• www.dbg.com

We would put the Desert Botanical Garden high on your to-do list. You might have seen botanical gardens before, but you probably haven't encountered one that celebrates the glory and variety of desert flora. You'll learn about dozens of varieties of cacti and succulents by winding through the garden's many nature trails. Often you'll find garden volunteers who have set up learning stations, perhaps even with hands-on activities. If you head to the garden in the spring, you will be amazed by the variety of cactus blooms, desert trees, shrubs, and flowers—which seems to include every color in the rainbow. Hours are 8 AM to 8 PM daily, except during the summer, when you can beat the heat by arriving at 7 AM. The center is closed on holidays. Admission is $7.50 for adults, $6.50 for seniors, $4 for teens 13 to 18, $1.50 for children ages 5 to 12, and free for those 4 or younger. Learn more about the garden in our Attractions chapter.

The Phoenix Zoo
Papago Park, 455 N. Galvin Pkwy., Phoenix
• (602) 273-1341
• www.phoenixzoo.org

The Phoenix Zoo is such a lively place that regular visitors have found they can head there several times a year and still find exhibits to explore. The 125-acre zoo is well organized and easy to traverse if you just have a few hours to spare, but we recommend making a day of it if the weather is pleasant. Each of the trails has a theme, such as the tropics, Africa, or the Arizona desert, and that's how you'll find any animals you're particularly interested in, from baboons to coyotes to zebras. Be on the lookout for the unfamiliar, too: Kori bustards, Mexican wolves, warthogs, and Chacoan peccaries. One of the zoo's most recent additions is the Forest of Uco, featuring spectacled bears. If you're new to Arizona, don't miss the zoo's Arizona Trail, with its unique exhibit of rattlesnakes, scorpions, and other creepy-crawlies— some of them viewed in a dark tunnel under special lights. The Children's Trail features a small butterfly garden and a farm area with hands-on activities. The Safari Train takes visitors on guided tours for a small fee. Hours are 9 AM to 5 PM daily from Labor Day to Memorial Day. In the summer, hours change to 7 AM to 4 PM. (In the summer, the earlier you go, the better.) Admission is $8.50 for adults, $7.50 for seniors, $4.25 for ages 3 to 12, and free for those 2 and younger. Check our Annual Events chapter for details on two of the zoo's largest events, the pageantry of the holiday ZooLights and the Halloween festivities of Boo! at the Zoo.

South Mountain Park Bike Trails
10919 S. Central Ave., Phoenix
• (602) 495-0222

If you've never had the experience of mountain biking in the desert, this is a great place to try it. The ridges and crests of South Mountain Park are higher than you think, so be ready for a workout. The average trail is 20 miles long, but along the way you will enjoy the vistas of the city, the desert brush and wildflowers, and interesting rocks. You'll see trail markings when you enter the park from Central Avenue. Be sure to pack plenty of water to avoid dehydration.

Southeast Valley

Hayden Butte
First St. and Mill Ave., Tempe
• (480) 350-5200

Not too grueling and not too easy, this hike up a craggy hill is just right for families with young children. Also known as A Mountain, the butte is popular with Arizona State University students, who get a kick out of constantly repainting the concrete "A" near the top. The hike up is quite steep in parts, but it only takes a half-hour. Watch for rocks with petroglyphs on the way. Be rewarded with great views of the Salt River and East Valley.

Northeast Valley

MacDonald's Ranch
26540 N. Scottsdale Rd., Scottsdale
• (480) 585-0239
• www.macdonaldsranch.com

Take a horseback ride among desert scrub and tall saguaros, with the McDowell Mountains as your backdrop. For decades, MacDonald's Ranch—a real ranch that raises

KIDSTUFF

Get an up-close-and-personal look at the Sonoran Desert at Rawhide by taking the train.

horses—has been teaching young people about these magnificent animals, through lessons and day rides. The ranch also specializes in cowboy cookouts on the trail to complete your Western adventure (groups of 10 or more). Reservations are recommended for the cookout, and the ranch suggests this activity for children ages seven and older. There are pony rides at the ranch for those younger than seven. Sample prices: A one-hour guided trail ride is $24 per person; a one-hour ride with a cowboy luncheon is $40 per person.

Out of Africa Wildlife Park
N. Fort McDowell Rd., Fountain Hills
• (480) 837-7779
• wwww.outofafricapark.com

Tigers in Arizona? This wildlife park has developed a natural habitat for white tigers and other species of predators, who star in the park's unrehearsed shows. The most popular show is Tiger Splash, where visitors can see tigers practicing hunting techniques as they splash in and out of the water with staff members. The park presents nine animal shows in all, featuring not just tigers but lions, coatis, foxes, bears, cougars, wolves, pythons, and exotic birds. Other features include a cafe and gift shop. To get to Out of Africa, take the Beeline Highway (State Route 87) north until you're 2 miles north of Shea Boulevard, then turn right on Fort McDowell Road. Winter hours (October 1 through Memorial Day) are 9:30 AM to 5 PM, Tuesday through Sunday. Summer hours are 9:30 AM to 5 PM, Wednesday through Sunday. Admission, which includes the shows, is $13.95 for adults, $12.95 for seniors, and $4.95 for children ages 3 to 12. Children 2 and younger get in free.

Northwest Valley

Wildlife World Zoo
1605 W. Northern Ave., Litchfield Park
• (623) 935-9453
• www.wildlifeworld.com

This scaled-down, no-frills zoo is a trek to reach, but it's worth seeing because of its unusual and rare animals—more than 200 species in all. For example, the new indoor-outdoor penguin exhibit features Black-footed penguins from Africa. Wildlife World's denizens are also easier to see than in some zoos, so visitors get a close-up look at rhinoceroses, llamas, tigers, lions, and antelopes. A new feature is the Australian Boat Ride, where you can ride a pon-

toon through the Outback and see emus, kangaroos, and cockatoos. Kids will get a kick out of the giraffe feeding station, where a platform puts them at eye-level with the giraffes where they can literally have these graceful creatures eating out of their hands. You can also feed small parrots called lories, which are partial to apple wedges. On-site amenities include a gift shop, a food service, and free parking. The zoo is open 9 AM to 5 PM daily, with admission prices of $10.95 for adults and $5.95 for children ages 3 to 12. Admission is free for children younger than 3.

Amusement Parks

Phoenix

Castles n' Coasters
Metrocenter, I-17 and Dunlap Ave., Phoenix
• (602) 997-7575

This amusement park catches your eye from Interstate 17 and the best way to get there is to take the Peoria exit. The park's name comes from its castle replica, which anchors the center of the amusement park, and the two roller coasters, one of which is Arizona's largest. If the thrills and chills of that double-loop coaster, Desert Storm, are too much, try the slightly tamer log ride, bumper boats, or NASCAR racers. The park also features a smaller coaster and carousel, along with four miniature golf courses. Inside the castle are video games and snack areas. Teens favor this amusement park as a hangout place on weekend nights, while younger kids enjoy having birthday parties there on weekend days. Castles n' Coasters opens at 10 AM year round, but hours for the rides are seasonal. Usually the rides run on Friday evenings, all day and until 11 PM on Saturday, and all day until 10 PM on Sunday. Call for hours on weekday evenings. Rides are priced individually (Desert Storm costs $4), or you can buy an unlimited ride pass for $18 or an unlimited ride and golf pass for $23.

Enchanted Island at Encanto Park
1202 W. Encanto Blvd., Phoenix
• (602) 254-2020
• www.enchantedisland.com

Encanto Park, a public area, stretches for several blocks between Thomas Road and Encanto Boulevard. Should you happen to meet any adults who are native Phoenicians, they will tell you this was the place to go in their childhood, particularly because of its resident amusement park, Enchanted Island. The park continues to be a favorite gathering place for families, especially those living in central Phoenix. Enchanted Island's most nostalgic attraction is a carousel that has graced the park since 1948. Another long-time favorite is the C.P. Huntington train that winds around the park. For more amusement, there's a pirate ship, kiddie roller coaster, rope climbing, bumper boats, action play stations, and more. There are also plenty of picnic areas adjacent to Enchanted Island. At Encanto's lake, try a little paddle boating, canoeing, or fishing. You can rent boats from Encanto Park Boat Rentals at (602) 254-1520. Enchanted Island hours vary, so call ahead. An unlimited ride pass costs $8.50 and individual rides cost 60 cents, but prices may go up.

Southeast Valley

Fiddlesticks Family Fun Park
1155 W. Elliot Rd., Tempe
• **(480) 961-0800**
8800 E. Indian Bend Rd., Scottsdale
• **(480) 951-6060**
• **www.fiddlesticksaz.com**
  The family that plays together will have

oodles of fun at Fiddlesticks, where the amusements include miniature golf, bumper boats, go-carts, batting cages, and video games. The Scottsdale location has all the above features, plus a new kiddie land, a new roller coaster, an elephant ride, and the new favorite among amusement parks aficionados—laser tag. The Tempe location has a lighted driving range popular with golfers of all ages. Families can buy value packages that allow entrance to a combination of attractions; the packages are $15 for adults and $11 for children under 59 inches tall. Hours vary so please call ahead.

Northeast Valley

CrackerJax
16001 N. Scottsdale Rd., Scottsdale
• **(480) 998-2800**
• **www.crackerjax.com**
  Miniature-golf aficionados like this place for its three courses of varying difficulties. You can also try your hand at real golf on the two-level driving range, which has enough space for 60 duffers. This amusement park also keeps kids young and old happy with bumper boats, go-carts, sand volleyball, batting cages, and video games and an arcade. You can load up on eats at the park grill and eatery. Park hours vary by

The family that plays together can stop by any of the Valley's entertainment venues and amusement parks, like Arizona-grown Fiddlesticks Family Fun Park.

Photo: courtesy of Fiddlesticks Family Fun Park

season, but generally it opens at 10 AM daily for golf and batting cages, with most rides operating by 4 PM. Rides start at 10 AM on Saturday and Sunday. The park stays open until 10 PM Sunday through Thursday and until midnight on Friday and Saturday. All-day passes are available and are sold according to your height: The smallest children pay $10, and from there it goes up to the adult price of $17.

Water Parks

To fight off the summer doldrums and beat the heat, many Valley families head to water parks. This area is fortunate to have three big ones—all packed with fun features and millions of gallons of cool, refreshing water. Parents and kids cool down with lots of soaking, splashing, sliding, and tubing. All three water parks are run by Golfland Entertainment Centers and are convenient to reach from anywhere in the Valley. The parks usually open Memorial Day weekend and remain so through Labor Day weekend. The less crowded days tend to be Monday through Wednesday.

We give admission prices for all three parks, but be ready for add-on costs, such as inner tube, inflatable raft or boogie board rentals; locker rentals; and the food and beverage tab, since rules prohibit bringing your own.

A couple of other tips: Consider wearing slip-on aqua shoes—the concrete surrounding the pools is hotter than you think. Also, be mindful of the ratings given to slides—1 through 4, with 4 being the fastest slide. Those fast slides require good swimming ability, not to mention nerves of steel. One last reminder: Wear a good sunscreen lotion and apply it hourly.

Admission prices change from year to year, but most recently they were $15.99 for those 12 and older and $12.99 for children ages 4 to 11. Children 3 and younger get in free. The water parks offer discounts for late admission, which is after 3 or 4 PM, depending on the park.

Phoenix

Waterworld Safari
4243 W. Pinnacle Peak Rd., Phoenix
• **(602) 581-8446**
• **www.golfland-sunsplash.com**

This water park with an African safari theme is popular with folks in the West Valley. Its newest attraction is the Zambezi River, a 1,100-foot-long lazy waterway that's perfect for re-

laxing. The wave pool is designed to give 10 minutes of calm and 10 minutes of wave action. Little ones have a great time on the easy slides and the rapids, curving waterways that zip you down to a shallow pool. The Jungle-Jim's children's play pool has a self-latching, fenced area. Lifeguards are on duty. For adventuresome older kids and adults, there are eight larger slides of the super-speedy, scream-eliciting variety. Hours are 10 AM to 8 PM, Monday through Thursday; 10 AM to 9 PM, Friday and Saturday; and 11 AM to 7 PM, Sunday.

Southeast Valley

Big Surf
1500 N. McClintock Dr., Tempe
• **(480) 947-7873**
• **www.golfland-sunsplash.com**

This almost 30-year-old park brings back fond memories for any adult who grew up in Phoenix. It's legendary as the place to hang out; it was one of the world's first artificial-wave pools and is still probably the largest in the world. The massive pool—as big as four football fields—lets you ride the waves every 90 seconds. Its surrounding landscaping and decor lend the park a Polynesian theme. Big Surf has 11 giant slides and assorted other slides. Little ones will enjoy a wading pool with sprinklers and easy slides. Hours are 10 AM to 6 PM, Monday through Saturday; and 11 AM to 7 PM, Sunday.

Golfland/Sunsplash
155 W. Hampton Ave., Mesa
• **(480) 834-8318**
• **www.golfland-sunsplash.com**

The gigantic wave pool here differs from Big Surf's—you get 10 minutes of calm and 10 minutes of wave action. Another feature that appeals to relaxation-seekers is a circuitous "river" that you can lazily float upon in your inner tube. The kiddie area is quite big, with easy concrete slides, a waterfall, sprinklers, and hoses for lots of safe water play. This Caribbean-theme park has 10 tube and giant slides. For indoor diversion, there's a huge arcade area with games for any skill level, which is a favorite date place for Valley teenagers. The park also has a new laser tag area. Also popular are the miniature golf courses adjacent to the arcade. The water park is open 10 AM to 8 PM, Monday through Thursday; 10 AM to 9 PM, Friday and Saturday; and 11 AM to 7 PM, Sunday. Golfland is open 10 AM to 10 PM, Sunday through

Rawhide's many kid-centered special events will delight all ages, such as its old fashioned Fourth of July.

Photo: Jean-Pierre Brietta, courtesy of Pinnacle Sonoran Properties

Thursday; and 10 AM to Midnight, Friday and Saturday.

Other Parks

Phoenix

Desert West Skateboard Plaza
Desert West Park, 6602 W. Encanto Blvd., Phoenix
• (602) 495-3700

When this skateboard park opened in 1997, Phoenix was the first city in Arizona to have such a park. It has been packed ever since with teens wanting to perfect their jumps and turns. The massive park features several bowls, a central four-sided pyramid and various ledges for the daredevil in you. It makes good sense to wear helmets and other protective gear, by the way. Hours are 7 AM to 9:45 PM daily. Admission is free.

Southeast Valley

Desert Breeze Railroad
Desert Breeze Park,
Ray Rd. and McClintock Dr., Chandler
• (480) 940-1685

Ride on a reproduction of an 1880s train in this small but pleasant park in a suburban neighborhood. When—or if—the tots should tire of that, there's plenty of playground equipment in the park and a new carousel. The train runs 10 AM to sunset, Wednesday through Sunday, and closes in July and August because of the heat. Amenities include a snack bar and a covered patio. A train ride costs $1.50, although infants and toddlers ride free. The carousel costs $1.25. A ten-ride pass is available for $12. Special seasonal rides are offered on Halloween and Christmas.

Northeast Valley

Indian Bend Wash Bike Path
Along Hayden Rd., Scottsdale
• (480) 994-2732

This is an easy, meandering bike path along a greenbelt, but the route stretches for 11 miles. So decide beforehand how much of it you want to tackle. There are several good starting points, such as north of downtown Scottsdale at Chaparral Park at Hayden and Jackrabbit Roads, or the Bike Stop Rest Area on Thomas Road between Miller and Hayden Roads. You can head north toward Shea Boulevard or south toward McKellips Road in Tempe. Along the way you'll meet many other bicyclists—this is a popular route because the greenbelt and its small lakes and golf courses make pleasant surroundings. In-line skaters, strollers, joggers, and dog walkers share the route. It makes dips here and there under major traffic arteries. The greenbelt is slightly below street level because it's the place that catches the flow of rainwater after big storms and thus prevents flooding of nearby homes.

McCormick-Stillman Railroad Park
7301 E. Indian Bend Rd., (Indian Bend and Scottsdale Rds.), Scottsdale
• (480) 994-2312

Scottsdale residents love their railroad park—it's often overflowing with people enjoying birthday parties and picnics on weekends. The park has added an antique carousel and clock tower. The resident train is a 5/12-scale model of the Rio Grande Western Railway, and it chugs a little over a mile through 30 acres of parkland. You board at Stillman Station, a replica of a historic train depot at Clifton, Arizona. Railroad buffs should head to the corner of the park housing displays of railroad memorabilia. There you'll find a Pullman car that was used by several United States presidents, a 1906 Baldwin locomotive, a 1914 Santa Fe baggage car, and a machine shop dating from 1903. For most of the year, rides on the train and carousel are offered daily, starting at 10 AM and running until 6:30 PM. On summer weekends, the hours are the same, but on summer weekdays, the train runs only from 4 to 8:30 PM. Tickets cost $1, with children younger than 3 riding free. Next to the carousel is a sandy playground with lots of climbing equipment and slides. A Southern Pacific Caboose houses a snack bar. In October, the park hosts its annual Railfair celebration, with displays, games, and other fun events for the entire family.

Southwest Valley

Crow's Dairy
10505 W. Broadway Rd., Tolleson
• (602) 936-4435
• www.crowsdairy.com

This is a fourth-generation, working dairy farm where families can pet and feed barnyard animals and watch milking demonstrations.

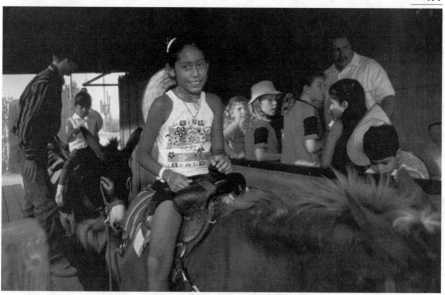

Burros rides always tempt the younger set at Rawhide.

Photo: Jean-Pierre Brietta, courtesy of Pinnacle Sonoran Properties

Never taken a hayride? Here's your chance. The park is open to the general public twice yearly, but any type of group—from families to corporations—can schedule tours from October through May, with a 20-head minimum. Admission during public openings is $4 per person, with all proceeds benefiting AASK (Aid to Adoption of Special Kids.)

Duncan Family Farms
17203 W. Indian School Rd., Goodyear
- **(623) 853-0111, (623) 853-9880**
- **www.duncanfamilyfarms.com**

Here's another working farm that welcomes kids and shares its use of state-of-the-art farming and environmental techniques. Attractions include a pick-your-own organic produce garden—featuring strawberries, blackberries, peaches, apples, plums, broccoli, and summer squash—rounded out by a petting zoo, a kiddie cattle-train ride around the barnyard, a farm-style play yard, and an area to gather fresh eggs. The Country Bakery & Market offers homemade pies, cookies, and orchard fruit bars. It has two celebrations a year, an October Pumpkin Festival and a June Cool Corn and Melon Celebration, with proceeds going to Arizona food banks. The farm is open Fridays through Saturdays, from October to mid-July. From October through June, hours run from 9 AM to 5 PM. From May through July, its hours run from 7 AM to 3 PM. It costs $3 for the wagon ride, tour, petting zoo, and so forth.

Annual Events

Thanks to El Sol, The Valley of the Sun bustles with outdoor festivals. The season of festivals and major outdoor events—including a number of arts and sports related events—usually begins in late October and runs through April. Throughout the year, the Valley plays host to many festivals celebrating diverse cultures—Mexican-American, Native American, Japanese, Scottish, Greek, you name it. These festivals not only reflect our unique heritage, but also show our desire to share it with all those around us.

The Valley's pleasant winters allow all kinds of holiday-related outdoor festivals, including the popular ZooLights at the Phoenix Zoo, and Las Noches de las Luminarias at the Desert Botanical Garden.

The event calendar drops off in the summer, when the triple-digit temperatures have driven out the tourists, as well as many residents. Hardy souls turn up the heat even higher by plunging into our great Cinco de Mayo festivals and celebrating our country's independence at the Valley's Fourth of July shows.

The Arizona Office of Tourism estimates that there are at least 4,000 events around the state annually. In the Phoenix area, that translates to several hundred large public gatherings a year. This chapter will bring you up to speed on several not-to-be-missed events, as well as a few smaller festivals that may pique your interest.

We have supplied approximate dates for these various events, but be aware that they are subject to change, as are admission prices.

January

Celebration of Fine Art
Chauncey Equestrian Center, 18500 N. Scottsdale Rd., Scottsdale
• (480) 443-7695
• www.celebrateart.com

This open-air exhibition and festival hoists its big white tents every year for about 11 weeks, starting in January. Touted as an outstanding art event, it provides a chance to see the on-site studios of more than 100 artists, including painters, sculptors, jewelers, photographers, weavers, and ceramists. One of the attractions of the event is the chance to see artists in action. It is usually open in daytime hours, and admission is $6.50, with discounts for seniors and children.

Barrett-Jackson Classic Car Auction
WestWorld, 16601 N. Pima Rd., Scottsdale
• (480) 503-5555
• www.barrettjackson.com

This show, rightly dubbed "the Oscars of the collector-car world," is an auction and show of 800 classic cars, almost all in excellent original or restored condition. Along with the Phoenix Open and the Arabian Horse Show, the Barrett-Jackson Classic is one of Scottsdale's top three events, attracting high-rolling automobile enthusiasts from around the world. In 1999, total sales exceeded $23

Balloons brighten the desert at events like the Balloon Race at Fountain Hills.

Photo: Courtesy of Phoenix Convention and Visitors Bureau

million, the highest mark in 10 years, and featured world-record bids for the following vehicles: a 1948 Tucker Sedan was purchased for $333,900; a 1970 Chevrolet Chevelle LS-6 convertible went for $111,300; and a 1956 Chevrolet Bel Air convertible brought $86,920. The top-selling automobile of the 29th annual event was a 1968 Ford GT 40 Mark I, which sold for $429,300. More than 140,000 people attended the event, including Major League Baseball Hall of Famers Reggie Jackson and Robin Yount, Van Halen bass guitarist Michael Anthony, Indianapolis 500 winners Arie Luyendyk and Tom Sneva, and country singer George Jones.

The classy event was rounded out with good eats, and those who could not take home the car of their dreams could at least pick up some automobile memorabilia. The event runs four days in mid-January, with daily general admission tickets costing $15 each, $10 for students and seniors (62 and over), $6 for youths ages 6 to 12, and free for children younger than 6. A four-day pass costs $50.

The Phoenix Open
Tournament Players Club of Scottsdale, 17020 N. Hayden Rd., Scottsdale
- **(480) 870-4431**
- **www.phoenixopen.com**

The Phoenix Open is considered the world's largest-attended golf tournament. And who wouldn't want to catch a glimpse of famous golfers in the beautiful setting of a Phoenix winter? The 2000 Open attracted 415,310 people, and players included Tom Lehman, Rocco Mediate, Robert Allenby, Brandt Jobe, Kirk Triplett, and Hal Sutton. In addition to being the place to be for serious and casual golfers, the Open is a highly successful fund-raiser. The sponsoring organization, The Thunderbirds, raises money

INSIDERS' TIP

If you are attending an outdoors festival or event, don't forget to take your umbrella. While it's true that the skies are perpetually blue in the Valley, those out-of-work umbrellas make marvelous sun shades.

for various Arizona charities, especially those bringing sports to disadvantaged youths. The tournament lasts four days, generally around the last weekend in January. But the event stretches to fill out the week with such things as celebrity tournaments, a Skills Extravaganza, a "Dream Day" of golf for inner-city youth, and a Special Olympics putting clinic. Tickets at the gate cost $20 per person; children 17 and younger are admitted free when accompanied by an adult. The TPC course is adjacent to the lovely Scottsdale Princess Resort (see our Resorts chapter).

West Valley Native American Arts Festival
West Valley Fine Arts Center, 387 Wigwam Blvd., Litchfield Park
• **(623) 935-6384**
• **www.wvfac.org**

This outdoor festival showcases more than 200 Native American artists and craftspeople from the Southwest. You'll find a wonderful array of jewelry, sculpture, weavings, and paintings plus hands-on crafts activities for children. Native American music and dance performances are also featured. The event is organized by the West Valley Fine Arts Council. Admission is $5 for adults, $4 for children 3 to 10; children under 3 are admitted free. Look for this two-day event the third weekend in January.

February

Scottsdale Indian Artists of America Show
Civic Center Mall, 7380 E. Second St., Scottsdale
• **(480) 945-5556, (520) 398-2226**

Since 1995, the Indian Artists of America juried exhibition has drawn 75 of the nation's finest potters, weavers, jewelers, sculptors, and painters, representing a number of tribes. Usually held on a Saturday and Sunday in early February, the show also spotlights Native American dancing and music, fashion shows, and bird of prey demonstrations. Admission is $8 for adults, and free for children 12 and younger.

Scottsdale Jaycees Parada del Sol
WestWorld, 16601 N. Pima Rd., Scottsdale
• **(480) 990-3179**
• **www.scottsdalejaycees.com**

Parada del Sol—or a walk in the sun—offers a chance for the increasingly cosmopolitan

Scottsdale to live up to a slogan it coined several decades ago: "The West's Most Western Town." Yes, there was a time when cowboys traveled the dirt roads into Scottsdale to hitch their horses on Main Street while they grabbed a beer at the saloon. This event, founded in 1959, celebrates this tradition. During Parada del Sol Week, cowboys, pioneer women, and mountain men reclaim their place in Scottsdale history. Events include the Hashknife Pony Express, in which riders deliver mail via horseback on a 225-mile ride from Holbrook to Scottsdale; the Parada del Sol Parade, a Saturday morning spectacular that's believed to be the world's largest and longest horse-drawn parade; the Parada del Sol Rodeo, four days of bronc-riding, steer roping, rodeo clowns, and more, sanctioned by the Professional Rodeo Cowboys Association; a Rodeo Dance; and a Trail's End Celebration, featuring food, drinks, kids activities, and gunfight performances. Parada del Sol events usually take place in late January or early February. The parade is free.

World Championship Hoop Dance Contest
Heard Museum, 2301 N. Central Ave., Phoenix
• **(602) 252-8840**
• **www.heard.org**

You won't see this too often: More than 40 Native American hoop dancers from the United States and Canada gathering annually for one of the few hoop dance competitions in the country. Originally, the hoop dance was part of a healing ceremony meant to restore balance and harmony. In Native American tradition, the hoop symbolizes the cycles of life. At this early February event, you'll see members of various tribes in their colorful buckskin costumes bearing jingling metal trinkets. Dancers use as many as 50 hoops to form shapes and suggest images, while showing off their fluid grace and precision.

Arizona Renaissance Festival
East of Apache Junction on U.S. Hwy. 60
• **(520) 463-2700**

Every winter brings a crowd of Henry VIII wannabes and shrews more shrewish than Shakespeare's Kate. Aha! It must be the performers in the annual Arizona Renaissance Festival. You can travel back in time starting in early February, with the festival continuing for eight weeks at a 30-acre village wholly decked out in the Renaissance look. And the 600 perfectly costumed, in-character performers surely aid the illusion. Actors, jugglers, clowns, acrobats, musicians, and singers can be found in every corner of the village. Knights joust three times a day in the tournament arena. Children can try medieval pursuits, such as archery and ax throwing, or ride ponies and camels. Booths all around feature crafts that were common in medieval times. Food includes humongous roasted turkey drumsticks, as well as steak on a stake, apple dumplings, Italian ices, and other treats. Admission is $15 for adults, $6 for children ages 5 to 12, and free for those younger than 5. Check advertisements for retailers selling discounted tickets. Signs will point you to the festival grounds from Interstate 60. The drive from central Phoenix is less than an hour.

Scottsdale Arabian Horse Show
WestWorld, 16601 N. Pima Rd., Scottsdale
• **(602) 515-1500**
• **www.scottsdaleshow.com**

Founded in 1955, the Scottsdale Arabian Horse Show is a huge event for Scottsdale and attracts more than 200,000 spectators. This is, in fact, one of the world's largest Arabian horse shows, with 2,000 of the world's finest steeds competing for more than $200,000 in prize and scholarship money. A main arena and two secondary arenas run simultaneous classes in halter, English pleasure, trail horse, hunter, jumper, dressage, Western pleasure, and other categories. But if you're thinking this show is just for horse lovers, you're wrong. Two huge tents become display space for more than 250 exhibitors from around the world selling clothing, jewelry, fine art, food, and horse accessories. The pomp and pageantry are enough for anyone's eyes to drink in. And there's always a chance of spotting celebrities. Seen at the show in previous years have been Wayne Newton, Beach Boy Al Jardine, and actor Patrick Swayze, to name a few. Daily admission to the 10-day extravaganza is $10 for adults, $7 for seniors, and free for children younger than 12. Look for it in mid-February.

Fountain Hills Great Fair
Avenue of the Fountains, Fountain Hills
• **(480) 837-1654**
• **www.fhchamberofcommerce.org**

The town of Fountain Hills looks forward each February to welcoming thousands to this three-day outdoor fair featuring the creations of almost 500 professional artists and craftspeople. Also on the bill are food courts, live entertainment, carnival rides, games, and an early morning hot-air balloon race—all taking place on the expansive park in the center of Fountain Hills. You can't miss it—this is where

you'll see one of the tallest fountains in the world, shooting 500 feet into the air at set intervals. Admission is free. From the intersection of Scottsdale Road and Shea Boulevard in north Scottsdale, head 12 miles east to Fountain Hills. Admission is free.

Matsuri: A Festival of Japan
Heritage and Science Park,
Seventh and Washington Sts., Phoenix
• **(602) 262-5029**

You will have many ethnic and cultural festivals to choose from during a Phoenix winter, but this is probably the loveliest of them. Since 1984, Matsuri organizers have brought together the sights and sounds of Japanese classical dancing, Taiko drummers, natives dressed in beautiful kimonos, and artists displaying unusual crafts. Martial arts play a big part in the festival, too, with demonstrations in judo, Shotokan karate, swordsmanship, and tae kwon do. Exhibits include bonsai demonstrations, origami folding, kite construction, fabric art, and cooking demonstrations. Booths serving Japanese food are in abundance. Matsuri usually takes place the fourth weekend in February and admission is free.

Arizona Scottish Gathering and Highland Games
Mesa Community College,
1833 W. Southern Ave., Mesa
• **(602) 431-0095**

Have a Gaelic old time at this celebration of all things Scottish. The two-day event in mid-February offers athletic events you've probably never heard of, such as the hammer throw and caber toss. On top of that are historical re-enactment groups, bagpipe and drum competitions, dances, and children's activities. One-day general admission passes are $11 for adults, $10 for seniors, $3 for children ages 5 to 11, and children younger than 5 are admitted free. The Scottish community of Phoenix has sponsored the gathering for 33 years.

Greek Festival
Chandler Community Center,
125 E. Commonwealth Ave., Chandler
• **(480) 899-3330**
• **www.stkatherine.org**

Immerse yourself in Greek folkways and food at the annual Greek Festival, held each year since 1985 in mid- to late February. You'll find live Greek music, dancing, wine, imported products, and carnival rides throughout this weekend-long festival. Specialty food items include baklava, calamari, and fresh lamb roasted on a spit. Proceeds benefit the St. Katherine Greek Orthodox Church. Admission is $2 for adults, with children younger than age 12 admitted free.

Lost Dutchman Days
Apache Junction Rodeo/Event Center, Lost Dutchman Blvd. at Tomahawk Rd., Apache Junction
• **(480) 982-3141**
• **www.apachejunctioncoc.com**

The legend of Jacob Waltz—the Lost Dutchman—and his futile quest for gold in the Superstition Mountains has been celebrated since 1964 in Apache Junction. Lost Dutchman Days features a parade, a senior pro rodeo, various vendors, a carnival, gold panning, and food booths. The event lasts for three days and is generally held around the end of February. Admission is free to most events, except the rodeo.

March

Heard Museum Guild Indian Fair & Market
Heard Museum, 2301 N. Central Ave., Phoenix
• **(602) 252-8840**
• **www.heard.org**

If you are in town the first weekend of March, heed this advice: You must go to the Guild Indian Fair & Market. Of the many events put on by the world-renowned Heard Museum, this is the best. As always over the past 40 years, the fair nurtures respect and admiration for the visual and performing arts of various tribes. More than 350 of the nation's finest Native American artists show their work. Plus you will see various tribal dances, with performers in full regalia, and hear a variety of Native American music. Children will have fun with craft activities, and the food booths are numerous, letting you choose among Native American, Mexican, and other fare. The event runs daytime hours on a Saturday and Sunday. Tickets are $6 for adults, and $3 for children ages 4 to 12. It's free for children younger than 4. Admission to the fair includes admission to the Heard's seven galleries.

Arizona Agriculture Day
Wesley Bolin Plaza, Washington St., and 17th Ave., Phoenix
• **(602) 659-7008**

Learn more about another side of Arizona—namely its role as one of the nation's largest producers of citrus fruits, vegetables, and cotton—at Arizona Agriculture Day, held the first part of March. Events include a produce derby, a celebrity cow-milking contest, music, commercial exhibits, and displays of large farm equipment. Admission is free. A farm-fresh barbecue lunch is offered for $1.

Cox Communications Air Show and Spectacular
Williams Gateway Airport, 6001 S. Power Rd., Mesa
• **(602) 774-9355**

With a slogan of "more fun at Mach 1," this air show presents historic planes along with fancy aerial stunts by sophisticated new planes and jets. Recent shows featured Stoli MiGs, the Cox Communications Parachute Team, and the USAF Thunderbirds. In addition to fly-by demonstrations, enjoy ground entertainment of various sorts. For comfortable seating, bring along lawn chairs and blankets. Admission ranges from $9 to $29 for adults, and $7 to $12 for children 12 and younger. Look for this event the first or second weekend in March.

Chandler Ostrich Festival
Downtown Chandler
• **(602) 842-8434**
• **www.ostrichfestival.com**

This wacky, three-day family festival hearkens back to the days of ostrich farms in the Valley, and was featured as a backdrop to the 1995 Whitney Houston movie, "Waiting to Exhale." From the streets of historic downtown Chandler, you'll be amused by ostrich-themed events, including jockeys riding ostriches as if they were thoroughbreds. Numerous food booths give you a chance to sample ostrich burgers—or something more familiar. There is a carnival midway and live entertainment. Three stages of entertainment feature a slate of national and local talent, playing anything from classic rock to Hispanic music. The Ostrich Festival usually takes place the second weekend in March, and admission is free. Seeing the ostrich races costs $3 for adults and $1 for children.

Scottsdale Arts Festival
Civic Center Mall, 7380 E. Second St., Scottsdale
• **(602) 994-ARTS**
• **www.scottsdalearts.org**

The work of more than 175 artists and artisans is featured in this juried outdoor show that is ranked among the top art festivals in the country. Adding to the ambiance are

Many Native Americans fashion beautiful pieces of jewelry and other art and crafts.

Photo: Paul Markow, courtesy of Scottsdale Convention and Visitors Bureau

musical performances on two stages, food and beverage booths, and an area for children. The event takes place on a Friday, Saturday, and Sunday in mid-March. Admission is free.

The National Festival of the West
WestWorld, 16601 N. Pima Rd., Scottsdale
• **(602) 996-4387**
• **www.festivalofthewest.com**

From old-time fur traders to modern-day ranching, this festival commemorates the romance, lore, and legend of the American cowboy and the settling of the American West. Over four days, the festival presents Western music and movies, cowboy poetry, and costume contests. Western heroes and peddlers dressed in period costumes stroll the festival grounds. Features include an exhibit of Western art and cowboy collectibles, the National Cowboy Mounted Shooting Championships, and ranch rodeo-style arena events. One of the highlights of the show is the Chuck Wagon Cook Off, in which chuck wagons from across the country come to compete for prizes. Visitors can sample their old-fashioned cooking. Each year in mid-March, the festival honors individuals who have helped preserve the Western lifestyle. Past honorees have included Gene Autry, Ben Johnson, and Denver Pyle. Admission is $10 for adults, and $3 for children.

Tempe Festival of the Arts
Downtown Tempe
• **(480) 967-4877**
• **www.millavenue.org**

You will marvel at the ingenuity of craftspeople as you wander through this three-day outdoor festival of juried works. Vendors show everything from jewelry and pottery to photography and blown glass. The streets of downtown Tempe, including several blocks of Mill Avenue, are blocked off to traffic for this pedestrian-friendly event. Adding to the festive atmosphere are street musicians and jugglers, food booths, and activities for kids. This event in the last weekend of March and a similar festival the first weekend of December are organized by the Mill Avenue Merchants Association. Both are well-attended, but crowds only add to the fun. Admission is free.

April

Xerox Southwest Salsa Challenge
Scottsdale Stadium,
Osborn Rd. and Civic Center Blvd.,
Scottsdale
• **(602) 955-3947**

Bring your taste buds to this event, where a saucy selection of some 50 salsas vie for the People's Choice Award in this annual benefit for the Hemophilia Association. The flavors span the salsa spectrum from sweet, fruit-flavored to four-alarm fire varieties. Celebrity judges award top honors in business, restaurant, and individual categories. The event also includes live musical entertainment. The last two years it has taken place on a Saturday in early April, but the date varies. It's usually a springtime event, though. Admission is $3 for adults and older kids, and free for children 12 and younger.

Sunday on Central
Central Ave., downtown Phoenix
• **(602) 534-FEST**

You might think the good people of Phoenix have gone crazy—whizzing down the middle of busy Central Avenue on bicycles, skateboards, in-line skates, and even on foot. Actually, they're celebrating Sunday on Central, during which all of Encanto Lane to Indian School Road (about 1.5 miles) is closed to traffic so that families can play on the street. The event occurs the second Sunday in April (unless it coincides with Easter) and includes musical entertainment, street performers, food vendors, crafts displays, and a pet parade. Of course, it's okay just to walk around if you're not on wheels. The daytime event is free.

Scottsdale Culinary Festival
Scottsdale Civic Center Mall,
7380 E. Second St., Scottsdale
• **(480) 945-7193**
• **www.scottsdaleleague-arts.org**

This long-running annual event is a weeklong salute to the culinary arts, held the middle of each April. Events include: Tour Culinaire, in which participants hop around town by trolley to progressively sample courses of a meal, which costs $150 per person; the

ANNUAL EVENTS

Both the young and the young-at-heart can learn more about our Western heritage at Festival of the West.

Photo: Courtesy of Festival of the West

Appetizer Cup, a competition among chefs, which costs $50 per person; an authors luncheon; Cooks and Corks, offering food demonstrations and wine tastings; and the event that fills the grassy mall to overflowing—the Great Arizona Picnic, offering food booths from dozens of Valley restaurateurs and caterers. The picnic takes place the second weekend of the festival. Live music on two outdoor stages goes on throughout the day and evening of that Saturday and Sunday, so there's plenty to excite the senses. Tasting coupons at the picnic are available individually, and there's usually a beer garden in one corner of the mall. For more information on this annual fundraising event, call the Scottsdale Center for the Arts box office at the above number, or call the sponsoring organization, the Scottsdale League for the Arts at (480) 945-7193.

Country Thunder USA
Queen Creek, near Schnepf Farms
- **(480) 966-9920**
- **www.countrythunder.com**

Country music fans from around the Southwest—as many as 30,000 per day—flock to this four-day festival. It's easy to see why: Recent performers included John Michael Montgomery, Jill Marie, Chris LeDoux, and Sawyer Brown. Country Thunder takes place in mid- to late April at a large campground site in Queen Creek, enabling those traveling in RVs to stay close to the festivities. There are activities for kids, shows of glowing hot air balloons, and food booths to go along with the concerts. Admission at the gate in 2000 was $99 for general admission for two for one day, with camping and VIP tickets costing considerably more. Discounted tickets are available in advance of the show.

May

Cinco de Mayo
Mesa Southwest Museum,
53 N. Macdonald St., Mesa
- **(480) 644-2230**
- **www.sw-museum.org**

Cinco de Mayo (Fifth of May) celebrates the victory of Mexican forces over the French in 1862. Mexican restaurants around the Valley go all out with fiestas and special meals. At Mesa Southwest Museum, the fun includes ethnic cuisine along with live entertainment, lectures on Mexican history, and authentic Mexican crafts. The event starts the Friday evening

closest to May 5 and runs through the next day. Admission is free.

Cinco de Mayo Festival
Patriot's Park, Central Ave. and
Washington St., Phoenix
- **(602) 279-4669**

The weekend near the fifth of May brings a Mexican-themed street celebration to downtown Phoenix. The live entertainment includes mariachi bands, folklorico dancers, and headliner acts from the United States and Mexico. Performers have included Laura Flores, Yolanda del Rio, and Freddy Fender. The celebration, which includes numerous food booths, children's activities, local bands, and various contests, usually begins about noon each day and continues into the late evening. Admission is $3 for adults, and free for children 12 and younger.

June

Cool Corn & Melon Celebration
Duncan Family Farms,
17203 W. Indian School Rd., Goodyear
- **(623) 853-0111**
- **www.duncanfamilyfarms.com**

This working farm celebrates the beginning of the summer harvest with tastings of several kinds of melons and corn. This family-oriented event features live Calypso bands, a water-play area, and a children's craft area. The farm's usual attractions are open, including a farm play yard, a petting zoo, and organic gardens where you pick your own produce. The festival starts early in the morning and runs past lunchtime. It's usually scheduled for the first weekend in June.

July

Fabulous Phoenix Fourth
State Capitol, 17th Ave. and
Washington St., Phoenix
- **(602) 534-FEST**

Patriotic hearts swell with pride at the sight of fireworks above Arizona's Capitol building. This is how the city of Phoenix celebrates the Fourth of July—with a 25-minute fireworks spectacular and numerous events scattered on 120 acres. Hear the oohs and aahs of the 250,000 people around you. The event begins at 4 PM, and features various stages of entertainment, food vendors, and crafts displays. In the past few years, Fabulous Phoenix Fourth has

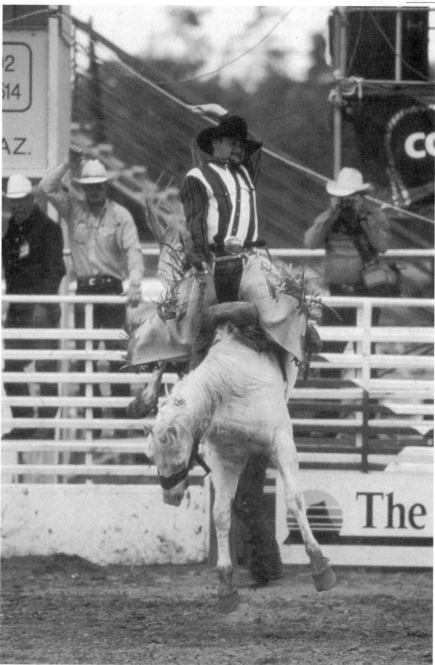

The wild and wooly West lives on in many Arizona annual events, like Frontier Days at the Yavapai County Fair.

Photo: Courtesy of Phoenix Convention and Visitors Bureau

managed to book top-name country entertainment, including The Dixie Chicks, Alabama, Toby Keith, and The Mavericks. Fireworks start at 9:30 PM. Admission is free.

Summer Spectacular Art Walk
Art district of downtown Scottsdale
• (602) 990-3939

For more than 10 years, shortly following the Fourth of July, the dozens of galleries of downtown Scottsdale collaborate on a Thursday evening Art Walk filled with artists' receptions, refreshments, musical entertainment, and other special events. An after-dark stroll through the galleries of Marshall Way, Main Street, and other avenues offers a good way to beat the heat, especially because the galleries roll out the red carpet by presenting works from nationally known artists. The Art Walk is free.

October

Sunday A'Fair
Scottsdale Civic Center Mall,
7380 E. Second St., Scottsdale
• (480) 994-ARTS
• www.scottsdalearts.org

Mini arts festivals, the Sunday A'Fairs make an appealing way to while away a Sunday afternoon on the grassy mall of Scottsdale Civic Center Mall. They feature outdoor concerts by well-known and emerging Valley musicians. Expect a variety of musical styles, including Cajun-zydeco, reggae, Delta blues, and mainstream pop. Also find Arizona-made arts and crafts and plenty of food and beverage booths. Admission is free, and the A'Fairs generally are held each Sunday afternoon from October through mid-April, unless a larger festival or special event is using the mall. Hours are noon to 4:30 PM.

Arizona State Fair
State Fairgrounds, 19th Ave. and
McDowell Rd., Phoenix
• (602) 268-FAIR, (602) 258-6711
• www.azstatefair.com

So much to do, so little time. Even though the Arizona State Fair runs for 18 day beginning in mid-October, it's easy to walk away feeling you haven't seen or done nearly enough. Just giving attention to the hundreds of agricultural, livestock, fine arts, crafts, and collectibles displays can take a day. But if you want just a daylong outing, then of course you need to leave time for enjoying the midway rides and games. Family favorites include the

Ferris wheels and a roller coaster. But there are plenty of other rides—tame and not so tame—to choose from. You also want time to indulge in barbecue, hot dogs, meat on a stick, Navajo frybread, cotton candy, and the many other treats sold at booths throughout the fair. Don't forget to peruse the fair's various merchant booths, especially those selling Indian jewelry and Mexican imported goods. We haven't even mentioned the live entertainment nightly in Veterans Memorial Coliseum at the fairgrounds. The lineup includes national headliners in country, rock, and pop. Expect to pay around $7.50 for adults, $4.50 for seniors 55 and older, $3.50 for youths 5 to 15, and free for kids younger than 5. Ride tickets and games cost extra. The concerts are free with admission; reserved seats for the concerts are available for an extra fee and can be purchased in advance. Check advertisements in local newspapers to see which Valley retail outlets are selling discount tickets or admission/ride package deals.

Cowboy Artists of America
Phoenix Art Museum
1625 N. Central Ave., Phoenix
• (602) 257-1222
• www.phxart.com

Magnificent sculptures in bronze and stone, oil paintings, and drawings—all portraying the people and animals of the American West with sensitivity and historical accuracy—are created for exclusive display each fall at the Phoenix Art Museum. The works of art are the creations of the more than two dozen members of Cowboy Artists of America, a prestigious group founded in 1965 by cowboy artists in Sedona. With some of the art works selling in the six figures, the sale has become the most prestigious in the country. The sale is a specially-ticketed event and a major fund raiser for the Museum. Following the sale, the artworks remain on exhibition at the Museum for viewing by the public

Boo! at the Zoo
Phoenix Zoo, 455 N. Galvin Pkwy.,
Phoenix
• (602) 273-1341
www.phoenixzoo.org

This is one of the Phoenix Zoo's most popular annual events—not surprising since it gives children a chance to come to the zoo in their Halloween costumes. And that provides a chance to scare a lion instead of vice versa. In addition to seeing regular zoo exhibits, kids can participate in hands-on activities and hear educational talks about animals from zoo staff. Zoo admission is $8.50 for adults, $7.50 for seniors, $4.25 for children ages 3 to 12, and free for children younger than 3.

November

Metris Thunderbird Balloon Classic
WestWorld of Scottsdale,
16601 N. Pima Rd., Scottsdale
- **(602) 978-7797**
- **www.t-birdballoonclassic.com**

Aficionados of hot-air ballooning know that this is one of the premier events on the national circuit. Launched in 1974, the classic features races with more than 130 balloons and, despite the huge crowds, it is definitely worth seeing. The corporate balloons are a show in themselves: Flying high in past years have been a Burger King Whopper, a Tony the Tiger, a Planters Mr. Peanut, and an Air Shamu, to name a few. Proceeds benefit scholarships at Thunderbird, the American Graduate School of International Management. The competitions usually take place early mornings on the first Saturday and Sunday of November. Related events—which include activities for kids, skydiving exhibitions, nighttime shows of glowing hot air balloons, and crafts booths—start the Friday evening before. Daily admission per event is $10 at the gate, with an all-events pass costing $25.

Glendale Celebration of Art & Antiques
Downtown Glendale
- **(623) 842-8434**

Set amid dozens of antique stores and the lawns of Murphy Park, this street festival features about 140 vendors of arts and crafts over a three-day weekend in mid- to late November. There's also live music; a KidZone with hands-on activities and rides for the little ones; and a beer tasting garden. Admission is free.

Glendale Glitters Holiday Light Extravaganza
Downtown Glendale
- **(623) 930-2299**

Glendale does indeed glitter around the holidays when you consider that all the buildings in a 10-block area are decked out in lights—more than one million of them. The light display extends into Murphy Park. In Catlin Court, an antique shopping district, the build-

ings sparkle with icicle lights. The lights are switched on the night following Thanksgiving, with a street festival that includes fireworks for good measure. The lights stay on until mid-January, when they go out in style during Glendale Glitter and Glow, another nighttime street festival, this time complemented by three dozen glowing hot-air balloons. Glendale Glitters events are free.

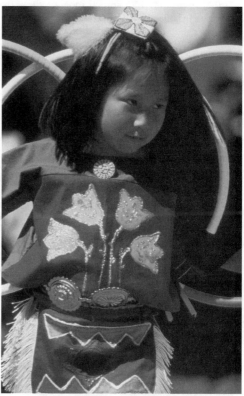

The Annual World Championship Hoop Dance Contest at the Heard Museum showcases Arizona talent.

Photo: Courtesy of Heard Museum

Simply Citrus
Center St. in downtown Mesa
- **(480) 644-2351**

If life gives you lemons, head out for this new Mesa festival, debuting November 2000, which celebrates the region's citrus-growing tradition. The family festival features music, games, activities, and entertainment by stunt teams, mini racecars, and even a yo-yo championship. Kids and adults can compete in bike rides and races, including an in-line skate race. The events are rounded out by a Citrus Ball, featuring swing dancing; a Sunday afternoon blues concert; and an evening fireworks and laser show.

Sun City Arts & Crafts Festival
Sundial Auditorium, 14801 N. 103rd St., Sun City
• **(623) 876-3000**

For more than 30 years, the seniors of Sun City have organized an annual show of their multifaceted talents in arts and crafts. Through clubs at the recreation centers of Sun City, seniors produce photography, calligraphy, ceramics, knitting, metalwork, lapidary, leatherwork, needlework, quilts, stained glass, woodworking, paintings, and more. Billed as the largest senior craft show in Arizona, the show always runs on Thanksgiving weekend in November. Admission is free.

December

Tempe Festival of the Arts
Streets of downtown Tempe
• **(480) 967-4877**

This arts and crafts extravaganza, founded in 1998, usually attracts a crowd as diverse as the artworks being shown. Cast your people-watching eye upon babies in strollers, senior citizens, young urban professionals, Arizona State University students, alternative hipsters, and others. Oh, the art is pretty eclectic too. This is a juried exhibition, so expect high-quality ceramics, photographs, glass art, sculpture, handmade toys, weavings, and jewelry galore. The Holiday Zone features seasonal crafts, including ornaments. Add to this carnival mood a variety of street performers, from jugglers to cellists to unicyclists. The main stages of entertainment feature locally known bands. The Mill Avenue Merchants Association-sponsored festival takes place annually on the first weekend of December. Admission is free.

APS Fiesta of Light Electric Light Parade
Central Ave., downtown Phoenix
• **(602) 261-8604**

Various holiday events are sponsored by the Phoenix Parks, Recreation, and Library Department, but none so well attended as this event, which has been held since 1987. The nighttime parade has been known to attract 300,000 curbside spectators along the three-mile route along Central Avenue, with another 300,000

people watching the local live broadcast. It's great fun, and while no one has actually counted the lights in the light parade, the number has been estimated at more than 1 million. Watch from 80 to 100 floats—some of them covered with as many as 50,000 lights. Also see a variety of light-covered vehicles, marching bands, clubs, and schools walking in groups—with almost everyone wearing battery-operated strings of lights. The parade is on the first Saturday of December starting at 7 PM, and admission is free.

Las Noches de las Luminarias
Desert Botanical Garden,
1201 N. Galvin Pkwy., Phoenix
• **(480) 941-1225**
• **www.dbg.org**

For more than 20 years, volunteers at the beautiful Desert Botanical Garden have marked the holiday season with Las Noches de las Luminarias. Southwestern-style luminarias are paper bags weighted down with sand, with each bag containing a lighted candle. It's a holiday tradition to place luminarias along a path to brighten the way in the dark nights of winter. At this three-night event, usually held the first weekend in December, the garden paths glow with 7,000 luminarias, which makes for quite a sight. Musical entertainment adds to the scene. This is a popular event, so buy tickets as soon as possible. Cost is $12.50 for adults, and $4 for children 5 to 12, with members getting a discount. Ticket are not sold at the door, and it's best to buy yours far in advance.

ZooLights
Phoenix Zoo, 455 N. Galvin Pkwy., Phoenix
• **(602) 273-1341**
• **www.phoenixzoo.org**

This is a delightful holiday-time outing for families and out-of-town visitors. The Phoenix Zoo strings more than 600,000 lights along the pathways and up in the trees. Look carefully, and you'll see light displays of butterflies, birds, spiders, snakes, and larger creatures. Some displays are "animated," such as frogs that jump across a lake, and some displays move in time to holiday music. Also captivating are the many costumed characters, the dancing trees, and Grandmother Oak, a talking tree. ZooLights hours are from 6 to 10 PM nightly from the first weekend in December to the second weekend in January (closed on Christmas Eve). Admission is $5 in advance, and $6 at the gate.

Pueblo Grande Museum Indian Market
South Mountain Park Activity Complex, 10919 S. Central Ave., Phoenix
- **(602) 495-0901**
- **www.pueblogrande.org**

For more than 20 years, the Pueblo Grande Museum in Phoenix, site of an ancient Hohokam village, has organized a wide-ranging outdoor exhibition of Native American arts and crafts. The show has become so popular—representing 450 artists from more than 60 tribes—it has moved to South Mountain Park. Most artwork is reasonably priced, and you have the satisfaction of knowing they are authentic. Those in the holiday mood will surely want to look for Native American-themed Christmas ornaments. The two-day event in mid-December also features native music and dance. Admission is $7 for adults; children younger than 12 are admitted free.

Victorian Holiday Celebration
Heritage Square, Monroe and Seventh Sts., Phoenix
- **(602) 262-5071**

The feeling of an old-fashioned Christmas is in store when you check out the displays and entertainment at Heritage Square for this weekend event in mid-December. The square, where some of Phoenix's earliest homes have been preserved, is a perfect setting. Enjoy arts and crafts, hands-on activities, carriage rides, train rides, puppet shows, and musical entertainment—all evoking days long ago. Admission is free.

Peoria's Oldtown Holiday Festival
Osuna Park, Oldtown Peoria
- **(623) 773-7198**
- **www.peoriaaz.com**

Since 1986, Peoria has been celebrating the season with an old fashioned Christmas celebration. Events and attractions include a Valley-wide high school choral contest, a snow area, a merchant scavenger hunt, cookie decorating, make-and-take crafts, and hay wagon rides. Santa wouldn't miss this for the world. The event runs one evening in early December, from 5 to 9 PM. Admission is free.

Tempe Tostitos Fiesta Bowl Block Party
Downtown Tempe
- **(480) 350-0900**
- **www.tostitosfiestabowl.com**

This is no neighborhood block party. Named one of the top eight places to spend New Year's Eve by *USA Today*, more than 150,000 people ring in the New Year in the Southwest's version of Times Square. Sponsored by Tostitos, the event officially welcomes the Fiesta Bowl football teams and their fans to Tempe. The city blocks off downtown streets and clears

ANNUAL EVENTS

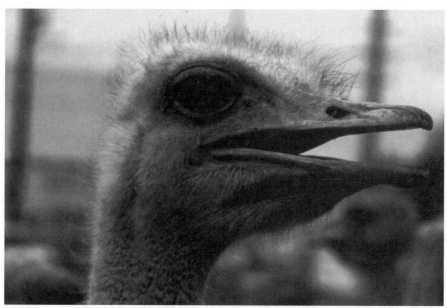

Ostriches take center stage at the Chandler Ostrich Festival in March.

Photo: Courtesy of Lido Communictions, Inc. and CK Event Enterprises the way for live entertainment from nationally known performers like Billy Idol, Sugar Ray, The B-52's, The Goo Goo Dolls, REO Speedwagon, and Lee Ann Rhimes. Food and beverage booths, kiddie rides, and fireworks displays round out the event, as well as a pep rally with each visiting team's marching band and drill squad. The action begins about 4 PM, with the pep rallies starting after dark. Two rounds of firework displays top the event, at 9 PM and again at midnight. Admission is $15, with additional charges to attend other Fiesta Bowl events.

INSIDERS' TIP

Bookaholics, beware. If you're in town late February, you're likely to hear the buzz about Phoenix's favorite used book sale: the Visiting Nurses Service Association Sale, which is held at the Arizona State Fairgrounds Exhibit Building. The Saturday and Sunday event features a half-million used (and new) books plus maps, magazines, videos, CDs, and books on tape. Admission is free, but, more important, books are cheap.

bowl game brings the Fiesta Bowl Parade, a lively spectacle of 20 or so floats plus dancers, equestrians, pompom groups, and walking groups from schools and clubs, all colorfully presented. Also in the spotlight are national award-winning high school marching bands. Past grand marshals include baseball great Ryne Sandberg, skater Kristi Yamaguchi, football player Danny White, and basketball player Charles Barkley. The parade, which heads down Central Avenue, usually takes place two to three days before the big game. The date varies from late December to early January. The free event is a big draw for residents and tourists alike, many of whom support one or the other team in the Fiesta Bowl by wearing the appropriate team colors. Expect a crowd of about 400,000, but there's plenty of room along the parade route, which runs for several blocks.

Fiesta Bowl Parade
Central Ave. in downtown Phoenix
• **(480) 350-0900**
• **www.tostitosfiestabowl.com**

The Fiesta Bowl college football game at Sun Devil Stadium in Tempe is the center of attention this time of year in the Valley. The

The Arts

If you look at the extensive selection of creative petroglyphs carved in stone by the Valley's first dwellers, you might come to the conclusion that Arizona has always inspired artists.

You'd be right. In addition to those early peoples, artists were among those who spearheaded Western expansion by painting the beauty of the region for all to see. In the 1850s, Henry Cheever Pratt, Seth Eastman, and John Russell Bartlett, landscape artists, were part of a border commission to survey the area. Other visual artists who worked in Arizona included well-known black and white photographer Ansel Adams; surrealistic German painter Max Ernst; and Maynard Dixon, a turn-of-the century post-Impressionist who used the mountains of Arizona as backdrops for his fanciful Greek scenes. The abstract artist Jackson Pollock spent some of his teenage years on his family's dairy farm in Phoenix, and he was one of the Works Projects Administration artists who worked in Arizona during the 1930s. Depression photographer Dorothea Lange, known for her heart-wrenching images of migrant farm workers, also found plenty of fodder in Arizona.

The city of Phoenix began building a foundation for arts and culture early in the century. The Heard Museum opened in 1929, the Phoenix Art Museum traces its beginnings to the 1930s, and the Phoenix Symphony just celebrated its 50th anniversary. Since the mid-1980s, the Valley of the Sun's arts community has matured. The Valley's economic boom has influenced the arts in much the same way a desert rain helps bring life to the desert. Nevertheless, the lure of the outdoors diverts much attention and funds away from the arts, so even top-ranked companies like Ballet Arizona find that maintaining a financial stability presents problems.

Despite the financial challenge, the arts—visual, music, drama, dance, and literature—play an important part in the Valley's quality of life. Artists in all mediums draw on the combination of ethnic, regional, and classical influences that stem from our unique heritage. If you take a gander in any gallery district, you'll find Native American pottery, katsinas (kachinas), jewelry, weaving, and more. Hispanic culture is well represented by dance and music, and its varied pottery styles—from Mata Ortiz to Oaxacan—can be found in many museums and shops.

Cowboy art is an important tradition in the Valley. The Cowboy Artists of America was founded in 1965 in Sedona, and its annual auction is a premiere Valley art event. Modern art has found a haven here as well, but perhaps the best combination of the two styles is the work of Ed Mell. The Arizona native draws on western themes for his cubist renditions in oil and bronze.

Another form of art that has allowed people around the world to enjoy Arizona's natural wonders is photography. The photographers of the magazine *Arizona Highways*—which just celebrated 75 years of publishing—have established the benchmark for this type of landscape work. Its first color cover featured a photograph taken by one of Arizona's famous politicians, Barry Goldwater, who was also a fine photographer who documented Native American life.

One of the top contemporary artists in the world hangs his hat near

LOOK FOR:
- **Theater**
- **Dinner Theater**
- **Music**
- **Dance**
- **Venues and Museums**
- **Visual Arts**
- **Arts Organizations**

Flagstaff. James Turrell uses light as a medium to produce optical illusions. One part science and one part creativity, his interactive sculptures warp viewers' perceptions of light, space, and matter. In addition to maintaining a constant flurry of exhibitions and installments around the world—such as a Skyspace proposed for the Scottsdale Center for the Arts—his passion has been funneled into his large-scale environmental project near Flagstaff. There, he has worked 27 years to bring The Roden Crater project to fruition. Planned for completion in fall of 2001, the celestial gallery will provide a complex array of viewing spaces from which visitors can experience the cosmos. His grand plan is expected to become another Arizona landmark.

As for theater, rarely does a week go by when there isn't something hot going on in regional and local theater or national touring productions. Many musicians and theater professionals from the East and West coasts have made the area home, and the Valley theater scene has blossomed to include an estimated 60 professional and community theater companies, ranging from the mainstream to experimental. Active theater departments on the main and west campuses of Arizona State University also enliven the scene. In Tempe, you can catch a variety of productions—small works, staged readings, video productions, and experimental works—at the Lyceum Theatre, the Prism Theatre, the Intelligent Stage, and Drama City. At ASU West, theater students stage their works in the University Center Building. The Valley has several theater companies whose works appeal to children, and we even have a puppet theater. These companies are listed in our Kidstuff chapter.

Community-level arts are alive and well too. The Sun Cities, for instance, have modern dance groups, choruses, all manner of arts classes, and a continuing slate of events at the Sundome and the Sun Cities Museum of Art.

Community arts centers are a focal point of cultural activity in several other cities in the Valley, including Scottsdale, Tempe, and Mesa. They not only host art exhibitions and live performances, but also have a community outreach goal to bring in families for classes and other events.

Observers say a healthy national economy and better marketing have helped boost attendance and revenues for symphonies and other classical music groups. After many rough years, the Phoenix Symphony is in a period of relative financial stability. The symphonies of smaller Valley cities, notably Mesa, Tempe, Sun City, and Scottsdale, continue to draw audiences.

Downtown Scottsdale boasts several thriving gallery districts. Visitors browse all they want during the Art Walk held on Thursday evenings.

Photo: Paul Markow, courtesy of Scottsdale Convention and Visitors Bureau

Arizona State University has a symphony, as well as chamber ensembles and a concert band. Around the Valley you'll find string quartets, Baroque music ensembles, and piano trios regularly playing at small venues. Arizona Opera has gone beyond traditional notions of opera to attract a new generation of fans. For those who like rock, pop, alternative, and New Age music, Phoenix will not disappoint. It attracts most of the major tours, from the Rolling Stones to Yanni. The jazz scene also sizzles, thanks to local music promoters who bring in regional and national artists known for classic jazz, easy-listening jazz, Dixieland, and other styles. (See our Nightlife chapter for jazz and pop music venues.)

Outside the Valley, art also flourishes. To the north, Sedona is home to approximately 200 working artists, many of whom have fled urban areas to draw inspiration from the town's red-rock vistas. A $9 million performing arts center, the Sedona Cultural Park, opened in 2000. Jerome, near Sedona, and Bisbee, to the south, are both former mining towns that have also retooled themselves as art communities. Tourists find plenty to see and do in these areas, as our chapter on Daytrips illustrates in more detail.

In this listing, we give an introduction to arts in the Valley—though a comprehensive listing would be longer than this book. You'll find contact information for many of the performing art organizations, as well as the venues where they usually perform.

Theater

Actors Theatre of Phoenix
- **(602) 253-6701,**
  (602) 252-8497 box office

Formed in 1984, this professional theater company goes by the slogan "theater that's just slightly off-center, off-Broadway, just downtown." After stints at different venues, ATOP has settled into the downtown Herberger Theater Center, 222 E. Monroe Street, Phoenix, as a resident company, performing on Stage West. It aims for five productions per season, and past hits include a "slightly off-center" version of *A Christmas Carol*, *The Complete History of America (abridged)*, and *Nixon's Nixon*. Ticket prices range from $25 to $32.

Arizona Jewish Theatre Company
444 W. Camelback Rd., Suite 208, Phoenix
- **(602) 264-0402**
- **www.azjewishtheatre.org**

As the only Jewish theater company in the state, the AJTC produces plays that reflect the Jewish experience and introduce Jewish culture to the community. The nonsectarian, nonprofit theater came into being in 1988 and performs at The Playhouse on the Park, 1850 North Central Avenue, inside the Viad Corporate Center in Phoenix. The company does both drama and comedy, and recent productions have included *I'm Not Rappaport* and *Talley's Folly*. It prides itself on its multicultural perspective, with cast and crew from all walks of life. Curtain Call, the company's educational division, provides a variety of theater workshops for children from all backgrounds, both during summer and after school. AJTC season subscrip-

tions or individual tickets ($24 to $26) are available. Performances are usually Thursday through Sunday evenings, with afternoon performances on Sunday.

Arizona Theatre Company
502 W. Roosevelt St., Phoenix
- **(602) 256-6899,**
  (602) 256-6995 box office
- **www.aztheatre.org**

"The equal of anything on Broadway." That's been said about productions of Arizona Theatre Company, the state's nonprofit resident theater, whose work increasingly has won national recognition. ATC annually puts on six main-stage productions in both Phoenix and Tucson. In Phoenix, the ATC performs at the Herberger Theater Center, 222 E. Monroe Street in downtown Phoenix. The company formed in Tucson in 1966 as the Arizona Civic Theatre, then in 1978 added performances in Phoenix and changed its name. David Ira Goldstein has served as artistic director since 1992. In choosing plays, ATC says its mission is to offer a broad range of theatrical styles, confront a spectrum of issues, and deepen ATC's commitment to cultural diversity. Recent productions included *The Mystery of Irma Vep*, a comedy, and the drama Side Man. Expect first-class costumes, lighting, and sound and stage design from ATC. Performances usually run Tuesday through Sunday, with a few matinees. Single-ticket prices range between $23 and $48; season subscriptions are available.

Black Theatre Troupe
333 E. Portland St., Phoenix
- **(602) 258-8128**

The Black Theatre Troupe performs four to

five productions a year at the Helen K. Mason Center for the Performing Arts, a modest stage in downtown Phoenix at Third and Portland Streets. Concentrating on productions that illuminate the African-American experience, this troupe's previous works include *Blues in the Night* and *Black Nativity*. Tickets range from $10 to $16.

Childsplay
• (602) 350-8101

Of all the theater companies for children that have blossomed in the Valley, this one stands out. Named by *American Theatre* magazine as one of the leading theaters in the nation for young audiences, its out-of-the-ordinary productions have been providing unforgettable experiences for children and adults alike since 1977. The award-winning troupe of adult professional actors is led by artistic director David Saar, who's not afraid to tackle serious subjects and bring them to a child's level of understanding. Comedies, musicals, and mainstream works, such as *Anne of Green Gables*, are all part of the Childsplay repertoire. Its production of *The Velveteen Rabbit* has become so popular that it's been presented every holiday season since the mid-1980s.

Childsplay's mission is "to create theater so strikingly original in form, content, or both, that it instills in young people an enduring awe, love, and respect for the medium, thus preserving imagination and wonder, the hallmarks of childhood." To that end, Childsplay tours to schools statewide and brings school groups to the theaters where it performs, including the Herberger Theater, 222 E. Monroe Street in Phoenix, (602) 252-8497; the Tempe Performing Arts Center, 132 E. Sixth Street in Tempe, (480) 350-8101; and the Scottsdale Center for the Arts, 7380 E. Second Street in Scottsdale, (480) 994-2787. Most public performances are on Friday evenings and Saturday and Sunday afternoons. Season subscriptions or individual tickets are available. Single-ticket prices range from $11 to $18.

Desert Foothills Theater
33606 N. 60th St.,
Cactus Shadows Fine Arts Center
• **(480) 488-1981**
• **www.azfcf.org**

The award-winning Desert Foothills Theater, which plays at the Cactus Shadows Fine Arts Center in Cave Creek, celebrates more than 25 years of community theater. It is sponsored by The Foothills Community Foundation. It puts on four performances a year, with shows

like *The Pirates of Penzance, You Can't Take it With You, Tomfoolery,* and *Escape from Papago Park*. Ticket prices range from $16 to $18, with students admitted for $9. The first Thursday of every run is free.

Ethington Theatre
3300 W. Camelback Rd., Phoenix
• **(602) 589-2871**

The resident theater of Grand Canyon University has added to the cultural life of the West Valley since 1950. Its student-faculty productions are known for being innovative and energetic. One season's ambitious productions for this small venue included *Tartuffe, The Mousetrap, Accidental Death of An Anarchist, Hansel & Gretel,* and *The Gondoliers*. Performances are usually Friday and Saturday evenings at 8 PM, with Sunday matinees at 2 PM. Admission is $10.

Phoenix Theatre
100 E. McDowell Rd., Phoenix
• **(602) 258-1974**
• **www.phoenixtheatre.net**

Organized in 1920, Phoenix Theatre claims to be the nation's oldest continually operating community theater. Known for many years as Phoenix Little Theatre, this group adopted a new moniker and expanded mission a few years ago and now operates from remodeled headquarters next to the Phoenix Art Museum. Its season runs September through May, and it presents productions that exhibit a commitment to little-known gems along with big-name works. Recent productions have included *Man of La Mancha, Arsenic and Old Lace, A Comedy of Errors,* and *Steel Magnolias*. A popular sidelight is the Cookie Company, a troupe that performs theater for children—and serves cookies too. Both troupes offer season subscriptions and individual tickets; call for prices.

Scottsdale Community Players
7020 E. Second St., Scottsdale
• **(480) 990-7405**
• **www.stagebrush.bizhosting.com**

One of the Valley's oldest community theaters, Scottsdale Community Players has been bringing down the house since 1952. Its stage is the Stagebrush Theater, a barn-like building in Old Town Scottsdale. It performs six regular season shows and two shows during the summer season. Recent performances have included *Guys and Dolls, The Diary of Anne Frank,* and the *Will Rogers Follies*. Individual tickets cost $18 for adults and $17 for seniors and students. The Stagebrush is also home to Greasepaint, a children's theater company.

Southwest Shakespeare Company
- **(480) 641-7039**

This is a modest company with only a few productions per season, but it can be a good way to spend an evening with the Bard. The company performs at the Mesa Amphitheatre, 201 N. Center Street in Mesa, (480) 644-2560. Recent productions have included *Hamlet* and *Romeo and Juliet*. Each production usually runs two weekends in a row. Season tickets cost $40; and individual tickets are $18 for adults, $14 for seniors and students; and group discounts are available.

Theater Works
9850 W. Peoria Ave., Peoria
- **(623) 815-1791,**
  (623) 815-7930 box office
- **www.theaterworks.org**

Theater Works came into being in 1986 to fill a void in the Northwest Valley. It bills itself as Arizona's largest community theater, offering comedies, dramas, and children's programs like *My Favorite Year*, *The Hobbit*, *One Flew Over the Cuckoo's Nest*, and *The Best Christmas Pageant Ever*. Ticket prices are kept low ($14 to $18), in keeping with the theater's mission of making high-caliber entertainment accessible to everyone. The season consists of seven shows presented September through May, plus four Summer Stock shows. Workshops and classes are popular with children in the community. Shows cost $7.50 for adults and $6 for children.

Dinner Theater

Max's Dinner Theatre
6727 N. 47th Ave., Glendale
- **(623) 937-1671**

Max's is an institution on the dinner theater scene, having been around for two decades. The Copperstate Players perform comedies both Friday and Saturday evenings. The dinner menu offers American fare. The cost is $29.95 per person.

Mystery Mansion
3950 E. Campbell Ave., Phoenix
- **(480)994-1520**
- **www.mysterymansion.com**

Treat yourself to food, laughs, and shivers at Mystery Mansion's production, *Murder at Greystone Manor*. This audience-participation murder mystery is complemented by a four-course Italian dinner, served by the adjoining Pronto Ristornte. The show and meal cost $33

and are offered every Friday and Saturday at 7:30 PM.

Music

Arizona Opera
4600 N. 12th St., Phoenix
- **(602) 266-7464**
- **www.azopera.com**

This is not your parents' opera—even the initially dubious cannot help but be impressed by the grand themes, costumes, and scenery they'll see and hear on the Arizona Opera stage. Its innovative productions rock the traditional opera world. It uses the latest in theatrical and technical advances, such as the use of subtitles (for those who need to brush up on Italian) and the use of rear projectors. The organization won international acclaim under long-time Director Glynn Ross. David Speers has taken over as general director and has attracted a number of rising stars to his stage. Recent productions have included *Carmen*, *The Barber of Seville*, *Don Carlo*, and *The Girl of the Golden West*. The opera plays October through March at Phoenix Symphony Hall, 225 E. Adams Street, Phoenix, and sometimes offers a Great Singer Series at The Orpheum Theatre, 203 W. Adams Street, Phoenix. If you can't catch them in Phoenix, you can also grab a show in Tucson—Arizona Opera duplicates its entire season there. Call the opera directly for tickets or Ticketmaster at (480) 784-4444. Season tickets are available, and individual tickets range from $19 to $69.

Phoenix Boys Choir
Helen C. Lincoln Center for the Phoenix Boys Choir, 1131 E. Missouri Ave., Phoenix
- **(602) 264-5328**
- **www.boyschoir.org**

This isn't just any boys choir, but one with an international audience, five recordings, awards, and alumni that have made their way as professional musicians. Its 180 members play in five choirs. They are mostly boys ages 7 to 14, but a fifth ensemble of 30 Boys Choir graduates sing as The Men of the Phoenix Boys Choir. Successful choir alumni include pop musician Richard Page, former lead singer of '80s pop stars, Mr. Mister; Carl Gayles, international pianist; Brian Kunnari, who arranges scores for Disney Studios; and Martin Davitch, who composed the theme music for "ER." Founded in 1948, the choir owes much to artistic director Harvey K. Smith, who has been at the helm since 1960, but retired recently. Artistic director Georg Stangelberger now takes the helm.

THE ARTS

The touring members of the choir have traveled to Austria, Paris, France, London, Taipei, Beijing, and Sydney. The choir's repertoire includes English choral classics, sacred music, folk music, jazz, show tunes, and holiday programs. In 1998, the choir received an AFIM "Indie" award for "Best recording of 1999" for its premiere of Penderecki's "Credo." Performances are held at Phoenix Symphony Hall, 225 East Adams Street in Phoenix; the Chandler Center for the Arts, 250 N. Arizona Avenue in Chandler; the Orpheum Theatre, 203 W. Adams Street in Phoenix; and Arizona State University West "La Sala", 4701 W. Thunderbird Road in Phoenix; Scottsdale Center for the Arts, 7830 E. Second Street, in Scottsdale; as well as several area churches. Individual tickets ($18 to $25) and season subscriptions are available.

Phoenix Chamber Music Society
• (602) 252-0095

Founded in 1961, the Phoenix Chamber Music Society had modest beginnings by bringing together a quartet of Phoenix Symphony Orchestra members for a small concert series. It has grown to host performances by chamber musicians from all over the world. The 2000-01 season's nine concerts included the Moscow Chamber Orchestra, the Munich Chamber Orchestra, and the Kempf Piano Trio. Performances are at the Scottsdale Center for the Arts, 7380 E. Second Street, and individual tickets are $20.

The Phoenix Symphony
455 N. Third St., Suite 390, Phoenix
• (602) 495-1117 office,
  (602) 262-7272 box office
• www.phoenixsymphony.org

The Phoenix Symphony has battled financial problems and indifference in the Valley, but it was recently commended by the National Endowment for the Arts for its high level of musicianship and successfully selling itself to tough Southwest audiences. Founded 52 years ago, it became a full-time symphony in

INSIDERS' TIP

Care for an art stroll through a large college campus? With walking shoes and a map in hand, head for Arizona State University in Tempe. There you'll find the Nelson Fine Arts Center, Gammage Auditorium, the Gallery of Design, the Computing Commons Gallery (computer-generated art), Northlight Gallery (photography), and the College of Law Art Collection. Or seek out student art at the Memorial Union Gallery, the Harry Wood Art Gallery, or Step Gallery 369. For a map to all these campus galleries, stop by the ASU Visitors Center at Rural Road and Apache Boulevard. For a recorded list of the day's activities at Arizona State University, including performances and art exhibits, call (480) 965-2ASU.

the 1980s and has won two recording awards from the American music industry, plus continental Europe's equivalent of the Grammy. In 1997–98, spirits were high as the Phoenix Symphony celebrated its 50th anniversary season. Hermann Michael came aboard as conductor and music director. A native of Germany, he has guest-conducted a number of U.S. orchestras over the years. His predecessors have included James Sedares in the early 1990s and Theo Alcantara through most of the 1980s. The 75 musicians of the Phoenix Symphony Orchestra play classics, chamber, and family concerts at Symphony Hall, 225 E. Adams Street, and provide music for Ballet Arizona, the Arizona State University Choral Union, and the Phoenix Boys Choir, along with other performance groups.

In the last decade, the symphony has produced three recordings, all of which spent time on *Billboard*'s classical music charts. Among its guest artists over the years are Pablo Casals, Van Cliburn, Yo-Yo Ma, Itzhak Perlman, and Wynton Marsalis. Doc Severinsen has served as principal pops conductor since 1982. The Phoenix Symphony's season runs September through May. Tickets are sold individually and by subscription and range in price from $18 to $45. Seats at special Family Concerts are available for $10 and $15, but make reservations early. Some concerts are preceded by lectures discussing the music to be performed.

Sun Cities Symphony of the West Valley
• (623) 972-4484 business,
  (623) 975-1900 Sundome Box Office

This organization recently celebrated its 30th anniversary. Performances are at the Sundome, 19403 R.H. Johnson Boulevard in Sun City West. James Yestadt, longtime music director and conductor, leads classical music programs that often feature well-known soloists, such as flutist Eugenia Zuckerman or violinist Eugene Fodor. The symphony also offers an annual pops concert. Classical concerts are preceded by a one-hour talks that delve deeply into the music to be featured. Tickets range in price from $15 to $25.

Dance

Ballet Arizona
3645 E. Indian School Rd., Phoenix
- **(602) 381-0184,**
  (602) 381-1096 box office
- **www.balletarizona.org**

With the introduction of a new artistic director, it looks like Ballet Arizona might just leap clear of its financial woes, though the fate of the ballet company still hangs in the balance. Ib Anderson, whose star shines so bright that the New York City Ballet's legendary George Balanchine created roles just for him, took the helm in 2000. Some of that stellar quality is sure to rub off on the company, which was founded in 1986 and is already one of Arizona's largest performing-arts companies. Its repertoire has included demanding classical ballet works, major 20th-century works, world premieres of new works, and cutting-edge choreography. Its annual performance of *The Nutcracker*—performed at Symphony Hall, 225 E. Adams St., Phoenix—draws thousands of families who might otherwise not be interested in ballet. In recent years, Ballet Arizona has made strides in community and educational outreach and in introducing cultural diversity to its performances. The Ballet Arizona School has more than 250 students. The company's major performance venues include the Orpheum Theatre, 203 W. Adams Street, Phoenix; and the Herberger Theatre, 222 E. Monroe Street, Phoenix. Season subscribers receive discounted rates on tickets; single tickets range from $16 to $42, with discounts for seniors and students.

Ballet Etudes
- **(480) 844-2788**

The dancers of Ballet Etudes are between ages 9 and 18. They're selected annually by open auditions and are expected to meet rigid standards of study, rehearsals, and performances, with the goal of emulating a professional ballet company. The young dancers receive training from professionals and vast stage experience. Members have gone on to study or perform with the Joffrey Ballet, Ballet West, and other prestigious organizations. The highlight of each season is *The Nutcracker*, presented on Thanksgiving weekend at the Chandler Center for the Arts, 250 N. Arizona Avenue in Chandler. Also attracting family audiences is the annual springtime production, *Dancing with Fairytale Favorites*, also at the Chandler Center. The company occasionally performs with the Phoenix Symphony and the Mesa Symphony Orchestra. Tickets are available from the Chandler Center box office, (480) 782-2680, for $9 to $12.

Center Dance Ensemble
231 W. Frier Dr., Phoenix
- **(602) 997-9027**
- **www.centerdance.com**

The Herberger Theater Center created the Center Dance Ensemble as its resident modern dance company in 1988. The small company of nine dancers has become highly respected under the leadership of Frances Smith Cohen, artistic director and choreographer. Cohen helped found the dance program at the University of Arizona in the early 1970s and has been an influential local dance teacher for many years. She received the Governor's Outstanding Artist Award in 1994. One of her greatest works with the ensemble has been *Snow Queen*, based on a Hans Christian Andersen fairy tale. Other works by Cohen have tackled issues such as the Holocaust and bigotry and have shown a willingness to experiment with many forms of music. The ensemble performs four times a year at the Herberger, 222 E. Monroe Street in Phoenix, and tickets are available from the center's box office. Admission is $18 for adults, $15 for seniors, and $7 for students.

Southwest Arts & Entertainment
2248 E. Christy Dr., Phoenix
- **(602) 482-6410**

As a nonprofit presenting organization, Southwest Dance still brings top-quality dance ensembles around the world, but it has recently changed its name

THE ARTS

Ballet Arizona's productions, such as Swan Lake, *bring world-class performances to the valley.*

Photo: courtesy of Ballet Arizona

and expanded its focus. It attracts world-class companies, from ballet to contemporary, such Ukrainian National Dance and Ballet Folklorico de Mexico. It also brings in world music, jazz, and other attractions to Arizona, such as the Preservation Hall Jazz Band. Venues include Phoenix Symphony Hall, 225 E. Adams Street in Phoenix; the Orpheum Theatre, 203 W. Adams Street in Phoenix; the Chandler Center for the Arts, 250 N. Arizona Avenue in Chandler; and The Cactus Shadows Fine Arts Center, 3606 N. 60th Street, Cave Creek. Single tickets, ranging from $20 to $40, are available from the Civic Plaza box offices for Phoenix performances, and from the Chandler Center box office or TicketMaster for Chandler performances. You also can order tickets at www.tickets.com or by calling (800) 905-3315.

Venues and Museums

Phoenix

Herberger Theater Center
222 E. Monroe St., Phoenix
• (602) 254-7399,
(602) 252-8497 box office
• wwww.herbergertheater.org

A block north of Phoenix Symphony Hall is a more recent addition to the growing list of performing arts venues in a revitalized downtown. The Herberger has two stages designed to provide an intimate theater experience. The Center Stage seats 802 on three levels, and Stage West seats 343 in a proscenium, or horseshoe, configuration on four levels. When the orchestra pit is not being used, it can be raised or lowered to accommodate set designs. Acoustics are designed to facilitate the spoken word, making the Herberger a popular venue for theater. With five resident companies and several rentals to community groups, the Herberger bursts with about 600 performances a year. The companies are Arizona Theatre Company,

Ballet Arizona, Actors Theatre of Phoenix, Center Dance Ensemble, and Childsplay. The Herberger is ADA compliant and it now has an infrared system for audio-described and listening-impaired systems. Concessions are available. An orientation for volunteers is held the first Saturday of every month.

Orpheum Theatre
203 W. Adams St., Phoenix
• (602) 252-9678,
(602) 262-7272 box office

Renovate it, and they will come. The Orpheum was built in 1929 as an ornate, art deco theater to showcase vaudeville acts and movies. Later it attracted Broadway shows and all kinds of stars. In the 1970s, it moved into Hispanic-theme concerts. But time was not kind to the Orpheum, which fell into disrepair and closed in the 1980s. Thanks to city bond funds and private donations, the theater reopened in early 1997, after $14.2 million in renovations. Visitors today can enjoy the architectural wonders of the Spanish Colonial Revival-style building. The winding staircases, embellished doors, gilded proscenium, murals, and starlight-painted ceiling are worth seeing. Technical amenities have been brought up to date as well. The theater has hosted Carol Channing in a production of *Hello Dolly*, international ballet stars, and regional theatrical productions. It has no resident company, but is used primarily

Dance, theater, and the arts are partners in the cultural environment of Phoenix.

Photo: Penny Keingartner

THE ARTS

by Southwest Dance, Theatre League, Ballet Arizona, JAM Theatricals, and Peoples Pops. The 1,400-seat Orpheum is another triumph in the revitalization of downtown Phoenix.

Symphony Hall
Phoenix Civic Plaza, 225 E. Adams St., Phoenix
• **(602) 262-6225**

The home of the Phoenix Symphony Orchestra and the Arizona Opera often hosts touring performers and Broadway shows as well. The hall, which has the largest proscenium stage downtown, is known for its good acoustics, plush interior, and stunning chandeliers. It seats 2,600 on the main floor and balcony. Symphony Hall faces a large terrace that's frequently the setting for city-sponsored festivals and outdoor concerts.

Southeast Valley

Chandler Center for the Arts
250 N. Arizona Ave., Chandler
• **(602) 786-2680 box office,**
  (602) 786-2682 administration
• **www.chandleraz.org**

The high-tech Center for the Arts, completed in 1984, has contributed to the coming of age of downtown Chandler. Its concerts, road shows, and theatrical productions draw

people into what not too long ago was a sleepy city center. The center is known for the "turntable" design of its auditorium—two seating sections in the rear rotate 180 degrees to face two more intimate stages. Walls move, too, meaning the center can run three events simultaneously. The Main Stage seats 1,560; the Little Theater, 365; and the Recital Hall, 255. State-of-the-art acoustics, expansive dressing rooms, a dance studio, a television studio, a scene shop, and tunnel access connecting stage areas are among its amenities. Past performers include Jay Leno, Crystal Gayle, the Stars of the Bolshoi, and Le Ballet National du Senegal. More than two dozen regional arts organizations regularly use the center. In addition to the more than 1,000 activities held each year in the three theaters, the center continuously runs visual arts exhibitions and educational programs. An adjunct of the center, the Vision Gallery, recently opened at 80 S. San Marcos Place in Chandler. The nonprofit Chandler Cultural Foundation manages the center for the City of Chandler.

Grady Gammage Memorial Auditorium
Arizona State University,
Gammage Pkwy. and Mill Ave., Tempe
• **(602) 965-3434**

One of the Valley's architectural jewels, Gammage was designed by Frank Lloyd Wright

Symphony fans have an excellent center for performances in Phoenix.

Photo: Penny Kleingartner

and completed in 1964. A redesigned adaptation of Wright's never-built Bagdad Opera House, 50 concrete columns support the round roof, which has a pattern of interlocking circles. A few years ago the 3,000-seat auditorium underwent an extensive renovation and continues to be known for its acoustic excellence as well as its beauty. This is the place to see touring Broadway shows, and in the past Gammage has hosted *Cats*, *The Phantom of the Opera*, *Rent*, and the recent revival of *Cabaret*. It also books smaller theatrical performances and pop and classical music concerts. The stage accommodates a full symphony orchestra and a massive pipe organ. You can catch a guided tour of Gammage daily; call ahead at (480) 965-4050 for an appointment.

School of Music Building
Arizona State University, Gammage Pkwy. and Mill Ave., Tempe
• **(480) 965-8863**

Frank Lloyd Wright's Taliesin Architects designed the Music Building to complement Gammage Auditorium (see the listing in this chapter). A Southwestern-style addition, completed in 1991, blends well with surrounding architecture. The building is home to Katzin Concert Hall, the Music Theatre, Recital Hall, and Organ Hall, which boasts a 1,800-pipe organ. The halls are used for a variety of performances, particularly concerts by students of ASU's up-and-coming music school.

Northeast Valley

Kerr Cultural Center
6110 N. Scottsdale Rd., Scottsdale
• **(480) 965-5377**
• **www.asukerr.com**

Tucked in amidst the glitzy resorts and shopping centers of Scottsdale Road, Kerr (pronounced CARE) Cultural Center is a 300-seat adobe studio built in 1959 by violist/arts patron Louise Lincoln Kerr. The studio was designed for chamber music, and such notables as Pablo Casals and Isaac Stern have played here. Today, Kerr's programming includes jazz, folk,

world music, theater, lectures, cameo theatrical events, and family concerts. It is run by Arizona State University. The entrance to Kerr is a little tricky. Follow the signs at the stoplight at Rose Lane near the Borgata Shopping Village.

Scottsdale Center for the Arts/ Scottsdale Museum of Contemporary Art
7380 E. Second St., Scottsdale
• **(480) 994-ARTS**
• **www.scottsdalearts.org**

The vibrant offerings by the Scottsdale Center for the Arts and its new Scottsdale Museum of Contemporary Art (SMoCA) contribute to the city's reputation as one of the nation's top art destinations. A cultural hub for the region, the SCA offers a first-rate venue for nationally-known performers. It hosts more than 60 music, dance, and theater performances, as well as several screenings of independent films throughout the season. Tony Award-winning star of Broadway Betty Buckley, Downbeat Lifetime Achievement jazz pianist Marian McPartland, virtuoso violinist Joshua Bell, the illusionist dance company Pilobolus, and Ireland's ever-popular Chieftains are just a few of the high energy talents that grace the stage of the center this season. Presentations by the Phoenix Chamber Music Society, the Phoenix Symphony Chamber Orchestra, and the Scottsdale Symphony Orchestra also can be heard on a regular basis.

Some concerts are held under the stars in the center's outdoor amphitheater, and on Sunday afternoons from October through March, the SCA presents Sunday A'Fair from noon to 4:30 PM when concerts and artist booths are offered free to the public outside on beautiful Scottsdale Civic Center.

Scottsdale Civic Center, an oasis of grassy lawns, beautiful flower gardens, fountains, and sculptures, is also the setting for the Scottsdale Arts Festival.

Opened in 1999, the stunning architecture of SMoCA's Gerard L. Cafesjian Pavilion, designed by Arizona's renowned Will Bruder, mirrors the top-quality

INSIDERS' TIP
One way that Valley residents while away the long, hot summers is to attend outdoor concerts—after the sun's gone down, of course. Concert series that are free or charge a small admission take place at several spots, including the Desert Botanical Garden, (602) 754-8134; Kiwanis Community Park in Tempe, (480) 350-5201; Murphy Park in downtown Glendale, (623) 930-2820; el Pedregal Festival Marketplace in Carefree, (480) 488-1072; and Encanto Park in Phoenix, (602) 262-6412.

THE ARTS

The new Scottsdale Museum of Contemporary Art was designed by renowned Arizona architect Will Bruder. Inside, visitors find the most recent innovations in contemporary art.

Photo: Bill Timmerman, courtesy of the Scottsdale Center for the Arts

art, architecture, and design on exhibit within its walls. The large diochric glass wall by New York artist James Carpenter incorporated into the exterior of the building, serves as a beacon to museum-goers. Visitors to SMoCA can experience exhibits like ALMOST WARM & FUZZY: Childhood and Contemporary Art, a delightful mix of innocence and nostalgia; an exhibition of works by internationally-acclaimed Flagstaff-based artist James Turrell, including an overview of the artist's monumental Roden Crater project and a new Turrell Skyspace; Donald Sultan's Pop-influenced, still-life images; and a retrospective of works by German sculptor Wolfgang Laib, among other shows. In April 1999, SMoCA was awarded the highest honor a museum can receive: accreditation by the American Association of Museums (AAM). Among more than 8,000 museums nationwide, only 750 have been accredited by the AAM Accreditation Commission.

The joy of shopping has not been overlooked at SCA and SMoCA. Each has an award-winning museum store that offers a selection of unusual and artsy objects. For the visitor's dining pleasure, Scottsdale Civic Center is ringed by a number of fine restaurants that include a gourmet coffee shop, Indian food, Spanish fare, and top-quality American cuisine.

The SCA and SMoCA are managed by the Scottsdale Cultural Council. Tickets can be purchased online through tickets.com, or by phone by calling (480) 994-ARTS (2787). Museum

hours are 10 AM to 5 PM, Tuesdays and Wednesdays; 10 AM to 8 PM, Thursdays, Fridays, and Saturdays; and noon to 5 PM, Sundays. The museum is closed on Monday. Admission is $5, $3 for students, and free for members and children 15 and younger. Admission is free on Thursdays, sponsored by *New Times*.

Northwest Valley

Second Stage West
Arizona State University West,
4701 W. Thunderbird Rd., Phoenix
• (602) 543-ARTS

Downstairs in the University Center Building at ASU West, this stage principally serves the Department of Interdisciplinary Arts and Performance. Though primarily a development space for works in progress by both students and well-known performers, you also can catch experimental and live performances.

Sundome Center for the Performing Arts
19403 R.H. Johnson Blvd., Sun City West
• (623) 975-1900

The largest single-level theater in the nation, the Sundome seats 7,033. It was completed in 1980 and over the years it has hosted such acts as Bob Hope, Tom Jones, and George Burns. In recent years it has added country music and mainstream pop acts to lure younger audiences. Still, it's a source of pride for the

The House of Native American Music

Canyon Records sits atop the Native American music mountain. It's not a very big mountain, mind you, but the Phoenix-based record company's position in this special segment makes Canyon a noteworthy presence in the national music scene.

Canyon Records' story is that of Ray Boley, an Anglo, and the two Native American musicians—Ed Lee Natay and R. Carlos Nakai–who changed his life.

In 1951, Boley opened Canyon Films, a company that made commercials and industrial films, after running his own recording studio in Phoenix for three years. That's when Phoenix Little Theatre, a local stage company, asked Boley to record some songs for a production.

Chances are that if you're not from a Native American reservation, you've never heard of Navajo singer Ed Lee Natay. Boley hadn't either. So when he first heard Natay sing traditional vocal chants, accompanying himself with a drum, Boley was awestruck. The theater job involved recording Natay performing four songs, but when the project was over, the music lingered in Boley's mind. He vowed to record an album of Natay's chanting. He did just that. Using a single microphone, Boley captured Natay and his drum for posterity. That album, Natay—Navajo Singer, was the first Canyon Records release.

Boley soon found out that almost nobody was recording Native American music, and the few companies that did—such as Folkways—did so for ethnographic purposes rather than for the love of music. That is, they weren't Native American records made for Native American people, but were marketed to those interested in learning how Native American music sounded. That's not what Canyon Records was about. For the next 20 years, Boley and his wife, Mary, made seeking out and recording Native American music their hobby, while Boley's main stock-in-trade remained the film company. They went to different tribes seeking different sounds, and Native Americans came to Canyon Records to hear their music. During that time, Canyon's catalog of albums was small, but quite a few singles were issued.

Although these were popular records, the Native American market itself was tiny. A record that sold 20,000 copies would have been a runaway hit. However, Boley's devotion to the music grew, and in 1971 he sold off the film company to concentrate on Canyon Records. In the next year, he and his wife nearly doubled the label's catalog of albums to a whopping 50 titles. They had recorded songs from many nations, including the Arapaho, Chippewa, Cree, Kiowa, Papago, and Pima. They recorded war dances, round dances, lullabies, and peyote chants. Boley was not a purist, and thus he went beyond tribal and traditional music to record modern entertainment such as "chicken scratch" music, which takes the European polka and gives it a tribal twist.

The Boleys opened their own retail store, Canyon Records and Arts, on December 2, 1972. The site, at 4143 N. 16th Street, perches across from the Phoenix Indian Hospital. Boley hired Numkena Associates, headed by Hopi architect Dennis Numkena, to design the building in the adobe brick and earth tone Southwestern Pueblo style. The opening was a gala affair, and 800 people from Arizona tribes attended. The building was blessed by a Catholic priest and an Apache medicine man. Although Canyon Records' products predominated, the Boleys also sold other Native American recordings, books, crafts, and

(Continued on next page)

artwork. Boley, preferring to work on the recording end, sold the retail part of the business to Bob Nuss in 1983. Nuss kept the Canyon Records and Arts name until July 1987, when the store became known as Drumbeat Indian Arts. Still, the store serves the same social function it has for many years, complete with a bulletin board that lists local Native American event and powwow information.

Enter R. Carlos Nakai. Boley met Nakai in the mid-1980s, when Canyon Records was already well established. As Natay had done 35 years earlier, Nakai changed everything for Boley. Nakai, of Navajo-Ute heritage, was trained as a classical trumpeter. However, he wanted to improvise, and although the ghosts of Louis Armstrong, Miles Davis, and Dizzy Gillespie might argue with him, Nakai felt he couldn't improvise on the trumpet. Nakai adapted the wooden flute—common among tribes of the Great Plains—to his musical needs. He played traditional Plains melodies and wrote and improvised his own haunting tunes. He even paired his wooden flute with synthesizers, creating a sound that fit comfortably into the then-mushrooming New Age category.

Once again, Boley was fascinated. He took a chance on Nakai, whose ideas deviated from traditional notions of Native American music, and the payoff was surprising. The market for Canyon Records products immediately expanded as Anglos began buying Nakai's music, which received exposure off the reservations. Today, Nakai can rightfully be called "the superstar of Native American music," having sold more than 2.5 million albums since he started recording in 1985. Nakai has more than 20 titles in his Canyon Records catalog and perhaps a dozen more on other labels. One album, Canyon Trilogy, has sold more than 500,000 copies worldwide. A prolific performer and composer, Nakai's efforts include those with a band called Jackalope and team-ups with other performers and composers. He opened the door for many more Native American performers to find their places in this new crossover market.

Boley retired from Canyon Records in 1992, selling the label to Robert Doyle. By the time he retired, the label had more than 400 titles in its catalog. The Phoenix Indian Center honored Boley with a benefit dinner on April 15, 1995. His willingness to record Native music helped preserve and promote traditional culture among Native Americans and, ultimately, to the world at large.

Under Doyle's management, Canyon Records continues to thrive and has expanded its offerings. In addition to Native American flute music, recent recordings have included nouveau flamenco, jazz, New Age, and even rap. You can find its recordings in the Valley under "World Beat" or "Native American" categories at Tower Records, 1110 W. Southern Avenue, Mesa; Drumbeat Indian Arts, 4143 N. 16th St., Suite 1, Phoenix; or at any Borders Books & Music stores. For more information about the label's catalog sales and tour details, or for general information about Native American music, call (800) 268-1141, or visit the web site at www.canyonrecords.com.

seniors of the Sun Cities. The Sundome operates under the aegis of Arizona State University.

Visual Arts

In the 1980s, the people of Phoenix got serious about raising the city's stature as a cultural center and approved a vast amount of bond money to help improve museums and libraries. One of the funding recipients was the Phoenix Art Museum, whose space had become severely cramped. A gleaming, $25 million remodeling of the museum was completed in 1996. Building design improvements by a well-known New York architectural firm have helped put the museum in the national art spotlight. Equally important are the exhibitions the museum has been able to mount in the past few years; these, too, have garnered national attention.

Any survey of the Valley visual arts scene has to include Scottsdale. With its dozens of galleries in the downtown arts district and elsewhere, Scottsdale is considered one of the top five art destinations in the nation. It competes with Santa Fe for top honors in promoting Southwestern art. Many well-known painters and sculptors live and work here, and the roster includes Native American artists who excel not only in painting and sculpture, but also jewelry, weaving, woodcarving, and pottery.

Museums and galleries are one way to immerse yourself in the Valley's fine arts scene. The area's many arts and crafts fairs are another. Always drawing crowds are the Heard Museum Guild Indian Fair and Market; the Scottsdale Arts Festival; the Old Town Tempe Festival of the Arts in the spring and fall; the Fountain Hills Great Fair; and the Indian Artists of America show in Scottsdale. Check our Annual Events chapter for details on these shows and others.

Art Centers

Southeast Valley

Mesa Arts Center
155 N. Center St., Mesa
• **(480) 644-2242**
• **www.mesaarts.com**

This arts center wears many hats in serving Arizona's third-largest city. It supports the visual-arts exhibitions of Mesa Contemporary Arts; the children's plays of Mesa Youtheatre; a series of outdoor concerts; more than 600 visual- and performing-arts classes for all ages, year-round; a film series; and special events. Many events, such as the Thanksgiving gospel-music festival and Cinco de Mayo, reach out to Mesa's diverse cultural communities. Examples of the concerts the center sponsors are the Out to Lunch series at Community Center Plaza; Concerts at the Amp at Mesa Amphitheatre; and Concerts in the Park at Dobson Ranch Park, all with free admission. Mesa Contemporary Arts is perhaps best known for its annual "Vahki" exhibition, which for 20 years has featured the best of contemporary American crafts through a national, juried show. The gallery is open noon to 8 PM, Tuesday through Friday; and noon to 5 PM on Saturday. The art exhibits rotate for several weeks at a time, and admission is free. Design plans for Mesa's new Arts and Entertainment Center are now under way. The new facility is expected to open in the fall of 2004, and will include four theaters, new art galleries, and per-

forming- and visual-arts classrooms. The new facility will replace the existing Mesa Arts Center, and will be located on the southeast corner of Center and Main Streets downtown.

Nelson Fine Arts Center
Arizona State University,
Mill Ave. and 10th St., Tempe
• **(480) 965-2787**
• **www.asuam.fa.asu.edu**

This is one of the newest and most impressive additions to the ASU campus—a highly modern building of textured purple-gray stucco designed by Antoine Predock, an internationally known architect who also designed Phoenix's Arizona Science Center (see our Attractions chapter). The Nelson Center has outdoor performance spaces, water features, and a 12-foot wall that serves as an outdoor projection screen. The center is home to the ASU Art Museum, known for its collections of nineteenth- and twentieth-century American paintings, Latin American art, and contemporary crafts. The galleries are open 10 AM to 9 PM on Tuesday; 10 AM to 5 PM, Wednesday through Saturday; and 1 to 5 PM on Sunday. The center is also home to the intimate Paul V. Galvin Playhouse and the University Dance Laboratory.

Northeast Valley

Cactus Shadows Fine Arts Center
33606 N. 60th St.,
south of Carefree Highway, Cave Creek
• **(480) 488-1105, (480) 488-1981 theater**

This arts center on the campus of Cactus Shadows High School serves the small but ever-growing communities of Cave Creek, Carefree, and far-north Scottsdale. The Foothills Community Foundation oversees programming, which includes exhibits by the area's professional artists and by public school students; four productions per season by the award-winning Desert Foothills Theater, (480) 488-1981; and plays by the high school drama club. Many dance performances are held here, such as work by the regional troupe Ballet Etudes. Every fall, the Missoula Children's Theater stops by on its world tour to produce a show with local kids. The center also hosts several of the concerts in Musicfest, (480) 488-0806, an annual classical music series for Foothills residents. Foothills Film Society, (480) 488-1090, offers an eclectic variety of independent films such as

Smoke Signals, Carnal Knowledge, and *Women in Love*. The center's hours and fees vary according to performances and exhibits, so call ahead.

Art Museums

Phoenix

Heard Museum
2301 N. Central Ave., Phoenix
• (480) 252-8840, (480) 252-8848
• www.heard.org

The world-famous Heard Museum is a must-see on your visit to the Valley. The museum's 10 spacious exhibit galleries offer valuable insight into Native American cultures and arts, both historical and modern. Its outdoor bricked courtyards, graced with traditional and contemporary Native American art, are a joy to see. The Heard Museum's recently completed 50,000-square-foot expansion nearly doubled its public spaces. New features include three galleries, a 400-seat auditorium, an education center, an expanded museum shop and bookstore, and an indoor/outdoor café. For simple enjoyment of Southwestern Indian baskets, pottery, rugs, sculpture, paintings, and artistic jewelry, plan to spend time in the Heard's many galleries and its shop. Also have a look at the Barry Goldwater collection of more than 400 Hopi katsinas (or kachinas). Contemporary paintings and other works by well-known artists are often on view in temporary exhibits. An especially good time to visit the Heard is during one of its special events, which are discussed in more detail in our Annual Events chapters. For more about the Heard, read our Attractions chapter. The Heard is now open daily, from 9:30 AM to 5 PM. Admission is $7 for adults, $6 for seniors, and $3 for children ages 4 to 12. Children younger than 4, museum members, and Native Americans get in free.

Phoenix Art Museum
1625 N. Central Ave., Phoenix
• (602) 257-1222, (602) 257-1880
• wwww.phxart.org

Back in the 1930s, when Phoenix was a much smaller town, surrealist painter Philip C. Curtis and others developed the Phoenix Art

INSIDERS' TIP

The art exhibits in the terminals of Sky Harbor International Airport are a wonderful diversion when waiting for a flight. In fact, Sky Harbor has one of the largest airport art programs in the United States, with at least 20 display areas and a permanent collection worth $2.1 million. Look for a variety of art media, along with historical and regional memorabilia, celebrating Arizona's heritage. For more information, call (602) 273-2006.

Center. With the postwar population boom, the city gradually became more serious about its cultural life, and the Phoenix Art Museum opened in 1959. Now the largest art museum in the Southwest, it mounts more than 20 exhibitions a year, including most of the blockbusters that tour the country. Recently, it has shown retrospectives on artists ranging from Norman Rockwell to photographer Annie Leibovitz. In 1996, the museum entered a new era with the completion of a $25 million expansion and renovation project that more than doubled its space to 160,000 square feet. The project also gave the museum some first-class improvements in lighting, wall space for massive works of art, an architecturally intriguing Great Hall, a state-of-the-art lecture hall, and better storage space.

The museum boasts more than 14,000 works in its permanent collection, including works on paper, paintings, textiles, and sculpture. Make time to visit the galleries with contemporary art; the Thorne Miniature Rooms showing historic interiors; the Art of Asia Gallery; the European Galleries; and the Western American Art Gallery. You'll be delighted by the prestigious, international array of artists, with works that date from 1600 to the present.

Children will enjoy the hands-on Art Works Gallery. Inquire with the museum about the schedule for art workshops for children and adults, docent talks, lectures, and special concerts. For refreshment, there's Eddie's Art Museum Cafe. For gifts, art books, jewelry, and many other items, stop in the Museum Store. The Phoenix Art Museum is open 10 AM to 5 PM, Tuesday through Sunday, and it stays open until 9 PM on Thursdays. Admission is $7 for adults, $5 for seniors and students, $2 for youths ages 6 to 18, and free for children younger than 6. Admission is free on Thursday.

Shemer Art Center and Museum
5005 E. Camelback Rd., Phoenix
• (602) 262-4727

This small museum makes an interesting side trip, as much for the building itself as for the artwork within it. The first house built in Arcadia (a stately neighborhood at the base of

The Heard Museum—the place to go to see Native American art—has one of the largest collections of Katsinas (or Kachina dolls) in the country. This Hopi Katsina, Poliimana, was made by Jimmie Kewantwytewa in the 1950s.

Photo: courtesy of the Heard Museum

Camelback Mountain), it houses galleries and art classrooms. The Santa Fe Mission-style, adobe structure was built in the 1920s and purchased in 1984 by Martha Shemer for donation to the city of Phoenix. It's been expanded and renovated over the years but maintains an "old Phoenix" character. Inside you'll find contemporary works by local artists and an intriguing 1890s miniature mansion for dolls. Bold steel sculptures and a citrus orchard enliven the center's grounds. The annual Sunday at Shemer family art festival in November is a popular event. In addition to a variety of art classes for all ages, the museum sponsors an Artists' Cafe series where local artists can keep abreast of trends and issues. Gallery hours are 10 AM to 9 PM on Monday; 10 AM to 5 PM, Wednesday through Friday; and 9 AM to 1 PM on Saturday. Admission is free.

Northeast Valley

Fleischer Museum
17207 N. Perimeter Dr., Scottsdale
• **(602) 585-3108**
• **www.fleischer.org**

Artists like Armin Hansen, Guy Rose, and Clarence Hinkle will be more familiar after you visit this museum dedicated to the California School of American Impressionism. These artists and others, influenced by French Impressionism, imbued their landscapes with an American character. The Fleischer salutes more than 80 artists in a collection of about 200 paintings. Special exhibitions survey related art movements, such as Russian Impressionism of the mid-twentieth century and the Connecticut School. Museum hours are 10 AM to 4 PM daily except holidays, and admission is free. Look for the Perimeter Center office complex near Frank Lloyd Wright Boulevard and Pima Road.

Heard Museum North
Scottsdale Rd. and Carefree Hwy., Scottsdale
• **(480) 488-9817**
• **www.heard.org**

Heard Museum North is an 8,500-square-foot branch of the Heard Museum. Opened in 1996 at el Pedregal Festival Marketplace near Carefree, it shows changing exhibitions of Native American art, hosts guest artists, and showcases special events. The small shop on the premises offers the highest-quality arts and crafts, purchased directly from Native American artists. Hours are 10 AM to 5:30 PM, Monday through Saturday; and noon to 5 PM, Sunday. Admission is $2 for adults, $1 children for ages 4 to 12, and free for those younger than 4. Entrance to the shop is free.

Northwest Valley

West Valley Art Museum
17420 N. Avenue of the Arts, Surprise
• **(623) 972-0635**
• **www.wvam.org**

The stately look of this midsize museum and its collections tells you the seniors of the Northwest Valley are pretty serious about their art. Exhibits change often; a gallery might have realistic landscapes one month and contemporary art another month. The stature of some of the shows is well worth the visit, as the museum often exhibits heavyweights like Leonard Baskin, the world famous sculpture and printmaker, and Philip C. Curtis, Arizona's surrealistic master. The museum's collection of ethnic costumes from more than 60 countries, acquired from all over the world, is worth seeing, as is the sculpture garden. The museum has an extensive permanent collection of the works of American realists George Resler and Henry Varnum Poor. The museum offers art classes, and it hosts a weekly series of concerts and art lectures called Artful Afternoons on Tuesdays. You'll find books, cards, and gifts in the small museum store. The Classic Café offers daily lunches and Sunday brunch. Hours are 10 AM to 4 PM, Tuesday through Sunday. Admission is $4 for adults, $3 for seniors, and $1 for students.

Galleries

So abundant are the art galleries in Scottsdale, Phoenix, and other parts of the Valley that we can't list them all here. Instead,

> ## INSIDERS' TIP
> Want to add to your enjoyment of an event? Many of the Valley's art venues and companies, such as the Phoenix Symphony and Ballet Etudes, have pre-performance talks that offer insight into the evening's program. Check for that availability when you order tickets.

THE ARTS

Art in the Public Eye

You don't need to go to a museum or gallery to see great art in the Valley – just look around. Not only will this keep travel-tired kids busy, but admission is free and the work can be enjoyed even if you are just passing by.

Dozens of artworks grace public spaces in the Valley, adding style in unexpected places. Gargantuan lizards, prickly pear cacti, and Native American motifs, jazz up the walls that line the Pima Freeway in a six-mile-long work called "The Path Most Traveled" by artist Carolyn Braaksma. Windswept metal trees and sculptural saguaros, conceived by artist Joe Tyler, transform six bus stops along Shea Avenue. Whimsical sculptures of trumpet flowers and hummingbird-attracting plants brighten the view of nursing home residents near Civic Center Boulevard and Earll Drive in the Hummingbird Sanctuary Garden, the brainstorm of artist Kevin Berry.

This visual feast illustrates the commitment of Valley residents to support the arts and beautify their cities, a notion that has gained momentum since the mid-1980s when many cities started investing in public art programs. In addition to adding some much-appreciated eye candy, the artwork you'll see is often utilitarian. Artists add their embellishments to the functional, infrastructure of civic works, such as sound barriers, bus stops, canals, and libraries. Even the unused areas surrounding interstate interchanges have designs formed from landscaping rock, sort of like sand painting on a giant scale.

The city of Scottsdale—whose residents approved a Percent for Art

(Continued on next page)

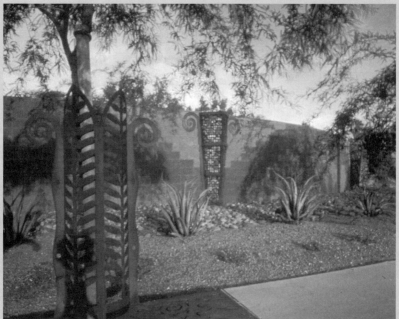

Keep your eyes open when you travel around the Valley, you never know what great artwork you'll see—such as this installation by artist Keven Berry, dubbed West Couplet.

Photo: Courtesy of the Scottsdale Center for the Arts

THE ARTS

Ordinance in 1985—boasts perhaps the most thriving public art program in the Valley. Since then, more than 35 public art projects have been created throughout the city, and many more are in the works, adding to the city's reputation as one of the top art destinations in the country. Take a stroll through the Scottsdale Civic Center Mall, 7380 E. Second Street, and you'll see a number of outstanding works. Nearly seven acres of gardens contains 16 works of art, including the beloved Windows on the West sculpture by artist Louise Nevelson. The mall provides a quiet retreat on weekdays; on weekends it buzzes with special events, like concerts, art fairs, and festivals.

The Scottsdale Center for the Arts also resides on the mall. In addition to its galleries, it will soon be exhibiting a piece by James Turrell. Considered to be one of the top ten contemporary artists in the world, this Flagstaff, Arizona, resident creates optical illusions with light and shadow. His skyscape, a viewing room for contemplating the sky's changing light, is expected to draw national attention.

A sample of other public art works in the Valley include:

• The 540-mural overlooking Tempe Town Lake from the wall of Loop 202, fashioned by Rebecca Ross and Jeff East from thousands of handmade tiles. The playful critters and images that represent the past, present, and future of the Salt River, were made with the help of Tempe schoolchildren.

• Michael Maglich's whimsical sculptures on the columns in front of Phoenix Civic Plaza, which pay tribute to Arizona's official neckwear, the bola tie.

• Marilyn Zwak's Native American-inspired wall relief for the Thomas Road bridge of the Squaw Peak Parkway.

• John Waddell's sculpture, Dance, which captures attention in front of the Herberger Theater. Waddell is a well-respected Arizona artist who works in bronze.

• Trevor Southey's 9-foot male nude, Full Life Reach, at Central Avenue and Washington Street.

• Doug Hyde's massive bronze Tribute to Arizona's Navajo Code Talkers is at Central Avenue and Thomas Road.

• Memorials to Vietnam and Korean War veterans at Wesley Bolin Plaza, 19th Avenue and Jefferson Street, next to the State Capitol.

• The 180-foot-long, bright green pedestrian bridge, designed to resemble a grasshopper, at Cave Creek Wash in Moon Valley Park, north of Coral Gables Drive.

For a map of self-guided tour and map to the city of Scottsdale's public art sites, contact the Scottsdale Cultural Council at (480) 994-ARTS.

we've given a small sampling of galleries to illustrate the area's diversity. You'll find spaces specializing in Native American art, modern art, Western art, objets d'art, eclectic art, and high-quality crafts. Many of the downtown Scottsdale galleries are open Thursday evenings for Art Walk. Some are closed Sundays.

Phoenix

Eleven East Ashland Gallery
11 E. Ashland Ave., Phoenix
• (602) 257-8543

Far from the glitz of downtown Scottsdale's arts district lies a small, independent art space that has been here 12 years. Eleven East Ashland

is in an old house in central Phoenix and has a reputation for showing talented local artists who prefer not to make the Scottsdale scene. Here you'll find unusual, thought-provoking paintings, photography, and mixed media works, as well as performance art. Gallery hours are limited to 5 to 9 PM on Wednesday, noon to 5 PM on Saturday, and other times by appointment.

Movimiento Artistico del Rio Salado (MARS)
126 S. Central Ave., Phoenix
• (602) 253-3541

The 1981 opening of this artist-run, non-profit art space located downtown helped established the city's alternative arts scene. The gallery has a good selection of works by Mexican-American/Chicano artists. One of its best annual shows is La Phoeniquera, which showcases work in all mediums by Arizona artists.

Northeast Valley

Bentley Gallery
4161 N. Marshall Way, Scottsdale
• (480) 946-6060

The Bentley specializes in abstract and minimalistic contemporary painting and sculpture, with a roster of artists that includes Pat Steir, Helen Frankenthaler, Martin Mull, and Vernon Fisher. This is where interior designers find marvelous steel sculptures. The gallery is open only during the day and is closed Sundays.

Gilbert Ortega Museum Gallery
3925 N. Scottsdale Rd., Scottsdale
• (480) 990-1808

You'll see the Gilbert Ortega name on several storefronts in Scottsdale. Ortega, a fourth-generation trader in Indian arts and crafts, boasts a dozen locations around the Valley. If you're in the market for authentic Native American jewelry, baskets, rugs, and pottery, it's a good idea to get a sense of the variety by stopping in at one of his stores. His newest location, listed here, is one-part retail store and one-part display area for several museum-quality pieces from Ortega's private collection.

Joan Cawley Gallery
7135 E. Main St., Scottsdale
• (480) 947-3548

Another veteran of the Scottsdale gallery scene, Joan Cawley showcases American contemporary and Southwestern art. Among the artists represented are Dick Phillips, R.C. Gorman, and Jean Ekman Adams. Another gallery is located at 1410 W 14th Street in Tempe, (480) 858-0920.

Materia/The Hand and the Spirit
4222 N. Marshall Way, Scottsdale
• (480) 949-1262

A gallery like this helps you appreciate the artistry and variety in the realm of crafts by showcasing the best work available. You'll find high-quality contemporary crafts in wood, ceramics, and glass, plus wearable art in jewelry and clothing.

Vanier on Marshall Way
4142 N. Marshall Way, Scottsdale
• (602) 945-0195

Formally the Joy Tash Gallery, the business is under new ownership but remains focused on contemporary art. Another mainstay of Scottsdale galleries, this space represents

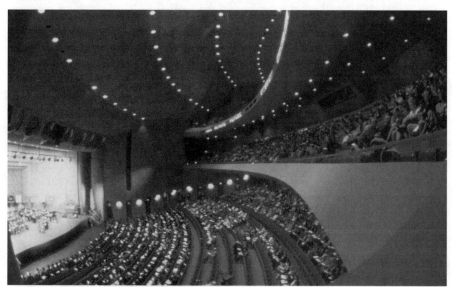

Grady Gammage Auditorium, on the Arizona State University Campus, was one of the last designs by architect Frank Lloyd Wright.

Photo: Jim Richardson, courtesy of Tempe Convention and Visitors Bureau

THE ARTS

several nationally known contemporary artists, including Larry Bell's mixed-media works, the studio art glass of Dale Chihuly, and bronzes by Arizona legend John Waddell.

Lovena Ohl Gallery
4251 N. Marshall Way, Scottsdale
• **(480) 945-8212**

The late Lovena Ohl is considered one of the pioneers in generating interest in Native American art. Her name has been revered among Southwestern art dealers and buyers for two decades. This gallery continues her efforts by representing such well-known artists as painter Michael Kabotie, Santa Clara potter Grace Medicine Flower, sculptor Larry Yazzie, and jeweler Harvey Begay.

Lisa Sette Gallery
4141 N. Marshall Way, Scottsdale
• **(480) 990-7342**

A gallery loved by serious contemporary collectors represents national and even international artists. Even those who don't know much about art will appreciate works such as those by William Wegman, whose clever dog photos have picked up commercial appeal. Other artists represented include Francis Whitehead, Fred Stonehouse, Marie Navarre, and Luis Gonzales.

May Gallery
The Borgata, 6166 N. Scottsdale Rd., Scottsdale
• **(480) 998-2424**

Located in the ritzy Borgata shopping village, the May Gallery features Realism, Impressionism, and Western works by leading artists. Its studio glass art is especially fine, and museum-quality Southwestern jewelry is available. The May Gallery has three other locations in the Valley.

Overland Gallery
7155 E. Main St., Scottsdale
• **(480) 947-1934**

Overland is known for its collection of early twentieth-century Russian paintings of everyday people, painted in the style of the Impressionists. This is the place to pick up Western and American representational art for your formal living spaces.

Riva Yares Gallery
3625 N. Bishop Ln., Scottsdale
• **(480) 947-3251**

The Yares Gallery is set a bit apart from the crowd, both geographically and philosophically

speaking. Two blocks south of most of the galleries, its high-tech exterior looks freshly transplanted from New York City. That metropolitan attitude carries over to the gallery's collection, which emphasizes abstract and contemporary art.

Suzanne Brown Galleries
7160 E. Main St., Scottsdale
• **(480) 945-8475**

One of Scottsdale's very first art dealers still wows them with a diverse collection of contemporary works. Two of the West's best landscape artists, Merrill Mahaffey and Ed Mell, are represented by Suzanne Brown.

Art Walks and Festivals

Evenings during the Valley's cooler months are a lovely time to be out walking, and evenings are a lovely time to stroll among the galleries in our art districts. Scottsdale galleries have a longstanding tradition of opening their doors to browsers on Thursday evenings. Central Phoenix art studios currently offer open houses and self-guided tours one Friday evening a month. Smaller-scale art walks have sprung up as well. You don't have to be a serious art buyer to go on an art walk. Artists and galleries appreciate the chance to introduce their works to a wider audience. Often the artists will be on hand, and many galleries serve light refreshments and feature great, live entertainment.

This section also includes information about a few of the big outdoor art exhibits held during tourist season. They, too, welcome browsers and art collectors alike.

Celebration of Fine Art
18500 N. Scottsdale Rd., Scottsdale
• **(480) 443-7695**

The open-air exhibition area called Celebration of Fine Art hoists its big white tents every year for about 11 weeks starting in January. It offers a chance to see the on-site studios of more than 100 artists, including painters, sculptors, jewelers, photographers, weavers, and ceramists. In previous years the tents have been in a prominent spot on Scottsdale Road just north of Camelback Road. In 1998, the show moved north to the grounds of the Chauncey Equestrian Center. It's usually open 10 AM to 6 PM daily during those 11 weeks, and admission is $6.50, with discounts for seniors and children.

Magic Bird Festivals
Locations vary
• (480) 488-2014

The Magic Bird Gallery in Cave Creek organizes outdoor arts and crafts festivals at several locations from October through April. The festivals usually feature dozens of booths, imported wares, food, music, and family entertainment. Locations include McDonald's Ranch, 26540 N. Scottsdale Road, Scottsdale; and the Peoria Sports Complex, 16101 N. 83rd Avenue, Peoria. Hours typically run from 10 AM to 5 PM, Friday through Sunday. Admission and parking are free.

Phoenix First Fridays
Downtown Phoenix
• (602) 256-7539

This art walk, held the first Friday of each month from October to June, is an opportunity to see mainstream and avant-garde artists. At Janet deBerge Lange's studio, for instance, see her complex assemblages of found objects. At Metropophobobia, catch performance art. The Melting Museum @ The Icehouse is an old cold-storage compound now used for large-scale experimental exhibitions. The participating studios are clustered in downtown Phoenix, but you'll need a car. Also along the self-guided tour find the Phoenix Art Museum and the MARS Artspace (see their listings in this chapter). First Friday hours are 7 to 10 PM. Call the sponsoring organization, Artlink, at the above number for a map of studios. Also inquire about Art Detour, an extended version of First Fridays, held each spring.

Scottsdale Art Walk
Various locations
• (480) 990-3939

If it's Thursday evening and the weather is pleasant (nine times out of 10 it is), several streets in downtown Scottsdale will be brimming with pedestrians hopping from gallery to gallery. Head for Marshall Way, Fifth Avenue, First Avenue, Main Street, and Craftsman Court and ogle artworks in many mediums, some of them worth thousands of dollars. The art walk is presented by the Scottsdale Gallery Association, and the 75-plus members open

their doors from 7 to 9 PM every Thursday. Also find free entertainment, refreshments, and artist demonstrations.

Hidden in the Hills Tour & Art Sale
Cave Creek
• (480) 488-3381

Once a year, the artists who live and work in the hills around Cave Creek open their studios for a public tour. The tour is presented by the Sonoran Arts League and represents about 40 artists and 19 studios. The event offers a chance to see interesting sculptures, paintings, glasswork, and pottery, some by nationally known artists. The event is usually held two weekends in November. Maps to the studios are available from area retailers or the Cave Creek Chamber of Commerce by calling the number listed.

Thunderbird Artists
15648 N. Eagles Nest Dr., Fountain Hills
• (480) 837-5637
• www.thunderbirdartists.com

Those interested in buying paintings or sculptures—especially in the Southwestern genre—should check out the juried fine art and fine crafts festivals organized by Thunderbird Artists. The group, which represents about 150 U.S. artists, often exhibits work in conjunction with themed festivals. The Carefree Fine Art & Wine Festival, held in November, January, and March, turns the streets of Carefree into one big art gallery. The Scottsdale Fine Art & Chocolate Festival, held in February, stimulates the senses with art spectacular sculptures and 20 chocolate booths. The free shows usually run on weekends from 10 AM to 5 PM.

INSIDERS' TIP

If you want a toe-tapping good time, check out the swinging sounds of Big Band music at joints like The Bash on Ash in Tempe or the Rockin' Horse in Scottsdale. Arizona bands to catch include the 18-piece orchestra of the Arizona Big Band, Midnight Blues, Heavenly 7, The Swing Tips, Studio 42, the Handgrenades, and the Kings of Pleasure. Tucson-based Slimstyle Records is the largest contemporary swing label in the country.

Arts Organizations

Arizona Commission on the Arts
417 W. Roosevelt St., Phoenix
• (602) 255-5882

Among the many good works of this

THE ARTS

Arizona artist Ed Mell is known for his stylized paintings and sculptures. His 1993 bronze,
Jack Knife, *graces downtown Scottsdale.*

Photo: Courtesy of the Scottsdale Center for the Arts

state-funded commission is its roster of state artists—in the visual and performing arts—who travel to schools and community centers. In addition, its grants help keep many small, multicultural art groups running. A monthly bulletin helps keep artists abreast of workshops and job opportunities.

COMPAS (Combined Metropolitan Phoenix Arts & Sciences)
3110 N. Central Ave., Phoenix
• (602) 287-9300

Founded in the early 1960s, COMPAS funds more than 40 art organizations and venues, fulfilling its slogan, "Giving a Hand to Our Cultural Community." Recipients have included the Phoenix Art Museum, the Heard Museum, the Phoenix Zoo, and the Desert Botanical Garden. Recently, COMPAS has expanded its grant-giving to include several other arts- and science-related nonprofit organizations, both large and small, particularly new ones. It holds two fundraising events annually.

Arizona Artists Guild
8912 N. 4th St., Phoenix
• (602) 944-9713

Founded in 1928, the Arizona Artists Guild provides a nurturing environment for artists. It meets the third Tuesday of each month, September through April, at 7:30 PM at the guild building. Meetings include talks and demonstrations by nationally known artists, which nonmembers can attend. Members with an interest in a specific medium, such as sculpting, get together regularly. Other activities include juried exhibitions, critique groups, and a fundraiser.

Phoenix Arts Commission
200 W. Washington St., 10th Fl., Phoenix
• (602) 262-4637

Since its creation in 1985 by Phoenix City Council, the Arts Commission's mandate has been to enhance the arts in Phoenix and raise the public's awareness and involvement in preserving, expanding, and enjoying the arts. The commission also directs a public art program—outdoor sculptures, murals, and other works—and fosters arts education in the schools. Many of the city's cultural activities are funded by matching grants from the commission. About two dozen citizens serve on the commission; city staff administers programs and services.

Scottsdale Artists' School
3720 N. Marshall Way, Scottsdale
• (480) 990-1422, (800) 333-5707
• www.scottsdaleartschool.org

For 15 years, the nonprofit Scottsdale Artists' School has been a small oasis of art instruction, attracting adults of all skill levels from all over the country and abroad. One reason the school is so popular is its roster of working artists who serve on the faculty. Students have a chance to learn portraiture, still-life painting, figure sculpture, and dozens of other techniques from artists well-regarded in their fields. Annual enrollment is more than 2,200, and early registration is recommended. Call the school to receive its annual schedule of classes.

Scottsdale Cultural Council
7380 E. 2nd St., Scottsdale
• (480) 994-2787
• www.scottsdalearts.org

The Scottsdale Cultural Council is a nonprofit arts management organization contracted by the City of Scottsdale to oversee its cultural affairs, including management of the Scottsdale Center for the Arts, SMoCA (Scottsdale Museum of Contemporary Art), the Scottsdale Public Art program, and the Scottsdale Arts Festival. The council has been recognized for its contributions to the community with accolades and awards, including an Arizona Humanities Council Distinguished Organization Award.

INSIDERS' TIP

The Valley's earliest art—petroglyphs—are being preserved. The City of Phoenix built a large retaining wall to preserve more than 160 petroglyphs at 19th Avenue and Greenway Road. In Tempe, find petroglyphs along the hike up "A" Mountain near Arizona State University. For more information on petroglyphs, visit the Deer Valley Rock Art Center in north Phoenix, or call (623) 582-8007.

West Valley Fine Arts Council
387 E. Wigwam Blvd., Litchfield Park
• (623) 935-6384
• www.wvfa.org

The arts scene in the far West Valley is small but poised to grow as new residents trickle in. Keeping on top of the situation is the West Valley Fine Arts Council, which was founded in 1989. It operated as the Cultural Arts

THE ARTS

Art festivals are popular in Arizona's mild climate. The Scottsdale Arts Festival is one of the biggest and best.

Photo: Courtesy of the Scottsdale Center for the Arts

Society West for 20 years before that. The council, which receives funding from COMPAS, the Arizona Commission on the Arts, and elsewhere, is entrusted with developing, enhancing, and promoting quality arts and arts education in an area that encompasses Litchfield Park, Avondale, Goodyear, Buckeye, and parts of west Phoenix, Glendale, and Peoria. The council's annual Native American Festival, a showcase of authentic crafts, music, and hands-on activities for families, generally kicks off with a performance by award-winning Native American flutist R. Carlos Nakai. Other events include a mariachi festival; the Phoenix Symphony pops concert; an annual jazz festival; and an annual youth arts festival.

Our Natural World

Weather forecasters don't have to work too hard in Phoenix. For more than 300 days of the average year, the forecast is sunshine. Visitors and newcomers soon find out, though, that the natural world of Phoenix offers much more than sun.

The desert's plants, birds, animals, and insects make a powerful impression on first-time Westerners. Black widows or scorpions may lurk in a dark recess of an unoccupied park bench. On the fringes of the city, drivers brake for brazen coyotes. Jackrabbits bound out of hiding in suburban neighborhoods. Tall saguaro cacti stand like sentinels in the popular desert landscapes around many homes. Those who opt for grass lawns will pull up a bounty of desert weeds. (People who try to tell you the desert is barren just aren't paying attention to the world around them.)

Sometimes it seems as though the developers who keep chewing up the desert at the rate of an acre an hour, as one local newspaper likes to say, don't see anything but a vast, flat, barren plain in the Valley of the Sun. Yet the selling point, especially for the fringe-area, upscale developments, is the pristine beauty of the unforgiving desert, the natural world that wins over the heart of a true desert dweller.

A Rocky Desert

Phoenix and the Valley of the Sun sit at the northern extreme of the Sonoran Desert, an ancient seabed that's now almost devoid of moisture. Mentioning a desert may call to mind movie panoramas of wind-blown sand dunes, but that's the wrong picture. Before humanity's intrusion, the Sonoran Desert was an endless tract of eroded, brown mountains punctuated by valleys of patchy desert grass, palo verde trees, saguaro cactus, and creosote bushes. The sand is brown, reddish-brown, or a gravelly gray. It doesn't accumulate in dunes or even seem like sand really, but rather a surface grit.

At a distance, the desert's precipitous mountains look like piles of precariously balanced rocks ready to come tumbling down if a crucial stone is pulled out. This is an illusion created by erosion. The topsoil has been stripped away by the eons, and today we view the bedrock, the skeleton of these mountains. The smoothness of their surfaces recalls their origins at the bottom of an ancient sea.

Other mountains, still brown, slope more gently toward the sky. More hospitable than the rock-faced giants, these mountains' sides are dotted with cacti, and the surfaces seem coarse and pebbly. Some of the mountains are relics of ancient volcanic activity, but today those forces of nature sleep soundly. Although Arizona is the next-door neighbor of seismically active California, it's relatively inactive as far as earthquakes are concerned.

The Lay of the Land

The Valley of the Sun, where Phoenix and its neighboring cities dwell, sits about 1,000 feet above sea level. Essentially, this is the Salt River Valley. The metropolitan area is bisected and bounded by rivers. The Salt River, or Rio Salado, cuts across the Valley, and easy access to its water for irrigation was Phoenix's initial reason for being. To the east of the Valley, the Salt meets the Verde River as both wend their ways down from mountain ranges. To the west, the Salt flows into the Gila River, which continues westward to the Colorado River on Arizona's border with California. Like a western boundary line for the Valley of the Sun, the Agua Fria River flows from the north into the Gila.

The nearly imperceptible slope of the Salt River Valley gives the Phoenix metroplex the appearance of a plain ringed by gigantic, jagged teeth, something like an impossibly huge bear trap.

Phoenix looks northwest to the Bradshaw Mountains; its topography to the north and east gradually rises to the steep ascent known as the Mogollon Rim (pronounced "muggy-OWN"). To the south, South Mountain creates a wall within the city only recently girdled by new housing developments spreading ever southward. The Sierra Estrella and the White Tank mountains rise to the southwest and west, respectively. The Superstitions float like heat-borne apparitions to the southeast, while the McDowell Mountains to the northeast could never be mistaken for a mirage.

Humanity has made South Mountain, which sits south of the Salt River, among the Valley's most identifiable summits. Broadcast towers blinking their red warnings to aircraft are clustered atop the mountain. On a clear night, they can be seen from the ground upwards of 50 miles away, like a homing beacon for returning travelers.

Other easily identified prominences include Camelback Mountain and Squaw Peak. As its name implies, Camelback huddles like a sleeping camel of the desert amid the northern Valley's suburban sprawl. Progressively more expensive estates climb not quite halfway up its side, ignored like fleas by the dozing giant. To the west, Squaw Peak provides a vexing sensitivity problem from a politically incorrect time. The name has been decried by many—but not all—Native American groups as derogatory. Its name may change, and the change

The desert and mountains surround Phoenix with rugged beauty.

Photo: Penny Kleingartner

Hummingbirds in the Valley:
A Blur of Feathers

Why not invite some of the prettiest desert dwellers into your own yard? Putting up a hummingbird feeder is an excellent way to make new friends with one or two of these tiny birds.

Once you decide to start looking for hummingbirds, you'll begin to see them just about everywhere. They live throughout the Valley and seem to follow regular routes each day, moving between flower to flower, feeder to feeder, on fairly regular schedules. Be sure to look at any red flowers (they love bright reds and pinks) but they'll visit flowers of all colors. Also look at the tops of pine trees and even along telephone lines. Hummingbirds spend part of their day sitting down (if you had to flap your wings that fast, you'd sit down, too.)

Two species are commonly seen in the Valley. The Anna's hummingbird (look for a flashy red head and throat) and the Black-chinned hummingbird (distinguished by a deep violet crown and extended bib) are regulars here. You'll see them darting between flowers only to pause and look around momentarily and then rocketing out of sight. They are fiercely possessive of feeders and will defend them from other hummingbirds in dramatic shows of aerobatics worthy of the movie *Top Gun*.

Most of the hummingbird's day is spent flying between flowers and feeders to eat, with pauses for sitting, napping, flirting, preening, and defending territory. They have a heart rate of 1,260 beats a minute. And to feed that metabolism, they require some 155,000 calories per day (compared to 3,500 for a 170-pound man). Scientists estimate that to match the energy requirements of a hummingbird, a human would have to consume 285 pounds of hamburgers a day.

The source for most of these calories is the sugar-packed nectar of flowers, with the occasional insect thrown in for variety and protein. To the dismay of spiders, hummingbirds are notorious for raiding the bugs from spider webs. The birds don't suck nectar from flowers. Instead they lap it up with long trough-shaped tongues at 13 licks per seconds.

With such a high metabolism, the birds do something odd each evening in order to survive the long night. Many hummingbirds slow their breathing and heart rates until they enter a state of hibernation until the morning. They sleep this way until warmed by the sunlight of dawn when their vital signs return to normal.

Hang your feeder somewhere where you can see it throughout the day (so you can enjoy their visits). Don't use the premixed feeder solutions sold in stores (the red dye in the solution is not needed and may harm the birds). Instead, make your own by boiling one part sugar to four parts water. Let it cool and fill up your feeder. Be sure to change the sugar water every two weeks or so, removing any black mold that may develop. A clean feeder is essential for the bird's health. Once a bird has adopted your feeder as its own, it will expect you to keep it filled. People tell stories about empty feeders and impatient birds darting up to house windows and hovering there, expectantly, reminding you that they are hungry.

Once you've hung the feeder, be patient. Keep an eye on it over the next several weeks and eventually a hummingbird will find it and adopt it as a regular watering spot. Hummingbirds have fixed routines, visiting certain flowers, flying to various yards, and it will take some time before the birds will find yours. After a few visits, they will add your sugar water to their daily routine and become regulars. The birds will soon become used to seeing you, too. You can get very close to them if you can hold still when they visit, as sudden movements will startle the birds. Eventually you and the hummingbirds can enjoy breakfast on the patio together. When that happens, you know that you've been accepted as a true desert dweller.

Once you've seen your first hummingbird, you might turn your attention to looking at some of the other birds that frequent the area. Here are some of the best places to see the local species.

Desert Botanical Gardens
1201 N. Galvin Parkway in Papago Park
• (602) 481-8134

Many desert birds, including hummingbirds, make their homes in the natural setting of this lovely garden. The Garden frequently sponsors a docent-led bird walk (call for times), but you don't have to take tour to see hummingbirds here, you just need a bit of patience.

The Phoenix Zoo
455 N. Galvin Parkway in Papago Park
• (602) 273-1341

Although the Phoenix Zoo does not officially have hummingbirds on display, they frequently can be seen buzzing around the grounds. During the warmer summer months, the Zoo opens at 7 AM and offers misted paths to cool visitors, Animal Encounters education shows, and even puppet shows that will delight kids and adults alike. The birds and animals are much more active in the morning hours and are easier to view. Come later in the day and they tend to be napping, often hidden from sight.

Maricopa Audubon Society Bird Hotline
• (480) 832-8745

Local birders maintain a telephone message that details the rare and unusual birds passing through the area. Calling it is like opening Christmas packages: you never know what surprises are coming your way.

Boyce Thompson Arboretum
US Hwy. 60, just three miles west of Superior
• (520) 689-2811

Only an hour from Phoenix, this remarkable series of gardens offers a wide range of habitat that attract birds of all kinds (including hummingbirds). Since the location is higher than the Valley, it is noticeably cooler during the summer and a terrific place to have a picnic, watch birds, and admire spectacular flowers.

could come quickly, or the issue could drag on for another century. Whatever the case, its conical shape makes it an easily recognizable spot on the Phoenix landscape.

From a distance, the Papago Buttes, which today overlook the Phoenix Zoo and the Desert Botanical Garden, look like smooth bumps separating Phoenix from Scottsdale and Tempe. Their reddish-brown surfaces make them look like close cousins to Camelback well to the north. Come closer and you'll see that those seemingly smooth surfaces are pockmarked by shallow openings.

Weather and Climate

You won't melt in Phoenix despite the heat of the desert. You can't literally fry eggs on the blacktop here, even though TV weather people try it for the camera every now and again at summer's high point. If you come here in summer, you will soon learn why people are fond of saying, "It's a dry heat."

OUR NATURAL WORLD

Desert cactus varieties make for an interesting visit to the Phoenician Resort garden.

Photo: Penny Kleingartner

Low humidity lets the summer mercury rise high. The hottest days peak at more than 120 degrees Fahrenheit. And summer ignores the calendar here, with 100-degree days sometimes stretching from May to October. On the upside, the lack of humidity means the shade of a leafy tree offers considerable relief. Swimmers emerging from a pool on a hot summer day may suddenly feel chilled because the water evaporates so quickly off their skin, supercooling them. This factor makes it possible to use a relatively inexpensive form of air conditioner, known technically as an evaporative cooler and popularly as a "swamp cooler," to cool homes for most of the summer. In these systems, a fan takes in hot outside air and then blows cool air created by the rapid evaporation of water soaked up by special pads. These coolers become ineffective when the dew point hits 55 degrees or higher. (The dew point is the temperature at which water vapor in the air will condense on an object. The lower the dew point, the less moisture there is in the air.) For Arizona, a dew point of 55 means the air is holding a high percentage of moisture. In the Valley, the dew point hits that level during the late-summer rainy season. As long as the air is dry, many say that 105 degrees in Phoenix is more comfortable than 95 degrees in a humid climate.

A desert left to itself undergoes vast temperature fluctuations each day. The scorching midday heat gives way to a chill in the dead of night. The desert doesn't have an insulating coat of humid air (dry heat makes way for dry cold) or a thick blanket of vegetation to hold the day's heat close during the night.

Such is not the case for the Valley of the Sun, except on its very fringes. A "heat sink" effect is a direct result of the Valley's staggering growth. In 1940, Phoenix was a cow town of 65,000 and Scottsdale was a hamlet of 1,000. Today, the Valley houses almost two million people. The sun beats down on pavement, sidewalks, buildings, and homes all day. These structures store the heat, and at night they radiate it back into the air. Average summer low temperatures have been climbing for decades, and it is not unusual to experience 100-degree temperatures well after dark. This is a major change from the days when agriculture was the dominant industry here.

Agriculture in the desert? Believe it or not, with irrigation provided by the federal Salt River Project, certain crops grow extremely well in this climate. Desert soil that had never seen the plow proved rich in nutrients. In 1915, soon after the completion of the Roosevelt Dam, which created Roosevelt Lake, Phoenix's primary water source, there were 250,000 acres of alfalfa, cotton, citrus, grain, and other crops under cultivation. The large number of irrigated fields provided significant cooling at night, although not the same degree of cooling that uncultivated desert affords because humidity moderates temperature extremes, and the irrigated fields were humid.

During the winter, temperatures still creep down to below freezing in the Valley's colder locations, and people have to protect frost-sensitive citrus and other plants and flowers. These low temperatures usually occur only in the dead of night and any accumulated frost or ice melts away by mid-morning. On very rare occasions, some snow may fall, but unless it falls in the area's higher elevations, it most often disappears as it hits the ground or even sooner. Valley dwellers can look out from their homes and see snow atop Four Peaks, the Superstitions, or the Bradshaws. They can smell the snow in the air, feel a little chill, and still work or play outside in shirtsleeves. The winter also is the most likely time to see fog in Phoenix, as cool air close to the ground holds the winter moisture.

Like the heat sink, the problems associated with the winter temperature inversion are directly related to the Valley's growth. During the winter, a warm air mass traps the cold air close to the surface like an invisible bowl held over the Valley, creating what the television weather reporter will call an "inversion layer." The surface air stagnates, and pollutants accumulate to unhealthy levels, waiting for a weather front to push them out. In an effort to fight this situation, Maricopa County declares no-burn days when wood-burning stoves and fireplaces, long popular accoutrements for Valley homes, may not be used. Also, the use of oxygenated fuels is mandated for Valley vehicles in the winter months. Ordinances banning the installation of wood-burning fireplaces in new construction have also been passed by Valley municipalities.

The Monsoon

During the late summer, humidity builds up into a rainy season, known locally as "the monsoon." The presence of the monsoon is not determined by the presence of storms but by the measure of moisture. When the average dew point hits 55 degrees for three days in a row, the monsoon season is considered to be up and running.

The flowering of the desert cactus is always dramatic and colorful.

Photo: David Moore Dupe, courtesy of Scottsdale Convention and Visitors Bureau

OUR NATURAL WORLD

Like its namesake in southern Asia, the Arizona monsoon depends on a shift in the prevailing winds. During the rest of the year, these winds come from the east, but as the monsoon builds, sometime in late June or early July, the prevailing winds begin to come out of the west. Moisture flows up through Mexico from the Pacific Ocean and the Gulf of California, stirring up torrential rains, impenetrable dust, and dazzling lightning.

To desert dwellers, the process can be excruciatingly gradual. One day, a single cloud is visible in the distant sky. The next day, perhaps, it's a few. Then, a few more and so on, until huge billows of storm-bearing cumulonimbus circle the Valley like huge, white anvils in the sky.

The surrounding mountains and the Valley's super hot air seem to form a barrier that has to be hammered away by the increasing strength of the monsoon system. Each day, the thunderheads creep closer but then dissipate in rain over the mountains. The Valley almost resists the incursion of these summer storms, even as Valley dwellers wish the tease would end and the rains begin. After all, the humidity is building, and desert living is at its most uncomfortable. Everyone anticipates the welcome release of the rain, knowing it will refresh the landscape and all that lives within. Finally, heaven's gates open.

INSIDERS' TIP

Don't panic at the bites of venomous bugs or snakes. Stay calm and call the Poison Center-Samaritan Regional Emergency Hotline, (602) 253-3334.

These storms cause flash flooding through the normally dry channels of washes and arroyos. In a matter of minutes, gentle trickles become hell-bent torrents that can sweep away the unwary. This is the natural course of storms in the desert where the vegetation is sparse and the underlying hardpan resists rapid percolation of the water. The hard ground refuses to absorb the water so it runs off, accumulating in the washes. The gathered waters flow rapidly to a low point—in this case the Salt River. The Valley's building boom aggravated those natural tendencies, and new developments are required to have flood-retention basins to stave off flash flooding in neighborhoods.

Although the Valley is occasionally surprised by morning blows, the monsoon storms generally occur in the late afternoons and early evenings after the atmosphere has had the whole day to saturate itself with moisture. The National Weather Service's storm warnings usually expire no later than midnight. In the wee hours of the morning, the cycle begins again as the moisture deposited earlier starts to evaporate and form clouds.

Often, the thunderstorms are preceded by pillars of blowing dust whipped up from the desert surface to thousands of feet in the air. An approaching dust storm looks like a tidal wave of airborne dirt and can make the daytime dark. In the worst case, visibility goes down to zero. In some rare instances, the dirt stays in the air even after the rain hits, and the water showers the surface with tiny blobs of mud.

There's no official measure of when the monsoon ends. The humidity suddenly stops anywhere from late August to mid-September, and weather observers recognize immediately that it's over for another year.

Compared with the monsoon storms, most other rains in the Valley are gentle. The unabashedly corny storytellers are fond of joking, "We had a 6-inch rain last night. The raindrops were 6 inches apart."

Some years, the monsoon season is much drier than others. Even less dependable is the winter rainy season, which can fluctuate wildly in intensity. Generally, the winter rains are soft. Yet the worst flooding in the 1980s and 1990s resulted from winter storms fanned by the Pacific Ocean weather condition known as El Niño. Despite all that stormy weather, the average annual rainfall is listed as a mere 7.66 inches.

The Desert as Garden

The winter rains make the spiny defensiveness of desert vegetation explode into colorful profusion in a too-short spring. The palo verde tree's bright-green bark and leafless, bony branches explode into bright yellow blooms. As the ironwood tree blossoms purple, the yucca wears white, the ocotillo sports red, and the saguaro crowns itself with waxy-white flowers high above the desert floor.

Varieties of cacti abound precisely because they are so well-adapted to the undependable rainfall of the desert. Cacti fall under the classification "succulents" because they store up water in preparation for bone-dry years. The girth of a century-old saguaro may be punctuated by a number of thin waists representing the various dry periods. The saguaro's circumference may increase by 20 percent during the monsoon season. The saguaro is among the largest of cacti, and mature saguaros can grow to be 50 feet tall and weigh up to 20 tons—98 percent of which is water. Aside from the Grand Canyon, the image of the saguaro with a pair of arms upraised as if startled or facing an armed burglar is the most familiar in Arizona—and the trademark of the Sonoran Desert. Its stunning white bloom is Arizona's state flower. The giant dwells only in the desert lowlands, below 3,600 feet. Sixty miles north of Phoenix, the saguaro disappear as the ground level rises. The saguaro is a suffering species, withered by the Valley of the Sun's air and noise pollution.

Another familiar sight is the barrel cactus, particularly since it's quite popular as a landscaping plant. The barrel cactus grows to about 5 feet tall. Its spines are not thin and fine like hair, yet they resemble hair in the way they cover the barrel's stubby body. This is the cactus a lost desert traveler could dig into for water.

Most people already know the prickly pear cactus. Although it is native to the Western Hemisphere's deserts, it can grow in less arid and colder climes. The prickly pear comes in 300 varieties that have been cultivated around the world. Unlike most cacti, it is not tubular. Its flat pads look like thorny, oval-shaped oven mitts. Fruit and flowers bud atop the edges of the pads.

The cholla (CHOY-uh), especially the breed known as the teddy-bear cholla (or jumping cactus), has numerous barbed spines, which make the plant look like an unkempt, hairy hermit. The spines dig into flesh and, because of their barbs, are hard to get out.

The Superstition Mountains, home of the fabled Lost Dutchman Mine, form the eastern edge of the Valley of the Sun.

Photo: Courtesy of Mesa Convention and Visitors Bureau

The jumping cactus likes to trick the unsuspecting: People tend to misjudge the spines, walk too close, and brush against them. The teddy-bear joints detach easily upon contact. First-timers will say the cactus jumped out to get them, hence the name. (Of course, it also makes you jump.) Botanists maintain that the cholla cannot jump; the rest of us are not so sure and remain wary.

Another desert plant that's popular in landscaping is the ocotillo (ah-ca-TEA-oh), which is not a succulent. Its strategy of defense against long dry periods is to remain dormant most of the time, its thorny arms like octopus tendrils praying for water. After a rain, its brown arms sprout thousands of tiny green leaves and then shed them to prevent water loss by transpiration.

The agave (uh-GAH-vay), or century plant, lives up to 75 years to bloom just once. Imagine artichoke leaves several feet long but opened up rather than clenched. At the end of its life, the agave sends up a stalk that might grow to be 30 feet high. The stalk holds the precious blooms, and once that work is done, the agave dies. Yuccas, which bear a close resemblance, also show up in desert landscaping.

The palo verde tree, a Spanish name that translates as "green pole," generally grows in desert

OUR NATURAL WORLD

washes. The state tree of Arizona, it bears leaves for a short time, but sheds them as the ocotillo does, to conserve water. Photosynthesis continues though. The tree's bark is green because of the presence of chlorophyll, the catalyst of photosynthesis, and the surface of the branches sustains the tree the way leaves do in other trees.

Mesquite (mess-KEET) trees are not native to the Sonoran Desert. They were imported from Texas, but they love it here. They can grow up to 30 feet tall, and their root systems will spread out as much as twice that distance to trap as much water as possible during a rain. Grazing cattle, eating the tree's beans and depositing them elsewhere in their droppings, helped the trees multiply rapidly in Arizona's rangeland.

The creosote bush dominates the Sonoran Desert, and its survival strategy seems to be birth control. The plants are widely spaced so that they don't vie with each other for water. Scientists believe this happens partly because the mature plants produce substances that inhibit seedlings.

Critters Great and Small

Without air conditioning and irrigation, only hardy creatures can survive the Sonoran Desert's extremes of climate. Before humanity got here, inhabitants developed their own means to cope with the desert's undependable rainfall and extreme heat. In a land where food is scarce for all creatures, they developed vicious defenses against becoming food themselves, whether the spiny barbs of the jumping cactus or the poisonous sting of the scorpion. The desert's bag of surprises for the unwary includes 16 species of rattlesnake and more than 20 species of scorpions, not to mention four species of skunk and the gila monster, the only species of poisonous lizard in the United States. Two poisonous spiders—the Arizona brown spider (cousin to the brown recluse) and the black widow—also make their home in the desert's dark spots, where flies serve as plentiful food.

As much as the mention of these creatures might raise goosebumps, there is tremendous beauty in them. The black shell of the black widow is almost luminescent, and the red hourglass shape on its belly offers aesthetic contrast. The black-and-orange skin of the gila monster looks like an exquisitely beaded belt.

INSIDERS' TIP

Saguaros and many other desert plants and trees on public lands are protected by law. Attempting to take them to landscape your yard or to give as gifts is illegal.

The relentless sun can heat the desert floor to 150 degrees, so many desert creatures are nocturnal. Foremost among these is the coyote. In Native American lore, the coyote is a wily trickster, but in the dead of night, a coyote's howls sound plaintive rather than self-assured. Perhaps the notion of being a trickster comes from the coyote's speed, which can fool those unfamiliar with it. Another factor in the coyote's trickster image is that coyotes hunt in packs in clever fashion. One will chase the prey while others rest, and then one of the rested will take up the pursuit if necessary. The prey never gets to rest, of course, and eventually tires. Coyotes also are opportunistic so they don't often work hard to find food. They eat carrion, diseased animals, and even plants. Coyotes are generally gray and weigh in at between 15 and 45 pounds. The Valley's relentless growth has driven back the coyote to the fringes for the most part. Outlying homeowners and campers know not to let domestic cats or small dogs out where they will become easy prey for the coyote.

After all those Warner Bros. cartoons, it's only natural to mention the roadrunner here. The birds are rarely seen in the Valley since they've mostly been driven out by settlement, but it doesn't take too much travel to see them.

Like the coyote, predators such as the mountain lion, the bobcat, and the badger don't hang around the Valley much, although it's within their range. Neither do elk and mule deer. Most of the remaining wildlife in the Valley is pretty good at hiding itself. Fleet-footed jackrabbits and cottontails may jump out of suburban hiding places. Rodents and squirrels do a good job of hiding out too. People don't see owls much, but they're up there, waiting to come out at night and catch some of those rodents. Any number of small lizards will dwell in your backyard, and toads will occasionally show up. Life near a small stream will turn up frogs as well.

The Valley's diversity of birds is great, but you're most likely to see pigeons, sparrows, finches, woodpeckers, doves, ducks, and geese. Every yard seems to have a mockingbird. Set out a hummingbird feeder, and the spoon-size birds will show up hungry. (It takes a lot of fuel to power those wings). The state bird is the cactus wren. It is the largest North American wren, but it prefers the open desert to the confines of civilization—although they frequently turn up in the Valley. It loves to nest in cholla, where its home is protected from predators by the cholla's spines. The gila woodpecker and the flicker, on the other hand, cut holes into a saguaro cactus and nest inside. Some hawks make their nests in the crook of the saguaro's arm, although they're not likely to do it in your backyard.

Bats also lurk here. Although feared by many, bats are prized by some for their ability to keep the insect population down. Some people even build bat houses—something like bird houses except they have space inside for the bats to hang upside down—to attract them.

INSIDERS' TIP

Don't drive off-road in the desert. It's unsafe, illegal, and can upset the desert's delicate balance of life.

Poisonous snakes such as the diamondback rattlesnake, which can grow to more than six feet long, prefer to stay away from humanity. However, Valley residents have occasionally found rattlesnakes on their doorsteps in the spring. Usually, such snakes are halfway dazed as they come out of hibernation and have wandered someplace they don't really want to be in search of a place to sun themselves. If you see one, don't assume it will give you a warning before it strikes. They are very quick and don't necessarily rattle their tails before striking. Call an animal-control officer. They're prepared for this.

Although pest extermination is a big business, the Valley still harbors the poisonous black widow and Arizona brown spider. The spiders don't need much maintenance in order to thrive. Just give them a dark place buzzing with flies. The black widow female is usually about a half-inch long, a glossy black with a red hourglass on her underside. The male is seldom seen and carries red marks along the sides of its abdomen. (Maybe he's seldom seen because the female has a habit of eating him after mating.) Widows will eat other spiders along with other insects and centipedes. They are easily provoked when guarding an egg sac but otherwise don't agitate too easily. Not strictly a desert dweller, the black widow is found in the warm regions of all 48 contiguous states, but its presence in the hard-bitten desert seems almost symbolic of the desert's cruel beauty. The spider's venom causes muscle spasms, and on rare occasions can be fatal.

The Arizona brown spider is about four-tenths of an inch long, with a yellow-orange hue and a violin shape on its back. Like a true desert dweller it is nocturnal, and it paralyzes small insects with its poison to trap them before feeding. Its bite is rarely fatal, but this is a creature you don't want in your house. They have been known to bite sleepers, leaving ugly round scars where the venom kills the skin.

INSIDERS' TIP

Slather on the sunscreen. The intense desert sun burns quickly, even in the winter.

If you want to get a human Valley dweller upset, talk about a scorpion bite. Scorpions don't bite. They sting. They have pincers that make them look something like tiny lobsters, but the sting is in the tail. Scorpions are found under rocks in the desert, so be careful if you're turning over a stone. Generally, the smaller the scorpion, the more dangerous its sting. The Centruroides sculpturatus is the deadliest in Arizona and can kill humans, although this rarely happens anymore. This tiny scorpion is distinguished by a thin tail and straw-colored body about two inches long.

A relative newcomer to the pantheon of Valley pests are the Africanized honeybees, commonly known as "killer bees." These bees arrived in Arizona from Mexico in the late 1980s and by the early 1990s had extended their range to include the Valley. They are uncommonly aggressive in defense of their hives and will swarm over a perceived intruder and sting relentlessly. Depending on the susceptibility of the victim, even the gentler European honeybee can kill, so the killer bees' threat is greatly exaggerated. Still, caution is advised. The basic preventive measure is to watch for bee activity and call a beekeeper if it appears that there's a hive forming on some part of your property.

Scary, but not dangerous, is a critter commonly known as a "sewer roach." These are big, brown beetles that can be about two to four inches long and look an awful lot like the common cockroach subjected to some evil nuclear experiment. They don't glow in the dark, but they crunch if you squish them.

OUR NATURAL WORLD

Parks and Recreation

With more than 300 days of sunshine, the Valley of the Sun provides perfect weather for playing outdoors. When the sun is just too hot or when the occasional rain falls, indoor recreational opportunities abound as well. A number of Phoenix municipal parks are in mountain surroundings, including South Mountain Park, the largest municipal park in the world. The mountain parks provide desert views for picnics, as well as such activities as hiking, mountain biking, and horseback riding. Even rock climbing is available within the city on the sheer walls of Camelback Mountain.

Of course, there are times when you'd rather cool off than sweat your way up a mountainside. As you might imagine, municipal pools are popular in the Valley's hot climate. Such commercial water parks as Big Surf, which has a wave pool to simulate the pounding of the sea, are another wet alternative. Nearby wilderness and lakes afford Valley residents and visitors easy access to boating and fishing as well, not exactly activities you'd expect to find in the desert, but certainly ones that provide hours of entertainment and some relief from the summer heat.

We have participatory sports leagues and tennis courts—and so many great golf courses we decided to dedicate a whole chapter to the subject (see our Golf chapter). In addition to sports and various forms of exercise, municipal parks and recreation departments and YMCAs offer a variety of relatively sedate leisure activities from dance lessons to quilting, too numerous to list here.

To give you an overview, we've divided this chapter into two sections. The first is Parks, in which we list the major parks in and around the Valley of the Sun and the variety of recreational offerings each offers. The second section is Recreation, which focuses on specific recreational activities, like horseback riding and soaring. For information on camping in the Valley, see our RV Parks and Campgrounds chapter.

Parks

National Forest

Tonto National Forest
Mesa District Ranger Station,
26 N. Macdonald St., Mesa
- **(480) 610-3300**
- **www.fs.fed.us**

Tonto National Forest is adjacent to the Valley, bordering north Scottsdale and Mesa, and Valley points in between. The forest covers nearly 3 million acres of wilderness, and the Forest Service says it is one of the most heavily visited National Forests. It covers rugged territory, rising from the desert into mountains covered with pine trees. (The elevations range from 1,300 to almost 8,000 feet.) There's no admission charge to enter the forest, although there are charges for camping and other activities.

Many Valley dwellers are attracted to the water-based activi-

*There's plenty of smooth sailing at Lake Pleasant Regional Park, where the members of the Arizona
Yacht Club gather each spring and fall for friendly regattas.*

Photo: Lori Pfeiffer

ties in the forest on the Verde and Salt Rivers and at such reservoirs as Saguaro Lake. They are also fond of the cool clime of Payson in summer. (See our write-ups on Saguaro Lake and Payson in the Daytrips chapter and our write-ups under the Boating, Fishing, and Tubing headings in this chapter.) The Forest Service says the white water on the upper stretches of the Salt River is world class.

Tonto National Forest offers 900 miles of hiking and equestrian trails. Those closer to the Valley are better suited to novices. Other trails are deep in remote areas and will prove challenging to the experienced hiker and rider.

It's always a good idea to check up on conditions and fire restrictions out in the wild before starting on a backcountry trip. The Mesa District Ranger Station offers a convenient place to pick up trail maps and other forest recreational information.

State Park

Lost Dutchman State Park
6109 N. Apache Tr., Apache Junction
• (602) 982-4485

Jacob Waltz, known as the "Dutchman,"

traveled through the Superstition Mountains east of the Valley in 1880s searching for gold. The name of the park is a bit of a misnomer because it makes it sound as though the Dutchman was lost. Waltz claimed he had found gold in the Superstitions, and as proof he used gold to buy supplies when he returned to civilization. Waltz always eluded anyone's attempts to follow him to the mine, and when he died, the location of the mine was "lost"—if it wasn't a figment of Waltz's imagination, which seems most likely. Ever since, people have searched for the "Lost Dutchman Mine." For the record, Waltz was German, not Dutch.

The park was established in 1977 after the U.S. Bureau of Land Management sold the Lost Dutchman Recreation Site to the state. The 320-acre park's facilities include a visitors center, picnic areas with tables and grills, a campground with 35 units, a dump station, trails, restrooms, showers, and group-use areas. Saguaros are everywhere in this desert park. At night, the lights of the Valley are visible. A hiking-equestrian trail leads into the rugged Superstition Wilderness area of the Tonto National Forest. Park rangers advise that the grade of the trail makes it tough on horses and recommend the park's lower-level trails, on which hiking, mountain-biking, and horseback riding are all permitted. The entrance fee is $4 per vehicle with up to four people. To get there, take the Superstition Freeway (Interstate 60) east to the Idaho Street (State Route 88) exit. When Ariz. 88 becomes the Apache Trail, follow it about 5 miles northeast to the park entrance.

Maricopa County Parks

The Maricopa County Parks system describes itself as the largest county parks system in the country. As such, it offers ample opportunities for fun—hiking, camping, swimming, and many other activities. Daily hours of operation vary, so call the county for the information at (602) 506-2930.

Adobe Dam Recreation Area
43rd Ave. and Pinnacle Peak Rd., Phoenix
• **(602) 506-2930**

This 1,526-acre county park includes a number of recreational facilities: the Victory Lane Sports Complex for softball, Waterworld water park, Arizona Kart Racing Association and Phoenix Kart Racing Association tracks, the 500 Club golf course, an airport for ultralight aircraft, and the Arizona Model Pilots Society complex. To get there, take Interstate 17 to the Pinnacle Peak Road exit and then head west to 43rd Avenue. There is no daily fee.

Cave Creek Recreation Area
37904 N. Cave Creek Pkwy., Cave Creek
• **(623) 465-0431**

This 2,922-acre county park is within the town of Cave Creek. Its entrance is on 32nd Street, 1.5 miles north of the Carefree Highway (State Route 74). Interesting rock formations and scenic views are the park's hallmarks. There are a number of old mine shafts in the park, and visitors are advised not to enter them because they are hazardous. The park includes 43 individual picnic sites available on a first-come, first-served basis. There are four large ramadas

INSIDERS' TIP
When you encounter wildlife in Arizona's back country, appreciate the encounter, but leave the animals alone. They will return the favor.

for group picnics, and these can be reserved for a fee. A group campground is available by reservation only, and a campground with 38 individual sites. There is also a horse-staging area. The park has six well-maintained trails, totaling 11 miles. All are multiuse, unless otherwise marked. The daily fee is $3 per vehicle. To get

there from downtown Phoenix, take Interstate 17 north to the Carefree Highway exit and head east to 32nd Street. You can also reach the park from north Phoenix by taking Cave Creek Road or from Scottsdale by taking Scottsdale Road. When you reach the Carefree Highway from either road, proceed west to 32nd Street.

Estrella Mountain Regional Park
W. Vineyard Ave., Goodyear
• **(623) 932-3811**

The 19,840-acre Estrella Park features 56 acres of turfed area with picnic tables, grills, restrooms, playground equipment, two lighted ballfields, and a rodeo arena. An amphitheater nestles against a hill overlooking the picnic area. Ten ramadas with electricity can be reserved. Group camping is available with reservations. Water is available in picnic areas. The park has 33 miles of trails for hiking, horseback riding, and biking. A new competitive track with two loops that total 11 miles has been added to the park. This track is intended for high-speed training for mountain bikers, equestrians, and runners. The daily fee is $3 per vehicle. To get there, take the Estrella Parkway exit south from I-10. About 5 miles south of I-10, head east on W. Vineyard Avenue. The park entrance will be on your right.

Lake Pleasant Regional Park
Ariz. Hwy. 74, Peoria
• **(520) 501-0107**

This is a 22,662-acre park surrounding Lake Pleasant, which was formed when the New Waddell Dam was built to store water brought into Maricopa County by the Central Arizona Project canal. The lake is 9,966 surface acres and 225 feet at its deepest point, and the park has two boat ramps—a 10-lane one at the south end of the lake and a 4-lane boat ramp accessible through the north entrance. Two campgrounds are open for tent or RV camping. Reservations are not accepted for the 144 sites, which have electrical and water hook-ups. Nearby restrooms have showers, and all sites have picnic tables and firepits. Shoreline camping is allowed in the summer and fall months. A new Desert Outdoor Center is available for rent by calling (520) 501-1730. There is no electricity or public telephone at the park. The park is open 24 hours a day, and the daily fee is $5 per vehicle plus $6 per car with watercraft. Located

20 miles northwest of Phoenix in Peoria, take State Route 74 to the Castle Hot Springs Road exit. Drive north approximately two miles on a paved road, til you hit the entrance to the main camping areas and the visitors center.

McDowell Mountain Regional Park
McDowell Mountain Rd.,
Maricopa County
• (480) 471-0173

This 21,099-acre park in the McDowell Mountains features 88 picnic tables, comfort stations, a youth-group camp area, and family and group campgrounds. The campgrounds offer 80 sites with a dump station, water, electricity, and shower facilities. Water is available in the picnic areas. There is a 14-night limit on camping, and advance registrations are required for the group and youth-group camp areas. The park features hiking, mountain-biking, and horseback-riding trails. A competitive track opened in 1998, which offers three loops of varying difficulty for competitive training away from recreational users. Mountain bikers, equestrians, and runners are invited to use this track. The daily fee is $3 per vehicle. To get there from downtown Phoenix, take Interstate10 east to Loop 202 (Red Mountain Freeway), continue heading east to Loop 101 (Pima Freeway), and head north to McDowell Road. Take McDowell Road east to the Beeline Highway (State Route 87). Follow the Beeline north to the Shea Boulevard exit that leads into Fountain Hills. Take Shea Boulevard to Fountain Hills Boulevard and turn north. The park entrance will be on your left a few miles outside of Fountain Hills.

Usery Mountain Recreation Area
Usery Pass Rd., Maricopa County
• (602) 984-0032

Usery Mountain Recreation Area is a 3,648-acre park on the edge of the Tonto National Forest and Pinal County. Just 12 miles northeast of Mesa via the Apache Trail, you know you're really in the desert here. The park features a 73-unit family campground, and a group campground that requires reservations. Water, electricity, showers, and a dump station are available. The facilities also include a reservations-only, group-picnic area, comfort stations. and 60 individual picnic sites with grills, tables, ramadas, and water. The facilities include an archery range, a horse-staging area, and a network of 11 trails, seven for hiking or horseback, the other four for hiking only. Closing times at the picnic areas, staging area, and archery range vary. The park is closed to all off-

road travel, and horseback riding is restricted to existing trails. The daily fee is $3 per vehicle. To get there from the Superstition Freeway (Interstate 60), take the Ellsworth Road exit north. Ellsworth Road becomes Usery Pass Road about four miles north of the highway. The southern boundary is a short distance north of McDowell Road; the main entrance will be on the right-hand side, about a mile farther on.

White Tank Mountain Regional Park
W. Olive Ave., Maricopa County
• (623) 935-2505

This park, among the White Tank Mountains just to the west of the Valley, seems almost a secret to Valley dwellers. It's rarely, if ever, crowded, which makes it a good place to enjoy the desert. The 26,692-acre park includes 260 picnic sites with grills, tables, ramadas, and restrooms; a 40-site campground; and a group campground that requires reservations. Three group picnic areas are available. The park also has a mountain bike race course and 29 miles of trails for hiking. Some trails lead to walls that are good for rock climbing. The park has two barrier-free trails, which led to petroglyphs in their natural setting and provide an opportunity for all to discover this unique site. Numerous petroglyph sites dot the park, and educators can provide information or guided hikes. The entry fee is $3 per vehicle. To get there from downtown Phoenix, take Interstate 10 west to Cotton Lane. Head north to Olive Avenue and then head 5 miles west to the park.

Municipal Parks

All the Valley's cities have parks. Some are lush and green, others revel in a rocky desert landscape. Some are not much more than a large lot with playground equipment, while others feature multiple ball fields and artificial lakes. We note some of the popular municipal parks in the following listings. The parks departments of each city can provide a complete list.

Phoenix

The Phoenix Parks, Recreation, and Library Department, (602) 262-6861, administers almost 26,000 acres of desert and mountain parkland within Phoenix's city limits. In addition to the standard picnic areas and recreational facilities, such as basketball courts and playgrounds, these desert parks offer more than 100 miles of trails for hiking, biking, and horseback-riding enthusiasts. Phoenix parks are open from 5:30 AM to midnight daily.

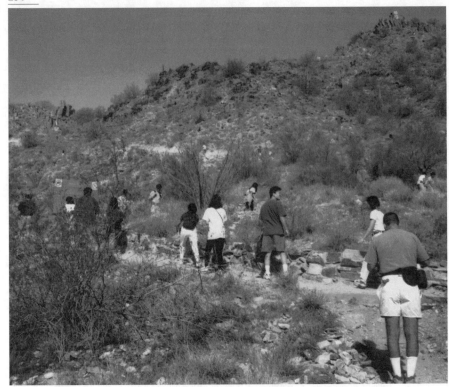

Hiking Squaw Peak offers even beginners a close–up view of desert surroundings.

Photo: Penny Kleingartner

Echo Canyon Recreation Area
E. McDonald Dr. at Tatum Blvd., Phoenix
• (602) 256-3110

When Phoenix was small, Camelback Mountain's south side was its familiar face and the north side was as mysterious as the dark side of the moon. The north side is where the Echo Canyon Recreation Area sits. The rock here, which rises some 200 feet in places, is redder than in most Phoenix mountain parks, except for Papago Park. This area doesn't have the usual park amenities—the only water available is a water fountain at the trailhead— just hiking trails and the opportunity to go rock climbing. The views of the city are wonderful and it lures experienced rock climbers and hikers. The upper portions of Cholla Trail become rugged, and may be unsuitable for small children. The park is open May through September, from 6 AM to 7:30 PM; and October through April, from 7 AM to 5:30 PM. See our Hiking and Biking section in this chapter.

Encanto Park
15th Ave. and Encanto Blvd., Phoenix
• (602) 262-6412

A lush, grassy enclave in the heart of Phoenix, Encanto Park is the easiest way for people caught up in the swirl of downtown business to take a breather. It's also a spot for family picnics and recreation. There's boating and fishing on the small lake, a children's amusement park, a lit basketball area, an exercise course, golf, handball and racquetball courts, a playground, a pool, and softball fields.

North Mountain Recreation Area
10600 N. Seventh St., Phoenix
• (602) 262-6696

Situated on and around North Mountain

> ## INSIDERS' TIP
>
> **Hikers, bikers, equestrians, and off-road motor-vehicle enthusiasts share many trails in Arizona's parks. They're urged to leave as little mark of their passing as possible and to show courtesy to one another.**

and covering a small section of the North Mountain Preserve, the North Mountain Recreation Area looks down over Sunnyslope and the major part of Phoenix to the south. It offers basketball and volleyball courts, a playground, a ramada and picnic area, restrooms, and hiking and riding trails.

Papago Park
Van Buren St. and Galvin Pkwy., Phoenix
• (602) 56-3220

Papago Park marks Phoenix's boundary with Scottsdale and Tempe. The reddish hue of its soil makes it seem more colorful than Phoenix's other desert parks. The air somehow seems crisper here too. Within the park boundaries sit the Phoenix Zoo, the Desert Botanical Garden, a lighted softball complex, a baseball complex, an archery range, fishing, a golf course, horseshoe pits, an orienteering course, ramadas and picnic areas, restrooms, volleyball courts, and hiking and riding trails. The views toward the rest of Phoenix and other parts of the Valley are gorgeous.

South Mountain Park
10919 S. Central Ave., Phoenix
• (602) 495-0222

At 17,000 acres, South Mountain Park is billed as the largest municipal park in the world. More important than that to Valley dwellers

and visitors, it offers an easy way to get an overview of the Valley. You can see virtually everywhere in the Valley from Dobbins Lookout, and a "compass" points you in the direction of such landmarks as Four Peaks, a mountaintop in Tonto National Forest to the northeast, and the Sierra Estrella, a mountain range to the southwest. This is also the best place in the Valley to see saguaro and other desert flora in their natural habitat. A park road hairpins up and down the mountain to serve both autos and daredevil bicyclists. In addition, the park offers an interpretive center to learn about all the desert flora and fauna; an activity complex; ramadas and picnic areas; restrooms; and a network of hiking and riding trails. See the Equestrian and Hiking and Biking sections in this chapter.

Squaw Peak Recreation Area
2701 E. Squaw Peak Ln., Phoenix
• (602) 262-6696

On the south end of Phoenix Mountains Preserve, a vast preserve of desert mountain land that sits just about mid-city as Phoenix's current boundaries are figured, Squaw Peak Recreation Area is one of the area's most popular desert parks. Although it has ramadas and picnic areas situated in a cul-de-sac below Squaw Peak, the main draw here is the hiking trails, particularly the Summit Trail, which

The McDowell Mountain Regional Park offers a prime wilderness experience near Scottsdale.

Photo: Courtesy of Scottsdale Convention and Visitors Bureau attracts joggers, hikers, and casual walkers in droves each morning. Travel even a short way up the mountainside here and the views of Phoenix are good, giving just about everyone the incentive to get to the summit and find out just how far they can see. See our Hiking and Biking section in this chapter.

Southeast Valley

Desert Breeze Park
Ray Rd. and McClintock Dr., Chandler
• **(480) 940-1685**

Desert Breeze Park is home to the Desert Breeze Railroad, described as a one-third size replica. The train, which features both a 1880-style locomotive and a modern diesel locomotive, takes passengers through a tunnel and around the lake in the park's center. The train runs 10 AM to sunset, Wednesday through Sunday, and closes in July and August because of the heat. Amenities include a snack bar and a covered patio. A train ride costs $1.50, although infants and toddlers ride free. The carousel costs $1.25. A ten-ride pass is available for $12. The depot is decorated like a Western village. A snack bar and a carousel ($1 per person) also provide entertainment. (More details on the railroad are available at (602) 940-1685.) The park has playground equipment and picnic areas that are available for rental through the

City of Chandler Community Services Department at the number above. Reservations are taken 12 months in advance. Nonresidents are charged more than Chandler residents for reservations. Fishing is also allowed. See our Fishing section in this chapter for more details.

Kiwanis Community Park
Mill Ave. and All America Way, Tempe
• **(480) 350-200**

The facilities at green Kiwanis Park, the biggest park in south Tempe, are extensive, including lighted softball/baseball fields, batting cages, lighted sand volleyball courts, a lighted basketball court, picnic tables, playground equipment, a lake, a wave pool, and a recreation center that includes 15 lighted tennis courts. For information on recreation center activities call (480) 350-5200. Boats rentals are available for Kiwanis Lake. Tempe residents may reserve picnic ramadas, ball fields and volleyball courts up to 11 months in advance by calling (480) 350-5200. Fishing is also permitted. See the Softball, Fishing, and Tennis writeups in this chapter for more details.

Red Mountain Park
7745 E. Brown Rd., Mesa
• **(480) 644-2351**

At Red Mountain Park, you get away into a marshland against the backdrop of the Super-

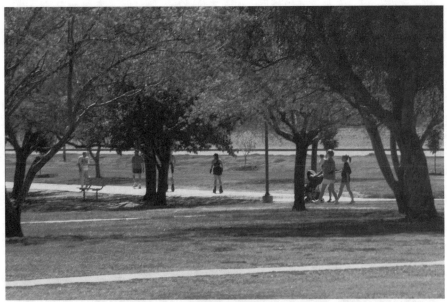

In-line skaters join baby strollers while enjoying the trail through Chaparral Park in Scottsdale on a pleasant March day.

Photo: Debbie Ross

stition Mountains. At the center of the park's artificial lake is a marsh environment where ducks and other birds hide out when they're not out on the water. The park offers picnic ramadas that can be reserved, playground equipment, a cement volleyball court, soccer fields, and basketball courts—all lighted. Reservations require a permit that must be obtained at least one business day in advance, and permits for Friday and Saturday use must be obtained by Thursday. For details, call (480) 644-4271. Across Brown Road and to the east of the main developed portion of the park is the park's lighted softball complex. Fishing is also permitted. See the Softball and Fishing write-ups in this chapter for more details.

Northeast Valley

Fountain Park
El Lago and Saguaro Blvds., Fountain Hills
• (623) 837-2003

A 30-acre park surrounds Fountain Lake, where Fountain Hills' namesake fountain can shoot water up to 560 feet into the air. Normally, the fountain's plume, created by two 600-horsepower turbine pumps, is 330 feet. (A third pump is kept idle as a backup, and it's only on the rare occasions when the third pump is turned on that the 560-foot stream is possible.) The fountain has a utilitarian purpose. It is used to help evaporate effluent (or treated wastewater). Through most of the year it operates for 15 minutes at the top of the hour from 10 AM to 9 PM. The schedule can increase during winter when there's more effluent to evaporate. The fountain's plume can be seen from the Beeline Highway shooting up over mountaintops. The park—a perfect place for picnicking on the grass, jogging, and playing on playground equipment—has been recently renovated, with new walking paths around the fountain's perimeter and new restroom facilities. Fountain Park is also a popular place for weddings and other group events, but reservations are required. For details, call the number above.

Indian Bend Wash
Along Hayden Rd., Scottsdale
• (480) 312-2304

The greenbelt that is Indian Bend Wash can be looked at as one huge park, although it's not. An 11-mile path used by bicyclists, joggers, walkers, and skaters connects a series of golf courses and city parks in one vast stretch of green, roughly through the center of Scottsdale. Four city parks sit among the golf courses: Chaparral Park, at 5401 N. Hayden Road; Indian School Park, at 4289 N. Hayden Road; Eldorado Park, at 2311 N. Miller Road; and Vista Del Camino Park, at 7700 E. Roosevelt Road. The facilities include softball fields, tennis courts, basketball courts, volleyball courts, playgrounds, and picnic areas. For more information on facilities, call the number above. See our Softball and Tennis sections in this chapter for more details on those activities. Both Chaparral and Eldorado Parks have municipal pools; see our Aquatics section for more details. Also see the Hiking and Biking section for details on those activities. Fishing is permitted at Chaparral Park; see our Fishing section.

McCormick-Stillman Railroad Park
Indian Bend and Scottsdale Rds., Scottsdale
• (602) 994-2312

The railroad at McCormick-Stillman Railroad Park is a 5/12-scale railroad modeled after the Rio Grande Western Railway. People board at Stillman Station, a replica of a historic Arizona train depot, and the train takes them on a mile-long ride through the 30-acre park. Also at the park are displays of railroad memorabilia, along with a Pullman car used by several United States presidents, a 1906 Baldwin locomotive, and a 1914 Santa Fe baggage car. The park features a playground and carousel. For most of the year, rides on the train and carousel are offered daily, starting at 10 AM and running until 6:30 PM. On summer weekends, the hours are the same, but on summer weekdays, the train runs only from 4 to 8:30 PM. Tickets cost $1, with children younger than 3 riding free. Next to the carousel is a sandy playground with lots of climbing equipment and slides. A Southern Pacific Caboose houses a snack bar. For most of the year, rides on the train and carousel are offered seven days a week starting at 10:15 AM and running until 8:30 PM. On summer weekends, the hours are the same, but on summer weekdays, the train runs only from 4 to 8:30 PM. Tickets are $1; rides are free to children younger than 3.

Northwest Valley

Bonsall Park
59th Ave. and Mountain View Rd., Glendale
• (623) 930-2820

Known to many Insiders as "Chicken Park," for the ranch that preceded it, Bonsall Park has attracted generations of families for picnics.

Activities include feeding the resident ducks or admiring the Air Force jet perched in simulated flight on concrete stand. The park's recent upgrades have made it even more attractive. Amenities include picnic tables, grills, a pool recreation center, and a new in-line skating rink. Courts for volleyball, tennis, and basketball are available.

Sahuaro Ranch Park
**59th Ave. and Mountain View Rd.,
Glendale**
• **(623) 930-2820**

Walk around Sahuaro Ranch Park for just a minute, and you're bound to run into a peacock or peahen. More than 50 of them roam freely around the grounds. About a century ago, Sahuaro Ranch began to bloom as a citrus orchard out in then-remote desert. Today, it is part of Glendale's mainstream. The park's major draw is the 60-acre recreation area that includes three daytime soccer fields and one lighted one, four lighted softball fields, four lighted sand volleyball courts, picnic areas with grills, nine lighted ramadas, a playground, and restrooms. The remainder of Sahuaro Ranch Park is a historical area that gives visitors a view of the orchard operation. It's buffered from the rest of the park by original citrus groves. A variety of buildings have been preserved or restored, such as the Adobe House and Guest House, which let visitors see the rustic furnishings of pioneer life. In addition, the ranch's Fruit Packing Shed was converted into an art gallery in 1995. The 80-acre park is open April through October from 6 AM to midnight daily, and from November through March from 6 AM to 10 PM daily.

Thunderbird Park
**59th Ave. and Mountain View Rd.,
Glendale**
• **(623) 930-2820**

Thunderbird Park boasts 1,185 acres of conservation park that offer great views of the northwest Valley. Part of Hedgpeth Ills, the natural desert park includes hiking, biking, and equestrian paths; covered picnic areas with grills; wildlife viewing areas; and a pond.

Southwest Valley

Staggs Park
**Litchfield Rd. and Villa Nueva Dr. S.,
Litchfield Park**
• **(623) 935-9040**

The Southwest Valley is still mostly rural and agricultural in character. Tiny (less than 3 square miles) Litchfield Park, the home of the Wigwam Resort, has been a shady, suburban residential oasis amid the vast tracts of farm and ranch land in the area. (New housing developments in neighboring Avondale and Goodyear are quickly changing things.) Staggs Park is, like the town, a sleepy little place. The park is shaped like a cane with the upper part of the cane surrounding the west end of the lake, and the length of the cane running along the north side of the lake. Residential properties line the south end of the lake. Across Litchfield Road sits a field with a baseball backstop and playground equipment. Fishing in the lake requires both a state license and a permit from the city. (No net fishing is allowed.) Boating also requires a permit.

Recreation

Aquatics

Swimming is big in the desert. What better way to stay cool, after all? The offerings include commercial amusement parks, municipal pools, and water-based parks such as Lake Pleasant Regional Park. Also big are aquatic activities such as kayaking and sailing, which can be done at Lake Pleasant.

Municipal Pools

Phoenix
Almost all the Valley's communities have at least one municipal pool, but Phoenix's system is extensive. Phoenix's Parks, Recreation and Library Department's Aquatic Section operates 28 pools citywide. Pools open for weekend swimming in May and are open seven days a week from the first Monday in June through Labor Day.

Admission for each pool is 50 cents for swimmers younger than 18 and older than 55, and $1.50 for everyone in between. All ages can swim for 25 cents each on weekdays after 6 PM (excluding holidays). Season passes are available for the summer as well.

Learn-to-swim programs, water-safety and specialty classes, and recreational team programs are offered throughout the summer at many of the pools. For more information on the city's aquatic programs, call the city's Swim Line at (602) 258-7946, or TDD (602) 262-6713.

Deer Valley, El Prado, Paradise Valley, and Starlight pools are equipped with waterslides. Many of the pools have diving boards. Most of them have separate wading pools for very young children. Paradise Valley pool has a large mushroom in its wading area, which provides a cool shower of water for the children to play in. For persons with disabilities, the city operates Telephone Pioneer pool. Telephone Pioneer is equipped with lifts, dry- and wet-access ramps, and a separate therapy pool. Lessons are available. Pool hours vary; call for hours of operation and directions if you need them.

Alkire Pool, 1617 W. Papago Street, Phoenix, (602) 261-8787

Cactus Pool, 3801 W. Cactus Road, Phoenix, (602) 262-6680

Cielito Pool, 4551 N. 35th Avenue, Phoenix, (602) 262-4752

Coronado Pool, 1717 N. 12th Street, Phoenix, (602) 262-6709

Cortez Pool, 3434 W. Dunlap Avenue, Phoenix, (602) 262-7107

Deer Valley Pool, 19400 N. 19th Avenue, Phoenix, (602) 534-1842

Eastlake Pool, 1548 E. Jefferson Street, Phoenix, (602) 261-8729

El Prado Pool, 6428 S. 19th Avenue, Phoenix, (602) 261-8638

Encanto Pool, 2125 N. 15th Avenue, Phoenix, (602) 261-8732

Falcon Pool, 3420 W. Roosevelt Street, Phoenix, (602) 262-6229

Grant Pool, 714 S. Second Avenue, Phoenix, (602) 261-8728

Harmon Pool, 1239 S. Fifth Avenue, Phoenix, (602) 261-8733

Hermoso Pool, 5749 S. 20th Street, Phoenix, (602) 261-8731

Holiday Pool, 4530 N. 67th Avenue, Phoenix, (602) 261-8031

Madison Pool, 1440 E. Glenrosa Avenue, Phoenix, (602) 262-6494

Marivue Pool, 5625 W. Osborn Road, Phoenix, (602) 261-8929

Maryvale Pool, 4444 N. 51st Avenue, Phoenix, (602) 262-6685

Mountain View Pool, 1104 E. Grovers Avenue, Phoenix, (602) 534-1347

Paradise Valley Pool, 17648 N. 40th Street, Phoenix, (602) 534-5161

Perry Pool, 3131 E. Windsor Avenue, Phoenix, (602) 262-7367

Pierce Pool, 2150 N. 46th Street, Phoenix, (602) 262-6199

INSIDERS' TIP

Newcomers seeking recreational opportunities for their children should check with the local school district. Many districts host after-school and summer recreational programs and can direct parents to such opportunities as Little League and other youth sports programs. Another good source is the local recreation department.

Roadrunner Pool, 3502 E. Cactus Road, Phoenix, (602) 262-6789

Roosevelt Pool, 6246 S. Seventh Street, Phoenix, (602) 262-6832

Starlight Pool, 7810 W. Osborn Road, Phoenix, (602) 495-2412

Sunnyslope Pool, 301 W. Dunlap Road, Phoenix, (602) 262-7165

Telephone Pioneer Pool, 1946 W. Morningside Drive, Phoenix, (602) 495-2404

University Pool, 1102 W. Van Buren Street, Phoenix, (602) 261-8730

Washington Pool, 6655 N. 23rd Avenue, Phoenix, (602) 262-7198

Southeast Valley

Chandler

Chandler has four municipal pools open from the last week of May through mid-August. Fees are 50 cents for kids 17 and younger, and $1.50 for adults. Lessons are available. Hours vary, so call ahead.

Desert Oasis Aquatic Center, 1400 W. Summit Place, Chandler, (480) 732-1061, (480) 732-1062

Arrowhead Meadows Pool, 1475 W. Erie Street, Chandler, (480) 732-1064

Folley Pool, 600 E. Fairview Street, (480) 732-1063

West Chandler Aquatic Center, 250 S. Kyrene Road, (480) 783-8261, (480) 783-8262

Gilbert

Fast-growing Gilbert has two municipal pools open from mid-May through mid-August. Fees are $1 for kids 18 and younger, and $1.75 for adults 19 and older. Swim passes are available through Gilbert Parks and Recreation, (480) 898-5665. Lessons are available. Call for hours.

Mesquite Aquatic Center, 100 W. Mesquite Street, Gilbert, (480) 503-6292

Gilbert Municipal Pool, 1016 N. Burk Street, Gilbert, (480) 926-1030

Mesa

Mesa's 13 municipal pools have been voted the "best in the nation." Pool hours vary at different times of the summer, so it's best to call Mesa Parks and Recreation, (480) 644-2351, for more details. Fees are 75 cents for kids 17 years and younger, and $1.50 for adults. Swim passes are also available at the Parks and Recreation number. Lessons are available. In 2003, look for a $19-million, indoor competitive, instructional, and therapeutic aquatics complex, the Mesa Indoor Aquatics Center, in Mesa Town Square.

Brimhall Junior High Pool, 4949 E. Southern Avenue, (480) 644-5087Carson Junior High Pool, 525 N. Westwood Street, Mesa, (480) 644-2374

Falcon Field Pool, 4800 E. Falcon Field Drive, Mesa, (480) 644-2375

Fremont Junior High Pool 1001 N. Power Road, Mesa, (480) 644-2369

Kino Junior High Pool, 894 N. Horne Street, Mesa, (480) 644-2376

Mesa Junior High Pool, 828 E. Broadway Road, Mesa, (480) 644-2377

Parkway Recreation Center Pool, 1753 E. Eighth Avenue, Mesa, (480) 644-2864

Poston Junior High Pool, 2433 E. Adobe Street, Mesa, (480) 644-2371

Powell Junior High Pool, 855 W. Eighth Avenue, Mesa, (480) 644-2378

Rhodes Junior High Pool, 1860 S. Longmore Road, Mesa, (480) 644-2550

Shepherd Junior High Pool, 1407 N. Alta Mesa Drive, Mesa, (480) 644-3037

Stapley Aquatics Complex, 3250 E. Hermosa Vista Drive, Mesa, (480) 644-4977

Taylor Junior High Pool, 705 S. 32nd Street, Mesa, (480) 644-3036

Tempe

Tempe has three outdoor municipal pools and the Kiwanis Park Wave Pool inside the Kiwanis Park Recreation Center. The pool season runs from the last week of May through mid-August. Hours vary, so it's best to call the pools at the phone numbers listed below. Fees for the outdoor pools are 75 cents for kids 6 to 17 years old, and $1.25 for adults. Lessons are available. Fees for the wave pool are $6 for adults, and $3 for children ages 3 through 17. In addition, the wave pool is open for "float-in" movies once a month in June, July, and August. For more information, call the city's Parks and Recreation office at (480) 350-5200, or TDD (480) 350-5050.

INSIDERS' TIP

On trips into the back country, Arizona State Parks officials recommend carrying along at least five gallons of water for drinking. They also recommend not going alone and always telling a responsible person what your backcountry travel plans are and provide a map if at all possible.

Clark Park Pool, 1730 S. Roosevelt Street, Tempe, (480) 350-5203

Escalante Pool, 2150 E. Orange Street, Tempe, (480) 350-5499

McClintock Pool, 1830 E. Del Rio Drive, (480) 350-5202

Kiwanis Park Wave Pool, 6111 S. All-America Way, Tempe, (480) 350-5201

Northeast Valley

Scottsdale

Scottsdale has three municipal pools open through the summer. Fees are $1.50 for adults, and $1 for kids 17 and younger. Lessons are available. Call for hours.

Cactus Pool, 7202 E. Cactus Road, Scottsdale, (480) 312-7967

Chaparral Pool, 5401 N. Hayden Road, Scottsdale, (480) 312-2361

Eldorado Pool, 2301 N. Miller Road, (480) 312-2483

Northwest Valley

Glendale

Glendale has a seven-pool system that operates from June through August. Schedules vary for each pool. For the full range of aquatic activities and swimming lessons offered, it's best to call (623) 930-2654 for information or the individual pools at the numbers listed below for schedule details.

Apollo Pool, 8045 N. 47th Avenue, Glendale, (623) 915-2713

Cactus Pool, 15500 N. 63rd Avenue, Glendale, (623) 412-5532

Cardinal Pool, 6350 W. Glendale Avenue, Glendale, (623) 915-1679

Community Pool, 6000 W. Olive Avenue, Glendale, (623) 915-2775

Ironwood Pool, 12603 N. 61st Avenue, Glendale, (623) 412-5868

O'Neil Pool, 6448 W. Missouri Avenue, Glendale, (623) 915-2803

Rose Lane Pool, 5003 W. Marlette Avenue, Glendale, (623) 930-7905

Peoria

Peoria Pool at Peoria High School, 11200 N. 83rd Avenue, Peoria, (623) 979-3456, is open from Memorial Day weekend through mid-

August on a daily basis and on weekends through Labor Day weekend. Fees are 50 cents for children 16 and younger, and $1.50 for swimmers 17 and older.

Tubing

Salt River Recreation Inc.
N. Bush Hwy. and Usery Pass Rd., Mesa
• **(480) 984-3305**
• **www.saltrivertubing.com**

Floating down the Salt River on an inner tube is one of the great joys of Valley life. This part of the Salt River, south of the Stewart Mountain Dam that forms Saguaro Lake and north of the confluence with the Verde River, is always running. You get a faster ride on days after a rain, and a slower ride when the weather's been dry a while. Park at the south end of the route, rent your tube (or bring your own), then ride a shuttle bus up to your desired starting point. The company has drop-off points for various lengths of ride. Allow yourself about three hours. Then, let the cool current carry you past desert scenery. When you've come to your route's end, you're right where you parked your car. Keep your car keys in something waterproof and attached to you. In some very minor white water, your rear end may skid on some rocks. Some people outfit their tubes with floating coolers and entertainment centers. We haven't seen a barbecue grill on a tube yet, but we're sure someone's working on it. Salt River Recreation is open from May 1 to October 1 each year, though days and hours of operation vary. Tube rental and shuttle bus service costs $10 per person. Children must be older than eight to rent an inner tube, and life jackets are recommended.

Water Parks

Water parks in the Valley are popular because they offer an active way to cool off. Some tips when you go, consider wearing slip-on aqua shoes—the concrete surrounding the pools is hotter than you think. Also, be mindful of the ratings given to slides—1 through 4, with 4 being the fastest slide. Don't forget to apply good sunscreen on the hour.

Admission prices change from year to year,

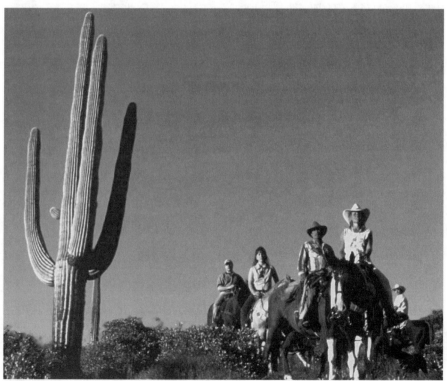

Soak up the desert's beauty by horseback.

Photo: Courtesy of Jessen Associates, Inc.

but most recently they were $15.99 for those 12 and older and $12.99 for children ages 4 to 11. Children 3 and younger get in free. The water parks offer discounts for late admission, which is after 3 or 4 PM, depending on the park.

Big Surf
1500 N. McClintock Dr., Tempe
- **(480) 947-7873**
- **www.golfland-sunsplash.com**

Big Surf lays claim to being the original water park in the Valley and is a legendary place to hang out. As big as four football fields, it probably still is the largest wave pool in the world. Its surrounding landscaping and decor lend the park a Polynesian theme. Big Surf has 11 giant slides and assorted other slides. Little ones will enjoy a wading pool with sprinklers and easy slides. Hours are 10 AM to 6 PM, Monday through Saturday; and 11 AM to 7 PM, Sunday.

Golfland/Sunsplash
155 W. Hampton Ave., Mesa
- **(480) 834-8318**
- **www.golfland-sunsplash.com**

Golfland/Sunsplash offers a miniature golf course and water-park combination. The park's waterslides are big fun. It also features a wave pool and a tunnel known as the Black Hole. Another feature that appeals to relaxation-seekers is a circuitous "river" that you can lazily float upon in your inner tube. The kiddie area has easy concrete slides, a waterfall, sprinklers, and hoses for lots of safe water play. This Caribbean-theme park has 10 tube and giant slides. For indoor diversion, there's a huge arcade area with games for any skill level, which is a favorite date place for Valley teenagers. The park also has a new laser tag area. Also popular are the miniature golf courses adjacent to the arcade. The water park is open 10 AM to 8 PM, Monday through Thursday; 10 AM to 9 PM, Friday and Saturday; and 11 AM to 7 PM, Sunday. Golfland is open 10 AM to 10 PM, Sunday through Thursday; and 10 AM to Midnight, Friday and Saturday.

Waterworld Safari Water Park
4243 W. Pinnacle Peak Rd., Phoenix
- **(602) 581-8446**
- **www.golfland-sunsplash.com**

Waterworld may be the best of the Valley's water parks. It's newer than the others and boasts the six-story Avalanche speed slide along with waterfalls, a wave pool, kiddie pools, and other slides for all levels of daring. Its newest

attraction is the Zambezi River, a 1,100-foot-long lazy waterway that's perfect for relaxing. The wave pool is designed to give 10 minutes of calm and 10 minutes of wave action. Little ones have a great time on the easy slides and the rapids, curving waterways that zip you down to a shallow pool. The Jungle-Jim's children's play pool has a self-latching, fenced area. Lifeguards are on duty. For adventuresome older kids and adults, there are eight larger slides. Hours are 10 AM to 8 PM, Monday through Thursday; 10 AM to 9 PM, Friday and Saturday; and 11 AM to 7 PM, Sunday.

Ballooning

A Aerozona Adventure
7418 E. Cortez St., Scottsdale
- **(480) 991-4260**
- **www.azballoon.com**

The owners of A Aerozona have been taking people aloft over State Trust lands between Cave Creek Road and 99th Avenue since 1974, and have garnered a perfect safety record. They have flights every day of the year, weather permitting. They arrange to meet you at the launch site about 15 minutes before dawn. After a dawn launch, you'll be floating anywhere from treetop level to 1,000 feet high over 200 miles of open desert the company leases. You'll touch down from 45 to 90 minutes later and enjoy a champagne brunch in the desert as you and other passengers reflect on the flight. Then, they drive you back to your car. *Bon Appetit* magazine rated A Aerozona Adventure as one of the best balloon rides in the country in 1991. Rates are $125 per person if you go to the launch site and $145 if you want to be picked up. Gift certificates and group rates are available. Reservations should be made one to three weeks before a flight. The owners recommend making reservations four weeks before a holiday flight. Late-afternoon flights are available from November through March.

Adventures Out West
Scottsdale
- **(602) 996-6100**
- **www.adventuresoutwest.com**

Adventures Out West has been flying people over the desert since 1973. The company offers what it calls the Five Star Vacation flight, which includes a 60 to 90 minute flight, brunch, and a videotape of the flight. It charges $110 per person if you drive out to the launch site and $140 if you want to be picked up. Group rates are

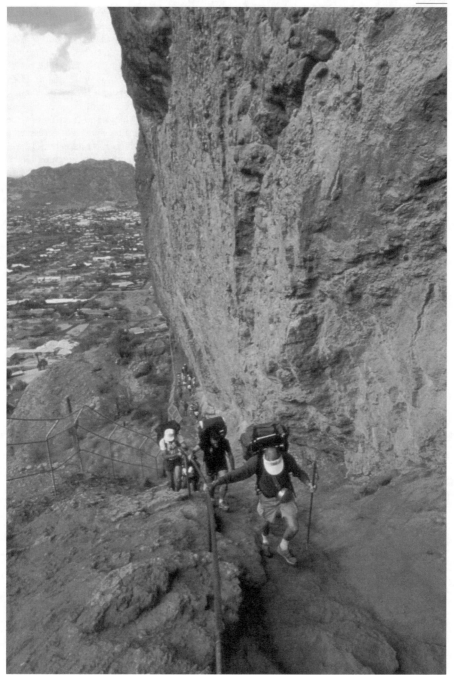

*Camelback Mountain offers a strenuous hike with great views—all in the center of the city.
Watch your step!*

Photo: Courtesy of Scottsdale Convention and Visitors Bureau also available. The company also offers a Basic Flight, which includes a one-hour flight and a small brunch. Flights take off from the Northeast Valley over State Trust lands every morning at sunrise and in the late afternoons from November through March. The company also offers flights that take off from the Southeast Valley and fly over housing and farmland south of the Valley. Call for reservations one to three weeks before flying.

Boating

Arizona is among the top states in per-capita boat ownership, another fact to add to your store of desert trivia. The opportunities to go boating in nearby waters include the most popular options of Lake Pleasant in the Northwest Valley and Saguaro Lake in the Tonto National Forest. If you don't own your own boat, boat rentals are available at a number of urban lakes, such as Kiwanis Park and Encanto Park. Check with each city's parks department for information. If you do go out in a speed boat or with jet skis, show courtesy to swimmers, water skiers, and those in kayaks, sailboats, and canoes.

In Arizona, all aquatic vehicles—from sailboards to Jet-Skis to large boats—must be registered with the Arizona Game and Fish Department. The only vehicles exempted are non-motorized inflatable boats that are less than 12 feet in length. Registration costs $4, plus the license tax of 45 cents per foot, up to 18 feet; and 68 cents per foot, for over 18 feet . Non-resident fees cost $20 for registration, plus a license tax of $2.90 per foot, up to 18 feet; and $5.50 per foot, for over 18 feet.

A life jacket is required for every person aboard, and those younger than 12 must wear their life jacket while aboard. Further information on boating licenses is available at the Arizona Game and Fish Department, 2222 W. Greenway Road, Phoenix, (602) 942-3000, or 7200 E. University Drive, Mesa, (480) 981-9400.

Lake Pleasant Regional Park
State Route 74, Peoria
• **(623) 566-3100 or (520) 501-3100**

From most parts of the Valley access to Lake Pleasant is fairly easy, which, of course, means crowds on weekends. But despite the rush of kamikaze jet skiers, the lake also is an abode for the members of the Arizona Yacht Club, who frequently use the lake as a venue for their weekend regattas. The lake, formed by the Waddell Dam, offers gorgeous views of the mountains surrounding it. The park crawls

with wildlife, including coyotes, burros, and a shy pair of nesting American Bald Eagles. The lake permits parasailing as well as boating. You pay $5 per motor vehicle to get into the park; $6 for vehicles pulling watercraft. The park's main entrance (the first as you come up from the Valley) gives access to a 10-lane boat ramp, which is adjacent to parking for 590 vehicles with boat trailers. The second (north) entrance is 3 miles past the first and gives access to a four-lane ramp, which has space for 112 vehicles with boat trailers. Both launching ramps are on the western shore of the lake. Before you come upon the main entrance, you'll pass Pleasant Harbor Road, which gives access to the Pleasant Harbor Marina on the lake's eastern shore. Lake Pleasant Watercraft rental, (623) 516-2397, offers boat storage and complete repair facilities. Camping and shower facilities are available.

Saguaro Lake Recreational Area
Off Bush Hwy., about 10 miles northeast of Mesa in Tonto National Forest
• **(480) 610-3300, (602) 225-5200**

Saguaro Lake is the closest of three lakes formed by dams along the Salt River. As such, it gets crowded on summer weekends, but it's still a great place to enjoy watery fun. There are two Forest Service boat-launch ramps on the north end of Saguaro Lake. You can come straight up and launch, park your land vehicle nearby and take the boat on out. When coming from Mesa, the launch ramps can be reached by taking the turn off Bush Highway for the Sheriff's Aid Station and the Saguaro Lake Marina. The lake is closed to parasailing (it's just as well since the surrounding mountains close off the lake from prevailing winds). Those with boats and jet skis should be considerate of water skiers and kayakers. For boat storage, call the marina at (480) 986-5596; for service and rentals, call (480) 986-0969. Boating maps are available at the Mesa District Ranger Station, 26 N. Macdonald Street, Mesa (480) 610-3300 and at the Tonto National Forest Office, 2324 E. McDowell Road, Phoenix (602) 225-5200. The entry fee is $4 per day, per vehicle, with $2 extra charged for watercraft.

Climbing

Camelback Mountain
Echo Canyon Recreation Area,
E. McDonald Dr. at Tatum Blvd., Phoenix
• **(602) 256-3110**

Camelback Mountain offers quick access to

great climbs in the Valley, but the crumbly sandstone walls make the situation a bit dicey. The 80-foot tower called the Praying Monk, one of the most popular climbs, offers a sheer angle, a great view of the Valley, and permanent—though aging—bolts fixed along the route. The east face is rated at a 5.4; the southeast corner at a 5.6. Hikers beware—do not climb these rocks without the proper gear, protection, and instruction.

Fishing

If you're 14 or older and plan to fish in Arizona, you need to be licensed by the state Game and Fish Department. Some local jurisdictions require a special permit as well, so it's good to check on local regulations before you decide to test out an interesting new fishing spot.

Licenses are issued annually to residents for a $12 fee, but several license options are available for non-residents. A tourist can pick up a one-day license for $8, a five-day license for $18.50, and a four-month license for $22. These licenses entitle you to catch warm-water fish in any body of water in the state, including the Valley's canals. To catch trout, you pay $10 more for an annual trout stamp.

The exception to this rule is the Urban Fishing program, which costs $12 annually for residents and visitors alike. An Urban Fishing License costs the same as the general fishing license, but it entitles you to fish only at certain park lakes in the Phoenix and Tucson areas. To fish anywhere else in the Valley or the state, you need the general license. The advantage of the urban fishing program is that the license fees pay for the stocking of these specific lakes with catfish in the summer and trout in the winter.

The Urban Fishing License covers fishing at these Valley parks: Cortez Park, 35th and Dunlap Avenues, Phoenix; Desert West Park, 6602 W. Encanto Boulevard, Phoenix; Encanto Park, 15th Avenue and Encanto Boulevard, Phoenix; Papago Park, Van Buren Street and Galvin Parkway, Phoenix; Chaparral Park, 5401 N. Hayden Road, Scottsdale; Canal Park, McKellips Road and College Avenue, Tempe; Kiwanis Community Park, Mill Avenue and All America Way, Tempe; Desert Breeze Park, Desert Breeze Parkway, Chandler; Red Mountain Park, 7745 E. Brown Road, Mesa; and Riverview Park, 2100 W. 8th Street, Mesa.

Further details on fishing licenses may be obtained from the Arizona Game and Fish Department, 2222 W. Greenway Road, Phoenix, (602) 942-3000, or 7200 E. University Drive, Mesa, (480) 981-9400.

Roosevelt Lake
Off the Apache Tr., Ariz. Hwy. 88, about 30 mi. northeast of Apache Junction in Tonto National Forest

Serious anglers recommend Roosevelt Lake because of its good fishing. Although it's a bit

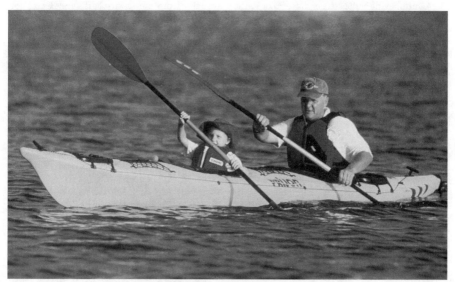

Kayaking offers a good way to get out and enjoy the parks. A good beginner's session can be found on the new Tempe Town Lake.

Photo: Courtesy of Tempe Convention and Visitors Bureau

of a haul from the Valley, you can easily do an overnight turnaround. From the Valley, Roosevelt Lake is the farthest of the four lakes formed by dams along the Salt River. Despite being the highest of the lakes, it's fairly warm because it's shallow. Thus, the fish grow well. Spring is the best time to catch bass up there. Catfish are best caught in the spring and summer. Crappies are abundant in spring. You can fish the lake year round, though, and still turn up some good catches.

Saguaro Lake
Off Bush Hwy., about 10 mi. northeast of Mesa in Tonto National Forest

Saguaro Lake is a challenging place for anglers because the lake is so popular. It's tough to make a good catch here. The best time to fish Saguaro Lake is in the winter, when most of the boating traffic dies down. Anglers who can't wait for winter will get up well before dawn or stay up into the wee hours to partake of Saguaro Lake's bounty of bass and catfish in some secluded cove.

Lake Pleasant
Off Ariz. Hwy. 74, Peoria

Lake Pleasant presents the angler with bass, catfish, and crappie. Again, because the lake is so popular, the serious, but bleary-eyed, angler is going to be out in the water well before dawn.

Hiking and Biking

A number of Valley cities have bike paths along urban streets; call the respective city parks and recreation departments for information and maps. More interesting because they are away from the roads are the paths along the canals through the Valley of the Sun. These canal paths are shared by bicyclists, hikers, joggers, horseback riders, and the occasional dog, but they generally offer a tranquil route through the Valley.

We can't emphasize enough, though, that you should take adequate water along with you for your trip. On the urban trails, where you can quickly turn off and hit a convenience store, this may not be much of a concern, but when you get more isolated, you want to keep well-hydrated, even in winter.

Indian Bend Wash Bike Path
Along Hayden Rd., Scottsdale
• **(602) 994-2732**

This bike path meanders for 11 miles along the sunken greenbelt constructed for flood con-

trol through the center of Scottsdale. It's not a challenging trail at all, but it offers the chance to quickly get out in some greenery and unwind. There are several good starting points, such as north of downtown Scottsdale at Chaparral Park at Hayden and Jackrabbit Roads, or the Bike Stop Rest Area on Thomas Road between Miller and Hayden Roads. The path ends at Shea Boulevard in the north and at McKellips Road, on the line with Tempe, in the south. You'll pass a number of public golf courses, small lakes, and municipal parks along the way. You won't have to worry about auto traffic, but pedestrians, skaters, and joggers share the path.

Sun Circle Trail
Maricopa County
• **(602) 506-2930**

The Sun Circle Trail incorporates paths along some major canals as it makes its 110-mile circle through the Valley. The trail—open to pedestrians, bicyclists, and horseback riders—was conceived and mapped by the Arizona State Horsemen's Association Trails Committee and then presented to the county Board of Supervisors back in the early 1960s. In 1965, the county obtained cooperation from the Salt River Project and the U.S. Department of the Interior to have the trail run alongside the canals. Parts of the trail remain unfinished, as flood-control clearance and rights of way are sought, but a good deal of the trail is continuous. Signs mark the trail at intervals. Maps are available from the county Parks and Recreation Department at the number above.

The Arizona Canal, a major part of the completed portion of the Sun Circle Trail, travels west from the Granite Reef Dam on the Salt River east of the Beeline Highway (State Route 87) across Scottsdale to roughly Hayden Road, and then it jogs south toward Indian School Road, which it parallels into Phoenix. Then, it heads northwest to Glendale and Thunderbird Peseo Park, where it terminates at approximately 75th Avenue and Thunderbird Road. Along the way, it passes such bike-friendly parks as the Phoenix Mountains Preserve, North Mountain Park, and Squaw Peak Park.

The southern portion of the Sun Circle Trail connects with the Arizona Canal path at the Granite Reef Dam. It travels southwestward along the South Canal, a bit south of the Salt River. The Sun Circle Trail then follows the Consolidated Canal eastward through Mesa and then south into Gilbert. The trail then turns west on the Western Canal, north of Elliot

Road, and travels through Chandler and into Tempe. When the Western Canal veers to the north near Tempe's Kiwanis Park, the trail continues westward into South Mountain Park in Phoenix.

Points of interest along the trail include Papago Park, Granite Reef, South Mountain Park, the Agua Fria River, and the Salt River Indian Reservation.

Grand Canal

Another attractive canal path is the Grand Canal. It travels across the Valley from where it emerges from an underground aqueduct southwest of the intersection of Washington Street and Mill Avenue in Tempe. The canal path heads northwestward into Phoenix, north of Indian School Road and past the Phoenix Indian Medical Center before it heads almost due west between Phoenix Central High School and Brophy College Preparatory School and then curves southwest. South of Indian School Road and I-17, the canal begins to travel west. It travels to the northwest a little north of 56th Avenue and Osborn Road. It travels into Glendale at 75th Avenue and Camelback Road, continuing northwest to Bethany Home Road and 83rd Avenue, where it heads due west to about 107th Avenue and ends.

Mormon and National Trails
South Mountain Park,
10919 S. Central Ave., Phoenix
• **(602) 495-0222**

These are fun trails for mountain biking, although they're shared by hikers, so be careful and courteous. From the mountain-bike point of view, Mormon Trail is a technical single track. The trail climbs to a mountain ridge, follows it, and then hooks up to the National Trail. At this point, a rider can choose to return to the trailhead by turning left down the National Trail. By turning right, you continue upward on the National Trail. At "the waterfall," bike riders are forced to carry their bikes up a short distance, and then it's 3 to 4 miles back to the parking lot. The bike ride down is very bumpy.

Summit Trail
Echo Canyon Recreation Area,
E. McDonald Dr. at Tatum Blvd., Phoenix
• **(602) 256-3110**

At 2,700 feet, Camelback Mountain happens to be the tallest in Phoenix, so its Summit Trail takes hikers to the top of the Valley's world. However, you don't get the reward of a

magnificent view without a little work. This is a popular place among overachievers, and the park rangers rate it a difficult hike. The mile-long path is steep with slippery patches of gravel, but it's well worth the effort.

Summit Trail at Squaw Peak
Squaw Peak Recreation Area,
2701 E. Squaw Peak Ln., Phoenix
• **(602) 262-6696**

We hesitate to mention the Summit Trail at Squaw Peak because it's already so popular and crowded. This 1.2-mile trail doesn't go as high as Camelback's Summit Trail (it's only 2,600 feet), and it isn't as difficult. However, the view is just as good.

Bicycle Rental and Repair

If you're visiting and want to use a bicycle to check out some of the trails, a few places rent bikes for that purpose. Most rent on a daily basis. The number of bike-rental places is diminishing due to insurance concerns and theft, so it's best to call and check first. All of the places here repair and sell bicycles as well.

Bike Chalet
5761 E. Brown Rd., Mesa
• **(480) 807-2944**
• **www.bikechalet.com**

This bike shop has a number of locations in the Valley, but only this location near the foothills of the Superstition Mountains handles rentals. It rents front-suspension mountain bikes ranging from $35 a day; dual-suspension mountain bikes, $40 a day; and road bikes for $25 a day.

Tempe Bicycle
330 W. University Dr., Tempe
• **(480) 966-6896**
• **www.tempebicycle.com**

Tempe Bicycle is just a bit off Mill Avenue in downtown Tempe. The shop rents nonsuspension bikes for $30 a day, front-suspended bikes for $40 a day, and full-suspension bikes for $40 to $50 a day. Special rates are available for weekly rentals.

Hockey

Although ice hockey in the desert seems a non sequitur, it's been popular in the Valley forever—or at least dating back to when the late, minor-league Phoenix Roadrunners came to town. Roller hockey made the game even more popular with kids. After the advent of in-line skates, kids could set up a net in their cul-de-sac and play, instead of having to find an ice rink or a roller rink willing to let them play.

Listed here are a number of rinks dedicated solely to in-line roller hockey. Look under Ice Skating and Roller Skating headings to find facilities that offer hockey leagues, in addition to open skating. Look in our Sports Organizations section for associations that help coordinate and promote hockey in the Valley.

In-line Hockey Rinks

Casey at the Bat
Union Hills Dr. and 40th St., Phoenix
• (480) 971-3224

Casey at the Bat is a sports complex that includes a roller rink for hockey league-only use. The nearby batting cages are available for use for $1 for 16 balls.

In-Line Hockey Rink
**Bonsall Park, 59th Ave. and
Bethany Home Rd., Glendale**
• (623) 930-2820

This City of Glendale-owned rink offers free open play by age group, as well as clinics on how to improve their game to both youth and adult hockey leagues. For details on hours, league schedules, and group reservations, call the number above.

Organizations

Desert Youth Hockey Association
1520 N. Hayden Rd., Scottsdale
• (602) 994-9119

This association organizes youth hockey leagues and tournaments and coordinates participation in national tournaments.

Valley of the Sun Hockey Association
Phoenix
• (602) 340-0001, ext. 301

The association organizes youth ice hockey leagues and tournaments.

Horseback Riding

Phoenix is not far removed from the Wild West, so you can bet that horseback riding remains dear to many folks out here. People who own horse properties out on the fringes of the Valley just get up on their horses and ride out into the rural area or wilderness nearby, which is not exactly advisable for people who don't

know an area. It's easy to get lost in the wilderness. If you ride from the stables listed below, you will have a trail guide regardless of your experience with horses. Also, remember to take plenty of water, especially in the wilderness areas.

Trail Information

Glendale Parks and Recreation Department
5850 W. Glendale Ave., Glendale
• (623) 930-2820

Thunderbird Park and Thunderbird Paseo Park both offer horseback riding trails. The trail at the Thunderbird Paseo Park links with the Arizona Canal, while the trails at Thunderbird Park are favored by many Valley equestrians. Call the number above for information and maps.

Lost Dutchman State Park
6109 N. Apache Tr., Apache Junction
• (602) 982-4485

With all those saguaros out there, you'll know you're in the Arizona desert at Lost Dutchman State Park. A hiking-equestrian trail leads into the rugged Superstition Wilderness area of the Tonto National Forest. Park rangers advise that the grade of the trail makes it tough on horses and recommend the park's lower-level trails, on which hiking, mountain-biking, and horseback riding are all permitted. The entrance fee is $4 per vehicle with up to four people. To get there, take the Superstition Freeway (Interstate 60) east to the Idaho Street (State Route 88) exit. When State Route 88 becomes the Apache Trail, follow it about 5 miles northeast to the park entrance.

Maricopa County Parks and Recreation Dept.
3475 W. Durango St., Phoenix
• (602) 506-2930

The county parks and recreation department can supply maps and information on the horseback trails at Estrella Mountain Regional Park, Usery Mountain Recreation Area and McDowell Mountain Regional Park. Maps can also be picked up at the parks' respective ranger stations. The department is also the place to go for maps and information on the Sun Circle Trail, which travels through urban areas and wilderness alongside the Arizona Canal and other major canals in the Valley. The Maricopa County Parks and Recreation Department has horseback riding concessionaires on or adjacent to the Cave Creek Recreation Area, (623) 465-0431; White Tank Mountain Regional Park, (623) 935-2505; Estrella Mountain Regional Park, (623) 932-3811; and Usery Mountain Recreation Area, (480) 984-0032. These outfits have special use permits that allow them to lead trips into the regional parks and recreational areas managed by Maricopa County.

Phoenix Parks, Recreation and Library Dept.
200 W. Washington St., Phoenix
• **(602) 262-6861**

North Mountain Recreation Area, Papago Park, and South Mountain Park all offer horseback riding trails, and they are very popular places to make a quick getaway into desert scenery without leaving the Valley. The department can provide maps to the trails.

Stables

Phoenix

Ponderosa Stables
10215 S. Central Ave., Phoenix
• **(602) 268-1261**
• **www.arizona-horses.com**

Ponderosa Stables offers horseback riding in South Mountain Park. The stables are open daily from 8 AM until dark. Trail rides are $17 per person per hour. A four-hour ride is $50 per person on weekdays, $52 on weekends. Ponderosa also gives riding lessons at $25 an hour per person. The lessons are one on one. Ponderosa's wranglers will also take groups out on cookout rides, featuring steak and chicken or hamburgers and hot dogs. There's an eight-person minimum on those, and reservations are needed. Another ride, called the T-Bone, takes place at sunset. Groups of two or more are taken on an hour ride over the mountains to the T-Bone Steakhouse, where they have dinner and then are guided back to the stables. The cost is $23 per person, and riders pay for their own meals at the steakhouse.

Southeast Valley

Papago Riding Stables
440 N. Scottsdale Rd., Tempe
• **(480) 966-9793**

Papago Riding Stables will take you on trails through the red rocks of Papago Park. Trail rides are $15 per hour, per person. The stables open at 8 AM each day, but the closing hours vary with the season and weather. In the summer,

the stables shut down at the hottest hours of the day and reopen in the late afternoon. It's best to call ahead for times.

Northeast Valley

MacDonald's Ranch
26540 N. Scottsdale Rd., Scottsdale
• **(480) 585-0239**
• **www.macdonaldsranch.com**

For decades, MacDonald's Ranch—a real ranch that raises horses—has been taking people through the magnificent McDowell Mountains. The ranch also specializes in cowboy cookouts on the trail to complete your Western adventure (groups of 10 or more). Reservations are recommended for the cookout, and the ranch suggests this activity for children ages seven and older. There are pony rides at the ranch for those younger than seven. Sample prices: A one-hour guided trail ride is $24 per person; a one-hour ride with a cowboy luncheon is $40 per person.

Southwest Valley

Wigwam Stables
13234 W. Indian Springs Rd., Avondale
• **(623) 853-0588**

You can head out into the scenic Estrella Mountains from these stables. Trail rides go for $15 per person for one hour, and $25 per person for two hours. Wigwam Stables can also arrange hayrides and cookouts with a steak dinner. Hayrides cost $150 per hour for a group up to 25 people. Overnight rides, with two meals and several hours of riding, cost $75 and, if you hanker to try your hand at cowboying, you can even work a cattle drive. Reservations are suggested. The stables are 8 AM to 5 PM every day of the year.

Ice Skating

Think about it. It's the middle of summer and you want to get some exercise, but you'd like to stay cool too. Ice skating is just the right prescription, and it's fun year round, even though you'll never see a frozen Valley pond.

Phoenix

Ice Chalet
3853 E. Thomas Rd., Phoenix
• **(602) 267-0591**
• **www.icechalet.com**

The Ice Chalet is open for skating and lessons. Located inside the Desert Palms Power

Center, it has public skating sessions during both days and evenings, with skating lessons on weekend afternoons. Days skating sessions are 1 to 4:30 PM, Monday through Friday; from noon to 3 PM, Saturdays; and from 1 to 4 PM on Sundays. Evening skating sessions are from 7 to 9 PM, Tuesdays and Thursdays; and 7 to 9 PM, Fridays and Saturdays. Admission is $5.50 for adults, $2.50 for children 6 and younger, and $2.50 for skate rental. Sunday afternoons, you can get a special family package for $24, which includes admission and skate rentals for a family of four.

Southeast Valley

Oceanside Ice Arena
1520 N. McClintock Dr., Tempe
• (602) 947-2470
• www.iskateaz.com

This facility, named for its location next to Big Surf water park, is open for skating and lessons. You can usually skate during the afternoons or evenings, but call ahead for hours. Admission is $4 for adults and $3 for children 12 and younger. Figure skate rentals are $3.50 and hockey skate rentals are $4.50. Inquire about lessons for beginning skaters or children's hockey. Adult leagues play there, too.

Northeast Valley

Alltel Ice Den
9375 E. Bell Rd., Scottsdale
• (480) 585-7465

The Phoenix Coyotes' practice ice rink is open for public skating several times a week. The ice is almost exactly like the America West Arena rink in downtown Phoenix, where the Coyotes play their home games. The facility offers figure skating and hockey programs for children and adults, plus a pro shop, concessions area, and restaurant. Public sessions vary by the season, but usually last two hours every weekday, with the addition of two-hour evening sessions Thursday through Sunday. Admission is $7 for adults and $5 for those 6 to 15, with skate rental being an additional $4 for hockey skates or $3 for figure skates. Kids un-

der 5 skate for $5, skate rental included. Friday and Saturday evening sessions cost $8. A family of four can skate on Wednesdays and Sundays for $28, skate rental included. Call for league information.

Jeep Tours

Desert Storm Hummer Tours
15525 N. 83rd Way, Scottsdale
• (480) 922-8868
• www.dshummer.com

Head out into the Four Peaks Wilderness Area of Tonto National Forest in one of the sturdiest 4 x 4 vehicles around, a Humvee. This vehicle can take you places a jeep couldn't, like 4,000 feet up the side of a 6,000-foot mountain. Humvees replaced the old military jeeps in 1979 and became available commercially in 1992. Desert Storm Hummer Tours has been in operation four years. It has six hummers leaving seven days a week for the Four Peaks Wilderness Area. For a four-hour tour, the price is $90 per person; children 12 and younger ride for $50 apiece. For resort or home pickup, the price is $100 per person. Call as early as possible for reservations in the busy season from October through June. In July through September, the company says it can usually take people who call the day they want to go.

Rafting

Desert Voyagers
Scottsdale
• (480) 998-7238
• www.desertvoyagers.com

Desert Voyagers can take you on a variety of raft rides in the desert rivers near the Valley. Funwater Floats take a half-day, with a two-hour float through the Tonto National Forest. The price is $55 per person. Or, for the same price, you can share a "Funyak" with someone and paddle behind one of the guided rafts on a Funwater Float. The company also offers the Best of Arizona, which combines a desert jeep tour with a raft trip for $105 per person, with a minimum of four people. Reservations are recommended.

Roller Skating

When it comes to roller skating, you can choose from rinks that allow in-line skating or those that are strictly the old-fashioned, roller-derby style skates. (The in-line rinks may also have hockey leagues.) The Valley has enough rinks to keep fans of both styles happy.

Phoenix

Rollero Family Roller Skating Center
7318 W. Indian School Rd., Phoenix
• (623) 846-1510
• www.rollero.com

Rollero has been in business for 45 years and maintains a family atmosphere. It's open on all major holidays, with open skating sessions on most nights of the week. Prices can vary daily, ranging from $1 to $8 per person depending on the day and time. There is no charge for skate rental. The schedule changes depending on the season and to accommodate private parties (Rollero specializes in birthday parties), so it's best to call ahead. Rollero does not allow in-line or street skates.

Southeast Valley

Surfside Skate
1625 E. Weber Rd., Tempe
• (480) 968-9600
• www.surfsideskateland.com

Tempe's Skateland is an indoor roller rink near Big Surf water park, and it offers in-line skating and skating lessons. Open skating sessions take place Friday through Sunday. Hours change to accommodate lessons and private parties, so call ahead. Admission ranges anywhere from $3.75 to $6.75, depending on the day, time, and activity. Skate rental is $1.75. Skateland also hosts artistic, speed skating, and youth hockey leagues, so call for more information.

Skateland
7 E. Southern Ave., Mesa
• (480) 833-7775

Mesa's Skateland is an indoor roller rink as well. It offers in-line skating and skating lessons. Open skating sessions take place Friday through Sunday. Hours change to accommodate lessons and private parties, so call ahead. Admission ranges from $1 with donation of an item on special skate nights, to $7 for regular skating. Regular skate rental is $2, and speed skates or in-line skates are available for $3.50. Skateland also hosts adult and youth hockey leagues, so call for league information.

Chandler Sports Spectrum
1101 W. Ray Rd., Chandler
• (480) 917-8634

The Chandler Sports Spectrum is an indoor in-line rink that offers open skating sessions that vary according to season. Admission is $5, and the price includes skate rental. A family rate of $10 for four family members is also available. The schedule changes to accommodate private parties and league schedules, so it's best to call ahead. The Spectrum also provides skating lessons, hockey lessons, open hockey for adults, and adult- and youth-league hockey.

Northwest Valley

Great Skate of Arizona
10054 N. 43rd Ave., Glendale
• (623) 842-1181

The Great Skate boasts the largest rink in Arizona, and it allows both in-line and roller-derby style skates. Afternoon open skating sessions go from 1 to 4 PM and are $4. The skating schedule changes regularly, so the Great Skate suggests you call ahead for the current schedule. Prices range from $3 to $6, and skate rental is included. The rink is available for private parties and also offers lessons.

Soaring

Arizona Soaring, Inc.
Estrella Sailport, Az. Hwy. 238,
Maricopa County
• (520) 568-2318, (800) 861-2318,
(480) 821-2903
• www.azsoaring.com

How about soaring silently through desert sky at about 4,000 feet? Although Estrella Sailport is well south of the Valley, you can see the Valley spreading northward from your perch. Weather and geography are kind to Estrella Sailport, offering conditions right for soaring almost every day of the year. Arizona Soaring is open 11 AM to 5 PM, Monday through Friday; and 9 AM to 5 PM, Saturday and Sunday. Sailplanes are taken up and released at 3,500 feet and, by riding the air currents, generally reach an altitude of about 5,000 to 6,000 feet. The high-performance craft can soar to 10,000 feet on a good day. A ride in a trainer lasts 20 minutes and cost $69.95 per person. A 20-minute ride in a high-performance sailplane costs $89.95, and a 40-minute ride costs $129.95. Daredevils may want to try the 15-minute aerobatic ride for $99.95. Arizona Soaring also offers longer rides and lessons. To get there, take Interstate 10 east to Exit 164 and head toward Maricopa. Follow the road for 15 miles and then turn west on State Route 238. You'll come upon Estrella Sailport 6.5 miles later.

Softball

Softball has been big in the Valley of the Sun ever since fast-pitch softball (the type with the windmill windup as opposed to slow underhand pitching) was a major spectator sport out here in the early twentieth century. Slow-pitch softball has been growing nationwide since the 1960s, and its growth in the Valley mirrors the national trend. When we talk softball as an adult recreational activity, it's slow-pitch that rules in the Valley. Fast-pitch is generally played by women's teams. Slow-pitch is generally played by men's and co-recreational teams.

If you've got a softball team, and you want to play more than an occasional pickup game, there are many different leagues and tournaments open. Company and industrial leagues, church leagues, and ethnic leagues are mostly closed to people outside those particular groups.

City leagues are open to all participants, sometimes with a residency requirement or restriction (i.e., teams that have no residents from the specific city may be last in line to be registered). Tournaments sponsored by the two major sanctioning bodies—the Amateur Softball Association and the United States Slo-Pitch Softball Association—are open to member teams.

Phoenix

Phoenix Parks, Recreation and Library Dept.
200 W. Washington St., Phoenix
• **(602) 262-6861**

Phoenix offers year-round league play for upper levels of competition at Rose Mofford Sports Complex, 9833 N. 25th Avenue, Phoenix, (602) 261-8011; and Papago Softball Complex, 6201 E. Oak Street, Phoenix, (602) 261-8841. Leagues vote on using ASA or USSSA rules. For other levels of competition, five geographical districts in the city field their own

leagues. Call the department for further information.

Southeast Valley

Chandler Community Services Department
125 E. Commonwealth Ave., Chandler
• **(480) 782-2727**

Chandler offers men's, women's, and co-recreational slow-pitch league play in winter, spring-summer, and fall seasons. The league plays by ASA rules. Games are played at the Snedigar Sportsplex, 4500 S. Basha Road, and Folley Memorial Park, 601 E. Frye Road. Registration information is available at the phone number above.

Gilbert Parks and Recreation Department
119 N. Gilbert Rd., Gilbert
• **(480) 503-6200**

Gilbert offers men's, women's, and co-recreational slow-pitch league play year round. The league plays by ASA rules. Games are held at Freestone Park, 10190 E. Juniper Avenue. Registration information is available at the phone number above.

Mesa Community Services Department Parks, Recreation and Cultural Division
125 N. Hobson St., Mesa
• **(480) 644-2677**

Mesa offers men's, women's, and co-recreational slow-pitch league play year round. The league plays by ASA rules. Games are held at Red Mountain Park's Softball Complex, 7808 E. Brown Road; Riverview Park, 2100 W. 8th Street; Ellsworth Park, 107 S. Horne Road, Mesa; and Kleinman Park, 710 S. Extension Avenue. Registration information is available at the phone number above.

Tempe Community Services
3500 S. Rural Rd., Tempe
• **(480) 350-5207**

Tempe offers men's, women's, and co-recreational slow-pitch league play in the spring, summer, and fall. The league plays by modified ASA rules. Games are held at Kiwanis Community Park softball fields on All America Way; Tempe's Papago Park, Curry Road and College Avenue; Daley Park, College Avenue and Encanto Drive; Tempe Diablo Stadium Complex, 2200 W. Alameda Drive; Clark Park, Roosevelt and 19th Streets; and Escalante Park, River Road and Orange Street. Registration information is available at the phone number above.

Northeast Valley

Scottsdale Community Services
7447 E. Indian School Rd., Scottsdale
• **(480) 994-7643**

Scottsdale offers men's, women's, and co-recreational slow-pitch league play year round. The league plays by ASA rules. Games are played at Horizon Park, 15440 N. 100th Street; Chaparral Park, 5401 N. Hayden Road; and Eldorado Park, 2311 N. Miller Road. Registration information is available at the phone number above.

Northwest Valley

Glendale Parks and Recreation
5850 W. Glendale Ave., Glendale
• **(623) 930-2820**

Glendale offers men's, women's, senior's, and co-recreational slow-pitch league play in spring and fall. In summer, Glendale offers co-recreational play only. The league plays by ASA rules. Games are played at Sahuaro Ranch Park, 59th Avenue and Mountain View Road; Foothills Park, 57th Avenue and Union Hills Drive; and Paseo Racquet Center, 63rd Avenue and Thunderbird Road. League and reservation information is available at the number above.

Peoria Community Services
8401 W. Monroe St., Peoria
• **(623) 412-7129**

Peoria offers men's, women's, and co-recreational slow-pitch league play in spring, summer, and fall. The league plays by ASA rules. Games are played at Varney Park, 11820 N. 81st Avenue. Reservation information is available at the number above.

Softball Organizations

American Softball Association State Chapter
Prescott
• **(520) 445-5725**

The American Softball Association sponsors a number of tournaments at such Valley ven-ues as the Rose Mofford Sports Complex and Victory Lane Sports Complex. You can get information on those and on tournaments held outside the Valley by calling the number above. Although the ASA is dedicated foremost to preserving fast-pitch softball, its rules for both fast-pitch and slow-pitch softball are observed by a number of Valley city softball leagues.

Tennis

Racquet sports have always been popular here, although not quite as popular as golf. Most of the parks and recreation departments offer tennis courts, many lighted after dark, that are available in local parks on a first-come, first-served, no-charge basis. Call the respective city parks department for a complete list of courts. The following are some of the public, pay facilities in the Valley.

Phoenix

Phoenix Tennis Center
6330 N. 21st Ave., Phoenix
• **(602) 249-3712**

The Phoenix Tennis center features 22 lighted, hard-surface tennis courts. It's best to call the day before you want to play to make reservations. Rates are $1.50 per person for 90 minutes. The facilities include lockers and showers.

Southeast Valley

Gene Autry Sports Complex
4125 E. McKellips Rd., Mesa
• **(480) 644-2149**

This new complex features 16 lighted tennis courts, a practice wall, showers, and a small pro shop. Drop in tennis hours are Monday through Saturday, at 7:30 AM; and Sunday at 6:30 PM. Hours of operation vary, so call ahead. Court rental is $4 during the day and $6 in the evening for singles play; doubles play cost $6 during the day and $8 during the evening.

Kiwanis Park Recreation Center
6111 S. All America Way, Tempe
• **(480) 350-5701**

The Kiwanis Park Recreation Center has 15 lighted hard courts. It has been recognized by the U.S. Tennis Association as one of the

INSIDERS' TIP
Practice Plus-One Boating, meaning what you take out on your boating trip be sure to bring back plus one—one piece of litter or debris, every time. If it floats, net it. If it blows out, go back and get it. Act ethically and responsibly to keep our waterways clean for the enjoyment of all.

outstanding public tennis facilities in the country. Fees are $4.50 per court for 90 minutes before 7 PM and $6 per court after 7 PM. The center also offers lessons and tennis leagues. Its hours are 7 AM to 10 PM, Monday through Thursday; 7 AM to 7 PM Friday; 8 AM to 6 PM, Saturday; and 8 AM to 9 PM, Sunday.

Northwest Valley

Paseo Racquet Center
6268 W. Thunderbird Rd., Glendale
• **(623) 979-1234**

The Paseo Racquet Center features 14 hard courts and one red-clay court, all lighted. The center opens at 7 AM in July and August and at 8 AM the rest of the year. It closes at 9:30 PM, Monday through Friday; and at 2 PM on Saturday and Sunday. Fees are $1.50 per person for 90 minutes. At night, add on a $2 light fee per court. The Paseo Racquet Center won an Out-

standing Public Facility award from the U.S. Tennis Association. Reservations are taken 24 hours in advance and are recommended. The facility has a pro shop, lockers, and showers. Group and private lessons are available. The center also hosts about 20 tournaments per year.

YMCA

YMCA Valley of the Sun
YMCA Metropolitan Office,
350 N. First St., Phoenix
• **(602) 257-5120**

The YMCA offers a wide variety of athletics, fitness, and sporting activities, from basketball leagues and in-line hockey to swimming pools and aerobics. The YMCA Valley of the Sun has 10 locations across the Valley.

Parks and Recreation Departments

The greatest single resource for finding information on park facilities, participatory sports leagues, fitness programs, and other recreational activities too numerous to list here is your municipal parks and recreation department.

In addition to fielding their own sports leagues, these departments also tend to rent facilities to outside organizations like Little League. Here's a list of the Valley's parks and recreation departments' information lines.

Chandler, (480) 782-2727
Gilbert, (480) 503-6200
Glendale, (623) 930-2820
Mesa, (480) 644-2351
Peoria, (623) 773-7137
Phoenix, (602) 262-6861
Scottsdale, (480) 312-2722
Tempe, (480) 350-5200

Golf

In Arizona, golf is life.

Golfers build their personal and work schedules around their tee times and build their houses around the golf course. Deal-makers and rock stars are often spotted on our links, and dozens of pro athletes live here in their off-seasons so they can be on the courses every day. Some people joke that the reason football free agents come to talk to the lowly Arizona Cardinals is because the golf is so good and plentiful here. People schedule business trips and conventions in the Valley, knowing that when the work is done, the golf course awaits.

Many communities are built around golf courses, boasting the course as an amenity just the way homeowners once boasted of indoor plumbing. In places such as the retirement haven Sun City, drivers will see diamond-shaped yellow road signs with the silhouette of a golf cart within, warning them of golf-cart crossings. Certainly, the number of retirees out here helps boost the numbers, but golf is played avidly by every age group in Arizona, the National Golf Foundation reported in a study for the Arizona Golf Association and the Arizona Department of Commerce.

The NGF study revealed that nearly half a million Arizona residents play golf in each year and that 13.5 percent of Arizona residents older than 12 play the sport. This rate of participation is greater than the rate in any other Sun Belt state, proof that golf is life in Arizona. In addition, the NGF looked at the visitors' market and estimated that more than 2 million visitors play golf here each year.

If there's a difference between older and younger golfers, it's the number of rounds they play. The NGF study learned residents age 60 and older play 35 percent of all golf rounds in Arizona. This age group averages 44.5 rounds per year, while people in the 40 to 49 age group play about 17.2 rounds a year, or about 17 percent of all rounds played.

Golf course construction, like every other kind of construction in the Valley, is booming. By the end of 2000, Arizona had more than 300 golf courses and 15 commercial driving ranges, and nearly 75 percent of the state's courses were open to the public. Arizona adds courses and makes additions to existing courses at an average of eight a year. Most of that construction is in the Valley.

In real estate terms, building a home along golf-course frontage property increases the value of both multifamily and single-family housing from 15 to 30 percent. Homes with extraordinary views and golf frontage, a combination found on many of the Valley's newer courses, can increase real-estate values anywhere from 50 to 200 percent. Putting the money issues aside, golf courses are just beautiful places to live beside. Sitting in your backyard, you can enjoy the illusion that all that nearby fairway is part of your yard. Of course, you may have to put up with occasional errant golf balls in your yard but balance that with the chance to enjoy the sweet smell of newly cut grass.

Golf began to take hold in Arizona when Harry Collis and Will Robinson designed a course at the San Marcos Golf Resort in Chandler back in 1912. Soon after, the Phoenix Country Club had a course as well. In those days, traditional Midwestern and Scottish links designs ruled

LOOK FOR:
- **Phoenix**
- **Southeast Valley**
- **Northeast Valley**
- **Southwest Valley**
- **Northwest Valley**

the courses, with lush greens transporting golfers out of the desert and back to the places they left—only without the snow to cramp their games.

Arizona's rapid growth has changed that trend. Growth makes water an increasingly scarce commodity in a desert environment, which affects the types of design and landscaping used by course architects. Even architects who design more traditional styles tend to surround the fairways with desert landscaping. The Arizona Department of Water Resources allows courses in the Phoenix area to have 90 acres of primary turf and 30 more acres of rough turf, which has a lower water-application rate. Course designs in Arizona have to account for circumstances that differ wildly from those in other golf meccas such as Florida and the Carolinas. The hostile desert environment, the rocky soil, and restrictions on water use have forced course architects to become creative with placing turf. Desert target courses tend to be among the most challenging available, and they really test the skills of the average golfer. You should count on spending some time looking for your ball out among the cactuses and brush.

With roughly 200 golf courses within 50 miles of downtown Phoenix, your golfing choices are plentiful. Many great course architects are represented here—Gary Panks, David Graham, Tom Weiskopf, Jay Morrish, Robert Trent Jones Jr., Tom Fazio, Pete Dye, even Arnold Palmer.

The Valley's near-constant sunshine makes year-round golf a pleasant prospect. Granted, it's a little tough in the summertime, but that's also the time when course traffic eases up considerably, and bargains are the rule. Summer is the perfect time to play all the courses you can't afford to try during the pricey peak season.

The high season for golf in the Valley is from late December through April. The weather for golf is at its best then, with sunshine and mild temperatures. The influx of winter visitors, who vie with full-time residents for time on the links, makes demand even greater. Because the law of supply and demand is in effect, you'll pay the highest fees in winter. The low season runs from May through August, and avid golfers

Designed by Ted Robinson, the Ocotillo Golf Club features 27 holes.

Photo: Courtesy of Mesa Convention and Visitors Bureau

who don't mind the heat can find fees reduced greatly. The cost of the extra sunscreen you'll need will eat up only a small fraction of the greens fees' savings. Some courses have different fees for short-lived shoulder seasons between the high and low seasons. These fees are usually 'tweeners, not as high as the high-season fees but higher than low-season fees. Some courses charge less on weekdays, when demand is lower than on weekends. For golf-planning purposes, assume that a weekend is Friday, Saturday, and Sunday and that weekdays are Monday through Thursday. These price breaks are noted in the listings below. All fees listed include a golf cart, unless otherwise noted.

Golf course pricing has begun to follow the lead of the airlines. A typical golf course will often change rates depending upon volume and timing. The greens fees we list were the fees from late 2000 through the summer of 2001 and are intended to help you determine the range of prices out there. No course contacted would announce exact fees for the 2001 season and beyond, so assume that fees will be higher than those listed here. Although we attempt to give representative prices for each season, a number of courses did not have year-round pricing information available. When there's a gap in seasonal pricing information, you can determine a price range from the fees for the other seasons at that course. So, unless price is no object, always ask about fees when reserving your tee time.

There is no easy rule to follow when reserving your tee time. The earliest you can reserve a tee time on most crowded municipal courses is three days in advance. At Papago, easily the busiest Phoenix municipal course, no advance reservations are taken, so people camp out in their cars to be first in line when the course opens for the day. On the other hand, Encanto, another busy Phoenix municipal course, proudly boasts they'll get walk-ups on the course within a half-hour. Some of the high-end semiprivate courses will allow you to book a tee time a month in advance, but you'll pay a hefty reservation fee because if they're going to hold a time for you that long they want to make sure you'll show up. Demand is high on those courses, and they want to keep things flowing smoothly. Remember the seasonal nature of demand too. In summer, some courses change their tee-time reservation policies. The best advice is to call a week to two weeks before you plan a golf outing, find out the reservation system of the course at that time, and make your plans accordingly. For information on the Valley's well-known golf tournaments, see our Spectator Sports chapter.

Phoenix

Ahwatukee Country Club
12432 S. 48th St., Phoenix
• (480) 893-1161

Ahwatukee Country Club boasts mature landscaping on its par 72, 6073-yard course. Johnny Bulla of Phoenix designed and built it in 1972, at a time when Ahwatukee was way out in the desert. Phoenix has grown to envelop the course, but 550 eucalyptus trees, palms, and Aleppo pines cloister it off from noisy distractions. Play this one straight: The rough is really rough, the fairways are lined with houses, and besides the trees, there's some water along the way.

The food and beverage area of the 10,000-square-foot dining facility was recently remodeled, and there's a new locker room as well. The high season (November through April) greens fees are $49 on weekdays and $69 on weekends. No firm plans have been announced, but Ahwatukee hopes to become a members-only club for the high season. When and if that takes place, the club would be open to public play from May through October. That's just as well because Ahwatukee is a great low-season bargain, and presumably would remain so. People can play there May through September for $12, plus the cost of the cart.

Arizona Biltmore Country Club
2400 E. Missouri Ave., Phoenix
• (602) 955-9655

The Arizona Biltmore has represented the upper crust of Valley accommodations for most of the century, and the Biltmore's Adobe course has been part of the amenities since 1932. The Links course, equally topnotch, offers a more modern alternative to the Adobe. These are semiprivate courses, with resort guests having priority on tee times.

As you might suspect from its age, the Adobe is a traditional 18-hole course. The par 72, 6122-yard course features landscaping that's an extension of the hotel grounds' lush green-ery. The signature hole is the No. 3, a 423-yard par 4 that features water before the hole, a bunker to the right, and a pine tree to the left.

The par 71, 5726-yard Links course wraps around the outer edge of the Biltmore grounds and offers good views of Camelback Mountain and downtown Phoenix in the distance. Seven lakes add challenges to your game.

Amenities include a clubhouse, pro shop, driving range, and the resort hotel's restaurant and swimming pool. The greens fees, cart included, are $98 in high season (January through June), $63 in the shoulder season (September through December), and $38 in the low season (July through August).

Cave Creek Golf Course
15202 N. 19th Ave., Phoenix
• (602) 866-8076

Averaging about 100,000 rounds a year, Cave Creek Golf Course surpassed Papago Park as the most popular Phoenix municipal golf course in recent years. Like the other Phoenix courses, this is a traditional 18-hole course. Very unlike the other courses, this land was once a landfill reclamation project. Cave Creek runs through the middle of the course, and nearby hills and mountains add color. The 6,290-yard, par 72 course is difficult, with the toughest being the 450-yard, par 4 No. 8 hole.

The greens fee in high season (October through May) is $27 for Phoenix residents and $37 for nonresidents, golf cart included. In low season (June through September) the greens fee is $20 for residents, and $21 for nonresidents. There are also discounts for seniors and juniors, and a variety of other discounted fees. Amenities at Cave Creek include a clubhouse, a pro shop, a driving range, putting and chipping greens, and a snack bar.

Encanto Golf Course
2745 N. 15th Ave., Phoenix
• (602) 253-3963

Encanto Park offers its surrounding homes a bucolic and green reprieve from desert dwelling, so it's only natural that its golf course, enhanced by mature palm and salt cedar trees, would do the same. The par 70, 6,173-yard municipal course was designed by William P. Bell and is a favorite among local golfers. Completed in 1935, Encanto is billed as the third oldest golf course in Arizona. Encanto has level, wide fairways and a limited number of hazards. The ambiance is relaxed and amiable, a perfect place for the average golfer to just enjoy being out there knocking the ball around. The course features eight par 4s that are more than 377 yards. Half of those are the last four holes, which are 430, 413, 400, and 403 yards.

The greens fee in high season (October through May) is $28 for Phoenix residents and $38 for nonresidents, golf cart included. In low season (June through September) the greens fee is $21 for residents and $22 for nonresidents. There are also discounts for seniors and juniors and a variety of other discounted fees. In addition to its clubhouse, golf shop, driving range, practice area and lessons, Encanto has a swimming pool, tennis court, and a reasonably priced restaurant called Mulligan's. No credit cards are accepted at this course.

Maryvale Golf Course
5902 W. Indian School Rd., Phoenix
• **(623) 846-4022**

When you're driving by Maryvale Golf Course with the windows rolled down late on a summer's night, you'll feel the temperature go down dramatically. Nighttime irrigation of the grass on this 18-hole traditional municipal course produces the natural air conditioning. Of course, it helps that eucalyptus, cottonwood, and palm trees shade the course as well. And let's not forget that there's water on the course. Designed by William F. Bell (who also designed San Diego's Torrey Pines course), Maryvale is not nearly as busy as Phoenix's other municipal courses, which makes it both a bargain and a mellow experience. The toughest hole is No. 3, a par 4 that's 421 yards, but generally speaking this 6191-yard, par 72 course is good for all skill levels.

Maryvale's amenities include a clubhouse, a pro shop, a driving range, a practice area, lessons, and a snack bar. The city touts the course's junior golf school, where many of the state's golf pros learned the game. The greens fee in high season (October through May) is $35 for Phoenix residents and $37 for nonresidents, golf cart included. In low season (June through September) the greens fees are $11 in morning and $9 in the afternoon for residents and $12 in morning and $9 in afternoon for nonresidents. There are also discounts for seniors and juniors, and a variety of other discounted fees. Credit cards are not accepted at this course.

Papago Golf Course
5595 E. Moreland St., Phoenix
• **(602) 275-8428**

This 6613-yard course undoubtedly is Phoenix's most attractive municipal golf course; as a result, it's very busy. Golfers play about 85,000 to 90,000 rounds a year at Papago. And why not? It's one of the best municipal courses anywhere. With the red rocks of the Papago Buttes dominating the views, golfers know full well they're in the desert Southwest even though they're walking through a traditional, tree-lined course. Designed by William F. Bell, the course features wide, flowing fairways and large, rolling greens. It's playable but challenging for the average player, with demanding doglegs and interesting holes. For instance, the finishing hole, a par 4, 443-yarder, doglegs uphill to a wide green. Papago is also the home of the Phoenix Open qualifying round. Amenities include a clubhouse, a pro shop, a driving range, a practice area, lessons, and the Double Eagle Cafe.

The greens fee in high season (October through May) is $30 for Phoenix residents and $31 for nonresidents, golf cart included. In low season (June through September) the greens fee is $23 for residents and $24 for nonresidents. There are also discounts for seniors and juniors and a variety of other discounted fees. Credit cards are not accepted at this course.

The Raven Golf Club at South Mountain
3636 E. Baseline Rd., Phoenix
• **(480) 243-3636**

The Raven, designed by David Graham and Gary Panks, opened in November 1995 on what

INSIDERS' TIP
A number of courses offer price breaks for twilight rounds. Duffers leave work early, grab their clubs, and play until sunset. Some courses offer special rates in the morning, others in the late afternoon. The mornings are cooler, even a bit cold in the winter. In summer, the late afternoon will be very hot, but doable if you're a fanatic (and drink lots of water).

used to be farmland at the base of South Mountain. It has quickly earned a favorable reputation for its enjoyable course layout and top-of-the-line service that rivals members-only clubs. A 6264-yard, par 72 course, The Raven offers well-manicured, wall-to-wall grass in the Midwestern traditional golf style. More than 6,000 pine trees line the wide, undulating fairways, giving the golfer a sense of solitude. The Raven is very playable, with challenging holes. The par 3 7th hole is very intimidating. It has water and sand all the way down the left-hand side of the fairway. The 18th hole, a par 4, is one of the best finishing holes around. A lake sits in front of the green and to the right is a three-tiered waterfall. South Mountain rises in the background, making it scenic as well.

The Raven plays host to the Southwest Section of the PGA Championship, the Western States Tour Championship, and the Arizona Golf Association's State Stroke Play Championship.

Greens fees in high season (December 25 through May 17) are $175, cart included. In the low season (June 1 through August 31), they're 70. In the two shoulder seasons, greens fees are $115. Amenities include a pro shop, a locker facility, indoor and outdoor dining, a learning-performance center, an outdoor pavilion, a putting green, and a chipping area.

Southeast Valley

Dobson Ranch Golf Course
2155 S. Dobson Rd., Mesa
• **(480) 644-2270**

Dobson Ranch, sequestered in a suburban Mesa neighborhood, rivals Phoenix's Cave Creek and Papago Park courses as one of the busiest in the state. Built in 1972, this 6176-yard, par 72 course is a very traditional, very playable, and forgiving course. Dobson Ranch is well-groomed with fast, often undulating greens. The layout is open, but the course features many trees to make it more scenic in a traditional vein. It's also an easy course to walk. The 8th hole, sitting next to a creek that runs down the whole right side of the course, is the signature hole. The sloped green of this par 4 hole sits among bunkers on three sides.

The course features a golf shop, a clubhouse, lessons, putting greens, a chipping area, a lighted driving range, and the Ranchhouse restaurant. The greens fee in high season (November 1 through March 31) is $35, including

GOLF

Golf is a specialty of the big resorts in the Valley of the Sun.

Photo: Courtesy of Hyatt Regency

cart. In the shoulder season (April 1 through May 30), the fee is $28, and in the low season (June through October), it's $18. Credit cards are not accepted.

Karsten Golf Course at ASU
1125 E. Rio Salado Pkwy., Tempe
• (480) 921-8070

Karsten, opened in 1989, was designed by Pete Dye to accommodate players of all skill levels. Dye molded desolate land near the usually dry Salt River bottom into a stunning Scottish style links course, with rolling hills, plenty of bunkers, and water. The 6,200-yard, par 72 course is adjacent to Tempe's Town Lake, a project that reclaimed the river bottom for use as an urban lake. Views of the manmade lake add beauty to the surroundings, which already provide a great view of ASU's Sun Devil Stadium leaning against A Mountain. With water lining the left-hand side, bunkers on the right-hand side and water on the approach, the 18th hole has a lot of character and has become a favorite.

Karsten serves as the practice facility for ASU's men's and women's golf teams and hosts NCAA and other regional championships. The amenities include a clubhouse and golf shop, a driving range and practice area, a private dining room, lessons, and the Trophy Room restaurant. In addition, the staff stresses service, treating players well in the fashion of the best resort courses.

Greens fees, golf cart included, in high season (January through April) are $88. In low season (June through September) they're $25. In the shoulder seasons, they're $45. Fees go up $10 for weekend (Friday through Sunday) play.

Ken McDonald Golf Course
800 E. Divot Dr., Tempe
• (480) 350-5250

Ken McDonald Golf Course is a traditional, municipal golf course in Tempe. As such, it sees quite a bit of use; it can host more than 98,700 rounds a year. This course prides itself on running a tight ship. Despite the volume of players, tee times are the times you will be hitting the ball off the first tee. The 6316-yard, par 72 course is like a little park tucked away in a suburban development. McDonald is so unassuming it shares a parking lot with the Tempe YMCA. The flat layout is easy to walk, and the tree-lined fairways make it desirable to do so. Playing here is not overly demanding either. The landing areas off the tees are relatively generous. One of the more interesting holes is No. 17, a par 3. There is water to the right, bunkers to both left and right, and the green undulates. This is no cheap shot.

Tempe residents have preference in reserving tee times. Greens fees, including golf carts, are $19 for residents, and $28 for nonresidents in the high season (November 1 through April 30). They are $11, and $20 in low season (May 1 through October 31).

The amenities include a pro shop, a clubhouse, lessons, club repair, practice areas, two putting greens, a chipping green, dining facilities, and Pete's 19th Hole snack shop.

Ocotillo Golf Club
3751 S. Clubhouse Dr., Chandler
• (480) 917-6660,
(888) 624-8899

A basic description of Ocotillo Golf Club would mention water, houses, and grass. Ocotillo's 27 holes—three separate nines called Blue, White, and Gold—feature 27 miles of shoreline. The nines are built on a traditional design, with 23 of the 27 holes involving water and houses surrounding the perimeter. Designed by Ted Robinson, Ocotillo opened in 1986 as something of a break from the beat-you-up target courses. Although the water threatens, the fairways are wide. The Blue course is shortest but has the most water, while the Gold has the least, making for the safest and easiest passage. The White is the toughest of the three. The Blue-White combination is a 6180-yard, par 71; the White-Gold combination is a 6297-yard par 71; and the Gold-Blue combination is a 6379-yard, par 72.,

The 4th hole on the Gold course is a par 4 with water down the left side and water on the approach to the green. It's very pretty but

INSIDERS' TIP

Diehard golfers should book early morning tee times in the summer and take advantage of the summer rates, which are quite a bit lower than the high season. You can get a lot of golf in before it grows too hot, and you don't have to compete with crowds of winter visitors for a good tee time. And don't be shy about slaking your thirst from the drinking fountains around the course and when the beverage cart stops—bottled water is always a good choice.

not too forgiving. Similarly, the 4th hole (par 4) on the White course carries water off the tee and water off the second shot. With a waterfall to the left of the green and the clubhouse behind the green to the right, this is the prettiest hole on the course. And guess what the 8th hole on the Blue course features? More water. It's a par 4 with water down the right-hand side and more water that you have to cross twice before the green.

The greens fees are $115, golf cart included, in the high season (January through March), $75 in the shoulder seasons (mid-April through May, October through December), and $45 in the low season (June through September).

Ocotillo has a 28,000-square-foot clubhouse facility that includes a restaurant, outdoor dining area, and special-events pavilion. The amenities also include a golf shop, lessons, a putting green, and a full driving range.

Sheraton San Marcos Golf Resort
100 N. Dakota St., Chandler
• (480) 963-3358

The San Marcos has a claim to being the oldest golf course in Arizona because its original nine, which is now where the Chandler Public Library sits, was built back in 1912 by Harry Collis and Will Robinson. The current 18-hole golf course is ancient by Arizona standards, too, having been opened by Collis in 1922. The San Marcos was a ritzy getaway when such celebrities as Fred Astaire, Bing Crosby, Errol Flynn, Clark Gable, and Jimmy Stewart played here in their heyday. Even Al Capone played here.

The 6116-yard, par 72 course is a traditional, Midwestern style, built long before current water restrictions began to limit the amount of turf. Because of its age, it has a mature ambiance and plenty of grass and trees, such as salt cedar, eucalyptus, willow, and palm, that offer shade from the desert sun.

Greens fees, including cart, are $95 in high season (January through March), and they go down to $55 after 2 PM each day. In low season (June through August), fees are $32. In the spring shoulder season (April through May), the fees are $45, and $30 after 2 PM each day. Weekend fees (Friday through Saturday) go up by $10. Fees for the fall shoulder season (September through December) were unavailable. Hotel guests have first dibs on tee times. The amenities include a clubhouse, pro shop, driving range, putting and chipping greens, and a restaurant.

Toka Sticks Golf Club
6001 S. Power Rd., Mesa
• (480) 988-9405

Toka Sticks began as an Air Force golf course as part of Williams Air Force Base. The Gila River Indian Community bought the course in 1996 and renamed it after a traditional field-hockey game played by the women of the Pima tribe. The Pimas upgraded the course to the tune of $2 million, adding new cart paths and bunkers and sprucing up the greens. The 6194-

GOLF

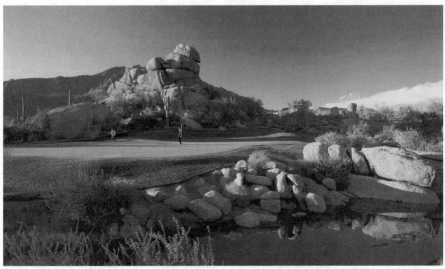

Desert golf combines spectacular beauty with challenging play.

Photo: Courtesy of The Boulders Resort

yard, par 72 traditional course was built in two phases. The Air Force built the first nine holes in the early 1950s, and the second nine, designed by civil engineers, were added in the early 1980s. The course is lined with trees such as eucalyptus and salt cedar. The toughest hole on the course—a par 5 of 541 yards—is saved for last. Amenities include a clubhouse, a pro shop, a driving range, putting and chipping greens, and a snack bar.

Greens fees are $50, including cart, in high season (December through March), $28 in the shoulder season (April through May), and $24 in low season (June through September).

Northeast Valley

The Golf Club at Eagle Mountain
14915 E. Eagle Mountain Pkwy.,
Fountain Hills
• (480) 816-1234

Eagle Mountain lets you look down on the East Valley as you golf. Perched as it is in the foothills of the McDowell Mountains, many prominent peaks add to the course's picturesque quality. Although Eagle Mountain is not a target course—there's grass from tee to green—its landscaping is nontraditional. When you're off the fairways and greens, you're in the desert where saguaros and desert scrub dot the surroundings. The 6191-yard, par 71 course, designed by Scott Miller and opened in January 1996, takes advantage of desert ravines to make the course, which wraps around Eagle Mountain, seem set apart rather than an expected part of the Eagle Mountain master-planned community. One of the best examples of the course's scenic charms is the closing hole. The tees are at the highest point on the golf course, with the green at the bottom of a slope. A lake and bunkers sit to the right, and the hole is framed by a dramatic view of Red Mountain.

Greens fees, including cart, in high season (December 26 through April 12) are $175 on weekends (Friday through Sunday), and $150 weekdays (Monday through Thursday). In the spring shoulder season (April through May), they are $125 on weekends, and $100 weekdays. In low season (mid May through Au-

gust), they are $100 on weekends, and $65 weekdays. In the fall shoulder season (September through December 15), fees are $135 on weekends and $105 weekdays.

The service and ambiance of Eagle Mountain are comparable to those of a private country club. The amenities include a clubhouse, a full practice facility, a golf shop, lessons, and The Grille restaurant.

Grayhawk Golf Club
8620 E. Thompson Peak Pkwy., Scottsdale
• (480) 502-1800

Grayhawk features two desert-style courses—Talon and Raptor. Set in the foothills in north Scottsdale, it offers views of the McDowell Mountains, Pinnacle Peak, and the Valley. The sheer beauty of the desert almost overwhelms the golf here. Talon, designed by David Graham and Gary Panks, is a 6391-yard, par 72 course. Despite its wide landing areas, Talon features 14 acres less grass than Raptor and plays more like a target course. Take for example, the 17th hole, a par 3 with an island green. Raptor, a 6620-yard, par 72 course designed by Tom Fazio, features its own challenges, such as the 16th hole. A lake and a creek run alongside this par 3 that plays anywhere from 185 yards to 200 yards. It's definitely challenging.

Greens fees, including cart, are $210 in high season (Christmas through Easter). Rates change almost every two weeks during the shoulder season from mid-April through early June, with the top rate being $170. In low season (June through September), the greens fees are $75 on weekends and $50 on weekdays.

Grayhawk features a 42,000-square-foot clubhouse, two dining areas, a golf shop, lessons, the Kostis-McCord Learning Center, and Phil's Grill. Phil Mickelson is the tour representative at Grayhawk.

Kierland Golf Club
15636 Clubgate Dr., Scottsdale
• (480) 922-9283

Kierland, which opened in 1996, features three nine-hole layouts—Ironwood, Acacia, and Mesquite—that golfers can combine for an 18-hole, par 72 round. Scott Miller designed a lush

GOLF

parkland with undulating greens for all three nines. Each layout, named for the predominant trees in its landscape, has its own identity. A wide-open topography allows for views of Pinnacle Peak, Camelback Mountain, and the McDowell Mountains. (In fact, the beginning holes are oriented to each of these landmarks.) Interestingly, Miller's design takes advantage of golden-colored native grasses—instead of

More than 6,000 trees line the fairways at the Raven Golf Club at South Mountain.

Photo: Courtesy of Mesa Convention and Visitors Bureau

rocks and cactus —to give strong definition to the fairways. So it looks like a target course but is less forgiving. With lakes at all three finishing holes and dry washes throughout the course, Kierland offers playability and drama. The yardages are: Ironwood-Acacia, 6247; Acacia-Mesquite, 6263; and Mesquite-Ironwood, 6298.

Amenities include a clubhouse, a pro shop, food and beverage service, a practice facility, and the *Golf Digest* Golf School under the direction of pros Mike and Sandy LaBauve.

Greens fees, including cart, are $125 in high season (January through April), $120 in the spring shoulder season (April through mid-June), $85 in the low season (mid-June through September), and $85 in the fall shoulder season (late September through early January).

The Phoenician Golf Club
6000 E. Camelback Rd., Scottsdale
• **(602) 423-2449**
Since luxury is the calling card of the Phoenician resort, no one should be surprised that its semiprivate, resort-golf experience is equally luxurious, featuring impeccably mani-

cured grass and gorgeous landscaping. The Phoenician has 27 holes, three distinct nines. These wrap around the resort so that they can be played in three 18-hole patterns. Before the Phoenician opened in 1988, a public course sat on this site, but it was completely redone for the resort. The Phoenician's facility opened with 18 holes designed by Homer Flint. Ted Robinson Sr. designed the other nine holes, which opened in 1996.

The Oasis Course lives up to its name with plenty of water features that please the eye but trouble golfers; the Desert Course is a challenging target course that skirts the base of Camelback Mountain; and the Canyon Course is lushly landscaped and undulates across the southern slope of Camelback. The three 18-hole combinations are each a par 70. The Oasis-Desert combination is 5842 yards; the Desert-Canyon combination is 5691 yards; and the Oasis-Canyon combination is 5839 yards.

The clubhouse and golf shop are as well-appointed as the resort's hotel. The package is completed by a driving range, club rentals, and lessons. Lessons can be augmented with the ASTAR video-analysis system, which offers a complex analysis of a player's swing.

Although winter is the high season, there's no set date when the winter rates begin because over-seeding with winter grass plays havoc with the schedule. Nonetheless, the high rates go into effect sometime after Labor Day. The high season rates, which include golf carts, are $150 for guests and $170 for nonguests. The low season rates, which kick in on June 21, are $90 for guests and $95 for nonguests. Hotel guests have tee-time priority.

Tournament Players Club of Scottsdale
17020 N. Hayden Rd., Scottsdale
• **(480) 585-4334**
• **www.playatpc.com**
As the home of the Phoenix Open, the Tournament Players Club of Scottsdale can be thought of as the premier professional challenge in the Valley. There are two courses at TPC—Stadium and Desert. The team of Tom Weiskopf and Jay Morrish designed the courses to take advantage of the desert setting and ex-

cellent views of the McDowell Mountains. Both courses feature lush fairways surrounded by desert landscaping and punctuated by lakes and bunkers. The 6049-yard, par 71 Stadium course is aptly named, using mounds and terracing to provide a stadium-like area for spectators to watch PGA Tour events such as the Phoenix Open. The Desert course, a 5339-yar, par 71, is more level than the Stadium course, and the greens are larger, making it more playable for the average golfer. Amenities include clubhouses, a golf shop, lessons, and the Grill Restaurant.

INSIDERS' TIP

Should you ever master all the Valley golf courses and grow bored with play, there is plenty more golf waiting to be played in Arizona. About 100 golf clubs await you outside the Valley of the Sun.

Stadium course greens fees, cart included, are $192 in high season (December to April 5); $192 in the high shoulder seasons (April 6 to May 3, October 19 to November 29); $160 in the low shoulder seasons (May 4 to May 31, August 31 to September 27, and October 12 to 18); and $85 in low season (June 1 to August 30).

Desert course greens fees, cart included, in high season (October 1 to May 3) are $40 for Maricopa County residents, and $50 for nonresidents. In the low season (May 4 to September 30), fees are $30 for Maricopa County residents, and $35 for nonresidents. There are also discounted rates for youngsters and seniors.

Troon North Golf Club
10320 E. Dynamite Blvd.,
Scottsdale
• **(480) 585-7700**

Troon North offers two courses—Monument and Pinnacle. Monument, the older of the courses, was designed by Tom Weiskopf and Jay Morrish before they went their separate ways. Weiskopf designed the Pinnacle course. Both of these courses are tough for the average player. *Golf Magazine* ranks Troon North among America's Top 100. It's ranked No. 1 in Arizona by *Golfweek* magazine.

Monument's flow through its 6636 yards is smooth, yet the par 72 course is a desert target style—very tough. Every hole presents a challenge. The 3rd hole is the Monument hole, a par 5 with a 25-foot tall boulder in the middle of the fairway. The ambiance—with views of the McDowell Mountains, Pinnacle Peak, and the Valley—convinces the golfer that the everyday world is far away. Pinnacle's front nine

are the most scenic holes at Troon North. For example, the 6th hole of this 6719-yard, par 72 course runs up the side of a hill where Pinnacle Peak dominates the background.

Troon North is a semi-private facility, and members have preference for booking tee times. Greens fees, including cart, are $215 in high season (January 15 through March) and $190 in the shoulder seasons (April through mid-June and September through October). In low season (mid-June through August), they're $140 Friday through Sunday and $85 Monday through Thursday. Troon also has a late-fall shoulder season (October 30 through January 28), when fees are $160.

The amenities include a clubhouse, a pro

In the shadow of Sun Devil Stadium, the Karsten Golf Course at ASU features Scottish-style links play.

Photo: Courtesy of Mesa Convention and Visitors Bureau

shop, a driving range, a practice area, lessons, dining facilities, conference rooms, and The Grill at Troon North.

Southwest Valley

The Wigwam Resort
451 N. Litchfield Rd.,
Litchfield Park
• **(623) 272-4653, (800) 909-4224**

The Wigwam Resort is another bastion of the old high life of Arizona resorts. Originally built as the private domain of Goodyear executives, the Wigwam is open to those who can pay the price for these elegantly rustic surroundings. And the same goes for its three golf courses. The Wigwam has earned *Golf Magazine*'s Silver Medal Resort honors and *Links Magazine*'s Best of Golf Award. In addition, the Gold course is ranked as the top resort course on *Golf Digest's* list of Arizona's Best Courses.

The Gold course features a traditional layout designed by Robert Trent Jones Sr. A 6492-yard, par 72 course, the Gold is a tough one to play with elevated greens, narrow landing areas, bunkers, and water. At 6030 yards, the par 72 Blue course is the shortest layout at the Wigwam, but that doesn't make it the easiest. It's a fairly unforgiving links-style course. The 6277-yard, par 70 Red course was designed by Arizona's Robert "Red" Lawrence and features lakes, creeks, and huge greens. It's a traditional layout that is something like comfort food compared with the others, although it still presents a challenge.

The Gold's greens fees are $110 in high season (January through April), $85 in the shoulder season (September 15 through January 7), and $80 in low season (April through August). The Blue's greens fees are $100 in high season, $75 in the shoulder season, and $70 in the low season. The Red's fees are $110 in high season, $85 in the shoulder season, and $80 in the low season. All fees include carts. Amenities include a clubhouse, pro shop, driving range, and practice area as well as tennis courts, dining facilities, and lessons.

INSIDERS' TIP

The Valley has plenty of golf stores but our favorite is In Celebration of Golf, (480) 951-4444, 7001 N. Scottsdale Rd., Ste. 172, Scottsdale. The décor compares favorably with the most stylish stores in Scottsdale. Of course they have men's and women's golf apparel, playing equipment, books, and indoor practice facilities, but they also have unusual golf antiques and even fine art with golfing themes. If you're looking for the right wallpaper for your study (complete with golf imagery), the home furnishings section has exactly what you're looking for. Be forewarned that if you go, you'll probably end up buying something.

Northwest Valley

The Legend at Arrowhead
21027 N. 67th Ave., Glendale
• (623) 561-1902

Arnold Palmer and Ed Seay designed this traditional, grass-from-tee-to-green course as the centerpiece of the master-planned Arrowhead Ranch community in Glendale. This relatively new area is booming because its gray-black hills and generous lots keep suburbia looking like the desert. Although The Legend is a traditional course featuring six lakes, it is built on those dark hills and can't be mistaken for a Midwestern-style course. This 6013-yard, par 72 course becomes much more difficult when played from the championship tees (7005 yards), but if you choose your tee boxes well, it can be very enjoyable. In fact, golf doesn't get any better than the 5th hole. It's a 426-yard, par 4 that's played from elevated tees to an hourglass-shaped green with water on the right.

Greens fees, cart included, in the high season (January through March) are $175 on weekends and $155 on weekdays. In the shoulder season (April through May), they're $135 on the weekend and $115 on weekdays. In the low season (June through September), they're $80. Amenities include a clubhouse, a pro shop, lessons, a driving range, and a practice area.

GOLF

Spectator Sports

Fall, winter, spring, or summer, sports fans won't have any trouble getting their fill of good things to see in Phoenix and the Valley of the Sun. The market is one of the few in the country to boast four big-league franchises—football's Arizona Cardinals, baseball's Arizona Diamondbacks, hockey's Phoenix Coyotes, and basketball's Phoenix Suns. In addition, the Valley had the honor of hosting Super Bowl XXX in 1996 and the NBA All-Star Game in 1995.

The Valley also welcomes Major League Baseball's Anaheim Angels, Oakland Athletics, Milwaukee Brewers, Chicago Cubs, San Francisco Giants, Seattle Mariners, and San Diego Padres for spring training in the Cactus League. The other teams in the league—the Diamondbacks, Colorado Rockies, and Chicago White Sox—play their home games in Tucson but are frequently in the Valley for games against their league opponents.

Bubbling just below that level in the Valley's sea of sports is the WNBA franchise, the Phoenix Mercury, and the two-time Arena Football champions, the Arizona Rattlers. Meanwhile, Major League Baseball's Arizona Fall Baseball League lets Valley dwellers and winter visitors get a peek at up-and-coming baseball players.

In addition to the professional sports, Arizona State University's Sun Devils field competitive teams in football (men's), basketball (men's and women's), baseball (men's) and fast-pitch softball (women's).

The Valley is also home to such annual events as the Phoenix Open, a natural in a place where golf is the preeminent participation sport, and the Fiesta Bowl, which hosted the first unified national college championship game in 1999. America West Arena in Phoenix was part of March Madness when it hosted the NCAA Western Regional tournament in 1999.

The Valley's biggest sports fiasco may well have been the Phoenix Grand Prix. All it did was tear up the streets of downtown Phoenix for weeks at a time in 1990 and 1991 before it moved out of town for lack of local interest. However, the Valley loves auto racing, and crowds of 100,000 show up on race day for the NASCAR Winston Cup Dura-Lube 500 at the relatively remote Phoenix International Raceway on the far west side of the Valley.

Arena Football

Arizona Rattlers
America West Arena,
201 E. Jefferson St., Phoenix
• **(602) 514-8300**
• **www.azrattlers.com**
    Ever since America West Arena

opened in 1992, the expansion team Arizona Rattlers have been a major participant in the Arena Football League. Football purists may scoff at the indoor arena game, which is played on a 50-yard field with eight players on the field, but tickets are very affordable and you will appreciate sitting in air-conditioned comfort. Players play offense and defense with the exception of the kicker, quarterback, offensive specialist, kick returner, and two defensive specialists. However, the speedy, offense-oriented contests pack about 16,000 fans into the arena on summer weekends. The off-field atmosphere is raucous, with lots of flashing lights, ear-splitting music, and sound effects. There are plenty of giveaways and half-time and pre-game festivities that feature the team mascot, Fang, a fierce-looking biker who rides into the arena on a huge Harley to rev up the crowd's response (and his motorcycle).

The Rattlers have played under coach Danny White, the former Dallas Cowboys quarterback, since their inception and have won two league championships (1994 and 1997). Rattlers' gear is available at the Team Shop in the arena. The team is involved in many community events and sponsors a flag-football tournament.

The Rattlers' 14-game season begins in May and ends in August. Season-ticket rates range from $75 to $295, which includes a preseason game and the first shot at buying playoff tickets. Single-game tickets range from $10 to $38.

Auto Racing

Firebird International Raceway
20000 Maricopa Rd., Chandler
• **(602) 266-0200**
• **www.firbirderaceway.com**

Drag racing rules at Firebird. Funny cars and jet dragsters roar around one of three tracks so the events are noisy and festive. The east track is 1.25 miles long and features 10 turns. The west track is 1.1 miles long with 11 turns. The Firebird Course is 1.6 miles with 14 turns. Drag racing is held most Friday nights throughout the year. Major annual events at Firebird include the NHRA National Time Trials, the NHRA ATSCO Nationals and the NHRA World Series of Drag Racing. Adjacent Firebird Lake also is the site of drag-boat racing. Admission varies with events. Firebird Raceway is

easily accessible from Interstate10, just west of the Maricopa Road exit.

Phoenix International Raceway
7602 S. 115th Ave., Phoenix
• **(602) 252-3833**
• **phoenixintlraceway.com**

Situated in view of the ruggedly gorgeous Estrella Mountains, Phoenix International Raceway serves as a setting for many TV commercials that highlight cars moving against a pristine desert backdrop. The track is in use 300 or more days a year for auto testing, driving schools, commercials, and, especially, the racing events.

The raceway, described as the fastest 1-mile oval in the world, opened in 1964 in an unincorporated part of Maricopa County about 30 miles west of downtown Phoenix. Back then its location was way, way out in the Valley, and even now, with tendrils of development creeping out that way, it remains an isolated desert experience. The NASCAR Winston Cup Dura-Lube 500, held in late October, draws about 100,000 people to the D-shaped track. The Indy Racing League's Dura-Lube 200 in mid-March draws about 35,000, as does the Skoal Bandit Racing Copper World Classic in late January. Schedules are available at the track's office in Phoenix. For ticket information, call (602) 252-2227.

To reach the track from Phoenix, go west on I-10 to 115th Avenue. Head south on 115th about 4 miles until 115th Avenue takes a turn to the west into Baseline Road.

Baseball

Arizona Diamondbacks
Bank One Ballpark, 401 E. Jefferson St., Phoenix
• **(602) 462-6500**
• **www.azdiamondbacks.com**

The Diamondbacks' story began with the Phoenix Suns basketball team. Suns owner Jerry Colangelo announced in 1993, the year his basketball team went to the NBA finals, that he

---

INSIDERS' TIP

As almost anywhere, parking is something of a hassle when you're trying to reach a sporting event. Football tailgaters have the right idea. Get to the event early and make a day of it. Most facilities have concession stands and restaurants to make it easier to pass the time before the event. If you're heading to Cardinals or Sun Devils events, there are numerous restaurants, taverns, and coffee shops within walking distance in downtown Tempe where you can enjoy a meal before or after the game. The same holds true for America West Arena and Bank One Ballpark events in downtown Phoenix.

SPECTATOR SPORTS

was putting together an ownership group to try to purchase a Major League Baseball franchise for Phoenix. In 1995, Colangelo received the franchise, which would start play in 1998.

Almost immediately, work began on Bank One Ballpark (affectionately dubbed BOB), a retractable-roof stadium with a natural-grass playing surface. It was built in the current MLB fashion to offer the old-time, single-use baseball stadium feel. At the same time, it is air-conditioned to make a capacity crowd of 48,569 comfortable during the summertime game schedule. BOB even boasts a swimming pool for patrons who want to stay wet during a game. The opening of the roof even has its own dramatic theme music. In 2000, the team revealed its mascot, D. Baxter Bobcat.

When former New York Yankees coach Buck Showalter signed on in 1995, 18 months before the Diamondbacks would play their first game, the tone was set for good, fundamental baseball. Alas, it was still an expansion team despite having a team of talented veterans—including gold glover Matt Williams at third base and former St. Louis ace Andy Benes pitching—and exciting prospects such as former Olympic first baseman Travis Lee. The Diamondbacks stuck to the bottom of the National League West division in 1998. The next year, the D-Backs, with the help of demon pitcher Randy Johnson, took the National League's Western Division Championship. For a new team, the Diamondbacks have quickly moved to the top ranks of the majors.

Season tickets range from $332 for the uppermost level to $4,565 for the Clubhouse level. Single-game tickets range from $4 to $55.

There are approximately 33,600 parking spaces available within a 15-minute walk of BOB, which (using a 1.5 persons per car average) would seem to mean there's enough parking for everyone. However, BOB is downtown. People work there on most days and thus take up parking spaces. The Diamondbacks' home schedule also will overlap with home games of the Phoenix Suns, Phoenix Coyotes, Phoenix Mercury, and Arizona Rattlers on many nights, which means an additional 10,000 to 19,000

Getting Tickets

TicketMaster is the major agency offering off-site sales of tickets to sporting events.

Most of the sports arenas also have their own box offices that will be happy to sell you tickets if they have them. When events are sold out, many people can locate seats by asking around and networking with coworkers who own tickets that they are unable to use. Etiquette demands that you repay the owner for the face value of the tickets. Be wary that this rule goes away during playoffs and important rivalry games. Then the value of the tickets is what the market will bear.

TicketMaster does add fees for credit-card service over the phone and for mailing. You can reach TicketMaster at (480) 784-4444.

Ticket Brokers

Don't call them scalpers, please. Reselling tickets at a handsome markup, a practice that's known as scalping elsewhere, is perfectly legal in Arizona. You just can't do it right outside the venue itself. So ticket brokers tend to park themselves about a block from any venue, asking passersby if they need to buy or sell tickets. If the brokers are overstocked, their markup tends to go down as the event gets closer.

Are those tickets real or counterfeit, though? There is no way to protect yourself from a ripoff in a situation like that. If you can't get tickets from the venue itself (either because it doesn't have the seats you want or because the show or game is sold out), you'll be better off visiting one of the 20 or so ticket brokers who are listed in the Phoenix Yellow Pages. There'll be someone at their offices who's accountable if your tickets turn out to be counterfeits.

A $3.50 ticket to a sold-out 1998 Arizona Diamondbacks vs. the Seattle Mariners game went for $15 at one of these ticket brokers' offices. We didn't feel scalped. We got to see Ken Griffey Jr. hit a home run after all.

people downtown on some game nights. Though parking hassles have been minimal, you should allow for extra time to park if you want to arrive in time for the national anthem. Shuttle buses operate from Park Central Mall. The shuttle fare is $3 per person.

The best way to get there from outlying areas is to take I-10 to the Seventh Street exit and head south to Washington Street. Then head west to Fourth Street, where BOB sits just one block south. Canny drivers will avoid parking headaches by getting downtown early and parking blocks away from the stadium. The walk will help burn off some of those hot dogs.

Cactus League
120 N. Center St., Mesa
• (480) 827-4700

The Cactus League is Arizona's wing of Major League Baseball's spring training. Ten teams begin working out in Arizona in the last week of February, which still counts as winter in all but baseball's peculiar logic. They play exhibition games against one another through March, when the regular season begins.

Compared with Florida, where the other 20 MLB teams take their training, Arizona is a relative newcomer. The Cactus League's roots stretch back to 1947 when the Cleveland Indians moved their spring training to Tucson and convinced the San Francisco Giants to hold theirs in Phoenix. In 1951, Del Webb, the builder who created Sun City, was a co-owner of the New York Yankees and had his team switch places with the Giants for one season of spring training. In 1952, the Chicago Cubs, dissatisfied with spring training on Catalina Island where they could get no other teams to come, settled in the Valley for spring training.

For most of the '50s and '60s, the Cactus League was anchored by the Indians, Giants, and Cubs, with a number of other teams, including the Boston Red Sox, Baltimore Orioles, and Houston Colt .45s, filling in a fourth slot. With the 1969 expansion, the Seattle Pilots and the San Diego Padres settled into the Cactus League as well. (Both are still in the league, although the Pilots are now known as the Milwaukee Brewers.) The league had eight teams for most of the '70s and '80s, seven in the Valley and one in Tucson.

In the late '80s, the original Cactus League team, the Cleveland Indians, packed its bags and moved to Florida, and the Arizona league looked in serious danger of collapse as Florida had passed legislation to make it more attractive for teams to hold spring training there. Even the Cubs, whose games were the highest-attended in spring training, were thinking of moving to the East Coast. A group of Valley boosters formed the Cactus League Association, and then-Gov. Rose Mofford created the Arizona Baseball Commission in efforts to keep spring training in Arizona.

With the addition of the Arizona Diamondbacks and Chicago White Sox, the Cactus League now stands at a healthy 10 teams in seven stadiums. The current teams have long-term leases, and all the stadiums are either new or have been renovated in the past decade.

The volunteer Cactus League Association says the economic impact of spring training on Arizona, thanks to the teams and fans who spend money here, is about $200 million annually.

Ticket information changes each spring. The Cactus League Association can provide league schedules and stadium locations, but has no hand in ticketing. For tickets, fans can call the individual teams or stadiums (see subsequent list), or Ticketmaster, (480) 784-4444, depending on which ticket agency covers games at a particular ballpark.

The league's current participants, their spring-training ballparks, and the phone numbers for each team's ticket office are:

Anaheim Angels, Tempe Diablo Stadium, 2200 W. Alameda Drive, Tempe, (480) 438-9300.

Arizona Diamondbacks and Chicago White Sox, Tucson Electric Park, 2400 E. Ajo Way, Tucson, (888) 683-3900.

Chicago Cubs, Hohokam Park, 1235 N. Center Street, Mesa, (480) 964-4467.

Colorado Rockies, Hi Corbett Field, E. Broadway Boulevard and Randolph Way, Tucson, (520) 327-9467.

Milwaukee Brewers, Maryvale Sports Complex, 51st Avenue and Indian School Road, Phoenix, (623) 247-7177.

Oakland Athletics, Phoenix Municipal

INSIDERS' TIP

Too many people forget that young children attend many sporting events and that little ears can hear adults spouting profanities. Most of the sporting venues have started taking a harder line in dealing with profanity, heckling, and general obnoxiousness. Why not check bad language at the door? Remember, it's just a game.

Phoenix: Sports Town USA

Why are Phoenix and the Valley of the Sun so big on sports? Is it something in the water? Is it the high proportion of Chicago-area transplants longing for their Bears, Bulls, Cubs, White Sox, and Blackhawks?

A cynic might say that the media here hyped sports into a big thing. The cynic would be right, but the media are just playing to the market.

Let's go in for a little pop psychology here and attribute the hold sports has on the Valley to the huge number of people who have relocated and are now seeking some kind of hook to make them feel Arizonan. Sports teams with their geographic names fill the bill easily. Relocating from the frozen north, many people feel like they're just camping out here in their initial years. As vast and spread out as it is, the Valley hardly seems settled if you've relocated from a megalopolis. With earning a living as their major preoccupation, many transplants have a hard time sinking roots in their communities. They buy the house and meet the neighbors, but the very architecture of homes built in the last two decades (the lack of front porches and cinder-block fences) combined with increasingly tight schedules keep casual neighborly contact—something you almost can't avoid back East—to a minimum. Although people often work hard to become part of their communities by forming neighborhood associations and block watches, the common denominators to conversations are often sports. Meet a stranger, and within three minutes one of you will remark about a sports team with a comment like, "How about those D-Backs last night!" Besides, people working that hard at everything need something to distract them.

When the Phoenix Suns landed Charles Barkley in 1992 and catalyzed the team to only its second run to the NBA finals, for the first time in almost anyone's memory strangers in the Valley had something to talk about besides the weather. The phrase "How about those Suns?" had the power to form instant bonds. When a Suns game was on, particularly once the playoffs started, everyone seemed to be tuned to KTAR listening to play-by-play announcer Al McCoy. In fact, if you were sitting at an intersection with the car radio on, you could expect passing pedestrians to wave and ask for the score.

But not everybody was sold. Many people in the Valley revel in keeping their old allegiances. When the Suns met the Bulls in the finals, it was not uncommon to see Bulls banners on cars and homes, although there were many more "Go Suns" markings out there. This old allegiance thing crosses many lines. Some love life in the Valley, but they hang on to their old team as a link to their old home, even though they don't want to shovel snow anymore. Others see the Valley as just a stopping-off point in their lives, and they'll stick with whatever city they really care about.

The oddest of these are the longtime Valley dwellers, some of them natives, who refuse to switch allegiance from the Dallas Cowboys to the Arizona Cardinals, which, by the way, is the only Arizona big-league franchise that doesn't play in downtown Phoenix. They say that before the Cardinals got here in 1988, the Cowboys were the team they followed and they see Dallas as their home team. When the Cowboys play the Cardinals, the only home game sure to sell out in a Cardinals season, the Cowboys' fans envelop the Cards' red-garbed fans in a sea of blue.

However, even those nay-sayers are a testament to the sports obsession in the Valley. After the Suns' big run, forests of backboards, portable and permanent, popped up seemingly overnight in the acres of tiled-roof Valley developments.

Of course, the pop psychology goes out the window when you consider that there isn't much home-team identification when it comes to motor sports and golf, which are both big in the Valley sports scene. So there must be another factor (or factors) to the sports craze here.

One of them is the environment. With its almost perpetual sunshine and low humidity, the Valley is a comfortable place to play sports almost year round. Even in the dog days of the summer monsoon, evening recreation is tolerable. Golfers golf. Kids shoot hoops. Tennis courts jam. Soccer leagues fill playgrounds. Softballers and Little Leaguers play on their respective diamonds. That's not to mention swimming, running, skiing, snowboarding, and mountain biking, all of which have their own adherents. Many, many Valley dwellers are active in their leisure time, and their participation in sports tends to make them more interested in them. Add in couch potato sports watchers, who probably outnumber the active types, and you've got an extremely fertile field for sports obsession.

One of the interesting things about the Valley's sports nuttiness is that it's one of the few things that unites the average citizens with Phoenix's movers and shakers. Valley boosters have been obsessed with getting major sports events, such as the Super Bowl, to town for decades—at least since the formation of the committee that created the Fiesta Bowl in 1969. Although many average Joes resent the deals the movers and shakers cut with sports franchises to build stadiums and arenas, many more follow the games.

In fact, the downtown redevelopment of Phoenix has hinged on the Suns' popularity. When owner Jerry Colangelo moved the team to its downtown America West Arena digs in 1992, smaller entrepreneurs began to see the value in opening such businesses as sports bars and restaurants downtown. The success of the Suns put Colangelo in the position to be the linchpin in turning the Winnipeg Jets NHL franchise into the Phoenix Coyotes, and to lure Major League Baseball here, making the Valley one of the few markets with four major-league teams. Colangelo also got Phoenix in on the ground floor of the WNBA, which seems likely to be a league of the future. With both the baseball stadium and arena drawing thousands downtown, redevelopment is in full swing. So much development raised the question of whether the Valley community can support all these teams. Signs seem to point to yes.

So, yeah, Phoenix is a sports town. Most definitely.

Bank One Ballpark, BOB, even boasts a pool for spectators attending games.

Photo: Penny Kleingartner

SPECTATOR SPORTS

Stadium, 5999 E. Van Buren Street, Phoenix, (602) 392-0217.

San Diego Padres and Seattle Mariners, Peoria Sports Complex, 16101 N. 83rd Avenue, Peoria, (623) 878-4337.

San Francisco Giants, Scottsdale Stadium, 7408 E. Osborn Road, Scottsdale, (480) 990-7972.

MLB's Arizona Fall Baseball League
10201 S. 51st St., Phoenix
- **(602) 496-6700**

Compared with spring training and the Diamondbacks, the Fall League is a well-kept secret with a total attendance of about 50,000 people at 138 games. Here's your chance to see the stars of tomorrow play. The league is totally owned by Major League Baseball so that each of the 30 teams has a piece of it.

A developmental league that began in October of 1992, the Fall League is essentially an all-star league of double-A and triple-A players. Each MLB team sends six such prospects to the league, and they are assigned to one of the league's five teams. About 400 of the players from 1992 through 1997 graduated to the majors, including such stars as the Los Angeles Dodgers' Mike Piazza and the Boston Red Sox's Nomar Garciaparra. In 1994, the league drew its biggest crowds ever because of double-A player Michael Jordan, who had already made his name in some other sport.

The schedule is set by about the middle of June, and the games are played from the beginning of October through November. Game times are 1:05 PM and 7:05 PM. Season passes and schedule details are available through the league office. Plenty of walk-up tickets ($4 for adults, $3 for seniors and children) are available on game days at the individual stadiums.

The teams and their stadiums are:

Grand Canyon Rafters and Scottsdale Scorpions, Scottsdale Stadium, 7408 E. Osborn Road, Scottsdale, (480) 941-1930.

Maryvale Saguaros, Maryvale Baseball Park, 3600 N. 51st. Ave., Phoenix, (623) 247-2727.

Peoria Javelinas, Peoria Sports Complex, 16101 N. 83rd Avenue, Peoria, (623) 486-2800.

Phoenix Desert Dogs, Phoenix Municipal Stadium, 5999 E. Van Buren Street, Phoenix, (602) 681-9363.

Basketball

Phoenix Mercury
America West Arena, 201 E. Jefferson St., Phoenix
- **(602)514-8333**
- **www.mercury.com**

In 1997, the WNBA's inaugural year, the Phoenix Mercury professional women's basketball team won the Western Conference title. The team drew an average attendance of 13,703, tops in the eight-team league. Team owner Jerry Colangelo, confident that there was an untapped market in women's basketball, hired Cheryl Miller to be head coach and general manager of the Mercury. Miller was known for building winning records as a coach at USC from 1993 to 1995. The Mercury had a 16-12 record the first year.

Since then, the WNBA has seen more expansion with two new teams and a 30-game regular-season schedule. The playoffs also changed from single-game semifinal and final rounds to two best-of-three series.

Fans of the Mercury are noisy and festive, making these games a lot of fun to attend. They raise the roof whenever a team hero like the 6'8" center Maria Stepanova swooshes another three-pointer. Don't leave during the fourth quarter because the post-games shows led by Cheryl Miller are worth staying for. With the dramatic vocal skills of a born-preacher, Miller speaks to the Mercury fans about the upcoming games and you can feel the energy of the crowd as they stand and dance to the funky music that accompanies Miller.

Ticket prices range from $10 to $80 per game, while season tickets range from $135 to $1,200 on the floor. Season tickets include a preseason game and first dibs on post-season tickets. The ticket office can be reached at (602) 252-9622.

> ## INSIDERS' TIP
> If you ever cried while watching the movie, *Black Beauty*, or love the film, *The Black Stallion*, you need to visit the annual Scottsdale Arabian Horse Show in mid-February. The event features popular horse events like dressage, English pleasure, and hunger jumper, along with hundreds of booths selling fine art, jewelry, clothing, and collectibles. It all happens at West World, 16601 N. Pima Rd., Scottdale. Daily tickets are $10 for adults and $5 for the kids. Call (602) 483-8800 or (602) 515-1500.

SPECTATOR SPORTS

If you have front row seating at the Bank One Ballpark, you'll have special access through these doors.

Photo: Penny Kleingartner

Phoenix Suns
America West Arena, 201 E. Jefferson St.
- **(602) 379-7900**
- **www.nba.com/suns**

The Phoenix Suns opened up shop in 1968 as an NBA expansion franchise, the first big-league club in Phoenix. Befitting an expansion franchise, their first few seasons were terrible. Their bad luck didn't end with a 16-66 mark in their first season. Thanks to the last-place finish, the Suns had the opportunity to flip a coin with expansion mates the Milwaukee Bucks to decide who would get the No. 1 pick in the 1969 draft. The Bucks won the toss and got Lew Alcindor (soon to be much better known as Kareem Abdul-Jabbar). In 1971, he led the

Bucks to the NBA Championship. The Suns are still waiting for their turn.

The team made a run to the finals in the 1975–76 season, parlaying up a 42–40 season record. When they met the Boston Celtics in the finals, the series was tied after four games. The Suns took Game 5 to triple overtime at the Boston Garden before losing to the Celtics. They lost the series in the next game. The NBA finals didn't see another triple overtime game for 17 years, until (guess who?) the Phoenix Suns met the Chicago Bulls in 1993. Although the Suns, led by the irrepressible Charles Barkley, won the triple overtime this time, the Bulls still prevailed in six games thanks to Michael Jordan. The list of impressive Suns players goes on to include Kevin Johnson, Dan Majerle, and current star Jason Kidd, a recent captain on the U.S. Olympic team.

The Suns have sold out America West Arena's 19,023 basketball seats ever since the arena was opened in the fall of 1992. Tickets range from $15 in the uppermost seats to $65 in the lower bowl, while club seats go for $90 per game. Season tickets range from $500 in the uppermost seats to four digits for the club seats. Season tickets include a subscription to *Fast Break* magazine and dibs on the post-season tickets. The Suns ticket office can be reached at (602) 379-7867.

College Sports

Arizona State University Sun Devils
Ticket Office, Sun Devil Stadium, Stadium Dr., Tempe
- **(480) 965-6006**

When the Sun Devils football team made its 1996 run to the Rose Bowl, it captivated the Valley, often outdrawing the NFL's Cardinals in the same stadium each fall weekend. Average home-game attendance was 63,884 that year.

The university's athletics programs have been an important part of the Valley's spectator sports spectrum since their inception. As is the case with most sports programs, the men's ball teams—football, basketball, and baseball—have the highest profile. However, there is a strong following for the school's women's basketball and softball teams as well.

ASU has 21 varsity sports and has won 129 total national championships, including 11 in women's golf and 5 in baseball. Former Sun Devils include "Mr. October" Reggie Jackson, former Dallas Cowboys quarterback and current Arizona Rattlers coach Danny White, and golfer Heather Farr, who died in 1993.

Football, far and away, is the dominant sport in terms of fan support and can fill Sun Devil Stadium's 73,379 seats. (Somehow they squeezed 74,963 people in to see ASU beat California, 35–7, on November 9, 1996.) The annual game with arch rival University of Ari-

zona is one of the most spirited and competitive events in college football.

Men's and women's basketball teams play at the University Activity Center, a 14,198-seat facility that was built in 1974 at a cost of $8 million. Baseball players try to knock it out of the park at Packard Stadium, a 7,875-capacity ballpark built in 1974. Softball pitchers do their windmill windup at Sun Devil Club Stadium, a 600-seat field. Track and field events take place at the Sun Angel Stadium/Joe Selleh Track, which has a 5,000-seat grandstand and movable bleachers that can accommodate another 4,000 for big events such as the annual Sun Angel Track Classic. There's an aquatic center for the swimming teams, and Karsten Golf Course at ASU gives the golf teams dedicated space for practice. The Sun Devil Ticket Office has information on all sports tickets at ASU.

Tostitos Fiesta Bowl
120 S. Ash Ave., Tempe
- **(480) 350-0900**
- **www.fiesta-bowl.com**

The Fiesta Bowl is part of the College Football Bowl Alliance, formed in 1997, to create a system to guarantee a true national championship game each year. The championship game rotates among the four members of the alliance, which, besides the Fiesta Bowl, includes the Sugar, Orange, and Rose Bowls.

The idea that the Valley should have a football bowl game was first floated in a speech by ASU president B. Homer Durham at an athletic awards banquet in 1968. Boosters seized on the idea and formed a group called the Arizona Sports Foundation. They prepared a pitch that emphasized that the Rose Bowl was the only bowl game being played outside of the South, that Arizona's climate would be a natural ally in the game's success and that a number of worthy Western Athletic Conference teams had been overlooked by the existing bowls. They also framed it as a charity event that would aid the fight against drug abuse. They made the pitch to the NCAA in 1970 and were turned down. The next year, though, the NCAA gave its approval.

The first Fiesta Bowl was played December

INSIDERS' TIP

Looking for baseball tickets? The Arizona Diamondbacks release 400 tickets on game days that sell for $1 each. The bargain pricing helps reduce scalping outside the ballpark but the seats are placed way up in the stratosphere, so bring binoculars if you have them. You'll have to pick these tickets up in person, so call first for details: (602) 462-6500.

SPECTATOR SPORTS

Best Seats In the House: Valley Sports Bars

The big game you wanted to see sold out? Tickets too expensive? Don't get angry, get smart! There's an inexpensive way to see most of the Valley games, and you're guaranteed a chance to get a good seat.

As a big time sports town, Phoenix and the Valley have a wide array of big-time sports bars. These are the friendly lounges that special-ize in sports as much as they do in pouring beverages and serving food. The atmosphere is always convivial and it's easy to make friends. After all, you all have the same thing in common—you're there for the games.

These cordial venues not only have immense video screens, they also have many of them, allowing the lucky viewers to watch all the college football games at the same time. With the advent of satellite dish technology, sports bars now have access to an unbelievable amount of sports action from around the country and from across the globe. In addition to the expected football, baseball, basketball, and hockey, you can also watch events like motor sports, skydiving, skate boarding, and even sumo wrestling from Japan. And they even rerun old games from years past so you can still watch your sport when it is out of season.

A few bars do charge a cover, but in return, you'll usually find nicer munchies and an upscale atmosphere. During the regular Monday Night football games, many sports bars host trivia contests and games of skill. You might find yourself throwing a nerf football at a basket across the room in hopes of getting a free appetizer or trying to predict the score for the next quarter.

The pleasures of the sports bar are many. The seats are always good. Beers by the bottle far exceed the quantity (and quality) of the offerings at the local stadiums and are far cheaper. Peanuts and assorted munchies are often free at the lounge and you'll have a have an entire menu at your fingertips for dining during the game. Perhaps you'll order up some hot wings or nachos as an appetizer—the options are extensive. You also can pay with a credit card. (Try asking the peanut vendor at the game to charge it!)

Perhaps the best thing about watching the game with other people at the bar is the feeling of camaraderie. You can cheer together and boo as a group. Like a good joke, the pleasures of the game are heightened when shared.

Go ahead and look closely at the those shots of the fans at the game. They look a little bit hot, don't they? Well, you're sitting in air-conditioned comfort in August watching the same game. So tip your glass in their direction and sit back with your buddies and enjoy the game.

Big Screens and Good Times

Ahwatukee

Famous Sam's Restaurant and Sports Bar
4142 E. Chandler Blvd.
(480) 706-5564

The Sports Bar, Pointe South Mountain Resort
7777 S. Pointe Parkway
(602) 431-6476

Shannon's Grill
1334 E. Chandler Blvd.
(480) 283-8750

The Vine Tavern & Eatery
4855 E. Warner Rd.
(480) 893-6525

(Continued on next page)

Cave Creek

Harold's Cave Creek Corral
6895 E. Cave Creek Rd.
(480) 893-6525

Chandler

Damon's
7450 W. Chandler Blvd.
(480) 961-7427

Draft House Sports Café
393 W. Warner Rd.
(480) 963-5520

Famous Sam's Restaurant & Sports Bar
940 N. Alma School Rd.
(480) 812-1177

First Round Draft
7200 W. Chandler Blvd.
(480) 961-3080

Gallagher's
2050 N. Alma School Rd.
(480) 963-0093

Hitts Sports Bar & Grill
6045 W. Chandler Blvd.
(480) 961-4488

The Stadium Club
2060 W. Chandler Blvd.
(480) 963-3866

Downtown Phoenix

America's Original Sports Bar
455 N. Third St.
(602) 252-2502

Cooper's Town
101 E. Jackson St.
(602) 253-7337

Jackson's On Third
245 E. Jackson St.
(602) 254-5303

Majerle's
44 N. Second St.
(602) 253-9004

Gilbert

Champions Sports Saloon
211 N. Gilbert Rd.
(480) 545-9669

The Dugout
3861 E. Baseline Rd.
(480) 497-0018

Famous Sam's Restaurant & Sports Bar
720 W. Ray Rd.
(480) 899-9804

First Round Draft
1520 W. Warner Rd.
(480) 497-2445

Mesquite Grill & Sports Bar
74 W. Baseline Rd.
(480) 892-0807

Mesa

Benchwarmers Grill
801 S. Power Rd.
(480) 854-8670

Famous Sam's Restaurant & Sports Bar
2860 E. Main St.
(480) 924-1305
430 N. Power Rd.
(480) 854-9400
2730 E. Baseline Rd.
(480) 497-1252

Papilions Too! Sports Bar & Restaurant
525 S. Gilbert Rd.
(480) 834-7680

Sluggo's Sports Grill
161 N. Centennial Way
(480) 844-8448

Three Cheers
5750 E. Main St.
(480) 985-1244

The Vine Tavern & Eatery
6110 E. Main St.
(480) 396-2472

Scottsdale

Bleacher's Sports Grill
6949 E. Shea Blvd.
(480) 948-9710

Brennan's Sports Bar
13610 N. Scottsdale Rd.
(480) 951-8837

Famous Sam's Sports Bar
7134 E. Thomas Rd.
(480) 994-4488

Goldie's Neighborhood Sports Vafe
10135 E. Via Linda
(480) 451-6269

J.J.'s Sports Cantina
409 N. Scottsdale Rd.
(480) 990-3477

Stooges Sports Pub
7901 E. Thomas Rd.
(480) 990-1114

Tempe

Ball Park Pub
1855 E. Guadalupe Rd.
(480) 838-9585

Champions Sports Bar
1825 E. Apache Blvd.
(480) 966-2896

Doc & Eddy's
909 E. Minton Dr.
(480) 831-0635

McDuffy's
230 W. Fifth St.
(480) 966-3490

Philly's Sports Bar & Grill
1826 N. Scottsdale Rd.
(480) 946-6666

Prankster's Gar & Brill
1024 E. Broadway Rd.
(480) 967-8875

SixShooters Sports Bar and Grill
705 S. Rural Rd.
(480) 551-6820

Skip & Jan's Sports Bar
7700 S. Priest Dr.
(480) 598-8611

The Vine Tavern & Eatery
801 E. Apache Blvd.
(480) 894-2662
975 E. Elliot Rd.
(480) 730-6313

West Valley

Max's Restaurant & Sports Lounge
6727 N. 47th Ave., Glendale
(623) 937-1671

SPECTATOR SPORTS

27, 1971, with ASU beating Florida State before a crowd of 51,098. CBS televised the Fiesta Bowl from 1974–77 and NBC took over in 1978. Over the years, the Fiesta Bowl spawned dozens of auxiliary events including the Fiesta Bowl Parade, four tennis events, a three-on-three basketball tournament, and a gigantic New Year's block party in downtown Tempe. In 1987, the Fiesta Bowl pitted top-ranked Miami against second-ranked Penn State in a national championship that sold out the stadium with a crowd of 73,098 and a television audience of 70 million. The Fiesta Bowl played host to the first unified National Championship Game in 1999, at Arizona State University's Sun Devil Stadium. Ticket and event information is available by calling (480) 350-0911.

Dog Racing

Phoenix Greyhound Park
3801 E. Washington St., Phoenix
• (602) 273-7181
Even people who never bet on the dogs can enjoy an evening out at Phoenix Greyhound Park. The ambiance at the clubhouse restaurant, with excellent views of the track and tableside TVs for watching the races and offtrack races around the country, is comfortable and, well, club-like. Dinners are buffet-style and a bargain at $10.95, and servers can even explain the betting to novices. If you choose instead to sit out in the grandstands, the trackside cafe is your food option.

The track was established in 1954 and underwent a $20 million renovation in 1990. The quarter-mile track is used for both 550-yard and 680-yard races all year long. (The track is only closed on Christmas Eve and Christmas.) Races from other tracks are also piped in, and off-track wagers are taken.

Admission is $3 for the air-conditioned clubhouse, and $1 for the grandstand. General parking is free every day. On Thursday through Sunday, valet parking is available for $2, and preferred parking close to the clubhouse is $1.

Football

Arizona Cardinals
8701 S. Hardy Dr., Tempe
- **(480) 379-0101**
- **www.azcardinals.com**

The short course in Arizona Cardinals history goes like this: 1899, Morgan Athletic Club (Chicago); 1900, Racine (Chicago) Normals; 1901–1921, Racine (Chicago) Cardinals; 1922–1959, Chicago Cardinals; 1960-1987, St. Louis Cardinals; 1988–1993, Phoenix Cardinals; 1994-present, Arizona Cardinals. That last name change puts the Cards at the front of the NFL Rolodex, which, unfortunately for long-suffering fans, is the only place they'll be a front-runner for the foreseeable future.

Locals cheer quarterback Jake "The Snake" Plummer and are keeping their fingers crossed that someday they may have a great team. The Cardinals last won an NFL championship in 1949 when they were still in Chicago. They've been to the postseason only rarely since and never since they moved to Tempe. The season begins during the warm summer months (so wear sunscreen to the games) and ends all too soon (for Cardinal devotees) in December.

The Cardinals play their home games at Arizona State University's Sun Devil Stadium on Stadium Drive in Tempe, the only NFL franchise playing in a college stadium. Ownership is trying to work a deal for its own stadium, which would significantly boost revenues. Public sentiment seems to be running against taxes to fund a new stadium until the team puts a winner on the field.

In 1997, Cardinals single-game tickets ranged from $30 in the south end-zone bleachers to $200 for 50-yard line loge seats, while season tickets ranged from $170 for the south end-zone to $1,800 for the 50-yard line loge. As the season progresses, the team will offer value packages that combine remaining games into lower priced tickets. The Cardinals ticket office can be reached at (602) 379-0102.

Stadium parking is offered for season ticket holders, and there are many lots close to the stadium that provide paid parking. Don't try to park in ASU lots, which require a campus parking decal.

Sun Devil Stadium is easily reached from U.S. Highway 60, where you can take either the Rural Road or Mill Avenue exits north. From Mill Avenue, the stadium is a right turn off Fifth Street straight onto Stadium Drive. From Rural Road, take a left on University Drive and then take a right onto Stadium Drive. However, you can avoid many headaches by parking some distance away in the lots and streets around Mill Avenue or Rural Road.

Golf Tournaments

Phoenix Open
7226 N. 16th St., Phoenix
- **(602) 870-0163**
- **www.pagatour.com**

The Phoenix Open is the one of the top-drawing sporting events in Arizona, not exactly a surprise since golf rules here. In 1998, the Open set a record of 467,600 in attendance for the weeklong event, held the third week of January at the Tournament Players Club of Scottsdale, 17020 N. Hayden Road, Scottsdale. The audience cheers local favorites like Tom Lehman and Mark Calcavecchia along like national names like Tiger Woods who made

---

INSIDERS' TIP

Perhaps the most serene spectator event is the annual Metris Thunderbird Balloon Classic. During the first weekend of November, more than a hundred hot air balloons are inflated and released with their crews. The balloons are made of brightly colored materials and often made in unusual shapes. You might see a giant cowboy boot gliding above you or an immense dog, so be sure to bring a camera. The event will have 60,000 spectators over the weekend, with live music in the evenings. The balloons set up at West World, 16601 N. Pima Rd., Scottsdale. For more information, visit their website: www.t-birdballoon.com.

a hole in one on the 16th hole. The celebrity events, held on Tuesday and Wednesdays, are also popular.

It wasn't always that way. Only about 600 people were in the gallery to see Ralph Guldahl finish five strokes better than John Perelli to win the tournament in 1932. The tournament was abandoned during the depths of the Depression but was revived by the special events committee of the Phoenix Chamber of Commerce in 1939. The committee was expanded to become the Thunderbirds, a service group that has been putting on the Phoenix Open ever since. The Thunderbird's put on the Thunderbird Collegiate Invitational and the Thunderbird Junior and Senior Golf Classics each summer. All of the Thunderbirds' efforts benefit the Special Olympics and such youth charities as the Boys and Girls Clubs and Make-A-Wish Foundation.

The Phoenix Open PGA event includes such pre-tournament activities as a Special Olympics putting contest, a junior golf clinic, four pro-am events, a pro-celebrity shootout, and a long-drive contest.

Prices are $20 for general admission each day. Children 17 and younger get in free with an adult. Information is available year round at the Thunderbirds office number listed above.

Standard Register Ping
1441 N. 12th St., Phoenix
• **(602) 495-4653**
• **www.standardregisterping.com**

For 16 years, the LPGA has been coming to the Moon Valley Country Club for this tournament, held the third week of March. At 6,435 yards, Moon Valley's course is the longest on the LPGA tour. With $850,000 in prize money, this has become the fifth-highest-ranked event on the tour. Local favorites are Dina Ammaccapane and Chris Johnson. Wednesday is the day for the Pro-Am. The event, which benefits the cancer-care efforts of the nonprofit Samaritan Hos-

pitals, draws about 125,000 spectators over the course of a week. Tickets are $15 a day and $50 for the full week. Moon Valley Country Club is on Moon Valley Road in Phoenix, north of the intersection of Thunderbird Road and Coral Gables Drive.

The Tradition at Desert Mountain
10550 E. Desert Hills Dr., Scottsdale
• **(480) 595-4070**

In 1992 The Tradition was officially designated by the Senior PGA Tour as the year's first major championship. That was the ultimate validation for an event that had only begun in 1989, after Lyle Anderson conceived the idea of establishing a major seniors championship in Arizona. Today, the weeklong event, played in the first week of April, draws more than 40,000 people.

The tournament itself is a 72-hole contest that takes up the last four days. The Tradition honors seniors who are past winners of the four major events of the PGA Tour and the Senior PGA Tour. Besides the tournament, there's the Countrywide Grand Tradition, an 18-hole, four-ball-stroke play (better ball) competition.

The tournament benefits such charities as the Telephone Pioneers of America, the Central Arizona Chapter of the Arthritis Foundation, Barrow Neurological Institute, Scottsdale HealthCare, and the Scottsdale Active 20/30 Club.

The Tradition is played at Cochise Golf Course at The Golf Club at Desert Mountain, which is 3 miles east of Carefree off Cave Creek Road. Season tickets are $100, and they're available through The Tradition office.

INSIDERS' TIP
Why wait in line at the ticket booth when you can avoid it with a little planning? If you order early enough, you can have tickets mailed to you and walk right through the turnstiles when you arrive for the event. Another approach is to order tickets beforehand and have them waiting at the will-call window where the lines are always shorter.

INSIDERS' TIP
Always bring sunscreen and a hat to outdoor events in Arizona. Sunburn can happen with less than 20 minutes' exposure.

Tennis

Franklin Templeton Tennis Classic
Princess Resort,
7575 E. Princess Dr.,
Scottsdale
• **(480) 473-4444**

The Franklin Templeton Tennis Classic is the ATP Tour event in Arizona and brings top

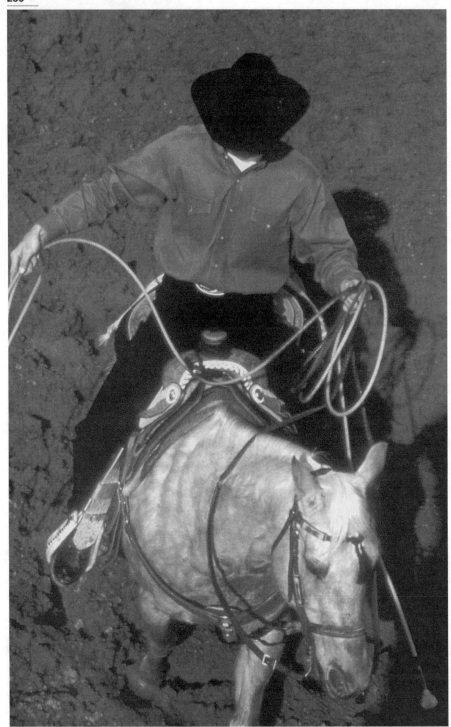

Rodeos are a long-time sporting tradition in Arizona, such as the Parada del Sol Rodeo held in Scottsdale each February.

Photo: Paul Markow, courtesy of Scottsdale Convention and Visitors Bureau

stars from around the world. The tournament, which draws about 50,000 people for the week, includes matches by 32 singles players and 16 doubles teams. Surrounding events include the annual draw party, celebrity auction, and the ATP Tour kids' day. Tickets range from $10 to $60 per match, and event packages range from $140 to $300. It is held the first week in March.

Hockey

Phoenix Coyotes
2 N. Central Ave., Phoenix
• **(602) 379-2800**
• **www.phoenixcoyotes.com**

Like so many others from the frozen north, the Winnipeg Jets flew the coop in 1996 for the unlikely hockey clime of Phoenix, becoming the Coyotes and playing at America West Arena. In their first two Phoenix seasons, they made the postseason, and fans dressed up entirely in white in what became known as "the whiteout" to help raise the team's spirit. (Be warned that you should wear white, too, if you don't want to hear about it during the game.) With capacity of 16,210 people, the arena's ice-hockey games average 96 percent of capacity making this one of the hottest tickets in town for one of the coolest sports.

Single-game tickets start at $11, and season-ticket prices start at $450, which includes all 41 regular-season games, four preseason contests, and first dibs on playoff tickets. Check out the paper and you'll see special offers on single tickets from time to time that sometimes include a drink and a hot dog. The ticket-office number is (602) 379-7825.

Horse Racing

Turf Paradise
19th Ave. and Bell Rd., Phoenix
• **(602) 942-1101**
• **www.turfparadise.com**

Riders up! Turf Paradise features live thoroughbred racing and betting on simulcast races from late September to early May. Although the main attraction is horse racing, the track's floral gardens, olive grove, three lakes, orchid trees, palm trees, and waterfall let the track live up to its name. The exotic avian wildlife includes swans, flamingos, and herons. The tranquil setting contrasts with the high adrenaline in the grandstand.

Walter Cluer announced he would build a horse track on the 1,400-acre site back in 1954, when the spot was many miles from Phoenix. Now, although encircled by growth, it maintains its desert oasis atmosphere.

Among the big days of the year is Super Saturday, held the first Saturday in February, featuring three major races—the Turf Paradise Breeders Cup, with a $150,000 purse; the Turf Paradise Derby, with a $100,000 purse; and the Arizona Oaks, with a $50,000 purse.

There are two restaurants in the clubhouse level—the Turf Club and the Clubhouse. The Turf Club has an elegant feel to it, while the Clubhouse is more casual. In addition there are two rooms for banquets and the top-level Director's Suite. All provide good views of the racing action. Admission is $1 for the grandstand and $5 for the clubhouse levels.

SPECTATOR SPORTS

Daytrips

Although enough hot spots abound within the Phoenix Metropolitan Area to keep visitors and residents busy, you would be remiss if you did not venture outside of the Valley to experience the rest of Arizona. Getting out of town on one of the Valley's crowded arterial roadways might seem like a hassle on a Saturday morning, but you will be amply rewarded. There's enough to do and see in Arizona that our state magazine, *Arizona Highways*, has been going strong for more than 75 years and has yet to run out of fascinating places and landscapes to feature. Moreover, the state's climate varies—from sunny desert to cool pine forests so that in the winter, you can literally golf in the morning in the Valley and ski in the afternoon in the White Mountains or Flagstaff.

The Grand Canyon is, of course, our top destination point, but there are plenty of other areas within a three-hour drive to discover. Of course, our foray into the rest of the state is only an introduction—to cover it thoroughly, we'd need to publish another book—so you might want to do further research into some of the areas that pique your interest. Destination points that are worthy of a visit, but require more than a day to do include Lake Powell, Canyon de Chelly, Monument Valley, and the Painted Desert in the northeast part of the state. Toward the east, the White Mountains offer ample skiing, hiking, and fishing opportunities. To the southeast, the frontier town of Tombstone and the mining-turned-artist community of Bisbee delight. In this chapter, we'll touch on some destination points closer to the Valley that can be done in a day, organizing our trips into those that can be reached via Interstate 17 and those that can be reached via Interstate 10.

Up Interstate 17

Arcosanti

Visitors may know about our famous architect, Frank Lloyd Wright, but few know about one of his students, Paolo Soleri, who has been gathering international acclaim for his experimental city that is the antithesis of Phoenix's urban sprawl. Arcosanti, about 50 miles north of Phoenix, is east of Interstate 17 at the Cordes Junction exit. This prototype city is compact and meant to leave little impact on the surrounding landscape—a refinement of Italian hill villages, where people live in clustered housing while the fields where they work stretch out for miles around.

The cement structures, while cast in futuristic geometric shapes, look rustic, at least in part because they're unfinished—something like a ghost town from tomorrow. Privately funded—with most of the legwork being done by students and volunteers—Arcosanti may never be completely finished. The environmentally sensitive philosophy behind the project has made it attractive to ecological idealists and artisans, and fascinates anyone interested in ways to solve the problems of diminishing energy resources and a dwindling supply of open land. Soleri has been internationally recognized for his innovative designs.

Some of the funding for the project comes from the sale of distinctive Soleri-designed wind bells, which are sold in the gift shop. Guided tours of Arcosanti take about an hour, but you can walk around the grounds, visit the cafe and bakery, and even stay overnight if you wish. For details, call (520) 632-7135.

Flagstaff

Flagstaff—140 miles north of Phoenix on Interstate 17—makes an easy daytrip from the Valley, but be aware that the two cities are practically polar opposites when it comes to weather. While you may be enjoying a round of golf in February in the Valley, the 52,000 residents of Flagstaff are likely to be hunkered down in their homes, staying warm by the fire. While Phoenix is one of the warmest cities in the nation, Flagstaff is one of the nation's snowiest cities, with 84 inches a year. Not surprisingly, the annual snowfall bodes well for Flagstaff's ski area, the Arizona Snowbowl, nestled in the San Francisco Peaks.

Come summer, Flagstaff is bustling with Valley residents escaping the blistering heat for the pines, the peaks, and temperatures that usually top out in the low 80s. Many Phoenicians have summer cabins in the Flagstaff area. The highway to the north continually dips and rises as the Sonoran hills become more mountainous, and the landscape of saguaro and cholla turns green with cottonwoods and other trees. After a drop down into the Verde Valley, you climb up into the thick forests of pine that form the gateway into Flagstaff, elevation 7,000 feet. The city's backdrop is the San Francisco Peaks, where you will find 12,643-foot Mount Humphreys, the highest point in Arizona.

Over the last decade, Flagstaff has made a lot of progress sprucing up its downtown. We recommend a day in downtown Flagstaff if you enjoy browsing arts and crafts stores and soaking up the historic ambiance of this major east-to-west railroad stop. Northern Arizona University is also interesting to see, as is the Museum of Northern Arizona. Probably, though, you will want to combine Flagstaff with two or three other sights in the northern and central parts of the state. See this section for descriptions of Sedona, Jerome, and Montezuma Castle, which are all within about a 90-minute driving radius of Flagstaff. The city also makes a good stopover point—either for dining, lodging, or both—if you are headed to the Grand Canyon. (For further information on these destinations, check out the *Insiders' Guide to the Grand Canyon*.)

Here's the lowdown on a few of Flagstaff's major attractions, places to stay, and restaurants.

The Arizona Snowbowl's ski season usually runs from December to mid-April. There are more than 30 trails and four chairlifts. In summer, those chairlifts turn into the Scenic Skyride, lifting you to an elevation of 11,500 feet. The ride is open daily mid-June through Labor Day and for a limited time through mid-October. The Snowbowl is 14 miles north of Flagstaff on State Route 180. For information call (520) 779-1951, or visit www.arizonasnowbowl.com. For the Snow Report call (520) 779-4577.

About a mile from downtown is Lowell Observatory, where the planet Pluto was discovered in 1930. Lowell has a visitors center, hands-on exhibits, tours, lectures, and sky shows. It is at 1400 W. Mars Hill Road, (520) 774-3358, or visit the Observatory at www.lowell.edu. The Northern Arizona University campus also has an observatory, offering weekly public viewing of the night sky. Their phone number is (520) 523-7170, or visit www.nau.edu.

The Museum of Northern Arizona, 3101 N. Fort Valley Road, (520) 774-5213 or www.musnaz.org, is a good place to learn about the anthropology, biology, and geology of the Colorado Plateau region. Also, there is often an exhibit focusing on Native American arts and crafts. The museum's short nature trail with its cliff overlooks is worth walking too.

Fairly close to Flagstaff are two interesting natural attractions: Sunset Crater Volcano National Monument, with nature trails through volcanic fields and lava flows; and Walnut Canyon National Monument, with a paved nature trail leading to Sinagua cliff dwellings built into steep canyon walls. Sunset Crater is 15 miles north of Flagstaff on State Route 89, (520) 526-0502. Walnut Canyon is 7 miles east of Flagstaff on Interstate 40, (520) 526-3367.

Lodging is plentiful in Flagstaff because of its ski industry and its reputation as an Arizona summer getaway. The city also is convenient for those traveling cross-country on Interstate 40. Reservations are essential in the height of summer. Radisson Woodlands Plaza Hotel, 1175 W. Route 66, (520) 773-8888, is one of the fancier spots in the city. Scenically situated in a ponderosa forest is the Little America Hotel, 2515 E. Butler Avenue, (520) 779-2741, (800) 865-1399.

Chain motels and hotels are well-represented and include the Days Inn at 2735 S. Woodlands Village Boulevard, (520) 779-1575; the Econo Lodge at 2480 E. Lucky Lane, (520) 774-7701; and the Quality Inn at 2000 S. Milton Road, (520) 774-8771, (800) 228-5151. A charming bed and breakfast is the Inn at 410 in a turn-of-the-century home. It's located at 410 N. Leroux Street, (520) 774-0088, (800) 774-2008. Campgrounds include the KOA Campground at 5803 N. Highway 89, (520) 526-9926, and the Fort Tuthill Coconino County Park Campground off Interstate 17 just south of Flagstaff, (520) 774-5139, October through April, or (520) 774-3464, May through September.

Flagstaff's dining choices have become more sophisticated over the years. Country French cuisine is served at Chez Marc, 503 N. Humphreys Street, (520) 774-1343, www.chezmarc.com. For American and continental food, try Buster's Restaurant & Bar, 1800 S. Milton Road, (520) 774-5155. For Italian food, try Pasto "Fine Italian Dining" at 19 E. Aspen Avenue, (520) 779-1937. Breakfasts are terrific at Brandy's Restaurant and Bakery, 1500 E. Cedar Avenue, (520) 779-2187, www.brandysrestaurant.com. As a college town, Flagstaff attracts coffeehouse intellectuals, artists, outdoors enthusiasts, and other free spirits. Their hangouts include Café Espress, Café-Bakery-Gallery, 16 N. San Francisco Street, (520) 774-0541, and Macy's, 14 S. Beaver Street, (520) 774-2243—which serve great vegetarian dishes, coffees, and pastries.

One of Flagstaff's major annual events is the Winterfest in February. Highlights include sled-dog races, sleigh and snowmobile rides, snow sculpture contests, concerts, art shows, winter stargazing, and various winter sports. For more information, call the Flagstaff Chamber of Commerce at (800) 842-7293. During the summer, you'll find various art and music programs like A Celebration of Native American Art held at the Northern Arizona University, (520) 774-5213, www.musnaz.org. The Wool Festival features sheep, goat, and llama shearing, animal shows, and demonstrations of spinning, felting, dyeing, and weaving. For more information, call the Arizona Historical Society Pioneer Museum at (520) 774-6275. In June, you won't want to miss the Pine Country Pro Rodeo at the Coconino County Fairgrounds, on State Route 89A, a few miles south of Flagstaff. For information call (520) 774-4505, or visit www.pinecountryprorodeo.com.

Find antique stores and art galleries downtown along the famous Route 66, San Francisco Street, and Beaver Street, as well as in other parts of town. Flagstaff Mall, at 4650 N. State Route 89, is northern Arizona's regional shopping mall, with more than 60 stores.

For more information, contact the Flagstaff Convention and Visitors Bureau at 211 W. Aspen Avenue, Flagstaff, AZ 86001, (520) 779-7611, www.flagstaffarizona.org, or from the Flagstaff Visitor Center, 1 E. U.S. Route 66, Flagstaff, AZ 86001, (800) 842-7293.

Grand Canyon

What's a visit to the Grand Canyon State without a visit to the Grand Canyon? We don't mean to be overbearing here, but if you have come all the way to Phoenix from the eastern half of the United States or abroad, go to the Grand Canyon! It is, after all, one of Mother Nature's most awe-inspiring sights.

If you only have the time to do the Canyon as a daytrip, do it, but pace yourself accordingly. The South Rim is about a five-hour drive from Phoenix, and half of the trip is on interstates. To get there, take Interstate 17 north for about two and a half hours to Flagstaff, then get on U.S. Highway 180, heading north, for about another two hours. All told, it's about 220 miles from Phoenix. Private vehicles pay $20 to enter Grand Canyon National Park. Many of the park's scenic overlooks are accessible by car but, because of the large number of visitors at the park, some are closed parts of the year and you should be prepared to catch a shuttle bus to the rim. The East Rim Drive (Highway 64) is open year around and follows the canyon rim for 26 miles east of Grand Canyon Village to Desert View, the park's east entrance. The West Rim Drive is closed to private automobiles from mid-March through Mid-October, during which times the park runs a free shuttle bus. When it is open, you can follow the rim for 8 miles from Grand Canyon Village west to Hermits Rest.

Backcountry hiking through the 1.2 million-acre Grand Canyon National Park requires a permit. The cost is $20 per person plus an additional $4 per person for each night you camp in the canyon. Write to: Backcountry Office, Grand Canyon National Park, P.O. Box 129, Grand Canyon, AZ 86023, or call (520) 638-7875. As part of an effort to promote hiker safety and

The Grand Canyon is a bit of a drive from Phoenix, but it is worth the trip to see such a wonder of nature.

Photo: Courtesy of the Phoenix Convention and Visitors Bureau emphasize the importance of packing enough water and food, the Park Service will send you a free video called "Hiking the Grand Canyon."

North Rim

Since the North Rim is quite a ways from Phoenix and is better reached from Colorado or Utah, we'll give only a quick overview and then focus on the south rim. To reach the North Rim from Phoenix, take Interstate 17 north to Flagstaff, then take Interstate 40 east to U.S. Highway 89 north. This is a mostly two-lane road of more than 100 miles through some rather desolate stretches of the Navajo and Hopi Reservations. But you're not done yet—at Bitter Springs, take U.S. Highway 89A west, cross the Colorado River at Navajo Bridge and continue on to Jacob Lake. Head south on State Route 67 through beautiful pine forests to the North Rim entrance. This is an all-day drive, but you will be rewarded with a more peaceful Grand Canyon experience. Park Service cabins are available for overnight lodging. For details on the North Rim, we recommend a look at the *Insiders' Guides to Southwestern Utah* and the *Grand Canyon*, or call Grand Canyon National Park at (520) 638-7888, www.thecanyon.com. Since the North Rim is a couple of thousand feet higher than the South Rim, many Park Service facilities there are open only from mid-March through late October.

South Rim

"I hiked the Grand Canyon!" proclaim T-shirts proudly worn by the hardy souls who make the daylong hike from the rim of the canyon to the Colorado River a mile below. The trails are more winding than a coiled snake; they are steep, rocky, and dusty—and rather dangerous in spots. We don't recommend a hike to the bottom if you're doing the canyon as a daytrip. But you can set out on the popular Bright Angel Trail for a spell just to see what it's like. Be sure to wear your best sneakers with treads, or better yet, hiking boots. Also, pack water and sunscreen. Hiking is only advised when it is not snowing or raining at the canyon. In fact, spring and fall are excellent times to see the South Rim because the crowds lessen a bit (actually, it's gotten to the point where there is no downtime for tourism here) and because the walking is easier in balmier weather. Summer temperatures at the canyon are about 80 degrees on the rim and about 100 degrees at Phantom Ranch along the Colorado River. However far you take the trail, remember that the hike back up will take almost twice as long as the hike down. If you don't feel like hiking, you can arrange to descend the canyon by mule.

Don't feel bad if you decide to skip the hiking altogether. The scenic drives give excellent views, and there are several observation points where you can get out of the car and take in the wonderment of it all. Unfortunately, pollution has made the canyon a little less photogenic than it used to be. To better capture the definition and depth of the red rocks, gray cliffs, and tree-studded mesas, try taking your pictures at sunrise or sunset.

If you want to learn more about the park or simply catch a shuttle bus, visit the new Canyon View Information Plaza, which opened October 2000. Here, visitors can catch their first glimpse of the canyon in relative serenity away from the noise of traffic. Here you can also get an overview of the park's recreational options, including information on the shuttle buses, biking, hiking, and ranger guided activities; In 2004, the park's mass transit system, including alternative fuel buses and light rail, will be completed. Visitors will also have access here to the Grand

INSIDERS' TIP

Kartchner Caverns near Benson in southeastern Arizona is one of Arizona's newest attractions. In 1974, two Arizona cavers discovered this pristine cave, which includes 13,000 feet of passages, rare multicolored formations, and two rooms as long as football fields. They explored the cave for two years before revealing their secret to the property owners. The public learned about the cavern in 1988, when Arizona State Parks purchased the property. The cave, a Discovery Center, hiking trails, hummingbird garden, and campgrounds, were opened to the public in 1999. The cavern's features include a thin stalactite "soda straw," which measures 21 feet long, nitrocalcite "cotton," and "birds nests" formed from rare quartz. Fossils from sloths, horses, and bears that roamed the area more than 40,000 years ago were also unearthed. The park is located 160 miles from Phoenix, nine miles south of Interstate 10 in Benson, Arizona. Reservations are required. For more information, call (520) 586-CAVE.

Canyon Greenway, a trail system, which will eventually extend from Canyon View Information Plaza to the future Grand Canyon Transit Center north of Tusayan, which is seven miles south of the South Rim.

We hope you'll do more research about the Grand Canyon if you plan an extended stay here. Here are a few other things to think about as you plan your trip:

After heavy rains, desert flowers can carpet the highway's edges.

Photo: Courtesy of Mesa Convention and Visitors Bureau

•If you take the Bright Angel or South Kaibab trail all the way down, you might consider arranging for overnight lodging at Phantom Ranch, which has bunkhouses, cabins, and a few other simple amenities to revive you after the hike. But reservations are a must; in fact, you should make them a year in advance. The number is (303) 297-2757.

•During the Canyon's busiest times, it's likely that portions of the scenic drive along the rim will be closed to private automobiles and you will be asked to take one of the free shuttle buses operated by the Park Service. It's part of an effort to reduce pollution and parking problems at this tourist Mecca, which receives more than 5 million visitors a year from all over the world. Eventually, the Park Service hopes to bring visitors in by light-rail mass transit from Tusayan, seven miles south of the South Rim.

•Have you considered taking a train to the Grand Canyon? From a depot in Williams, west of Flagstaff, you can catch the scenic Grand Canyon Railway to the South Rim. For information, call (520) 635-4061 or (800) 843-8724.

•Still other ways to see the canyon include small airplane and helicopter flights; mule rides; motor-coach tours; white-water rafting trips; mountain biking; and guided walks with a park ranger.

•Lodging at Grand Canyon Village ranges from rustic cabins ($46 per night and up) to Western-style lodges ($73 to $124 per night) to the historic El Tovar Hotel ($116 per night and up). The El Tovar, dating from 1905, recently underwent $1 million worth of renovations. Once visited by the likes of former President Theodore Roosevelt and Western writer Zane Grey, many of the rooms offer wonderful views. The hotel decor resembles an elegant hunting lodge, with massive wood-beam ceilings, fireplaces, and chandeliers. All reservations are made by calling (303) 29-PARKS, faxing (303) 297-3175, or visiting www.grandcanyonlodges.com. The hotel and lodges have various high-end restaurants, steakhouses, cocktail lounges, coffee shops, and cafeterias. You can also find several reasonably priced restaurants and motels in Tusayan. Campers should call the Grand Canyon National Park Campgrounds at (800) 365-2267 for reservations.

•See the Grand Canyon on a seven-story IMAX screen at the Grand Canyon National

If you travel anywhere near Native American reservations, you might have an opportunity to buy some jewelry or crafts at a roadside table.

Photo: Peter Pfeiffer

Geographic Theater in Tusayan, seven miles south of the South Rim. A film called *The Hidden Secrets* gives a history of the 277 mile long canyon, including the story of Major John Wesley Powell and his trip down the Colorado River in 1869. For information, call (520) 638-2203.

For a Trip Planner and other information, write to Grand Canyon National Park at P.O. Box 129, Grand Canyon, AZ 86023, call (520) 638-7888, or visit www.thecanyon.com.

Jerome

Approximately 130 miles north of Phoenix in the Central Arizona hills, Jerome has evolved from a mile-high ghost town into an eclectic artist community. Browse art galleries, sip latte at an outdoor café, and admire the buildings that survived Jerome's long-gone heyday as a copper mining town. To get there from Phoenix, head north on Interstate 17 , then take State Route 260 west until you hit State Route 89A, which will pass through the small towns of Cottonwood and Clarkdale. Jerome beckons you from high upon its precarious perch on the side of Cleopatra Hill, overlooking the Verde Valley. The short, steep, and winding drive provides plenty of fun.

Miners struck it rich in Jerome in the mid-1800s. The population boomed in the 1920s to about 15,000, but that didn't last. Today, Jerome's population totals about 500 residents.

Don't expect a ghost town in the sense that it's devoid of people. Actually, they come in droves, especially on weekends with good weather. Jerome is a popular daytrip for Phoenix residents. And word has gotten out—along with the Arizona license plates, don't be surprised to see plates from all over the country. Jerome also seems to be on the A list for motorcyclists.

While in Jerome, wander around to the historic buildings, or what's left of them. A "traveling jail" still stands, even though a dynamite explosion in the 1920s moved it to about 200 feet from its original foundation. The mansion of mining king "Rawhide Jimmy" Douglas has been turned into Jerome State Historic Park. Old photographs and exhibits of the region's copper mining days can be seen at the Jerome Historical Society Mine Museum, Main Street and Jerome Avenue, (520) 634-5477. The Gold King Mine Museum, Perkinsville Road, (520) 634-0053, has a replica of a mine shaft. Several of Jerome's historic homes open each May for the town's annual home tour. Call the Jerome Chamber of Commerce for more information about the tour or any other aspect of the town. The chamber can be reached at 50 N. Main Street, Jerome, (520) 634-2900.

You might want to combine a trip to Jerome with a look at Tuzigoot National Monument near Clarkdale, where you'll see the ruins of a 100-room pueblo inhabited by the Sinagua from the twelfth to fifteenth centuries. For information call (520) 634-5564. Also, Clarkdale is the departure point for the Verde Canyon Railroad, which affords a scenic, 40-mile round trip through cottonwood groves and desert mesas. For more information, contact the Cottonwood/Verde Valley Chamber of Commerce at 1010 S. Main Street, Cottonwood, (520) 634-7593, or visit www.chamber.verdevalley.com. You can also call the railroad directly at (800) 320-0718 or visit www.verdecanyonrr.com.

Both Jerome and the Cottonwood area have plenty of lodging. Choices include: The Inn at Jerome, 309 N. Main Street, (520) 634-5094, (800) 634-5094; the Ghost City Inn, 541 N. Main Street, (520) 63-GHOST; and the Surgeon's House, 100 Hill Street, (520) 639-1452, (800) 639-1452, a bed and breakfast converted from the home of a mining company surgeon. All of these inns are several decades old but have been carefully restored. In Cottonwood, try the Best Western Cottonwood Inn, 993 S. Main Street, (520) 634-5575 or (800) 258-1234.

For dining, your options include chain restaurants in Cottonwood and Clarkdale. In Jerome, take your pick of several reasonably priced cafes along Main Street. One interesting restaurant is The English Kitchen on Jerome Avenue, (520) 634-2132, which claims to be the oldest continually operating restaurant in Arizona. It was originally built in 1899 by Charley Hong, an immigrant from China, and served miners and travelers alike.

INSIDERS' TIP

Seniors 62 or older may obtain a Golden Age Passport for a one-time fee of $10, which grants them free admission for life to all National Park Service sites in the country. Annual Grand Canyon passports, valid for the calendar year, are available for $40. Those who are physically or mentally challenged may apply in person for a Golden Access Passport, which also offers free admission for life to all our National Parks. The rest of us can purchase The National Parks Pass for $50, which is good for a year of unlimited entries to all the National Parks. For more information, call (888) GO-PARKS or visit www.nationalparks.org.

Montezuma Castle National Monument

A nice side trip on the way up to Flagstaff or Sedona is Montezuma Castle National Monument. These cliff dwellings, the best preserved of Arizona's ancient structures, had nothing to do with Montezuma and the Aztecs. However, early white settlers thought they did and thus misnamed them after the Aztec ruler.

The buildings are relics of the Sinagua, a Native American tribe that vanished without a trace in the 1300s. You can't enter these pueblos, but Montezuma Castle is a startling sight. As you come upon it from the trail, you see a cave high up in the cliffside holding a five-story stone building, defying our modern sense of where a building should be. Obviously, these ancient peoples had more sense than we did because this building and its mud-plastered walls have been virtually untouched by the elements in the intervening years. The other ancient building at this location, which stands so much more sensibly at the bottom of the cliff, has been weathered by rain and wind.

There is a visitors center with exhibits of artifacts from the pueblos. Admission to Montezuma Castle is $2 for adults and free for kids 16 and younger. It is open year round. To get there, take Exit 289 east off I-17 and follow the signs. For details call (520) 567-3322.

DAYTRIPS

Prescott

Arizona's first capital, Prescott (pronounced press-KIT) sprang up amid the nation's largest contiguous forest of ponderosa pines back in 1863, shortly after gold was discovered in the nearby hills. Today, Prescott is the county seat of Yavapai County (named after a local Native

American tribe) and an easy two- to two-and-a-half hour trip from Phoenix. Take Interstate 17 north to the Cordes Junction exit and then head west on State Route 69 until the junction with State Route 89, where a quick jog south puts you in the heart of the city.

State Route 69 wends through pretty, mountainous country on the way to Prescott. Most of the highway has been widened to four lanes in recent years to accommodate local residential traffic and the increasing number of visitors from the Valley. You'll pass the tall smokestack of a long-abandoned smelter in the one-time mining town of Mayer. A fairly natural stopping point is Young's Farm in Dewey at the junction with State Route 169. This is the place for fresh produce. Its coffee shop and bakery are open daily. For more information, call (520) 632-7272 or visit www.youngsfarminc.com.

Just before the turn onto State Route 89, you traverse the Yavapai Reservation, where casino gambling adds another attraction for Prescott visitors.

A more challenging "back way" from the west Valley offers a scenic ride through the ponderosas of Prescott National Forest. Take Grand Avenue northwest to Wickenburg. In Wickenburg, Interstate 60 splits off to the west. From that point, continue northwest for about seven miles and take the turnoff for State Route 89 and the town of Congress. From Congress, State Route 89 climbs northeast up steep Yarnell Hill. The view back toward Wickenburg becomes a bird's-eye view panorama, and the scenery near Yarnell Hill quickly becomes mountainous evergreen forest. State Route 89 brings you into Prescott on Montezuma Street, which is better known as Whiskey Row.

If you choose to take this route for a daytrip, it's advisable to take it one way, either into or out of Prescott, and to use the Interstate 17 route for the other portion of the trip. The back way adds an hour or more, mostly because you're heading farther west and then cutting back to Prescott. Mountain switchbacks tend to slow the progress of even the most intrepid driver.

Young professionals are likely to motor up to Prescott on the weekend to soak up the local nightlife around Whiskey Row (so named because it used to be where all the town's saloons and bawdy houses were), stay the night, and then head back down to the Valley. Despite the appearance of the smart set, Prescott offers plenty of attractions for families as well. The city boasts 525 buildings listed on the National Register of Historic Places—a pleasant contrast to the Valley's penchant for tearing down any building that's been up for a while.

Courthouse Plaza—bounded by Gurley Street on the north, Montezuma Street on the west, Goodwin Street on the south and Cortez Street on the east—is the heart of Prescott. Tree-shaded and cool (Prescott averages about 20 degrees cooler than Phoenix), the plaza invites visitors to dawdle while checking out the courthouse, which dates back to Prescott's stint as the Territorial capital.

Prescott's pace feels slower than the Valley's. The restored, brick buildings that house the restaurants, antiques stores, saloons, and other businesses around the plaza are authentic reminders of Arizona's Wild West days. Shopping for antiques certainly fits the setting.

To get a full appreciation of Prescott's past, visit the Sharlot Hall Museum, two blocks west of the plaza at 415 W. Gurley Street, (520) 445-3122, www.sharlot.org. Sharlot Hall came to the territory at age 12 in 1882. Her fascination with Arizona, its history, and artifacts led her to become the official Territorial historian in 1909. The museum she opened in 1928 encompasses the original Governor's Mansion, a log home built in 1864, two 1870s vintage homes, and such utilitarian buildings as a blacksmith's shop and a schoolhouse, among others. The Sharlot Hall Building, opened in 1934, is itself old enough to be considered historic in this neck of the woods. It houses the museum's exhibits on Prescott and Native American history. The museum also is host to major annual events such as the Folk Arts Festival during the first weekend of June, the Arizona Cowboy Poets Gathering held the third weekend in August, and the Indian Arts Market held the first weekend of October. From April through October, the museum is open 10 AM to 5 PM Monday through Saturday, and 1 to 5 PM Sunday. From November through March, it closes at 4 PM, except Sundays. There is no admission fee, but donations are accepted.

Another Prescott museum, The Smoki Museum, 147 N. Arizona Street, (520) 445-1230, www.smok.com, displays artifacts from many Native American tribes, include clothing, ornaments, and ceremonial paraphernalia from the Sioux, Apache, and Woodland tribes. Many items in the collection were donated by Arizona son Barry Goldwater, who was a member of the Smoki People.

Of the many annual events in Prescott, the Frontier Days/World's Oldest Rodeo celebration around the Fourth of July is the city's biggest draw. Prescott also plays host to the Cowboy Poets

Gathering in August, an Intertribal Powwow in June, and the Yavapai County Fair in September.

Prescott's setting at the edge of a mountain-studded plain makes it a natural spot for hiking, fishing, boating, and other activities that take in the scenery. Off Thumb Butte Road west of Downtown, Thumb Butte—which resembles a giant thumb—offers a picnic area and hiking trails. North of town, on State Route 89, the Granite Dells, giant slabs of yellowish-brown granite, rise on both sides of the highway. Sparse vegetation clings to the sides of these smooth, rounded rock towers, which will take much longer to wear away than the soil that once covered them.

As you might expect, the nearby Prescott National Forest is well worth a visit for hiking and camping. Last June, area trail advocates dedicated the 5.5-mile "Prescott Peavine Trail," formerly known as the Santa Fe, Prescott, and Phoenix Railway. The railway was known as the "Peavine" because its circuitous route through the "Granite Dells," large red rock outcroppings that resembled a pea vine. In the 1980s, Prescott area trail advocates recognized the potential of converting the abandoned railway to a non-motorized recreation trail.

Maps and information are available at the Prescott National Forest Main Office, 344 S. Cortez Street, (520) 771-4700.

If you want to spend the night in Prescott, the Hassayampa Inn at 122 E. Gurley Street, (520) 778-9434, (800) 322-1927, one of Prescott's many historic buildings, offers accommodations in the $100-a-night range. The Hotel St. Michael, 205 W. Gurley Street, (520) 776-1999, (800) 678-3757, offers accommodations in the $50-per-night range. It sits next door to a Whiskey Row cowboy bar, and a ghost supposedly haunts the building—possibly because the cowboys are keeping it awake.

If you want to grab a bite while you're in Prescott, forget all the national fast-food outlets and check out Kendall's Famous Burgers and Ice Cream, 113 S. Cortez Street, (520) 778-3658.

Take a Pink Jeep Tour in Sedona and you'll see the landscape from a whole different angle.

Photo: Peter Pfeiffer

DAYTRIPS

The burgers are big and tasty. For Southwestern-style prime rib, go to Murphy's at 201 N. Cortez Street, (520) 445-4044. Situated in one of Prescott's many historic buildings, Murphy's is very popular with folks in Prescott, and reservations are recommended for lunch and dinner, especially on the weekends. Murphy's offers its own microbrews and private-label wine too. To dine elegantly, the Peacock Room at the Hassayampa Inn, 122 E. Gurley Street, (520) 778-9434, ext. 104, is the place for continental cuisine.

These are just a few of the accommodations, activities, and points of interest in Prescott. For more information, contact the Prescott Chamber of Commerce, 117 W. Goodwin Street, (520) 445-2000, (800) 266-7534, or visit www.prescott.org.

Sedona

The artist's community of Sedona, named after one of the town's original settlers, Sedona Schnebly, nestles among towering red rocks that form one of the most beautiful spots in Arizona. The rock formations are imbued with deep hues from iron oxides, their names— Cathedral Rock, Bell Rock, the Cockscomb Spires—inspire flights of fancy. A top tourist attraction, Sedona nevertheless offers plenty of places to sequester oneself from the madding crowd. Some locals and many visitors believe that the area's natural electromagnetic field—dubbed "vortexes"—have rejuvenating properties. Decide for yourself by making the fairly easy, two-hour drive to Sedona from Phoenix. Follow Interstate 17 north to State Route 179, then turn west toward Sedona.

You'll find plenty to do by walking through town, especially if you like arts and crafts. Possessing much the same ambiance as the Scottsdale art scene, Sedona's galleries showcase topnotch paintings and sculptures in a variety of media, from Native American arts and crafts to modern studio art glass. One celebrity artist to check out is Robert Shields, once a member of the popular mime duo Shields and Yarnell, whose fanciful creations are showcased in his studio, Robert Shields Design, (520) 204-2123. Altogether, Sedona has more than three dozen galleries, which congregate not only along the main road, State Route 89A, but also at Tlaquepaque Arts and Crafts Village, (520) 282-4838, a re-creation of an old Mexican village graced with all manner of galleries. Tlaquepaque is located on your left just off State Route 179 on your way into town.

The Tlaquepaque Arts and Crafts Village in Sedona offers an abundance of nice shops nestled in the re-creation of a Mexican Village.

Photo: Peter Pfeiffer

Another must-see is the Sedona Arts Center, (520) 282-3809, in the center of town, which has changing exhibits by regional artists and frequent theatrical and musical performances.

Sedona's weather is usually pleasant throughout much of the year, but be warned that it does snow there in the winter, and summer temperatures can go as high as 100 degrees. Because of the nice weather, outdoor festivals are popular. One new venue is the city's new $9 million Sedona Cultural Park, 250 Cultural Park Place; (520) 282-0747 or (800) 780-ARTS, which features an outdoor amphitheater and arts education center. Some of the town's biggest annual events involve the performing arts: the Sedona International Film Festival in March; the Sedona Chamber Music Festival in May, (520) 526-2256; and Sedona Jazz on the Rocks in September, (520) 282-1985. In December, folks come from all around Arizona to see Sedona Red Rock Christmas Fantasy, whose more than one million lights illuminate several acres at Los Abrigados Resort.

If you feel spiritually uplifted after your visit, that's probably because Sedona's vortexes , which draw believers in New Age philosophies about healing and enlightenment. There are said to be about a dozen such vortexes, including ones at Cathedral Rock and Bell Rock. Nonbelievers can still enjoy some of the earthly delights in massages and spas offered by Sedona's New Age stores and traditional resorts.

INSIDERS' TIP

The much-lauded Arizona Trail, a 790-mile recreation trail cutting through the state from Utah in the north to Mexico in the south, is nearly complete. So far, 600 miles have been completed and it will be finished by the end of 2002. The trail is open to hikers, equestrians, mountain bicyclists, cross-country skiers, and other outdoor enthusiasts. The trail links up with the Grand Canyon, the San Francisco Peaks, the Mogollon Rim, Saguaro National Park, and other important sites. For a map and more information, write the Arizona Trail Association at P.O. Box 36736, Phoenix, AZ 85067; phone (602) 252-4794; or visit www.aztrail.org.

If the city shops make you feel fenced in, plenty of outdoor activities abound. Stop by the Sedona Heritage Museum, at 735 Jordan Road, Sedona Historical Park; (520) 282-7038, for a peek at Sedona's past, including its location as a site for old Western films. Hiking along Oak Creek Canyon is popular, as is splashing and enjoying the creek's natural water slide at Slide Rock State Park. Northern Light Balloon Expeditions runs hot-air flights above Sedona; call (800) 230-6222. Jeep tours, four-wheeling, and horseback riding are fun too. There are several companies in town offering excursions, but the oldest one is Pink Jeep Tours at (520) 282-5000. If you drive a high-clearance vehicle, try Schnebly Hill Road, which connects Sedona with Interstate 17 and Flagstaff and offers great views of the red rocks and Verde Valley.

You might be tempted to stay overnight in Sedona (maybe it's those vortexes pulling you in), and if so, your choices will run the gamut from luxury golf resorts to intimate inns to chain motels. Known for a long time to Phoenix residents wishing to splurge on a romantic getaway is L'Auberge de Sedona, re-creating a French country inn at 301 L'Auberge Lane, (520) 282-1661, (800) 272-6777. We also recommend Junipine Resort on State Route 89A, (520) 282-3375, (800) 742-7463; Los Abrigados Resort, 160 Portal Lane, (520) 282-1777, (800) 521-3131; and Poco Diablo Resort, 1752 State Route 179, (520) 282-7333, (800) 528-4275.

There are several nice bed and breakfasts, some along Oak Creek Canyon north of town. Look into the Lodge at Sedona, 125 Kallof Place, (520) 204-1942; The Territorial House, 65 Piki Drive, (520) 204-2737 or (800) 801-2737; Canyon Villa Bed & Breakfast Inn, 125 Canyon Circle Drive, (520) 284-1226, (800) 453-1166; or the Inn on Oak Creek, 556 State Route 179, (520) 282-7896, (800) 499-7896. The budget-conscious traveler might consider the Comfort Inn Sedona, 725 State Route 179, (520) 282-3132, (800) 228-5150, or the Sedona Super 8 Motel, 2545 State Route 89A, (520) 282-1533, (800) 858-7245. The Manzanita Campground in Oak Creek Canyon is small but scenic. It has about 20 sites for non-RV campers—there are no hookups, but you will find tables, grills, toilets, and drinking water. The phone number is (520) 282-4119. There are also several Forest Service Campgrounds along Oak Creek, north of Sedona.

At last count, Sedona had more than 60 restaurants covering the spectrum from fast food to Mexican to gourmet. We heartily recommend the Heartline Cafe, 1610 W. State Route 89A, (520) 282-0785, which serves up exquisite continental cuisine.

The Sedona-Oak Creek Canyon Chamber of Commerce can be reached at P.O. Box 478, Sedona, AZ 86339, (520) 282-7336 or (800) 288-7722.

DAYTRIPS

Up the Beeline Highway (State Route 87)

Payson

Located approximately 95 miles away from downtown Phoenix, Payson is the closest summer getaway for people in the East Valley. From downtown, you get on the Red Mountain Freeway (202 east) to its junction with State Route 87. It's a simple buzz north up the Beeline Highway, through the Salt River Pima-Maricopa and Fort McDowell Yavapai Reservations, through the Mazatzal (pronounced, believe it or not, ma-tah-zall) Mountains and into the pine forest coolness of Payson.

At an elevation of 5,000 feet, the temperature in Payson is typically 20 degrees lower than in the Valley. The Payson area also enjoys about 21 inches of rain a year, about three times the Valley's annual rainfall. Payson sits in the Tonto Basin, about 20 miles south of the Mogollon Rim, the steep lip of a 7,000-foot plateau that stretches eastward to New Mexico. The Rim separates Arizona's northern plateau area from the state's central and southern regions. The huge rock wall stands like a shorter Grand Canyon wall. The Rim dominates the landscape, hence the Payson area is also known as Rim Country.

Founded in 1882 as a mining settlement, Payson has gone through phases as a ranching and lumber town. Today, tourism and retirement industries dominate the local economy. You'll find 15 antiques shops in the area, nine motels, a number of bed and breakfasts, cabin facilities, nine RV parks, and six campgrounds.

Payson bills itself as the Festival Capital of Arizona, and the annual events in Payson include the World's Oldest Continuous Rodeo in August. (Say, isn't that what Prescott called its rodeo? We'll just let them fight it out!) There are a number of other festivals as well, including the Arizona State Old Time Fiddlers' Contest in September.

Set in the middle of the Tonto National Forest, Payson is a place to enjoy outdoor activities year round. It's a place to view spring wildflowers, to stay relatively cool in summer, to view colorful foliage in the fall, and to do cross-country skiing in winter. The area's mountains, lakes, and streams lure anglers, bird watchers, boaters, campers, hikers, horseback riders, hunters, swimmers, and water skiers.

Western novelist Zane Grey fell in love with the Rim Country and wrote and set many of his cowboy novels in this region. He built a hunting lodge near Payson in 1920, writing there often. For many years after his death in 1939, the cabin was preserved as a historic site featuring exhibits on the novelist and the Wild West. Unfortunately, it was one of 61 homes that burned down in the Dude forest fire in 1990, the effects of which still can be seen outside Payson, where the forest slowly grows back. The Zane Grey cabin site is now owned by a private developer and no longer open to the public, but you can find plenty of Zane Grey history in Payson proper.

In fact, the Rim Country Museum, 700 Green Valley Parkway, (520) 474-3483, has plans to re-create the Zane Grey cabin on its grounds in Payson. This would complement its exhibits on Grey. The museum, which has exhibits on all aspects of the area's history from pre-Columbian Indian times through today, resides in the original Tonto National Forest Ranger Station, built in 1907. Admission is $3 for adults, $2.50 for senior citizens, $2 for youths 13 to 17, and free for kids 12 and younger. It's open from noon to 4 PM Wednesday through Sunday, and closed on holidays.

There's more Zane Grey memorabilia at the Zane Grey Museum, 503 W. Main Street, (520) 474-6243. You can view photographs documenting Grey's days in the Rim Country, plus movie posters, first editions, and foreign-language printings of Grey's books. Guns and Indian artifacts are also on display. The museum is open 10 AM to 3 PM daily, except Sundays. Admission is free.

Attractions near Payson include the Payson Zoo, (520) 474-5435, which features about 40 animals—not counting the peacocks, pheasant, and other birds on hand. The zoo takes in animals that have no other home—orphans from the wild, unwanted circus and zoo animals, and wild animals confiscated from private owners. You get a close-up view of the animals—which include bears, baboons, and an African lion—as the zookeeper gives you a tour. The zoo is open 10 AM to 3 PM daily, except Thursday. Admission is $4 for adults and $1 for children 12 years

It may be sunny in the Valley, but there's snow elsewhere in Arizona during the winter. This snowman came to life near Flagstaff.

Photo: Brian Winter, courtesy of the Flagstaff Convention and Visitors Bureau

DAYTRIPS

old and younger. To get there, take State Route 260 about 6.5 miles east of Payson and then head south on Lion Springs Road to the zoo.

While you're out that way, you may want to tour the Tonto Creek Fish Hatchery, (520) 478-4200. It's a 17-mile drive from Payson to the turnoff to the hatchery on State Route 260., The road is marked with a sign and you'll turn north on Forest Service Road 289. The hatchery has been stocking Rim Country creeks and lakes with trout for 50 years. You can tour their facility free of charge from 8 AM to 4 PM seven days a week, excluding holidays. Stop by their visitor's center where you'll learn more about the whole process.

Down the same road as the hatchery is the Tonto Creek campground. The campground's upper section features 9 sites, while the lower has 17. You're in the forest out here—nestled amid ponderosas, junipers, and oaks. Tonto Creek flows nearby, and it's stocked with rainbow trout. This is a rustic site with no toilets or electricity. It's open April 1 through October 30. The fee for camping is $8 per day.

Payson is just 10 miles south of Tonto Natural Bridge State Park, on State Route 87, (520) 476-4202. The natural rock formation that gives the park its name is the largest travertine, or limestone, bridge in the world. The bridge is 400 feet wide and 180 feet high and crosses a 150-foot-wide canyon. In fact it is so big, that when you arrive at the old lodge and park your car you have no idea that you actually are on the bridge. Viewpoints are easily accessible, but most exciting is a steep climb down a trail at the side of the canyon wall, which will lead you under the bridge. The site was discovered by prospector David Gowan in 1877 during a skirmish with Apaches. A lodge that Gowan's nephew built in 1927 has been restored on the site. Admission is $7 a carload. Hours vary, so call ahead.

On the way to Tonto Natural Bridge, you may want to check out the Shoofly Indian Ruin. It's just north of Payson, off State Route 87 on Houston Mesa Road. The only remains of this ancient settlement are primitive rock pit houses, abandoned by their residents about A.D. 1250. No one knows why, or where they went.

About 19 miles north of Payson on State Route 87 is the town of Strawberry, home of the oldest schoolhouse in Arizona. Turn left at Strawberry Lodge in the center of town and about 1.5 miles later, you'll find the log schoolhouse, built in 1884. The last classes were held there in 1916.

Strawberry is just below the Rim. You can climb State Route 87 another 10 miles to the top

The San Francisco Peaks near Flagstaff provide plenty of recreational opportunities for outdoors enthusiasts.

of the Rim. Watch for the signs to Forest Road 300, which turns off to the east. This gravel road, maintained only in summer and passable by passenger car, offers spectacular lookouts from the edge of the Rim as well as picnic areas and campgrounds. It also affords access to a number of lakes that are great for fishing. If you follow the road for its entire 45-mile length, you'll end up on State Route 260, approximately 30 miles east of Payson.

Anglers can pick up information on good fishing locations in Rim Country lakes and streams (as well as other information on Payson area attractions and activities) by visiting the Rim Country Regional Chamber of Commerce at the corner of State Route 87 and Main Street, (520) 474-4515 or (800) 672-9766.

For hikers, a number of trails wander through the area. One popular trail is the Highline National Recreational Trail, which travels for 51 miles beneath the Mogollon Rim. Some trails branch off from the Highline up to the Rim itself. From the Pine Trailhead, 15 miles north of Payson off State Route. 87, the Highline heads toward the 260 Trailhead, 27 miles east of Payson off State Route 260. For more details on trails in the Tonto National Forest, pick up trail guides available at the U.S. Forest Service Ranger's District Office at 1009 E. State Route 260 in Payson, (520) 474-7900. The office also has information on nearby Forest Service campgrounds.

If you want to wrap up the day with gambling at a one-armed bandit or a game of chance, there's the Mazatzal Casino, a half-mile south of Payson on the east side of State Route 87 at milepost 251, (520) 474-6044 or (800) 777-7529. The casino is run by the Tonto Apache tribe.

If you want to stay the night, lodgings include the Rim Country Inn, in the $70 to $100 double-occupancy range, at the corner of State Route 87 and Phoenix Street, (520) 474-4526, and the Best Western Paysonglo Lodge, with rooms ranging from $55 to $110 double occupancy, at 1005 S. Beeline Highway (State Route 87), (520) 474-2382. Remember, though, if you want to stay in Payson over a summer weekend when things are really hopping, you'll need to make reservations well in advance. For more information, call the Rim Country Regional Chamber of Commerce, (520) 474-4515 or (800) 672-9766, or visit www.rimcountrychamber.com.

At lunchtime, check out the Small Café at the Twin Pine Shopping Center, Beeline Highway and State Route 87, (520) 474-4209, which serves sandwiches, soups, and salads. At the Oaks Restaurant and Lounge, 302 W. Main Street, (520) 474-1929, you'll find well-prepared steaks and seafood for dinner and a good selection of hot and cold sandwiches for lunch. Reservations are suggested. (It's closed on Monday and Tuesday.)

INSIDERS' TIP

When you are traveling on Native American land, be respectful. Don't take any pictures without permission, and be sure to inquire about all the necessary permits and licenses if you plan on going hiking, hunting, or fishing. Keep in mind that dances are often part of religious ceremonies and visitors should have the same deference they would in church. Alcohol is not permitted on reservations. For more information on enjoying Native American destinations, contact the Arizona Office of Tourism at (602) 230-7733. You can also call the Arizona American Indian Tourism Association at (520) 523-7320.

Saguaro Lake

Boating, Jet-Skiing, fishing, picnicking, and camping can be enjoyed at a number of different lakes around Phoenix. One of our favorites is Saguaro Lake, about an hour-and-a-half drive out of the central part of the Valley. From Scottsdale, take Shea Boulevard east to Fountain Hills, then catch State Route 87 going north. About 10 miles past Fort McDowell Casino, you will see the signs directing you to Saguaro Lake. You can also get to State Route 87 (nicknamed the Beeline Highway) from Mesa, where Country Club Drive turns into the Beeline as it heads north.

Saguaro Lake is part of a chain of four lakes formed by Salt River dams that have been built in Tonto National Forest over several decades of the twentieth century. The most famous of these dams is Roosevelt Dam. Completed in 1911, it is the world's largest masonry dam, constructed entirely of quarry stone. The dams provide the Valley of the Sun with hydroelectric power, irrigation, and flood control. Roosevelt Lake is the easternmost of the four lakes, and the chain moves to the west with Apache and Canyon Lakes, then Saguaro—the second-smallest at 1,200 acres.

Anglers catch bass and trout in Saguaro. Jet-skiers and motorboaters ply the elongated

DAYTRIPS

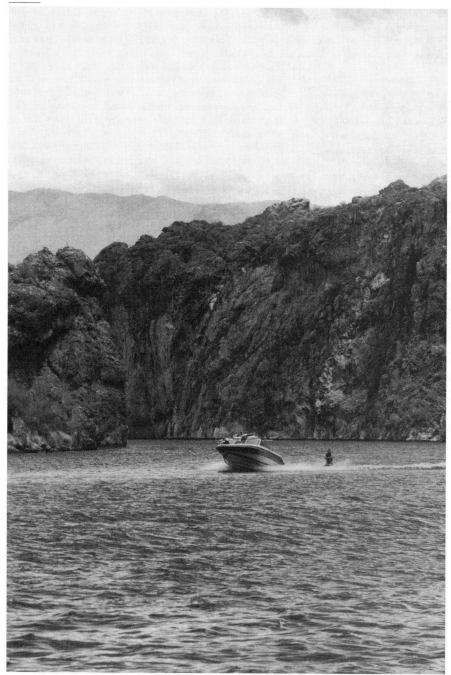

10-mile-long Saquaro Lake provides a watersport paradise for those who enjoy wet sports.

Photo: Debbie Ross

stretches of the lake with wild and wet abandon. If none of these pursuits appeals to you, consider a one-and-a-half-hour paddleboat cruise on the Desert Belle. It allows you to see much of the lake's 22-mile shoreline, and the captain provides occasional commentary to enhance your visit. You have your choice of sitting in an open or covered area. The weather will be a bit cooler than in the Valley, and you'll get a breeze off the lake, so dress appropriately. The scenery is an intriguing juxtaposition of rocky desert outcroppings against the blue water. You will pass dozens of rock formations, narrow canyons and caves as well as cliffs streaked with black varnish where waterfalls once cascaded. Flora includes many varieties of cacti, desert trees, and, in the spring, a good smattering of desert wildflowers. As a rarity, saguaro cacti grow close to the shore with branching arms. Wildlife sightings are part of the fun. It's not unusual to see coyotes, javelinas, rabbits, squirrels, mule deer, and bighorn sheep. Birds are quite abundant, and if you're lucky you'll see turkey vultures, hawks, owls, blue herons, and even bald eagles. In fall, October through January, the Desert Belle leaves the dock at 12:30 PM Wednesday through Sunday. In high season (February through April) the cruise is offered at 12:30 and 2:30 PM daily. In summer (May through August) the gears shift to a sunset cruise, at 5:30 PM only, on Saturday and Sunday. The cost is $12 for adults and $7 for children. If you're not picnicking for this daytrip, we suggest lunch at the Lakeshore Restaurant, (480) 984-5311, which is open daily where you can get a nice view of the lake and marina from the patio. For more information on the Lakeshore Restaurant or the Desert Belle, call (480) 984-5311 or visit www.saguarolake.net.

Information on other amenities at Saguaro Lake is also available from the Tonto National Forest Service by writing P.O. Box 5348, Phoenix, AZ 85010, or calling (602) 225-5200. Those with boats and jet skis should be considerate of water skiers and kayakers. For boat storage, call the marina at (480) 986-5596; for service and rentals, call (480) 986-0969. Boating maps are available at the Mesa District Ranger Station, 26 N. Macdonald Street, Mesa (480) 610-3300 and at the Tonto National Forest Office, 2324 E. McDowell Road, Phoenix (602) 225-5200. The entry fee is $4 per day, per vehicle, with $2 extra charged for watercraft.

Canyon Lake also offers cruises, in this case aboard the Dolly Steamboat, a 100-foot replica of an old double-decker riverboat. You have to take a different route to reach Canyon Lake, which lies 16 miles north of Apache Junction off State Route 88, also called the Apache Trail. Cruise times vary by season, but generally the 90-minute Nature Cruise, which costs $14 plus tax, departs at noon and 2 PM daily. The Twilight Dinner Cruise varies depending on the season and costs $39.95. Call ahead for the latest prices, schedules, and reservations at (480) 827-9144 or visit www.dollysteamboat.com.

Down Interstate 10

Tucson

For a look at Arizona's second-largest city, you need only drive about two hours southeast of Phoenix on Interstate 10. The distance is 115 miles, and Arizonans joke that it is the most boring drive in the state. Luckily, the 75-mph speed limit helps you breeze past the desert scrub toward the more interesting sight of Tucson's Santa Catalina Mountains. One stop to consider along the way, though, is Picacho Peak, near Eloy, site of Arizona's only Civil War battle. It is commemorated with a monument and a flagpole.

Like Phoenix, Tucson is a highly livable desert metropolis seeing tremendous growth. It has beautiful residential developments, a respectable cultural scene, and a healthy economy. Plus, it's in a lovely setting surrounded by five mountain ranges, including the blue-tinged Santa Catalinas.

Tucson encompasses 800,000 people in a metropolitan area of 500 square miles. Its residents by and large love their "Old Pueblo," preferring it over Phoenix, which they see as being way too urbanized and sprawling. You'll often hear residents of the two cities banter over which place is better.

Tucson does seem to have a slight advantage concerning weather. It boasts 350 days of sunshine a year, compared with Phoenix's 300 days. Also, those familiar with both cities say the summer daytime heat is somewhat less oppressive, and the nights are crisper in Tucson, although 105 degrees in June is not uncommon. Tucson is 1,000 feet higher than Phoenix, which partially explains the weather difference. Winters feel a bit more like winter thanks to the sight of snowcaps on the surrounding mountains. As expected, for at least six months of the year, Tucson's weather is wonderful.

Tucson makes a great daytrip from Phoenix, but its scenery, major attractions, and resorts make it a fine vacation destination in and of itself. What follows are several suggestions on making the most of your excursion. For further details, see the *Insiders' Guide to Tucson*.

If we had to name two things you must see while you are in the area, they would be the Arizona-Sonoran Desert Museum and Mission San Xavier del Bac. So plan your day with that tip in mind.

The Arizona-Sonoran Desert Museum is about 10 miles west of Tucson at 2021 N. Kinney Road. It offers a terrific immersion in the plant and animal life of the desert, with more than 300 types of plants and 1,300 kinds of animals in a natural landscape. One exhibit features nocturnal desert dwellers such as kit foxes and tarantulas. An underwater viewing area lets you see beavers, river otters, and desert fishes. There's also a hummingbird aviary and a prairie dog colony. A walk-through cave leads you to an exhibit of gems and minerals from this region. All around are blooming desert gardens and displays of cacti. Admission is $9.95 for adults, $1.75 for children ages 6 to 12, and free for children younger than 6. Hours are 8:30 AM to 5 PM in the fall and winter and 7:30 AM to 5 PM in the spring and summer. From June through September, the museum is open until 10 PM on Saturday nights. For more information, call (520) 883-1380 or visit www.desertmuseum.org.

The mission at San Xavier del Bac is easy to reach from Interstate 19. Heading south about 10 miles from Tucson, look for the San Xavier Road exit. Its gleaming white towers and domes are unmistakable. Against a clear blue sky, this mission—dating from 1783—makes a one-of-a-kind image, so be sure to bring your camera. The interior architecture is wonderful as well, thanks to many years of meticulous restoration work. Called the "Sistine Chapel of North America," the

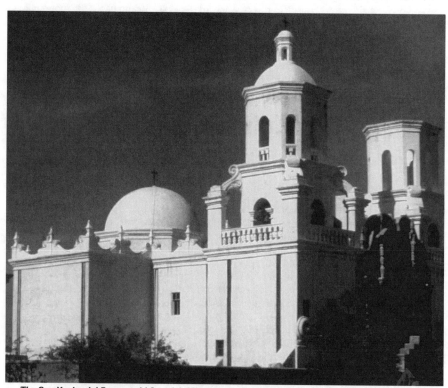

The San Xavier del Bac, an old Spanish Mission near Tucson, is known as the "White Dove of the Desert." It's a must-see for its unique architecture, frescoes, and statues.

Photo: Peter Pfeiffer

DAYTRIPS

mission features artwork on practically every square inch and in practically every nook and cranny. This includes paintings, frescoes, and statues. Arizonans know the mission as the "White Dove of the Desert." As you wander around, learn about the Jesuit missionary and explorer Father Eusebio Francisco Kino and other men of the cloth who served here. Located on the Tohono O'odham Reservation, the mission is one of the last Spanish churches still serving its Native American parishioners. The mission is open for view during daytime hours, and no admission is charged, although donations are welcome. Masses are held each morning and four times on Sundays. For more information, call (520) 294-2624.

If you're exploring Tucson by car, try to fit in a drive to Saguaro National Park, where you will find the largest concentration of saguaro cacti in the state and in the world, for that matter, since saguaros only grow in the Sonoran Desert. For the western district, or the area surrounding the Tucson Mountains, exit at Ina Road from Interstate 10 and drive west, following the signs. For the eastern district, or the area surrounding the Rincon Mountains, continue on I-10 until you reach southern Tucson, then take Houghton Road north and follow the signs for about 8 miles. The western district's number is (520) 733-5158; the eastern district's is (520) 733-5153.

For a taste of the Old West, one of the best bets in Arizona is Old Tucson Studios, originally built as a set for the movie *Arizona* in 1939. It has since been used as the backdrop for more than 200 movies, TV shows, commercials, and documentaries. Old Tucson is tourist-friendly, with lots of staged gunfights, stunt shows, trail rides, costumed characters, tours of movie sites, films, old-fashioned shops, stagecoach rides, cowboy-style dinners, and saloons. It's 12 miles west of Tucson, next to Saguaro National Park's western entrance. The address is 201 S. Kinney Road. In the winter, hours are generally 10 AM to 6 PM, Tuesdays through Sundays. Admission is $14.95 for adults, $9.45 for children ages 4 to 11, and free for children younger than 4. For more information, call (520) 883-0100 or visit www.oldtuscon.com.

Another Tucson-area attraction worth considering is the Pima Air & Space Museum, 6000 E. Valencia Road, (520) 574-0462 or (520) 574-9658, www.pimaair.org. It has more than 180 civilian and military airplanes on display. It's open from 9 AM to 5 PM daily, with admission costs of $7.50 for adults, $6.50 for seniors and military, $4 for children ages 7 to 12, and free for those younger than 10.

The University of Arizona also makes an interesting stop. Highlights of the campus include the planetarium and observatory at the Flandrau Science Center, (520) 621-4515; the Ansel Adams and Alfred Steilitz collection at the Center for Creative Photography, (520) 621-7968; and the exhibits on Native American cultures at the Arizona State Museum, (520) 621-6302.

If you don't mind going a little farther afield, the Columbia University Biosphere 2 Center in Oracle is worth seeing. About 30 miles north of Tucson on State Route 77, Biosphere 2 is the new incarnation of Biosphere 1, which you may remember as the place where several scientists lived under a roof of glass and steel in a small version of Earth and its various climates. The scientists no longer live there; it is now a research center with daily tours and plenty of interesting exhibits, including ones on global warming and rainforest plant life. Admission is $12.95 for adults, $8.95 for youth 13 to 16, $6 for children ages 6 to 12, and free for children younger than 6. For more information call (520) 896-6400 or visit www.biosphere2.com.

INSIDERS' TIP

Being a desert area doesn't keep Arizona from having a winter. Valley winters are mild, so we have to remind ourselves when we're traveling to northern Arizona that snows can be heavy and unexpected. Tire chains are recommended for those making winter trips into the Mogollon Rim country or up to Prescott or Flagstaff. Check the travel weather reports on television or call the state Department of Public Safety for reports on highway conditions along your route at (602) 651-2400, extension 7623.

INSIDERS' TIP

For more than 30 years, the city of Casa Grande, between Phoenix and Tucson, has hosted a Native American powwow called O'odham Tash each February. Events include parades, a queen's pageant, Native American music and dance, a carnival, a rodeo, and arts and crafts displays—all put together by various Southwestern tribes. For more information, call (520) 836-4723 or (800) 916-1515.

DAYTRIPS

Colossal Cave, one of the largest dry caverns in the world, is 20 miles east of Tucson, (520) 647-7275. The Titan Missile Museum, about 30 miles south of Tucson, features a tour of the underground silo housing the world's only Titan II ICBM. The phone number is (520) 625-7736. Tombstone, with its famed OK Corral, is about 70 miles southeast of Tucson. Call (520) 457-3456 for information or visit www.tombstoneaz.com. Even Nogales, Mexico, with its border-town ambiance, is within reach by going 60 miles south of Tucson on Interstate 19.

In addition, a trip to Tucson puts you closer to Arizona's winemaking region. Yes, the desert soil, cultivated just right, can produce grapevines that yield premium, award-winning red and white wines. Wineries that offer tours and tastings include the Dark Mountain Brewery and Winery in Vail, (520) 762-5777, www.darkmountainbrewery.com, and Sonoita Vineyards in Elgin, (520) 297-2850. You can also call the Arizona Wine Commission for more information on Arizona's wine industry at (602) 542-0877.

Tucson is known as the "Astronomy Capital of the World," thanks in large part to clear desert night skies and to Kitt Peak National Observatory, which houses the largest collection of telescopes anywhere, including the largest solar telescope. You can find it about 50 miles south-west of Tucson via a steep and winding mountain road. The visitors center at the observatory is open from 9 AM to 4 PM daily and offers guided tours. Inquire about evening stargazing programs. For information call (520) 318-8726. The Flandrau Science Center at the University of Arizona also offers programs in its planetarium and public observatory. Call (520) 621-4515 or visit www.flandrau.org.

Hiking enthusiasts can head up to Sabino Canyon in north Tucson. From Interstate 10, exit east on Grant Road, then take the Tanque Verde Road turnoff. Tanque Verde leads to Sabino Canyon Road and the visitors center. The Sabino Canyon Recreation Area can be reached by calling (520) 749-8700.

Although Tucson's event calendar is not quite as lively as Phoenix's, you might be on the watch for several major events. In February, try to attend the Tucson Gem & Mineral Show, an international exposition, (520) 624-1817. Also in February is the huge, PRCA-sanctioned rodeo La Fiesta de los Vaqueros, preceded by the world's largest non-motorized parade, (520) 741-2233. Throughout March, look out for spring training baseball at Hi Corbett Field and Tucson Electric Park for the Colorado Rockies, the Chicago White Sox, and, last but not least, the Arizona Diamondbacks, (888) 683-3900.

Shopping is a good diversion in Tucson, thanks to a mix of major metropolitan malls and cozy boutique districts. Foothills Mall at Ina Road and La Cholla Boulevard, (520) 219-0650, offers several outlet stores, a movie theater, a brewery, and an indoor games and rides area for children. Park Place is at 5870 E. Broadway Boulevard, (520) 748-1222. And the Tucson Mall is at 4500 N. Oracle Road, (520) 293-7330. Old Town Tucson, near Main Avenue and Franklin Street, is a quaint place for browsing, and shops have a good selection of Native American and South-western arts and crafts. Old Town Artisans, a marketplace dating from the 1850s, can be reached at (520) 623-6024 or by visiting www.oldtownartisans.com. Also, several great little shops are clustered on Fourth Avenue. For studio glass art check out the work of Arizona master Tom Philabaum at Philabaum Contemporary Art Glass at 711 S. Sixth Avenue, (520) 884-7404. Tucson's Antique Mall is at 3130 E. Grant Road, (520) 326-3070.

Should you decide to stay overnight in Tucson, the city has a good selection of chain hotels and motels, including Courtyard Marriott, with locations near the airport at 2505 Executive Drive, (520) 573-0000, or at the Tucson Williams Center, 201 S. Williams Boulevard, (520) 745-2393. Another possibility is The Hilton Tucson East at 7600 E. Broadway Road, (520) 721-5600, with 233 rooms in an atrium-style upscale hotel. Tucson also has several nice bed and breakfasts, including Casa Alegre at 316 E. Speedway Boulevard, (520) 628-1800 or (800) 628-5654, and the El Presidio Inn, 297 N. Main Avenue, (520) 623-6151, (800) 349-6151.

First-class resorts help feed Tucson's tourism industry. Those with a national reputation include the Arizona Inn, a restored hotel dating from 1930. It is at 2200 E. Elm Street, (520) 325-1541, (800) 93301093, or www.arizonainn.com. Spa enthusiasts can't go wrong with Canyon Ranch and its full slate of fitness activities, nutrition counseling, beauty treatments, and gour-met meals. It's tucked away at 8600 E. Rockcliff Road, (520) 749-9000, (800) 742-9000, or www.canyonranch.com. Golf resorts, all brimming with amenities, include: Loews Ventana Canyon Resort, 7000 N. Resort Drive, (520) 299-2020, (800) 234-5117, or www.loweshotels.com; the Sheraton El Conquistador Resort, 10000 N. Oracle Road, (520) 544-5000, (800) 325-7832, or www.sheratonelconquistador; and the Westin La Paloma, 3800 E. Sunrise Drive,

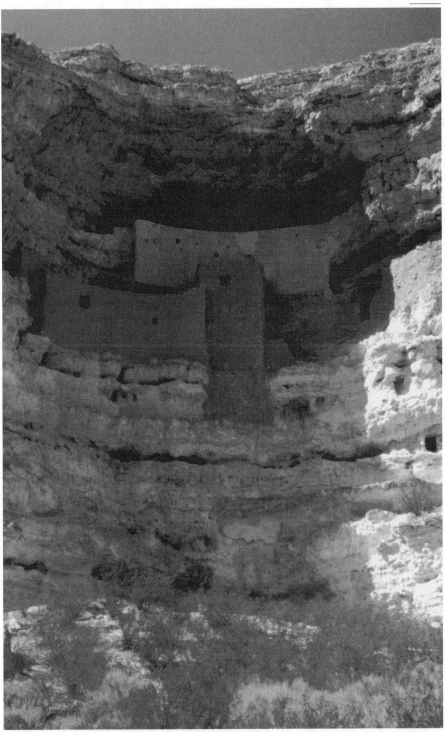

Montezuma Castle National Monument is one of the most well-preserved structures built by Arizona's ancient settlers, the Sinagua.

Photo: Peter Pfeiffer

DAYTRIPS

(520) 742-6000, (800) 937-8461, or www.westin.com. Expect rooms at these resorts to go for at least $200 a night double occupancy in high season.

Restaurant options are plentiful in Tucson. Two of the best-known upscale dining rooms are the Ventana Room, 7000 N. Resort Drive, (520) 299-2020, and The Tack Room, 7300 E. Vactor Ranch Trail, (520) 722-2800. Quite popular is the Southwestern fare at the Cafe Terra Cotta, 4310 N. Campbell Avenue, (520) 577-8100. Mexican restaurants are a good option: Check out El Charro Mexican Cafe, the oldest family-operated Mexican restaurant in the United States, at 311 N. Court Avenue, (520) 622-1922; or Lerua's Fine Mexican Food, 2005 E. Broadway Boulevard, (520) 624-0322. Or tap into the University of Arizona scene with a visit to Gentle Ben's Brewing Co., 865 E. University Boulevard, (520) 624-4177 or www.gentlebens.com, a bar and restaurant with several of its own brews on tap.

Detailed information on Tucson's many attractions, restaurants, accommodations, and shopping can be obtained by calling or writing the Metropolitan Tucson Convention & Visitors Bureau, 130 S. Scott Avenue, (800) 638-8350 or by visiting www.visittucson.org.

INSIDERS' TIP

When driving out of the Valley into other parts of the state, travelers can be surprised at how cool it is at their destination. When the elevation is 5,000 feet above the Valley floor, the temperature drops quickly, so dress accordingly. Even if you stay within the Valley, the desert floor does not retain its heat during the night and you can freeze.

DAYTRIPS

Neighborhoods and Real Estate

LOOK FOR:
- **Neighborhoods**
- **Apartment Living**
- **Relocation Services**
- **Real Estate Agencies**

With growth eating up the desert at the rate of an acre an hour, it's a buyer's market in Phoenix and the Valley of the Sun. Developers are busy building new homes on the far edges of the Valley and with many people moving to the area, real estate is a booming industry.

In 1999, the median price of a home in the Valley was $136,098. Compare that to houses in Sarasota, Florida, which will run you $161,160 or housing in San Diego which goes for $236,544. With a median price of $105,000, resale homes in the Valley are also a bargain. Figures from the National Association of Realtors in January 1998 showed that a 2,200-square-foot single-family home with four bedrooms, two baths, a family room, and a two-car garage that would be priced at $422,800 in Nassau County, New York, would run about $105,000 in Phoenix.

The state has one of the lowest income-tax structures in America. During the last decade, the state reduced income tax by 31%. Couple that with the relatively low property taxes—the average property tax rate in Maricopa County in 1997 was $13.13 per $100 of assessed valuation—and buying and keeping a home in the Valley becomes a terrific bargain. Maricopa County collects property taxes for itself, the state, cities, school districts, the community college district, the Central Arizona Water Conservation District, and any other taxing districts within which a residence is located. (The average tax figure cited is a blend of all of these.) Residential property is assessed at 10 percent of current value, so that a $105,000 home would be assessed at $10,500. At the average $13.13 per $100, the annual taxes on that home would be $1,378.65. Not bad, eh?

In this chapter, we take a look at the Valley's booming real estate scene. We introduce you to some of the Valley's well-known neighborhoods and to some of the area's established real estate agents who can help you find the perfect home, should you like the Valley so much you decide to move here. The Valley is known for its retirement communities, and we have listed those in greater detail in our Retirement chapter. For information on Valley school districts, see our Education and Childcare chapter.

Neighborhoods

Most Valley housing is relatively new and, consequently, so are most neighborhoods. The neighborhoods that people can pick out by name usually have some history to them. Phoenix, at least partly because of the way it has annexed unincorporated communities, has neighborhoods with names. In Phoenix, neighborhoods such as Encanto, Arcadia, Maryvale, Paradise Valley, and Sunnyslope are among the best known.

To the rest of the Valley, a neighborhood usually is the name of a development. With so many new developments popping up, any listing would quickly become a litany of names and features without any context. It's much more useful to think of the Valley outside of Phoenix in geographic terms. North and South Scottsdale are distinct from one another, so are North and South Tempe and East and West Mesa. The neighborhoods and developments within each geographic area are very similar.

With very few exceptions, the great truth about Valley development is that the farther you get from the Valley's core, the houses being built are bigger and the landscaping is more desert-like.

The oldest Valley neighborhoods were built to help the residents forget they were in the desert. Greenery abounds thanks to lawn irrigation. In these neighborhoods, lawns were often sunk an inch or two below the surrounding sidewalks and bounded by grass-covered mounds. The lawns are flooded at night so that they look a bit like rice paddies. They stay green.

As time went on, the Valley became more water-conscious. The neighborhoods built in the 1950s through the 1970s saw a mixture of green lawns and desert landscaping, with grass lawns still tending to outnumber the desert landscapes. By and large, these neighborhoods are full of ranch-style houses built without basements on concrete pads. Because the elements (except for the sun) were relatively kind to autos, many homes built in that era featured car ports rather than garages. Most of these homes were built in cozy proximity for young, blue-collar and lower-middle-class families.

The developments built in the past 15 to 20 years tend to have a more spacious feeling. Two-story houses have become more common. Garages are the norm. The developments themselves have sunken greenbelts for flood protection, which opens up the landscape of a neighborhood. The greenbelts become places to jog, walk the dog, ride your bike, or just meander. Many newer developments are built around artificial lakes or golf courses to add a touch of cool, green relief to the surroundings. On the higher end of the price scale, some communities are gated and have their own security.

Homeowner associations have become more common, both in older neighborhoods and in new developments. In new developments especially, they act as a form of low-level government, enforcing various restrictions in the property deeds in an effort to keep property values up for all association members. Enforcement is usually through fines, after the homeowner has been given some warnings. The associations use their dues to keep up common areas, such as greenbelts and roadside landscaping. Restrictions can be as loose as making sure that all the houses are painted in a similar palette of colors or as tight as not allowing outdoor speakers in a patio area. Outdoor remodeling and building additions often have to be reviewed by the associations in order to ensure that they comply with the deed restrictions. This is in addition to any review procedure that a city might have.

The associations evolved because of the vast differences in neighborhood upkeep, especially in Phoenix proper. You can drive down one half-mile of a street in a development and find nothing but immaculately kept homes and landscapes, and then proceed the next half-mile through blocks of badly kept rentals. The associations help keep this patchwork from developing any further.

INSIDERS' TIP

When the summers heat up, many seniors keep on with their exercise programs by walking at the air-conditioned shopping malls. The doors open early in the morning (before the stores) and people walk the cool sidewalks. It's a great opportunity to make new friends and stay healthy at the same time.

Phoenix

Sprawling for more than 400 square miles, the City of Phoenix encompasses many neighborhoods. The following are some of the more identifiable.

Ahwatukee

Sitting south of South Mountain, Ahwatukee is an area that saw most of its growth in the 1980s and '90s. Terracotta roofs and stucco predominate, and the neighborhood is generally

The full moon competes with a glittering Phoenix skyline.

Photo: Courtesy of Jessen Associates, Inc.

NEIGHBORHOODS
AND REAL ESTATE

walled off from the main streets, with a few entry points. This is a neighborhood full of young urban professionals and slightly older families. Be warned that commuter traffic during rush hour can be slow. The housing, generally single-story or two-story homes and a wide variety of upscale apartments and town homes, ranges from the moderately priced to the expensive.

Arcadia

The Arcadia area is one of the more mature neighborhoods. Sitting beside Camelback Mountain and stretching to Scottsdale, this neighborhood developed mostly in the postwar era. Within its confines a mix of wood-frame, brick, and painted cinder-block homes can be found. The landscaping is mature, and the streets are lined with trees, making it an attractive area for middle-class families and young urban professionals. The houses have more character than many of the homes built in later years.

Downtown Phoenix

Downtown Phoenix is undergoing a revitalization spearheaded by the location of two major venues in the area: America West Arena and Bank One Ballpark. This has brought an explosion of interest in opening businesses—particularly restaurants, coffeehouses, and nightclubs—that could take advantage of the sudden influx of nighttime foot traffic in the area.

What little housing there was in the area before downtown's resurgence was older and housed mostly lower-income people. This housing, generally small, single-story houses with mature, water-intensive grass-and-tree landscaping, is gradually being torn down to make way for upscale condominium and townhouse sorts of housing. However, it is an area where concerns about crime and personal safety are legitimate. The changes in demographics mean that the old social fabric is being torn apart, and a new one has yet to emerge. You have to question whether this is a neighborhood in the traditional sense or just a section of the city with some housing in it.

The main advantage of living here is being close to downtown jobs, and the principal disadvantage is that downtown is becoming something of an adult Disneyland, an entertainment theme park without such essential services as grocery or drug stores. From America West Arena, which generally is seen as the southern end of downtown, there is one grocery store within a two-mile radius, and beyond that you have to travel a bit for more. Considering the pace of change, this could become a very desirable neighborhood very quickly.

INSIDERS' TIP

Besides the real estate classifieds of *The Arizona Republic* and *The Tribune*, a number of publications can aid home shoppers. Look for *Homes & Land, The Real Estate Book, Homes Illustrated, Harmon Homes,* and *Home Buying Choices. Home Buying Choices* covers the entire Valley in one publication, and the rest offer several editions zoned to specific areas. All of them include photos of the houses. They're all available for free at various grocery and convenience stores, usually in racks by the exits so they're easy to grab on the way out.

Encanto

The neighborhood around Encanto Park, which forms a good portion of the square mile defined by Seventh Avenue, Thomas Road, 19th Avenue, and McDowell Road, is very good-looking. The homes are older, dating from as far back as the 1920s, and feature mature landscaping. There's a sense of being in an oasis that has a bit of a Midwestern look. Unlike developments built after water restrictions came in, this is a neighborhood that relies on grass for landscaping rather than desert styles. Being in a relatively flat area of central Phoenix that is only a few miles from the Salt River, the neighborhood's trees and grass insulate and isolate the area. You don't notice the surrounding mountains so much here, just the neighborhood. As a desirable little enclave close to downtown Phoenix, Encanto's housing is relatively expensive, filling the neighborhood with professionals and their families. The Encanto neighborhood is of a similar character to a number of neighborhoods within five miles of downtown Phoenix, including the Willo, Coronado, and Phoenix Country Club neighborhoods.

Chris-Town

By and large, the homes in the area around Chris-Town are affordable and close to the amenities of downtown and the state fairgrounds. The neighborhood streets, developed from the '50s through the '70s, are wider than those in older neighborhoods such as Encanto, so it doesn't seem so isolated from the desert.

The postwar housing reflects a suburban imperative. Single-story structures, either of wood-frame or painted cinder-block construction, dominate, with mature landscaping and grass-blanketed yards. If not for the palm trees and desert mountains visible in the distance, this would be a suburban area that would fit comfortably in any part of the country.

In many ways, the Chris-Town area is mirrored east of Central Avenue by similar unnamed neighborhoods (or neighborhoods whose names are obscure) and west of I-17 by the vast Maryvale neighborhood. They present a line of demarcation between the old Phoenix of the '50s, with its working-class ambiance, and the outlying upper middle-class areas (often defined by desert landscaping) farther out from the city's core.

> ## INSIDERS' TIP
>
> Arizona housing is being built at a fantastic rate. Developments are spreading into the desert at more than an acre an hour. The newer developments offer more of a desert flavor than the older neighborhoods, but established neighborhoods already have their own distinctive cultures and flavors, which can be a good source of support during any transition.

Maryvale

Maryvale has become almost synonymous with the west side of Phoenix. In actuality, Maryvale was a 1950s development by builder John F. Long. (He named it after his wife, Mary.) The units were affordable for young families, looking something like desert versions of the house in the Dick Van Dyke Show. The streets were broader than the old cozy developments like Encanto, but the general suburban desert feeling was the same. Occasionally, you see some desert landscaping, but most reminders of the desert are the occasional cactus or saguaro that's part of a conventional grass lawn. Maryvale still attracts working-class and lower-middle-class folks.

Many builders followed Long's lead in subsequent decades, and the effect is a similar style of single-story tract housing for many miles around. The only difference is that with newer developments, desert landscaping began to catch up with and rival the predominance of grass lawns.

Some areas of Maryvale have deteriorated and face high crime, although west-side business has been growing since the completion of I-10. The housing, which depended on lower-cost materials for its affordability, goes south very quickly when not maintained properly. That desert sun is murder on asphalt shingles and sprayed-paint exteriors.

Desert Sky Pavilion, an open-air entertainment amphitheater that opened on Maryvale's west side in 1990, helped fuel a major economic revitalization of the area. The then-moribund Westridge Mall, which is across Encanto Boulevard from the amphitheater, has since been renamed Desert Sky Mall and is thriving. The area also managed to attract a spring-training baseball complex that opened in 1998.

Metrocenter

The area around Metrocenter mall, which runs alongside I-17 from the Arizona Canal to Peoria Avenue, is newer than Chris-Town. Looked at as a geological exercise, this neighborhood reflects the next strata in the Valley's growth. The developments around the mall are more likely to feel like suburban enclaves than those in Chris-Town. The Metrocenter neighborhood's

NEIGHBORHOODS AND REAL ESTATE

streets feature more twists and turns that keep nonresidents from cutting through, a legitimate concern in light of the mall's heavy traffic. Here some desert landscaping starts to creep in among the suburban lawnscape. The landscaping is mature, and houses may be just a tad farther apart. Again, single-story structures dominate, and there is less of the painted cinder-block and more of the wood-frame type of house. By and large, this area is a bedroom community for middle-class families of professionals who work downtown or in nearby office-industrial parks.

North Central

From the 1920s on, an address along the northern parts of Central Avenue meant the occupants were wealthy. Keep in mind that northern is a relative term. The city has expanded far to the north of Northern Avenue, which once was the northern boundary of the city. This well-heeled section of Central Avenue begins at Camelback Road on the south and extends to just north of Northern Avenue. Houses here were built over a long period. Some reflect an older, more-stately style, while others are upscale suburban ranch houses. The streets are narrow and cozy. You'll find a tree-shaded walking path on both sides of Central Avenue, the remains of an old riding trail for horses. The landscaping is mostly a lush green. The neighborhood is upscale and filled with professionals.

Sunnyslope

Sunnyslope began as a place where indigent people came to seek cures for lung ailments. The Valley's dry climate made it the perfect place for such cures, but cure-seekers were banned from pitching tents in Phoenix proper. So they went north to around Dunlap and Central Avenues to the foothills where they would sit on the "sunny slopes" and recover their health. Eventually a sanatorium was built there, and a small, thriving lower-middle-class community arose.

The beauty of Sunnyslope is that the neighborhood feels cozy. It's a strange perception because the houses aren't really any closer together than elsewhere. Perhaps the maturity of the landscaping and the way the community nestles at the foot of the North Mountain Preserve makes it feel more enclosed than some other areas. Homes in the area mainly are ranch style, and the character of the neighborhood is generally middle class.

Paradise Valley

The Paradise Valley neighborhood of Phoenix borders on the town of Paradise Valley, but don't confuse the two. They're very different. The Paradise Valley neighborhood is a visually busy area that creeps up to the north end of North Mountain. It also rises toward the foothills to the north. Houses here are peopled by blue- and white-collar type. The construction is generally single-story tract homes, with many taking advantage of desert landscaping, which tends to become more of the norm in the areas immediately around Phoenix's mountains.

South Phoenix

Technically, South Phoenix would include Ahwatukee and an extremely wide variety of houses and neighborhoods. Farms, ranches, nurseries, orchards, and industrial parks, as well as the luxurious area around the Pointe South Mountain Resort—all are part of South Phoenix.

Unfortunately, in popular parlance, South Phoenix is the wrong side of the tracks—actually, the wrong side of the Salt River. Some (and we stress the word "some") sections of South Phoenix come as close as you'll find to an urban war zone in the Valley.

There's a strong effort among community members to fight blight and crime. South Phoenix, like many other Valley areas, is an area of suburban tract homes, many of them built in the past 20 to 30 years. A few developers are rediscovering the area and building pockets of upscale homes near the base of the South Mountain. These developments offer great values on mountain-view housing. Even when you exclude the more luxurious areas of South Phoenix, the income levels vary widely, from middle class to poor.

Southeast Valley

Chandler

Chandler has a small core with some housing that dates back to the city's founding. Chandler didn't see an immediate postwar growth boom, and thus remained a largely agricultural community until residential developments began sprouting at a good clip in the late 1970s and early 1980s. Again, the newer developments are predominantly of the tile-roof and stucco style, but there are also wood-frame neighborhoods and neighborhoods akin to Maryvale. Chandler is attractive to young families and middle-class professionals, particularly since Intel became a major employer here.

Gilbert

Like Chandler, Gilbert had been an agricultural community for most of its existence. Then in the 1980s, residential development started to boom. So, the vast majority of housing in Gilbert is relatively new, which means tile roofs and stucco. The older places in town are a mixture of horse properties and small ranches. The city of Gilbert attracts young families and middle-class professionals.

Mesa

At 122 square miles, Mesa is not as vast as Phoenix. Still, the east-west drive across Mesa is long and makes the city seem to stretch on forever. Most of the city's growth in the past two to three decades has been in housing developments that spread eastward from the more mature area surrounding downtown.

Downtown Mesa—The center of downtown spreads out from the intersection of Center and Main Streets. The streets are wide and lined with trees. There's plenty of space for parking, and a number of the streets are wide enough so that you can park diagonally head on to the curb. Many of the streets have substantial grassy medians. Much of the housing is from before World War II. Exteriors of red brick, painted brick, and painted cinderblock and stucco are the norm here. The area ranges from middle class to blue-collar.

East Mesa—The eastern portion of Mesa is a progression of new housing developments. The farther east you travel, the stucco and tile-roof style that predominates in the Valley's new developments is just as predominant here. However, you're also more likely to see wood-frame housing reminiscent of the East or Midwest here than you are in other new areas. These new suburban developments are encroaching upon older areas that contain horse properties and little clusters of old trailer parks and rentals. The area also includes huge trailer-park complexes, such as Leisure World.

The spaces between the old development clusters and the new are still fairly wide open as you near Apache Junction and the Superstition Mountains. These older areas grew up around the old alignment of U.S. Highway 60, which followed Main Street and the Apache Trail to points east. (Main Street becomes Apache Trail as it heads east of Power Road.) The new alignment of US 60 along the Superstition Highway, and the completion of the highway through Mesa makes it an easy hour's drive to downtown Phoenix, thus fueling the building boom.

With the addition of Williams Gateway Airport, the growth of east Mesa has also expanded southward, again with new developments of tile-roof and stucco housing. The area features a mixture of young families and middle-class professionals.

West Mesa—Much of this area was developed from the 1960s through the 1970s and features suburban housing tracts that are similar to the Maryvale, Chris-Town, and MetroCenter areas of Phoenix. You'll find a mix of lawns and desert landscaping here and more shingle roofs than tile. The vast majority of homes are single story. The developments are very similar in character to those in neighboring areas of Tempe. The area's residents include young families, blue-collar workers, and middle-class professionals.

INSIDERS' TIP

If yours is a low-income household, you can learn about the many services and programs available to you in Arizona by obtaining the *People's InfoGuide*. Published by the Arizona Community Action Association, it lists senior services along with places to go for assistance with employment and training, healthcare, housing, understanding Social Security benefits, and help in paying utilities. For the annually updated guide, write the association at 202 E. McDowell Road, Suite 255, Phoenix, AZ 85004.

Tempe

Although there are many smaller neighborhoods in Tempe, the city breaks down into essentially three areas—north of the Salt River, the Arizona State University area, and south Tempe.

The area north of the Salt River resembles and is adjacent to south Scottsdale. A quick rise from the river toward the Papago Buttes gives the well-kept, single-story tract housing an attractive background. The neighborhoods up here are pretty well settled with mature landscaping, usually grass and palm trees.

Redevelopment and the addition of Tempe's Town Lake have changed the face of downtown Tempe, which is adjacent to the ASU campus south of the Salt River. The neighborhoods surrounding downtown and ASU are older areas, with mature trees and grass landscaping. The wood-frame and brick houses are small but have individual character. These are pleasant and shady neighborhoods of old-time flavor, almost a stereotype of the college town. The area attracts students and faculty.

South of Southern Avenue, Tempe essentially becomes the land of red tile roofs and stucco. Housing here tends to start from the low $100,000s, and in some enclaves goes well beyond that. As you move south, the lots grow larger with a few horse properties and even pricier homes. So the area attracts middle-class, upper-middle-class, and, depending on the development, a few wealthy folk.

Northeast Valley

Fountain Hills

Isolated from the rest of the Valley by the ridge of the McDowell Mountains, Fountain Hills revels in its small-town atmosphere. Residents swear by the friendliness of neighbors. In 1997, *Parenting* magazine featured Fountain Hills in an article called "10 Great Places to Raise A Family." A planned community, Fountain Hills set its sights on retirees when it opened in 1970. The area had previously been a cattle ranch. The houses were intended to be small to fit the needs of the retired couple. Life would center on the golf course that wends its way through town along Saguaro Boulevard and on Fountain Park, where the world's tallest fountain can send a jet of water up to 560 feet into the air. The town's master developer, MCO Properties Inc., says that the market changed and demanded larger houses. Most of what's available in Fountain Hills is of the stucco and tile-roof variety, but there's more variation within that style than you'll see in many recent developments. Fountain Hills is attractive to older families, professionals, and retirees.

Scottsdale

Scottsdale essentially is two cities—north and south—that are divided by the downtown area. The southern portion of the city is the area developed from the '50s through the '70s as a result of booming employment in aerospace and other industries. Palm trees dot the landscape and let the sun shine through. The housing, mostly single-family tract homes, is affordable and has been, for the most part, well maintained. It's an area that attracts faculty and students from nearby ASU as well as middle-class families.

As you move northward, the housing values rise from the low $100,000s up to infinity (or at least close). New developments of the red-tile roof and stucco variety seem to be going up constantly, eating up more of the pristine desert that two decades ago wasn't even part of the city. These are all upscale developments, some of them featuring artificial lakes, others dependent on golf courses, and all basking in the splendor of the nearby mountains. You can't forget you're in the desert up here, even though most of the subdivisions have plenty of trees and greenery.

Paradise Valley

Now, if you really want to go upscale, check out the town of Paradise Valley, which is adjacent to (but not to be confused with) the Paradise Valley neighborhood of Phoenix. Surrounded by Phoenix and Scottsdale, this community boasts a vast array of well-to-do celebrities, including "Family Circle" cartoonist Bil Keane and rock star Alice Cooper—talk about diversity! With the reddish-brown rock of Camelback and Mummy Mountains dominating the hilly landscape, this is a place where desert landscaping abounds. Many of the houses, all single-family dwellings and anything but tract homes, are done in variations of Mexican home architecture, giving them a cool quality in the bright heat of the sun. People with money are buying up perfectly good older homes, tearing them down and building mansions on the expensive earth. The spaces between houses seem vast and are peppered with desert plants.

Northwest Valley

Glendale

Glendale has three faces. The part of Glendale that bounds the north-central section of Phoenix is much like that part of Phoenix in character. As you go north from the Glendale line at Camelback Road and 43rd Avenue, the developments get newer. The southern end is much like the Chris-Town neighborhood of Phoenix, giving way to developments more like those around MetroCenter. The southern end has more young families, and in the northern end more established professionals predominate.

Downtown Glendale has been through quite a face-lift in recent years. It has a charming, small-town quality that belies the city's status as the third largest in the Valley. This is where you'll find the city's oldest prewar houses (some of them pre-World War I), a number of them being reclaimed by professionals who like their charm. As with most housing from the Valley's early days, red brick and white stucco are the norm.

Then, there's the rest of Glendale, which has boomed and expanded over the past two to three decades to the southwest and to the north. The growth has been in areas that once were covered with farm fields and orchards. True to the character of most suburban development in the area, there is much tile-roof and stucco. Given that Glendale once had a reputation as a blue-collar town—old industrial parks dot Glendale's south end—the new development is surprising. For it's not only middle-class, but also upper middle-class in character. Arrowhead Ranch in northwestern Glendale typifies this up-and-coming face of the city. The 4,000-acre development features artificial lakes with 14 miles of shoreline and two championship golf courses was essentially a stopping point on the drive up Grand Avenue to Wickenburg in the days when Peoria was virtually all agricultural. Much of Peoria's commercial development is along Grand Avenue.

The housing developments that have exploded across Peoria in the past two to three decades are mostly of the tile-roof and stucco variety with desert landscaping, although you'll also find some wood-frame styles mixed in. The city is attractive to both younger and older families.

NEIGHBORHOODS AND REAL ESTATE

Surprise

Surprise officials say that a new home is completed in Surprise every three and a half hours, so the old town is quickly disappearing. Surprise has attracted new development as young families look farther from the Valley's core to find lower-cost property. Now, Surprise also includes the latest of developer Del Webb's retirement communities, Sun City Grand, which is quickly adding retirees to the mix.

Sun City

Sun City is a well-planned retirement community that offers every amenity to its residents. Life here revolves around the golf courses and recreation centers, where senior citizens defy old stereotypes with an active lifestyle. The 1,200 acres of golf links create belts of green relief among houses that were built from 1960 through 1980. Sun City is an unincorporated area of Maricopa County. (See our Retirement chapter for more about Sun City.)

Sun City West

Separated from Sun City by the usually dry Agua Fria River, the Sun City West retirement community opened when Sun City was just about built out in 1980. Sun City West is a bit grander in scale than Sun City. The houses are bigger and essentially for more well-to-do seniors. Sun City West also reflects a general housing trend in the Valley toward bigger, less-crowded development. However, in its basics, Sun City West is much like Sun City, revolving around its golf courses and recreation centers. Sun City West is an unincorporated area of Maricopa County. (See our Retirement chapter.)

Youngtown

Youngtown opened in 1954 and was incorporated in 1960. It, too, is a well-planned retire-

The beautiful mansions of old Phoenix are a reminder of this city's history.

Photo: Penny Kleingartner

ment community, and the housing, of 1950s through 1960s vintage, reflects the retirement imperatives of the time—simple, small ranch houses. The retirees here typically have less income than in Sun City and Sun City West. It has much more of a small-town atmosphere than either Sun City or Sun City West, which seem more like resorts than towns.

Southwest Valley

The Southwest Valley continues to be primarily dependent on agriculture, but it's clear that planning departments and developers see what is called the Western Gateway Area—Avondale, Buckeye, Goodyear, Litchfield Park, and Tolleson —as an area ripe for residential development.

Avondale

Avondale retains a small-town feeling, at least partly because planners are attempting to keep the city's growth manageable. Because of its proximity to Goodyear, most of Avondale's older housing was built during World War II and the decades afterward to house workers at the Goodyear Co. So Avondale is essentially an agricultural community with pockets of suburban neighborhoods. New development, aimed at young families and professionals, is heading in the tile-roof and stucco direction. The city recently annexed the rural area that includes Phoenix International Raceway, an area of large, relatively isolated homes.

Buckeye

Buckeye is a small farming community as far as population goes, but it encompasses about 100 square miles. Similar to Goodyear, most of Buckeye's housing is contained in a small town center. Being on the far western fringe of the Valley, where development essentially stops and desert wilderness begins, Buckeye has plenty of opportunity to incorporate even more land. I-10 puts Buckeye about 30 to 45 minutes from downtown Phoenix, making it desirable to anyone who wants to get away from the hustle and bustle of Phoenix.

Goodyear

Because of the dominance of the Goodyear plant, Goodyear has always had a company-town feeling to it. The city's older, single-family housing essentially was built for workers. The fields where the company once planted the cotton it used in tire cords have given way to other agricultural uses over the years. The new developments tend to attract young families and professionals, many of whom commute to Phoenix.

Litchfield Park

As Valley sizes go, Litchfield Park is a small town both in size and population. Its streets are shady, and the homes are generally upscale for this part of the Valley. No walls separate Litchfield Park from the rest of the Valley, but it nonetheless feels like an enclave. The town has developed over the past three decades in the shadow of the Wigwam Resort, which remains Litchfield Park's top employer. Litchfield Park attracts older families, professionals, and retirees.

Tolleson

Tolleson is a largely Hispanic small town with mostly single-family homes akin to the style in Maryvale, which shouldn't be too surprising since it's just south of there. Like the other communities in the Southwest Valley, Tolleson has been dominated by farming. Its character is

NEIGHBORHOODS AND REAL ESTATE

changing because, with relatively low property values and good access to I-10, companies are buying land for shipping/warehouse facilities.

Apartment Living

Extensive growth in the Valley has put an upward pressure on the rents charged by apartment complexes. Still, the Valley remains a very affordable place for renters. Very broadly speaking, good one-bedroom units with a minimum six-month lease range from the low $400s per month in Phoenix to $900-plus monthly in north Scottsdale.

Apartment Finders
3554 W. Northern Ave., Phoenix
• (602) 841-5055

In business since 1981, Apartment Finders has a computer network that offers current information on more than 200,000 units in the Valley of the Sun. The information available includes floor plans, amenities, school information, and other details. The company's licensed agents can help find long-term and short-term leases for winter visitors and corporate relocators. They even escort apartment seekers to the properties. The company is paid by the property owners, so its services to renters are free. It has five offices (three in Phoenix, one each in Tempe and Mesa) serving the entire Valley. The Valley-wide number for the company is (602) 957-7000.

Apartments & More
5835 N. 16th St., Phoenix
• (602) 279-9578

Apartments & More opened its doors in 1989 and works with several hundred apartment communities in the Valley. The agency has nine offices serving the entire Valley of the Sun. The agents can help find long- and short-term leases and will escort potential renters to the properties. Information includes floor plans, lease terms, and move-in costs, among other details. The service is free to prospective renters.

Relocation Services

Arizona Insights Relocation Center Inc.
3610 N. 44th St., Phoenix
• (602) 952-2177, (800) 899-7356
• www.aptfind.com

Arizona Insights has been in business since 1982 to help corporate transferees, new hires, and candidates. Services include an area orientation, home-finding and rental assistance, temporary housing, spouse/partner career assistance, and school counseling. It's a one-stop center for information on relocating to the Valley. It also offers the same services to Valley residents seeking to relocate worldwide.

Real Estate Agencies

Century 21 A.M. Realty
227 E. Baseline Rd., Tempe
• (480) 831-1114

Century 21 A.M. Realty opened its doors in 1980 and is the oldest Century 21 franchise in Maricopa County. Based in Tempe, the agency focuses on Tempe and the east Valley, although it can find and sell homes across the Valley. Through Century 21 and the VIP Referral System, the agency can accept and refer relocation clients worldwide. Century 21 has dozens of independently owned and operated affiliates in the Valley that offer similar services.

Coldwell Banker Success Realty
6808 E. Camelback Rd., Scottsdale
• (480) 481-8400

Success Realty has more than 11 sales offices serving every portion of the Valley of the Sun. It is the largest multi-office company within the Coldwell Banker Real Estate Corporation affiliate network in Arizona. Founded in 1950, Success Realty, in-

INSIDERS' TIP

Look across the Valley and you'll see a sea of red-roof tiles. Developers take their knocks for building so many homes with tile roofs and stucco walls, but there are advantages to such construction. The stucco is applied to wire mesh over insulating foam panels for added insulation from the summer heat, which helps reduce utility bills. The tile roofs stand up to intense desert sun better than any other roofing surface. The average owner will never have to re-roof a tile-roofed house.

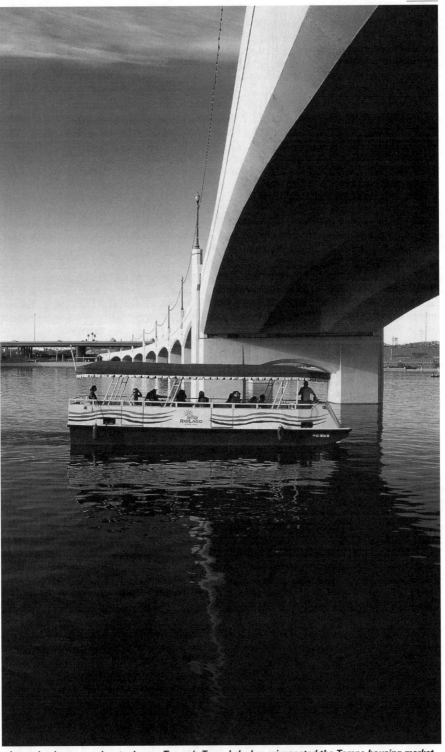

Attracting boaters and water lovers, Tempe's Town Lake has rejuvenated the Tempe housing market.

Photo: Courtesy of Mesa Convention and Visitors Bureau

NEIGHBORHOODS
AND REAL ESTATE

cluding its offices in Tucson, employs more than 1,400 real-estate professionals. The company has a full-fledged relocation division. The Coldwell Banker network includes a number of other firms serving every part of the Valley with similar real estate sales, rentals, and relocation services.

ERA Encore Realty
678 E. Thunderbird Rd., Phoenix
• **(602) 938-2000**

Encore Realty is one of the top 50 offices in sales in ERA's international franchise network of 2,600 real-estate offices. Based in Phoenix, Encore handles sales in all areas of the Valley with more than 40 agents. Encore agents are members of the National Corporate Relocation Council and the Employee Relocation Council. Encore is also a member of the National Military Broker Network and specializes in meeting the needs of service members from Luke Air Force Base.

John Hall and Associates
11211 N. Tatum Blvd., Ste. 200, Phoenix
• **(602) 953-4000**

John Hall and Associates, in business in Arizona since 1974, has seven offices and more than 800 real estate professionals covering the Valley. As a member of RELO, an international network of more than 1,200 firms with more than 14,000 offices internationally, the agency provides relocation and referral assistance to families moving around the county or the world.

Keller Williams Realty Southwest Region
1250 E. Baseline Rd., Tempe
• **(480) 839-3555**

Keller Williams Realty maintains nine sales offices in the Valley of the Sun—in north Phoenix, Ahwatukee, and Scottsdale. The firm provides local sales and relocation services as part of the Keller Williams network.

MCO Realty Inc.
9617 N. Saguaro Blvd., Fountain Hills
• **(602) 837-2500**

You can't miss MCO Realty, because its two-story headquarters stand prominently at the busy intersection of Saguaro and Shea Bou-

levards. A wholly owned subsidiary of MCO Properties, the master developer of Fountain Hills, MCO Realty focuses on selling both new and resale homes as well as custom home sites in Fountain Hills.

Molly Bridgeman Realty
7206 N. 55th Ave., Glendale
• **(623) 934-0095**

Molly Bridgeman loves Glendale and Peoria, and she puts her money where her mouth is. Most of her properties are in the Northwest Valley. Bridgeman has been in Arizona real estate for 20 years and has had her own agency for the past 15 years. Her office, a remodeled 1913 red-brick house in downtown Glendale, is near the Catlin Court antique-store district. The six-agent office handles new homes, resales, relocation services, and property management for investors.

> ## INSIDERS' TIP
> To find out which adult-care homes for assisted living are licensed by the state of Arizona, contact the Office of Home and Community-Based Licensure, Department of Health Services, 1647 E. Morten Avenue, Phoenix, (602) 255-1199.

Russ Lyon Realty
6710 N. Scottsdale Rd., Scottsdale
• **(480) 367-6030**
• **www.russlyon.com**

Russ Lyon Realty, a Valley firm that opened for business in 1947, has more than 350 sales associates in nine sales offices based in Ahwatukee, Carefree-Cave Creek, Phoenix, Paradise Valley, and north Scottsdale. It also is an affiliate of Sotheby's International Realty, specializing in luxury properties.

Realty Executives
301 E. Bethany Home Rd., Phoenix
• **(602) 604-0615**

This is the uptown Phoenix office of the Realty Executives franchise operation, which was born in the city in 1965. Today, there are 460 Realty Executives franchises in five countries. Reflecting its hometown roots, Realty Executives has 55 of its independently owned and operated franchises in the Valley of the Sun, as well as its corporate headquarters.

RE/MAX All Stars
8079 N. 85th Way, Scottsdale
• **(480) 998-6000**

RE/MAX All Stars is one of 20 RE/MAX offices across the Valley of the Sun. It offers full-service real estate sales and service and relocation services through RE/MAX's international network.

A pool is an added plus when Arizona's summer gets into the upper digits.

Photo: Scottsdale Convention and Visitors Bureau

West USA Realty
3101 W. Peoria, Phoenix
• **(602) 866-7099**

West USA Realty is a Phoenix firm that opened its doors in April of 1986 and has since grown to a network of six offices and 1,100 real estate professionals in the Valley. This office serves Phoenix and Glendale, while others are based in far north and midtown Phoenix, Paradise Valley, Scottsdale, and Mesa.

Why USA Penelope Realty
Waddell
• **(623) 935-3804**

Penelope C. Myer has been in real estate for more than a decade, and has had her own agency for the past four. Although she sells homes Valleywide, she concentrates on the west Valley and specializes in residential and retirement properties. The three-agent office sells horse properties and offers relocation services as well.

Retirement

In Phoenix, you can talk to retirees who have traveled the world—for leisure, business, or military service—people who know they have a wealth of choices for a retirement nest, and they'll tell you why they chose this city above everywhere else: climate, of course. Tired of shoveling snow and skidding on ice, many retirees opt for the Valley of the Sun. They also like the fact that Phoenix is so welcoming to seniors. The cost of living is relatively low, the people are friendly, there's plenty to do, and the active retirement communities here have gained international fame.

That's not to say Phoenix's population is overwhelmingly seniors. The percentage of Maricopa County permanent residents who are 65 and older, 12.5 percent, is about the same as the national percentage. But the winter months do bring in a ton of golden-aged folks, and the smiles on their faces tell you how happy they are to be away—temporarily, at least—from the frigid Midwest, Northeast, and Canada.

We call these part-time winter residents, who are usually at least 50 years old, snowbirds—although the chamber-of-commerce types prefer the term "winter visitors." Snowbirds flock to a variety of Valley roosts—apartments and condos with short leases, relatives' homes, their own part-time homes, and, most notably, mobile homes and RV parks. In many cases, they find enclaves of like-minded seniors, easing their way into feeling at home in the big city.

Seniors tend to congregate on the fringes of the metropolitan area. In Apache Junction, in the far southeast Valley, for instance, there are literally dozens of mobile home and RV parks that attract the older set, those here either year round or part of the year. Diagonally across the Valley, in the far northwest, is the world-famous, first-of-its-kind Sun City, along with similar age-restricted communities marketed as havens for seniors.

One enclave for the mature set is Youngtown, about 12 miles northwest of Phoenix. Technically, Youngtown—not Sun City—was the nation's first master-planned retirement community, established in 1954 and welcoming residents in 1960. It shies away from the glitz of Sun City and instead prefers to remain a quiet, incorporated town of 3,000. Recently, it repealed an ordinance that had been in place for many years requiring at least one member of each household to be 55 or older.

Here in the Valley, part-time and permanent residents alike defy the stereotype of crotchety, stay-at-home "old people." As long as they're blessed with good physical and mental health, seniors remain actively engaged in intellectual, recreational, and community pursuits—and glorious, year-round golf.

Active retirement communities fit many to a T. Developers across the Valley have poured millions of dollars into championship golf courses and recreation centers that complement comfortable—and in many cases, luxury—homes. Ever since Sun City, the golf-resort concept has been copied or elaborated upon by several Valley developers. The concept seems to be even stronger in the late '90s as baby boomers mature.

If you're in your second childhood, you will be amazed by the diversions here. Note that travel becomes a major part of the lives of seniors. Often they join their retirement community on tours to exotic places arranged by organizations. Or they're looking for adventure from the seats of their motor homes and recreational vehicles. Or perhaps it's classic car road rallies and motorcycle clubs that beckon them.

Some seniors are born again as exercise fanatics and many embrace active lifestyles. You'll find more than 4,000 participants in the Valley's Senior Olympics. And we're talking medalists in sprinting, swimming, cycling, tennis, fitness walking, powerlifting, and more.

Many in the 55-plus crowd, though they may have chosen to settle down in neighborhoods with people of their age and interests, do choose to continue working, part-time or full-time. Volunteer work is another option, and communities such as the Sun Cities and Sun Lakes are known for the mighty volunteer corps they send out to social service agencies, hospitals, and schools. Add to that your choice of arts and crafts clubs and hobby groups geared to seniors around the Valley.

There are a number of ways for a newcomer to make friends, notably the "state clubs." At many retirement communities, clubs have formed to represent every state in the union, not to mention some foreign countries. Folks with any kind of tie to a club's state or country can join in on picnics and other social events.

Not all the Valley's senior citizens choose a Sun City-like lifestyle, of course. You might decide you don't like the homogenous feel of living only near other seniors, or you might find the pristinely kept streets and houses a little too tidy for your tastes. You might decide you don't want to live in a place quite so active, or perhaps the country-club life is not your scene.

Many seniors live in the older neighborhoods of Phoenix, in homes they bought when their families were younger. Now they live side by side with younger couples starting their families. Many have chosen neighborhoods where they can downsize to garden apartments, patio homes, condominiums, or mobile homes. Even within the 55-plus communities, there are options besides owning a single-family home. Especially popular for cost-saving reasons are villas, which are virtually maintenance-free and often lie adjacent to golf courses or greenbelts.

In addition, Phoenix is a desirable place for seniors who need a bit of assistance because there are so many options. Several new and established complexes offer "active independent living," where seniors can enjoy one- or two-bedroom suites, with some meals provided, as well as health aides, housekeeping, swimming pools, and planned activities.

For those not living in retirement communities, the Valley's many senior centers can become the avenue to keeping active. The centers are well-spread geographically across the Valley, and they are bustling with bingo games, dances, holiday parties, intergenerational get-togethers, and educational programs.

As a 55-plus volunteer at the Sun City West Visitors Center said after reeling off a long list of the area's amenities, "If you're bored, it's your own fault."

Active-adult Communities

Ever wonder how "active adult" became the catch phrase for seniors-only communities? The concept of vibrant retiree neighborhoods—where grannies biding their time on rockers are far from the norm—got its start in the Valley of the Sun. In 1960, pioneer builder Del Webb completed Sun City, a tidy community of homes northwest of Phoenix. Sun City homes were built on circular streets, with major roads bisecting those streets and leading the way to clusters of activity—shops, banks, and recreation centers as well as acres and acres of golf courses. Now, the community is so self-contained that many residents prefer to get around in golf carts instead of cars. Cultural life flourishes thanks to the 7,000-seat Sundome Center for the Performing Arts as well as a well-tended art museum and various musical, dance, and theatrical groups. And, over the years, the place has filled to the brim with social groups catering to a wealth of interests. The requirement to buying into this paradise: At least one member of the family has to be 55 or older, and no one younger than 18 is allowed, except for visits.

The concept has taken off like Arnold Palmer with a 9-iron. Developers' billboards all over the Valley display the happy faces of couples that look just barely older than 55—playing golf, swimming, reveling in a lifestyle that, supposedly, is "like being on vacation every day!" At 38,000 residents, Sun City remains the largest retirement community in the country, and it set the standard for other active-adult communities from Florida to California.

After Sun City, Del Webb Corp. followed up with two other communities in the northwest

Valley, opening Sun City West in the late 1970s and launching Sun City Grand in 1996. In the southeast Valley, Robson Communities got on the bandwagon with Sun Lakes in the 1970s. More than a dozen other active-retirement communities—designed by different developers but offering similar amenities—dot the Valley, mainly in the suburbs. Here's a quick rundown of those by Robson and Del Webb, the two leaders in the concept, followed by the names of Valley developers whose projects include 55-and-older communities.

Sun City
• (623) 583-0692

When you're comparing Valley retirement communities, you'll find Sun City gains favor for being a tad closer to the lifeblood of Phoenix and big-city amenities. Also, many seniors like the mature character of its homes. The majority of houses and condominiums are in the $50,000 to $100,000 range, with spacious homes on a lake or golf course going for as much as $275,000. A couple of vital statistics: Population in 1995 was just over 38,000, and median age that year was 74.5.

Run by a volunteer group called the Sun City Ambassadors, the Sun City Visitors Center, 9903 W. Bell Road (Promenade Center), (623) 977-5000, (800) 437-8146, is chock full of pamphlets, maps, fliers, and magazines describing the dozens of recreational opportunities, housing options, social clubs, and more for would-be residents. It's also the place to arrange for a guided tour. Hours are 9 AM to 4 PM Monday through Saturday.

Sun Cities Information and Referral, 9451 N. 99th Avenue, Sun City, (623) 974-4713, has volunteers on hand to answer general questions about amenities, services, and housing in Sun City, Sun City West, and Sun City Grand, and to make referrals when more information is needed.

Sun City's seven recreation centers are conveniently dispersed around town. A look around will tell you in an instant that residents in these parts don't like sitting still. The centers encompass seven swimming pools (six outdoor and one indoor); two libraries; a variety of classes in crafts, hobbies, and fine arts; square dancing and ballroom dancing; fitness rooms; and bowling alleys. Add to that therapy pools, lawn bowling, tennis courts, miniature golf, and shuffleboard. Eight golf courses belong to the recreation centers, and three belong to private country clubs. The recreation centers are: Bell Recreation Center, 16828 N. 99th Avenue, (623) 876-3040; Fairway, 10620 W. Peoria Avenue, (623) 876-3044; Marinette, 9860 W. Union Hills Drive, (623) 876-3054; Mountain View, 9749 N. 107th Avenue, (623) 876-3042; Oakmont, 10725 W. Oakmont, (623) 876-3046; Sundial, 14801 N. 103rd Ave., (623) 876-3048;

and Lakeview, 10626 W. Thunderbird Boulevard, (623) 876-3000.

Sun City residents have formed several organizations and clubs. For instance, Sun Cities Volunteer Placement Services, 14475 R.H. Johnson Boulevard, Sun City West, (623) 546-1774, is for retirees with time to make a difference. It's the place to get matched with a nonprofit agency for volunteer positions such as library aide, tutor, museum host, hospital aide, and errand runner for less active neighbors.

The motto "Keeping Sun City Beautiful" rings true thanks to the more than 300 Sun City residents who volunteer for the Sun City Prides, P.O. Box 1463, Sun City, AZ 85372, (623) 972-6558. They spend untold hours picking up litter, raking the landscaped medians, trimming bushes, painting the trunks of the community's 1,800 orange trees, caring for the automatic watering systems, and reporting needed street repairs. County government officials once estimated the Prides' services to be worth more than $500,000 a year. The Sun City Sheriff's Posse, volunteers coordinated by the Maricopa County Sheriff's Office, helps Sun City maintain one of the lowest crime rates for a U.S. city of its size. Posse members help with neighborhood watches, search and rescue, and home-security surveys.

Sun City West
13950 Meeker Blvd., Sun City West
• (623) 546-5000

Buoyed by the success of Sun City, Del Webb Corp. moved two miles west in the early 1970s to begin building a second active-adult community. The first homes were completed in 1978, and final construction through 1998 is expected to bring the total to 17,000 homes. The population is about 31,000 so far. Like its neighbor, Sun City West is self-contained, with dozens of shops, banks, restaurants, several golf courses, four recreation centers, and a hospital. In the same vein, it mandates that at least one member of a household be 55 or older. Because it's a newer community, though, its median age tends to be about five years younger than in Sun City. Home prices range from $60,000 to $400,000. Many of the more expensive homes are built facing a golf course.

Sun City West also has a Sheriff's Posse to keep crime down and a Prides volunteer organization to keep neighborhoods tidy. It calls itself "Flag City U.S.A." owing to the hundreds of American flags lining the major thoroughfare, R.H. Johnson Boulevard, under the guidance of the local American Legion post.

In addition, the community is in the limelight each holiday season when homeowners decorate driveways and sidewalks with more than 200,000 luminarias—a Christmas-in-the-desert tradition of candles inside paper bags weighted down with sand. Proceeds from the sale of luminarias go toward the Sun City West Community Services Center.

The residents' get-up-and-go attitude is reflected in the diversity of clubs and social groups at their disposal. A club list from the visitors center, for instance, lists almost 100 organizations, from the Agriculture Club to the Yoga Club. Folks regularly get together for jazz dancing, water therapy, bicycling, and other sports.

And don't forget the ubiquitous golfing. The community has nine golf courses, seven of which are owned by the residents. One is a public course, and another is part of a private country club.

The Property Owners and Residents Association, 13815 Camino del Sol, (623) 584-4288, is Sun City West's watchdog over legislative and governmental matters affecting retirees and their pocketbooks. It also runs town halls with community leaders, provides consumer information, raises funds for charity, and answers gardening questions.

Sun City West's four recreation centers are R.H. Johnson Recreation Center, 19803 R.H. Johnson Boulevard, (623) 584-2050; Beardsley Park, 12755 Beardsley Drive, (623) 584-6078; Fred P. Kuentz Recreation Center, 14401 R.H. Johnson Boulevard, (623) 546-0737; and Palm Ridge, 13800 W. Deer Valley Road, (623) 214-1398. Amenities include an Olympic-size swimming pool at each of the centers as well as tennis, bowling, billiards, racquetball, miniature golf, fitness rooms, slow-pitch softball, and horseshoes. Social halls host various kinds of dancing, bingo, and other weekly activities. Arts and crafts rooms let rec center members try their hands at ceramics, stained glass, painting, woodworking, and many other endeavors.

The Sun City West Visitors Center, 13823 W. Camino del Sol, (623) 214-8629, (800) 482-3798, is a good first stop for potential residents. Members of the Sun City West Ambassadors are ready and waiting to answer questions, show you an informational video, and direct you to the walls lined with fliers, pamphlets, maps, and other take-home information. The center will also arrange tours of the community. It's open from 9 AM to 4 PM Monday through Saturday and from 12:30 to 4 PM Sunday.

Sun City Grand
19726 N. Remington Dr., Surprise
• **(623) 546-5149, (800) 341-6121**

By 1996, it was time for Del Webb Corp. to capitalize even further on the active retirement living concept. When completed, Sun City Grand in the city of Surprise, just west of Sun City West, will encompass 9,500 homes. All the features that the other Sun Cities are famous for are here, too, but the overall look will be a definite '90s one, with upgrades on amenities and lots of Southwestern architectural style. That means red-tiled roofs and neutral tones of stucco. The community buildings are a classy terra cotta with copper and turquoise accents.

As of late 1997, 18 model homes were open for view at the development, which will be building for the next nine years. Home prices start in the low $90,000s and go up to the low $200,000s.

Sun Lakes Resort Community
25025 S. E.J. Robson Blvd., Sun Lakes
• **(480) 895-9600**

On the opposite end of the Valley from the Sun Cities lies the community of Sun Lakes—similar in its 55-plus concept but with an overall feeling that seniors are "getting away from it all" even more so. Sun Lakes, which has grown to more than 10,000 people, is about 20 miles from downtown Phoenix, but is still considered part of the Valley because of its proximity to Interstate 10. As you're heading southeast to Tucson, Sun Lakes springs out of agricultural fields like an oasis of towering trees and ample golf courses. Here, too, seniors find plenty of ways to have fun and stay busy with social clubs, recreation opportunities, places of worship, and performing arts.

You'll find bingo, bocce ball, bell choirs, rock hounding, fishing, travel groups, support groups, pinochle, ballroom dancing, rug weaving—to name just a few of the hundreds of activities listed at clubhouses and in community newspapers. Every major holiday brings some kind of get-together at the community centers.

Sun Lakes was conceived about 30 years ago when developer Ed Robson envisioned an active-adult community with a "youthful spirit." The community was built in three phases, beginning in 1972, and homes are still going up, with the aim of bringing the population to 20,000.

Its 3,500 acres are basically organized around the five country clubs, called Sun Lakes, Cottonwood, Palo Verde, Ironwood, and Oakwood. Many of the streets are circular, with the golf courses and lakes as the focal points. Housing runs the gamut from luxury villas and modest garden homes to townhouses and mobile homes. The homes going up now range in price from $120,000 to $256,000.

Although the growing city of Chandler and regional shopping malls are fairly close to home, Sun Lakes residents can get much of their shopping done within the community. Supermarkets, banks, professional offices, a health center, and specialty shops are at the major intersections.

Like Sun City, this community has organized a Sheriff's Posse that aids in neighborhood watches. The posse also sponsors driving classes for seniors.

INSIDERS' TIP

You know you're in an Arizona retirement community when . . . yellow diamond street signs warn you of oncoming golf carts.

SunBird Resort Community
6250 SunBird Blvd., Chandler
• (480) 732-1000

This is Robson Communities' smaller version of Sun Lakes, and it's just a few miles to the east. Golf, tennis, swimming, and other recreation outlets as well as community gatherings and hobby groups all fall into the formula, although on a smaller scale. Home prices range from $77,000 to $140,000.

Other Communities

Arizona Traditions
7001 N. Scottsdale Rd., Ste. 2050, Scottsdale
• (480) 483-0006
administration, (623) 546-5613 sales

Continental Homes, one of the Valley's largest builders, is completing an 1,800-home, active-adult community in Surprise, on Bell Road about 5 miles west of Grand Avenue. Arizona Traditions recently won top honors in a National Association of Homebuilders survey of active-adult communities. Eleven models are offered, with prices starting in the $90,000s.

Senior living in Phoenix offers residents an abundance of activities.

Photo: Penny Kleingartner

It's a gated community with an 18-hole golf course and a community center offering not only swimming and tennis, but also a computer room, woodworking shop, crafts classes, and a fitness center.

Farnsworth Development Co.
2150 S. Farnsworth Dr., Mesa
• (480) 832-6200

Farnsworth has built four 55-plus communities, all in Mesa. Dreamland is near University Drive and Recker Road; Sunland Village is near Broadway and Greenfield roads; Sunland Village East is near Baseline and Sossaman Roads; and the newest, Sunland Springs Village, is near Baseline and Signal Butte Roads. The latter two developments are the largest, with an anticipated 2,500 homes and 3,000 condominiums upon completion in 15 years.

Leisure World
908 S. Power Rd., Mesa
• (480) 832-7451

One of the more established active-adult communities, Leisure World consists of 2,600 homes and 4,500 residents. It has two large recreation centers, two 18-hole golf courses, security gates, a 24-hour mobile patrol, and minibuses that shuttle to nearby shopping centers. Resale homes are two- or three-bedroom. You can also choose from one-, two-, or three-bedroom condominiums, garden homes, and duplexes, with prices starting in the $80,000s.

Pebble Creek Resort Community
3639 Clubhouse Dr., Goodyear
• (602) 935-6700, (800) 795-4663

The far west Valley's wide-open spaces are giving way to residential uses, including this 55-plus community about 15 miles west of downtown. It's two miles north of I-10 from the Pebble Creek Parkway exit. Phase I, nearing completion, will have about 2,000 single-family homes, and Phase II is expected to eventually include more than 4,000 single-family homes. There are 12 model homes, with various options for customizing them. Selling prices are in the $100,000 to low-$300,000 range. An 18-hole golf course winds through the development, and two more courses are planned for Phase II. You'll also find a country club, a restaurant, swimming, tennis, and an arts and crafts building.

INSIDERS' TIP
To find out which adult-care homes for assisted living are licensed by the state of Arizona, contact the Office of Home and Community-Based Licensure, Department of Health Services, 1647 E. Morten Avenue, Phoenix, (602) 255-1199.

Springfield Active Adult Community
6495 S. St. Andrews Blvd., Chandler
• (480) 802-6999

Pulte Homes entered the market for active-retirement communities in 1997 with Springfield, at McQueen and Riggs Roads in Chandler. Upon completion Springfield will have 740 single-family homes, with easy access to a 14,000-square-foot recreation center that offers two swimming pools, a spa, and tennis courts. The nearby golf course is semiprivate, with Springfield residents getting preferred tee times. Seven models of homes are available, with prices ranging from the high $80,000s to the low $180,000s.

Ventana Lakes
10874 W. Chino Dr., Peoria
• (623) 566-2734, (800) 846-5828

This community by Lennar Homes is near 99th Avenue and Beardsley Road near the city of Peoria. Made up of all single-family homes, Ventana Lakes is expected to be completed in three to four years. Nine models are available, with prices ranging from the mid-$90,000s to the $150,000s. The community boasts artificial lakes and 26 acres of links. The clubhouse offers many kinds of activities for the 55-and-older residents.

Westbrook Village
8805 W. Union Hills Dr., Peoria
• (602) 933-0181

Completed this year, Westbrook Village by UDC Homes includes about 3,800 single-family homes. It's an active-adult community open to those 40 and older. No children are allowed as permanent residents. Amenities include two championship golf courses, a golf club, and two recreation centers with swimming, tennis, and arts and crafts classes.

Mobile-home Communities

With its alluring climate and longstanding reputation as a haven for seniors, the Valley of the Sun has developed a variety of lifestyle options for those ready to settle into retirement. Age-restricted (55-plus) mobile-home communities are an option to consider. Like the Sun Cities and Sun Lakes, many of these parks are happy to assist you in your pursuit of an active retirement full of recreation and socializing. If quiet and solitude are more to your liking, they can accommodate that, too. Plus, mobile-home parks are usually the more economical route.

Mobile-home parks in the Valley number literally in the hundreds and can accommodate as few as two dozen homes or as many as 600. The new term for mobile homes is manufactured homes, referring to the large, prefabricated homes trucked into a community from a factory. Once a site is chosen, the homes pretty much stay put for decades until they're replaced by newer models.

Manufactured homes are said to be the hottest trend in the U.S. housing market, accounting for 34 percent of all homes sold in 1995. The Valley of the Sun is keeping up with the trend, judging from the number of manufactured-home communities developing on its fringes. Their architectural amenities rival those of custom homes, yet manufactured homes can save buyers 25 to 50 percent per square foot. At Crescent Run in Mesa, for instance, home prices range from $50,000 for a 964-square-foot model to the $80,000s for a 1,794-square-foot model. But also factor in the cost of leasing space for the manufactured home.

Mobile and manufactured homes are a favorite roost of snowbirds. And each mobile-home community varies in its ratio of permanent residents (those who brave the summer) to winter residents, who tend to stay from three to eight months each year and either leave their homes vacant during the summer or rent them out.

The following list describes several of the larger 55-plus mobile- and manufactured-home parks scattered around the Valley. Being larger, they are more likely to offer their residents a potpourri of leisure ac-

tivities and social groups. Amenities typically include heated pools, billiards, shuffleboard, tennis courts, card groups, bingo games, holiday-themed parties, and even small golf courses.

INSIDERS' TIP
Potential home buyers should know: Many retirement communities have either wholly or partially de-annexed themselves from school districts so that they don't have to pay the districts' property taxes. It's a controversial subject with many Valley residents of all ages.

INSIDERS' TIP
When the summers heat up, many seniors keep on with their exercise programs by walking at the air-conditioned shopping malls. The doors open early in the morning (before the stores) and people walk the cool sidewalks. It's a great opportunity to make new friends and stay healthy at the same time.

Southeast Valley

Crescent Run
8500 E. Southern Ave., Mesa
• (480) 373-8500, (800) 437-9910
• www.crescentrun.com

An 11,000-square-foot recreation center is the centerpiece of this community of 110 (and growing) manufactured homes. It's also a gated community, with amenities that run the gamut from pools, golf, and tennis to craft rooms, exercise classes, and a library. On the grounds is an eight-acre park with a natural grass amphitheater.

Hacienda de Valencia
201 S. Greenfield Rd., Mesa
• (480) 832-6081

The Hacienda has room for 365 mobile homes. Amenities include two pools, a hot tub, a horseshoe pit, a gazebo area for barbecues, a social hall, a card room, a billiards room, and an exercise room.

La Casa Blanca
2208 W. Baseline Rd., Apache Junction
• (480) 983-1344

This gated, 198-space community has pools and other recreation amenities and hosts hiking and golfing trips, potlucks, and lectures. About 70 percent of the residents call it home all year. A sister community, La Casa Blanca East, has just opened nearby, with 207 spaces.

Las Palmas
215 N. Power Rd., Mesa
• (480) 396-2172

Las Palmas is huge—539 spaces to be exact. Recreation facilities include swimming and therapy pools, with a continuous roster of planned activities within the community.

The Meadows
2401 W. Southern Ave., Tempe
• **(602) 438-1865**

This manufactured-home community boasts lush landscaping and room for 391 houses. A guard stands at the front entrance. For recreation, there are a clubhouse, pool, sauna, exercise room, shuffleboard, and areas for cards and billiards. Many planned activities are available.

Palmas del Sol Country Club
6209 E. McKellips Rd., Mesa
• **(480) 641-3385**

Tennis, anyone? There are courts aplenty here, along with pools, hot tubs, and shuffleboard. The manufactured-home sites number 467.

Northeast Valley

Paradise Peak West
3901 E. Pinnacle Peak Rd., Phoenix
• **(480) 946-2299**

Boasting a view of the McDowell Mountains, this community has 415 spaces for manufactured homes. It's known for its nine-hole golf course.

Roadrunner Lake Resort
1149 N. 92nd St., Scottsdale
• **(480) 945-0787**

This 627-space community promotes resort living with a driving range, a miniature golf course, a pool, a hot tub, and shuffleboard as well as many activities in its large clubhouse.

Shadow Mountain Village
8780 E. McKellips Rd., Scottsdale
• **(480) 947-8393**

Conveniently located near the new Pima and Red Mountain Freeways, this community has 589 spaces and a number of recreational amenities, including a tennis court, a horseshoe pit, shuffleboard, pools, and hot tubs, an indoor sauna, exercise equipment, and billiards, all located in and around three clubhouses. Planned activities include holiday parties, pancake breakfasts, and dances.

Northwest Valley

Apollo Village
10701 N. 99th Ave., Peoria
• **(623) 933-0166**

Apollo Village is relatively compact at 238 spaces, but it's large enough to offer a clubhouse, pool, hot tub, picnic area, car wash bay, library, and beauty shop.

Blue Sky Mobile Home Estates
4800 W. Ocotillo Rd., Glendale
• **(623) 939-5425**

Blue Sky has only 160 spaces but plenty of amenities—a clubhouse, pool, hot tub, exercise room, billiards area, and library. Add to

Leisure World, like many retirement areas, offers a complete community.

Photo: Penny Kleingartner

that weekly live music, lots of bunco and bingo games, potlucks, breakfasts, and art classes.

Friendly Village of Orangewood
2650 W. Union Hills Dr., Phoenix
• **(623) 869-7498**

This gated community likes the fact that it's 75 percent permanent residents—a fairly high number among mobile-home communities. In addition to planned activities, residents enjoy the village's five-hole golf course, pool, hot tub, shuffleboard, and other recreational opportunities.

Grand Missouri Mobile Home Park
4400 W. Missouri Ave., Glendale
• **(623) 937-7721**

Retirees with an interest in crafts will find company here in the various classes offered. Planned activities include bingo games and potlucks; exercise options include swimming and therapy pools, shuffleboard, and aerobics. The park has 303 spaces.

Palm Shadows Mobile Home Park
7300 N. 51st Ave., Glendale
• **(623) 934-1308**

Bingo every night? You'll find it here, along with horseshoes, shuffleboard, billiards, pools, and spas. Palm Shadows also has an auditorium. A mix of winter and permanent residents occupy the 300 spaces.

Information and Assistance for Seniors

Valleywide

American Association of Retired Persons
302 N. First Ave., Ste. 410, Phoenix
• **(602) 256-2277**

AARP is a nonprofit, nonpartisan service organization for people 50 and older. By design and mission, AARP helps members achieve goals of independence, dignity, and purpose. There are several active AARP chapters in the

Valley. The number above is for the statewide office, which can put you in touch with local groups.

Area Agency on Aging
1366 E. Thomas Rd., Phoenix
• **(602) 264-2255**

The Area Agency on Aging's Region One office serves the elderly and disabled adults in all of Maricopa County. It administers contracts with various services and agencies for benefits assistance, transportation, counseling, home repair, assisting the homebound, recreation, socialization, and respite services, etc. It also runs specialized programs, for instance, dealing with elder abuse prevention or assisting someone in making the transition from hospital to home. In addition, the Area Agency on Aging advocates on behalf of the elderly, provides information and referral services, and runs a Senior Help Line, (602) 264-HELP.

The AAA publishes a list and provides information on the Valley's more than three dozen senior centers. The centers are bustling with activities, including recreation, arts and crafts, hobby clubs, health screenings, and educational and intergenerational programs. Plus, they regularly provide nutritious meals and opportunities for socializing. The directory is available by calling (602) 264-4357.

The senior centers reach out to all areas of the Valley and to all income levels. Some are freestanding, and some are housed in churches or YMCAs. A few are affiliated with ethnic communities such as the Chinese Senior Center, Chicanos Por La Causa Senior Center, the Jewish Community Center, and the Phoenix Indian Center. A few are run by city parks and recreation divisions. And a handful have their own support organizations to raise funds to provide even better services. At Los Olivos Senior Center in east Phoenix, seniors enjoy regularly scheduled bingo, dancing, singing groups, walking groups, and coffeehouses.

Arizona Senior Citizens Law Project
1818 S. 16th St., Phoenix
• **(602) 252-6710**

This service helps people who have prob-

INSIDERS' TIP

Arizona works hard at welcoming retirees to the Grand Canyon state. The helpful (and free) publication, *Arizona Living, A Guide to Active Retirement*, is published by the Arizona Department of Commerce/Office of Senior Industries Development. It's a terrific resource, filled with articles and a wide variety of contact information that will help you learn more about retirement in Arizona. For retirement relocation information and to obtain a copy, call (800) 937-9995.

lems concerning government benefits, housing, consumer affairs, wills, probates, guardianship, and other legal matters. Financial accommodations are made for those in hospitals or nursing homes and for those seeking the reduced-fee services of a private attorney.

Beatitudes Center DOAR (Developing Older Adult Resources)
555 W. Glendale Ave., Phoenix
• (602) 274-5022

This organization lends a hand in a variety of ways, including a nursing/ministry network, a library with books and videos related to aging, care-giver support groups, a volunteer base that makes home visits and phone calls to seniors living on their own, and an interfaith volunteer network that runs errands and does small home repairs for those in need.

Foundation for Senior Living
77 E. Thomas Rd., Phoenix
• (602) 285-1800

The Foundation's aim is to protect seniors as well as adults with disabilities from institutional placement that may be both costly and inappropriate. Its many flexible, individualized, personal care programs are the means to do that, through counseling, adult day care, home healthcare, and low-cost remodeling, apartments and supervised private homes geared to their needs, and through senior centers. Another important program is OASIS (Older Adult Services and Information System), which offers seniors many cultural and educational activities such as outings to museums and discussion roundtables.

Phoenix Advocacy and Counseling for the Elderly
200 W. Washington St., Phoenix
• (602) 262-6631

PACE is open to Phoenix residents 60 and older who need help with or referrals for food, clothing, counseling, assistive devices, insurance bills, housing, transportation, and legal aid. It is a City of Phoenix program.

Samaritan Health Systems Older Adult Services
7575 E. Earl Dr., Scottsdale
• (480) 254-4357

The Samaritan hospital and behavioral health chain in the Valley runs a referral service and help line for seniors. Other services include a clinic for geriatric and psychiatric evaluations and an Alzheimer's program at Casa Teresa, at the behavioral health clinic in Scottsdale.

Northwest Valley Interfaith Services Inc.
Sun City
• (623) 584-4999

This agency provides a number of services, including adult day care, in-home respite care,

The senior community finds the desert surroundings enjoyable, whether they stay for the winter season or live in the area year round.

Photo: Courtesy of Jensen Associates

grocery shopping and transportation help, and counseling on options in assisted living and long-term care.

Northwest Valley Regional Community Council
12425 W. Bell Rd., Surprise
• (623) 583-4100

The council publishes a directory of long-term care options in the Northwest Valley that lists nursing homes, supervisory care homes, home health agencies, and hospices. A $3 donation is asked.

Meals on Wheels
Sun City
• (623) 974-9430
Sun City West
• (623) 214-4233

Residents of the Sun Cities and Youngtown who are unable to prepare their own meals are eligible for this service. Hot and cold meals are prepared, then delivered by volunteer drivers for a nominal fee.

Sun Health
13041 N. Del Webb Blvd., Sun City
• (623) 972-4064

Many of the healthcare services in the Sun Cities come under the aegis of Sun Health, including Boswell Memorial Hospital in Sun City and Del E. Webb Memorial Hospital in Sun City West. Sun Health also runs a physician referral service, a community education program, and hospice and home healthcare services.

Educational Opportunities

Southeast Valley

Mesa Community College
1833 W. Southern Ave., Mesa
• (480) 461-7000

Mesa Community College reaches out to retirees with a program called New Frontiers for Learning in Retirement. Of interest to seniors are classes in computers, history, Spanish, and more.

Sun Lakes Education Center
25105 S. Alma School Rd.
• (480) 802-8000

An arm of Chandler-Gilbert Community College, this center offers a variety of noncredit classes, including Spanish, creative writing, financial planning, Southwest history, art, fitness, and nutrition.

Northeast Valley

Scottsdale Community College
9000 E. Chaparral Rd., Scottsdale
• (480) 423-6000

The college's Senior Adult Program offers courses of interest to seniors, along with lecture series and special events. Choose from courses on history, the environment, religion, English literature, contemporary cinema, computers, yoga, and "cerebral aerobics." The program also sponsors 55-Alive driving classes and a Silver Striders walking club. Call the program directly at (480) 423-6559.

Northwest Valley

ASU Lifelong Learning Programs—Sun Cities
19403 R.H. Johnson Blvd., Sun City West
• (623) 546-9659

Offered by Arizona State University's College of Extended Education, the Lifelong Learning classes run the gamut from travel lectures and tai chi to conversational Spanish and computer literacy. Residents have their pick of about 10 locations for these low-cost classes. ASU also offers Elderhostel, an international travel and learning program for mature travelers.

Rio Sun Cities
12535 W. Smokey Dr., Surprise
• (623) 583-0548

With support from Rio Salado College, seniors can take a number of noncredit classes by enrolling in R.I.S.E. (Rio Institute for Senior Education). The program asks for a nominal

INSIDERS' TIP

If yours is a low-income household, you can learn about the many services and programs available to you in Arizona by obtaining the *People's InfoGuide*. Published by the Arizona Community Action Association. It lists senior services along with places to go for assistance with employment and training, healthcare, housing, understanding Social Security benefits, and help in paying utilities. For the annually updated guide, write the association at 202 E. McDowell Road, Suite 255, Phoenix, AZ 85004.

annual fee and lets you take any class, from Spanish to handwriting analysis to literature appreciation. A few for-credit computer classes are also available.

Volunteer Opportunities

Arizona Emeritus
1366 E. Thomas Rd., Phoenix
• (602) 264-2255

Emeritus professionals such as former lawyers, teachers, scientists, engineers, accountants, and business managers are recruited into a variety of volunteer positions through this new program run by the Area Agency on Aging.

RetiredSenior Volunteer Program
1366 E. Thomas Rd., Phoenix
• (602) 264-8878 West Valley,

RSVP assists people 55 and older in discovering uses for their creativity, energy, and expertise. Volunteers are placed with nonprofit organizations and public agencies.

SCORE
2828 N. Central Ave., Phoenix
• (602) 640-2329

The Service Corps of Retired Executives consists of volunteers giving time as mentors to those wanting to start their own businesses.

Volunteer Bureau of the Sun Cities
14475 R.H. Johnson Blvd., Sun City West
• (623) 546-1774

The Volunteer Bureau is a placement service, and among the many organizations served by Bureau volunteers are AARP, Habitat for Humanity, the Arizona Humane Society, and Northwest Valley schools.

Volunteer Center of Maricopa County
1515 E. Osborn Rd., Phoenix
• (602) 263-9736

The center works with more than 750 nonprofit and public agencies, such as the Salvation Army, the Association of Arizona Food Banks, and local hospitals.

Job Opportunities

Age Works & C-POW+ER
1366 E. Thomas Rd., Phoenix
• (602) 264-4357

These two programs, affiliated with the Area Agency on Aging, work together to help persons 50 and older find work.

Plus-50 Placement Center
5119 N. 19th Ave., Phoenix
• (602) 246-0260

Operating on funds from the United Way, grants, and contributions, this nonprofit job placement and counseling service is geared to those 50 and older. There is no charge for placement on the part of the employer or employee. Plus-50 has offices in north Phoenix, Glendale, Mesa, Scottsdale, Sunnyslope, and Tempe.

Frequently Called Numbers

The Phoenix area has an ever-growing number of community services that, if not directly related to seniors, can still be of help. Here are the telephone numbers for 10 important resources:
AARP—(602) 256-2277
Alzheimer's Association Helpline—(602) 528-0550
Area Agency on Aging Help Line—(602) 264-2255
Foundation for Senior Living—(602) 285-1800
Catholic Social Services—(602) 285-1999
City of Phoenix Human Services Department—(602) 262-4520
Community Information & Referral—(602) 263-8856
Senior Helpline—(602) 264-4357
Sun Cities Information and Referral—(623) 214-1340
Welcome Wagon—(602) 951-6731

Healthcare

If you have adequate healthcare coverage, you'll be glad to know that Phoenix and the Valley of the Sun are home to a number of nationally prominent healthcare facilities such as Barrow Neurological Institute, the Arizona Heart Institute, and the Mayo Clinic, among others. This reflects a forward-looking attitude toward healthcare innovations that the Valley has maintained since the earliest days of Maricopa Medical Center, the oldest healthcare institution in the Valley, which was established in 1883. That said, most Insiders will tell you that healthcare is not always available to everyone in the Valley. Nearly one in four Arizonans, and 20 percent of Arizona's children, don't have health insurance. And, if you are from the Midwest and you are trying to get into see a doctor, don't expect the same-day service you would get from your practitioner at home. With a 460 to 1 resident-to-doctor ratio in Phoenix, it's obvious that Valley doctors are pressed for time.

Phoenix's early hospitals emerged from a need to combat various epidemics—small pox for Maricopa Medical Center, and tuberculosis for St. Joseph's Hospital and Medical Center, John C. Lincoln Hospital, and Good Samaritan Regional Medical Center.

The Valley embraced chiropractic, osteopathic, and holistic medicine before more traditional parts of the country did, and it has become home to Midwestern University's College of Osteopathic Medicine in Glendale.

The Valley also had the first free-standing, outpatient surgical center in the nation. Innovative techniques such as radial keratotomy and other eye procedures quickly became popular here.

INSIDERS' TIP

Many hospitals offer community education classes on all aspects of staying healthy, from childcare tips to maintaining a healthy heart. Call a hospital nearest you for more information.

Sports medicine as a separate discipline had its roots here in the work that Dr. Paul Steingard did as the first team physician of the Phoenix Suns. Steingard developed ways to help his athletes recover faster from injuries and helped them learn how to prevent injuries. (Of course, it helped that his patients were highly motivated to stay in the games.) By the early '70s, Steingard's own clinic had become the first sports medicine practice in Arizona. Today the Steingard Medical Group, 15830 North 19th Avenue in Phoenix, (602) 336-1966, does both sports medicine and general practice, and is leading the way in making highschool sports safe for teens by offering free annual physicals, and doing research on teens at risk for sudden cardiac death.

Another innovative practice in the Valley is the Arizona Reproductive Medicine & Gynecology, Ltd., , 2850 N. 24th Street, Phoenix, (602) 468-3840, www.conceive.com, which offers advanced help for infertile couples. Doctors there are able to help couples achieve pregnancy by using cutting-edge technology to help harvest the eggs and sperm necessary for in vitro fertilization. The Mayo Clinic Scottsdale also offers technology such as in vitro fertilization for childless couples.

Today, all of the hospitals feature state-of-the-art equipment and the latest ideas in patient care—such as single rooms where mothers can go through labor, delivery, and recovery in relative comfort, instead of being wheeled around from the labor area to the delivery room and then to the recovery room. Most of them also offer preventive medicine, either in the form of classes or wellness programs. In this chapter, we give you a selection of Valley hospitals, as well as some walk-in clinics, emergency numbers, and mental health resources. We also touch briefly on alternative medicine in the Valley.

Hospitals

Phoenix

Arizona Heart Hospital
1930 E. Thomas Rd., Phoenix
- **(602) 532-1000**
- **www.azheart.com**

The 59-bed Arizona Heart Hospital, dedicated to the diagnosis and treatment of heart disease, opened in early 1998, and has received international recognition for its work. It has close ties to the Arizona Heart Institute (see next listing), and its medical director and founder is Dr. Edward B. Diethrich. The facility was built to function as an advanced coronary-care unit. The hospital has three operating rooms, four cardiac catheterization and electrophysiology labs, 13 recovery beds, 14 outpatient beds, eight trauma/observation rooms, and a 24-hour heart emergency center.

Arizona Heart Institute
2632 N. 20th St., Phoenix
- **(602) 266-2200, (800) 345-4278**
- **www.azheart.com**

In 1971, Dr. Edward B. Diethrich founded the Arizona Heart Institute, the nation's first freestanding outpatient clinic devoted to the prevention, detection, and treatment of cardiovascular diseases.

Affiliated with The Arizona Heart Institute, its multi-specialty outpatient facility is dedicated to the prevention, detection, and treatment of cardiovascular, pulmonary, and neurological disorders. It specializes in advanced non-surgical interventional therapies that replace traditional scalpel and suture treatment for heart and blood vessel disease, and trains physicians and treats patients from around the world.

The clinic is available 24 hours for urgent care, and it offers airport pickup and nearby hotel accommodations for families of out-of-town patients. Treatments include advanced alternatives to surgery, angioplasty, cardiac rehabilitation, general medical care, cardiovascular and thoracic surgery, pulmonology, checkups, and preventive medicine, among others.

Barrow Neurological Institute
St. Joseph's Hospital and Medical Center, 350 W. Thomas Rd., Phoenix
- **(602) 406-3000**
- **www.thebni.com**

Recently named by *U.S. News and World Reports* as one of the nation's best neurological hospitals in the nation, Barrow Neurological Institute was launched at St. Joseph's Hospital in 1962 as advances in brain surgery and neurology made such a center feasible. The institute treats aneurysms, vascular tumors, malformations, occlusions, ischemia, epilepsy, chronic pain, and trauma. Barrow is one of the largest neuroscience centers in the Southwest, with six surgical suites, a post-anesthesia care area, a 16-bed intensive-care unit, a 24-bed neurological-care unit, a 24-bed intermediate-care area, a 38-bed neuro-rehabilitation inpatient unit, a five-bed epilepsy monitoring unit, a subacute rehabilitation unit, and outpatient neurology specialty clinics. A pediatric neurosurgery section helps children with complex conditions such as spina bifida, cerebral palsy, craniofacial abnormalities, brain tumors, and head injuries. The institute is part of a Level I Trauma Center for brain and spinal-cord injury victims in central Arizona. It is also a teaching hospital and a research facility. Treatments pioneered at Barrow are now being used around the world.

INSIDERS' TIP

911 is for life-threatening emergencies only. This may seem like a no-brainer, but 911 operators are often called by people who don't understand this. Please, don't get in the way of someone else's rescue. If something is non-life threatening, seek help at a walk-in clinic or emergency room.

HEALTHCARE

Good Samaritan Regional Medical Center

1111 E. McDowell Rd., Phoenix
• **(602) 239-2000**
• **www.bannerhealthaz.com**

Good Samaritan began its days as a tuberculosis sanitarium, the Deaconess Hospital and Home, which was founded by a Methodist group in 1911. In 1928, it was renamed Good Samaritan Hospital and began to offer a wider range of services to the local community. Today, Good Samaritan Regional Medical Center, popularly known as Good Sam, is one of the largest hospitals in Arizona with 570 beds. It also is the home of Phoenix Children's Hospital, although that hospital will be moving into its own facilities in the middle of 2001 (see separate listing). Good Sam has 570 licensed beds and 1,800 physicians representing 45 different specialties. It features 16 inpatient operating suites and 8 outpatient operating suites. The hospital leads the state in heart procedures. Two 15-bed inpatient units are devoted to the needs of orthopedic patients. The hospital offers maternity services, care for high-risk pregnancy and postpartum patients, a sleep-disorders program, rehabilitation, and outpatient services. More babies are born at Good Sam than at any other hospital in the state.

The hospital has 123 beds in 11 units dedicated to intensive-care and intermediate-care services. Good Sam's emergency room trauma center treats patients from around the Southwest and Mexico. Good Sam has the state's first positron emission tomography (PET) scanner, which is used to monitor the chemical activity of living cells within tissue. The hospital's oncology services include a bone-marrow transplantation program run in conjunction with the City of Hope National Medical Center in Los Angeles. Good Sam has offered kidney transplants since 1977. The campus also houses the Samaritan Institute of Reproductive Medicine and Samaritan Behavioral Health Center—Good Samaritan, which offers both inpatient and outpatient mental-health services. The Samaritan Regional Poison Control Center also is on campus. Its phone number is 253-3334.

Hacienda de Los Angeles

1402 E. South Mountain Ave., Phoenix
• **(602) 243-4231**
• **www.haciendainc.org**

Hacienda de Los Angeles is a long-term residential care and hospital-to-home transition center serving infants, children, and young adults. It was founded in 1967 by Eileen Butler, who shared her mobile home on South Mountain to care for these patients. In 1970, a group of supporters called the Madrinas secured funding for a proper facility, and in 1976 Hacienda de Los Angeles moved to its current location. The hospital serves patients who have genetic disorders, or have suffered from birth trauma, physical abuse, or accidents such as near-drowning, and car accidents. The hospital-to-home transition program is meant to speed recovery and the patient's return home. A respite-care program provides short-term care (including medical services and recreation) to allow the families of the patients to take a respite from caregiving, usually to attend to other matters. The long-term care program is a home away from home for chronically ill patients. Services include medical and therapeutic care, on-campus and public-school education, social and recreational activities, respiratory therapy, and physical, occupational, and speech therapy.

John C. Lincoln Hospital–North Mountain

250 E. Dunlap Ave., Phoenix
• **(602) 943-2381**

John C. Lincoln Hospital has its roots in the Desert Mission Sanitarium, which was opened by the Presbyterian Church in then-remote Sunnyslope to serve poor people who were ailing from tuberculosis. It grew through the years and became John C. Lincoln Hospital. Today, it's a 262-bed facility that provides Level I trauma and emergency services, cardiopulmonary programs, general surgery, oncology services, obstetric services, health information, and outpatient services. Part of its legacy as a one-time tuberculosis sanitarium are the respiratory wellness and pulmonary rehabilitation programs, which combine exercise and education to make daily life easier for people with chronic conditions such as emphysema. John C. Lincoln's Level I trauma center is one of five in the Valley, but it is the only one serving north Phoenix. The birthing center at the hospital was designed by women, and it features private rooms with whirlpool tubs and a quiet, calming atmosphere. The hospital also houses the Lincoln Institute for Sports Medicine, which serves both professional and amateur athletes with injury-prevention and rehabilitation programs.

John C. Lincoln Hospital–Deer Valley

19829 N. 27th Ave., Phoenix
• **(623) 879-6100**

The Deer Valley location of John C. Lincoln

Hospital began its days as Phoenix General Hospital, and for most of its existence it has been known as Phoenix General Hospital and Medical Center. It was purchased by John C. Lincoln Health Network in 1997. The hospital's 262-bed facility offers inpatient and outpatient medical and surgical care. Doctors perform diagnostic and therapeutic ambulatory surgery. The hospital also offers obstetrics, gynecology, cardiology, open-heart surgery, a cardiac catheterization laboratory, internal medicine, general surgery, intensive-care and coronary-care units, pulmonology, urology, orthopedics, and sports medicine.

Los Niños Hospital
2303 E. Thomas Rd., Phoenix
• **(602) 954-7311**
• **www.losninoshospital.com**

This 15-bed facility opened in 1994. The children's hospital offers medical care for children suffering from a variety of ailments. It specializes in acute care for infants, children and teens, including medical monitoring, urgent care, and transitional care. The hospital also offers physical, occupational and speech therapy, and training to prepare family members and others for patients' post-hospital care. Los Niños Hospital allows 24-hour visitation by parents and encourages them to spend the night. The hospital is locally owned and features a cheerful, home-like setting.

Maricopa Medical Center
2601 E. Roosevelt St., Phoenix
• **(602) 344-5011**

Maricopa Medical Center was honored in 1999 as one of the best hospitals in the country by *U.S. News and World Report*. The original Maricopa County Hospital was built at Seventh Avenue and Roosevelt Street in 1883 to handle smallpox victims. The site was very close to downtown Phoenix even then, so the county was pressured to move the contagious patients farther out. The county bought a site at 35th Avenue and Durango Street in 1885, where the hospital was built. By the early 1960s, the Valley had outgrown its existing hospitals, and a $10.8 million bond issue was approved to fund a new 425-bed county hospital. Site selection dragged into the late 1960s, when a document was uncovered showing the county owned a site at Roosevelt and 24th Streets. The new hospital opened in 1971. A regional burn unit was established at Maricopa County Hospital in 1965. The unit continues to serve all of Arizona and parts of surrounding states, and has

recently been renovated. This was also the first Arizona hospital to establish a Level I Trauma Unit to handle all types of life-threatening injuries and emergencies.

The 541-bed hospital also features the only emergency center in Phoenix dedicated to the special needs of children, a pediatric intensive-care unit, a neonatal intensive-care unit, three adult intensive-care units, and a family birthing center, among other services. A psychiatric annex contains another 92 beds for patients requiring mental health care. Maricopa Medical Center is a teaching hospital affiliated with the University of Arizona College of Medicine, Arizona State University, and the Mayo Graduate School of Medicine.

Maryvale Hospital Medical Center
5102 W. Campbell Ave., Phoenix
• **(602) 848-5000**

Maryvale Community Hospital opened with 60 beds in 1961 to serve the needs brought on by the first wave of explosive growth in the Maryvale area. Samaritan Health System bought the hospital in 1968, renaming it Maryvale Samaritan Hospital, and built the current, 239-bed hospital in 1978. In 1998, the hospital was acquired by Vanguard Health Systems and renamed Maryvale Hospital Medical Center. The hospital serves west Phoenix and the Southwest Valley. The emergency department includes a chest-pain center and urgent-care services. The childbirth center offers each patient a private room for labor, delivery, recovery, and postpartum care. The hospital has a 16-bed special-care unit for oncology, cardiology, medical, and surgical patients needing intensive services. The hospital has six operating rooms where both inpatient and outpatient surgeries are performed. The hospital also has a 26-bed skilled nursing facility and oncology and rehabilitation services. Its outpatient therapeutic aquatics program is nationally recognized.

Paradise Valley Hospital
3929 E. Bell Rd., Phoenix
• **(602) 923-5000**
• **www.paradisevalleyhospital.com**

As the Northeast Valley grew in the early 1980s, the need for a hospital became apparent. This 162-bed facility was built in 1983 to serve an area within a 10-mile radius of 40th Street and Bell Road. Today, there are more than 600 physicians on its staff. Paradise Valley Hospital features the only 24-hour, hospital-based emergency room in the far Northeast

Valley. The hospital has five surgical suites available for outpatient procedures and general surgeries. The diagnostic imaging department features an open scan MRI unit. Paradise Valley Hospital also has a Women's Center that provides women's healthcare services and includes a labor and delivery center. In addition to recovery units for orthopedic, oncology, and pediatric patients, the hospital also has a 14-bed intensive-care and coronary-care unit. The hospital offers outpatient surgery, rehabilitation services, home care, sinus laser treatment, spinal treatment, and hyperbaric wound treatment.

Phoenix Baptist Hospital and Medical Center
2000 West Bethany Home Road, Phoenix
• **(602) 249-0212**
• **www.baptisthealth.com**

Phoenix Baptist Hospital began as a small children's hospital in 1963. As the Valley grew, the hospital expanded its focus to all-purpose care for patients of all ages. Phoenix Baptist is a 217-bed facility that offers general medical and surgical services, an emergency room, an intensive-care and coronary-care unit, oncology services, a cardiology center, the Center for Arthritis and Joint Replacement, a mammography center, maternity services with labor-delivery-recovery-postpartum suites, and a perinatal department that can handle premature infants. Phoenix Baptist also houses a six-bed hospice unit and provides home healthcare.

Phoenix Children's Hospital
1111 E. McDowell Rd., Phoenix
• **(602) 239-2400**
• **www.phxchildrens.com**

The concept of a children's hospital had languished for about a decade when, in 1978, the Maricopa County Pediatric Society began considering ways to make the concept a reality. In 1980, a group of community leaders joined the pediatric doctors to form the nonprofit Phoenix Children's Hospital Inc. The founders decided that Phoenix Children's Hospital would best accomplish its mission in conjunction with an existing hospital, and hospitals throughout the Valley were invited to submit proposals. A blue ribbon committee accepted a proposal from Good Samaritan Regional Medical Center. Phoenix Children's Hospital opened in 1983 in space leased from Good Samaritan. There were no construction or equipment costs incurred. Instead, Good Samaritan transferred its pediatric services and beds to Phoenix Children's Hospital through the lease arrangement.

Phoenix Children's Hospital has outgrown its facility at Good Samaritan and, in mid-2001, will be relocating to a new hospital renovated especially for the treatment of children, though the neonatal intensive care unit will remain at Good Samaritan. This new hospital, which will be located at the former Phoenix Regional Medical Center site on Thomas Road and the Squaw Peak Parkway, will be one of the nation's largest children's hospitals. The new hospital will have about 300 beds, playrooms, school rooms, and family sleep areas in patient rooms and throughout the hospital.

The current 225-bed facility includes a 21-bed pediatric critical-care unit, a 14-bed subacute unit, a 59-bassinet newborn intensive-care nursery, two nurseries for stabilizing newborns, an 18-bed psychiatric unit, and 74 general pediatrics beds. The hospital employs 39 pediatricians and pediatric subspecialists who work exclusively for the hospital. More than 690 community physicians are members of the staff. The hospital also trains pediatric residents. Nearly half of all the beds at the hospital are devoted to critical care for youngsters suffering from trauma and acute illness or who have had complex surgeries. The hospital also offers outpatient services.

Phoenix Indian Medical Center, United States Department of Health and Human Services
4212 N. 16th St., Phoenix
• **(602) 263-1200**
• **www.ihs.gov**

The Phoenix Indian Medical Center started its days as a tuberculosis sanitarium for Native American children. The sanitarium opened in 1909 on land owned by the Phoenix Indian School, and it was administered by the school until 1931. After a few years as an independent facility, the sanitarium administration changed its mission, deciding to serve adults as well as children, and Phoenix Indian Hospital was born. Today, it serves the medical needs of six Native American communities with a population 45,000 under the aegis of the Phoenix Area Indian Health Services. The hospital has 137 acute-care beds and a complete array of health services. Because diabetes has become a scourge for tribal members, the National Institutes of Health maintains a National Institute of Diabetes, Digestive, and Kidney Diseases at the hospital. The hospital's Auxiliary Association provides scholarships for Native American students who are pursuing education in the health field. The auxiliary also purchases equipment for various departments and donates time and money to hospital-sponsored community events.

Phoenix Memorial Hospital
1201 S. Seventh Ave., Phoenix
- **(602) 258-5111**
- **www.phxmemorialhospital.com**

Phoenix Memorial Hospital has been honored as one of the most innovative hospital medical centers in the country. It began as St. Monica's Mission, Arizona's first maternity-care clinic, in 1934. In 1944, the hospital began the first interracial nurses training program west of the Mississippi. In 1951, the hospital opened the region's only polio treatment center, a unit with 40 iron-lung machines. The hospital opened the Southwest Cancer Institute in 1961, serving all of Arizona and parts of Nevada and New Mexico. The hospital offers cardiac catheterization, open-heart surgery, and cardiac rehabilitation; critical-care and intensive-care units; orthopedics and joint replacement; women's services including maternity, well-woman care, and mammography; a nurse-midwifery program; pediatrics; physical, occupational, and speech therapy; a rehabilitation center; a comprehensive cancer services center; and skilled-nursing and hospice units. Its new Del E. Webb Cancer Treatment Center, which is under construction, will provide state-of-the-art cancer treatment, community outreach, and education.

St. Joseph's Hospital and Medical Center
350 W. Thomas Rd., Phoenix
- **(602) 406-3000**
- **www.mha.chw.edu**

The Sisters of Mercy came from Ireland to Phoenix in 1892 to teach. When they got here, they were moved by the suffering of tuberculosis victims. By 1895, the sisters had raised enough money to rent a six-room cottage at Fourth and Polk Streets, where the original St. Joseph's Sanitarium was established. A year later, the sisters were forced to find larger quarters and changed the name to St. Joseph's Hospital. As the city grew, so did the hospital. The sisters opened a school of nursing in 1910. They moved the hospital to its current location in 1953, and it continued to grow, adding a kidney dialysis unit in 1956, the Barrow Neurological Institute in 1962 (see listing), a coronary-care unit in 1965, a neonatal intensive-care unit in 1967, a respiratory intensive-care unit in 1968, and pediatric intensive-care unit in 1972. The hospital also changed its name to add the words "medical center" to reflect its expanded role. On his trip to Phoenix in 1987, Pope John Paul II visited the hospital.

HEALTHCARE

Valley Lutheran hospital is an example of the high quality of medical facilities.

Photo: Penny Kleingartner

The Sisters of Mercy continue to guide the institution in partnership with secular hospital professionals. Its services include 475 beds for acute patients, a Level I trauma center, general surgery, hyberbaric medicine, maternity services, the Muhammad Ali Parkinson's Research Center, outpatient surgery, a pain center, a home-care unit, an adult-day hospital, an audiology center, behavioral and developmental pediatrics, a blood bank, a cardiac catheterization lab, cardiac rehabilitation, a child-abuse assessment center, dialysis, general medical education, and much more. In 1999, *U.S. News and World Report* ranked St. Joe's among the best hospitals in several specialties, including the eighth best hospital in the United States for neurology and neurosurgery. The hospital is one of the Catholic Healthcare West properties.

St. Luke's Medical Center
1800 E. Van Buren St., Phoenix
• **(602) 251-8100**

St. Luke's Medical Center opened in 1907 as the St. Luke's Home serving tuberculosis patients. Tuberculosis was pretty well under control in 1949, when St. Luke's expanded its mission. As St. Luke's Hospital, the facility specialized in respiratory and cardiovascular diseases as well as general medicine and surgery. Today, St. Luke's Medical Center is a 241-bed facility that provides services and programs in cardiology, pulmonology, orthopedics, general medicine and surgery, neuroscience, emergency medicine, gastroenterology, oncology, and ophthalmology. Facilities include the Charles A. Barrow Heart Lung Center, the Jane Eslick Johnson Physical Rehabilitation Center, and the Prentice Eye Center.

Surgicenter
1040 E. McDowell Rd., Phoenix
• **(602) 258-1521**

Dr. Wallace Reed and Dr. John Ford opened Surgicenter, the first outpatient surgery center in the nation, in 1970. The current facility, rebuilt in 1993, has eight operating suites—including two endoscopy units—as well as four overnight-care rooms. Patients are referred by their surgeons.

Carl T. Hayden Veterans Affairs Medical Center
650 E. Indian School Rd., Phoenix
• **(602) 277-5551**
• **www.va.gov**

In 1947, Senator Carl T. Hayden was approached by a group of Maricopa County residents who felt that Phoenix needed a hospital to serve veterans recently returned from World War II. A land deal was arranged with the Phoenix Indian School for a 27-acre parcel on the northwestern corner of Seventh Street and Indian School Road. Today, approximately 250,000 veterans live in Maricopa County, and the 300-bed facility serves about 35,000 of them annually through its programs. It is also a teaching and research hospital. Its services include an emergency life-support unit, a 104-bed nursing-home care unit, services for homeless veterans, a substance-abuse disorders program, and a post-traumatic stress disorder program. General medical and surgical services are offered, as are mental health and behavioral science services, physical medicine, rehabilitation, and neurology. In addition, the hospital has its own pharmacy and complete laboratory services. A 60,000-square-foot ambulatory-care center opened in 1998.

Southeast Valley

Chandler Regional Hospital
475 S. Dobson Rd., Chandler
• **(480) 963-4561**
• **www.crhaz.com**

A citizens group established Maricopa County Hospital District #1 in 1961 and, through it, built Chandler Regional Hospital. The 149-bed facility provides all private rooms. Its major services include an emergency center featuring Level II trauma care, an intensive-care unit, inpatient and outpatient surgery, physical rehabilitation services, a pediatrics unit, and cardiopulmonary services. A major expansion of its Birth Center, which features labor delivery-recovery rooms, was completed in 1999. In addition, the East Valley Regional Cancer Center, which offers comprehensive oncology services, is on the campus. The hospital has begun construction of a $20-million Ambulatory Surgery and Imaging Center to expand the hospital's emergency, surgery, and diagnostic imaging services.

Desert Samaritan Medical Center
1400 S. Dobson Rd., Mesa
• **(480) 835-3000**
• **www.samaritanaz.com**

Desert Samaritan Hospital opened in 1973, but its roots go back to 1921 when Genevieve LeSueur donated her two-story, 12-room house to become Mesa Southside District Hospital. As Mesa grew, so did the hospital. By 1958, it had moved to Main Street and Country Club

HEALTHCARE

Drive and expanded to become a complete hospital facility with operating rooms, a recovery room, and emergency room. In 1968, Southside merged with Good Samaritan Hospital, and Samaritan Health Service was born. The corporation built Desert Samaritan (or Desert Sam, as it's popularly known) to replace Southside Hospital. Desert Sam primarily serves Mesa, Tempe, Chandler, Gilbert, and Apache Junction. A full-service community hospital, Desert Sam has 400 private rooms. It features a Level II emergency room with 53 beds and an urgent-care center with 8 beds. Desert Sam also features 16 private labor-delivery-recovery rooms. It has a pediatric intensive-care unit and neonatal intensive-care units in its pediatric center. More than 6,000 inpatient surgeries and 10,000 outpatient surgeries are performed each year at Desert Sam, including more than 650 open-heart surgeries. The hospital also has a radiation oncology department, 64 critical-care and intermediate-care beds, a 32-bed orthopedic and neurology unit, and a sleep disorders center. Desert Sam offers various therapy programs, such as aquatic therapy, and community health education classes.

Mesa General Hospital Medical Center
515 N. Mesa Dr., Mesa
• (480) 969-9111

Mesa General Hospital opened in 1965 as a physician-owned community hospital. Today, it is a 124-bed facility that offers a full range of services, including an emergency room, an intensive-care unit, maternity services, outpatient surgery, and services. It is home to the Arizona Diagnostic and Surgical Center as well as a pain-medicine center.

Mesa Lutheran Hospital
525 W. Brown Rd., Mesa
• (480) 834-1211

Mesa Lutheran Hospital opened in 1963 with 165 beds. Today, Mesa Lutheran is a 375-bed hospital, including a 60-bed skilled-nursing facility. Its services include an emergency room, obstetrical services, a joint-replacement program, a women's health center, and general medical and surgical services. The hospital's cardiovascular program provides diagnosis, treatment and rehabilitation, and about 400 open-heart surgeries per year are performed. The John J. Rhodes Rehabilitation Institute and the Behavioral Health Institute, which offers inpatient and outpatient psychological services, are also on campus.

Tempe St. Luke's Hospital
1500 S. Mill Ave., Tempe
• (480) 968-9411

Tempe St. Luke's Hospital opened in 1946 as a small, 10-bed community hospital in the home of Dr. Ernest Pohle. It remains the only acute-care hospital in Tempe. A 110-bed facility, Tempe St. Luke's has an emergency room, general surgery, maternity and women's

The Scottsdale Mayo Clinic attracts patients from around the world.

Photo: Penny Kleingartner

services departments, a radiology lab, and out-patient surgery. Also on the hospital campus is a 63,000-square-foot medical office complex housing more than 40 specialized medical practices.

Valley Lutheran Hospital
6644 E. Baywood Ave., Mesa
• **(480) 981-2000**

Valley Lutheran Hospital opened in 1984 with 120 beds. It has grown into a 231-bed, full-service hospital providing general surgery and medical care, critical care, and maternity care. The hospital has an emergency room, a women's health center, a joint-replacement program, and a kidney-stone management program.

Northeast Valley

Mayo Clinic Hospital
5777 E. Mayo Blvd., Scottsdale
• **(480) 515-6296**
• **www.mayo.edu**

The latest addition to the Valley's hospital scene is the Mayo Clinic Hospital, which opened in 1998. It is the first hospital planned, designed, and built by the Mayo Clinic. A 178-bed facility, its focus is to provide inpatient care to support the 62 medical and surgical specialties practiced at the Mayo Clinic Scottsdale (see next entry). The hospital has 112 medical-surgical beds, 20 critical-care beds, 6 beds in a short-stay unit, 24 skilled-nursing beds, and 16 rehabilitation beds. It also has an emergency room and a full-service clinical laboratory, an intensive-care unit, inpatient dialysis, a bone-marrow transplant facility, and a sleep studies lab for the diagnosis and treatment of sleep disorders. The hospital recently added a liver and kidney transplant program, which has performed 35 liver transplants and 14 kidney transplants over the past year, with success rates higher than the national average. In March 2000, it also added Arizona's first liver dialysis unit.

> ## INSIDERS' TIP
> If you have a sick child, you might want to check out The Emily Center, a pediatric health library at Phoenix Children's Hospital. Founded 10 years ago by the family of Emily Anderson—who lost her life to leukemia at age 6—The Emily Center is the most comprehensive pediatric health library in the southwest. It is open to the general public and provides accurate and up-to-date information on children's health and diseases. It is open from 9 AM to 5 PM, at the PCH Outpatient Building, 909 E. Brill Street, Phoenix. You can also ask the staff questions by calling them directly at (602) 239-6902, or through e-mail at emilyc@phxchildrens.com.

Mayo Clinic Scottsdale
13400 E. Shea Blvd., Scottsdale
• **(480) 301-8000**
• **www.mayo.edu**

Mayo Clinic Scottsdale opened in 1987 and, owing to the Mayo Clinic reputation, it serves a varied clientele. About 50 percent of the patients come from the Valley, 25 percent from the rest of Arizona, and the rest come from across the United States and the world. It is a multi-specialty outpatient clinic with 240 exam rooms, an outpatient surgery center with 5 operating rooms, a full-service laboratory, a pharmacy, a patient-education library, and an endoscopy suite. About 90 percent of the clinic's patients are self-referred. The clinic is also a center for ongoing research in such areas as molecular genetics and cellular and molecular biology. Clinical research trials give patients access to the latest medical treatments. It is also a teaching institution. Sixty-two medical and surgical specialties are practiced at the clinic, which includes the state's first bone-marrow transplant program, a breast clinic, a cancer genetics clinic, critical-care medicine, a diabetes clinic, a gastrointestinal endoscopy program, a sleep disorders center, state-of-the-art radiation therapy, and more.

Scottsdale Healthcare Osborn
7400 E. Osborn Rd., Scottsdale
• **(480) 675-4000**
• **www.shc.org**

City Hospital of Scottsdale was founded in 1962 as a 120-bed facility. As the Northeast Valley grew, so did the hospital and its mission. For most of its existence, it has been known as Scottsdale Memorial Hospital, but in 1998 changed its name to Scottsdale Healthcare Osborn. It is a 328-bed, full-service hospital, known for its cardiovascular medicine, obstetrics, orthopedics, and oncology services. Its emergency department is a Level I trauma center that serves the East Valley and much of south central Arizona. The hospital also provides an urgent-care center; outpatient surgery and recovery care; inpatient and outpatient facilities for physical, occupational, and speech therapy; a 60-bed skilled-nursing facility; a cardiac center; nine operating suites, including two specifically equipped for open-heart surgery; a critical-care unit; a 16-bed obstetrics unit with seven labor-delivery-recovery rooms; and a Level II nursery. The hospital also houses hyperbaric oxygen treatment, adult day care, an outpatient cardiopulmonary rehabilitation and fitness center, pediatric services, an outpatient surgery center with a dedicated recovery care nursing unit, and primary care through the Family Practice Center.

Scottsdale Healthcare Shea
9003 E. Shea Blvd., Scottsdale
- **(480) 860-3000**
- **www.shc.org**

Scottsdale Healthcare Shea, consistently ranked among top hospitals in the nation, is a 242-bed hospital that features all private rooms and is known for its cardiology, oncology, and women's and children's services. The hospital's Kenneth M. Piper Outpatient Surgery Center offers surgical specialties, such as reconstructive, orthopedic, urology, and gynecology, and houses the Scottsdale Healthcare Reproductive Medicine program. The Piper Center contains eight operating rooms and a nine-room overnight-services pavilion to serve patients requiring post-surgery observation, pain control, or IV therapy. The hospital also has an emergency room and an urgent-care unit, cardiology services that include open-heart surgery, cardiac catheterization, and inpatient and outpatient cardiac rehabilitation facilities. The hospital also has an intensive-care unit, medical and surgical services, obstetric services, a bone-marrow transplant unit, a 24-bed oncology unit, a sleep disorders center, and an epilepsy monitoring center. Also available through the hospital are pediatric services; outpatient physical, occupational and speech therapy; laboratory services; and lithotripsy, a special treatment for kidney stones.

Northwest Valley

Arrowhead Community Hospital and Medical Center
18701 N. 67th Ave., Glendale
- **(623) 561-1000**
- **www.baptisthealth.com**

This 104-bed facility has served the North-

west Valley since 1988. It offers general medicine and surgery services, an emergency room, intensive-care and coronary-care units, a cardiac center, oncology services, a mammography center, labor-delivery-recovery-postpartum suites, a perinatal department, and a postpartum follow-up program for high-risk families. Arrowhead's women's health center offers health screenings, health education, and preventive medicine. In addition, the hospital has an arthritis and joint replacement center. Outpatient services and home healthcare are available. Arrowhead also houses the Valley's first hospital-based plastic-surgery center. It recently expanded its facilities, adding two additional operating rooms, 14 labor, delivery, recovery, and postpartum rooms, and 15 patient rooms in the emergency department.

Glendale Samaritan Surgicenter
5757 W. Thunderbird Rd., Ste. E150, Glendale
- **(602) 843-1900**

Glendale Samaritan Surgicenter is an ambulatory outpatient surgical facility. Patients are referred to the facility by their primary-care physicians.

Sun Health Boswell Memorial Hospital
10401 Thunderbird Blvd., Sun City
- **(623) 977-7211**
- **www.sunhealth.org**

When Boswell Memorial Hospital was built in 1970, Sun City was a long way from Glendale, Peoria, and the mainstream of the Valley. Reflecting the nature of the retirement community, Boswell focused on adult care and medicine. As the Northwest Valley has grown, Boswell has maintained that focus. This 319-bed community hospital provides inpatient and outpatient medical and surgical services as well as a skilled-nursing facility. Boswell offers an emergency center, an outpatient center, a cancer program, cardiovascular surgery, an intensive-care unit, and extended-care and rehabilitation services. A new addition for Boswell's heart hospital, completed in 2000, includes expanded catheterization labs and office space on site for cardiologists and surgeons.

Sun Health Del E. Webb Memorial Hospital
14502 W. Meeker Blvd., Sun City West
- **(623) 214-4000**
- **www.sunhealth.org**

The 208-bed Del E. Webb hospital, built in

1988, serves the retirement communities of the Northwest Valley. Focused on medicine for adults, the hospital offers an emergency center, general medical and surgical services, a cardiac-catheterization laboratory, outpatient surgery and services, rehabilitation services, medical-psychiatric services, mobile MRI and lithotripsy services, and extended-care facilities. It is the site for the Sun Health Pain Management Center and the Adult Behavioral Center. Of hospitals in the nation, it has been ranked number two in cost-containment management.

Thunderbird Samaritan Medical Center
5555 W. Thunderbird Rd., Glendale
- **(623) 588-5555**
- **www.bannerhealth.com**

Northwest Hospital—Glendale's first hospital—opened in 1960. In 1983, when it had outgrown its original site, the hospital moved to its current location and was renamed Thunderbird Samaritan Medical Center. The 318-bed hospital primarily serves residents of the Northwest Valley. Its emergency department features 21 fully equipped treatment rooms. The hospital also offers a complete range of gynecological and obstetrical services, including a labor, delivery, and recovery unit, and a nursery that provides expert care for premature infants. The hospital has seven operating rooms, including two suites for open heart surgery. Thunderbird Samaritan offers general surgery, orthopedics, pediatrics, pulmonary care, a critical-care and intensive-care unit, an oncology and urology unit, occupational therapy and rehabilitation services, cardiac care, and renal care. There is also a sleep-disorders program, an outpatient center, and a hospice program. In addition, Samaritan Behavioral Health Center–Thunderbird Campus offers psychiatric, behavioral-health, and substance-abuse treatment for adults on an inpatient basis. The hospital began a $50 million expansion in the summer of 2000.

Walk-in Clinics

Walk-in clinics come in a number of flavors. If the clinic doesn't have the word "urgent" in its name somewhere, then the clinic generally will turn out to be a general practice that accepts walk-in patients. Most of these general-practice clinics work the Monday through Friday, 9 AM to 5 PM shift. The urgent-care clinics tend to work the odd hours (some offer 24-hour services), and they're geared to handle accidents and conditions that need immediate care but are not life threatening. They're not the place to go if you think you're having a heart attack, but a good place to go if you think you've broken a limb. Call beforehand to ascertain hours and what insurance carriers are covered. In addition, many of the hospitals such as Mayo Clinic, Chandler Regional Hospital, the Samaritan group, and others have affiliated walk-in, general-practice clinics, and a call to the hospital can help you find a good clinic. (Most of the hospitals also have lines for doctor referrals.) The following list is not complete, but representative.

Phoenix

Ahwatukee Foothills Health Center, 4545 E. Chandler Boulevard, Phoenix, (480) 961-2300

Jesse Owens Urgent Care Center, 325 E. Baseline Road, Phoenix, (602) 243-4251

HealthSouth Medical Clinic, 2010 N. 75th Avenue, Phoenix, (623) 245-6695

Southeast Valley

Desert Samaritan Urgent Care, 4530 E. Ray Road, Gilbert, (480) 598-7500

Gilbert Health Center, 1501 N. Gilbert Road, Gilbert, (480) 503-2011

Minor Medical Care Center, 4427 S. Rural Road, Suite 1, Tempe, (480) 838-2289.

Sun Lakes Health Center, 10440 E. Riggs Road, Sun Lakes, (480) 802-6500

Northeast Valley

Primary Care Walk-In Center, 8102 E. McDowell Road, Scottsdale, (480) 946-3800

HealthSouth Medical Clinic, 10355 N. Scottsdale Road, Scottsdale, (480) 991-9358

Mayo Clinic Hospital–Urgent Care Facility, 5777 E. Mayo Boulevard, Scottsdale, (480) 342-1776

Northwest Valley

Sun Health Surprise Health Center, 12425 W. Bell Road, Building A, Suite 103, Surprise, (602) 815-2900.

Mental Health

Mental-health services are available at a number of the hospitals listed in this chapter, and through the services and hospitals listed below.

Arizona State Hospital, 2500 E. Van Buren Street, Phoenix, (602) 244-1331, (800) 242-7837

Behavioral Health Institute, Lutheran Health Care Network, 500 W. 10th Place, Suite 141, Mesa, (480) 461-2175

Charter Behavioral Health System of Arizona - Glendale, 6015 W. Peoria Avenue, Glendale, (623) 878-7878

Charter Behavioral Health System of Arizona–East Valley, 2190 N. Grace Boulevard, Chandler, (480) 899-8989

St. Luke's Behavioral Health Center, 1800 E. Van Buren Street, Phoenix, (602) 251-8535

Alternative Healthcare

Ever since settlers started coming to the Valley of the Sun in the 1800s, interest in alternative healthcare has been high. Back then, it was difficult to find practitioners well-versed in medical science anyway, so home cures, folk cures-and even out-and-out quackery-often filled healthcare needs that included bullet wounds, rattlesnake bites, and tuberculosis. By 1870, Arizona's settlers numbered 10,000, with 22 doctors to serve them. The few doctors out here had to live life on the road, traveling from settlement to settlement to treat people.

The first doctors in Arizona were undoubtedly Native American medicine men. A number of frontier doctors incorporated the many herbal and botanical cures that the medicine men used because they worked. Science has only recently begun to verify what these frontier doctors knew by experience. Today, herbal and botanical cures from many different cultures, including that of Native Americans, are considered part of the vast umbrella known as "alternative"—and even mainstream—healthcare.

The Valley offers a full range of alternative medical services, that complement or step outside the bounds of traditional Western medical practices. For example, chiropractors are virtually mainstream practitioners in Arizona and The Yellow Pages listings for chiropractors fill 17 pages. You'll also find homeopaths, naturopaths, acupuncturists, aromatherapists, massage therapists, bioelectric therapists, and just about any other practitioner of alternative medicine you can think of.

Unfortunately, alternative medicine is a vast and decentralized realm, and there are no authoritative referral sources in the Valley. So the best sources for finding an alternative-medicine practitioner are the phone book and word of mouth. You can also often stop by a local health food store to get recommendations on practitioners in the region.

The best advice we can offer is similar to what we would give when seeking a conventional medical practitioner. Find out where the physician studied, how long the physician has been practicing, and whether the physician is licensed with the state. Then, check with the licensing boards for any complaints. Arizona licensing boards include the Board of Chiropractic Examiners, 5060 N. 19th Avenue, Phoenix, (602) 255-1444; the Board of Homeopathic Medical Examiners, 1400 W. Washington Street, Phoenix, (602) 542-3095; and the Naturopathic Physicians Board of Examiners, 1400 W. Washington Street, Phoenix (602) 542-3095.

INSIDERS' TIP

Don't underestimate the power of the Arizona sun. Skin cancer danger is very real in Arizona, so you should always apply a heavy-duty sun block when you go out—and this goes double for the small tykes. Wearing a light, long-sleeved shirt will also help, and donning a hat when you go for a hike will also help combat heat stroke. Succumbing to dehydration is also easy here, even in the winter. Try to drink at least eight cups of water a day—even more during periods of heavy activity. Heat stroke can kill, so if you are someone you know succumbs to the heat, seek medical attention immediately.

HEALTHCARE

Education and Childcare

There's much to praise about the education scene in the Phoenix area: the ever-improving Arizona State University, one of the largest community college systems in the nation, and private schools whose fame reaches beyond Arizona's borders. In comparison, though, the Valley's public school system is not as dynamic as it could or should be for such a large metropolitan area. There are many bright spots—progressive, high-minded elementary and secondary schools in the urban core as well as in suburban areas. But those who rank livable cities say Phoenix's public schools are part of the reason the city doesn't make it to the top echelon.

Looking at Arizona public schools as a whole, you will learn that they lag behind many other states for a number of reasons: Arizona ranks last nationally in per-pupil spending our high school dropout rate is the second worst in the nation, and we have the fifth-largest class sizes in the nation—as many as 35 pupils in some classrooms. In addition, because of the exponential population growth, Arizona is plagued by teacher shortages and a building crunch.

If you talk to Phoenix area residents with young children, you'll find that many of them shop school districts as much as they do real estate when they are ready to move into new homes. (Homebuyers should consult our Real Estate chapter.) Certain districts have excellent reputations, while others limp along because of inequities in Arizona's system for school funding. Some schools have enough money to build swimming pools and topnotch computer labs, while others get by with barebones classrooms and the simplest of gymnasiums. Since statehood in 1912, Arizona schools have relied on bonds, repaid through property taxes, to build and improve schools. In 1994, the Arizona Supreme Court ruled that funding school construction through local property taxes was unconstitutional because of the disparities it created among classrooms. The Arizona Legislature has been struggling with the school financing issue ever since.

In this chapter we start our list of educational facilities with public and private universities, including Arizona State University, which for many years played second banana to the University of Arizona in Tucson. Some would argue that the two schools are now about equal.

Those looking for a community college will find an impressive selection in the Phoenix area. The Maricopa Community College District of 10 colleges is the second largest such district in the country. It draws 200,000 students, some of whom like the cost savings versus a four-year university and some of whom seek the specialized skills and training that community colleges can offer. Community colleges are also a great way to gather prerequisite classes before launching into a bachelor's degree at another institution. The colleges represent a wide range of ages and ethnic groups, and students include retirees, homemakers, and those seeking a career change.

Education opportunities trickle down to the youngest of Arizonans too. The Valley of the Sun has a number of good preschool programs, including ones endorsed by the National Association for the Education of Young Children, Montessori programs, and parent-cooperative programs. See the Childcare section of this chapter for important phone numbers as well as information on finding babysitters, nannies, and child-care centers.

Education

Public and Private Universities

Arizona State University

From a humble teachers college at the turn of the century, Arizona State University has grown to a multipurpose institution of 49,700 students on three campuses. It has undergone several name changes over the decades. It started out as Tempe Normal School in the 1890s, later became Arizona State Teachers College, then Arizona State College, until becoming Arizona State University in 1958. Recently, the university edged into the list of the 10 largest universities in the nation. ASU is very much a part of the Valley community based on its contributions toward education, research, business, and the arts. The campuses are a source of pride for local residents, because ASU has been able to continually ascend in the ratings of universities nationwide. In addition, ASU continues to improve in reputation as a research university. For instance, it has been highly involved in the Mars Pathfinder project.

In athletics, ASU is known for having an excellent overall program, one that rises to the national rankings in not only football, but also basketball, baseball, wrestling, swimming, gymnastics, and golf. The football team went to the Rose Bowl in 1996 and 1997. The teams' mascot, Sparky, is the maroon-and-gold Sun Devil, an impish-looking devil complete with pitchfork. Topnotch athletic amenities include Sun Devil Stadium, the Karsten golf course, and the Plummer Aquatic Center.

ASU has a variety of student organizations, including those that have religious or ethnic affiliations and certain political or environmental interests.

The ASU library system boasts 3.1 million volumes, making it the 37th largest research library in the United States and Canada, according to the Association of Research Libraries. Hayden Library on the main campus houses the Arizona Collection and research sites in Chicano and Native American studies. A two-level underground addition to Hayden opened in 1989. Also on campus are the Noble Science & Engineering Library, housing a vast map collection and data on U.S. patents, and law, music, and video research libraries.

ASU's newspaper, *State Republic*, is published Monday through Friday. A literary magazine called *Hayden's Ferry Review* comes out twice a year and highlights local and national writers and artists. It is considered one of the best literary magazines in the country.

The Arizona Board of Regents is the governing board for the state's public university system, which also includes the University of Arizona in Tucson and Northern Arizona University in Flagstaff.

Here we give overviews of the main campus and newer branches in the West and East Valley.

ASU, Main Campus
University Dr. and Mill Ave., Tempe
• **(480) 965-9011**
• **www.asu.edu**

With 44,000 students taking day and evening classes, the main campus is by far the focal point of the ASU system. The 650-acre campus takes up several city blocks in downtown Tempe, and it regulates the pulse of the city. When the students leave for the summer, the usually bustling Mill Avenue falls quiet. There's little open space and landscaping between campus buildings and Tempe businesses, so there's an overall feeling that this is an urban, commuter campus. On the other hand, the interior of the campus has several malls—wide, tree-lined pedestrian walkways—that give that feeling of seclusion and seriousness associated with institutions of higher learning. Plus, there are 13 residence halls and ASU-run apartment complexes, proving that the campus is a good mix of commuters and those who hang out close to campus.

Architecture buffs should have a look at Grady Gammage Memorial Auditorium on Mill Avenue, a grandly executed circular building with lighted ramps leading out from it. It was the last public building designed by Frank Lloyd Wright. Nearby, you will see the round and tiered Music Building and the futuristic Nelson Fine Arts Center.

ASU Main students pursue a choice of 86 undergraduate degrees, 97 master's degrees, and 52 doctoral or terminal degree programs. The colleges ASU is best known for are in liberal arts and sciences, fine arts, architecture, and environmental design, business, nursing, and education. To keep up with technology, the campus has five computing sites for use by students, faculty, and staff. The huge Computing Commons is near the center of campus.

ASU West
4701 W. Thunderbird Rd., Phoenix
• **(623) 543-5500**
• **www.west.asu.edu**

Established in 1984 to serve the West Valley, ASU West continues to grow. The modern-looking campus includes computer-linked classrooms, a library, a bookstore, a fitness center, a child-care center, and a cafeteria. Technopolis is a student computing access center. ASU West's 5,000 undergraduate and graduate students pursue degrees in the College of Arts and Sciences, Education, the School of Management, and the Division of Collabora-

tive Programs. Studies in Human Services lead to degrees in the administration of justice, communications studies, recreation and tourism, and social work.

ASU East
6001 S. Power Rd., Mesa
• **(480) 727-3278**
• **www.east.asu.edu**

This is ASU's newest campus, which took over part of the former Williams Air Force Base. It's the home campus for ASU's School of Technology and its school of Agribusiness and Resource Management.

ASU Extended Campus
502 E. Monroe Ave., Phoenix
• **(602) 965-3986**

Based in the Mercado Center in downtown Phoenix, the Extended Campus makes classes and programs available Valleywide by offering them at off-campus sites, over television, or by correspondence. These are for-credit classes to work toward degrees. Because the classes are offered at a variety of times—days, evenings and weekends—they appeal to older workers wanting to continue their education.

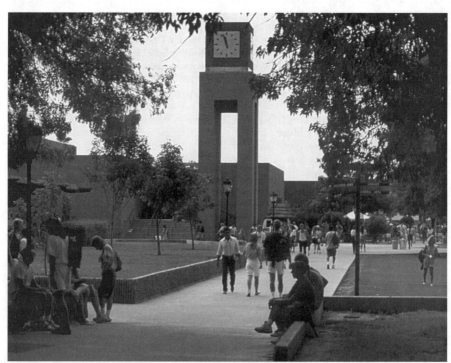

The Maricopa Community College District is one of the largest in the country. Here students enjoy the lush campus of Mesa Community College.

Photo: Courtesy of MCCD

Grand Canyon University

3300 W. Camelback Rd., Phoenix
• (602) 249-3300, (800) 800-9776
• www.grand-canyon.edu

The 2,100-student Grand Canyon University is Arizona's only private, traditional, Christian liberal arts institution. It has 60 programs of study, all with a Christian perspective. The six colleges are nursing, liberal arts, science/allied health, business, continuing studies, and education. The university is continually ranked among the best private liberal arts programs in the nation in surveys by *U.S. News & World Report*. The 90-acre campus, lined with palm trees and featuring fairly modern red-brick buildings, is easily accessible from busy Camelback Road in west Phoenix. The student population is a mix of commuting students, those transferring from other colleges and first-time college students living on campus. There is one residence hall, or the university can arrange for apartment housing. The university says it has a broad religious and ethnic representation, with students from all over the country and all over the world. In athletics, Grand Canyon has competed for national collegiate titles in baseball and basketball.

University of Phoenix

4605 E. Elwood St., Phoenix
• (602) 966-7400
• www.phoenix.edu
Northwest Campus, 15601 N. 28th Ave.,
Phoenix
• (602) 863-2600
East Valley Campus,
1811 S. Alma School Rd., Mesa
• (480) 831-8510
Scottsdale Campus, 7001 N. Scottsdale Rd.,
Scottsdale
• (4802) 922-8228
Southbank Campus,
3600 E. University Dr., Tempe
• (480) 470-1065

The Arizona-based University of Phoenix has recently risen to the distinction of being the nation's largest for-profit, accredited university, thanks to a student population of 40,000 on campuses in 12 states. There are 10,000 students in Arizona. The University of Phoenix bills itself as the nation's leading university for working adults, with degree programs in areas such as business, information systems, counseling, nursing, and education. An important note, though: The university accepts only gainfully employed students 23 and older. A recent study indicated that nearly half of all higher-education students are in this age group. Flexible scheduling of classes allows working professionals to earn degrees or certifications without interrupting their careers. This means weekend and evening classes, usually lasting for compressed amounts of time compared with similar classes at traditional universities.

Community Colleges

Maricopa Community Colleges

2411 W. 14th St., Tempe
• (480) 731-8000
• www.maricopa.edu

Ten colleges in Maricopa County are organized into the Maricopa Community College District, which is the largest provider of postsecondary education in Arizona. It is the second-largest community college district in the country. The district formed in 1962 with a single college and has since grown to serve more than 200,000 students annually in credit and noncredit programs. Students have their choice of professional, occupational, special interest, and continuing education programs. In other words, you can study just about anything somewhere within the Maricopa Community College system. Many students attending Arizona State University have taken prerequisites in the liberal arts and other subjects at a community college, either before starting at ASU or while at ASU. The student population also includes a fair number of older women re-entering the work force, retirees, young people still deciding on careers, and people just interested in a class or two to expand their knowledge. Some of the more interesting programs and classes include: culinary arts, equine science, hotel-restaurant management, film-making, and commerce. Of course, you will also find such familiar programs as business/computer information systems, counseling, communications, arts and sciences, and library/media science.

Campuses, for the most part, have a few thousand students, but some are smaller. District growth has enabled campuses to build not only classroom buildings, but also such things as fitness centers, child-care centers, and computer labs.

Flexible scheduling and evening classes help accommodate working adults. Rio Salado Community College is known as the college without walls, because most of the classes take place at nontraditional sites such as office buildings and shopping malls. Some of its campuses also offer distance learning via the Internet, fax, and regular mail. As such, it helps make the community college experience accessible to everyone.

The community colleges pride themselves on being able to serve every corner of the Valley. For addresses and phone numbers, call the district's 24-hour hotline at (480) 731-8333.

Other Higher Education Institutions

East Valley Institute of Technology
1601 W. Main St., Mesa
• **(480) 461-4173**

EVIT is Arizona's first regional, technological public school district, open to students in 10th through 12th grade from throughout the East Valley. It's free for those students, although adults out of high school pay a small tuition. The idea is to prepare students for immediate employment in such areas as health occupations, commercial art, computer programming, electronics, drafting, construction, plumbing, and many other areas of business and industry. Students typically spend half the school day at their regular school and half at EVIT.

Scottsdale Culinary Institute
8100 E. Camelback Rd., Suite 1001, Scottsdale
• **(480) 990-3773, (800) 848-2433**
• **www.scichefs.com**

The reason we mention this small school is that Scottsdale—with its many resorts, hotels, and fine restaurants—is a natural location for training chefs and offers a Le Cordon Bleu Culinary program. Graduates have gone on to great jobs, locally and elsewhere, as sous chefs, pastry chefs, and banquet managers. The institute, in operation since 1986, offers an associate's degree at an intensive, 15-month pace, with mostly hands-on learning. Average class size is 15 students per chef instructor. The Institute's L'Ecole Restaurant, rated three stars by Mobil, is a classroom, laboratory, and public restaurant. The restaurant is opened limited hours Monday through Friday.

Thunderbird–The American Graduate School of International Management
15249 N. 59th Ave., Glendale
• **(602) 978-7210**
• **www.t-bird.edu**

This private graduate school enjoys a global reputation as one of the top school of international business. It was established in 1946 on the principle that to do business on a global scale, one must be able to combine functional business skills—such as finance and marketing—with the ability to understand the culture, language, and business climate of one's customers and business associates. To that end, Thunderbird offers a three-part curriculum: the study of one or more languages, international studies, and international business. Students have their choice of studying Arabic, Chinese, French, German, Japanese, Portuguese, Russian, or Spanish. International students may opt for thorough training in English as a Second Language. Many international students are sent here by their home country's graduate schools or corporations for further polishing in the ways of international business. All students earn a master's in international management. Thunderbird, with 1,400 full-time students in 2000, bills itself as the oldest graduate management school in the United States devoted exclusively to the education of college graduates for international careers. It also boasts a large multimedia library called the International Business Information Centre. Tracking of graduates shows that most go into marketing/sales, finance/accounting, or consulting and work in the manufacturing and financial services sectors. The school says it has 32,000 alumni working in 12,000 companies, represented in 135 countries, making for an impressive global network of contacts for graduates. About 5,000 students go through the school's non-degreed executive programs, which offer short-term training, certification, and continuing education. The average age of Thunderbird students is 28, while the average for the executive programs is 36. Thunderbird has campuses in Tokyo, Japan and Archamps, France.

Valley School Districts

The Valley is a crazy quilt of almost 40 school districts. Some districts—especially in central Phoenix—are at a disadvantage in regard to academic programs, staffing, facilities, and amenities. Certain schools have been found to be substandard. On the other hand, districts in the suburbs with high growth typically enjoy excellent facilities and amenities, along with all kinds of extra programs to expand students' knowledge. Homebuyers flock to these newer areas, which leads to one drawback—overcrowding when supply can't keep up with demand.

It is these kinds of inequities that the Arizona Legislature is struggling to address, not only in the Phoenix area, but around the state. Education officials also express concerns about Arizona's student-teacher ratios and wish our high school graduation rates could be better, although they are about on par with the national rate.

In 1997, Arizona schools started giving the Stanford 9 Achievement test to selected grades and found that overall scores were less than glowing when compared to national scores on the standardized test, which looks at reading, math, and vocabulary. Some individual schools scored well, though, especially sites in Scottsdale, Paradise Valley, and areas of the southeast Valley.

Arizona's open-enrollment law means that you can send your child to a public school outside of your home district, provided that school has room. Deadlines for open enrollment are usually early in the calendar year. Call the school district you are interested in for more information. The only state requirements for enrolling your children in public school are birth certificates and immunization records. Some individual districts, however, require a proof of residency. State law requires children to be 5 before September 1 to start kindergarten.

Paradise Valley Unified School District
15002 N. 32nd St., Phoenix
- **(602) 867-5104**
- **www.pvusd.k12.az.us**

This district—the state's third-largest—encompasses all kinds of neighborhoods, from low-income housing to multimillion-dollar hillside homes. Some parts of the district are seeing high growth, and most of the schools were built in the last 16 years. Organized in 1919, the district became a unified elementary and high school district in 1976 and currently boasts 27 elementary schools, 5 middle schools, and 4 high schools. It also runs two alternative schools. There are 32,250 students in all. An alternative elementary/middle school and one alternative high school are also available. In March 1994, voters approved a bond election

INSIDERS' TIP

The Arizona State University Visitors Center at the corner of Apache Boulevard and Rural Road in Tempe can provide you with maps of campus and brochures about ASU programs. The visitors center also houses the alumni office. Hours are 8:15 AM to 4:45 PM Monday through Friday. Diagonally across the intersection is the Tempe Chamber of Commerce, with other information to help you find your way around.

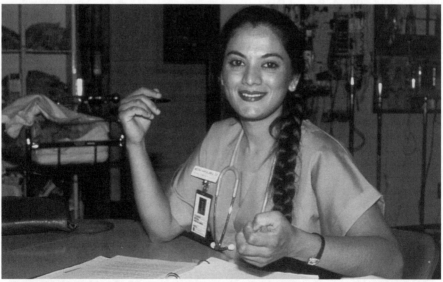

The medical profession also demands many students, and the Maricopa Community College District fills those slots.

Photo: Courtesy of MCCD

totaling $135 million for the construction of five new elementary schools, one new middle school, and one new high school.

Peoria Unified School District
6330 W. Thunderbird Rd., Glendale
- **(623) 486-6000**
- **www.peoriaud.k12.az.us**

Several Northwest Valley neighborhoods feed into the Peoria Unified School District, which encompasses 102 square miles starting at 51st Avenue, west to 115th Avenue. As Arizona's fourth-largest district in terms of enrollment, Peoria Unified School District boasts 25 elementary schools, with 2 more under construction, and 5 high schools, serving more than 27,000 students. Interestingly, 28 of the 29 schools have been built since 1972, indicating what a high-growth area this has been. Many of the older schools have received campus improvements, due to community support for the 1996 bond election. The district states its goal as providing all students "with sound academic opportunities to further their full academic, emotional, physical, social, and vocational potential." In 1999, the Peoria district completed the state's first Challenger Learning Center, one of about 30 around the world dedicated to space-themed programs in remembrance of the space shuttle Challenger. The center is located on the campus of Sunrise Mountain High School in Peoria. For more information, call (623) 322-2001 or visit www.azchallenger.org.

Phoenix Union High School District
4502 N. Central Ave., Phoenix
- **(602) 271-3100**
- **www.phxhs.k12.az.us**

Phoenix Union is the fourth largest high school district in the nation, serving more than 21,000 students, but what sets this district apart from other high school districts in the Valley is its 14 magnet programs. The magnet concept is how the district complies with a federal court order to desegregate its schools. The 10 comprehensive high schools, 2 alternative schools, and numerous alternative programs are monitored for ethnic and racial balance. Students often choose schools outside their neighborhoods because they're interested in a certain program at another school. Whatever their choice, they receive free transportation to that school. A magnet school, as described by the district, provides both specialized and advanced preparation to students with special needs or ambitions. In addition to specialized courses, the schools offer a full slate of basic curriculum, athletics, clubs, and student government.

Here are a few examples of magnet programs: medical and health studies at Alhambra High School in west Phoenix; computer studies at Carl Hayden High School in west Phoenix; an international baccalaureate program for college-bound students at North High School in central Phoenix; and performing and visual arts studies at South Mountain High School in south Phoenix. For 24 years the district's student's SAT score averages have remained above the national average.

The district also has a vocational-technical school with flexible scheduling called Metro Tech. It's at 1900 W. Thomas Road; the phone number is (602) 271-2620.

Scottsdale Unified School District
3811 N. 44th St., Phoenix
- **(480) 952-6100**

This district of 26,000 students celebrated its centennial in 1997. It enjoys a good reputation, although you may find newer schools in the growth areas of north Scottsdale are at an advantage in facilities and programs over older schools in south Scottsdale. The district incorporates Scottsdale as well as portions of east Phoenix and has 17 elementary schools, 2 K-8 schools, 5 middle schools, and 5 high schools. One of the elementary schools is a "learning center," where the emphases are on hands-on learning, whole-language reading, and cross-grade classrooms in a multicultural environment. Another elementary school focuses on back-to-basics instruction.

Charter Schools

Arizona is a leader in the concept of charter schools—state-funded K through 12 schools that market their specialized programs and offer Arizonans a choice besides traditional public schools for free education.

Arizona law defines a charter school as "a public school established by contract with a district governing board, the State Board of Education or the State Board for Charter Schools to provide learning that will improve pupil achievement." In addition, charter schools "provide additional academic choices for parents and pupils." Charter school statutes support flexibility and innovation in operations and structure, including governance, scheduling, curriculum, and instructional methodologies. Arizona's charter school laws are said to be among the most liberal in the nation.

Thus charter schools are owned and operated by private individuals or companies, but funded by taxpayers, to the tune of about $4,700 per student. Figures from 2000 show that about 50,000 Valley children attend more than 400 charter schools, and the number continues to rise.

In the past few years, many charter schools have sprung up in new buildings or have taken the place of existing schools. They are an eclectic bunch, and they receive state funding as long as they comply with the laws set up for them.

Charter schools advertise various focuses; examples are science/technology, back-to-basics, workplace skills, Montessori, college-preparatory, the arts, and integrated approaches. Most charter schools stick to either kindergarten through 8th grade enrollment or high school students. They are in a variety of neighborhoods; some take hundreds of students and others are as small as 50 students.

For a list of charter schools, call the Arizona Department of Education Charter School Unit at (602) 542-5094, or visit www. ade.state.az.us.

INSIDERS' TIP

If want to learn a new skill but aren't interested in earning college credit, consider auditing a course at a regular college or signing up for a community education class. Whether you want to paint or learn how to write your family history, your local city library or parks and recreation department should have information on community classes. If you look in The Yellow Pages, you can also find schools for everything from ballroom dancing to horseshoeing.

Private and Parochial Schools

You will be awash in choices if private schools are your preferred route. The Valley is home to several dozen. In addition, there are a good Catholic, Protestant, Jewish, and Islamic schools whose focus is also on religion.

There's an enormous tuition range, with some of the parochial schools asking for a $1,000 to $3,000 annual tuition, mid-range private

EDUCATION AND CHILDCARE

With many top restaurants in the country, the Valley of the Sun is a natural place for cooking schools. Here would-be bakers train at Scottsdale Community College.

Photo: Michael Isaac, courtesy of SCC

Schools in Phoenix range from historic to modern.

Photo: Penny Kleingartner

schools asking about $5,000 annually, and the more exclusive private schools asking for as much as $11,000 annually. Some schools test students prior to admitting them and may ask for interviews as well. You'll also find that siblings of current students have the edge in admissions. Ask about financial assistance; some schools offer scholarships or can set up flexible payment plans.

All Saints' Episcopal Day School
6300 N. Central Ave., Phoenix
• **(602) 274-4866**

All Saints' philosophy is to identify academically talented youth and develop their abilities through a curriculum that balances academic excellence, physical education, and spiritual awareness. There are many enriching programs, such as computers and drama, as well as extracurricular activities, such as chorus, sports, and community service. The school has been around since 1963 and now serves kindergartners through 8th graders. The student–teacher ratio is 9 to 1, with a maximum class size of 22.

Brophy College Preparatory
4701 N. Central Ave., Phoenix
• **(602) 264-5291**
• **www.brophyprep.org**

Brophy is part of a lovely campus at Central Avenue and Camelback Road that includes

St. Francis Xavier, a historically significant Catholic church. The boys-only school opened in 1928 and serves grades 9 through 12 in a college-preparatory program with some religious instruction. Typically, 99 percent of graduates go directly to higher education. The student–teacher ratio is 25 to 1.

Phoenix Country Day School
3901 E. Stanford Dr., Paradise Valley
• **(602) 955-8200**
• **www.pcds.org**

This is a popular option for Northeast Valley parents who want and can afford the private school experience. The school opened in 1961 and has expanded over the years to a sprawling campus near Camelback Mountain. It's open to preschoolers through 12th graders. It calls itself a student-centered school and has many electives and extracurricular activities. The student–teacher ratio is 10 to 1, with a maximum class size of 15. Current enrollment is 700.

Rancho Solano Private Schools
5656 E. Greenway, Scottsdale
• **(480) 996-7002**
• **www.ranchosolano.com**

Founded in 1954, Rancho Solano has four campuses in the Valley, including one in Scottsdale. It's open to preschoolers through

8th graders, and adheres to the philosophy that basic skills and appropriate study habits—mixed in with lots of activities, a positive attitude, and fun—are necessary to accomplish optimum personal, educational, and career goals. Rancho Solano has a college-preparatory focus, with arts, athletics, and bilingual education as pluses. The student–teacher ratio is 20 to 1. The schools are popular, so expect a waiting list to get in.

Scottsdale Christian Academy
14400 N. Tatum Blvd., Phoenix
• **(602) 992-5100**
• **www.scottsdalechristian.org**

The Scottsdale Christian Academy is quite large, with topnotch facilities on a sprawling campus in north Phoenix. Current enrollment is nearly 1,000 students, ages preschool through high school. All students must sign a statement of faith in Christianity before admission. Older students receive a college-preparatory curriculum, and athletic programs are popular here.

Tesseract
4800 E. Doubletree Ranch Rd.,
Paradise Valley
• **(480) 991-1770**

The word "Tesseract" comes from Madeleine L'Engle's book *A Wrinkle in Time* and refers to a fifth-dimensional learning experience. Tesseract Group, a Minneapolis-based chain of private and charter schools, opened this Paradise Valley school 10 years ago and recently opened new campuses in north Scottsdale and the Ahwatukee area of south Phoenix. The schools feature an "inquiry-based way of learning" that emphasizes self-esteem and communication skills for preschoolers through 8th-graders. The student–teacher ratis 12 to 1.

Childcare

You are sure to find the type of childcare you're looking for in an enterprising area like the Valley of the Sun. There are hundreds of options in day-care centers, in-home care, and preschools.

One of the best ways to start your search is by talking to your neighbors who have children. Usually, you will want something close to home for a day-care center or preschool, and neighbors will be able to recommend nearby places. When seeking out childcare, be sure to ask the provider about hours of operation, full-time versus part-time care, and cleanliness and safety standards. Look for a variety of toys and playground equipment and colorful surroundings. Beyond that, of course, you'll want to know whether it's a place where your child will have ample opportunities to learn, develop socially, and generally have fun. Find out if a preschool program tends to be open-ended and child-oriented or more academically oriented with a structured curriculum. The Valley has a number of parent-cooperative programs in which parents volunteer a few hours a week in the center. Many of these are affiliated with churches and temples.

To find a state-licensed day-care program, contact the following offices. For centers and family childcare homes serving more than five children, call the Department of Health Services Office of Childcare Licensure at (602) 674-4220. For family childcare homes serving one to four children, call the Department of Economic Security's Childcare Administration at (602) 542-4248. You can search the files of preschools that interest you and find out if there have been any complaints or violations listed against them, but remember, not all childcare facilities are required to have state licenses.

You might also want to contact Arizona Childcare Resources and Referral, which runs a resource and referral service and other programs in support of childcare for all income levels. Call (800) 308-9000, or visit www.arizonachildcare.org.

Another source of information is the Valley of the Sun Association for the Education of Young Children, which operates under the aegis of the nonprofit community group, Organization Southwest Human Development; the phone number is (602) 266-3065 or visit www.swhd.org. The association can tell you whether a preschool is accredited by the National Academy of Early Childhood Programs, which is a voluntary accreditation program. Preschools are evaluated for teacher–child

INSIDERS' TIP

The Arizona Commission for Post-Secondary Education publishes a directory of the state's private and public colleges and universities. The College and Career Guide costs $5 and may be obtained by writing the commission at 2020 N. Central Avenue, Suite 275, Phoenix, AZ 85004, or by calling (602) 229-2591. The directory is also available in the state's public libraries.

EDUCATION AND CHILDCARE

ratios, availability of enriching toys and activities, cleanliness, safety, and other matters.

Montessori programs are well represented in the Phoenix area, with more than two dozen schools listing themselves as having a Montessori philosophy. That philosophy embraces learning activities that are related to real-life experiences and that are highly interactive and hands-on. The various schools cater to toddlers, preschoolers, and elementary school-age children. For more information on Montessori schools in the Valley, contact the Foundation for Montessori Education, 9215 N. 14th St., Phoenix, at (602) 395-0292.

Among the childcare chains operating in the Valley are: American Childcare Centers, (602) 993-6070; Children's World Learning Centers, (480) 785-7887; Childtime Children's Centers, www.childtime.com; KinderCare Learning Centers, www.kindercare.com; La Petite Acad-

emy, www.lapetite.com; and Sunrise Preschools, (480) 860-1611.

If you're looking for in-home care provided by a babysitter or nanny, try calling one of the Valley's many nanny referral agencies. Two longtime companies are Nanny Finders, (602) 944-2229, and Peace of Mind Referral Service, (480)732-1234. Agencies will help you find a live-in nanny or someone who works in your home full time or part-time. The agencies will have done various background checks on potential babysitters before setting up interviews with you.

If you're a visitor in town seeking babysitting services, your hotel or resort can put you in touch with a number of caregivers. One Valley company that specializes in serving the tourist market is the Granny Company, (602) 956-4040.

INSIDERS' TIP

If you are looking for information on how schools stack up, call the Arizona School Report Card Program at (602) 542-5022.

Important Phone Numbers

Here are several addresses and phone numbers you might find helpful as you research the education scene in the Valley.

Arizona Department of Education, 1535 W. Jefferson Street, Phoenix, (602) 542-5057

County Superintendent of Schools, 301 W. Jefferson Street, Phoenix, (602) 506-3866

North Central Association Office of Accreditation, College of Education, University of Arizona, Tucson, (520) 621-7847

Arizona Congress of Parents and Teachers/PTA, 2721 N. Seventh Avenue, Phoenix, (602) 279-1811

Arizona Private School Association, (602) 254-5199

State Department of Education Charter School Unit, 1535 W. Jefferson Street, Phoenix, (602) 542-5094

Media

For the longest time Phoenix media was a parochial entity. But with the booming growth of the '80s and '90s came an influx of non-Arizonans writing and reporting the Valley's news. Growth made the pool of reporters and editors more cosmopolitan, a trait that sometimes stood at odds with what the audience wanted.

The local television news is dominated by happy talk. You would be hard-pressed to figure out what is Arizonan about these broadcasts, except when the anchors gloat about the sunny winter weather after the East and Midwest are snowed in. Local news is a rare commodity on all but a few radio stations.

But the media isn't just the news, it's entertainment as well. On TV, local non-news broadcasts are rare, but radio is driven by its local personalities. It's probably on radio that we get the truest media reflection of this community and its diverse interests and concerns.

LOOK FOR:
• **Newspapers**
• **Magazines**
• **Radio**
• **Television**

Newspapers

There are scores of newspapers across the Valley covering the minutiae of the neighborhoods—the potlucks and the PTA meetings, the open houses and the class reunions. It would be impossible for us to list and describe all the neighborhood papers, many of them freebies that show up on people's driveways. The following list covers English-language newspapers that have circulations of more than a few thousand.

Dailies

The Arizona Republic
200 E. Van Buren St., Phoenix
• **(602) 444-8000**
• **www.arizonarepublic.com**
The Arizona Republic is the big gun in town and has been the largest paper in Arizona since 1915. With a circulation that tops 491,000 daily and 600,000 on Sunday, it penetrates the Phoenix market like no other newspaper, magazine, television or radio station. Politically conservative, the paper was founded in May 1890 as The Arizona Republican by territorial Governor Lewis Wolfley and Attorney General Clark Churchill. The paper was as partisan as its name. The name changed to The Arizona Republic in 1930. Since its growth rested on the Valley's growth, the paper has consistently acted as a booster for business interests. On the plus side, that meant championing statehood. Yet oddly enough for a pro-growth cheerleader, the paper stood against freeways until the metropolitan area almost choked on its size. The Republic was influential enough to get its way on such issues for many years.

The paper was owned by Central Newspapers Inc., an Indianapolis-based corporation founded in 1934 by Eugene C. Pulliam, Dan Quayle's grandfather. This year, the Gannett newspaper chain purchased the paper, so expect to see substantial changes to the staff and editorial approach to daily news. The Republic has a Pulitzer Prize winner on staff: political cartoonist Steve Benson. The paper's only other Pulitzer was also won by a cartoonist, the late Reg Manning.

In 1997, the paper began publishing *The Rep*, a tabloid-size entertainment guide to compete with *Phoenix New Times* and the *Tribune's* "Get Out". It appears in *The Republic* on Thursdays and is circulated separately for free in boxes across the Valley—often beside the boxes offering *New Times* and "Get Out."

The *Sunday Republic* features *Parade* magazine as a mark of distinction. *The Republic* publishes an annual best-of-the-Valley section called "AZ Best" in November.

The Tribune
120 W. First Ave., Mesa
• **(480 898-6500**
• **www.aztrib.com**

The *Tribune* grew to its present size, circulation 112,000, when the previous owners bought the city newspapers of Chandler, Gilbert, Scottsdale, and Tempe. They retained the names of those papers on the front page, offering each community a locally focused cover, while other sections—such as entertainment and lifestyle sections—were common to all editions.

After being bought by Thomson Newspapers in 1996, *The Tribune* began aggressively flexing its muscle in an attempt to make itself the main newspaper in the cities it served. *The Republic* still penetrated deeper in the Southeast Valley than *The Tribune*.

Thomson streamlined the zoning process, changing the nameplate to *The Tribune* on a common edition that serves the Southeast Valley. The Northeast Valley edition became the *Scottsdale Tribune*.

Early in 1997, *The Tribune* began publishing "Get Out," an entertainment and recreation guide. It appears as a section of *The Tribune* on Thursday and is distributed independent of the paper for free. The Sunday edition of *The Tribune* carries *USA Weekend* magazine.

In Arizona terms, *The Tribune's* political stance is conservative to moderate, although "Get Out" has received complaints for being socially (if not politically) left of center.

The Sun City Daily News Sun
10102 W. Santa Fe Dr., Sun City
• **(623) 977-8351**

The mainstay of this afternoon paper is the local news in the Sun Cities. Thomson Newspapers bought this daily in 1998 but has not incorporated it into the zoning system of *The Tribune*.

Weeklies

Arizona Business Gazette
200 E. Van Buren St., Phoenix
• **(602) 444-7300**

The *Business Gazette*, published by the same parent company as *The Arizona Republic*, downsized during 1997, becoming essentially a vehicle for legal advertising. The news copy it contains focuses on the always-burgeoning Arizona business scene.

Arizona Capitol Times
14 N. 18th Ave., Phoenix
• **(602) 258-7026**

Arizona Capitol Times focuses on the goings-on at the State Capitol. The news coverage is straightforward with few graphic geegaws filling the pages. Among its features is a listing of bills being considered and passed. Some stories focus on issues, but all have the state government at their center. It is published weekly, with an extra year-end wrap-up issue.

Arizona Informant
1746 E. Madison St., Phoenix
• **(602) 257-9300**

The *Arizona Informant* is the major African-American newspaper in the Valley, with a circulation of about 10,000. A booster of the African-American community, the paper keeps an eye on race and social issues. Besides a general news section, it breaks down its coverage into sections on business, women, youth, sports, entertainment, health, and religion.

The Business Journal Serving Phoenix and the Valley of the Sun
3030 N. Central Ave., Phoenix
• **(602) 230-8400**

One of a chain of Business Journals across the United States, the Phoenix edition focuses on the Valley's business scene, trends, and local business figures.

Independent Newspapers
11000 N. Scottsdale Rd., Scottsdale
• **(480) 483-0977**

Independent Newspapers is a chain that

> **INSIDERS' TIP**
> **What's happening around town this weekend? You've three reliable sources for information on concerts, special events, and the bar scene in the weekly *New Times*, *The Arizona Republic's* "The Rep", and the *Tribune's* "Get Out." These tabloids are distributed free.**

publishes eight community weeklies across the Valley. The primary concern of the papers is the very local news and human-interest stories that the big papers tend to miss.

The papers are: *Apache Junction Independent* and the *East Mesa Independent*, 201 W. Apache Trail, Apache Junction, (480) 982-7799; the *Gilbert Independent* and *Chandler/Sun Lakes Independent*, 375 E. Elliott Road, Chandler, (480) 497-0048; the *Paradise Valley Independent* and *Town of Paradise Valley Independent*, 11000 N. Scottsdale Road, Scottsdale (480) 483-0977; and *Sun Cities Independent* and *Arrowhead Ranch Independent*, 10327 W. Coggins Drive, Sun City, (623) 972-6101.

Jewish News of Greater Phoenix
1625 E. Northern Ave., Phoenix
• **(602) 870-9470**

An independent journal of the Jewish community in Arizona, the *Jewish News* focuses on covering the diverse segments of the local community. It augments its local coverage with Jewish news wire stories to provide news on national and international events important to the community. The paper publishes many special sections in the course of the year on such themes as fashion, back to school, and finance. It publishes an annual Community Directory that is especially helpful to Jewish newcomers to Phoenix.

> ## INSIDERS' TIP
> **Don't expect to hear the phrase "Film at 11" in Phoenix. The late evening news comes on at 10 PM. (This town goes to bed early.)**

Phoenix New Times
1201 E. Jefferson St., Phoenix
• **(602) 271-0040**

New Times started out as an underground newspaper, but today is part of Phoenix's mainstream. Still, a booster it is not. The feature writers at *New Times* work on extended investigative stories on topics that often are not covered in the mainstream papers. People routinely turn to its "Flashes" column for the current juice on local public figures and to read the latest installment in the paper's running feud with *The Arizona Republic*. The meat and potatoes of the paper are magazine-length stories featuring in-depth reporting on government

The Arizona Republic is the biggest newspaper in town and has been since 1915.

Photo: Penny Kleingartner

MEDIA

malfeasance and public affairs (often the same thing) and social issues, such as the crystal meth epidemic, as well as the occasional major profile of local artists and performers and quirky attractions and people in the Valley. The dessert course is its comprehensive guide to Valley dining, events, arts, and nightlife. The "Best of Phoenix" issue, which appears in the fall, is an excellent reference guide and worth keeping around on a shelf to look at throughout the year when you're thinking about what to do and where to eat. You'll find awards for the best fish tacos, best used-book stores, and best public art work in town.

Phoenix New Times, which is distributed free, is the flagship paper of a chain of weeklies that includes *WestWord* in Denver, *Los Angeles New Times*, and the *Houston Press*.

Magazines

With the rapid population growth in the area, Phoenix recently has become a growing magazine market. New publications appear on magazine racks only to disappear within a year or two, only to be replaced by new magazines in pursuit of readers and advertising dollars. Out of all the churn, a few general-circulation magazines capture the Valley's flavor in print.

INSIDERS' TIP

It's only natural that radio station KTAR is the Valley's full-time news station. It was launched by *The Arizona Republican* on February 4, 1930.

Arizona Business Magazine
3111 N. Central Ave., Phoenix
• **(602) 277-6045**

This bimonthly magazine offers profiles of businesses across the state, but its primary focus is those in the Valley. The magazine also covers many issues that affect business, such as the impact of water policy on growth.

Arizona Highways
2039 W. Lewis Ave., Phoenix
• **(602) 712-2200**

Published by the Arizona Department of Transportation for the last 75 years, *Arizona Highways* is the state magazine with the highest profile nationally and even internationally. Essentially a travel magazine about our fair state, the photography is among the best anywhere. The prose attempts to match the vistas for color and excitement. Once you move here, it is fun to give your distant relatives a subscription so they can learn about your new home (and turn green with envy).

Harnett's Sports Arizona
67 E. Weldon., Phoenix
• **(602) 279-7999**

With four major-league teams, major college athletics at Arizona State University and the University of Arizona, baseball spring training, and plenty of golf, golf, golf, this state deserves a magazine devoted exclusively to its sports scene. The bimonthly *Sports Arizona* fills the bill. The best issue so far focused on the 50 greatest athletes from Arizona, including Danny White, who holds a number of Dallas Cowboys' records from his early '80s stint as their quarterback, and Olympic gymnast Kerri Strug.

PHOENIX Magazine
4041 N. Central Ave., Phoenix
• **(602) 234-0840**

PHOENIX Magazine aims for the sass and excitement of other big-city magazines, but the monthly magazine actually achieves something better—conversations with its readers. The subjects of those conversations are all over the map—quiet hiking trails and a trip down Indian School Road on the one hand, and a discussion of grandparents who kidnap their grandchildren on the other. In addition, you'll find plenty on Valley dining, a good events calendar, and a column that blends bright and hip short items called "The PHXFiles."

Phoenix Home and Garden
4041 N. Central Ave., Phoenix
• **(602) 234-0840**

Phoenix Home and Garden is upscale, dahling. It's fun to look at the homes and gardens of the well-to-do and wonder how to afford all this marvelous excess. The monthly's focus is on Southwestern decorating style, from lagoon-type pools and vaulted ceilings to stucco walls and terra cotta roofs. The gardening section is a solid resource for learning how to plant (and sustain) flowers and veggies in the desert climate.

Radio

Phoenix radio is volatile, and the landscape is littered with new formats that failed. Although the primary motivation for format changes is usually the sale of a station, some longtime owners have changed formats on their stations repeatedly, searching for the key to winning in a very competitive market. Even as this is being written, local stations are changing formats and searching for the highest ratings.

Listening to the radio is a popular hobby for Valley locals. With many people stuck in their cars for commutes that range from 20 minutes to more than an hour, people tend to find their favorite stations and stay with them. The five top stations in the Valley are country station KNIX-FM (102.5), talk station KTAR-AM (620), urban/top 40 station KKFR-FM (92.3), smooth jazz station KYOT-FM (95.9) and oldies station KOOL-FM (94.5), which demonstrates the diversity of Phoenix's listening audience.

Longtime market leaders are talk-news station KTAR, which carries the ever-popular Phoenix Suns basketball games all season; blue-collar rocker KUPD, propelled by morning jock Dave Pratt's decades of success; urban-contemporary KKFR, better known as Power 92; adult rocker KDKB; easy-listening KOY; and adult-contemporary KESZ, better known as KEZ and noted for morning personalities Beth McDonald and Bill Austin. Public radio station KJZZ has served its niche for many years and for the past few has been primarily a NPR talk-radio station, with acoustic jazz music filling in the off-hours. A second public radio station, KBAQ, programs classical music and features opera broadcasts on Saturday afternoons. Unfortunately, its weak signal does not reach all parts of the Valley.

Because the Valley is so large, a number of stations simulcast on two frequencies to cover the entire Valley.

INSIDERS' TIP

The first issue of *The Arizona Republican*, a partisan paper, was published May 19, 1890. In the opposing Democrat camp was *The Arizona Gazette*, which later became *The Phoenix Gazette*. In 1930, within a week of shortening *Republican* to *Republic*, the paper's owners bought *The Phoenix Gazette*. The purchase left *The Arizona Republic* as Phoenix's major player, with *The Phoenix Gazette* chugging along as a small afternoon daily until its closure in January 1997.

FM Stations

KNAI/KPHF 88.3
Spanish regional/Christian
KEAR 88.9 (Christian)
KBAQ 89.5(Classical)
KFLR 90.3 (Christian)
KGCB 90 (Christian)
KJZZ 91.5 (NPR news/talk/jazz)
KKFR 92.3 (Urban Top 40)
KDKB 93.3 (Album rock)
KSWG 94.1 (Country)
KOOL 94.5 (Oldies)
KYOT 95.5 (Contemporary jazz)
KLVA 96.3/105.5 (Christian)
KMXP 96.9 (Rock adult contemporary)
KRXS 97.3 (Album alternative)
KUPD 97.9 (Album rock)
KKLT 98.7 (Adult contemporary)
KBZG 99.3/104.3 (R&B oldies)
KESZ 99.9 (Adult contemporary)
KDDJ 100.3 (Modern rock)
KSLX 100.7 (Classic rock)
KESP 101.1 (Classic hits)
KZON 101.5 (Rock alternative)
KNIX 102.5 (Country)
KLNZ 103.5 (Spanish regional)
KPTY 103.9 (Top 40)
KZZP 104.7 (Contemporary hits)
KMYL 105.3 (Adult standards)
KHOT 105.9 (Spanish regional)
KEDJ 106.3 (Modern rock)
KMJK 106.9/92.7 (Urban adult contemporary)
KVVA 107.1 (Spanish contemporary)
KMLE 107.9 (Country)

AM Stations

KGME 550 (Sports/talk)
KSAZ 580 (Adult standards)
KTAR 620 (News/talk)
KIDR 740 (Spanish news/talk)
KMVP 860 (Sports)
KFYI 910 (News/talk)
KCTK 960 (News/talk)
KCTK 960 (News/talk)
KXEG 1010 (Gospel)
KDUS 10650 (Sports)
KFNX 1100 (Talk)
KCKY 1150 (Spanish)
KMYL 1190 (Adult standards)
KOY 1230 (Adult standards)
KTKP 1280 (News/talk)
KXAM 1310 (Talk)
KPXQ 1360 (Religion)
KSUN 1400 (Spanish)
KSLX 1440 (Classic rock)
KPHX 1480 (Spanish)
KFNN 1510 (Business)
KASA 1540 (Christian/Spanish)

KMIK 1580 (Children)

Television

Phoenix television includes affiliates of all four major networks as well as PBS, UPN, and the WB network. Channels 45 and 61, the stations that offer the limited platter of WB and UPN network offerings, are otherwise independent stations. Channel 45 has retained the rights to air Phoenix Suns basketball, Channel 61 airs Phoenix Coyotes hockey, and Channel 3 airs Arizona Diamondbacks baseball.

Cable television is available in most areas of the Valley, with about 50 percent of TV households wired in. All local broadcast outlets are carried on cable, unless otherwise noted in the listings below.

Local Stations

KTVK Channel 3 (Independent)
KPHO Channel 5 (CBS)
KAET Channel 8 (PBS)
KSAZ Channel 10 (Fox)
KPNX Channel 12 (NBC)
KNXV Channel 15 (ABC)
KPAZ Channel 21 (TBN-Religious)
KTVW Channel 33 (Univision-Spanish language)
LDTP Channel 39 (Daystar)

KUTP Channel 45 (UPN)
KPPX Channel 51 (PAX)
KUSK Channels 55 and 57 (Independent)
KASW Channel 61 (WB)
KDR Channel 64 (Telemundo-Spanish language)

Low-Power UHF Stations

The FCC approved low-power outlets to increase the availability of alternative television programming in markets like the Valley. KBI Channel 39 has family network and religious programming, while BOX Channel 58 Video Jukebox, or The Box, is an interactive station. Viewers call up and order (for a price) the video they want played. It is not carried on cable.

Cable TV Companies

Cox Communications, 17602 N. Black Canyon Highway, Phoenix, (602) 277-1000, serves most of Phoenix and the Valley.

Cable America Corp., 350 E. 10th Drive, Mesa, (480) 461-0715, serves portions of Mesa and eastern Maricopa County.

Insight Communications, 21200 N. Black Canyon Highway, Phoenix, (602) 582-8282, serves northwest Phoenix and much of the west Valley.

Worship

In a typical suburban development on the far west side of Phoenix, everything is as it should be. Palm trees shade the rows of tract houses, kids race bicycles along the low-traffic streets, soccer moms rush children to their games, and a pair of orange-clad Buddhist monks tend a little garden plot beside a home.

Whoa! Hold on there! Buddhist monks in the 'burbs?

Phoenix sometimes seems insecure about its position as a world-class city. If Valley boosters really wanted to demonstrate how cosmopolitan the Valley of the Sun is, they would boast about its religious scene. In this arena, the Valley is as diverse as the United Nations. Whatever your religion, or lack thereof, there is a place for you in the Valley.

The simple fact is that when you attract people from around the world, most of them bring their religions along with them. Our fair Valley holds more than 1,700 houses of worship—churches, synagogues, mosques, shrines, reading rooms, halls, and temples.

The latest breakdown on affiliations shows that 20 percent of the Valley's residents are Roman Catholic, while the mainline Protestant denominations—Lutheran, Methodist, Episcopalian, Presbyterian, and Assemblies of God—represent 17 percent. Baptists make up 9 percent, Mormons about 7 percent, and Jews about 2 percent. The remaining 45 percent is split among many smaller Christian sects, Muslims, Buddhists, Sikhs, New Agers, pagans, agnostics, and atheists.

The same study found that about 80 percent of the Valley's population is interested in learning about faiths other than their own, which indicates more than a passing interest in matters of faith among an astounding chunk of the population.

Surprisingly, despite such widespread interest and the diversity of faiths and adherents, there is no centralized source of religious information that's adequate for everybody. *The Arizona Republic* carries "Religion Roundup" in the "Religion" section of its Saturday editions, listing special worship services, concerts, and meetings occurring Valleywide, but not regular worship schedules. In the East Valley, *The Tribune* offers a similar listing in its Saturday "Religion" section.

The best bet for people seeking a place to worship, whether as a visitor or as a resident, may be the Yellow Pages. Its most recent edition carried 19 pages of church listings, covering more than 125 denominations—and that's not to mention the separate listings for synagogues and mosques.

All of this means that the subsequent overviews are necessarily incomplete. We mean no disrespect, particularly in the daunting section on "Protestant Congregations." The diverse histories of each mainline Protestant and Baptist subgroup in the Valley could fill a tome twice the size of our humble guide. We have instead opted to mention a few representative churches that we hope will offer our readers an introduction into the diversity of worship in the Valley.

Roman Catholic Influence

Roman Catholics represent the largest identifiable religious group in

LOOK FOR:
* **Roman Catholic Influence**
* **Mormon's Second Home**
* **Protestants in General**
* **The Jewish Community**
* **Muslims**
* **Buddhists**
* **Many Others**

the Valley. Within that group, there is quite a bit of diversity. There are parishes of Maronite (Lebanese) and other Eastern Rite Catholic Churches, among other ethnic churches.

Before Phoenix began to develop, Catholic missionaries had nearly 300 years of history in the Southwest, seeking to convert Native Americans and ministering to the needs of the Hispanic Catholic community. As more people settled in the Valley, Hispanics and Mexican-Americans were the first big block of Catholics, although other groups of ethnic Catholics moved in quickly. Disadvantaged and, due to prejudice, essentially shut out of the Anglo power structure, the Hispanic community forged its own subculture, and much of its communal life revolved around the first St. Mary's Church.

In 1915, a new St. Mary's Church was built. The church's style was like an exalted version of the mission churches found in isolated outposts throughout the Southwest. Spanish-influenced, the church's stained-glass windows, artwork, high ceilings, and wooden pews hark back to the pre-Vatican II world of Catholic worship.

In the mid-1980s, Pope John Paul II elevated St. Mary's Church to the rank of a minor basilica, a special status within the church. John Paul II made it a point to speak from the front balcony of the basilica when he visited Phoenix in 1987. And well he might, since the basilica sits across Monroe Street from the Phoenix Civic Plaza. In fact, St. Mary's Basilica stands out in Phoenix's redeveloping downtown, and is renowned for its stained-glass windows imported from Germany. Its address is 231 N. Third Street in Phoenix, but the church's front entrance sits on Monroe Street. A gift shop sits at the street level, near the stairs to the main entrance. The basilica is open Monday through Friday, from 9 AM to 2 PM, with longer hours on Thursday and Saturday for 5 PM masses. Admission is free. For more information, call (602) 252-7651. It's best to sign up for tours ahead of time.

There are about 89 Catholic parishes and 28 missions in the Valley as well as support services and charitable efforts. For more information, contact The Catholic Diocese of Phoenix, 400 E. Monroe Street, Phoenix, (602) 257-0030, www.diocesephoenix.org.

Mormons' Second Home

The true home of the Mormons is Utah, but Mesa—and to a lesser extent, the rest of the Valley—is a sort of second home to the Church of Jesus Christ of Latter-Day Saints. The Latter-

An annual Christmas pageant at the Mormon Temple attracts 80,000 visitors.

Photo: Penny Kleingartner

Day Saints' Arizona Temple was the most impressive structure in Mesa when it was built in 1927.

At that time, prejudice against Mormons was high elsewhere in the Valley, but Mesa, which Mormon farmers settled in May of 1878, was the city of their own making. They were influenced by the plan of Salt Lake City, and plotted out wide streets, squares, and big lots. Prejudice in Mexico also forced an exodus of Mormon settlers from south of the border into the Valley in 1912.

Today, Mormons are dispersed throughout the Valley, but the East Valley—including Mesa, Gilbert, and Chandler—still is the major bastion of the LDS church in Arizona.

The temple, a large, bright cube atop a rectangle, sits on Lesueur Street in Mesa. Old photos show that when it was built, the structure was out in the middle of nowhere, but downtown Mesa has grown around it. That's not to say that the city has swallowed the building—Mesa's well-planned spaciousness has left it impressive. Its Christmas lighting display draws many visitors, and since 1938, church members have presented an annual pageant, *Jesus the Christ*, that attracts more than 100,000 visitors.

In addition to worship, the Mormons have support services and missionary programs and charitable programs. The Mormon general information number is (480) 964-7164.

Protestants in General

When you add the percentages of Catholics, Mormons, Baptists, and mainline Protestants, it's clear that Christian churches dominate the religious landscape of Phoenix. Beyond the Catholics and the Mormons, who may be the most readily identifiable groups, the variety of adherents to Jesus and the Gospels is great.

From the independent gospel churches that dot the disadvantaged neighborhoods, to the cluster of African Methodist Episcopal congregations in South Phoenix, to scores of Baptist, Lutheran, Methodist, Presbyterian, and Episcopal congregations throughout the Valley, Christian worship is huge. What follows is the barest tip of what's out there.

According to those in the know, the Community Church of Joy in Glendale is admired nationwide for its successful growth into a mega-congregation. The sanctuary, built in 1983, only holds 1,000 people, so the church holds multiple services to accommodate its growing membership, which has hit 11,000 people. The Lutheran congregation bills itself as "a friendly place that really believes in you." The church, affiliated with the Evangelical Lutheran Church in America (ELCA), uses a contemporary worship style, including music, dance, drama, and multimedia, to reach beyond the traditional church-going public. For more information, call (623) 561-0500.

A similarly huge congregation is North Phoenix Baptist Church, 5757 N. Central Avenue, a Southern Baptist congregation. With more than 7,000 members, this church prides itself on the theatrical production values of its services. Its worship services are aired on local TV. The church melds drama, video montages, and live music into services that have received great word of mouth and always pack the church's ample parking lot. For more information, call the church at (602) 707-5757 or visit www.npbc.org.

Episcopalians who want to learn more about their worship options in the Valley should contact the local diocese. The headquarters of the Episcopal Diocese of Arizona is at 114 W. Roosevelt Street in Phoenix, (602) 254-0976, www.episcopal-az.org.

Many churches have gay and lesbian ministries, but a very few have principally gay and lesbian membership. Two of the largest such congregations in Phoenix are the Community Church of Hope, 4400 N. Central Avenue in Phoenix, (602) 234-2180,

> **INSIDERS' TIP**
>
> The Yaqui Lenten and Easter ceremonies are held at the Yaqui Temple and Ceremonial Grounds at Priest Road and 56th Street , south of Baseline Road, in Guadalupe. Dating from the 1600s, this colorful religious ceremony mixes Catholic beliefs and Native American traditions, through symbolic processions, prayer, music, and dance. Ceremonies begin on Holy Thursday at 7 PM, with a Mass of the Lord's Supper and a procession. A communion is held on Good Friday at 7 PM, and liturgy is held on Holy Saturday at 7 PM with a mass and the lighting of the Easter fire. Masses are held on Easter Sunday at 9:30 AM in English, and at 8 and 11 AM in Spanish. Everyone is welcome, but because it is a religious ceremony, no cameras are allowed and visitors are asked to be respectful.

WORSHIP

www.communitychurchofhope.com, and Gentle Shepherd Metropolitan Community Church. The latter has offices at 3201 N. 16th Street in Phoenix. Services are held in the Grand Ballroom at the Quality Hotel & Resort, 3600 N. Second Avenue in Phoenix.

If you are looking to explore your individual path spirituality in an open, rational, and liberal environment, check out the Unitarian UU Church at 17540 North Avenue of the Arts, Surprise, (623) 875-2550, or one of the three other Unitarian Universalist churches in the Valley.

The Jewish Community

By 1870, Jews were a visible minority in Phoenix. Unlike the case in many other cities, overt discrimination against them was rarely seen. Barry Goldwater's ancestors were among the prominent Jewish families in the Valley.

By the 1880s, worship services were being held in private homes around the city. In 1922, Temple Beth Israel, built at Second and Culver Streets, became the first synagogue in Phoenix. A Reform synagogue, Temple Beth Israel is now at 10460 N. 56th Street in Phoenix, (480) 951-0323. Its facilities include the Sylvia Plotkin Judaica Museum, www.sylviaplotkinjudaicamuseum.org, which features a permanent collection of historical and contemporary ceremonial objects used to observe basic holidays and lifecycle events, including Shabbat candlesticks, Seder plates, and Kiddush cups. The museum also has a reconstructed

Some Phoenix church buildings reflect the Spanish heritage of the region.

Photo: Penny Kleingartner

WORSHIP

Tunisian synagogue, and features two to three temporary exhibits per year. The museum is open Tuesday through Friday, 10 AM to 3 PM.; and Sunday on special occasions.

Phoenix's Jewish community numbers about 70,000, and it is diverse in spirit. There are Orthodox, Conservative, Reform, Jewish Renewal, and Humanistic congregations in the Valley of the Sun.

The Jewish Federation of Greater Phoenix conducts the annual UJC/Federation Campaign to benefit the United Jewish Appeal and local social services. Its constituent agencies include three Jewish community centers, the Jewish Family and Children's Service, and the Bureau of Jewish Education of Greater Phoenix, among others. The federation's offices are at 32 W. Coolidge Street, Phoenix, (602) 274-1800, or visit www.jewishphoenix.org.

Jewish News of Greater Phoenix publishes an annual directory of Jewish congregations, agencies, services, and schools in the Valley. The cost is $9. It's available at the Jewish News office, 1625 E. Northern Avenue, Phoenix, (602) 870-9470, www.jewishaz.com.

Muslims

With increased immigration from the Middle East, Africa, and Asia, the Islamic community in the Valley of the Sun is also growing. Adherents also include many African-American converts to Islam.

The Islamic Cultural Center, 131 E. Sixth Street, Tempe, (480) 894-6070, with its minaret, stands out in downtown Tempe. The cultural center and mosque work hard to fight stereotypes while raising Valley awareness of what Muslims believe. The congregation includes immigrants and first-generation members as well as American converts. Located as it is near Arizona State University, the center's air of scholarly prayerfulness is a welcome relief from the hustle and bustle.

There are a handful of other mosques in the Valley, and the Islamic Cultural Center can provide information on those.

INSIDERS' TIP

The Franciscan Renewal Center, 5802 East Lincoln Drive, Scottsdale, (480) 948-7460, www.sbfranciscans.org offers retreats and classes. Although it's a Catholic institution, it's open to anyone. Classes have included studies of Islam, taught by a representative of the Islamic Cultural Center, and even tai chi. Its 20 acres of desert space between Camelback and Mummy Mountains offers a spiritually refreshing place for a retreat, and has conference rooms for groups as large as 120 people.

Buddhists

Buddhism first found its way to Phoenix via an influx of Chinese railroad workers and the community that formed around them as they settled here. Many of their descendants remained, and Chinatown flourished in Phoenix until the early 1930s.

INSIDERS' TIP

The Arizona Ecumenical Council is a nonprofit umbrella group for about 700 churches in the state that sponsors programs to help solve social problems such as homelessness, domestic violence, hunger, and teenage pregnancy. It also sponsors gun safety programs. For more information, contact the council at (602) 468-3818.

Successive waves of Asian immigration to the Valley helped broaden Buddhism's reach here. In the early 1980s, the Thai community began a growth spurt that prompted establishment of Wat Promkunaram, a temple in west Phoenix.

The oldest Buddhist congregation in the state is the Arizona Buddhist Temple, established out of the concerns of a smaller Asian immigrant group—the Japanese. Only a few hundred Japanese resided in the Valley when the Arizona Buddhist Temple was established in 1932. The temple became central to the small group's community life. Today, the temple, at 4142 W. Clarendon Avenue in Phoenix, (602) 278-0036, serves not only an immigrant community, but also Western followers.

Possibly the saddest day in the state of Arizona's religious history, however, involved Wat Promkunaram. Nine Thai monks were slaughtered at the temple at 17212 W. Maryland Avenue, on the far west side

WORSHIP

of the Valley, in 1991. The mass murder raised questions, particularly among the Thai community here and in Thailand, of whether modern-day Arizonans were religiously tolerant. Locally, though, most people were shocked at the bloody crime in the temple. Wat Promkunaram had been established three years earlier to meet the needs of Thai immigrants, and it continues to serve them. To contact Wat Promkunaram call (623) 935-2276 or visit www.watprom.iirt.net. Services are open to everyone on Saturdays at 10 AM.

Many Others

There are many other religious and spiritual disciplines practiced in the Valley of the Sun. Most of them have arrived in the past few decades. Phoenix is the site of Yogi Paramahansa Yogananda's only U.S. temple outside California. The Self-Realization Fellowship Temple and Ashram Center offers services on Sundays and Thursdays that mix Hindu mysticism with discussions on Western scriptures at 6111 N. Central Avenue in Phoenix, (602) 279-6140.

Phoenix also has a Sikh community with a number of American adherents. Many of them can be found at congregational services at the Kundalini Yoga Center, 2302 N. Ninth Street, Phoenix, (602) 271-4480. Classes are seven days a week in the evening. Call ahead to register.

Another aspect of life in the Southwest is the rise of New Age religious and spiritual groups. Because of the blend of sources for their beliefs and practices, it is sometimes difficult to distinguish New Age believers from practitioners of Eastern mysticism, American Indian religions, pagan, and Wiccan ideas, but it is precisely the blending of these ancient beliefs into new forms that marks New Age. Because of this diversity of practices, it's difficult to find a characteristic group or church to profile here. Suffice it to say that there are numerous groups of this type listed in the phone book. Another source of information on these groups are the various New Age stores, where meeting places and times are often posted.

INSIDERS' TIP

Habitat for Humanity works with local religious groups to help build housing for the poor. The Valley of the Sun office is at 1432 East Saint Catherine Avenue, Phoenix, (602) 268-9022.

Index